Corrections

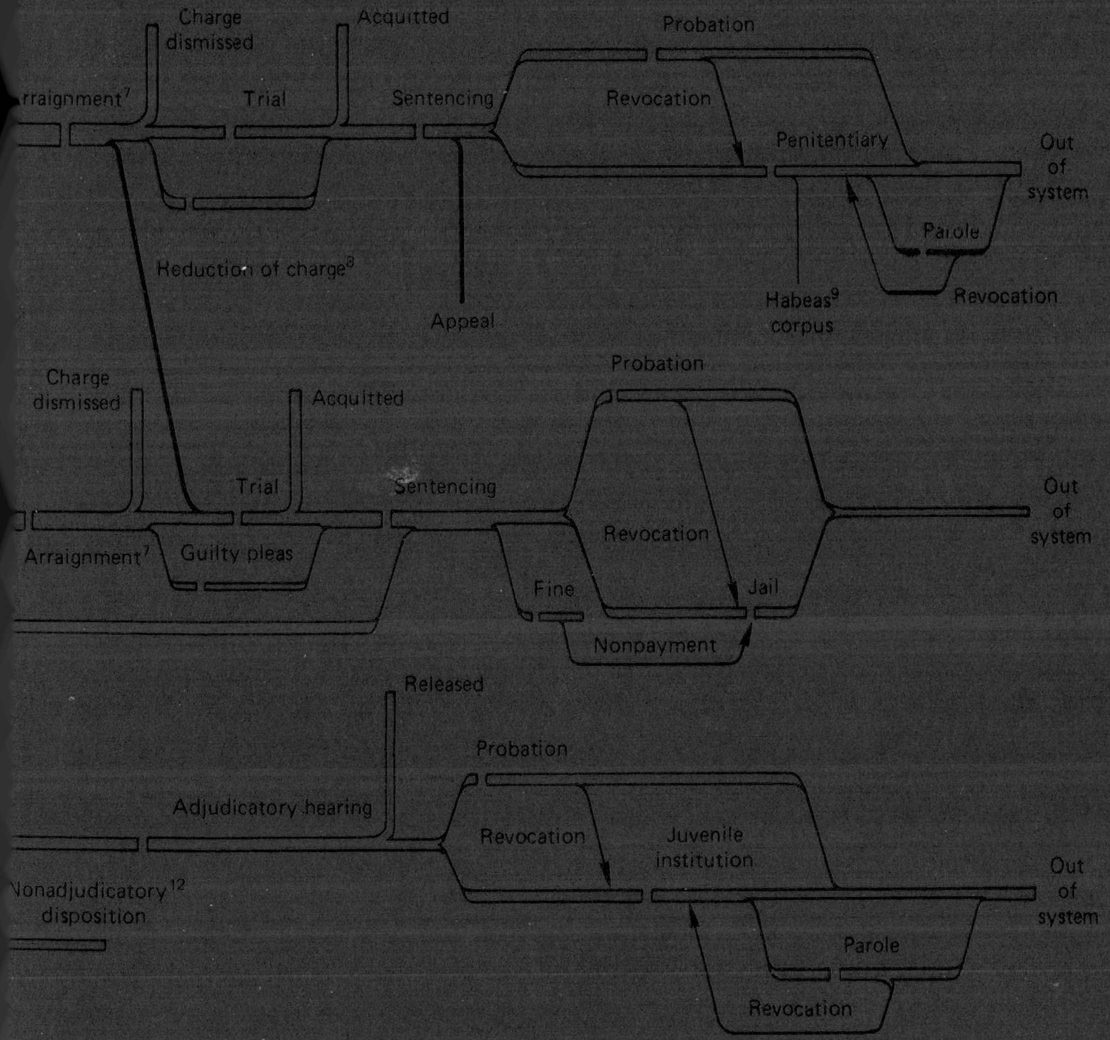

Arraignment[7] — Charge dismissed — Trial — Acquitted — Sentencing — Probation — Revocation — Penitentiary — Out of system
Reduction of charge[8]
Appeal
Habeas[9] corpus — Parole — Revocation

Arraignment[7] — Charge dismissed — Guilty pleas — Trial — Acquitted — Sentencing — Probation — Revocation — Fine — Nonpayment — Jail — Out of system

Nonadjudicatory[12] disposition — Adjudicatory hearing — Released — Probation — Revocation — Juvenile institution — Parole — Revocation — Out of system

7 Appearance for plea. Defendent elects trial by judge or jury. If available, counsel for indigent usually appointed here in felonies. Often not at all in other cases.

8 Charge may be reduced at any time prior to trial in return for plea of guilty or for other reasons.

9 Challenge on constitutional grounds to legality of detention. May be sought at any point in process.

10 Police often hold informal hearings, dismiss or adjust many cases without further processing.

11 Probation officer decides desirability of further court action.

12 Welfare agency, social services, counseling, medical care, etc., for cases where judicatory handling not needed.

Introduction to CRIMINAL JUSTICE

SECOND EDITION

NEIL C. CHAMELIN
Florida Police Standards and Training Commission

VERNON B. FOX
Florida State University

PAUL M. WHISENAND
California State University, Long Branch

Prentice-Hall, Inc., Englewood Cliffs, N.J. 07632

Library of Congress Cataloging in Publication Data

CHAMELIN, NEIL C., 1942–
    Introduction to criminal justice.

    Includes bibliographies and index.
    1. Criminal justice, Administration of—United States. I. Fox, Vernon Brittain, 1916– joint author. II. Whisenand, Paul M., joint author. III. Title.
HV8138.C49–1979   364   78-10291
ISBN 0-13-480145-8

Editorial/production supervision and interior design by Kim Field
Cover design by Mark Binn
Manufacturing buyer: John Hall

Prentice-Hall Series in Criminal Justice
James D. Stinchcomb, *Series Editor*

© 1979 by Prentice-Hall, Inc., Englewood Cliffs, N.J. 07632

All rights reserved. No part of this book
may be reproduced in any form or
by any means without permission in writing
from the publisher.

Printed in the United States of America

10 9 8 7 6 5 4 3 2 1

PRENTICE-HALL INTERNATIONAL, INC., *London*
PRENTICE-HALL OF AUSTRALIA PTY. LIMITED, *Sydney*
PRENTICE-HALL OF CANADA, LTD., *Toronto*
PRENTICE-HALL OF INDIA PRIVATE LIMITED, *New Delhi*
PRENTICE-HALL OF JAPAN, INC., *Tokyo*
PRENTICE-HALL OF SOUTHEAST ASIA PTE. LTD., *Singapore*
WHITEHALL BOOKS LIMITED, *Wellington, New Zealand*

Contents

Preface

Introduction 1

    The Prevalence of Crime 2

    Approaches to the Crime Problem 3

    The Study of Crime and the Criminal Justice System 5

    Approaches to the Identification of the Causes of Crime 6

    Objectives of the Criminal Justice System 12

    Summary 14

PART I THE POLICE SUBSYSTEM

1 Our Criminal Justice System 17

    The Subsystems: An Overview 18

    A "Typical" Crime in a Typical Local Government Setting 20

    The Challenge, Risk, and Fear of Crime 22

    The Cost of Crime Reduction 27

    Crime Reduction: The Transcendent Criminal Justice System Goal 30

Priority Crimes Cause Priority Programs   37
What Follows . . .   41
Suggested References   41

2 The Police Role   43

Overview   44
Our Police   44
Our Police in Action   45
Police Goals   46
History of the Police   49
Federal Response to Crime   57
Federal Policing   59
State Policing   73
Local Policing   81
Intergovernmental Coordination   90
Learning Exercises   90
Suggested References   91

3 Program Operations: Patrol   94

Overview   95
Patrol . . . the Backbone of Policing   95
Patrol Activities   98
Patrol Programs   105
Team Policing   111
The Role of the Patrol Officer   116
Learning Exercises   118
Suggested References   119

4 Program Operations: Specialist Units   121

Overview   122
The Need for Specialists   122

Criminal Investigation   125

Youth Services   130

Narcotics and Drug Abuse   133

Vice Control   136

Traffic Safety   139

Special Enforcement   142

Jail (Custody)   143

Crime Prevention/Community Relations   144

Civil (Court Support)   151

Learning Exercises   151

Suggested References   152

5 Police Administration   154

Overview   155

Management = Responsibility   155

The Management Component   164

Support Specialist Components   174

Learning Exercises   184

Suggested References   185

6 Community Crime Prevention   188

Overview   189

Crime Prevention and the Public   189

Citizen Responsiveness   190

The Delivery of Public Services   192

Community Crime Prevention Programs   195

Community Crime Prevention: An Epilogue—Placebo, Panacea, or Path?   203

Learning Exercises   203

Suggested References   204

Applying Your Knowledge: Law Enforcement   205

PART II CRIMINAL LAW AND THE COURTS 207

7 Historical and Moral Perspectives on Criminal Law 209

Overview 210
The Development of Legal Systems 211
The Enactment of Crimes 211
Theories of Punishment 212
Classification of Crimes 213
Parties to Crimes 214
Act and Intent 215
The Rules of Evidence and the Jury System 217
Moral Considerations and Law 220
Summary 226
Learning Exercises 226
Suggested References 227

8 Survey of Constitutional Principles 229

Overview 230
The Development of the Constitution 231
The Constitution as a Grant of Power 232
Amending the Constitution 233
State Constitutions as a Limitation on Power 234
Constitutional Interpretation of Statutes 234
The Bill of Rights 235
The Evolution of the Fourteenth Amendment 236
The Bill of Rights and the Criminal Justice System 239
The Constitution and Criminal Justice 251
Summary 252
Learning Exercises 252
Suggested References 253

9 Courts in the United States 254

Overview 255

The Development of Courts 255

The Supreme Court of the United States 256

The Supreme Court as a Political Entity 257

Lower Federal Courts 262

State and Local Courts 264

The Lower Courts 266

Juvenile Courts 270

Summary 274

Learning Exercises 274

Suggested References 275

10 The Processes of Criminal Justice 277

Overview 278

Pretrial Processes 279

Trial Processes 287

Post-trial Processes 297

Summary 301

Learning Exercises 302

Suggested References 303

11 Toward Judicial Reform 306

Overview 307

Law Reform 309

Unification of State Court Systems 309

A Need for Better Administration 311

Improved State-Federal Court Relations 312

Quality of Personnel 312

Court Procedures and Practices 314

Summary 319

Learning Exercises 320

Suggested References 321

Applying Your Knowledge: Courts 322

PART III CORRECTIONS

12 Development of Corrections 327

Overview 328

History of Corrections 330

Emergence of Corrections 334

Keeping Criminals as Public Policy 337

Capital Punishment 338

Brief Review of Criminology—Theory and Research 341

Summary 343

Learning Exercises 344

Suggested References 345

13 Jails 346

Overview 347

Jails and Stockades 348

Jail Administration and Operation 353

Lockups 355

Misdemeanants 355

Volunteers in Jail 357

Jail and Release on Own Recognizance 357

Houses of Correction 358

Summary 358

Learning Exercises 359

Suggested References 360

14 Probation 362

Overview 363
Presentence Investigation 366
Supervision of Probationers 368
Probation Subsidy Legislation 370
Conclusions 371
Learning Exercises 371
Suggested References 372

15 Prisons and Correctional Institutions 373

Overview 374
Types of Institutions 375
Objectives of the Institution 377
Organization and Administration 380
Custody 381
Court Intervention in Prisons 384
Treatment 388
Conclusions 394
Learning Exercises 395
Suggested References 396

16 Institutional Society 398

Overview 399
The People 400
Society 404
Culture 405
The Factions 408
Customs and Folkways 408
Staff Society 408

Effects of Institutionalization   409

Conclusions   411

Learning Exercises   411

Suggested References   412

17 Community-Based Corrections   414

Overview   415

Diversion Programs   418

Halfway Houses   419

Work Release, Study Release, and Furloughs   420

Ex-offender Groups   421

Private Community-Based Corrections   422

Conclusions   422

Learning Exercises   423

Suggested References   424

18 Juvenile Corrections   425

Overview   426

Juvenile Detention   427

Juvenile Training Schools   427

Juvenile Aftercare   430

Juvenile Justice and Delinquency Prevention Act of 1974   431

Conclusions   433

Learning Exercises   433

Suggested References   434

19 Parole and other Release Procedures 436

Overview 437

Selection for Parole 439

Prerelease Programs 422

Supervision of Parolees 444

Combined Probation and Parole Services 447

Problems with Parole 447

Other Releases from Prison 449

Summary 450

Learning Exercises 450

Suggested References 451

20 The Criminal Justice System in Transition 453

Urban Policy Development and the Criminal Justice System 456

The Reality and Mythology of the Criminal Justice System 457

The Manpower Base for Criminal Justice Operations 458

The Impact of Standards and Goals 461

Policing at the Crossroads 462

Gathering the Wayward Juvenile 465

The Perplexities of Prisons and Jails 467

The Propriety of the Way the Law Is Ruled 469

Applying Your Knowledge: Corrections 471

Appendix: The Constitution of the United States 473

Glossary of Frequently Used Terms in the Criminal Justice System 484

Index 495

Preface

The study of criminal justice as a separate discipline is fairly new. Before its inception, the problems related to crime were explored in two different areas. The study of sociology addressed the causes and origins of crime. The study of law emphasized the application of criminal law to offenders. The need to look at criminal justice as a unity became apparent as the result of two major studies. These were the Wickersham Commission Reports in 1931 and the President's Commission on Law Enforcement and Criminal Justice in 1967.

Because the criminal justice system has roots in many areas, it is extremely large and its structure and functions can be very complex. However, the extent of the system should not intimidate the beginning student. Its organization and processes can be understood through diligent efforts. This book has been written to simplify those efforts and to make sure that they are rewarded.

In one sense, the size of the system makes its study attractive. There is so much diversity within the criminal justice system that regardless of your background and interests you are likely to find something that you will consider stimulating, satisfying, and challenging. The text has been arranged to help you:

- become familiar with the vocabulary of the system—terms and basic concepts,
- understand what drives the major components of the system—Law Enforcement, Courts, and Corrections—and what makes them work, or falter,
- become acquainted with the issues and problems of the system from which change eventually flows, no matter how slowly
- understand the importance of individual decision making in the criminal justice process

apply the knowledge learned about the system for further professional study and growth

This book is divided into three principal sections and a total of twenty chapters. A quick, initial reading of the table of contents is suggested to grasp the scope of the text and the outline of the structure of the criminal justice system itself.

To further assist the student's learning experience, this book possesses certain distinctive features:

Selected chapter illustrations, tables, and charts help to illuminate important points in the text

Chapter overviews inventory and condense significant statements in the text.

Key terms, at the end of each chapter, contain concepts, terms, and names that should be mastered in order to progressively build a criminal justice vocabulary.

The learning exercises that follow each chapter are designed to engage the student in serious thought based upon information developed in the text and perhaps other reading. They often demand outside work and thought, not casual reactions.

Applying Your Knowledge sections are found at the end of each major part of the book. The *Issues* may spotlight some unresolved or controversial problem in the criminal justice system. The *Cases* largely reflect some decision-making requirement by a member of the system. *Cases/Issues* should develop lively debates among students and help them to appreciate the strategic dilemmas and tactical challenges to the system.

Extensive footnoting provides references that the authors have used to document or explain statements in the text. They are often starting points for further reading on a particular subject.

An appendix following the final chapter containing the entire Constitution of the United States is a handy reference for all students.

The glossary at the end of the book includes definitions of key items for the development of a standard vocabulary for criminal justice.

The authors sincerely believe that if students read the text faithfully and carefully and approach the learning aids methodically, they will be rewarded by finding the study of the criminal justice system temptingly profitable and consistently engrossing.

The authors wish to express a special note of appreciation to Frank McKernan who helped in many ways to coordinate our efforts, thus providing a well-integrated and more cohesive text.

The voyage starts promptly!

NEIL C. CHAMELIN
VERNON B. FOX
PAUL M. WHISENAND

Introduction

The Prevalence of Crime
Approaches to the Crime Problem
The Study of Crime and the Criminal Justice System
Approaches to the Identification of the Causes of Crime
Objectives of the Criminal Justice System
Summary

THE PREVALENCE OF CRIME

Crime recognizes no geographical boundaries. It respects no social or economic class. It is timeless, ageless, and disturbingly dynamic. It not only works within the fabric of the established community but also keeps pace with the outer fringes of technological development. As the nation pushes farther into the frontiers of a new computer world, for example, crime follows relentlessly to corrupt that world for illicit gain and advantage. It erupts violently by taking new forms, such as air piracy or hostage taking, plaguing the everyday lives of citizens and confronting law enforcement agencies, often unexpectedly, with new and aggravating challenges. It intrudes into the street corner, the darkened alley, the home, and the corporate boardroom or government office with equal ease. It possesses the insidious ability to increase a citizen's fear. In the more crowded cities, almost half of their citizens are afraid to walk the streets at night and almost 20 percent live in some degree of apprehension about their own safety even within the confines of their own homes.

The crime clocks developed annually by the FBI tick away with merciless regularity. Violent crimes (murder, forcible rape, robbery, and assault to kill), because of their intensely personal intrusions on citizen safety and well-being, produce persistent fear. Murder alone occurs every twenty-eight minutes. In a 1977 study of the Cleveland metropolitan area, murder moved ahead of disease and accidents as the major cause of death of young nonwhite males. Forcible rape happens once in every nine minutes, and aggravated assault, an appalling every sixty-four seconds. While citizens express increasing concern about the safety of their homes and business, the crime clock underlines and pays terrible heed to their anxiety: Robbery occurs once every seventy-five seconds; burglary, once every ten seconds; and larceny-theft, once every five seconds.[1]

Recent studies have begun to reflect society's fear of the more dangerous criminal, the consistent repeater, the career criminal who considers his activities, much as law-abiding citizens look upon their work, as an occupation pursued for "wages" and personal satisfaction. Such criminals weigh their chance-taking and risks. They are more likely to be operating in the realm of crimes against property where the statistics support their personal resolve.

A recent report indicates that the most dangerous criminals have been involved in serious crime since childhood, while the amateur criminals are usually

---

[1] The FBI crime clocks are found in U.S. Department of Justice, Federal Bureau of Investigation, *Crime in the United States, Uniform Crime Reports 1976* (Washington, D.C.: U.S. Government Printing Office, 1977), p. 6. The Cleveland study on murder is found in the *New England Journal of Medicine,* September 1977.

those who take up crime later in life. Intensive offenders commit ten times as many crimes as intermittent offenders and yet possess sparse arrest records in comparison to their extreme activity and dangerousness. They work mostly as loners, carefully plotting their crimes, often learning their trade before the age of thirteen.[2]

Demographically the perpetrators of violent crime are mostly males between the ages of fifteen and twenty-four—those at the lower end of the occupational scale, the poor, the unemployed, concentrated for the most part in the blighted, crowded areas of large cities where they largely feed upon their neighbors who, as victims, more often than not live in fear of even reporting crimes committed on their persons or property.

APPROACHES TO THE CRIME PROBLEM

The national response to crime in the past two decades has been a combination of extreme alarm and gross uneasiness, followed by more sober reflection on what the nation seemingly must live with and how it can best evaluate what can be done well in order to curb crime's growth.

The decade of the 1960s followed two paths that to many seemed paradoxical. On the one hand, the increasing crescendo of riots, violent dissent, assassinations, and the initiation of air piracy in 1961 led to the creation of a whole spate of commissions to study these many manifestations of crime in order to determine causes and propose solutions. At the same time, the Supreme Court intensified its efforts to guarantee individual rights involved in the criminal justice process.

The commissions tackled some of the most urgent problems: The Advisory Commission on Intergovernmental Relations (1968) discussed the breakdown of the sense of community and its ultimate effect upon crime. The National Advisory Commission on Civil Disorders (1968) examined the causes of recent riots. The great watershed of criminal justice study was the President's Commission on Law Enforcement and the Administration of Justice (1967).[3] The multivolume reports issued by this commission became the hallmark for defining and activating the criminal justice system (CJS). The Commission pressed for a further in-depth examination of CJS weaknesses, for a continuous evaluation of CJS functions and processes, and for some immediate pressing changes. This study became the benchmark for measuring progress during the 1970s in law enforcement, court procedures, and corrections activities. The National Commission on the Causes and Prevention of Violence (1969) addressed the problems of handguns and recommended major changes in the machinery for administering justice. Two other

[2] For a discussion of the youth origins of career criminals see the Rand Corporation, *Criminal Careers of Habitual Felons,* Study No. R2144 (Santa Monica, Calif.: The Rand Corporation 1977).

[3] See the President's Commission on Law Enforcement and the Administration of Justice, *The Challenge of Crime in a Free Society* (Washington, D.C.: U.S. Government Printing Office, 1967). Pp. 293-301 contain a summary of recommendations.

commissions working in the 1960s produced reports in the early 1970s. The President's Commission on Campus Violence (1970) addressed a newly developed phenomenon in American life which had preoccupied citizens in the 1960s. The National Commission on Reform of Federal Criminal Laws in its initial report in 1970 dealt with recommendations for the overhaul of the federal criminal code.

The 1960s likewise experienced a series of Supreme Court decisions to expand the rights of the accused and to focus more directly on the assurance of due process of law. A citation of a few of these decisions illustrates the direction of the Court.[4] In *Mapp v. Ohio* the Court ruled that evidence obtained in violation of the search and seizure provisions of the Fourth Amendment is not admissible in a state court. In *Escobedo v. Illinois* the Court ruled that the refusal by the police to allow an accused person to consult with his lawyer was in violation of the Sixth Amendment. In *Gideon v. Wainwright* the Court stated that indigent defendants must be provided with counsel in noncapital cases. In *Miranda v. Arizona* the Court ruled that an individual held by the police for interrogation must be informed by law enforcement agencies that his right of counsel includes the right to have his lawyer present during questioning while in custody. Countering the practice of juvenile courts—that is, treating juvenile trials as essentially civil, with the judge a substitute for parents, without affording the protections accorded to adults—the Court *In re Gault* said that juveniles must be given most of the protections of the Bill of Rights. These would include a timely notice of charges, right to counsel if a charge may result in incarceration, right to confront and cross-examine witnesses, a warning against self-incrimination, and the right to remain silent.

The 1970s were notable for producing a critical in-depth examination of almost every facet of the criminal justice system; a follow-up of many of the problems raised in the 1960s; an attack by scholars on traditional procedures or new procedures that did not appear to work; an attempt at prescription, at standards and goals to be developed and implemented to accelerate progress in improving the criminal justice system; and a sharper isolation of major issues to clear the deck for the resolution of such problems as defining the future function of the prison and ending disparities in sentencing.

For example, two major studies examined almost the entire spectrum of the criminal justice system in order to improve the quality of operations and to set new targets for advancing the system. The first of these studies was incorporated into the *Reports of the National Advisory Commission on Criminal Justice Standards and Goals*. These studies took their basic cues from the work of the 1960s and set concrete goals for achieving many of the concepts, ideas, and procedures advanced during that previous decade. Beginning in 1973 and continuing through 1977 successive reports were issued on *Criminal Justice Systems, A National Strat-*

---

[4] Cases cited are *Mapp v. Ohio* 367 U.S. 643 (1961); *Escobedo v. Illinois* 378 U.S. 478 (1964); *Gideon v. Wainwright* 372 U.S. 335 (1963); *Miranda v. Arizona* 384 U.S. 436 (1966); and *In re Gault* 387 U.S. 167 (1967).

egy to Reduce Crime, Police, Courts, Corrections, Community Crime Prevention, Juvenile Justice and Delinquency Prevention, and *Disorders and Terrorism.* Many of these standards have been or are being selectively incorporated into local and state laws, regulations, or procedures.

The second major study, by the American Bar Association, began in 1968 and continued into 1973. It developed seventeen separate volumes on standards almost exclusively for the judicial process. One volume published in 1973 included standards for the *Urban Police Function.* Again these standards are influencing the judicial system in its attempt to increase its effectiveness and efficiency.

Finally, the 1970s saw the criminal justice system reexamining with great vigor changes in the methods and purpose of imprisonment, treatment, and sentencing. For example, the state of Massachusetts abolished state institutions for the custody of juveniles, and the federal government, in its correctional facility at Buttner, North Carolina, began an experimental program modifying the treatment concepts and prisoner management procedures that had long been standard in prison systems. The federal government moved toward the regulation of sentencing procedures in order to introduce more uniformity among judges in their sentencing practices in regard to the type and amount of punishment decreed for similar offenses. Finally, greater attention was given to the methods for planning and organizing the criminal justice system itself through a combination of both state and federal efforts.

THE STUDY OF CRIME AND THE CRIMINAL JUSTICE SYSTEM

Criminology as a discipline for the study of crime did not emerge until the nineteenth century. The modern criminologist is now concerned about the etiology or causes and origins of crime; its dimensions; its prevalence; the trends in national, regional, and local crime; the origins of the definitions of acts that criminal law labels as crime; and the responses of the criminal justice system to the suppression of crime and the managing of offenders. The criminologist is interested in the advanced scientific means for the study of crime through empirically developed evidence. Criminologists and other professional personnel who study the criminal justice system utilize a variety of disciplines including sociology, anthropology, law, psychology, and psychiatry in their efforts. Because law enforcement and corrections originally had no clearly developed body of knowledge of their own, they initially drew heavily upon a variety of disciplines to help solve their problems.

Within the past few decades, however, there has developed a body of criminal justice knowledge that can be considered as the foundation of a criminal justice discipline. The clustering of this knowledge within the confines of the criminal justice system, as described in this book, has encouraged a more authoritative, methodical, and regularized acquisition of new knowledge directed at system problems through empirical research and the gradual establishment of a carefully designed data base. This body of knowledge is further being utilized to increase system identity and to enlarge the criminal justice discipline through the education of professional criminal justice personnel who will operate the system and direct its research and development needs.

APPROACHES TO THE IDENTIFICATION OF THE CAUSES OF CRIME

Today, when we search for causes of crime we must first recognize that those acts that society considers criminal are embodied into law. In the United States, the Congress and the state legislatures decide what is a criminal act. As the nation grew more urban, more industrialized, more technological, and generally more compressed, the social and economic structure changed. Such changes produced new interrelationships that placed individuals in closer proximity with one another. The problems of human relationships intensified, expanding the possibilities of crimes against persons. In addition, as commercial and industrial activities grew larger in these compact urban areas, the opportunities for crime against property also grew. Thus society in its effort to protect itself passed more laws to cope with new conditions. For example, as our computer technology grew more complex it provided a new arena for dishonest programmers to appropriate money not rightfully theirs or to steal technical specifications. Society then created new laws necessitated by the advent of a new piece of technological equipment. America now surpasses all other nations in the number of criminal laws on the books.

The great emphasis in early times was not upon what caused crime but what punishment to prescribe for the crimes committed. The harshness of such punishment occupied the thoughts of the late eighteenth- and nineteenth-century theorists who were considered to be the early criminologists. Their work on theories of punishment led directly to consideration of the larger issue, the causes of crime.

The *classical school* held that individuals were born with a free will and the capability to make choices that would give them pain or pleasure. They consequently could choose of their own free will to commit an illegal act or avoid such an act. Forbidden acts were described by the law which was to be impartial but rigid. Punishment was to fit the crime. The *positive school* held that crime could not be defined narrowly through legal means alone and under a concept of individual choice. The causes of crime were deep-seated and were determined rather by an individual's physical makeup and personality as well as his social and economic environment. Once these causes were isolated they could be treated. Thus punishment was to fit the criminal and not, as the classicists held, solely the crime.

The positive school helped to open up the scientific study of the causes of crime as well as the treatment of individuals in correctional settings. It aided in fostering separate approaches to the study of causation: the *physiological,* the *biological,* the *psychiatric,* the *psychological,* the *sociological,* and the *economic.* Such theories about crime causation looked at the individual and his physical and psychological composition, or the external forces that were likely to influence his behavior, or a combination of both.[5]

The Focus on the Individual

Ancient and medieval society blamed the unacceptable behavior in individuals upon the possession of the body by demons. Thus demons had to be cast out to protect society. It was then not accidental that later theories would continue to center their attention on the individual in their search for crime causation. The *physiological* approach centered its attention on the physical features and the bodily contours. Cranial measurements lead to the location of certain bumps. Such protrusions were thought to influence the way in which one individual might behave toward another. The fishy eye, the low-sloping forehead, the receding chin, thin lips, the long skinny neck, thick hair, and tattoo marks were identified as crime-prone indicators.

Further exploration of the body structure identified certain types—the round, the muscular, and the lean—and assigned certain temperaments to such types. Round and soft persons were determined to be more relaxed. Muscular persons demonstrated more assertiveness. The lean were rigid. Within such configurations some studies attempted to demonstrate that delinquency was somewhat more prevalent among those whose physiques were more muscular and athletic and who possessed more aggressiveness.[6] Generally most studies dealing with the individual's physiognomy have, however, produced little in discovering causes.

Probing more deeply into the individual, students of crime causation moved into the *biological* approach by, for example, studying genetic endowment. They theorized that criminal tendencies were inherited. Thus, individuals possessing certain structures in their genetic makeup were thought to be more likely to commit a crime. Much speculation dealt with feeble-mindedness in its relationship to crime. Abnormal sex chromosome combinations were also found to be related to criminality. The XYY combination, sometimes identified as the "supermale" pattern, has been found in criminal populations more frequently than expected from its representation in the general population. For example, Richard Speck, the individual who murdered eight nurses in Chicago in 1968, was an XYY. The more violent in prison populations tend to be similarly identified. However, such persons are also found more disproportionately in professional athletics. While there

---

[5] Some general works on causation are Stephen Schafer, *Theories in Criminology* (New York: Random House, 1969); George B. Vold, *Theoretical Criminology* (New York: Oxford University Press, 1958); and Sawyer F. Sylvester, Jr., ed., *The Heritage of Modern Criminology* (Cambridge, Mass.: Schenkman Publishing Co., 1972).

[6] See William H. Sheldon, *Varieties of Delinquent Youth* (New York: Harper and Brothers, 1949).

appears to be some relationship of the XYY to aggression, the relationship to crime, however, remains inconclusive.[7]

The modern *psychiatric* approach to crime causation attempts to search an individual's genetic or biological predisposition, the influence of his psychological and biochemical processes and his ongoing series of life experiences, beginning with the prenatal period and extending through childhood to the present environment and cultural pressures. Psychiatrists contend that conscious mental processes and behavior that can be defined, observed, and measured represent only the tip of the iceberg and that the major part of human behavior is subconscious. Some psychiatrists utilize the techniques of *psychoanalysis* to study these subconscious motivations as the basis for identifying deviant behavior. The wars within the subconscious may produce psychoses such as paranoia or drifts away from reality, hallucinations, or delusions of persecution or loftiness. When such conditions surface and predominate, psychiatrists believe that some persons are more likely to commit a crime. Individuals pushed by some misplaced aggression, for example, may be impelled to rape, steal, or set fire to a dwelling. Others who lose contact with reality or with any comprehension of right or wrong may commit crimes ranging from bilking to murder. Those who have delusions of persecution may be predisposed toward assault.

In the *psychological* approach to crime causation, psychologists developed explanations of deviant behavior, statistical measures of normalcy, and patterns of individual deviance. Their work has largely centered more on the possibilities of predicting crime than on the causes of crime itself. Their tools have been intelligence, attitude, and aptitude tests and the isolation of personality traits. Emphasis has been given primarily to the latter area in an attempt to develop profiles from scales of hysteria, paranoia, psychopathic personality, and other traits in order to identify delinquents. However, the perplexing problem is that research personnel find more similarities than dissimilarities between the nondelinquent and the delinquent. Critics feel that personality trait studies based upon objective tests do not, as yet, contribute significantly to predicting delinquency.

The Focus on the Environment

Modern studies of crime causation have increasingly emphasized the social and environmental influences. The *sociological* approach generally deals with the social group; group behavior; the impact of geography, industrialization, and urbanization; the alienation of individuals from normal social relationships; the despair and frustration of remaining stationary in a mobile world; the breakdown in family solidarity; and the pressures of ethnic and racial conflict.

Early studies of juvenile gangs, for example, indicated that a majority of crime occurred in and was committed by persons from the crumbling, de-

---

[7] See Richard G. Fox, "The XYY Offender: A Modern Myth?" *Journal of Criminal Law, Criminology and Police Science*, Vol. 62 (March 1971), pp. 59–73.

teriorated, confined areas between the economic center and the industrialized and commercial area of the city. Crime and delinquency declined with the distance from the city hall. In recent years, a general decentralization of industry and commerce has now produced a proportional increase in crime and delinquency in more suburban areas. The general principle then appears to be that crime and delinquency follows industry and commerce in terms of *geographical* areas.

When gangs were formed in areas of high delinquency, it was found that they retained a stature of permanency despite changing membership, passing their value system to the new members. Individuals who find dissatisfaction in a normal group relationship often discover that it may be more satisfying to transfer their loyalty to these organizations.

The family no longer transmits accepted social and moral standards. New racial and ethnic groups gradually displace the former inhabitants of certain spaces in older neighborhoods. Changes occur in who controls the old neighborhood (the power structure). Jobs grow scarce. Individuals are caught in the welter of social change. In order to satisfy their needs, those who cannot break away from their current environment generally seek the new group ties provided by gangs to satisfy their aspirations and goals. In the process they assume a role that conforms to the standards of the new group. Thus *peer pressure,* if it is aimed at illegal efforts, may insist that new recruits engage in petty theft, burglary, or extortion in order to gain peer acceptance and, in the process, help them to achieve some goal or satisfaction.

Part of the problem of crime causation in a social setting is that not all people living in deteriorating communities become criminals. Some emphasis must be given to other influences on why some do and others do not commit a crime. Some individuals are satisfied with their lot and are able to cope. Others have strong moral and family ties despite their burden. Still others are ill, old, and immobile. Other individuals display a persistent desire for upward mobility involving the *economic* approach to crime. The press, TV, or just the daily observations of life in large communities reveal how materialistic and economically competitive society happens to be. The good life can be achieved through the possession of money and goods. If an individual evaluates his chances of legitimately obtaining some measure of this good life as very small given his present condition, he may decide that he must achieve it by other means. He must compete. Even if an adequate job is not available, extralegal opportunities to add a measure of wealth or personal possessions still abound. There are numerous stores, banks, and defenseless old people all around. If despair and the economic yoke make one persistently heavy laden, wrath and indignation may lead to a lone act of burglary or robbery to somewhat help redress the imbalance in economic status.

Some of this criminal behavior results from a condition described by a peculiar word: *anomie.*[8] It is often used to denote alienation or dissociation from an

---

[8] Anomie is discussed in Robert K. Merton, *Social Theory and Social Structure,* enl. ed. (New York: Free Press, 1968).

individual's cultural group. Its basic concept is normlessness and conflict between some people, individually or in groups, and the established society and social groups. Thus criminal behavior may grow out of the difference between what culture says are ways that society is to be organized and operated and how wants and desires are to be fulfilled, and what one's peculiar social structure actually permits. Thus, for example, to break out of the restrictive social status some means other than those at hand seem necessary. When such alienation is present, the criminal act may occur, but not always. Some individuals just retreat and give up. Others sink into despair or into drugs and alcoholism which may predispose them toward a defined criminal act. Still others seek to change what they consider repressive conditions through a kind of rebellion that may take the form of legitimate group protest efforts or manifest itself in illegal assaults on others. Finally, there may be those who are innovative and may use illegal business practices, such as a petty investment racket involving old people, to achieve their goals. When such acts prove to be successful and satisfying, they may form the basis for a criminal career.

Another sociological concept, known as *differential association,* holds that criminal behavior is indeed learned rather than inherited.[9] Many influences in the biological, psychological, or social past of an individual may create a tendency toward delinquency, but the situation as it exists at the moment is the determining factor. If an individual is disposed toward committing a criminal act, he learns the techniques or the "how" of crime from an intimate organization or group with which he may associate.[10] Such associations may vary in terms of frequency, intensity, and duration. One theory holds that high delinquency areas tend to have more delinquents because they provide more opportunities for association with delinquents. Likewise, prisons breed more crimes because learning is facilitated by contact with other experienced criminals. On the other hand, crime rates may vary from one area to another because many individuals may not have ready access to such learning situations. They may not have illegitimate opportunities open to them and must, in their goal seeking, rely upon legitimate means (the theory of *differential opportunity*).[11]

All learning leading to a criminal act may not, however, be learned within a criminally inclined group. For example, a computer programmer may have acquired his skill at a legitimate business school and expanded it through work in a reputable and large banking business. However, once the skill is learned, the programmer may perceive an alternate use influenced by some economic or socially determining factor. He then uses that skill cleverly but fraudulently to divert

---

[9] Differential association is discussed in Edwin H. Sutherland and Donald R. Cressey, *Criminology,* 9th ed. (Philadelphia: Lippincott, 1974), pp. 75–91.

[10] See Frederic M. Thrasher, *The Gang,* abr. ed. (Chicago: University of Chicago Press, 1927, 1963).

[11] See Richard A. Cloward and Lloyd E. Ohlin, *Delinquency and Opportunity: A Theory of Delinquent Gangs* (New York: Free Press, 1960).

funds to a bogus account from which he makes discreet but illegal withdrawals. The condition that triggers the illegal act is situational.

A final approach to causation is known as *labeling*.[12]

> The process of making the criminal is a process of tagging, defining, identifying, segregating, describing, emphasizing, making conscious and self-conscious; it becomes a way of stimulating, suggesting, emphasizing, and evoking the very traits that are complained of.[13]

A teacher, law enforcement officer, or a social group may thus label an individual as a delinquent. Such labeling may, the theory maintains, manufacture delinquency and lead persistently and insidiously to a criminal act. But labeling often depends upon when an act was committed, who was involved, and the results of the act. Thus, in one social setting an impoverished drunk is picked up and labeled a disturber of the peace and vagrant. In another situation, amid a similar public disturbance, a friend quietly takes a drunk back to his comfortable home for recuperation, amply protected by his own social structure.

The theory is also expanded to hold that the politically dominant group in society establishes and administers criminal law. Crime is not necessarily behavior oriented. Crime is what those in authority define as a crime at a given point in time. For example, the prohibition amendment to the U.S. Constitution led to a whole structure of criminal acts under which, in the 1920s, America's "beer baron," Al Capone, was one of the nation's most wanted criminals. But when that amendment was repealed, and the manufacture, distribution, and sale of alcoholic beverages was decriminalized—except for local options, ordinances, and licenses—many previously criminal acts became acceptable business practice. Basically the larger social norm and the legal norm were in conflict and the former prevailed. All kinds of labelings suddenly disappeared.

In assessing the selected concepts and theories we have briefly described, it should be noted that the many empirical studies undertaken to test these theories have generally concluded that most of them are tenuous at best. Some theories do provide frameworks within which conscientious and scientific assessments can be made. Others, such as the concept that some individuals are born criminals, are wholly discredited. The basic problems of causation studies involve providing acceptable definitions of crime and delinquency, sufficient detail in spelling out theories, adequate methodologies for studying the concepts, accurate systems for prediction, and assurances that findings are not equally applicable to noncriminal as well as criminal groups.

Sir Leon Radzinowicz, the British criminologist, sums up the dilemma:

> Seldom, if ever, does a single explanation provide more than a partial truth. It is not a matter of "either-or," or even of "both," but a convergence of many factors which constantly affect each other. Moreover, crime covers a wide range of behavior which

---

[12] See Walter R. Gove, *The Labelling of Deviance* (New York: Halstead Press, 1975).
[13] Frank Tennenbaum, *Crime and Delinquency* (Boston: Ginn, 1938), pp. 19–20.

can no more be covered by a single explanation than disease. And even if the search for explanations is narrowed to particular categories of crime, it is still unlikely to lead to a single "cause," since very different meanings and motivations can be behind what at first seems a precise legal definition. That applies to all forms of crime, from murder to petty theft.[14]

OBJECTIVES OF THE CRIMINAL JUSTICE SYSTEM

The structure of the criminal justice system as it exists today did not appear suddenly as an instantly created unity. It is a product of the evolutionary process of history; changing as society became more humane; accommodating the new demands of industrialized communities; balancing human rights with group rights; defining criminal acts more and more precisely; and making institutional changes to reflect the progress of history and the moral demands of the community.

The CJS as it has evolved in present-day society may be described as now having seven major objectives.

First, it is established to contain and to reduce crime by increasing the risks of crime, reducing the opportunities for crime to occur, promoting crime prevention activities in the community, stimulating more precise studies on crime causation, and ensuring that judicial process is prompt and fair in its decisions. The National Advisory Commission on Criminal Justice Standards and Goals (1973) advocated very specific targets in crime reduction. It recommended a 50 percent reduction in high-fear crimes by 1983. Reductions were to concentrate in five areas: homicide (25 percent), forcible rape (25 percent), aggravated assault (25 percent), robbery (50 percent), and burglary (50 percent).[15]

Second, the CJS is to ensure that both the rights of the accused and the rights of victims are fully recognized in the criminal justice process. During the 1960s and early 1970s the Supreme Court rendered a whole series of decisions, as we have seen, to ensure that the rights of the accused were guaranteed by due process. During the 1970s the judicial process began to recognize the rights of the victim through compensation and remuneration as well as the more humane treatment of victims of rape. Victimization studies have attempted to determine the extent of nonreported personal and property offenses, alerting the criminal justice system to the seriousness of victim problems not appearing in official statistics on the growth of crime.

Third, the CJS is to improve the means of ensuring public safety by employing all the products of modern technology that might assist in sharpening the system's capabilities for apprehension and disposition of cases. These include the utilization of the most modern communication systems and crime fighting equipment and the employment of computers to speed crime detection and case prepa-

[14] Sir Leon Radzinowicz and Joan King, *The Growth of Crime* (New York: Basic Books, 1977), p. 93.
[15] National Advisory Commission on Standards and Goals, *A National Strategy to Reduce Crime* (Washington, D.C.: U.S. Government Printing Office, 1973). See goals for crime reduction following p. xv.

ration and movement, and to add quality and speed to the decision-making process among all components of the system.

Fourth, the CJS must plan for the future. It must anticipate the growing and changing needs for preserving community safety, project manpower and resource requirements to meet these needs, and evolve new tactical and strategic methods for combatting the changing patterns of crime. An insidious and elusive characteristic of crime is its capability of invading almost unannounced any part of the realm of human activity. Examples of new crime patterns include the use of air piracy often for political means, hostage taking for revenge and return of political prisoners, the assault on computers for private financial gain, and the invasion of private and corporate files for political or technological intelligence.

Fifth, the CJS is charged with bringing citizens closer to its operations, inviting them to share in its problems, and to help in crime prevention. Critics have maintained that, in the past, the CJS has been too autonomous, too secretive, and too remote and exclusive, as though it had a separate life of its own beyond the corporate body of the community. Public perceptions are often limited to the officer writing a traffic ticket; to the press statements on the misuse of police power; to the guard slamming the prison door and a feeling of utter isolation from what goes on within the correctional process; to the prosecutor or defense attorney remonstrating before a TV jury. Other distortions especially in law enforcement have also been spawned by television to further color public attitudes. Citizen participation in the CJS as an objective appears to require more initiatives upon the part of personnel within the CJS to invite such participation. The Commission on Standards and Goals recommended that police community programs encourage more citizen involvement by working more fully with troubled youth, by helping to establish additional youth services bureaus, and by sponsoring or ensuring the establishment of more social services to help prevent crime. Initiatives by the three components of the system—law enforcement, courts, and corrections—in helping to break the understanding and communications barrier between the CJS and citizens are likewise thought to lead to greater citizen demand for system improvements through elected officials.

Sixth, the CJS must be humane in its decision-making processes. This often generates more controversy and debate than any other objective. Bound up in it are such issues as adherence to due process, alternatives to custody, bail practices, plea bargaining, and the nature of punishment and rehabilitation. Perhaps the problem of punishment best illustrates some of the dilemma of "humaneness": John Rawls proposes that a "person is said to suffer punishment whenever he is legally deprived of some of the normal rights of a citizen on the ground that he has violated a rule of law, provided that deprivation is carried out by recognized legal authorities of the state, that the rule of law clearly specifies both the offense and the statute were on the books prior to the time of offense."[16] This definition reflects

---

[16] John Rawls, "The Concepts of Rules," in *The Philosophy of Punishment,* ed. H. B. Action (New York: St. Martins, 1969), pp. 111–12.

the broad philosophical and precise legal dimensions of punishment. But it leaves the whole issue of humaneness up to the recognized legal authorities of the state in carrying out deprivation. The degree of humaneness in the criminal justice process is often then a matter of public policy; of the management of the law enforcement, judicial, and correctional processes; and of the leadership, education, and training of those in the system who make decisions.

Seventh, the CJS must undertake under the most modern and scientific means such research, development, and evaluation that will permit: (1) the determination of what systems, procedures, and methods work best for improving the functions of the various components of the system; (2) the creation of a body of verified knowledge that will assist the decision-making processes, help to formulate the right questions to ask for system study and improvement, and provide the basis for the professional education of individuals within the system; and (3) the development of a basis for modification and change in criminal laws as well as the modification of public policies relating to the management of the criminal justice system.

In the achievement of these objectives the CJS pays heed to those individuals, happenings, executive decisions, or legislative actions that might serve as change agents. Normally change agents first define issues and then maintain a capability for offering solutions for a particular problem. Change agents may be operators of the system, research personnel, or public occurrences that compel immediate modification of an operation. Normally once an issue is created it forms the basis for debate and resolution.

To achieve the above objectives the criminal justice system must first be recognized as a system. It possesses interlocking, interrelated, and interdependent components—the law enforcement agencies, the judicial process, and the correctional facilities. This volume is an introduction to how this system now functions, together with its current strengths and weaknesses.

SUMMARY

This introduction has included some observations on the prevalence of crime, the study of crime and the multiple causes of crime, and the objectives of the criminal justice system. This brief review, it is hoped, will establish some perspective on why the system exists. The next chapter discusses the structural framework in which criminal justice operates as a system. Succeeding chapters in turn analyze the functions and operations of the principal components of the system—law enforcement, courts, and corrections.

PART I

The Police Subsystem

1
Our Criminal Justice System

The Subsystems: An Overview
A "Typical" Crime in a Typical Local Government Setting
The Challenge, Risk, and Fear of Crime
The Cost of Crime Reduction
Crime Reduction: The Transcendent Criminal Justice System Goal
Priority Crimes Cause Priority Programs
What Follows. . . .
Suggested References

This nation's *system* for the *delivery* of *criminal justice services* is but one of a multitude of systems. Are we not born into and through a hospital system? Medical and dental systems are a part of our early life. Most of our citizens experience at least thirteen years in an educational system. Many of us affiliate with a religious system. And eventually we are employed by a system that strives to produce products, goods, or services. In taking inventory, we can easily cite a large number of systems or organizations that daily impact our thinking and behavior. They are categorized in many ways such as: biological (e.g., our physical selves); financial (e.g., the banking system); technical (e.g., computer systems); aerospace (e.g., space satellites); industrial (e.g., automobile production); government (e.g., criminal justice); and so on. Our focus from this point forward is on the unique characteristics, goals, and complex relationships of one highly important and unusually visible system—the *criminal justice system* (CJS).

Before proceeding with other matters we should stop for a moment and analyze this term *system*. A brief definition of a system is: a set of component parts (e.g., organizations, bureaus, units, etc.) that enter into mutual transactions (e.g., things and people going back and forth) and possess common goals (e.g., social justice, community peace, and constitutional liberty). You will soon find that the components comprising the American CJS are pulled from all levels of government—federal, state, and local. Additionally, they either directly or indirectly represent various branches of our government—legislative, judicial, and executive. Because of this mixture, our CJS is occasionally referred to as "fragmented," "a nonsystem," or "in need of systematizing."

While admittedly it is somewhat loosely connected, we believe that our CJS is, in fact, a real system. To put it another way, our CJS is a viable and functioning reality that generates a variety of valuable services. At issue, however, are the means for (1) improving the effectiveness of the component parts, and (2) implementing the definition and rank ordering of goals. In the section that follows we will take a summary look at the three major components or *subsystems* of our CJS.

THE SUBSYSTEMS: AN OVERVIEW

The criminal justice system comprises three subsystems: police, courts, and corrections. Each subsystem in turn contains various divisions. For example, the police component by definition includes city, county, state, and federal policing agencies. More by interaction than definition, the police also include special-purpose and private police officers. Thus, we immediately observe within a single subsystem that four levels of government (or five, if regional police agencies are included), as well as both public and private sectors of our society contribute to making up the police subsystem. Similar complexity is found in the courts and corrections subsystems.

Illustrations may help us in our attempt to better understand the CJS. To begin with, let us view the CJS as an operation or activity. All systems have input, processing, and output. For example, the corrections subsystem has as one of its primary inputs convicted offenders (an output from the courts). In turn, it processes and tries to rehabilitate the offender for a period of time, and then outputs him into society. This sequence is illustrated below.

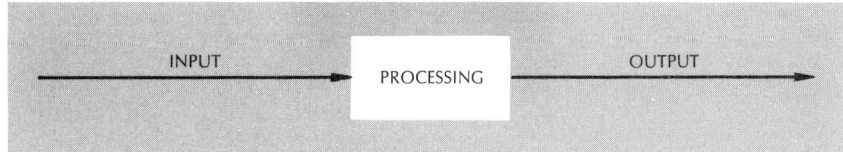

Even the most fundamental system often uses some portion of its output as input. In the normal sense of *system,* this is done deliberately so that output can serve somehow to control the input or the process. Such a system attribute is referred to as a "feedback loop" as shown below:

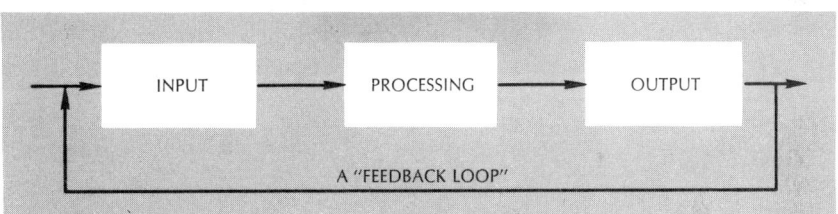

Going back to our example, if the released offender is convicted of another crime and is returned to a correctional facility, this serves as feedback to the CJS.

A simple criminal justice model becomes a larger illustration of this input-processing-output sequence:

The normal input to the criminal justice system is by means of law enforcement—shown here as "Police Service." The central process of this system is adjudication, shown as "Court Process." The third part, which creates the output by making people suitable to leave the system, is the "Corrections Process." Each of these, of course, has a number of major functional components, which interrelate essentially as shown in the next diagram. The circle in the diagram represents society. Its basic elements—potential inputs for the CJS system—are people. These are the small circles inside the large circle. Some of the small circles contain an x. These represent people with certain sets of characteristics who, presumably, are attracted to the system. The figure on the inside cover of this text combines and expands the above diagrams into a comprehensive view of the CJS.

Given these primary concepts, one may then attempt to understand the CJS. People, the system's basic elements, may be considered as part of a county or city. Most cities are within, or considered a part of, a county. Further, as the most fundamental element of the criminal justice system, the county contains all facets of the system—police, courts, and corrections. The county usually has major responsibilities under the state constitution for adjudication, public defense, and incarceration upon adjudication.

Keep in mind, however, that police, courts, and corrections exist also at the state and federal levels of government. What we are indicating at this point is that the majority of the CJS activities occur at the local (city and county) level of government.

A "TYPICAL" CRIME IN A TYPICAL LOCAL GOVERNMENT SETTING

What activates the criminal justice system? That is, what is it that sets the process into motion? Regardless of the level of government, it is a criminal offense (or what is presumed to be an offense) that energizes the CJS. Normally it starts with

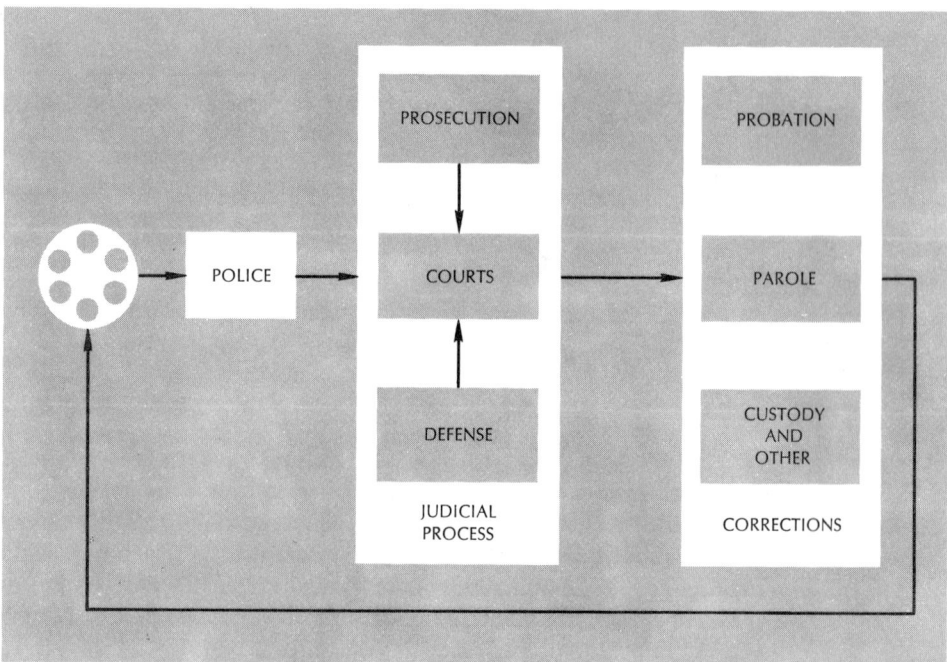

the police for they are the most frequent point of entry or contact. Depending on the decisions made at this point, the other two subsystems may or may not be put in gear. Keep in mind that police (and, to a lesser extent, the courts and corrections) often provide *noncriminal* services (e.g., family dispute intervention, missing persons searches, and traffic control).

Although there are many variations, let us hypothetically imagine that a burglary takes place within a city and the police department is called. To begin with, the police conduct an investigation and make a report. If identifiable property is involved, the investigating officer may, at his discretion, send out a teletype to likely adjacent areas and may notify the State Bureau of Criminal Identification and Investigation and the FBI's National Crime Information Center. Evidence is gathered that the suspect lives not in the city but in the county. A city policeman goes to the county sheriff and the two proceed together in the matter. They interrogate the suspect and secure a search warrant and a warrant for arrest from the municipal court. The suspect is then arrested and informed of his constitutional rights. The stolen property is located and inventoried. Property and suspect are taken to the city or county jail. The suspect is booked; if he does not make bail, he is placed in a cell. The property is also booked. Next, city and/or county officers interrogate the suspect who, in this case, makes a confession that may be recorded on color film and recording tape. As soon as the court convenes, the suspect is arraigned. Once arraigned, he is moved from the city jail to the county jail, where he will stay until he comes to trial or makes bail. The suspect is then indicted at a preliminary hearing held by a lower court. The next step is a superior court hearing where he makes his plea—in this event, guilty. A probation officer makes a recommendation based on several factors, including the fact that this defendant has been involved in similar incidents in the past. The judge then sentences the defendant to a stay in a state prison or county correctional facility. The offender enters the facility, is classified into some institutional program of work, study, and perhaps treatment, and begins his stated term. He remains until his term is up, or until he has been granted parole, then reenters the community. If on parole he will remain under some form of surveillance until the term of parole is ended. Meanwhile, if he violates his parole he is subject to revocation and return to prison. Otherwise, he enters society without further obligation.

Goals and Subgoals

The criminal justice system exists because society has in general decided that it is important to enforce the standards of human conduct so necessary to protecting individuals, their property, and the community. It seeks to fulfill its goals of protection and *service* through enforcement and assistance by reducing the risk and fear of crime; and apprehending, prosecuting, convicting, and sentencing those individuals who violate the rules and laws as promulgated by our society. The CJS may punish the offender for his violation by removing him from society and simultaneously may try to dissuade him through rehabilitation from repeating asocial acts. Both steps seek to deter people from committing criminal offenses. The first serves as a warning to other potential offenders—"If you commit the same or other criminal act, look at what may happen to you." The second may help the jailed person to realize that adhering to societal norms and laws is preferable to the loss of his freedom.

The subgoals are spread among the three subsystems. The police are responsible for controlling crime and maintaining order. The courts are responsible for judging the suspected offender by determining innocence or guilt. (It should be noted that the prosecution and defense are an integral part of this subsystem.) Finally, the goal of the corrections subsystem is institutionalizing and/or monitoring the activities of the offender and rehabilitating him to full and useful participation in society.

THE CHALLENGE, RISK, AND FEAR OF CRIME

The federal, state, and local governments in cooperation with many citizen groups have recently mounted the most comprehensive and vigorous attack on crime in the history of the country. Expanding and improving existing programs, adding new ones, and increasing federal support of state and local law enforcement efforts are concrete steps now being taken to support this attack. While crime continues to be *a local problem* primarily requiring *local solutions*, the federal government is becoming more directly involved in addressing the causes of crime and in enforcement against crime. Let us now examine the dangers and impact of crime on our society.

Crime and the *fear* of crime are causing major changes in the life styles of many of us. As a result, the strength and quality of life in our population centers is deteriorating. Stimulated by the reports of persistently growing crime rates and the fear that we may become a part of those crime statistics, we tend to move to the relative security of the suburbs and express a reluctance to return to the city to shop or to dine or to find entertainment. This exodus to the suburbs, in turn, undermines the tax base of the core cities, hence making it more difficult to furnish the services necessary to break the terrible cycle of poverty and despair that nurtures urban and suburban crime. For those of us left behind, there is the omnipresence of crime and criminals.

The Challenge

Crime is not a recent factor in American life. Administrators, politicians, scholars, and commissions have over a long period of time documented the growth and complexity of the crime problem in the United States—its causes, its costs (now estimated at over $90 billion a year), and its destructive effects on society. They have recognized the likelihood of damage to a person's property and well-being, and people's fear of unprovoked, unpredictable violence. Clearly the crime about which the nation is perturbed, the kind of crime that is accelerating, is crime against people and property; and it is often attended by violence—robberies, larcenies, assaults, and thefts of all kinds. This is not to say that Americans are indifferent to other types of criminal offenses. There is, and should be, concern over such white-collar crimes as tax fraud or price fixing, the corruption of public officials, such victimless crimes as gambling or prostitution, and the lawlessness of collective violence. (See Figure 1–1.) However, we are, it appears, most alarmed about, and feel immediately threatened by, crimes against person and property—crimes that you and I fear we might fall victim to.

The crime rate continues to climb, although there are a few bright spots we

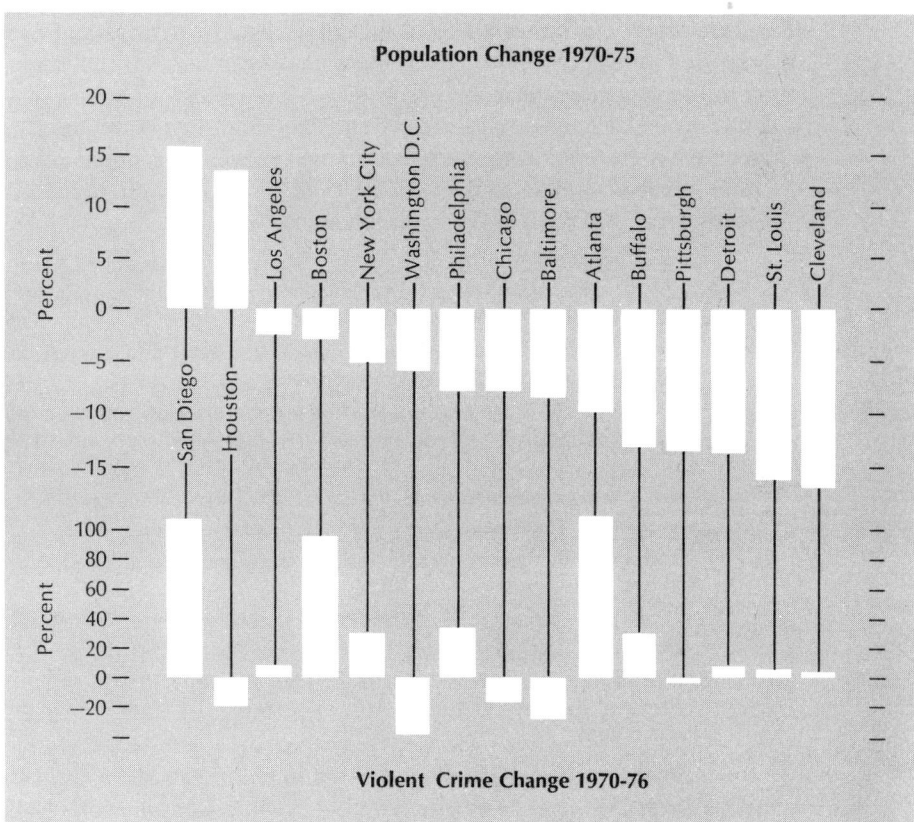

FIGURE 1–1   The ailing cities among these fifteen all lost both population and private jobs between 1970 and 1975. In New York, jobs disappeared at more than twice the rate of population decline; in Philadelphia the ratio was about 1.5 to 1. In ten of the fifteen cities, violent crime was higher during the first nine months of 1976 than for the comparable period of 1970, though the trend was down last year.

Source: "The High Cost of Cities," *Fortune*, March 1977, p. 198.

can point to where it has not increased as rapidly as in the past, or where a brief and unexplained dip has occurred. However, we must remind ourselves that crime statistics are reported rates only. For a number of reasons, we often bear the impact of crime in private.

The Risk and Threat of Crime

There are currently two methods of measuring national crime rates: the Uniform Crime Report (UCR), compiled annually by the FBI, and the National Victimization Survey, developed by LEAA. The UCR has a fundamental limitation of being based on reports from police departments. Thus it enumerates only those crimes known to the police. Victimization surveys, made since 1966 in various cities, report that at least half of all crimes against persons and property are not reported to the police. Moreover, there have been findings that some local law enforcement agencies have not recorded fully the extent of crimes that are reported by citizens, or have not accurately classified and defined reported offenses. Consequently, the victimization survey is now believed by some practitioners to give a more precise estimate of the volume, type, and cost of crime than the UCR. For example, a 1976 LEAA victimization survey revealed:

> Crimes measured by the surveys resulted in an estimated 37.7 million victimizations of persons, households, and businesses across the nation in 1973, including both completed and attempted offenses.
>
> The less serious type of offenses, namely personal and household larcenies, accounted for some three-fifths of the total.
>
> Rape, robbery of persons and businesses, and assault—offenses that involve personal confrontation and violence or its threat—made up some 15 percent of the crimes.
>
> With a victimization rate of 204 per 1,000 establishments, burglary of business places posed the greatest threat among targets at risk.
>
> The 5.5 million violent personal crimes translated to a rate of 34 per 1,000 persons age twelve and over.
>
> Among the relevant crimes, the least frequent was rape, for which women had a rate of 2 per 1,000.
>
> The less serious (or costly) forms of personal robbery and assault, as well as of household burglary and larceny, outnumbered the more serious forms of each of these crimes.

The fear of crime is now producing in many American cities an epidemic of silent terror. At this time no emotional or economic barometer is totally capable of measuring the fear of crime—but, one merely has to observe the rapid exodus from the cities, the strangling of businesses, and the mistrust between people to realize that, regardless of the lack of a precise method to measure it, it is present! In conclusion, then, crime is with us; it has us frightened, and we seem more interested than ever before in mounting a counterattack. Significantly, the key feature of the counterattack includes an effective criminal justice system.

Crime and Criminal Behavior

Crime has proliferated because it is the most (in some instances *only*) rewarding way of life available to those involved. While the problem is clearly evident—crime and more crime—we remain puzzled and thus frustrated on two subjects: (1) What causes crime? and (2) How can we stop (reduce) it? Let us for a few minutes think about some of the more plausible reasons for crime flourishing in our society.

To begin with, is it not a paradox that crime has risen the fastest in this country at a time when prosperity is likewise on the increase? In other words affluence is not reducing crime—or welfare, or drug abuse, or youth unemployment, or social unrest. Accusatory fingers are being pointed in every direction. Within the criminal justice system, for one example, the three components are at times highly critical of one another, arguing over who ought to receive the major share of the blame for spiraling crime rates in the midst of improving economic and social conditions. Out of such arguments it becomes apparent that three key factors were missing from many of the various programs designed to curtail crime: (1) a sense of community, (2) a sound understanding of human nature, and (3) reasonable expectations.

The first, a sense of community—a sharing of cultural and social values—is in open and direct conflict with crime. They are hostile forces in that one impedes if not bars the other. Crime—especially predatory crime—hampers the formation and maintenance of a community. One effect of crime is to cause us to act independently. Present-day crime is an internal threat that attacks certain standards (such as wealth, education, and fairness) and life styles (where one shops, recreates, and participates). It disrupts both formal and informal ties. The mutual enemy is, therefore, not an external one which would generate group solidarity. On the contrary, the culprit is felt to be nearby, internal, and hence capable of easily injuring the community's self-protection mechanisms. However, despite people's fears, a feeling and *acting* of neighborhood can occur with time and acculturation. To this end community "representation," "participation," and "accountability" have recently been assigned high-level priority by both citizenry and politicians. Growing common understanding and agreed-upon standards and values are beginning to forge new communities and strengthen existing ones. It is from the sense of belonging to such a community that we are able to take one step toward the restraint of criminal behavior.

The second factor, our conception of "man" or human nature, varies according to who is doing the intellectualizing. Psychologists, sociologists, political scientists, psychiatrists, criminologists, and public opinion have differing perspectives on human values, needs, attitudes, and interests. Without really knowing what they are we have valiantly searched for programs that will erase the "root causes of crime." Recently, however, our focus has shifted from the elusive roots to the criminal himself, and the ways he can be deterred from crime. People steal because the *benefits* are seen by some to exceed the costs or *risks* of stealing as compared to the benefits of working. Therefore, the risk of detection, apprehension, and penalty (cost) must be shown to be greater than the anticipated proceeds or benefits. It is not primarily the harshness of justice that deters but, more important, the certainty that it will prevail.

This brings us to the third point—our expectations of the criminal justice system. Unfortunately, society has overestimated its capacity for dealing with crime. Making the CJS perfect or getting it to operate the way we think it ought to is an ongoing and difficult task. Our expectations of this system have lacked moderation. No simple medicine is available to cure its ills. Nonetheless, the majority of us envision our CJS as being 100 percent healthy and effective. We are deluded and thus frequently disappointed. Our false expectations, in turn, are expressed as frustration, if not criticism (e.g., "Good grief we've added more police, improved the courts, and built more correctional institutions but crime is still with us.") For this reason it is important to keep in mind that our CJS is a relatively new institution and deserving of more patience than we have expressed toward it. In summary, community participation *linked* to a more accurate understanding of what drives us individually and as a group of people *linked* to an ever-maturing CJS will create an above-average chance (not promise) of less crime in the years to come.

Legal Parameters

Our Founding Fathers laid a cornerstone of justice that has given rise to a structure of exacting legal rules and procedures. While overtly straightforward, in practice we find that the prime instrument for delivering justice depends heavily on discretionary powers. The reality of judicial discretion fails to mesh with the more rigid precepts. As a consequence, our courts are plagued with uncertainty over criminal and civil statutes, adjudicative procedures, and sentencing practices. Moreover, while the court's main purpose is to decide on the guilt or innocence of the accused, in reality it devotes equal if not more time to the question of the sentence!

Our English ties in connection with our own unique democratic-jurist values produced two types of law, civil and criminal. Civil law deals with one *individual* seeking redress against another for some wrongful act or injury (e.g., a traffic accident), while criminal law centers on wrongful acts or injuries (e.g., causing a traffic accident while under the influence of alcohol) wherein the *state* serves as the victim or public agent. In this instance the redress involves punishment and/or rehabilitation. Typically criminal law and sanctions are (1) more punitive, (2) more difficult to impose because the burden of proof is greater, and (3) substantive in nature.

Let us explore the meaning of "substantive criminal law." First, mere thought without a guilty act is insufficient for establishing criminal liability. Second, a crime requires an intent to harm a victim, or behavior so wrong as to imply a desire to inflict harm (e.g., property theft, physical assault, arson, extortion, bribery, and so on). Third, crimes are assigned to one of two categories depending on their gravity: felonies and misdemeanors. The former carry a more severe penalty—generally one year or more under state supervision and perhaps an attached fine. The latter are punishable by fine only (as in the case of traffic citations) and/or county/city supervision for a year or less. The offender's state of mind has a strong influence on deciding how serious the crime is as well as the type of penalty. To illustrate, if a person should commit a homicide on another, the answer to the question, "Did he intend to kill the individual or was it by accident?" distinguishes between the crimes of murder and manslaughter. Fourth, there are principles of defense that must be followed. Mistake of fact ("I honestly thought the property was mine and therefore I took it with me"), if proven, can remove criminal intent. Further, if a person is forced (psychologically or physically) to commit a crime, he is not held blameworthy. Self-defense, once established as justifiable and reasonable, can remove guilt. Youthful age and insanity are often used as defenses by those charged with crime.

Finally, the use or abuse of criminal procedures will determine whether or not there is fair and efficient administration of justice. Basically, criminal procedures are standards for ensuring us of our "due process" rights once within adjudicative process. Significantly, in 1945 this nation's Supreme Court formalized a set of Federal Criminal Procedure rules. Many states have adopted these rules and thus there is considerable uniformity among them. Since criminal procedure rules are essentially derived from the U.S. Constitution, let us look at some of our constitutional rights as a defendant. Our due process rights include: (1) the right to remain silent, (2) the right to a speedy arraignment, (3) the right to counsel (and free counsel if indigent), (4) the right to receive notice of charges, (5) the right to bail, (6) the right to plead guilty or innocent, (7) the right to a speedy public trial, (8) the right to present and cross-examine witnesses, (9) the right to an impartial judge and jury, (10) the right to be free from arbitrary and capricious decisions, and (11) the right to be free from cruel and unusual punishment.

A prominent and perplexing issue in substantive criminal law today is that of "plea-bargaining." This is a process whereby criminal convictions are resolved *before* reaching the trial stage through a voluntary plea of guilty on the part of the defendant. The defendant normally receives a lower charge (e.g., robbery reduced to grand theft), and a reduced sentence. The *majority* of the criminal cases include a plea that has been negotiated between the prosecution and defense attorneys and agreed to by the accused. More will be said about this practice later on in the text.

THE COST OF CRIME REDUCTION

The *commission of crime,* the *reduction of crime,* the *cost of reducing crime,* and the *cost of processing criminals* center primarily at the local government level. However, there are major federal and state efforts to assist local authorities both directly and indirectly in coping with the adverse impacts of crime. Direct efforts include programs and agencies such as the Federal Bureau of Investigation, the Drug Enforcement Assistance Administration, state criminal investigation units, criminal justice information systems, and the like. Indirect efforts include the infusion of funds to support state and local criminal justice planning, operational programs, and research projects. In recent years federal and state governments have vastly expanded their commitment to reducing crime and processing criminals by direct intervention—and to sharing in its cost at the local level. The remainder of this section examines the dollar figures that support this contention.

To start with, federal outlays for crime reduction *more than doubled* between the years of 1968 and 1971. By the end of fiscal year (FY) 1972, the amount spent on crime reduction programs had more than tripled, reflecting the extent of the many and diverse crime reduction programs initiated and enlarged under the auspices of the federal government.

A 1976 survey of public "Expenditure and Employment Data for the Criminal Justice System (1978)" in the United States showed that direct expenditure in fiscal year 1976 amounted to $19,681 million—an increase of $2432 million (14.1 percent) over fiscal year 1975. Increases in direct expenditure occurred at all levels of government with the state governments showing a 12.8 percent increase over 1975, followed closely by the federal government (up 12.0 percent) and local governments (up 15.1 percent).

As shown in Table 1-1, fiscal 1976 continued the upward trend established over the period 1971-76 in which criminal justice expenditure by all levels of government in the United States increased by 87.1 percent! During that six-year period, the federal government increased its criminal justice direct expenditure by 101.6 percent, state governments by 94.1 percent, and local governments by 81.6 percent.

In October 1975 there were 1,050,503 criminal justice employees on a full-time equivalent basis. This was 39,298 more employees than there were in October 1974, an increase of 3.9 percent. State governments' criminal justice employment increased by 4.2 percent, followed by local governments (up 4.0 percent), and the federal government (up 2.5 percent). However, the rate of growth from 1974 to 1975 was the lowest in recent years as seen in Table 1-2.

During the five-year period 1971-75 there was a 21.9 percent increase in full-time equivalent criminal justice employment in the United States. This cumulative increase was shared by all levels of government with the state governments experiencing an increase of 27.9 percent, the federal government an increase of 24.0 percent, and local governments an increase of 19.5 percent.

As in the past, local governments accounted for more expenditure and employment in the criminal justice field than the federal and state governments combined (see Tables 1-3 and 1-4). Of the nation's $17,249 million direct expenditure for criminal justice purposes in 1975, $10,449 million (60.6 percent) was expended by local governments. In addition, 691,159 full-time equivalent employees (65.8 percent) were working in local criminal justice activities. Reflecting the fact that law enforcement is essentially a local government responsibility, $6,813

TABLE 1-1 Total criminal justice direct expenditure and percent change by level of government, fiscal years 1971-1976

Level of government	Amount (millions of dollars)						Percent increase or decrease (−)				
	1971	1972	1973	1974	1975	1976	1971 to 1972	1972 to 1973	1973 to 1974	1974 to 1975	1975 to 1976	1971 to 1976
Total	10,517	11,732	13,007	14,851	17,249	19,681	11.6	10.9	14.2	16.1	14.1	87.1
Federal	¹1,215	1,502	1,651	1,859	2,188	2,450	¹23.6	9.9	12.6	17.7	12.0	¹101.6
State	2,681	2,948	3,304	3,900	4,612	5,204	10.0	12.1	18.0	18.3	12.8	94.1
Local	6,621	7,281	8,052	9,092	10,449	12,027	10.0	10.6	12.9	14.9	15.1	81.6

Note: Detail may not add to total due to rounding.

¹The Federal expenditure amount shown for 1971 does not include data for the Office of Building Security Services of the Federal Reserve System; the Judicial, Prevention and Enforcement Services Division of the Bureau of Indian Affairs; or the Center for Studies of Crime and Delinquency at the National Institute of Mental Health, as these agencies were not included in the 1971 survey.

TABLE 1-2 Total full-time equivalent criminal justice employees and percent change, by level of government, October 1971–October 1976

Level of government	Number of employees					
	October 1971	October 1972	October 1973	October 1974	October 1975	October 1976
Total	861,776	898,305	945,309	1,011,205	1,050,503	1,079,892
Federal	¹77,523	85,222	87,139	93,755	96,136	99,553
State	205,859	216,603	232,299	252,588	263,208	272,488
Local	578,394	596,480	625,871	664,862	691,159	707,851

Level of government	Percent increase or decrease (−)					
	October 1971 to October 1972	October 1972 to October 1973	October 1973 to October 1974	October 1974 to October 1975	October 1975 to October 1976	October 1971 to October 1976
Total	4.2	5.2	7.0	3.9	2.8	25.3
Federal	¹9.9	2.2	7.6	2.5	3.6	¹28.4
State	5.2	7.2	8.7	4.2	3.5	32.4
Local	3.1	4.9	6.2	4.0	2.4	22.4

¹The Federal employment figure shown for October 1971 does not include employees of the Office of Building Security Services of the Federal Reserve System; the Judicial, Prevention and Enforcement Services Division of the Bureau of Indian Affairs; or the Center for Studies of Crime and Delinquency at the National Institute of Mental Health, as these agencies were not canvassed in the 1971 survey.

million (65.2 percent) of local government direct expenditures and 463,404 (67.0 percent) of their full-time equivalent employment was for police protection activities.

State governments spent 43.5 percent of their $4,612 million direct expenditure in the corrections field. In addition, close to half (48.2 percent) of the 263,208 full-time equivalent criminal justice employees of state governments were engaged in correctional activities. Figure 1–2 reports on the large urban city governments per capita expenditures for fiscal 1975–76. It revealed that the police costs are, in nearly every case, the highest single expense.

CRIME REDUCTION: THE TRANSCENDENT CRIMINAL JUSTICE SYSTEM GOAL

Our existing social problems and the costs associated with them necessitate a two-pronged response. First, we should approach the crime problem with realistic optimism—realistic in understanding the gravity of the problem and the level of effort required to successfully combat it, and optimism regarding our ability to do so. Second, we should set definitive and attainable goals—definitive to the extent that the goals aim our resources toward the desired ends; and attainable in that, while challenging, they are capable of being accomplished within an established time-frame. We are asserting, therefore, that our nation can reduce, within reasonable limits, the social and economic damage caused by all forms of crime. At the same time, particular attention must be focussed on reducing those crimes considered most threatening to individual citizens—the violent crimes of homicide (murder and nonnegligent manslaughter), forcible rape, robbery, and aggravated assault, and the property crime of burglary. We are not suggesting that other crimes such as forgery, bribery, extortion and drug trafficking be ignored. On the contrary, they certainly pose a threat, although not as much of a physical threat as those cited above. We are recommending, however, that the so-called crimes potentially of high personal physical risk be given greater priority. Let us now move on and address the question of "Why?"

Why These Five Crimes?

The five crimes cited above are particularly grave when perpetrated by one person on another. In such instances, an extra dimension is present—fear. Thus, when these crimes are committed, they can be termed as "high-fear" crimes.

The National Advisory Commission on Criminal Justice Standards and Goals (1973) proposed a two-level attack on these five crimes. First, the rate of "high-fear" (stranger-related) crimes should be cut in half by 1983. Second, regardless of whether the crime is committed by a relative, acquaintance, or stranger, the crime rates should be cut by 1983 as follows:

>   Homicide (murder and nonnegligent manslaughter)—at least 25 percent
>   Forcible rape—at least 25 percent
>   Aggravated assault—at least 25 percent
>   Robbery—at least 50 percent
>   Burglary—at least 50 percent

The Commission admitted that the selection of these crimes and percentages of reduction will stimulate the doubts of skeptics, but they submit that their proposal is reasonable. They define what we can hope for, not necessarily what we can expect.

Why Establish Quantitative Goals?

The use of numerical values gives a dimension to goal-setting that has been lacking in prior recommendations for reducing crime. Previously, government reports and political leaders have engaged in broad concepts such as: Crime should be controlled and reduced; administration of the criminal justice system should be improved; public expenditures on the system should be increased; we should re-

TABLE 1-3 Percent distribution of expenditure for the criminal justice system, by level of government, fiscal year 1976

Activity[1]	Amount (in thousands of dollars)				Percent distribution			
	All governments[1]	Federal Government[2]	State governments	Local governments[1]		Federal Government[2]	State governments	Local governments[1]
Total criminal justice system[3]	19,681,409	3,322,073	5,986,650	12,068,308		(X)	(X)	(X)
Direct expenditure	19,681,409	2,450,229	5,204,226	12,026,954		12.5	26.4	61.1
Intergovernmental expenditure	([3])	871,844	782,424	133,855		(X)	(X)	(X)
Police protection[3]	11,028,244	1,615,714	1,789,471	7,723,588		(X)	(X)	(X)
Direct expenditure	11,028,244	1,611,640	1,696,460	7,720,144		14.6	15.4	70.0
Intergovernmental expenditure	([3])	4,074	93,011	59,390		(X)	(X)	(X)
Judicial[3]	2,428,472	219,445	663,068	1,633,645		(X)	(X)	(X)
Direct expenditure	2,428,472	219,445	585,151	1,623,876		9.0	24.1	66.9
Intergovernmental expenditure	([3])	-	77,917	18,123		(X)	(X)	(X)
Legal services and prosecution[3]	1,047,929	149,402	253,591	653,502		(X)	(X)	(X)
Direct expenditure	1,047,929	149,402	247,723	650,804		14.3	23.6	62.1
Intergovernmental expenditure	([3])	-	5,868	3,142		(X)	(X)	(X)

Public defense[3]	331,102	103,718	78,622	157,364	(X)	(X)	(X)	(X)	(X)
Direct expenditure	331,102	103,718	70,139	157,245	31.3	21.2	47.5		
Intergovernmental expenditure	([3])	-	8,483	1,279	(X)	(X)	(X)		
Corrections[3]	4,385,512	285,973	2,589,609	1,678,879	(X)	(X)	(X)		
Direct expenditure	4,385,512	256,352	2,474,783	1,654,377	5.9	56.4	37.7		
Intergovernmental expenditure	([3])	29,621	114,826	49,547	(X)	(X)	(X)		
Other criminal justice[3]	460,150	947,821	612,289	221,329	(X)	(X)	(X)		
Direct expenditure	460,150	109,672	129,970	220,508	23.8	28.3	47.9		
Intergovernmental expenditure	([3])	838,149	482,319	2,374	(X)	(X)	(X)		

- Represents zero or rounds to zero.
X Not applicable.
[1] Local governments data are estimates subject to sampling variation; see text for data limitations
[2] Federal Government data is for the fiscal period beginning July 1, 1975 and ending June 30, 1976. Data for the transition quarter from July 1, 1976 to September 30, 1976 are displayed separately.
[3] The total line for each sector, and for the total Criminal Justice System, excludes duplicative intergovernmental expenditure amounts. This was done to avoid the artificial inflation which would result if an intergovernmental expenditure amount for one government is tabulated and then counted again when the recipient government (s) ultimately expend (s) that amount. The intergovernmental expenditure lines are not totaled for the same reason.

TABLE 1-4 Percent distribution of employment and payrolls for the criminal justice system, by level of government, October 1976

Activity	Amount (in thousands of dollars)				Percent distribution			
	All governments[1]	Federal Government	State governments	Local governments[1]	Federal Government	State governments	Local governments[1]
Total criminal justice system:							
Total employees	1,148,262	100,771	283,049	764,442	8.8	24.6	66.6
Full-time employees	1,049,750	99,016	267,685	683,049	9.4	25.5	65.1
Full-time equivalent employees	1,079,892	99,553	272,488	707,851	9.2	25.2	65.5
October payroll	1,277,120	159,726	311,636	805,719	12.5	24.4	63.1
Police protection:							
Total employees	670,724	72,301	97,887	500,536	10.8	14.6	74.6
Full-time employees	617,132	71,207	89,175	456,750	11.5	14.4	74.0
Full-time equivalent employees	628,347	71,421	90,884	466,042	11.4	14.5	74.1
October payroll	772,867	113,497	105,620	553,750	14.7	13.7	71.6
Judicial:							
Total employees	151,074	7,578	28,535	114,998	5.0	18.9	76.1
Full-time employees	127,736	7,473	25,629	94,667	5.9	20.1	74.1
Full-time equivalent employees	137,451	7,531	27,516	102,442	5.5	20.0	74.5
October payroll	154,466	13,733	42,786	97,948	8.9	27.7	63.4
Legal services and prosecution:							
Total employees	64,860	7,008	13,665	43,304	10.8	21.1	68.1
Full-time employees	54,473	6,821	12,984	34,668	12.5	23.8	63.6
Full-time equivalent employees	59,306	6,928	13,227	39,153	11.7	22.3	66.0
October payroll	77,140	12,427	17,623	47,050	16.1	22.8	61.0

Public defense:						
Total employees	7,623	219	2,912	4,492	2.9	38.2	58.9
Full-time employees	6,735	219	2,809	3,707	3.3	41.7	55.0
Full-time equivalent employees	7,255	219	2,843	4,193	3.0	39.2	57.8
October payroll	9,821	407	3,624	5,790	4.1	36.9	59.0
Corrections:						
Total employees	246,376	11,869	136,400	98,107	4.8	55.4	39.8
Full-time employees	235,625	11,634	133,520	90,471	4.9	56.7	38.4
Full-time equivalent employees	239,293	11,717	134,420	93,156	4.9	56.2	38.9
October payroll	252,890	16,938	137,928	98,024	6.7	54.5	38.8
Other criminal justice:						
Total employees	8,451	1,796	3,650	3,005	21.3	43.2	35.6
Full-time employees	8,049	1,662	3,568	2,819	20.6	44.3	35.0
Full-time equivalent employees	8,240	1,737	3,598	2,905	21.1	43.7	35.2
October payroll	9,935	2,724	4,054	3,157	27.4	40.8	31.8

[1]Local governments data are estimates subject to sampling variation.

Per Capita Municipal Spending (fiscal 1975)

Cities	Police	Fire	Sanitation (except sewerage)	Highways (except capital outlay)	Parks and Recreation	All Functions (except capital outlay)	Total Debt
Houston	$36.38	$27.47	$9.72	$5.55	$13.61	$155.30	$494.80
Atlanta	61.57	28.50	26.28	18.19	36.73	286.21	1,237.28
Pittsburgh	42.29	28.12	18.15	12.22	21.86	206.18	287.34
St. Louis	77.40	24.05	8.40	10.56	3.05	355.71	304.11
San Diego	34.08	18.17	8.81	9.12	40.16	186.48	188.01
Cleveland	62.08	36.13	18.06	17.62	11.75	301.49	596.68
Baltimore	79.09	39.77	39.55	29.96	30.11	822.94	643.64
Chicago	77.41	25.65	20.66	18.88	3.14	266.24	411.12
Los Angeles	74.21	30.19	13.23	16.35	18.02	246.74	837.31
Philadelphia	79.51	26.80	24.74	14.94	25.87	421.51	700.71
Detroit	88.47	30.23	20.28	13.10	24.88	369.95	550.42
Washington D.C.	135.36	40.33	33.86	30.53	30.07	1,709.78	1,570.63
Buffalo	56.43	42.58	16.49	10.20	20.12	604.48	710.85
Boston	104.99	55.96	19.83	14.31	30.01	912.77	846.11
New York City	73.42	30.06	29.93	14.48	19.80	1,330.44	1,934.64

FIGURE 1-2   Total costs of big-city government vary widely because counties, states, or independent districts often provide such expensive services as schools, hospitals, and welfare. New York City spends $378 per capita annually for welfare (and pays 25 percent of that out of its own empty pockets) while Baltimore spends only $156. Comparisons of costs for police, firemen, and the other items shown above are more meaningful because most localities meet these expenses entirely with their own revenues.

Source: "The High Cost of Cities," *Fortune*, March 1977, p. 198.

double our efforts to eliminate the causes of crime, such as poverty, discrimination, urban blight, and disease; planning should be improved; additional research should be undertaken; citizens should become more involved; and so forth. Regrettably, these broad statements do not easily translate into action. What, for example, does it mean to say that crime should be reduced? Which crimes? What is to be reduced—the rate, the actual number, the economic and social impact, or something else? How great a reduction is possible? How great a reduction is acceptable? How do state and local governments, criminal justice agencies, and citizens go about realizing these goals? And how is it possible to tell if a goal has been achieved?

These are not academic questions. They have real consequences in time, dollars, and lives. Goals are most helpful when they are measurable, when at the end of a specific period *actual achievements* can be compared with *desired achievements* and an assessment of the reasons for gaps can be made. For citizens, goals to reduce crime serve as a gauge for measuring the effectiveness of CJS operations and of other public service programs. For legislators, goals are guides to funding; for operating agencies, they provide a rationale for the allocation of personnel and equipment.

PRIORITY CRIMES CAUSE PRIORITY PROGRAMS

The five *high priority crimes* generate a need for *high priority programs* that are capable of reducing them. The National Advisory Commission on Criminal Justice Standards and Goals has proposed the following four priorities:

- Preventing juvenile delinquency
- Improving delivery of social services
- Reducing delays in the criminal justice process
- Securing more citizen participation in the criminal justice system

Before elaborating on each one of the four recommendations, we will briefly cover a process vital for their eventual implementation—program planning.

Program Planning

Planning is the identification of desired futures or goals, and the selection of approaches to their fulfillment. One of the enduring questions of this country, a subject of constant debate and endless analysis, is how a large system—a criminal justice system—can best plan, monitor, and direct operations spread over the three fundamentally different branches of government and throughout many separate jurisdictions. A number of commissions and research studies (cited and examined in later chapters) have proposed an answer in costly and elaborate management mechanisms and operating procedures. Through the use of central planning staff, intensified reporting procedures, and huge mounds of computer data, our CJS managers hope to gain more control and an improved interface among their disparate agencies. In other words, planning or more specifically *CJS planning* is being concentrated on as an instrument for better linking the three CJS subsystems.

A few years ago, phrases such as "CJS planning" or "crime-oriented planning" did not exist in the lexicon of CJS managers or public officials. In 1967, the President's Commission on Law Enforcement and the Administration of Justice recommended that statewide and city CJS planning units be established. The Commission's underlying concern for a CJS planning capability was that the various subsystems would eventually coordinate rather than conflict in their efforts to control and prevent crime.

This expressed hope for a CJS planning mechanism came to fruition in the Omnibus Crime Control and Safe Streets Act of 1968. The Safe Streets Act gave birth to the Law Enforcement Assistance Administration (LEAA) within the

United States Department of Justice. Essentially LEAA was appropriated funds for CJS planning and grants. In order to be eligible for federal dollars, each state had to create a *state* criminal justice *planning agency* (SPA). The SPAs, in turn, are required to generate an annual comprehensive plan for approval by LEAA. Once approved, the SPAs receive block grants (a lump sum) for funding various criminal justice projects. All fifty states have SPAs today as do also American Samoa, Guam, the District of Columbia, Puerto Rico and the Virgin Islands. Most of the SPAs have formed *regional* planning councils so as to more properly address local criminal justice needs. The SPAs and regional councils have appointed boards with CJS, public official, and citizen representation. Professional criminal justice planning staff are responsible for plan preparation and, when approved by the SPA or council, implementation and evaluation. Before leaving the subject of LEAA it is important to recognize that this agency performs many other criminal justice functions including the distribution of juvenile delinquency funds, research and impact evaluation studies, national reference service, student loans and grants, and civil rights monitoring.

Finally, in 1973 the National Advisory Commission on Criminal Justice Standards and Goals added still further support for CJS planning by recommending that the following tools be acquired: program budgeting, system-wide evaluation, project performance, and integrated computer-based criminal justice information systems. Much remains to be accomplished in the way of CJS planning. Nevertheless, important cornerstones have been carefully laid in order to construct the desired planning process. The requirement for multiyear state plans and comprehensive offender tracking information systems are but two examples.

Priority: Preventing Juvenile Delinquency

The highest attention should be given to preventing juvenile delinquency, to minimizing the involvement of young offenders in the juvenile and criminal justice system, and to reintegrating them into the community. By 1983 the rate of delinquency cases coming before the courts involving offenses that would be crimes if committed by adults should be cut to half the 1973 rate.

We have numerical evidence that street crime is primarily a young person's caper. More than half the persons arrested for violent crime in 1976 were under twenty-four years of age, with one-fifth being under eighteen. For burglary, over half of the 1976 arrests involved youths under eighteen. Moreover, there is statistical data showing that the majority of ordinary crimes against person and property is committed by young people who have had *previous* contact with the criminal justice system or juvenile justice system. Increased efforts must be made to intervene in this cycle of recidivism at the earliest possible point. One approach is to reduce the time involvement of the offender in the CJS. "Minimized involvement" is not a cute term for the coddling of criminals. It merely means that we should use the means of controlling and supervising the criminal offender that will best serve to remove him from the recidivism cycle and, at the same time, protect the community. Hard data purports that the further and the longer an offender penetrates into the criminal justice process, the more difficult it becomes to divert him from the CJS in the future.

We tend to learn from those closest to us. Regrettably, prisons and jails that throw together juveniles, first offenders, and hardened criminals have been found to be "schools of crime." Also, we tend to become what we are told or expect to be. The stigma of involvement with the CJS, even if only in the informal processes of juvenile justice, frequently separates persons from lawful society and can make further training or employment difficult.

The U.S. Department of Health, Education, and Welfare, which collects information on juvenile courts, estimates that about 40 percent of cases disposed of by courts, are cases of running away, truancy, and other offenses termed "status crimes" that would not be crimes if committed by an adult. As indicated, these are referred to as juvenile status offenses. The remaining 60-odd percent of cases estimated to be disposed of by juvenile or family courts are nonstatus crimes (or those that would be crimes if committed by adults). It is the rate of these cases on which we should concentrate.

Priority: Improving Delivery of Social Services

Public agencies should improve the delivery of all social services to citizens, particularly to those groups that contribute higher than average proportions of their numbers to crime statistics.

We are confronted with irrefutable proof that crime occurs with greater frequency where poverty, illiteracy, and unemployment exist, and where medical, recreational, and mental health resources are deficient. When unemployment rates among our youth in poverty areas of central cities are well above the norm, crime is omnipresent. It is impossible for us not to draw conclusions about the interdependency between jobs and crime. Does anyone doubt that the effective and responsive delivery of public services dealing with our individual economic well-being will contribute to a reduction in crime?

Undoubtedly, a meaningful and lasting improvement of social services to the degree necessary to abate crime will take years and not a few months. Building career education programs into elementary and secondary school curricula, for example, cannot be accomplished in the next two or three years; but we must start now if our nation is to attain desired benefits at the end of ten years or more. Likewise, our communities must accept and adjust to the diversity of drug abuse and alcohol problems, and the need for a variety of alternative treatment tactics. We must be willing to meet the costs of such treatment—not only because it will lessen crime, but also because effective treatment is fundamental to attacking an increasingly serious national health problem.

Priority: Reducing Delays in the Criminal Justice Process

Delays in the adjudication and disposition of cases must be greatly reduced and the period between arrest and trial must be reduced to the shortest possible time.

In recent years, backlogs and delays in our courts have been repeatedly exposed. Many courts in large cities and counties have professed delays of 500 to 1,000 days from arrest to trial and final disposition. Our legislatures, as well as judges, defense attorneys, and prosecutors, must assume some of the responsibility for this problem. Sluggishness in the criminal justice process corrodes law enforcement efforts and in turn creates a feeling of injustice in offender, victim, and citizen alike.

The harmful effects of judicial delays are significant. The number of defendants temporarily in jail and awaiting trial has reached dangerous proportions, and holding facilities are inadequate and overcrowded. Pretrial incarceration is costly to the individual, for it precludes his earning an income and, in fact, may cause him to lose his job. Extended incarceration caused by judicial delay is also costly to us as taxpayers, since pretrial detainees must be housed and supervised.

The pressures of heavy backlogs are linked to the controversial practice of *plea bargaining.* When confronted with an overwhelming caseload, we often find prosecutors seeking to avoid time-consuming trials by disposing of felony indictment (through negotiated guilty pleas) to less serious felonies or misdemeanors. Whether we view this situation from a rehabilitation, deterrence, or workload perspective, plea bargaining is a low visibility practice that can be gradually stopped if less burdensome court caseloads are achieved.

Priority: Increasing Citizen Participation

Citizens should participate in activities to control crime in their community, and criminal justice agencies should actively encourage citizen participation.

Out of necessity, the criminal justice system relies on citizen participation. The majority of crimes do not come to the attention of our police until they are reported by us. Without the active cooperation of citizen jurors and witnesses, our judicial process cannot operate. Further, institutional education and training programs will not be helpful to the offender if he cannot find employment in the community when he is released. Moreover, even our best-trained and equipped police agencies will continue to fail in combating crime if we do not take basic precautionary measures to protect ourselves by reducing our vulnerability to crime.

Our cooperation with our police has great potential, but is underdeveloped at the present. In 1970, 18 percent of the households in the United States adopted some form of home protection—special locks, lights, alarms, watchdogs, and/or weapons. Cannot our police agencies perform a useful service by actively disseminating its crime prevention knowledge to citizens? It is not necessary to "sell" self-protection to most of us, certainly not to those of us who have been victimized. Nevertheless, in many jurisdictions, there is an absence of outreach programs for crime prevention.

All of our agencies can do much in their operations to entice us to support their activities. This suggests, for example, that our police can process citizen complaints efficiently and courteously; that courts can minimize the time lost by jurors and witnesses; that corrections can operate its institutions to permit the community reasonable access to those incarcerated. These are minimums. Criminal justice agencies can do much more, if they earnestly attempt to: They can explain their role to ordinary citizens; and depict how we can participate in community crime prevention. But first our criminal justice agencies *must understand* and *respect us* and the communities they serve.

WHAT FOLLOWS. . .

This should be a meaningful section of the text since it is directed at you in your capacity as a present or future participant in the criminal justice system, whether as a practitioner or concerned citizen. Hopefully, by this early point in the book you have enhanced your interest in and developed a concern for a CJS that in fact deals in *justice* for all and is effectively interrelated as a total *system*. The CJS as it presently stands needs improvement and perhaps you are or will be in a position to assist it in perfecting its inputs, processing, and outputs.

Your participation within or assistance to the CJS can be internal or external. Internally, the CJS is in need of qualified and dedicated employees ranging from police officers to judges to corrections officers. Externally, the CJS is seeking the support and involvement of citizens in roles varying from reserve police officers to volunteer public defenders to volunteer case workers. If you are interested, your role would be challenging, exciting, and rewarding whether it was internal or external. Although commanding and demanding, we can assure you that the CJS would welcome your involvement.

SUGGESTED REFERENCES

AMERICAN BAR ASSOCIATION. *Standards Relating to the Urban Police Function,* Chicago: American Bar Association, 1973.

AMERICAN CRIMINAL LAW REVIEW. "A Symposium: Economic Crimes." *American Criminal Law Review,* Spring 1977, pp. 635–821.

BERS, MELVIN K. *The Penetration of Legitimate Business by Organized Crime—An Analysis.* Washington, D.C.: U.S. Government Printing Office, 1970.

FORST, MARTIN L. "To What Extent Should the Criminal Justice System Be A System." *Crime and Delinquency,* Vol. 23 (October 1977), pp. 403–16.

GERBER, RUDOLPH J. *Contemporary Issues in Criminal Justice.* Port Washington, N.J.: Kennikat Press, 1976.

GIBBONS, DON C., et al. *Criminal Justice Planning: An Introduction.* Englewood Cliffs, N.J.: Prentice-Hall, 1977.

GIBBONS, DON C., and BLAKE, GERALD F. "Perspectives in Criminology and Criminal Justice: The Implications for Higher Education Programs." *Criminal Justice Review,* Vol. 2 (Spring 1977), pp. 23–40.

MORRIS, NORVAL, and HAWKINS, GORDON. *Letter to the President on Crime Control.* Chicago: University of Chicago Press, 1977.

PARKER, DON B. *Crime By Computer.* New York: Scribner, 1976.

RADZINOWICZ, SIR LEON, and KING, JOAN. *The Growth of Crime: The International Experience.* New York: Basic Books, 1977.

────── "Concepts of Crime." *London Times Literary Supplement,* September 26, 1975.

RADZINOWICZ, SIR LEON, and WOLFGANG, MARVIN E. *Crime and Justice.* 2nd rev. ed. Vol. 1, *The Criminal in Society.* New York: Basic Books, 1977.

SCHUR, EDWIN M. *Crimes Without Victims: Deviant Behavior and Public Policy.* Englewood Cliffs, N.J.: Prentice-Hall, 1969.

SKOLER, DANIEL L. *Organizing the Non-System: Governmental Structuring of the Criminal Justice System.* Lexington, Mass.: Lexington Books, 1974.

TAYLOR, J.; WALTON, P.; and YOUNG, J., eds. *Critical Criminology.* London: Routledge and Kegan Paul, 1974.

WHITESIDE, THOMAS. "Annals of Crime" (Computers) in *The New Yorker,* August 22 and 29, 1977.

YATES, DOUGLAS. *The Ungovernable City.* Cambridge, Mass.: M.I.T. Press, 1977.

2

The Police Role

Overview
Our Police
Our Police in Action
Police Goals
History of the Police
Federal Response to Crime
Federal Policing
State Policing
Local Policing
Intergovernmental Coordination
Learning Exercises
Suggested References

OVERVIEW

The late 1960s gave rise to a nationwide effort to enhance the quantity and quality of our law enforcement services. A significantly expanded policing role for the federal and state governments is but one result of this commitment. In particular, one can observe an expanded purview in federal planning and grants, and statewide training, criminalistics, data processing, planning, specialized investigations (e.g., narcotics and organized crime), and crime prevention.

While the authority and import of federal and state programs are on the ascent, policing our nation continues to be primarily a local government responsibility. Police agencies ranging in size from a single part-time employee to thousands of full-time personnel constitute a loosely structured system of local policing. Many changes and advancements have recently occurred in city and county policing but perhaps the most meaningful is the expansion of the crime-fighting goal to encompass that of general government services. Other significant changes and encouraging improvements can be observed in the county sheriff agencies and private police organizations.

Sustained enhancements in efficiency and effectiveness are in the offing due to the recent promulgation of standards of achievement, productivity measures, and evaluation requirements. Random changes are now being subjected to the rigors of planned change and program evaluation.

OUR POLICE

When spoken or thought, the concept of a "police force" or "police officer" can conjure a varying set of emotions ranging from fear to relief. If one has committed a wrongful act, then the police usually present a threat. Alternatively, if one is in need of help, then the police typically are a welcomed sight. *Concern, change,* and *complexity* surround their existence and role in modern society. In part, our police are experiencing problems and frustration due to the ambiguity of their role. Also, in part, we have failed to recognize that our police are a fairly new societal invention. Most of our institutions (military, medicine, law, education, industry, etc.) have had hundreds of years to mature and achieve a sense of mission. The police, on the contrary, are a creature of English society in the second quarter of the nineteenth century. Hence, we find that their role is yet being tested and shaped.

If our attitudes and expectations regarding our police are inconsistent, we should not be alarmed or discouraged. In the short course of nearly fourteen decades we have witnessed our police system grow to an institution that now spans three levels of government (federal, state, and local). Moreover, we have seen our police form a closer working partnership with two other criminal justice components, courts and corrections. Shaping a role and set of functions out of this set of circumstances is clearly not simple. After all, our police have been assigned the responsibility for legitimately administering nonnegotiable coercive force in controlling and preventing crime and maintaining order. As a consequence of their newness and challenging demands made on them, we would propose that while on occasion our police are deserving of our criticism, they are likewise worthy of our compliments and respect.

OUR POLICE IN ACTION

We have repeatedly used the term "role" by which we mean "expected behavior." In order to concisely examine the police role, we draw upon a standard promulgated by the National Advisory Commission on Criminal Justice Standards and Goals (NAC).[1]

Standard 1.1

THE POLICE FUNCTION

Every police chief executive immediately should develop written policy, based on policies of the governing body that provides formal authority for the police function, and should set forth the objectives and priorities that will guide the agency's delivery of police services. Agency policy should articulate the role of the agency in the protection of constitutional guarantees, the enforcement of the law, and the provision of services necessary to reduce crime, to maintain public order, and to respond to the needs of the community.

    1. Every police chief executive should acknowledge that the basic purpose of the police is the maintenance of public order and the control of conduct legislatively defined as crime. The basic purpose may not limit the police role, but should be central to its full definition.

    2. Every police chief executive should identify those crimes on which police resources will be concentrated. In the allocation of resources, those crimes that are most serious, stimulate the greatest fear, and cause the greatest economic losses should be afforded the highest priority.

    3. Every police chief executive should recognize that some government services that are not essentially a police function are, under some circumstances, appropriately performed by the police. Such services include those provided in the interest of effective government or in response to established community needs. A chief executive:

        a. Should determine if the service to be provided has a relationship to the ob-

---

[1] National Advisory Commission on Criminal Justice Standards and Goals (NAC), *Police* (Washington, D.C.: U.S. Government Printing Office, 1973), pp. 12, 13, 17, 21, 22.

jectives established by the police agency. If not, the chief executive should resist that service becoming a duty of the agency;

    b. Should determine the budgetary cost of the service; and

    c. Should inform the public and its representatives of the projected effect that provision of the service by the police will have on the ability of the agency to continue the present level of enforcement services.

    d. If the service must be provided by the police agency, it should be placed in perspective with all other agency services and it should be considered when establishing priorities for the delivery of all police services.

    e. The service should be made a part of the agency's police role until such time as it is no longer necessary for the police agency to perform the service.

4. In connection with the preparation of their budgets, all police agencies should study and revise annually the objectives and priorities which have been established for the enforcement of laws and the delivery of services.

5. Every police agency should determine the scope and availability of other government services and public and private social services, and develop its ability to make effective referrals to those services.

The police role as described by the standard is commonly interpreted as one of crime control and order maintenance. However, we far too frequently ignore the obvious—our police provide a wide variety of services, *most* of which are noncriminal or general government in nature. Traffic direction, lost children services, emergency health care, referral services, and general citizen information are cases in point. Indeed, the majority of police work involves the latter type of activities. Only 10 to 15 percent of what a police officer does pertains to crime reduction. Yet, crime control remains the more pivotal component of the role.

> Whenever crime is discussed, the role of the police is conspicuously identified. Thoughtful students of police administration, as well as most observers of the crime phenomenon who view the problem systematically, realize that the police have been assigned a disproportionate amount of responsibility for both the present level of crime and the efforts to cope with it in the future. Nevertheless, the police role is obviously significant in considering short-range solutions to the crime problem.[2]

From the police role has been forged a set of police goals. We now turn to a description of these goals.

POLICE GOALS

Our local police agencies, although differing in many aspects, have become highly uniform in what they would like to achieve, or in their *goals*. The majority of police managers would concur that they have three main goals (1) to enforce the law, (2) to maintain order, and (3) to provide police service. The goals of any organization serve a number of purposes. The most fundamental of all purposes is that of

---

[2] O. W. Wilson and Roy McLaren, *Police Administration,* 4th ed. (New York: McGraw-Hill, 1977), p. 14.

justifying the existence of the organization. In other words, the goal of "law enforcement" provides, in part, the reason for developing and sustaining an organization that is designed to pursue that particular goal. As mentioned, organizational goals have more than a single purpose. Goals provide:

- A desired future state of affairs
- Guidelines for activity
- Standards for ascertaining effectiveness
- Source of legitimacy (reason for existence)

Because a *goal* is a condition that we seek, once a goal is accomplished, an organization could lose its reason for existing. Consequently, as goals are approached, often we see organizations either changing or adding new goals in order to survive.

Multiple Goals

A common characteristic of modern organizations is that they pursue more than a single goal. Certainly, the police are a case in point. "To protect and serve," maintain order, control crime, and so on serve as illustrations of police goals. On one hand, organizations that serve more than one goal do so more effectively than single-purpose organizations. The reasons are that serving one goal frequently increases achievement of another goal (the "apprehension of offenders" tends to "repress criminal activity") and there is improved occupational appeal because the job has more variety (a policeman could be a patrol-generalist, traffic specialist, juvenile officer specialist, and so forth). On the other hand, having more than one goal to achieve presents an opportunity for goal conflict. (For example, the "repression of criminal activity" can conflict with "building community support" in that the frequent stopping and questioning of people by the police often upsets the community.)

The Goals of the Police

A local law enforcement organization exists to deal, for the most part, with the actions and behavior of people. Early in their history, the police focused on those actions and behavior that were criminal in nature. Obviously, the police organization has evolved into much more than a law enforcement agency of local government. Thus, the police, in the course of their institutional growth and development, have added new goals and *modified* the older or traditional goals. In general, to the earlier goal of law enforcement has been added that of order maintenance. Moreover, concurrent with the additions and modifications of goals, lately we see goal statements being enlarged to include socially desirable ways of attaining them. (See Table 2–1.)

TABLE 2-1 Police Goals

Existing Police Goals	Modern (or Emerging) Police Goals
Prevention of criminality	Protect life and property
Repression of crime	Prevention of crime
Apprehension of offenders	Enforce laws
Recovery of stolen property	Detect, apprehend, and detail suspected offenders
Regulation of noncriminal conduct	Provide equitable administration of the law
	Promote respect for law and the criminal justice system
	Provide emergency services
	Reduce the opportunity to commit crime
	Maintain social order
	Protect individual freedom and privacy
	Provide personal and community services of a noncriminal and nonemergency nature

Source: This list of existing goals is drawn from a research effort entitled Project STAR. See *Project STAR Survey of Role Perceptions for Operational Criminal Justice Personnel: Data Summary* (Sacramento, Calif.: American Justice Institute, 1972), p. 44. Project STAR (Systems and Training Analysis of the Requirements for Criminal Justice Personnel) was a three-year, $2.3-million effort primarily by the LEAA and involving the states of California, Michigan, New Jersey, and Texas. The project, which began May 1, 1971, involved a comprehensive research effort to define roles, functions, and objectives as well as knowledge and skill requirements for operational criminal justice personnel. Based upon this research, educational curriculum recommendations and training packages were developed.

Operational criminal justice positions included in the project's scope are police officer, prosecuting attorney, defense attorney, judge, probation officer, parole officer, and correctional officer. The significant roles that these positions play are being identified through analysis of the data collected in role perception surveys of operational personnel and the public; position papers on anticipated future roles; a paper on past, present, and future American social trends as they related to the requirements placed on the criminal justice system; on observations of these operational positions in a work environment; and on discussions with criminal justice system representatives and clients in participating states.

From all this, you should conclude that goals are constantly changing. And, with the accelerating rate of change in modern society, we find that organizational goals are more transitory than ever—that they change much more often than necessary to justify the existence of organizations and they undergo necessary changes to keep pace with the society. Certainly, this state of affairs is evident within the police organization. Hence, a statement of police goals must be assessed in terms of its relevancy. Such a statement is provided above. The list differentiates between existing and modern or emerging police goals. We propose that local police agencies seek to effectively discharge those goals categorized as being modern.

HISTORY OF THE POLICE

The face of America has changed since colonial days from a collection of predominantly rural and independent jurisdictions to an industrialized, urban nation.[3] Yet in several respects, law enforcement has not kept pace with this change. As America has grown and policing has become correspondingly complex, the existing law enforcement system has not always been altered to meet the needs of a mechanized and metropolitan society.

Over the years, the proliferation of independent and, for the most part, local policing units has led to an overlapping of responsibilities and a duplication of effort, causing problems in police administration and in the coordination of efforts to apprehend criminals. America is a nation of small, decentralized police forces.

Other problems have plagued the police over the years. Forces have lacked an adequate number of sufficiently qualified personnel. Unattractive salaries and working conditions and a general lack of public support have hindered police development. The need for harmonious police-community relations has been a persistent problem—one which, unfortunately, has not been widely recognized until recently. Community relations problems are nothing new; they have existed since American cities were divided into subsocieties by the waves of immigrants from western, and later eastern, Europe, who started settling in urban centers before the turn of the century.

To understand better the prevailing problems that police agencies face today, it is helpful to examine their development in England as well as in the United States. There are many weaknesses in the existing system that stem from practices developed in the rural colonies and from the colonial philosophy of law enforcement.

Early History of English Law Enforcement

France and other continental countries maintained professional police forces as early as the seventeenth century. But England, fearing the oppression these forces had brought about in many of the continental countries, did not begin to create police organizations until the nineteenth century. Moreover, England, in its early history, did not maintain a permanent army of paid soldiers that could enforce criminal laws when not engaged in guarding the country's borders against invaders. The cost of developing a force specifically for peace-keeping duties was believed to be too high for the royal purse. Private citizens could do the job cheaper if given a few shillings reward for arrests. This simple law enforcement expedient,

---

[3] Rather than "re-invent the wheel," this section is drawn in part from a condensed, yet comprehensive, historical review of the American police contained in the President's Commission on Law Enforcement and the Administration of Justice, *Task Force Report: The Police* (Washington, D.C.: U.S. Government Printing Office, 1967), pp. 3–7.

which had begun with Alfred the Great (870–901), can be recognized as the forerunner of American police agencies.

Primarily, the system encouraged mutual responsibility among local citizens' associations, which were pledged to maintain law and order;[4] it was called the "mutual pledge" system. Every man was responsible not only for his own actions but also for those of his neighbors. It was each citizen's duty to raise the "hue and cry" when a crime was committed, to collect his neighbors, and to pursue a criminal who fled from the district. If such a group failed to apprehend the lawbreaker, all were fined by the Crown.

The king placed this mutual responsibility for group police action upon ten-family groups. Each of these was known as a "tithing." From the tithing, there subsequently developed the "hundred," comprised of ten tithings. From this developed the first real police officer—the constable.[5] He was appointed by a local nobleman and placed in charge of the weapons and equipment of each hundred.

Soon, the hundreds were grouped to form a "shire," a geographical area equivalent to a county.[6] A "shire-reeve"—lineal antecedent of tens of thousands of sheriffs to come—thus came into being, appointed by the Crown to supervise each county. The constable's breadth of authority remained limited to his original hundred. The shire-reeve was responsible to the local nobleman in ensuring that the citizens enforced the law effectively. From his original supervisory post, the sheriff soon branched out to take part in the pursuit and apprehension of lawbreakers.

It was during the reign of Edward I (1272–1307) that the first official police forces were created in the large towns of England. These were called the "watch and ward," and were responsible for protecting property against fire, guarding the gates, and arresting those who committed offenses between sunset and daybreak. At the same time, the constable became the primary law enforcement officer in all towns throughout England.

In 1326, to supplement the shire-reeve mutual pledge system, Edward II created the office of justice of the peace. The justices, originally noblemen, were appointed by the Crown to assist the sheriff in policing the county. This led in time to their taking on local judicial functions, in line with the primary duty of keeping the peace in their separate jurisdictions.

The constable, who retained the responsibility of serving as a major official within the pledge system, meanwhile gained in importance. He became an assistant to the justice, responsible for supervising the night watchmen, inquiring into offenses, serving summonses, executing warrants, and taking charge of prisoners.[7] It was here that the formal separation between judge and police officer developed.

As law enforcement increasingly became the responsibility of the central government in fourteenth-century England, the justice, as the appointee of the

---

[4] Daniel Devlin, *Police Procedure, Administration and Organization* (London: Butterworth & Co., 1966), p. 3.
[5] *Ibid.*, p. 49.
[6] *Ibid.*
[7] *Ibid.*, p. 6.

king, exercised a greater degree of control over the locally appointed constables. By the end of the century, the constable no longer functioned independently as an official of the pledge system. Rather, he was obliged to serve the justice. This essentially set the justice-constable patterns for the next five hundred years. The "justice [remained] the superior, the constable the inferior, conservator of the peace"[8] until the second quarter of the nineteenth century. Meanwhile, over these years the local pledge system continued to decline. Community support languished, and with considerable reason.[9]

But as the local pledge system was declining, innovations in policing were cropping up in the emerging cities of the seventeenth and eighteenth centuries. Those first law enforcement officers were increasingly assisted by a paid nightwatch force. Although this force was nominally responsible for guarding the cities against thieves and vandals, apparently they were not effective. Reportedly, they did little more than roam the streets at night, periodically calling out the condition of the weather, the hour, and the fact that "all was well."

Industrialization in England

While England remained essentially a rural country, the dominance of the justice of the peace in law enforcement machinery aroused little formal opposition. But with the advent of the Industrial Revolution at the end of the 1700s, families by the thousands began traveling to factory towns to find work. Inevitably, as the cities grew, established patterns of life changed, and unprecedented social disorder resulted. Law enforcement became a much more complex enterprise.

Government and citizens alike responded to this need for better law enforcement. A number of fragmented civic associations, such as the Bow Street Horse and Foot Patrol, were formed to police the streets and highways leading out of London and the government passed statutes creating public offices, later to be known as police offices. Each of these housed three paid justices of the peace, who were authorized to employ six paid constables. These new posts thus helped to centralize law enforcement operations within a small area.

By the beginning of the nineteenth century, nine police offices had been established within the metropolitan area of London, but there was little apparent effort to coordinate their independent law enforcement activities. This was reportedly due to the fact that each office refused to communicate with another for fear that the other might take credit for detecting and apprehending an offender.

In London especially, these weaknesses combined to make the police forces seemingly powerless to combat crime. Highwaymen on the road, thieves lurking in the cities, daily bank robberies, and juvenile delinquency all presented major

---

[8] Royal Commission on the Police, *Royal Commission on the Police 1962, Final Report* (London: Her Majesty's Stationery Office, 1962), p. 12.
[9] *Ibid*, p. 7.

law enforcement problems.[10] However, out of this difficult situation emerged a unique remedy to discourage thieves from attacking citizens. In the early 1800s, gaslights were introduced on the streets of London.

Many of the experiments in law enforcement before 1820 failed "because no scheme could reconcile the freedom of action of individuals with the security of persons and property."[11] In 1822, Sir Robert Peel, England's new Home Secretary, contended that although better policing could not eliminate crime, the poor quality of police contributed to social disorder. Seven years later, he introduced and guided through Parliament an "Act for Improving the Police In and Near the Metropolis." This led to the first organized British metropolitan police force. Structured along the lines of a military unit, the one-thousand man force was the first one to wear a definite uniform. The men were commanded by two magistrates, later called commissioners, who were given administrative but not judicial duties. Ultimately, the responsibility for equipping, paying, maintaining, and to a certain degree supervising the "bobbies," as they later became known, was invested in the Home Secretary. Because he was made accountable to the Parliament "for the exercise of his authority over the Metropolitan police, it could [thus] be said that the new force was under the ultimate control of a democratically elected Parliament."[12]

Availability of competent manpower, then as today, became an immediate problem. It was difficult to recruit suitable men to serve in the "new police" because the salaries were poor and the commissioners selective. And there were other harassments. Parliament objected to appropriating government funds to maintain a police force. The radicals were afraid of tyranny. The aristocracy, though willing to accept the protection of such a force, was disgruntled because the commissioners refused to abide by the traditional rules of patronage in making appointments.

Nevertheless, the London metropolitan police proved so effective in suppressing crime and apprehending criminals that within five years the provinces, which were experiencing increasing crime problems and violent riots, asked London for policing help.[13] Shortly after, Parliament enacted a series of police reform bills. Among them, one empowered justices of the peace in 1839 to establish police forces in the counties; in 1856, another required every borough and county to have a police force.

As regular police forces developed, the justices of the peace voluntarily relinquished their law enforcement duties and confined themselves to deciding questions of law. Before this change occurred, the police had served as the agents of the powerful justices and had consequently used the justices' authority to carry on investigations of those in custody. When the justices relinquished their law en-

---

[10] *Ibid.,* p. 59.
[11] *Ibid.,* p. 10.
[12] *Ibid.,* p. 16.
[13] Christopher Hibbert, *The Roots of Evil* (London: Weidenfeld and Nicolson, 1963), pp. 125–28.

forcement powers, the legislature gave no consideration as to what, if any, investigative responsibilities should be transferred to the police. As a result, the statutes for law enforcement officers that remain on the books today contain little recognition of the broad discretion that police continue to exercise.[14]

Law Enforcement in the American Colonies

American colonists in the seventeenth and eighteenth centuries naturally brought to America the law enforcement structure with which they were familiar in England. The transfer of the offices of constable and sheriff to rural American areas, which included most colonial territory, was accomplished with little change in structure of the offices. Drawing upon the pattern of the mutual pledge system, the constable was made responsible for law enforcement in towns, and the sheriff took charge of policing the counties. The Crown-appointed governors bestowed these offices on large landowners who were loyal to the king. After the revolution, sheriffs and constables tended to be selected by popular elections, patronage then being on the wane.

In many colonial cities, the colonists adopted the British constabulary-nightwatch system. As early as 1636, Boston had night watchmen in addition to a military guard. New York and Philadelphia soon developed a similar nightwatch system. The New York nightwatchmen were known as the "Rattlewatch," because they carried rattles on their rounds to remind those who needed reminding of their watchful purpose.

Urbanization in the United States

As American towns grew in size and population during the first half of the nineteenth century, the constable was unable to cope with the increasing disorder. As in England years before, lawlessness became more prevalent:

> New York City was alleged to be the most crime-ridden city in the world, with Philadelphia, Baltimore and Cincinnati not far behind. . . . Gangs of youthful rowdies in the larger cities . . . threatened to destroy the American reputation for respect for law. . . . Before their boisterous demonstrations the crude police forces of the day were often helpless.[15]

Again, as in England, many American cities began to develop organized metropolitan police forces of their own. Philadelphia was one of the first. In 1833, a wealthy philanthropist left a will that provided for the financing of a competent

---

[14] Edward J. Barrett, Jr., "Police Practices and the Law—From Arrest to Release or Charge," *California Law Review,* Vol. 50 (March 1962), pp. 17–18.

[15] Arthur Charles Coe, "The Irrepressible Conflict, 1859–1865," *A History of American Life in 12 Volumes,* Vol. 8, Arthur M. Schlesinger, Sr., and Dixon Ryan Fox, eds. (New York: Macmillan, 1934), pp. 154–55.

police force in Philadelphia. Stimulated by this contribution, the city government passed an ordinance providing for a twenty-four-man police force, to work by day, and 120 nightwatchmen. The force was unfortunately short-lived because the ordinance was repealed less than two years later.

In 1838, Boston created a day police force to supplement the nightwatch, and other cities soon followed its lead. Crime, cities were finding, was no respecter of daylight. There were certain inherent difficulties, however, in these early two-shift police systems. Keen rivalries existed between the day and night shifts, and separate administrations supervised each shift. Recognizing the evils of separate police forces, the New York Legislature passed a law in 1844 that authorized creating the first unified day and night police, thus abolishing its nightwatch system. Ten years later, Boston consolidated its nightwatch with the day police.

Following the New York model, other cities developed their own unified police forces during the next decade. By the 1870s, the nation's largest cities had full-time police forces. And by the 1900s, there were few cities of consequence without such unified forces. These forces gradually came under the control of a chief or commissioner, often appointed by the mayor, sometimes with the consent of the city council, and sometimes elected by the people.

These first formal police forces in American cities were faced with many of the problems that police continue to confront today. Police officers became the objects of disrespect. The need for larger staffs required the police to compromise personnel standards in order to fill the ranks. Police salaries were among the lowest in local government service, a factor that precluded attracting sufficient numbers of high-standard candidates. It is small wonder that the police were not respected, were not notably successful, and were not known for their vitality and progressiveness. Moreover, the police mission in the mid-1800s precluded any brilliance.

> The aim of the police departments was merely to keep a city superficially clean and to keep everything quiet that [was] likely to arouse public [ire].[16]

Many of the problems that troubled the first organized metropolitan police forces can perhaps be traced to a single root—political control. As one authority has explained:

> Rotation in office enjoyed so much popular favor that police posts of both high and low degree were constantly changing hands with political fixers determining the price and conditions of each change. . . . The whole police question simply churned about in the public mind and eventually became identified with the corruption and degradation of the city politics and local governments of the period.[17]

---

[16] Arthur M. Schlesinger, Sr., "The Rise of the City, 1878–1898," *The History of American Life in 12 Volumes,* Vol. 10, Arthur M. Schlesinger, Sr., and Dixon Ryan Fox, eds. (New York: Macmillan, 1934), p. 115.

[17] Bruce Smith, Sr., *Police Systems in the United States,* 2nd rev. ed. (New York: Harper Bros., 1960), pp. 105–6.

In an attempt to alleviate these problems, responsible leaders created police administrative boards to replace the control exercised over police affairs by mayors or city councils. These boards were given the responsibility of appointing police administrators and managing police affairs. Unfortunately, this attempt to cure political meddling was unsuccessful perhaps because the judges, lawyers, and local businessmen who comprised the administrative boards were inexpert in dealing with the board problems of the police.

Another attempt was made at police reform during the close of the nineteenth century. Noting that poor policing tended to occur mainly in urban areas, the state legislatures, which were dominated by rural legislators, required that police administrators be appointed by authority of the state. Thus, state control became an alternative to local control of law enforcement. This move brought little success, for many problems had not been anticipated:

> For one thing, the theory of the state control . . . was not uniformly applied. It was primarily directed at the larger cities, by legislature seeking to [perpetuate] rural domination in public affairs.[18]

In spite of increased state control, the large city continued to pay for its police service, and police costs rose. One reason was that police boards were not even indirectly responsible to the local taxpaying public that they served. In cases where the state and city governments were not allied politically, friction increased. It increased further when the state-appointed administrator instituted policy out of harmony with the views of the majority of the city population. It was not until the first decades of the twentieth century that cities regained control of police forces in all but a few cases.[19]

After these sincere attempts at reform, police forces grew in size and expanded in function. However, there was very little analysis of the changes in society that made expansion necessary nor of the effect such changes would work upon the role of the police. Civil service proved helpful; spreading to local police agencies and alleviating some of the more serious problems of political interference. The concept of merit employment, which some reformers had been proposing, was embraced by some forces.

One of the most notable police advancements of the 1920s was the advent of police training schools, even though on a somewhat modest basis. In the early 1900s, the new policeman learned chiefly in the school of experience:

> Thus, for the most part, the average American city depends almost entirely for the training of its police recruits upon such casual instruction as older officials may be able and willing to give.[20]

---

[18] *Ibid.*, p. 186.
[19] *Ibid.*, pp. 186–87.
[20] Elmer D. Graper, *American Police Administration* (New York: Macmillan, 1921), pp. 109–10.

State and Federal Law Enforcement Agencies

Although a state police force known as the "Texas Rangers" was organized in 1835 to supplement Texas' military forces, modern state police organizations did not emerge until the turn of the century. In 1905, the governor of Pennsylvania, in the absence of an effective sheriff-constable system, created the first state force. Its initial purpose was to cope with a public dispute between labor and management. Soon, such continuing factors as the inadequacy of local policing by constables and sheriffs and the inability or unwillingness of city police forces to pursue lawbreakers beyond their jurisdictional limits convinced state legislatures of the need for statewide police forces.[21]

The majority of state departments were established shortly after World War I to deal with the increasing problem of auto traffic and the accompanying wave of car thefts. Today, all states except Hawaii have some form of state law enforcement body. Although some state agencies are restricted to the functions of enforcing traffic laws and protecting life and property on the highways, others have been given general policing authority in criminal matters throughout the state.

The role of the federal government in law enforcement has developed in a sporadic and highly specialized manner. Federal law enforcement actually started in 1789, when the Revenue Cutter Service was established to help prevent smuggling. In 1836, Congress authorized the Postmaster General to pay salaries to agents who would investigate infringements involving postal matters. Among the more important law enforcement responsibilities later recognized by Congress were internal revenue investigation and narcotics control. Congress authorized a force of twenty-five detectives in 1868 and increased the number in 1915. In 1924, J. Edgar Hoover organized the Federal Bureau of Investigation in the Justice Department.[22]

With the expansion of interstate movement of people and goods, and federal involvement in all aspects of life, the responsibilities of federal agencies have increased significantly within the last few years. These federal agencies are responsible to departments of the national government. The Treasury Department's Secret Service is, for example, charged with the protection of the President and with investigating counterfeiting and forgery of federal documents. Civilian departmental agencies, with the sole exception of the FBI, function under civil service regulations.[23]

The manpower and jurisdiction of the FBI have increased greatly since its establishment. Some of the statutes that have been responsible for this expansion are the National Stolen Property Act, the Federal Kidnapping Act, the Hobbs Act (extortion), the Fugitive Felon Act, the White Slave Act, the National Bank Rob-

---

[21] *Ibid.*, pp. 147–50.

[22] *Ibid.*, pp. 67–68. In regard to the history of the police *investigative* function, we encourage you to consult the first chapter in Richard H. Ward, *Introduction to Criminal Investigation* (Reading, Mass.: Addison-Wesley Publishing Company, 1975).

[23] John Coatman, *Police* (London: Oxford University Press, 1959), p. 50.

bery Act, federal interstate gambling laws, and the Dyer Act, which brings automobiles stolen and taken across any state border within the FBI's jurisdiction. Recent passage of strong federal legislation has enhanced the FBI's role in the enforcement of civil rights.

Modernization

Serious study of police reform in America began in 1919. The problems exposed then and those faced by police agencies today are similar in many respects. For example, in 1931 the Wickersham Commission noted that the average police chief's term of office was too short, and that his responsibility to political officials made his position insecure. The commission also felt that there was a lack of competent, efficient, and honest patrolmen. It said that no intensive effort was being made to educate, train, and discipline prospective officers, or to eliminate those shown to be incompetent. The Wickersham Commission found that with perhaps two exceptions, police forces in cities above 300,000 population had neither an adequate communications system nor the equipment necessary to enforce the law effectively. It said that the police task was made much more difficult by the excessively rapid growth of our cities in the past half century, and by the tendency of different ethnic groups to retain their language and customs in large cities. Finally, the commission said, there were too many duties cast upon each officer and patrolman.[24] The Missouri Crime Commission reported that in a typical American city the police were expected to be familiar with and enforce 30,000 federal, state, or local enactments!

Despite the complexity of these problems, many hopeful improvements have occurred in the past few decades. Some cities, counties, and states have taken great strides in streamlining their operations through reorganization and increased use of technology and the use of modern techniques to detect and apprehend criminal offenders. Others are on the threshold of modernization. But many departments remain static. These static departments obviously constitute a burden on the machinery of justice, and are detrimental to the process of achieving a truly professional police service.

FEDERAL RESPONSE TO CRIME

As we stress throughout this book, most crime in the nation is state and local crime. It remains the basic responsibility of state and local governments to protect the citizen in his or her daily life. The Constitution recognizes the practicality and desirability of this division of responsibility. The federal and state governments have found it necessary to increase their enforcement activities, their assistance to

---

[24] National Commission on Law Observance and Enforcement, *Report on the Police* (Washington, D.C.: U.S. Government Printing Office, 1931), pp. 5–7.

local operations, and their coordinative mechanisms. The federal government has taken the following action.[25]

First, an effort of unprecedented magnitude was launched against narcotic addiction and drug abuse. New offices were established to coordinate federal efforts and to enforce criminal laws against traffickers at all levels. A Cabinet-level committee was formed to coordinate efforts to reduce the flow of heroin into the country. Rigorous new customs inspection procedures were implemented to stop the importation of heroin. The Department of Defense initiated special programs to treat GIs who had become narcotics users.

Second, the government ordered an all-out assault on organized crime. Department of Justice strike forces increased from seven to eighteen since the beginning of 1969. A Cabinet committee was formed to coordinate all federal efforts against organized crime. Funding support for state-level organized-crime prevention programs was doubled. Staff manpower in the Organized Crime and Racketeering Section of the Department of Justice increased from 68 in 1968 to 134 in the spring of 1972. The number of assistant United States attorneys, who handle much of the prosecution workload, increased by 40 percent. The Organized Crime Control Act of 1970, proposed by the Administration, developed a comprehensive approach involving special grand juries, witness immunity and protection, illegal gambling prosecution, and witness detention.

Third, new juvenile delinquency legislation was implemented that established an interdepartmental council to coordinate, for the first time, all federal programs in this area. Funding for state juvenile delinquency prevention programs assumed a high priority.

Fourth, the role of the Law Enforcement Assistance Administration (LEAA) was greatly expanded as follows. Massive increases in funds were proposed for state and municipal crime reduction programs, raising LEAA funding from $63 million in FY (fiscal year) 1969 to $641 million in FY 1979. LEAA provides funds, policy guidance, and technical expertise for states and cities across the board—in police services, courts, and corrections programs, in organized-crime prevention and civil disorders programs, and, increasingly, in juvenile delinquency and narcotics and dangerous-drug programs. A major new LEAA effort, the High Impact Anticrime Program—is aimed at sharply reducing street crime and burglaries in our nation's major cities.

Fifth, a large-scale program to improve the federal corrections system was ordered. A landmark national conference on corrections was convened. An interagency council to coordinate federal efforts in corrections was formed. A major new funding program through which LEAA is assisting states in upgrading their correctional facilities and programs has been approved.

---

[25] Most of the information in this section is derived from the Attorney General's First Annual Report, *Federal Law Enforcement and Criminal Justice Assistance Activities* (Washington, D.C.: U.S. Government Printing Office, 1972).

Sixth, on numerous occasions the federal government has created special commissions to study or investigate problems confronting parts or all of our country.

Seventh, the government undertook a large number of other programs: to increase the number of FBI agents; to protect the environment through more vigorous prosecution of those violating federal antipollution laws; to develop the first public defender service in the federal court system; to bring federal law on narcotics, marjuana, and dangerous drugs more into line with current scientific knowledge; and to increase support of the Community Relations Service in its efforts to help communities resolve disputes and difficulties arising out of discrimination based on race, color, or national origin.

FEDERAL POLICING

Once again *most crime in the United States is state and local crime.* Recent federal programs have had a dual nature: first, to expand and enhance all federal law enforcement and crime prevention efforts; second, to make available to state and local governments immense amounts of financial and technical assistance for the improvement of their own anticrime programs.

As a consequence, a new spirit of cooperation has spread through federal, state, and local law enforcement and criminal justice agencies. Federal assistance from LEAA and other agencies has helped to instill and stimulate this spirit. Local demands for action and reform have helped give this spirit its strength.

The result of this new federal-state-local cooperation is salutary. It means a more precise pinpointing of responsibilities in government. The federal government is providing leadership and funds. State governments are allocating federal assistance to cities and are reforming their criminal codes and their corrections systems. Local police departments and criminal justice agencies are mounting major efforts against crime at its very roots.[26]

The federal government has undertaken the most massive and sustained attack on crime in the history of the nation.[27] That attack utilizes the full range and force of federal authority:

1. Federal investigators and prosecutors are enforcing federal criminal laws vigorously.
2. The government is assisting state and local governments on an unprecedented scale in meeting their responsibilities to prevent and reduce street crime and other common crimes.
3. The federal government is coping with such crimes as airplane piracy, international narcotics trafficking, organized crime, civil disorders, and similar crimes that states and cities are unable to combat.

[26] Attorney General's First Annual Report, *Federal Law Enforcement and Criminal Justice Assistance Activities* (Washington, D.C.: U.S. Government Printing Office, 1972), p. vii.

[27] The main portion of this section is drawn from the Attorney General's First Annual Report, pp. 1–20.

In brief, the federal program is coordinated by departments and agencies working together at the highest levels to formulate policies related to their common interests and to eliminate duplication of effort. They share information or technical know-how, and their agents work together on interdepartmental enforcement teams.

Legal Powers: Source and Scope of Federal Authority

At the time of the founding of the Republic, the states exercised virtually exclusive jurisdiction over all crimes. That was altogether appropriate to the conditions of the time. The federal government exercised jurisdiction over such crimes as treason, piracy, revenue violations, customs offenses, and postal crimes, but little more. As the nation grew in population and complexity, as it grew geographically, as the economy developed, and as opportunity for abuses increased, so state jurisdiction was seen to need an increased but still complementary effort by the federal government. During the latter part of the eighteenth century and all of the nineteenth century, this dual approach to criminal conduct developed and matured. The present posture of criminal law jurisdiction in the United States is consistent with that intended by the Founding Fathers: The states retain jurisdiction over crimes committed within the state that are local in nature; the federal government has jurisdiction over certain crimes that involve interstate commerce, taxes, assaults on federal and foreign officials, and the like.

The federal government traditionally has fulfilled the function of assisting states in their efforts to prevent and control crime. This assistance began with such activities as the aid given by the Armed Services to states faced with civil disorders. It now includes, for example, the funding program of the Law Enforcement Assistance Administration and the unique laboratory facilities of the Federal Bureau of Investigation, and the Drug Enforcement Administration, all within the Department of Justice; and the Bureau of Alcohol, Tobacco, and Firearms of the Department of the Treasury. Yet, federal efforts remain auxiliary to state efforts in combating the crime problem. The common crimes, such as murder, rape, robbery, burglary, fraud, prostitution, obscenity, extortion, and usury remain largely state crimes. Even where federal jurisdiction exists, the Congress has limited federal involvement, for example by enacting such provisions as that requiring that at least $5,000 worth of certain kinds of stolen property be involved before it is a federal offense to transport that property in interstate commerce (18 U.S.C. 2314).

The federal government has jurisdiction over crimes that are national in nature, such as crimes involving national security, immigration and naturalization, operations of the government itself, internal revenue and customs matters, civil rights, and regulatory matters. The federal government also complements state law where common crimes such as theft, inciting to riot, and kidnapping may involve interstate commerce; here, federal power is brought to bear to apprehend and punish the violator where no state could effectively extend its jurisdiction to do so.

POWERS OF THE CONGRESS

Because there are no common law crimes against the United States, only those acts that the Congress forbids and punishes are federal crimes. These acts now number in the many hundreds, and most legislation relating to them is found in Title 18 of the United States Code.

The powers of the Congress to forbid and punish conduct derive from several sources in the Constitution. Only three clauses, however, other than the impeachment clause, actually mention crimes that the Congress enacts legislation to punish. Two of these are in Article 1, Section 8. The first, Clause 6, empowers the Congress ". . . To define and punish Piracies and Felonies committed on the high Seas, and Offences against the Law of Nations. . . ." This clause contains the only specific grant of constitutional power to the Congress to prohibit and punish offenses committed outside the territorial limits of the United States. The third reference is found in Article III, Section 3, defining treason:

> Treason against the United States, shall consist only in levying War against them, or in adhering to their Enemies, giving them Aid and Comfort. No Person shall be convicted of Treason unless on the Testimony of two Witnesses to the same overt Act, or on Confession in open Court.
>
> The Congress shall have Power to declare the Punishment of Treason, but no Attainder of Treason shall work Corruption of Blood, or Forfeiture except during the Life of the Person attainted.

The broad sweep of the power of the Congress to prohibit and punish certain acts derives from Article I, Section 8, Clause 18 of the Constitution, which states that the Congress shall have power:

> . . . To make all Laws which shall be necessary and proper for carrying into Execution the foregoing Powers, and all other Powers vested by this Constitution in the Government of the United States, or in any Department or Officer thereof.

This clause is referred to variously as the "necessary and proper" clause or the "coefficient" clause. It constitutes a broad grant of power from the people to the Congress to carry out its responsibilities, which include providing for the collection of taxes and duties, the regulation of interstate and foreign commerce, rules of naturalization and laws on bankruptcies, the coinage of money, the establishment of post offices, and the calling forth of Armed Forces to suppress insurrection.

That this clause is a broad grant of power, and not a limiting restraint, was established in *McCulloch v. Maryland*,[28] in which Chief Justice Marshall said of the powers of the Congress under this clause:

---

[28] 4 Wheat. 316 (1819).

> Let the end be legitimate, let it be within the scope of the Constitution, and all means which are appropriate, which are plainly adapted to that end, which are not prohibited, but consist with the letter and spirit of the Constitution, are constitutional.[29]

It has long been universally conceded that the Congress has the power to create, define, and punish crimes and offenses when necessary to carry out its constitutional duties and responsibilities.

POWERS OF THE PRESIDENT

The law enforcement power of the President is found in Article II, Section 3, of the Constitution, which requires that the President ". . . shall take Care that the Laws be faithfully executed. . . ." As it has in regard to the "necessary and proper" clause, the Supreme Court has read this clause as a broad grant of authority. It has said that the reference to laws in this clause encompasses not only statutes enacted by the Congress but also ". . . the rights, duties, and obligations growing out of the Constitution itself, our international relations, and all the protection implied by the nature of government under the Constitution."[30] This duty of the President is taken to include, therefore, the powers of investigation and prosecution of violations of federal criminal law and the power to take appropriate steps to prevent the violation of federal law.

POWERS OF THE JUDICIARY

The Constitution establishes the federal judiciary in Article III, Section 1:

> The judicial Power of the United States, shall be vested in one supreme Court, and in such inferior Courts as the Congress may from time to time ordain and establish. The Judges, both of the supreme and inferior Courts, shall hold their Offices during good Behaviour, and shall, at stated Times, receive for their Services, a Compensation, which shall not be diminished during their Continuance in Office.

The notion of "judicial power" is a complex one, and the phrase is not defined in the Constitution. In summary, however, it is taken to mean the power brought to bear by the court on a specific case when the court has taken jurisdiction over that case. That power includes the power to order an arrest, to order punishment for contempt, to enforce the orders and subpoenas of an administrative agency, and to prevent injustices, among others.

Coordinating Federal Policies and Activities

The executive branch has taken the initiative in many areas to assure that the vast resources of the federal government and the diversity of programs on all fronts of the national effort against crime are coordinated. Under its direction, many interagency committees to coordinate federal policies and activities in areas relating

---

[29] 4 Wheat. at 421.
[30] *In re Neagle,* 135, U.S. 1, 64 (1890).

to crime reduction have been formed. These interagency councils and committees formulate policy for a concerted and coordinated attack on the problems in their areas of responsibility. They work to identify problems, eliminate duplication of effort, integrate knowledge, and formulate strategies to combat criminal activity. During fiscal year 1971, coordinating committees were operative in the areas of juvenile delinquency, organized crime, international narcotics traffic, drug abuse, correction, air security, cargo security, communications, and urban information.

JUVENILE DELINQUENCY

The 1971 amendments to the Juvenile Delinquency Prevention and Control Act of 1968 created the Interdepartmental Council to Coordinate Federal Juvenile Delinquency Programs. The Council is composed of five major members, representing the Departments of Justice; Labor; Housing and Urban Development; and Health, Education, and Welfare. The Council also has three minor members: The Departments of Agriculture, the Interior, and Transportation, and two ex-officio members: the Office of Management and Budget and the Special Action Office for Drug Abuse Prevention. The Attorney General is chairman of the council, and he has delegated this function to the Administrator of the Law Enforcement Assistance Administration. The Council has set up three task forces composed of members of participating agencies whose purpose is to study coordination of efforts, evaluation of programs, and management techniques.

ORGANIZED CRIME

By executive order, the National Council on Organized Crime was created on June 4, 1970. Composed of Cabinet-level officials, the council provides guidance, strategy, and coordination on a national level in the fight against organized crime. It operates primarily in the area of policy formulation, such as deciding on the location of new strike forces. Membership in the council consists of the Attorney General, who serves as chairman, the Secretaries of the Treasury and Labor, the Postmaster General, and the Chairman of the Securities and Exchange Commission. Other Department of Justice members are the Assistant Attorneys General in charge of the Criminal Division and of the Tax Division; the Chief of the Organized Crime and Racketeering Section of the Criminal Division; the Commissioner of the Immigration and Naturalization Service; the Director of the Drug and Enforcement Administration; the Director of the Federal Bureau of Investigation; and the Administrator of the Law Enforcement Assistance Administration. Other members from the Department of the Treasury are the Assistant Secretaries for Enforcement and Operations and for Tax Policy; the Commissioners of the Bureau of Customs and of the Internal Revenue Service; the Director of the United States Secret Service; and the Chief Counsel of the Internal Revenue Service.

The Council has set up six regular staff committees to analyze current needs and efforts in their areas and to suggest methods of remedying problems. The areas of responsibility are narcotics; gambling rackets; infiltration of business;

labor; state and local efforts against organized crime; and counterfeit and stolen funds, securities, and credit cards.

DRUG ENFORCEMENT ADMINISTRATION

The Drug Enforcement Administration (DEA) is the sole federal law enforcement agency charged with the responsibility of combatting drug abuse. The administration was established July 1, 1973, by Presidential Reorganization Plan No. 2 of 1973. It resulted from the merger of the Bureau of Narcotics and Dangerous Drugs, the Office for Drug Abuse Law Enforcement, the Office of National Narcotics Intelligence, those elements of the Bureau of Customs that had drug investigative responsibilities, and those functions of the Office of Science and Technology that were drug enforcement related. The administration was established to control more effectively narcotic and dangerous-drug abuse through enforcement and prevention. In carrying out its mission, DEA cooperates with other federal agencies; foreign, state, and local governments; private industry; and other organizations.

The Drug Enforcement Administration is responsible for the *enforcement* of the laws and statutes relating to narcotic drugs, marijuana, depressants, stimulants, and the hallucinogenic drugs. Its objectives are to reach all levels of source of supply and to apprehend the greatest quantity of illegal drugs before they reach the user. To achieve its mission, the Administration has stationed highly trained agents along the many and varied routes of illicit traffic, both in the United States and in foreign countries. The DEA has thirteen domestic regional offices and six foreign area offices. Additionally, it has eighty-four district offices throughout the United States and overseas.

The administration also regulates the legal trade in narcotics and dangerous drugs. This includes establishing import, export, and manufacturing quotas for these controlled drugs.

Drug manufacturers, distributors, practitioners, and other persons responsible for handling, dispensing, or prescribing narcotics and dangerous drugs are subject to periodic inspections by DEA compliance investigators who check for record keeping and security safeguards of controlled substances. Such supervision of legitimate trade insures an adequate supply of drugs for medicinal purposes and research, and at the same time it is instrumental in preventing diversion of drugs into illicit channels.

Intelligence is an essential element in the success of any enforcement agency. DEA has an Office of Intelligence staffed by experienced criminal investigators and intelligence analysts. Each DEA regional office in the domestic United States and in foreign countries has assigned to it a regional intelligence unit. All information concerning narcotics and dangerous-drug trafficking organizations and individuals is furnished to the Office of Intelligence, where it is collated, analyzed, and disseminated in form of a finished intelligence product.

The administration's National Training Institute conducts intensive *training* in narcotics and dangerous-drug law enforcement for law enforcement officers from agencies throughout the United States and the world. Ten-week schools are conducted in which police officers receive training similar to that which DEA special agents receive. In addition, they are introduced to management concepts that will enable them to develop and lead drug investigative units and organize drug prevention programs in their own communities. Specialized two-week schools offer eighty hours of instruction to state, county, and city officers in the basic techniques of narcotics and dangerous-drug investigation. These schools are held at the administration's National Training Institute in Washington and at field locations throughout the United States.

Another area of responsibility for DEA is *drug abuse prevention* for those within the criminal justice system. As part of its program to make citizens aware of the hazards of narcotics and dangerous drugs, the agency provides factual information through literature, speakers, films, and displays to a variety of organizations, those in the criminal justice system, and to the general public. It also works closely with educators, as well as with local, state, and national government agencies, law enforcement officials, and organizations in planning and conducting abuse prevention programs. An effort is made to conduct these activities at the regional level whenever possible.

Investigation

Investigation of violations of federal laws are handled by a number of federal agencies. The FBI investigates all federal offenses with the exception of those that have been assigned by legislative enactment or administrative action to some other federal agency. Jurisdiction covers some 185 investigative matters. The FBI, as the principal investigative arm of the Department of Justice, collects evidence in cases where the United States may be a party of interest.

Enforcement of narcotics laws is the responsibility of the DEA. Bureau efforts center on apprehending international and domestic middle- and high-level traffickers, especially those with organized crime connections.

Investigators of the Immigration and Naturalization Service (INS), part of the Department of Justice, are authorized to investigate aliens or persons believed to be aliens, and to make arrests for felonies that have been committed in violation of the immigration laws. INS conducts investigations of aliens involved in organized crime, narcotics trafficking, and subversion or other criminal activities.

Within the Department of the Treasury, the IRS, the Bureau of Customs, the Bureau of Alcohol, Tobacco, and Firearms, and the United States Secret Service have investigative responsibility. Investigative functions in IRS fall to the intelligence division, the internal security division, and the alcohol, tobacco, and firearms division, which since July 1, 1972, has been reorganized as an independent bureau within the Department of the Treasury.

The intelligence division conducts investigations regarding violations of the tax laws of the United States. Together with the audit division, it conducts investigations and examinations under the Treasury/IRS Narcotics Traffickers Program. The program was initiated during fiscal year 1971 to coordinate on a national scale intensive tax investigations of middle- and upper-echelon narcotics traffickers and financiers. The objective is to disrupt the narcotics distribution system by prosecuting those guilty of criminal tax violations and to reduce their profits and working capital by assessing and collecting taxes and penalties on unreported income from the narcotics traffic. The internal security division investigates efforts to corrupt or compromise IRS personnel. It has authority to conduct criminal and administrative investigations, to execute and serve search and arrest warrants, and to serve federal subpoenas and summonses. The division also initiates prosecution.

The Bureau of Customs conducts investigations involving the smuggling of articles into the United States. This includes a major enforcement responsibility with respect to the smuggling of narcotics.

The Secret Service conducts investigations involving counterfeiting, and forging and altering government obligations. The Secret Service also has enforcement responsibility with respect to the protection of the President, the Vice President, and certain other persons provided for by statute.

The Bureau of Alcohol, Tobacco, and Firearms enforces the criminal provisions of federal law dealing with: the manufacture and sale of illicit alcohol; the unlawful possession and transportation of firearms under the Gun Control Act of 1968, and Title VII of the Safe Streets Act; and the unlawful use and transportation of explosives under Title XI of the Organized Crime Control Act of 1970.

Responsibility for protection of the mails rests with the Postal Inspection Service of the United States Postal Service. The head of the Postal Inspection Service executes policies, regulations, and procedures governing all investigations of a criminal nature and maintains liaison with other federal enforcement agencies.

The Department of Agriculture maintains the Office of the Inspector General, which acts as its primary law enforcement and investigative arm. The office investigates criminal violations under statutes establishing department programs, violations of the United States criminal code relating to those programs, and non-criminal violations of those programs. The office mainly investigates violations connected with price-supported commodities, loan programs, and the Federal Meat Inspection Act.

The United States Park Police of the Department of the Interior has enforcement responsibilities on national parklands in Washington, D.C. They have the *same* enforcement and investigative powers as the Metropolitan Police Department. In national parkland outside the nation's Capital, park rangers enforce the pertinent rules and regulations. The authority of the park rangers varies with the location of the parkland, however. In some areas, parkland is exclusively under the jurisdiction of the federal government. In other areas, jurisdiction is either partial, concurrent with the states, or proprietary. Park rangers are often deputized as county officials with authority to make arrests for violations not otherwise covered in their normal areas of responsibility.

Areas of Cooperation

In addition to high-level coordinating committees, cooperation among federal departments and agencies takes a variety of forms, including interagency enforcement groups; contractual agreements between departments or agencies; and areas in which two or more departments or agencies have concurrent jurisdiction.

CONCURRENT JURISDICTION

Departments and agencies occasionally share responsibility for enforcing a federal statute. For example, the Bureau of Alcohol, Tobacco, and Firearms (BATF) of the Department of the Treasury (which prior to July 1, 1972, was a division of the IRS) and the FBI have concurrent responsibility for enforcing Title XI of the Organized Crime Control Act of 1970, pertaining to explosives-connected offenses. The Postal Inspection Service has investigative jurisdiction over bombs and explosives sent through the mails or directed at postal facilities. BATF and the FBI recently adopted temporary guidelines allocating investigative responsibilities. Under these guidelines, the FBI is authorized to make a full investigation of bombings directed at federal property, at a federal function other than property or functions of the Department of the Treasury, which are the responsibility of BATF, or at a diplomatic facility; and bombings on college campuses if a non-Treasury federal function or property is involved. BATF is responsible for crimes relating to interstate transportation or receipt of explosives with unlawful intent, bomb threat, or false information through an instrument of commerce, and possession of explosives in a building used by the United States, only where Department of the Treasury property or functions are involved. BATF has sole responsibility for administering the regulatory provisions of the act.

Another example of concurrent jurisdiction involves the Narcotic Addict Rehabilitation Act of 1966, under which the Bureau of Prisons of the Department of Justice administers the provisions of Title II, which provides for treatment of narcotics addicts who are federal prisoners. The National Institute of Mental Health (NIMH) in the Department of Health, Education, and Welfare administers Titles I and III, which provide for civil commitment to the Surgeon General of narcotics addicts charged with certain nonviolent crimes who desire to be committed, and for the treatment of narcotics addicts who are not charged with criminal offenses but who themselves apply for rehabilitation.

INTERAGENCY AGREEMENTS

Federal departments and agencies occasionally enter into agreements with other departments and agencies to conduct special projects. The National Institute of Law Enforcement and Criminal Justice, part of the LEAA, has entered into a number of these, including several with the Department of Commerce. Under such agreements, the Bureau of the Census conducted projects to compile statistics on various aspects of the criminal justice system. Under another agreement, the National Bureau of Standards was commissioned to develop voluntary performance standards to help law enforcement agencies select, evaluate, and procure equipment.

INFORMATION SHARING

Various federal departments and agencies provide information on a regular ad hoc basis to other elements of the federal government. The National Crime Information Center, maintained by the FBI, stores data concerning stolen property or wanted persons, which is immediately available to any agency tied into the computer-based system. Additionally, agencies that discover evidence relating to organized crime in the course of their activities may relay this information to other interested departments or agencies.

COORDINATED ENFORCEMENT ACTIVITIES

To provide a concentrated preventive, investigative, or prosecutive effort against areas of criminal activity, various departments and agencies have pooled resources to form coordinated enforcement groups. Strike forces to combat organized crime are the premier example of this cooperation. Coordinated through the Organized Crime and Racketeering Section of the Criminal Division of the Department of Justice, the strike forces are composed of agents from the DEA; the Labor-Management Services Administration of the Department of Labor; IRS; the Bureau of Alcohol, Tobacco, and Firearms; the United States Secret Service; and the Bureau of Customs of the Department of the Treasury; the United States Postal Service; and the Securities and Exchange Commission. There are usually five attorneys from the Organized Crime and Racketeering Section on each strike force.

Still another example of coordinated enforcement activity is the air security program. The original air guard force was drawn from the Department of the Treasury, the Federal Aviation Administration, the FBI, and the Department of Defense. A permanent sky marshal force was formed shortly afterward, staffed with personnel from the Bureau of Customs in the Department of the Treasury. The United States Marshals Service, part of the Department of Justice, helps in the air security effort by providing personnel to conduct preboard screening on the ground.

Federal Assistance Activities

Although the national effort against crime in the United States is primarily the responsibility of state and local governments, the federal government has an extensive role in aiding state and local law enforcement activities. Every Cabinet-level department and many federal agencies have programs or services that aid law enforcement functions on the state and local level. Some agencies, such as the FBI, have provided expert assistance to state and local law enforcement for many years. Other agencies have developed assistance programs only recently.

Federal aid includes financial and technical assistance, the education and training of personnel, and the sharing of information. These federal programs are directed toward upgrading the effectiveness of police departments, courts, correctional facilities, and other parts of the criminal justice system. The federal government, recognizing the need for increased federal aid to state and local law enforcement agencies to fight crime, has greatly increased the funding levels of LEAA. Federal criminal justice assistance is directed toward eight main areas of state and local needs: police, courts, juvenile delinquency, drug abuse, personnel training, corrections, research and technology, and information exchange. A brief summary of federal activities in these areas follows.

LAW ENFORCEMENT ASSISTANCE ADMINISTRATION

The first major effort by the federal government to provide large-scale financial assistance for the prevention and reduction of crime at the state and city levels began with passage of the Omnibus Crime Control and Safe Streets Act of 1968 (P.L. 90–351). That act created the Law Enforcement Assistance Administration (LEAA), in the Department of Justice, in order to provide funds and guidance for state and local crime prevention and reduction programs. The mission of LEAA included undertaking research in law enforcement and criminal justice, providing educational assistance for law enforcement personnel, and developing other programs, such as those now operating in statistics and systems analysis. In FY 1971, the basic act was amended to provide a new funding program to assist states in upgrading their corrections systems. In early 1978 a significant change to restructure LEAA was proposed. Basically a new organization would be created—the National Institute of Justice. The Institute would assume most of the major functions currently performed by LEAA, the National Institute of Correction, and the Federal Justice Research Center.

In establishing the LEAA, Congress set up the funding so that grants would be awarded in lump sums to the states. The recipient states in turn allocate funds, according to a plan submitted beforehand to the LEAA, for their own law enforcement and criminal justice projects at the state, county, and city levels. This approach acknowledges that law enforcement is largely the responsibility of state and local jurisdictions. It also recognizes that solutions to most crime problems are best and most effectively worked out at the state and local level.

All fifty-five jurisdictions funded by LEAA block grants have State Planning Agencies (SPAs), which are required by law to be established as the official recipient agency for federal funds on behalf of the state. The fifty-five jurisdictions consist of the fifty states and American Samoa, the District of Columbia, Guam, Puerto Rico, and the Virgin Islands.

POLICE

Through LEAA and other offices, the federal government provides a wide range of support for various aspects of police work. LEAA grants funds for training and equipping state and local police forces and sponsors conferences for law enforcement officials. The FBI will conduct tests in the FBI laboratory for other law enforcement agencies and will also provide information contained in its fingerprint files. The National Crime Information Center (NCIC) keeps records on stolen property and fugitives. FBI instructors give training assistance at law enforcement schools, and conduct courses in special areas such as bomb disposal and bank robbery prevention. Agents of DEA cooperate with state and local police in criminal investigation of drug cases, and in the enforcement of laws pertaining to the sale of drugs.

The Department of Defense, although generally prohibited from enforcing criminal laws, is authorized to aid state and local police, under certain conditions, in quelling civil disorders. The Bureau of Alcohol, Tobacco, and Firearms, a part of the Department of the Treasury, provides assistance to state and local law enforcement agencies through its laboratory analysis. It also assists in tracing guns and explosives and in conducting investigations.

JUVENILE DELINQUENCY

Offices in the Department of Health, Education, and Welfare (HEW) and LEAA provide the majority of federal grants designed to combat juvenile delinquency and to rehabilitate young offenders. The Youth Development and Delinquency Prevention Administration (YDDPA) of HEW awards grants to states for planning programs to combat juvenile delinquency. It helps young offenders adust to their communities upon release. YDDPA also awards grants for training personnel in the field of delinquency prevention and rehabilitation.

The Office of Education in HEW funds vocational training programs for youths in correctional facilities and awards grants for research on youth studies, which include delinquency.

DRUG ABUSE

Another area in which the federal government has substantially expanded its assistance programs is in aid to combat drug abuse. Efforts here are primarily in prevention and rehabilitation. LEAA aids state and local agencies in areas of drug law enforcement, and drug abuse education, treatment, and rehabilitation. In cities with a high addiction rate, discretionary grants may be awarded for more intensive programs. The DEA holds training programs for state and local law enforcement officers, tests and analyzes evidence to be submitted in court cases, participates in criminal investigations, and directs pilot projects for involving community leaders in drug prevention.

RESEARCH AND TECHNOLOGY

Law enforcement today requires the use of new technology to combat crime. In this field, the federal government provides a variety of laboratory services, develops new tools and techniques for fighting crime, and funds further research. Three federal offices give laboratory services to state and local police. These services include analysis of evidence to be used in criminal court cases. The FBI, the DEA, and the Bureau of Alcohol, Tobacco, and Firearms furnish such aid. Finally, LEAA awards grants for various research and technology programs in crime control methods. It also sponsors studies that collect statistics and other basic information on crime.

Commissions

Until very recently, the criminal justice system was essentially ignored by political scientists, students of public administration, and the general public, though perhaps not local politicians. College textbooks on political science devoted only cursory attention to CJS problems, and the scholarly journals largely ignored them. The CJS was mentioned incidentally, of course, in articles on civil liberties and the criminal law; and it was a central figure in occasional exposés of alleged corruption and brutality in newspapers and popular magazines. But as the focus of careful study—of how the CJS operates and why, what the implications of these findings are for the distribution of power in a democracy, and what changes are desirable and feasible—the CJS long escaped the critical attention of students of politics and administrative behavior.

This long-standing state of neglect is now ending. Violence and crime, urban riots, speedier trials, inmate rehabilitation, charges of harassment and brutality in the ghetto, the use of more sophisticated methods of invading privacy—in all these areas there is increased public concern, and in all of them the CJS is centrally involved. Neither the general public nor the student of public affairs now views the CJS as an unimportant instrument whose policies and procedures can be disregarded as long as they are "efficient" in meeting society's goals. The goals of the CJS have been compared by special commissions to those of the society it serves.

One response to the needed improvement of the CJS has been the creation of special commissions. More than thirty years ago, the Wickersham Commission described the scandalous way in which justice was being administered in many of the country's lower courts, and urged that they be abolished; few of them have been abolished, and many of the remaining ones are still a scandal.[31] Following

---

[31] This commission was also known as the National Commission on Law Observance and Enforcement and published fourteen reports: No. 1—*Preliminary Report on Observance and Enforcement of Prohibition,* No. 2—*Report on the Enforcement of the Prohibition Laws of the United States,* No. 3—*Report on Criminal Statistics,* No. 4—*Report on Prosecution,* No. 5—*Report on the Enforcement of the Deportation Laws of the United States,* No. 6—*Report on the Child Offender in the Federal System of Justice,* No. 7—*Progress Report on the Study of the Federal Courts,* No. 8—*Report on Criminal Procedure,* No. 10—*Report on Crime and the Foreign Born,* No. 11—*Report on Lawlessness in Law Enforcement,* No. 12—*Report on the Cost of Crime,* No. 13—*Report on the Causes of Crime,* and No. 14—*Report on Police* (Washington, D.C.: U.S. Department of Justice, 1931).

the Commission's reports, came a series of more specific studies and surveys.[32] The 1960s saw a rebirth of commissions focusing on the CJS.[33] The most prominent are two Presidential Commissions—the Crime Commission, which reported in 1967, and the Riot Commission, which submitted its report early in 1968.[34] These two groups outlined several dozen proposals relating to police-ghetto relations and other areas of concern in the criminal justice system.

Among the recommendations emerging from the commissions were improved screening of police candidates to eliminate those with undesirable personality characteristics; particular care in selecting police for duty in ghetto areas; sharply increased lateral entry, especially to supervisory and specialist positions; more education and training, particularly in nontechnical subjects; and a greater police role in areas outside the traditional law enforcement pattern.

The commissions have grown to be more specific in their focus and recommended changes. The American Bar Association and the National Advisory Commission on Criminal Justice Standards and Goals are two prime examples.[35] The former has created eighteen reports covering such subjects as *Post-Conviction Remedies* (Vol. 2), *Electronic Surveillance* (Vol. 11), and *Function of the Police* (Vol. 17). The ultimate goal of the Advisory Commission's work is as simple to state as it is difficult to accomplish: to reduce crime through a combined effort of federal, state, and local governments. Unlike many of its predecessors, the Commission did not undertake a research program to codify existing reforms in the criminal justice field. Rather, it developed standards that looked toward new di-

---

[32] Attorney General's Conference on Crime, *Proceedings* (Washington, D.C.: U.S. Government Printing Office, December, 1934), and Attorney General's Survey of Release Procedures, Vol. 1—*Digest of Federal and State Laws on Release Procedures,* Vol. 2—*Probation,* Vol. 3—*Pardon,* Vol. 4—*Parole,* and Vol. 5—*Prisons* (Washington, D.C.: U.S. Department of Justice, 1939).

[33] President's Commission on Civil Rights, Vol. 1—*Voting,* Vol. 2—*Education,* Vol. 3—*Employment,* Vol. 4—*Housing,* and Vol. 5—*Justice* (Washington, D.C.: U.S. Government Printing Office, 1961). Attorney General's Committee on Poverty and the Administration of Federal Criminal Justice, *Poverty and the Administration of Federal Criminal Justice* (Washington, D.C.: U.S. Government Printing Office, 1963). National Conference on Bail and Criminal Justice, *Proceedings and Interim Report* (Washington, D.C.: Office of the Attorney General, 1965).

[34] President's Commission on Law Enforcement and the Administration of Justice, Vol. 1—*The Challenge of Crime in a Free Society,* Vol. 2—*Task Force Report: Assessment of Crime,* Vol. 3—*Task Force Report: Corrections,* Vol. 4—*Task Force Report: The Courts,* Vol. 5—*Task Force Report: Drunkenness,* Vol. 6—*Task Force Report: Juvenile Delinquency,* Vol. 7—*Task Force Report: Narcotics and Drug Abuse,* Vol. 8—*Task Force Report: Organized Crime,* Vol. 9—*Task Force Report: The Police,* and Vol. 10—*Task Force Report: Science and Technology* (Washington, D.C.: U.S. Government Printing Office, 1967). National Advisory Commission on Civil Disorders, "Kerner Report," Vol. 1—*Report,* and Vol. 2—*Supplemental Studies* (Washington, D.C.: U.S. Government Printing Office, 1968).

[35] American Bar Association Project on Standards for Criminal Justice (Chicago: American Bar Association), 18 Vols.; and the National Advisory Commission on Criminal Justice Standards and Goals (Washington, D.C.: Law Enforcement Assistance Administration, 1973). The titles of the reports are *A National Strategy to Reduce Crime, Criminal Justice System, Police, Courts, Corrections, Community Crime Prevention, Proceedings of the National Conference on Criminal Justice.*

mensions and directions of growth unhampered by past practices that are no longer relevant or acceptable. The Commission's attitude was that as existing laws or procedures need to be upgraded or eliminated, then state legislatures and state and local agencies should consider implementing such change. Similarly, new technological advances were reviewed for their applicability to law enforcement. Always of foremost importance to the Commission was the wisdom of the Constitution in balancing the needs of our society with the rights of all its members.

Clearly, the 1970s have been a decade for evaluating and implementing CJS standards that are intended to improve its operations and impact on crime.

STATE POLICING

The Federal Omnibus Crime Control and Safe Streets Act of 1968 placed renewed strength in and emphasis on the role of our states in coordinating and assisting local police agencies.[36] Additionally, more resources, new legislation, and innovative programs have enlarged both the role and capability of the state police. Remember, the state's involvement in policing differs from state policing. The former essentially means that state government in general is tending toward more active support and participation of local policing. The most outstanding examples are the state-wide criminal justice planning agencies (formed under the 1968 act) for the planning and distribution of federal and state money to state and local criminal justice agencies to reduce crime. The latter denotes a state police agency or agencies that provide services ranging from full-scale basic police operations to criminal investigation, crime laboratory, data processing, training, statewide communications, and highway traffic patrol.

Most state police agencies are restricted to the enforcement of specific laws or providing services in certain geographical areas. About one-half of the state police agencies (forty-nine states have police agencies) are assigned highway patrol duties as their main responsibility. Slightly over one-half of the state police departments have state-wide investigative powers and crime laboratory facilities. Again, however, the state and the state police agencies are rapidly expanding their ability to assist local departments and take direct police action. Perhaps the best example of this is the growing size and importance of state narcotic agencies.

The State's Regulatory Power

Our states direct or constrain the structure and performance of the police function through statutory or constitutional provisions regarding: (1) the election of various types of law enforcement officials; (2) the mandating of police personnel and pension requirements and minimum standards for police recruitment; and (3)

---

[36] This section is drawn in part from the Advisory Commission on Intergovernmental Relations, *State-Local Relations in the Criminal Justice System* (Washington, D.C.: U.S. Government Printing Office, 1971), pp. 82–87.

legal rules on the local powers of police in such matters as arrest and search and seizure.

In regard to the first point, forty-eight states regulate the election of various law enforcement officials, though several states allow optional provision of election or appointment under various forms of home-rule charters. Nearly all the states dictate that the county sheriffs be elected. Second, some states have also stipulated that local police meet mandatory employee qualifications before they receive permanent appointment. Third, the state places restrictions on the exercise of the local police power through its criminal code. Thus, only a state may provide powers of out-of-state arrest and pursuit. And only a state may make statutory provisions regarding the scope of police powers in the matter of arrest and search and seizure. Also of consequence, states are the prime movers in agreeing to interstate compacts and uniform laws in the area of crime control. These compacts and uniform laws increase the effectiveness of police work, especially in interstate situations.

State Police Services

States not only prescribe conditions under which the local police function is exercised, they also provide direct police services in all the states except Hawaii. State police forces range from a few hundred to many thousands. On the average, state forces account for 10 to 15 percent of total police employment within a state.

The forty-nine state police forces exhibit a wide variety of assigned tasks (see Table 2–2). Thus, state forces in Alabama, Oklahoma, and North Carolina

TABLE 2-2 Selected Characteristics of State Police Departments: 1968

State	Time Spent on		Particular Type of State Police Responsibilities					
	Traffic Services	Criminal Investig.	State-wide Crime	General State Patrol	Unincorporated Area Patrol	Statewide Investig.	Investig. Upon Request
Alabama	90.0%	6.4%		X			X
Alaska	25.0	35.0	X	X		X	
Arizona	45.0	.2		X			
Arkansas	60.0	10.0	X	X		X	
California	88.0	1.0		X	X		
Colorado	80.0	—		X			
Connecticut	30.0	19.0	X	X		X	
Delaware	47.3	41.8	X	X		X	

TABLE 2-2 (Continued)

State	Time Spent on		Particular Type of State Police Responsibilities				
	Traffic Services	Criminal Investig.	State-wide Crime	General State Patrol	Unincorporated Area Patrol	Statewide Investig.	Investig. Upon Request
Florida	86.0	1.0		X		X	
Georgia	50.0	10.0	X	X		X	
Hawaii			No State Police Force				
Idaho	53.0	2.0	X	X			X
Illinois	76.4	6.8	X	X		X	
Indiana	55.0	11.0	X	X	X	X	
Iowa	80.0	5.0		X			
Kansas	62.0	10.0		X			
Kentucky	82.0	10.0		X		X	
Louisiana	86.5	—	X	X			
Maine	80.0	15.0	X	X		X	
Maryland	80.0	15.0	X	X	X		
Massachusetts	NA	NA	X	X		X	
Michigan	30.0	29.0	X	X		X	
Minnesota	72.0	—		X			X
Mississippi	70.0	20.0			X		X
Missouri	67.9	4.2		X		X	
Montana	75.0	3.0		X			X
Nebraska	68.7	8.2	X	X		X	
Nevada	70.0	—			X		
New Hampshire	69.0	11.0	X	X		X	
New Jersey	41.5	23.3	X	X		X	
New Mexico	68.8	8.1	X	X		X	
New York	46.2	39.7	X	X		X	
North Carolina	95.0	.5			X		
North Dakota	81.3	1.0		X		X	
Ohio	80.0	2.0	X	X	X	X	
Oklahoma	93.0	2.0			X		X
Oregon	70.2	8.4	X	X		X	
Pennsylvania	59.8	22.6	X	X		X	
Rhode Island	NA	NA	X	X		X	
South Carolina	90.0	—			X		
South Dakota	60.0	5.0		X			
Tennessee	85.0	5.0			X		X
Texas	62.0	28.0	X	X		X	
Utah	66.7	3.8		X			
Vermont	60.0	30.0	X		X		
Virginia	81.9	10.8	X	X		X	
Washington	87.0	9.0		X			
West Virginia	51.6	14.6	X	X		X	
Wisconsin	87.0	—					
Wyoming	73.7	—		X			
Total States			26	41	11	26	7

TABLE 2-2 (Continued)

State	Training Local Police	Statewide Criminal Responsibility	Laboratory Services for Local Police	Investigating Complaints about Local Police	Provide for Local Radio-Comm.	Radio-Comm. with Local Police	Provision of Teletypewriter System
Alabama	X	X					X
Alaska			X	X			
Arizona					X	X	X
Arkansas	X	X	X				X
California		X	X				
Colorado	X						X
Connecticut	X	X	X				X
Delaware	X	X					X
Florida		X	X				X
Georgia	X		X	X	X		X
Hawaii	No State Police Force						
Idaho							X
Illinois		X	X	X			X
Indiana		X	X				
Iowa		X	X				X
Kansas		X	X				X
Kentucky		X	X				X
Louisiana		X	X				
Maine	X	X	X	X			X
Maryland	X	X	X	X		X	X
Massachusetts	X	X	X		X		X
Michigan		X	X	X			X
Minnesota	X	X					X
Mississippi		X	X				
Missouri	X	X	X			X	X
Montana				X			X
Nebraska		X	X	X	X		X
Nevada						X	X
New Hampshire	X	X	X		X	X	X
New Jersey	X	X	X				X
New Mexico	X			X			X
New York		X	X	X			X
North Carolina		X	X				
North Dakota						X	X
Ohio							X
Oklahoma		X	X				X
Oregon	X	X	X				X
Pennsylvania		X	X				X
Rhode Island	X		X			X	X
South Carolina		X	X				X
South Dakota		X					

76

TABLE 2-2 (Continued)

State	Training Local Police	Statewide Criminal Responsibility	Laboratory Services for Local Police	Investigating Complaints about Local Police	Provide for Local Radio-Comm.	Radio-Comm. with Local Police	Provision of Teletypewriter System
Tennessee		X	X				
Texas	X	X	X	X	X		X
Utah					X		X
Vermont			X				
Virginia						X	X
Washington							X
West Virginia		X	X				X
Wisconsin		X	X				X
Wyoming					X		X
Total States	17	33	33	11	8	8	40

Source: Advisory Commission on Intergovernmental Relations, State-Local Relations in the Criminal Justice System (Washington, D.C.: U.S. Government Printing Office, 1971), p. 33.

devote more than 90 percent of their time to general highway patrol duty, those in New York and Delaware spend 40 percent of their time in statewide criminal investigation. Seven states restrict state police patrol solely to unincorporated areas, and only twenty-six states give their police forces state-wide investigative responsibilities. Of course, the limited character of many state police departments is due to the manner in which states organize their public safety responsibilities. Overall, it appears that only a relatively small number of state police agencies have full range of police responsibilities.

Figure 2–1 depicts the organizational structure of a state police agency that can be categorized as "partial service" with its major commitment to traffic, criminalistics and data processing/telecommunications. A so-called "full service" agency would also include the uniform patrol and investigative functions.

State Assistance

States also may furnish a range of technical and financial assistance to local police departments. Several state police and state investigation bureaus provide investigative services to localities on request (see the standard below). Approximately 20 percent of the states offer state police-sponsored training to local governments. Over one-third have central crime laboratories that often provide technical assistance to local agencies. The National Advisory Commission on

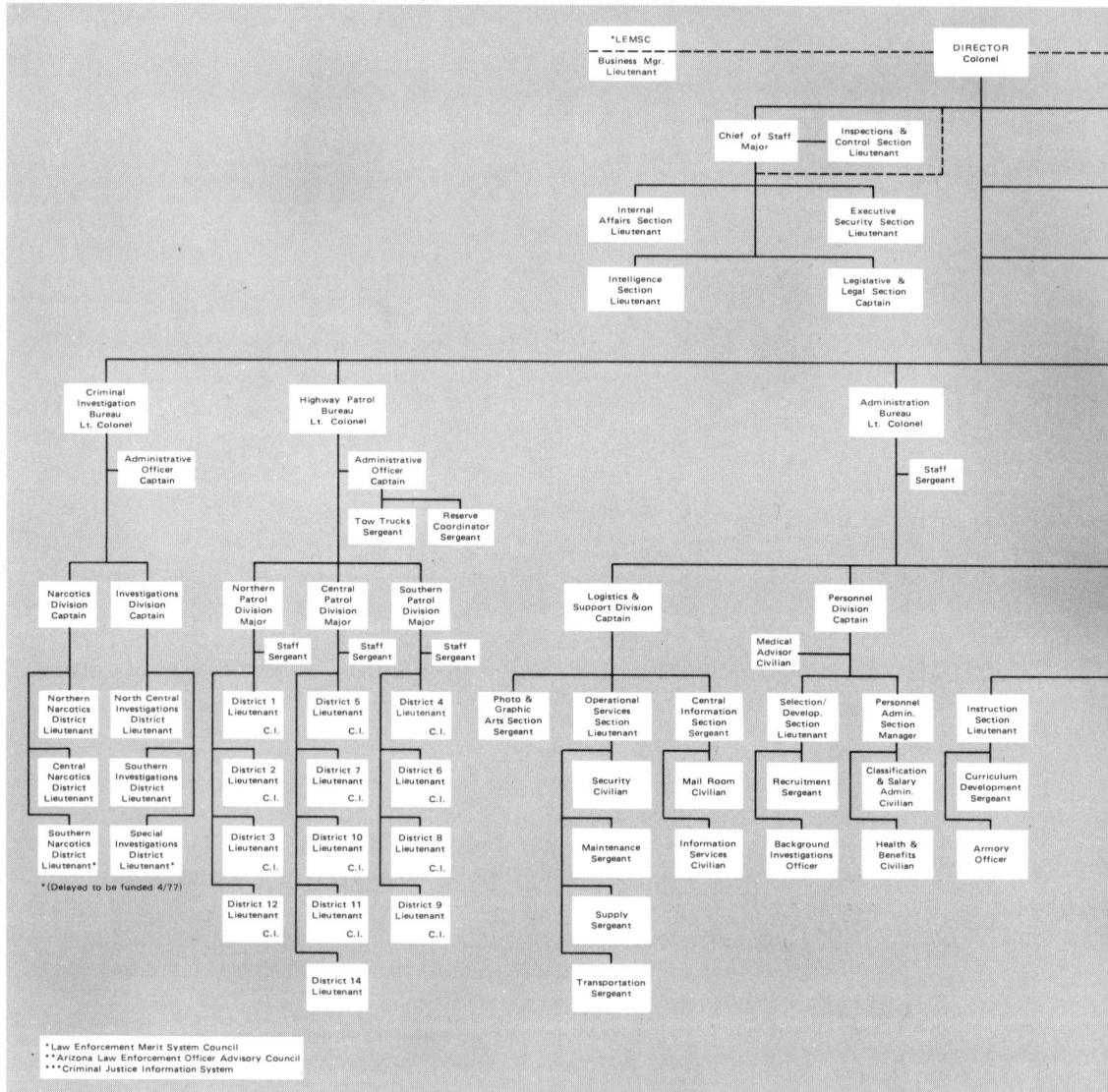

FIGURE 2-1   State of Arizona Department of Public Safety Organizational Structure

Criminal Justice supports such state assistance, in that it indicates that the states should establish a consolidated criminal laboratory system composed of local, regional, or state facilities capable of providing the most advanced forensic science services to police agencies. Further, it feels that every police agency should immediately ensure that it has access to at least one laboratory facility capable of timely and efficient processing of physical evidence.[37]

[37] National Advisory Commission on Criminal Justice Standards and Goals, *Working Papers from the National Conference on Criminal Justice* (Washington, D.C.: Law Enforcement Assistance Administration, January 1973), p. 71.

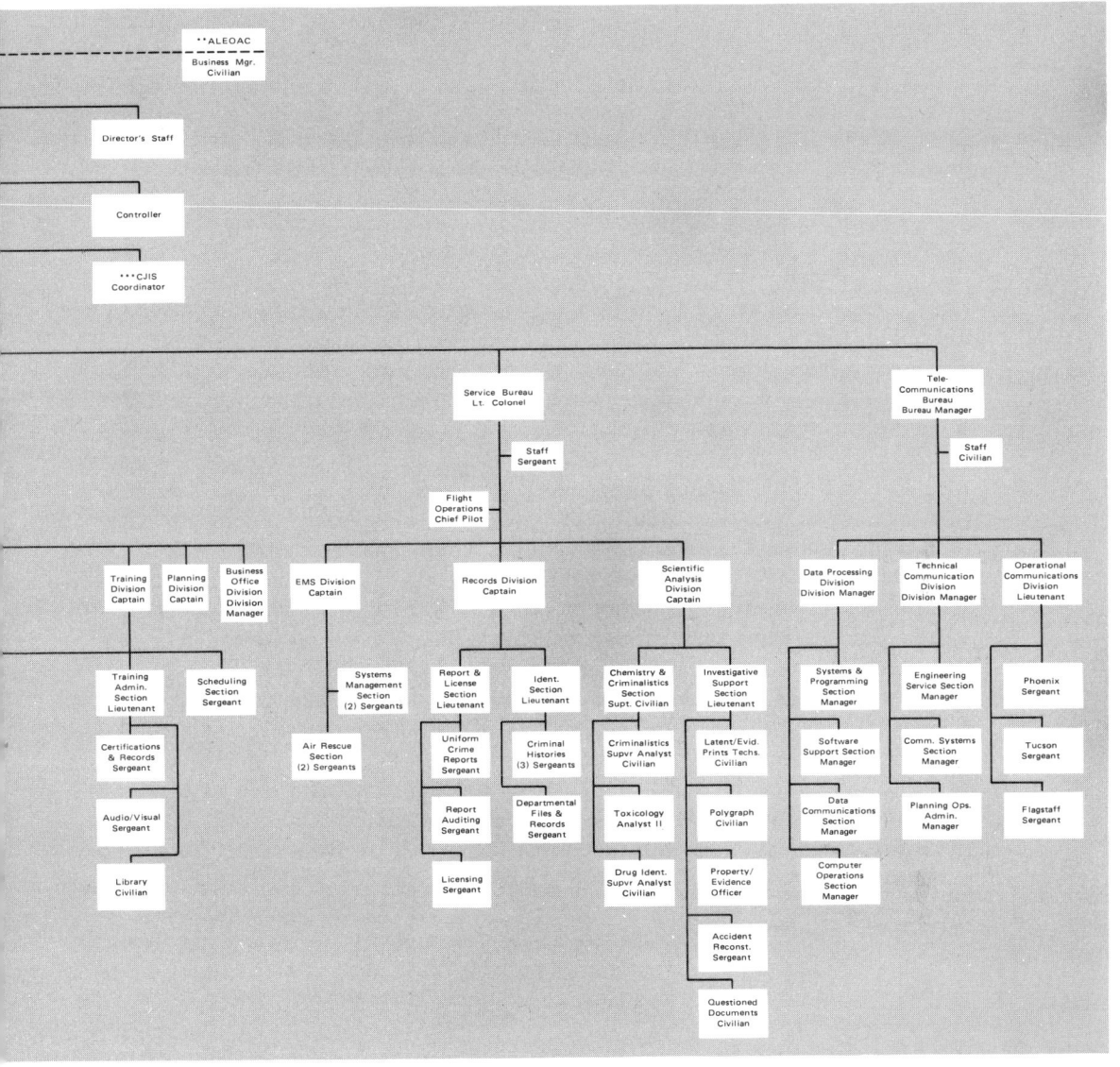

Standard 9.4

STATE SPECIALISTS

Every State, by 1975, should provide, upon the request of any local police agency in the State, specialists to assist in the investigation of crimes and other incidents that may require extensive or highly specialized investigative resources not otherwise available to the local agency. The State may also fund regional operational specialist activities. The State or regional specialists should not provide everyday needs to local law enforcement.

1. Every State should provide trained specialists who are properly equipped to assist local police agencies. Where appropriate, the State should provide funds to combine or consolidate local special investigative resources.

2. Every State should publish and distribute to every local police agency in the State the request procedure for obtaining specialists.

3. Every State should insure that its specialists pursue the investigation in complete cooperation with and support of the local agency.[38]

A few state police agencies may investigate complaints of local police corruption. Almost all the fifty states authorize their state agencies to provide supportive communications and information services to localities on request. (See Table 2-3 as an example.) Such aid allows local agencies to use the expertise of state agencies and thereby avoid incurring extra costs in the provision of specialized services. Again, over one-third have police standards commissions that administer statewide training programs. The majority of these agencies determine mandatory training standards for local policemen. Many of the commissions offer their programs at no cost to participating localities, and some states provide partial reimbursement to localities for the officer's salary while he is in training. States also broaden the capability of individual local agencies by providing other technical aids. Thus, some states provide extensive criminal identification and investigative services to local police departments. Again, the National Advisory Commission lends weight to this role by recommending that the states should provide, upon the request by any local police agency in the state, specialists to assist in the investigation of crimes and other incidents that may require extensive or highly specialized investigative resources not otherwise available to the local agency. The state may also finance regional operational specialist activities. Further, the commission recommended that the state or regional specialists should not provide everyday needs to local law enforcement.[39]

The states also furnish some form of fiscal aid for local police operations. As mentioned previously, the most outstanding example can be seen in the various state-wide planning agencies that were established under the Safe Streets Act of 1968.

Concluding Remarks

In summary, the police function is a *shared* responsibility of state and local government. In very broad terms, local governments produce the bulk of police work, and state governments have more limited, specialized police duties. Local governments generally perform patrol and general investigation duties; state governments perform highway patrol and, in some cases, render centralized supportive services (that is, central crime laboratories and criminal records centers) to local

---

[38] National Advisory Commission on Criminal Justice Standards and Goals, *Police*, p. 219.

[39] National Advisory Commission on Criminal Justice Standards and Goals, *Working Papers*, p. 69.

agencies. State police agencies are playing a larger role in training, crime laboratory, and communications assistance to local police departments, and local governments cooperate with state agencies in matters of criminal records, criminal investigation, and organized-crime control. Keep in mind, however, that the bulk of police personnel and expenditures still are provided at the local level, and some of the country's most sophisticated police forces are local forces. They represent the "front end" of police protection in the state-local police system.

LOCAL POLICING

The term *local* denotes city and county "policing" or police and sheriff departments. At this point, a more theoretical discussion of the functions and responsibilities of the local police is presented. Remember, local policing varies in many ways and rightly so. Please cast aside the idea that there is "one best way" to structure and plan a police agency.

Police Services

Both state and local police departments normally provide a "package of activities" in police work. These activities fall into two main categories: (1) program services, which include general patrol, traffic supervision, criminal investigation, juvenile work, and criminal intelligence activities; and (2) support services, which include police recruitment and training, internal control, planning and research, public information activities, records and communications activities, jail management, and crime laboratory services of "criminalistics."

The size of a police department, the extent and type of criminal activities it must deal with, and whether it is in a central city, suburb, or rural area all affect the department's ability to perform the various facets of its police work. To illustrate, a small police force must often combine its investigative and intelligence activities in one division or forego such activities altogether. A larger police department, on the other hand, may have separate divisions for investigative and intelligence operations and be able to employ various types of skilled personnel, such as evidence technicians. Police work is also affected by location. A community bisected by large arterial roads will have a greater traffic responsibility than another community that is more "off the beaten path." Finally, the amount and type of crime a police force must deal with will affect its police work. Communities having frequent racial disturbances will have more sophisticated community relations programs than racially homogeneous communities.

PROGRAM SERVICES

Local police and sheriff departments usually perform several distinct types of line operations or program services. These include general patrol, traffic supervision, criminal investigation, juvenile delinquency control, and undercover criminal intelligence work. The size of the department usually determines whether

TABLE 2–3 Information Available from the State of California Division of Law Enforcement

Description	Provisions
AUTOMATED PROPERTY SYSTEM The Automated Property System (APS) is a computerized repository of serialized property which has been reported as stolen, pawned, lost, found, under observation of evidence.	The APS provides law enforcement agencies with a rapid method of identifying serialized property reported under several categories. It also aids in the identification of the criminal in his attempt to dispose of stolen property across jurisdictional boundaries and through pawn shops. It also aids in the recovery of lost property. When a local agency enters an item of property that has been pawned, found or reported as lost or stolen, the system automatically checks all property already in file for a matching entry. If no hit is made, the item becomes a part of the file and is itself searched against subsequent entries or inquiries. If a hit is made, the entering and/or inquiring agency is automatically notified by a terminal printout.
MANUAL PROPERTY IDENTIFICATION SYSTEMS In addition to the Automated Property System (APS), the Property Identification Unit maintains manual files to aid in identification of property and persons who frequently pawn or sell property.	1. *Suspicious Pledgors' Name Index File (SPIN)* Reports of pawn and buy transactions are maintained alphabetically by the pledgor's names in a manual file. This file assists in identifying persons who frequently pawn or sell property. The file contains pawn tickets received from California law enforcement agencies pursuant to Section 11108 of the Penal Code. When a pledgor pawns large amounts of property (especially in different shops and cities) he becomes a "Suspicious Pledgor." His name is then searched in our master name index for a criminal record. The pawned property is searched in both the automated and manual systems for possible stolen reports. If stolen property is located and the suspicious pledgor is identified as having a criminal record, the concerned agencies are notified. Agencies are also notified if a suspicious pledgor does not have a criminal record but has pawned large amounts of property. The SPIN file is dependent upon pawn and buy reports contributed by local agencies. All reports containing serialized and nonserialized articles should be forwarded to the Bureau of Identification. If one desires to know if a particular suspect has been pawning or selling property, one may request a search of the SPIN file by a teletype or telephone call to the Property Identification Unit. 2. *Stolen Non-Automated Property File (SNAP)* Information pertaining to nonserialized stolen, lost, found, or under observation property that cannot be entered into the automated systems is recorded on index cards and filed by description. All property indexed into the SNAP file must have a unique

description or characteristic which makes it possible to identify. SNAP is a limited and restricted file. The types of property maintained in the SNAP file are antiques, collections (such as coins or stamps), art objects, ornate jewelry, precious stones, expensive furs, safes, and job lots of property stolen from stores, warehouses, or trucks.

Upon request, suspected stolen property that is not identified in the automated property file may be searched in the SNAP file for possible connection with a stolen report. The name of the reporting agency and case number can be provided.

3. *Inscription File*

The inscription file consists of stolen, lost, found, evidence, under observation, pawn or buy articles that have inscriptions. Inscription data is recorded on index cards.

The inscription cards are filed in alphabetical order according to the wording of the inscription. New inscription cards are checked for possible hook-ups with previous information in file. The file can be searched by inscription only. The interested law enforcement agencies are notified of the hook-ups by letter or teletype.

STOLEN BICYCLE SYSTEM

The Stolen Bicycle System (SBS) is a computerized repository of serialized bicycles which are reported stolen, lost, pawned, found, and under observation.

The SBS provides law enforcement agencies with a rapid method of identifying stolen or recovered bicycles. It provides a single file in which to search and store data on stolen or lost bicycles which have serial numbers. The ability to request special searches by reporting agency, bicycle make or a combination thereof also exists.

AUTOMATED FIREARMS SYSTEM

The Automated Firearms System (AFS) is a computerized repository of serialized firearm information.

AFS provides law enforcement agencies with a rapid method of identifying firearms. There are two files in AFS, namely the Law Enforcement File and the Historical File.

STOLEN VEHICLE SYSTEM

The Stolen Vehicle System (SVS) is a computerized repository of vehicle information of interest to law enforcement agencies.

The SVS provides law enforcement agencies with a rapid method of reporting and identifying stolen vehicles, vehicle parts, felony vehicles, stolen license plates, stored vehicles, lost vehicles, repossessed vehicles and vehicles associated with missing persons. Stolen vehicles, parts and license plates and felony vehicles are automatically placed in the NCIC file. All other entries are maintained only in SVS.

WANTED PERSONS SYSTEM

The Wanted Persons System (WPS) is a computerized repository of subjects for whom a warrant has been issued or a temporary (48-hour) want has been entered.

The WPS provides a rapid method to determine if a person is wanted by another agency. The file does not contain warrant abstracts, but is a "pointer" file describes the wanted person and names the wanting agencies. All "hits" must be verified with the wanting agencies.

TABLE 2–3 (continued)

Description	Provisions
CHILD ABUSE UNIT The Department of Justice maintains a central statewide file to correlate child abuse and neglect cases.	The file contains and provides reports of child beating, child neglect, assaults on children, death reports of children, incest and child molestation where a member of the family is involved. The file consists of the names of suspects, parents, victims, babysitters and other children mentioned in the reports. Upon receipt of a child abuse report, the names of the persons involved are entered into the file and compared with the existing names in the file. Local agencies are notified of matches in accordance with Section 11161.5 of the Penal Code.
MISSING PERSONS AND UNIDENTIFIED DECEASED UNIT The Department of Justice maintains two central statewide files containing identification data on (1) missing persons and on (2) unidentified deceased.	The file provides a means by which law enforcement agencies can obtain assistance on a state level in locating missing persons and identifying deceased persons. The missing persons information is compared with the unidentified deceased file. When matching information is found, the concerned agencies are notified.
SEX AND NARCOTIC REGISTRANT UNIT The Department of Justice maintains a central statewide file of persons who have been convicted of specific sex and narcotic offenses.	Persons convicted of certain narcotic violations (see Section 11590, Health and Safety Code) are required by law to register with the police agency in the jurisdiction where they reside for a period of five years after the date of sentence, custody or from end of the probation or parole. An alphabetic name file of these registrants is maintained in the Bureau of Identification. Persons convicted of certain sex offenses (see Section 290 of the Penal Code) are required by law to register with the police agency in the jurisdiction where they reside for life unless relieved from this responsibility through appropriate judicial process. An alphabetic name file of these registrants is maintained in the Bureau of Identification.

COMMAND CENTER—RECORD INQUIRY UNIT

The Department of Justice Command Center is a manual expedite unit whose primary function is to provide criminal record information to law enforcement and criminal justice agencies on a timely and continual basis. The unit is manned twenty-four hours per day, seven days per week.

In addition to providing criminal record information to authorized agencies on a need-to-know basis, the Command Center provides assistance in the use of the Wanted Persons System, Criminal History System, Automated Property System, Firearms System, Stolen Bicycle System, Stolen Vehicle System and format assistances for CLETS, LEDS, and NLETS.

COMMUNICATION CENTER

The Department of Justice Communication Center receives all teletype requests for record checks, APBs and direct responses to various units within the Department of Justice. The Communication Center is also the California Control Center for NLETS. The Communication Center is manned twenty-four hours per day, seven days per week.

The Communication Center provides formal instructions for the CLETS and the NLETS systems to users in the field who need assistance. Also, nationwide and regional broadcast requests are intercepted and scanned to determine if they meet the proper criteria. They are either broadcast on the CLETS or NLETS system, or a rejection notice is sent to the originator. Improperly addressed messages are examined, corrected and retransmitted. If the addressed agency does not have a CLETS terminal the originator is advised that the message cannot be delivered.

Courtesy: Division of Law Enforcement, State Attorney General, State of California (1978) various line operations have a distinct identity within the agency. Smaller departments often do not have separate divisions for various line operations. In general, larger departments perform their line operations in a more specialized fashion. Thus, larger police departments more often are able to delegate traffic supervision to civilian personnel, employ a greater number of specialized vehicles in their police work, and provide more in-service training to their policemen in handling mass violence.

The scope of program services that departments perform also may differ among localities. General patrol in a resort community may consist of protecting unoccupied property and discouraging vagrancy. General patrol in a large city or county is more dynamic, involving the prevention of such serious crimes as robbery, assault, or grand larceny. Similarly, criminal investigation may not have a separate status in smaller departments. Sophisticated criminal investigation can demand a full-time officer who is trained in the basic principles of criminal detection and who has working relationships with the local prosecutor. Specialization in criminal investigation may also be necessary to determine the *modus operandi* of certain types of crime. Therefore, investigation may be a separate line function in a large department, although this is not an altogether healthy development in the local police function as it can create an artificial division between the patrol and investigative function. Further, juvenile work and criminal inteligence operations are provided only by larger police departments in any systematic fashion. With the greater availability of resources and specially trained personnel, larger agencies can accord these line operations separate status. Smaller communities usually lack the funds and personnel for such operations as juvenile work, and often obtain criminal intelligence from either large city/county, state, or federal agencies.

SUPPORT SERVICES

Support services include such activities as police recruitment and training, internal controls and inspection, planning and research, public information, community relations activities, information processing, communications, jail operations, and crime laboratory. These operations support the program services of the municipal police department. Again, the scope of these services often depends on the size of the police department. Smaller departments generally do not have the money or manpower to invest in these services nor are such services always essential to such departments.

Although most departments have recruitment and training programs, those that are smaller in size typically rely on other, larger agencies to provide basic training. Smaller departments also often have only ad hoc internal control or planning and research capability. Larger police departments will have separate internal control divisions and may have planning and research activities that can provide a police department with alternative programs for combating crime. Another staff service is in the area of community relations. Here again, only the larger departments are apt to implement full-scale programs.

Almost all departments have at least rudimentary record-keeping capacity. There have been continuing improvements in more sophisticated systems of crime reporting, and most local police systems have a basic record-keeping capability that is linked to a state and national crime reporting system (for example, the FBI's National Crime Information Center).

Jail management is another support function of municipal police and county sheriffs. Local jails are used for such purposes as (1) short-term confinement of criminals and misdemeanants serving sentences of less than one year; (2) preventive detention of people awaiting trial; and (3) "lockups" for minor offenders, mainly public drunkards. Police and sheriffs' departments also perform criminal laboratory services that aid in the evidence-gathering activities inherent to the police function. Laboratory services, however, are more centralized than most other police functions. Quite often, many local departments receive their laboratory services from state or federal sources, though some of the larger local departments have renowned crime laboratories.

The County Sheriff:
From Cowboy Hats to Computers

The role and responsibility of the county sheriff is undergoing sweeping changes. The elective office, once belittled as a politician-police fiasco, is in the process of recouping prominence and a professional police status. We witness professional, well-trained police managers being elected by an aware electorate to the office of sheriff. Because of the political power that comes with a mandate from the *people,* the sheriff is finding himself in a better position to *resist* political pressure from a *person.* The combination of police services and regionalization of crime fighting efforts causes the sheriff to be looked at more and more for solutions to the problems of improved operations among jurisdictions and economy of scale. In the former case, some sheriffs are providing leadership in regional crime operations such as a multiagency attack on drug abuse. In the latter case, the sheriffs are furnishing by contract full or partial police services to cities within the county.

The day of the one- or two-man sheriff's agencies is yet with us, but is coming to a close. With consolidation of operations becoming more imperative, it appears that either the sheriff or a combination of city police agencies will survive in the future. As of this writing, the sheriff (elected or appointed) has an even greater chance of fulfilling the need for furnishing full-scale police services to one or more jurisdictions within a county or region.

Private Policing

> Over the past few years, the public police have received a great deal of attention and serious study; the private police have not. But today, of roughly 800,000 public and private security personnel in the United States, only half are public police officers.

And expenditures on public police (counting the costs of security devices as well as personnel) account for only roughly half of the $8.7 billion spent annually on both public and private security.[40]

It is held that private security services (provided by high-quality personnel and equipment) effectively complement the public police by providing security and other related services in areas and situations where the police do not—either because public police are not given adequate resources or because they are legally constrained from doing so. This view also holds that current controls and regulation are adequate because private police seldom abuse their powers. The other view holds that the private security "industry" feeds on fear and provides ineffective security services by untrained, low-quality personnel who are a potential danger to the public and who, in fact, abuse their limited powers. This view also holds that current controls on, and regulations of, private police are inadequate. Thus, we find ample reason to describe the role and extent of private policing.

THE ROLE AND FUNCTIONS OF THE PRIVATE POLICE

Public and private security forces are highly diverse. They may be categorized in several ways: by who employs them—a public agency or a private business, institution, or individual; by the degree of police powers they possess; or by the functions they perform. In this test, we utilize all three ways of categorizing security forces, as appropriate to the discussion at hand. The terms *private police* and *private security forces and security personnel* are used in this text to include all types of private organizations and individuals providing all types of security-related services, including investigation, guard patrol, lie detection, alarm, and armored transportation.

Within the private sector, there are a variety of security forces. They are either *contract forces* providing security services for a fee, or *in-house forces,* not for hire, providing services exclusively for the business institution or individual that employs them. Contract security agencies provide one or more of the following personnel services: guard; roving patrol (on foot or in cars); armored-car escort; central station alarm; and various investigative functions, such as credit, insurance, and preemployment background checks, and investigations in connection with civil and criminal court proceedings. Guard, patrol, investigative, and alarm services are also provided by in-house forces. Both types of security personnel are used by a wide variety of consumers, including individual citizens, banks, retail establishments, insurance companies, and other financial institutions, hospitals, industrial firms, educational institutions, and apartment houses, and at recreational events. Most private security personnel have no peace officer powers.

---

[40] James S. Kakalik and Sorrel Wildhorn, *Private Police in the United States: Findings and Recommendations,* Vol. 1 (Washington, D.C.: U.S. Government Printing Office, 1972), p. viii. The majority of the thinking expressed about private policing is derived from this benchmark document.

In some cases, the public and private sectors overlap. A small fraction of the privately employed security personnel, which we shall call *special police,* are granted either full or limited public powers by virtue of being deputized or commissioned by local police or state agencies. The police powers of these special forces generally may be exercised only while they are on duty at a specified geographic location, such as their employer's or client's property. Another not uncommon situation is for public policemen to accept supplementary second jobs as private security personnel. These moonlighting public police generally retain their full police powers even while working for the private employers.

Today, certain general principles have emerged that in practice define the roles of and relations between public law enforcement and private security in the United States. With some notable exceptions in which responsibilities overlap, these principles are:

1. The public police have the primary responsibility for maintaining order, enforcing the laws, preventing crime, investigating crimes, and apprehending criminals.
2. Public property is policed primarily by public police.
3. Policing private property is the primary responsibility of the owner, the management, or the homeowners, all of whom may provide or purchase private security services and equipment.
4. The private police are primarily concerned with crime prevention and detection, rather than crime investigation or criminal apprehension.
5. When invited or called, public police will enter private property for the purposes of restoring order and enforcing the law.
6. When they have not been called, public police may enter private property, if this is necessary to stop a crime from being committed or to make an arrest. Depending on crime patterns, they sometimes patrol private property that is readily accessible to the public, such as shopping center parking lots.
7. The public police can, and sometimes do, advise owners, managers, and homeowners with regard to crime prevention measures; that is, they play the role of consultants in encouraging crime prevention.

As a general rule, then, private police are usually concerned with the prevention and detection of crime on private property and the gathering of information for use by the client or client organization. Public police are primarily concerned with the public interest and with events in public areas; they have responsibility for the prevention of serious crime against the person; they have responsibility for apprehension of criminals; and they respond to urgent calls and requests from the public. Therefore, most private security services in our society complement public police services. But in some situations, such as in residential patrol or stakeouts by public police on private property, their roles are supplementary. Generally speaking, however, under current arrangements such supplementary roles involve only a small portion of the efforts of both public police and private police. Reserve and other special-purpose public police, on the other hand, typically supplement the public police forces because they generally perform some or all of the public police functions.

INTERGOVERNMENTAL COORDINATION

Coordinating activities of the various policing agencies is a significant and commanding chore. Laws differ, rules differ, goals differ, and jurisdictional expectations differ. Nonetheless, the various levels of policing, in order to be effective, must combine their efforts into a singular program that is targeted towards commonly agreed upon ends—an endeavor considerably more ambitious than placing man on the moon.

What is being done (or anticipated) to develop a unified front in policing our society in an individually humane and socially efficient way? The immediate response is, not enough. However, meaningful steps have been or are being taken to construct an integrated effort. Without a great deal of elaboration, we cite the following:

Planning. Those involved in federal, state, and local police work are developing and implementing definitive plans for improved levels of coordination (e.g., LEAA, regional planning councils, community-based coordinating councils, interagency strike forces, etc.).

Information System Sharing. Computer-based police information systems are being designed, implemented, and used for accurately and rapidly sharing time-relevant data. It is now feasible for a police officer to ask questions of a nationwide (NCIC) data base.

Professionalization/Education. The police are not today a profession. However, we propose that they soon (by 1990?) will become so. Professionalization denotes many things including: goal consensus, ethics, standardization, and an above-average occupational status. In total, they serve to undersign a mutually supportive approach to policing our nation.

LEARNING EXERCISES

Issues to Be Discussed

1. Since the police are a relatively new institution, what growing pains should they anticipate as they mature and move toward a professional status?
2. What can be done to better assess the ability of our police to attain their stated and implicit goals?
3. Of the various *federal* policing roles, which is the most crucial today in terms of crime reduction?
4. Of the various *state* policing roles, which is the most crucial today in terms of crime reduction?
5. Secure sufficient copies of the Federal Omnibus Crime Control and Safe Streets Act of 1968 in order that the class can be divided into subgroups of five members each. The groups are to: (1) assess the intent of the act, and (2) briefly summarize what they believe to be its most significant features. In turn, the entire class is to reach consensus on what are the more important aspects of the legislation.

Group Activity

Divide the class into groups of five members each. Imagine that each group has $1 million to spend. Each group is to independently allocate that amount among (or purchase) given police goals (see Table 2-1, emerging goals). For example, they may elect to appropriate $100,000 to "maintain social order." Once they have completed their deliberations, each group is to reveal its decisions along with a summary explanation.

Field Activity

Visit the local criminal justice planning agency and review their current plan and dollar allocations. (If no agency is close, then write for the plan.) Do the plan and monies appropriated have any particular emphasis? Write a synopsis of the plan along with your evaluation.

Key Terms

American Bar Association Project on Standards for Criminal Justice (ABA Standards)
Drug Enforcement Administration (DEA)
Federal Bureau of Investigation (FBI)
Goal
Intergovernmental Coordination
Law Enforcement Assistance Administration (LEAA)
Local law enforcement
National Advisory Commission on Criminal Justice Standards and Goals (NAC)
Private policing
Program services
Role
Support services

SUGGESTED REFERENCES

AMERICAN BAR ASSOCIATION, Project on Standards for Criminal Justice. *The Urban Police Function.* New York: American Bar Association, 1973.

BITTNER, EGON. *The Functions of the Police in Modern Society.* Chevy Chase, Md.: National Institute of Mental Health, 1970.

BOPP, WILLIAM, and SCHULTZ, DONALD. *A Short History of American Law Enforcement.* Springfield, Ill.: Charles C Thomas, 1972.

CLARK, RAMSEY. *Crime in America.* New York: Simon & Schuster, 1970.

CLONINGER, DALE O. *The Economics of Crime and Law Enforcement.* Sarasota, Fla.: University Print, 1975.

COHEN, BERNARD. *The Police International Administration of Justice in New York City.* New York: Rand Institute, 1970.

DUNFORD, FRANKLYN W. "Police Diversion: An Illusion?" *Criminology,* (November 1977), pp. 335-51.

GARMIRE, BERNARD L., et al. *Municipal Police Administration.* 8th ed. Washington, D.C.: International City Management Association, 1977.

GOLDSMITH, JACK, AND GOLDSMITH, SHAWN S. *The Police Community: The Dimensions of a Subculture.* Pacific Palisades, Calif.: Palisades Publishers, 1974.

GOLDSTEIN, HERMAN. *Policing in a Free Society.* Cambridge, Mass.: Ballinger Publishing Co., 1977.

MANNING, PETER K. *Police Work: The Social Organization of Policy.* New York: McGraw-Hill, 1977.

MOORE, HARRY W., JR., ed. *Critical Issues in Law Enforcement.* Cincinnati: W. H. Anderson, 1972.

MORRIS, NORWALL, AND HAWKINS, GORDON. *The Honest Politician's Guide to Crime Control.* Chicago: University of Chicago Press, 1969.

MUIR, WILLIAM K. *Police: Streetcorner Politicians.* Chicago: University of Chicago Press, 1977.

NATIONAL ADVISORY COMMISSION ON CRIMINAL JUSTICE STANDARDS AND GOALS. *Criminal Justice System.* Washington, D.C.: U.S. Government Printing Office, 1973.

———. *A National Strategy to Reduce Crime.* Washington, D.C.: U.S. Government Printing Office, 1973.

———. *Police.* Washington, D.C.: U.S. Government Printing Office, 1973.

PRESIDENT'S COMMISSION ON LAW ENFORCEMENT AND THE ADMINISTRATION OF JUSTICE. *The Challenge of Crime in a Free Society.* Washington D.C.: U.S. Government Printing Office, 1967.

———. *Task Force Report: The Police.* Washington, D.C.: U.S. Government Printing Office, 1967.

QUINNEY, RICHARD. *The Social Reality of Crime.* Boston: Little, Brown, 1970.

RADZINOWICZ, SIR LEON, AND WOLFGANG, MARVIN E., eds. *Crime and Justice,* Vol. 2. *The Criminal in the Arms of the Law.* 2nd rev. ed. New York: Basic Books, 1977.

RECKLESS, WALTER C. *The Crime Problem.* 5th ed. New York: Appleton-Century-Crofts, 1973.

RUBENSTEIN, JONATHAN. *City Police.* New York: Farrar, Straus & Giroux, 1973.

RUCHELMAN, LEONARD. *Police Politics: A Comparative Study of Three Cities.* Cambridge, Mass.: Ballinger Publishing Co., 1974.

SKOLNICK, JEROME H. *Justice Without Trial: Law Enforcement in a Democratic Society.* 2nd ed. New York: John Wiley, 1975.

SMITH, BRUCE, JR. *Police Systems in the United States.* New York: Harper & Row, 1960.

SULLIVAN, JOHN R. *Introduction to Police Science.* New York: McGraw-Hill, 1971.

SUTHERLAND, EDWIN, AND CRESSEY, DONALD R. *Criminology.* 9th ed. Philadelphia, Pa.: Lippincott, 1974.

Toch, Haus. *Police, Prisons and the Problem of Violence.* Washington, D.C.: U.S. Government Printing Office, 1977.

———; Grant, J. Douglas; and Galvin, Raymond T. *Agents of Change: A Study in Police Reform.* New York: John Wiley, 1975.

Walker, Samuel. *A Critical History of Police Reform: The Emergence of Professionalism.* Lexington, Mass.: Lexington Books, 1977.

Wileman, Fred A. *Guidelines for Discretion: Five Models for Local Law Enforcement Agencies.* Madison, Wis.: University of Wisconsin Institute of Government Affairs, 1970.

Wilson, James Q. *Thinking About Crime.* New York: Basic Books, 1975.

———. *Varieties of Police Behavior.* Cambridge, Mass.: Harvard University Press, 1968.

Wilson, O. W., and McLaren, Roy C. *Police Administration.* 4th ed. New York: McGraw-Hill, 1977.

3
Program Operations: Patrol

Overview
Patrol . . . the Backbone of Policing
Patrol Activities
Patrol Programs
Team Policing
The Role of the Patrol Officer
Learning Exercises
Suggested References

OVERVIEW

Police patrol is the most fundamental of all police functions. It varies in application from totally random to precisely specified enforcement objectives; from reactive to proactive responses in providing services; from a foot beat officer to a radio car officer; from helicopters to horseback; and from jurisdiction-wide accountability to delineated areas of accountability (team policing). The patrol officer is expected to perform the wide range of police tasks including crime prevention, apprehension and detention of criminal offenders, criminal investigations, traffic enforcement and accident investigation, crowd control, and general government services. Recent experimentation has disclosed that in some instances a modified work week is advantageous to patrol deployment. Another development of considerable import is team policing—the arrangement of patrol officers (and in some cases investigators) into permanent teams that are in turn assigned a given geographical area in which they are given full responsibility for the provision of all crime control and prevention efforts.

PATROL . . . THE BACKBONE OF POLICING

The expression "backbone of the police department" is commonly used to indicate the critical importance of the patrol officer to the agency and the community. Figure 3-1 depicts a police patrol model or "delivery system." The patrol offfiicer typically is viewed as a generalist in police matters. For example:

> Under *traditional* (emphasis added) police organization, the initial responsibility for confronting the entire range of police problems rests with the patrolman. Along with responding to criminal behavior, the patrolman is responsible for such matters as enforcing traffic regulations and for performing a myriad of services for the public. On any tour of duty a patrolman may confront a burglary in progress, an incapacitated drunk, an injured or ill person, a violation of a littering ordinance, an unlicensed peddler, a suspicious person, a traffic violation, a person locked out of his residence, or a domestic dispute.[1]

Note the term *traditional* in the above quotation. It should be understood that the so-called modern police organization finds its patrol officers performing the same tasks cited by the Crime Commission Report (1967). Yet, two major distinctions can be made between the existing and the emerging role of the patrol officer. First, the patrol officer is being recognized and *treated* as a "specialist" in

---

[1] The President's Commission on Law Enforcement and the Administration of Justice, *Task Force Report: The Police* (Washington, D.C.: U.S. Government Printing Office, 1967), p. 3.

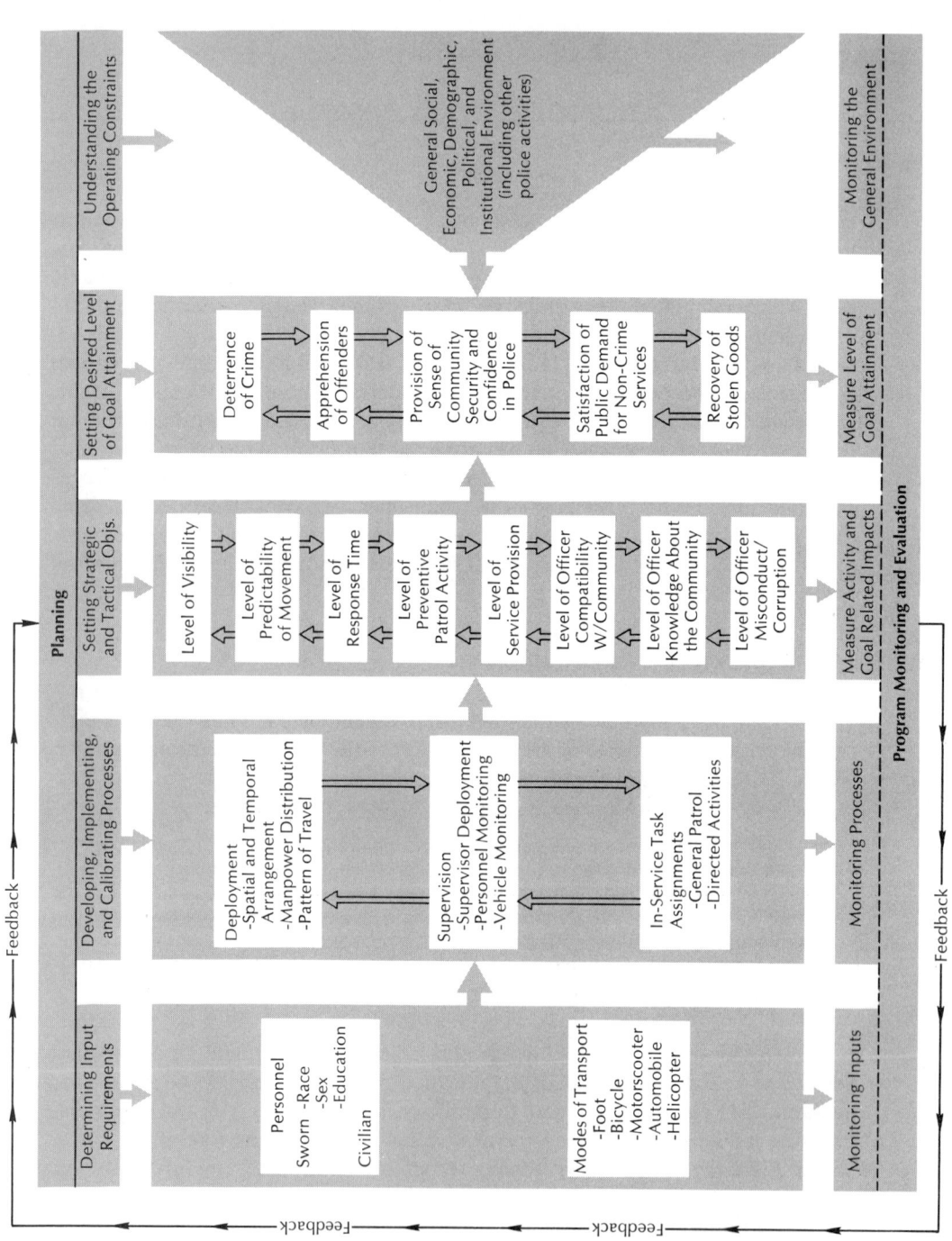

FIGURE 3–1 A Model Patrol System

Source: Theodore H. Schell et al., *Traditional Preventive Patrol: Phase I Summary Report* (Washington, D.C.: U.S. Government Printing Office, 1976), p. 3.

"generalism." Second, the patrol officer is similarly being recognized and *treated* as the cornerstone for building an effective police organization. Let us consider each of the two points in more detail.

To begin with, police patrol is especially important, complicated, conspicuous, and delicate. *Important,* because it provides twenty-four hour, seven-day-a-week protection and service to the community. *Complicated,* because it has well over three thousand tasks to perform.[2] *Conspicuous,* because it performs over three thousand tasks *in public,* and, *delicate,* because it must effect law and order with liberty, equality, and justice. Would anyone wonder, then, why the patrol officer is now being viewed as a specialist in generalism? Does not the vast majority of success or failure in crime prevention, apprehension of offenders, criminal investigations, police community relations, and so on depend on the activities of the patrol officer? Regretfully, far too often greater status and pay is attached to the position of specialist. Thus, many police officers approach a patrol assignment as merely a waiting period until they can achieve a specialist's position or a promotion. Fortunately, one can now detect a reaction to such thinking and practices. Police organizations are in the process of restoring a sense of prestige and equal economic rewards to the patrol assignment. The notion of the patrol officer as a specialist generalist is growing. The eventual results will significantly improve police work. James Q. Wilson best sums up this thinking when he writes:

> Enlarging the job of the patrolman is currently much in vogue for reasons of both morale and effectiveness. Reversing the past tendency to take away from the patrolman various tasks and give them to specialized units (detectives, juvenile officers, community relations specialist, narcotics investigators) should have, in the view of many, the effect of making the patrolman's tasks personally more satisfying and organizationally more effective. The officer will have a wider range of duties, greater freedom to schedule his own time, and accordingly higher morale; at the same time, he will be able to carry out follow-up investigations on the spot and provide more services to the citizen and provide them without the interruptions arising from other radio calls.[3]

The emergence of patrol specialists has resulted in enhanced recognition and appreciation of the patrol officer. To the citizen, the uniformed patrol officer is the police department. Further, he is viewed as representing general local government. Few citizens have any contact with other local departments (personnel, finance, planning, public works, and so on) and therefore frequently accept what the policeman does as speaking and acting for all government services. Although admittedly the complexities of the job and the growing scale of the police organization have caused a trend toward the establishment of specialized police units

---

[2] Project STAR has developed a series of role expectations for police personnel. Each of the roles involves a large array of tasks. See *Survey of Role Perceptions for Operational Criminal Justice Personnel: Data Summary* (Santa Cruz, Calif.: Davis Publishing Company, 1974).

[3] James Q. Wilson, "The Future Policeman" in *Future Roles of Criminal Justice Personnel* (Marina Del Rey, Calif.: American Justice Institute, 1972), p. 20. Wilson continued, however, by relating that job specialization has been verified as producing certain operational efficiencies. Enhanced generalization, on the other hand, has yet to be scientifically proven operationally effective.

(juvenile, detectives, narcotics, police-community relations, and so forth), the central and critical functions of patrol have not diminished. On the contrary, the *importance of effective patrol operations increases daily.* Police administrators, police researchers, and police educators are presently in the process of rediscovering and reemphasizing the effectiveness and prestige of the patrol force. Perhaps more pointedly, the patrol officer is the most critical person in the police organization.

> While *civility* and *humaneness* are *desirable qualities in any person,* and their possession *may be indispensable for competent police work, they do not suffice.* The opposite of the crude policeman is not one imbued with civic virtues and possessed of a polite manner; instead, he is the *informed, deliberating,* and *technically efficient* professional who knows that he must operate within the limits set by a moral and legal trust.[4]

PATROL ACTIVITIES

The multitude of tasks performed by a patrol officer can be grouped into ten major activities.[5] A discussion of each category follows.

General Preventive Patrol

General preventive patrol is the movement of a patrol officer (by foot, auto, bicycle, aircraft, or other means) over his assigned beat; it is designed to make the police officer "omnipresent." Omnipresence is important for two reasons. First, the citizen has an opportunity to communicate with a representative of local government. The citizen sees his government in action. Consequently, the mere presence of the officer partially fulfills the department's goal of furnishing general local government services. Second, the omnipresence of a patrolman inhibits the potential criminal. Disorders are less likely to occur when a police officer is nearby. Thus, we see that many of the goals of the police organization are served by general preventive patrol.

What is the patrol officer doing while on general preventive patrol? He is *waiting* for a call for police service from either a radio or an individual and *watching* for conditions that are in need of police service. The former is *reactive* in that the call for his services stems from a source that he must respond to. The latter is *proactive* because the patrolman is seeking to initiate remedial action in order to solve a particular problem. Watching or observing most completely describes the patrol officer's job. Clearly, his effectiveness depends on what he observes. The scope and sureness of his observation influence his ability to detect community

[4] Egon Bittner, *The Functions of the Police in Modern Society* (Chevy Chase, Md.: National Institute of Mental Health, 1970), p. 121.

[5] This section is drawn, with modifications, from the text by Paul M. Whisenand and James L. Cline, *Patrol Operations* (Englewood Cliffs, N.J.: Prentice-Hall, 1971), pp. 10–17.

hazards, to detect offenders, to know the habits of people living on his beat, and to be familiar with the residential and commercial districts that are the most frequent scenes of crime and disorder. The patrol officer, in effect, is the eyes and ears of the department. Through his observation of the assigned area he becomes the focal point of police operations, enabling him to quickly provide needed services.

As for the overall effectiveness of preventive patrol, a recent Kansas City, Missouri, experiment has raised some interesting questions. The Kansas City Police Department, the Police Foundation, and the Urban Institute conducted an eighteen-month study of preventive patrol.[6] The city was divided into a series of zones each having a different level of patrol activity. In the so-called "proactive" zones additional preventive patrol resources were assigned. In the "reactive" zones all preventive patrol forces were withdrawn (only called-for services were furnished). Other zones became control zones (no change in the level of patrol service). The striking results were: (1) The crime level in the proactive zones was not appreciably reduced; and (2) crime did not increase in the reactive zones. Although a landmark social scientific study, it failed to address a number of points and thus must be accepted on a highly cautionary basis. Perhaps the most significant outcome is that many police agencies are more carefully allocating, assigning, and supervising patrol units in terms of specific missions.

Planned Law Enforcement Patrol

Planned law enforcement patrol is sometimes referred to as selective patrol, or, better still, searching. Planned patrol is based on the use of statistical data. When used properly, these data have a predictive capability. Hence, crime and noncrime data can be processed for the creation of a law enforcement patrol plan. This plan attempts to deploy the patrol resources in the most effective pattern for apprehending criminals.[7] Technological machinery, such as the computer, is being used to establish the patrol plans. In fact, some departments have successfully experimented with the assignment of a called-for police service before the event actually happens—the patrol unit is sent to a given area based on the prediction that a crime will soon occur.

Planned law enforcement patrol should not be considered as a substitute for general patrol; both should be used. General preventive patrol, however, remains the more prevalent activity. Planned law enforcement patrol has proven effective, for example, in instances of high felony rates, traffic infractions, and traffic accidents. The next section of this chapter will discuss in more detail the innovative means for developing planned law enforcement patrol operations.

[6] George L. Kelling et. al., *The Kansas City Preventive Patrol Experiment: A Summary Report* (Washington, D.C.: Police Foundation, 1974).

[7] The subject of planned patrol is extensively covered in Kenneth W. Webb et al., *Specialized Patrol Projects* (Washington, D.C.: Law Enforcement Assistance Administration, 1977).

Called-for Services: Emergency

When the patrol officer is either dispatched to or observes a called-for service (CFS), his scope of observation is automatically limited to a particular event. He focuses on the resolution of the conditions that caused the complaining person to request police assistance or situation to require such aid. His first task is to arrive at the location of the CFS safely. In the case of an emergency CFS, the response time becomes critical in terms of life, property, and apprehension of the offender. Records establish that response time—the speed with which police can arrive at a crime scene—plays a large role in apprehension. The patrolman is our best tool for improving response time. Hence, a greater expenditure of funds is warranted in order to reduce the total response time in the apprehension process or preservation of life. Computerized communications, command, and control systems are one answer. Personal mobile radio extenders (walkie-talkies) are one more aid. Another is the use of police patrol helicopters. Emergency CFSs are major crimes (robbery, murder, assault with a deadly weapon, suicide attempts, and so on), disorders, or general emergencies (childbirth, fires, and so forth) that demand immediate attention and the making of accurate decisions under considerable pressure.

Called-for Services: Nonemergency

In a nonemergency called-for service, the response time becomes less critical. Naturally, every effort must be made to arrive as soon as possible. The *vast majority* of CFSs are nonemergency. The patrol officer will be involved in neighborhood and family quarrels,[8] in questionable (but often not criminal) business disputes, and in cases that are grounds for civil action in court. Because cases of this type can lead to criminal acts, he must make every effort to adjust and settle such disputes peacefully by explanation of the laws or regulations involved and by common sense. Often, he will refer the complaining persons to the proper agencies or individuals for a resolution of their difficulties. Other nonemergency incidents include caring for persons who are injured, sick, or lost; caring for or destroying injured, vicious, or strayed animals; and referring sick or destitute persons to welfare agencies. Further, the patrolman will assist other city agencies by providing information and preparing reports. In summary, a nonemergency CFS covers everything from the handling of a potential crime to the offering of advice on how to get one's cat out of a tree. Although such problems are seemingly unimportant, they are, in fact, extremely serious to the person who requested police service. The

---

[8] Experienced patrol officers are well aware of the potential dangers to themselves and the quarreling parties in a family dispute. In some departments, specialized patrol units have been established to resolve family arguments. The training for handling such occurrences is described in Morton Bard, *Training Police as Specialists in Family Crisis Intervention* (Washington, D.C.: U.S. Government Printing Office, 1970).

community evaluates its police agency both on the handling of criminal and noncriminal events. Because most citizens come to know their police department through the handling of noncriminal events, the attitude toward its effectiveness is heavily weighted on noncriminal matters. Regretfully, far too often the department solely relies on criminal statistics and fails to report the wealth of vital nonemergency services provided to the community. And, the single most important person in providing both emergency and nonemergency CFSs is the patrol officer.

Apprehension and Detention

When to apprehend (arrest) or detain (place in temporary custody) a suspected offender (in the case of juveniles, the individual is commonly referred to as "subject") is a grave decision even for an experienced and highly trained patrol officer. Certainly, existing laws provide a useful guideline—note the word *guideline*. Added to this guideline is another element—the necessity for sound judgment. A patrol officer's knowledge of penal statutes, case law, rules of evidence, plus his *judgment* will lead him to effect an arrest in one case; in another similar case, he may warn or advise the involved individuals.

A proper arrest serves as both a basis and a start for the successful movement of a suspected offender through the criminal justice system. A poor arrest leads to early failure in any determination of a suspected offender's guilt or innocence. A good arrest is even more valuable because of its efficiency. Figure 3–2 depicts the steps in the apprehension and arresting of an offender.

Investigation

The patrol officer conducts investigations of both criminal and noncriminal events. Some result from a called-for service; others grow out of observation by the patrolman of conditions or situations on his beat. Investigations range from gathering evidence on a robbery to investigating prowlers and other suspicious persons, or to stopping automobiles driven in a suspicious manner. As with arrests, the most efficient police service occurs when the patrol officer conducts the investigation as far as his competency and time allows. Major investigations that require the expenditure of long periods of time in solving one offense, for example murder, are normally assigned to a detective who specializes in homicide or crimes against the person. Also, vice and narcotics investigations are best assigned to specialized units. The patrol officer, however, does have the responsibility to detect and investigate vice and narcotic situations on his beat. Clearly, he maintains a general responsibility for all investigations. Effective investigation and clearance of cases by patrol officers conserves time, reduces the number of specialists required, and *increases* the chances of a successful investigation.

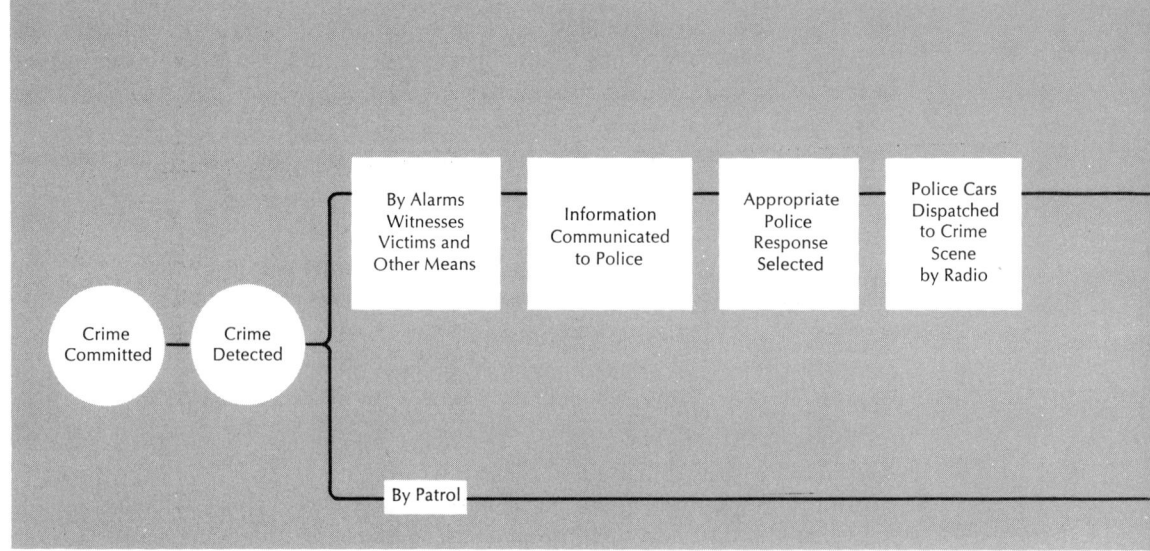

FIGURE 3-2 The Apprehension and Arrest Process
Source: The President's Commission on Law Enforcement and the Administration of Justice, *Task Force Report: The Police*. (Washington, D.C.: U.S. Government Printing Office, 1967), pp. 58-59.

Traffic

The patrol officer is usually a welcome sight at the scene of a traffic accident. The opposite is normally true during the issuance of a traffic citation. Even though some police organizations have created specialized units to handle their traffic problems, traffic enforcement and accident investigation still continue as primary patrol activities. The mere omnipresence of a patrol vehicle acts as a deterrent to those who might intentionally violate a traffic law or accidently operate a vehicle in an unsafe manner.

The issuance of a traffic citation to a person seldom results in a sincere "Thank you! I deserved that." In other words, traffic enforcement typically creates vexation for the recipient. Most people seldom have an opportunity to observe the many emergency and nonemergency services provided by a police department. Rarely does the citizen witness officers engaged in suppressing major criminal activities. Many people, however, have either received a traffic citation or observed an officer issuing one. The least a citation means to the motorist is an economic loss. Being cited hurts not only his pocketbook but his pride and driving record (a poor driving record can mean the loss of an operator's license). Consequently, the motorist is extremely sensitive to methods used by the police to enforce traffic laws. Citizens carefully scrutinize the apprehending officer's conduct during the issuance of a citation. If the violator is favorably impressed, he will usually not comment. If the driver is irritated by the officer's actions or attitude, however, he

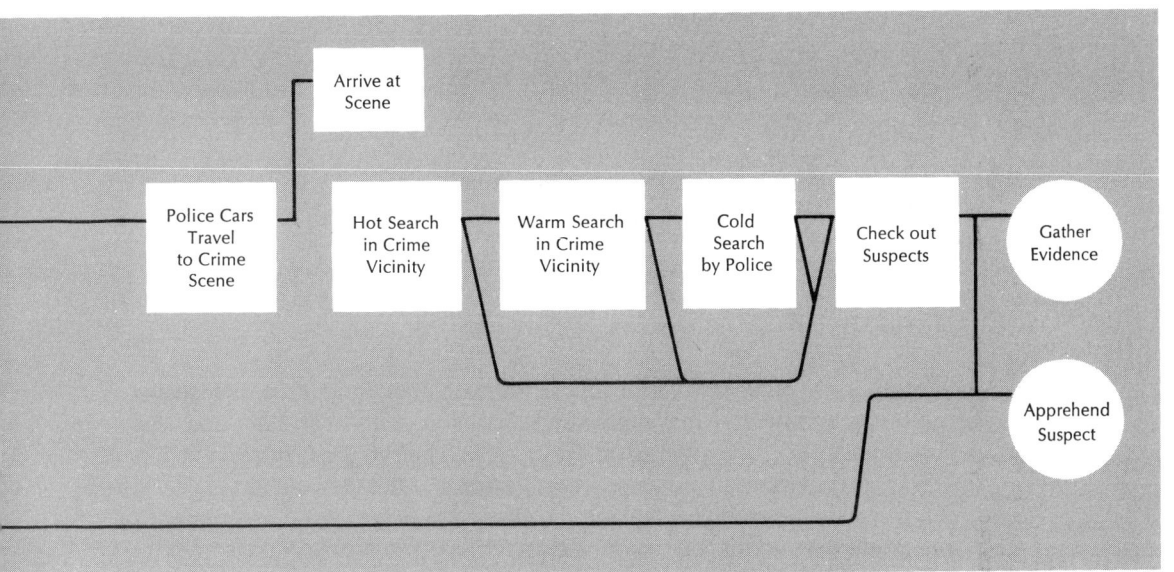

generally will publicly express his disapproval. When thinking of traffic enforcement, remember that the success of a police department's efforts to secure traffic safety and to relieve traffic congestion depends more on public support than rigid enforcement practices. The public's opinions, based on observations of officers' activities and behavior, mainly determine the degree of this support.

Crowd Control and Civil Disorder

To a patrol officer, any large gathering of individuals, whatever its reason, is a possible source of trouble.[9] Public demonstrations can be the forerunners of civil disorder. Skillful leadership and knowledge of crowd psychology by agitators can turn a seemingly harmless and peaceful group of people into a destructive mob. Poor judgment and overreaction to crowd behavior by the patrol officer can similarly turn a "seemingly harmless and peaceful group of people into a destructive mob"! Skillful leadership and proper action by the patrol officer can do much to defuse a potential civil disorder. The patrol officer should recognize that a group of people is not necessarily the same thing as a mob of people. Such a distinction

---

[9] Currently there is a large number of monographs, studies, and research reports devoted to the subject of riots or civil disorders. The most extensive, if not most prominent, report of late is the *National Advisory Commission on Civil Disorders* (Washington, D.C.: U.S. Government Printing Office, 1968).

between various types of crowds is necessary because they do not all require the active intervention of police. *Knowing when not to intervene is just as important as knowing when and how much police authority to apply.* To draw an analogy from an accepted profession, patrol officers must develop the attitude of physicians who take pride in employing all available means to avoid surgery, and who, when surgery is mandatory, take pride in making the smallest possible incision. This is to say, if *all* efforts fail to keep the peace then, and only then, should force be used to restore the lost peace.

Community Relations

Police-community relations (PCR) will be discussed in Chapter 4 as a specialized function. As mentioned at that point, PCR is everyone's job and not exclusively the responsibility of a few experts on the subject. The proper attitude on the part of a few PCR officers will in some way overcome crudeness on the part of the more numerous patrol officers. Hence, PCR can be a specialized assignment but in every instance is an activity to be performed by all officers. PCR is one of the most vigorously advocated developments to occur within the last ten years in police work, and rightfully so![10]

Also discussed later is the reality of the patrol officer representing all local government to the community. He can build or destroy supportive relationships among the public and its government. Remember, do not confuse community relations with public relations (the use of media to build an image of the department), or crime prevention programs (procedures designed to reduce the opportunity of motivation for crimes), or race relations (efforts to reduce racial prejudice between the police and minority groups). Effective PCR is, in essence, effective human relations. The public experiences favorable police-community relations by favorable police-community *relationships*. In other words, police-community relations are based on: (1) positive and unpartial acts (the police initiate the interaction) intended to assist members of the community; and (2) the maintenance of an open channel of communications between all citizens and their police. Undoubtedly, the most meaningful way to accomplish this twofold activity is through the patrol officer. Healthy PCR can be simply and primarily the output of good patrol work.

Information Processing

Information is the lifeblood of any law enforcement agency. Name and address files, fingerprint records, location indicators, and intelligence and investigation leads are all examples of data found in the files of most local police agencies.

---

[10] Examples of various PCR approaches are examined by Lee P. Brown, "PCR Typology: Orientation of Police Community Relations," *The Police Chief,* Vol. 38 (March 1971), pp. 16–21.

Added to these, and of equal use, are the files of prosecutors, probation and parole agencies, and state and federal investigative agencies. Where does most of this information originate? From the patrol officer. The patrol officer spends considerable time on the generation of information needed for the operating and managing of the department. Keep in mind that the "second" major problem for local law enforcement (the first is good personnel) is centered in the collection, analysis, and utilization of police-oriented data designed to support police officers in fulfilling the goals of the organization. Not so much the amount as the type of information produced and available is critical to the effective functioning of the department. Therefore, both the quantity and quality of information collected, processed (report writing), and communicated by the patrol officer are essential to the overall success of the department.

Further, in regard to information, the patrol officer acts as a community data resource center. This is to say that the line officer is frequently asked to provide advice, directions, and a host of other things all related to information. A day does not pass that a patrol officer is not asked "Where is . . .?" or "This is my problem—what should I do?" Hence, it is obvious that the performance of all police services, as well as the patrol activities, hinges on information.

PATROL PROGRAMS

Patrol programs are basically comprised of people, tools, and an allocation plan. As mentioned repeatedly, the most valuable of the three components is the human one. The selection, training, and integrity of police personnel is the cornerstone of the department's success. But patrol personnel also need tools for handling assigned responsibilities. Further, the patrol officers must be efficiently allocated in the community.

Historically, police patrol was accomplished on foot. Mass-produced automobiles and motorcycles have made the patrolman mobile. Currently, some agencies, such as the Michigan State Police, Los Angeles County Sheriff's Department, Kansas City Police Department, and the California Highway Patrol, have added fixed-wing aircraft and helicopters to the list of tools. Of course, large bodies of water or rivers must be patrolled by marine equipment. Some departments continue to use horses, four-wheel-drive vehicles, and bicycles for patrol as needs dictate.

Selecting the patrol tool best suited to protect a community and to derive at the same time maximum usefulness from personnel is a daily challenge to police managers. The various types of patrol are:

1. Foot
2. Automobile
3. Aircraft
4. Motorcycle
5. Horse

6. Dog
7. Boat
8. Bicycle
9. Television

The above tools can be, and often are, used in combination with one another. For example, television is now used along with the foot patrol officer, or placed in aircraft to assist ground-based police managers to make decisions during natural disasters or civil disorders. Other tools such as computers and automated dispatching systems were covered earlier but in reality should be revised as patrol "tools."

The effectiveness of these patrol types is a direct result of their capacity for being conspicuous. Conspicuousness gives the impression of omnipresence, which in turn prevents crime. The principal benefit of patrol still remains preventive: discouraging people who are motivated to commit crimes. Granted, prevention could be vastly increased by placing a policeman on every corner. Street crimes would be reduced because of the potential offender's fear of apprehension. Even indoor crimes such as burglary might be lessened by the increased probability of detection through pervasive police presence. But few citizens would tolerate living under police observation that intense; moreover, very few jurisdictions could afford it. The remainder of this section is devoted to these issues and other programs as well. To begin with, however, let us briefly examine the subject of "allocation."

Resource Allocation

When the police manager is informed of the number of patrol officers and types of equipment, his next step is to *plan* for their efficient use, that is, to allocate his resources effectively.[11] The first standard of allocation relates to the assignment of the patrol force throughout a twenty-four-hour period on the basis of the hourly need for police service. The second standard is the formulation of reporting districts. The third standard involves the division of the total area into beats, with the size of each beat determined by the need for police service. The information for making decisions on allocation stems from past, present, and predicted called-for police services. From this information, the department can properly assign its resources. The selection, the weighting (for example, the prediction that one beat will experience four serious crimes is given greater weight than the prediction that another beat will probably experience four calls for disturbing the peace), and the

[11] There is a growing body of literature on patrol allocation. The most exhaustive treatment to date is contained in the text by Richard G. Larson, *Urban Police Patrol Analysis* (Cambridge, Mass.: M.I.T. Press, 1972). Further, many computer-based information systems are in existence or being developed to facilitate rapid and accurate resource allocation. The Glendale (California) Police Department's Real-Time Data Capture system is programmed to effectively allocate police personnel.

processing of the information can be highly complicated and include mathematical models and influential statistics.

Essentially, the effective allocation of police resources takes into account four dimensions of CFS: time, location, frequency, and type. Although all four dimensions tend to influence the beat plans directly, reporting districts remain unchangeable. Reporting districts comprise a beat. They serve as the data base for the three patrol approaches. To explain, beats change, reporting districts do not. All four dimensions are analyzed with existing information from the reporting districts in order to structure the beats. The first approach forms beat plans on the amount of time spent in performing police services. The second and third approaches advocate that beat plans be determined by *location* and *frequency* of called-for services. The fourth and somewhat unique approach makes resource allocations to the areas of greatest hazard to bring about substantial reduction of actual and potential crime and disorder in these areas. The remaining area of the community receives only sufficient resources to cope with unanticipated emergencies. This fourth approach is more innovative and is referred to as fluid patrol, or the Tucson Plan. Finally, which of the four dimensions is most important? All four. Time, location, frequency, and type of called-for services should all influence the beat plan. Sufficient fluidity must be built into the allocation of resources so that, when necessary, concentrated patrol operations can result in selected reporting districts.

Many police departments either have made, or are in the process of making, more effective use of their patrol officers. These agencies are achieving maximum utilization from field personnel because they:

1. Distribute available patrol officers according to the most critical need for their services.
2. Improve supervision of the field force.
3. Improve coordination of effort among patrol personnel.
4. Improve patrol techniques by critically analyzing the need for such plans as foot patrol and two-man motor patrols.
5. Modernize report preparation and duplicating techniques.
6. Relieve patrol officers of menial tasks.

Foot Patrol Programs

There is good reason for "getting the police officer back on the beat" in high crime- and disorder-rate areas. This can be done without depriving him of the many advantages of radio-equipped vehicles. Due to advanced technology, foot officers can be equipped with small transistorized portable police radio transmitting-receiving equipment. Such portable radio devices can also serve to expand the operational area of radio-car personnel by permitting them to engage in extensive foot patrol and to range well away from their vehicles without sacrificing contact with headquarters. Because most radio-car patrolmen are forced to remain near the car's radio awaiting an assignment, most patrol officers have few chances to develop supportive relationships with people living on their beat.

The decision to use foot patrols should be made only after careful analysis because it can be a highly expensive type of coverage and geographically restrictive in nature. Where jurisdictions are not economically able to justify foot patrols, the police officer assigned to a radio car should be made aware that, in reality and practice, he is a foot patrol officer who possesses a vehicle for quick, nonfatiguing transportation from one point to another. Radio-car patrol officers can serve effectively as the community relations people of the police department only when out of their cars; yet they still can be subject to immediate recall and assignment. Consequently, when the patrol force is allocated on a basis of need, the police officer will, in fact, be "on the beat," *accessible* to the citizens of his community and providing protection for them. Such plans as the "team car" or "neighborhood car" are operationally designed to provide a direct, containing, and supportive interface between the officer(s) and community members. More will be said about these plans later.

One-Person and Two-Person Radio-Car Patrol Programs

Although which type of patrol to use is usually a lively, contested issue, today the trend is away from the use of two-man cars and toward the far greater use of one-man patrols. Police managers agree, however, that the resolution of the one-man versus two-man issue for their community lies with the police needs of that particular community. Where feasible, one-man radio car units should be used. A two-man unit is required when there are too many critical incidents for a single officer to handle in a densely populated area, a high frequency of situations in which patrol officers are likely to be assaulted, and a high prospect of disorderly behavior that can be prevented only by the action of two or more officers. If these conditions do not exist, two-man units are probably not required. Again, such decisions must be made by the agency and, regardless of the patrol practice, departments should regularly evaluate it to determine if changes are required.

Police Helicopter and Fixed-Wing Aircraft Patrol Programs

The importance of helicopters to improving patrol operations *is* relatively new but fairly well established. The use of aircraft by local police organizations is certainly not new; there is record of fixed-wing aircraft regularly operated as police vehicles since 1929. The development and perfection of helicopter equipment was stimulated primarily by World War II. In 1947, the New York City Police Department purchased the first helicopter for use in police operations. Since that date, a large number of federal, state, and local police agencies have established helicopter patrol units by either purchase or lease arrangements.

Police helicopter patrol is intended to provide local law enforcement agencies with a means for increasing the rate of apprehension and reducing the opportunities for criminal offenses. It accomplishes this function by being used in direct prevention and apprehension of suspected offenders. The researched and tested capabilities of a police patrol helicopter are:[12]

1. Improved preventive patrol capabilities
2. Increased probabilities of apprehension
3. More effective riot and disaster control
4. Increased security of police personnel
5. Innovative means for enlarging the significance of police communications, command, and control systems
6. Enhanced community service and support through increased visibility of the police to the public

Much is under development with police patrol helicopters and fixed-wing aircraft, and even more will be accomplished in the coming years. In the use of a helicopter or aircraft vehicle, the police have the means for creating sophisticated coordination between airborne and ground operational patrol units. The multidimensional capabilities of the helicopter and other aircraft now make such coordination not only possible, but imperative. High-speed chase of offender vehicles by police has become unnecessary now that aerial units are available. As supportive police equipment has improved technologically, patrol effectiveness from the air has been effectively extended into all types of called-for services with surprisingly positive results.

Crime Specific Programs (Special Enforcement Teams)

The 1970s opened with a large-scale attack by the federal government, state-wide criminal justice planning agencies, and local law enforcement organizations on reducing certain types of major crimes. Most often cited as being the target of a massive endeavor to measurably decrease criminal behavior were the crimes of robbery, burglary, grand theft, auto burglaries, and in general stranger-to-stranger street crimes.[13] The police have named the units responsible for concentrated efforts on certain "specific" crimes as "selective enforcement," "metropolitan," "tactical," and "crime specific." Their organizational location has varied between specialized and generalist components. Although their location and in-

---

[12] A compilation of current research findings can be found in Paul M. Whisenand and George M. Medak, "Police Helicopter Patrol," *Management Information Service* (Washington, D.C.: International City Management Association, October 1971).

[13] A brief overview of six crime specific programs is contained in the article by Joanne Rockwell, "Crime Specific . . . An Answer?" *Police Chief,* Vol. 39 (September 1972), pp. 38–43.

tended target crimes may differ, the primary goal is fixed—to discernibly reduce a particular type of crime (in some cases it may be two or three specific offenses). Invariably, the crimes are of a major consequence (felonies) to the public.

It appears that crime specific programs will continue to hold the interest and hopes of the police departments for an indefinite period of time. Their evaluation, that is, the impact of the effort on the specific crime, will decide how long police resources will be committed to such programs. The means for implementing that program will vary according to the individual police agency. Yet, it presently looks as if more and more of the crime specific programs will be located in, staffed by, and the responsibility of the patrol division. Consequently, a certain number of patrol officers are destined to be assigned the duty of dramatically decreasing the number of specific criminal occurrences. Their deployment will be exclusively based on the frequency, time, location, and severity of a particular crime(s). In all probability, they will use a variety of dress, patrol tools, and operational techniques to accomplish their identical objectives. In summary, to *permanent random* patrol we are witnessing the addition of *temporary specified* patrol. To repeat a point made earlier in this chapter, generalized (permanent and random) patrol will at all times remain at the foundation of any police department.

The Modified Workweek Program

The police are experiencing, as are other private and public organizations, what appears to be a growing national trend toward the adoption of a shorter workweek along with enlarged workday.[14] The plans vary in title and configuration. Hence, one observes the four-day, forty-hour week (or Four/Forty, Ten-Plan, Four/Ten) being substituted for the traditional five-day, forty-hour week. In some instances, although by far more rare, we find some organizations using a three-day, thirty-six-hour week. Although considerable variations are either in existence or being proposed, two generalizations are reasonable at this time. One, many organizations have changed or are contemplating changing the dimensions of their workweek. Two, the early findings seem to indicate great interest in the direction of the Four/Forty, and especially as it relates to patrol work.

The four-day, forty-hour workweek is a fairly simple reallocation of work hours from five days to four days. In effect, an employee will work forty hours in four days. The original number of work hours is maintained, for the most part, but because they are grouped differently, there is a change in the impact of the hours on the performance of the agency and on the utility of the employees' leisure.

Broadly, the Four/Forty Plan is presently viewed as providing the following:

[14] For a comprehensive analysis of the Four/Forty Workweek see the research study by Paul M. Whisenand, George M. Medak, and Bradley L. Gates, "The Four-Day, Forty-Hour Workweek," *1972 Municipal Year Book* (Washington, D.C.: International City Management Association, 1972), p. 24.

1. It *increases* field patrol deployment during peak activity periods.
2. It increases the efficiency of the patrol division and ultimately of the department.
3. It increases department morale.
4. It is more economical than the five-day, eight-hour workweek.
5. It may increase personnel off-duty problems.

The repetition of responses, extolling the positive effects of the Four/Forty Plan on all aspects of officers' lives, cannot readily be minimized by those administrators still operating under the classic workweek. In an age where strikes by public employees are becoming increasingly prevalent, the Four/Forty Plan may serve to lessen those extreme grievances and complaints about working conditions that prompt such strikes. To date, the Four/Forty Plan has been an innovative test of manpower deployment for law enforcement agencies. Thus far, the plan has not been sufficiently experimented with or analyzed to allow us to formulate further conclusions about its merits and disadvantages. More explicitly, the Four/Forty Plan has not withstood the most important test—time. There are apparent and immediate advantages, to be sure, but the plan's total impact has not been sufficiently revealed. There is one question yet to be answered. Will the Four/Forty Plan, over an extended period of time, create serious unforeseen problems, or will it be flexible enough to satisfy organizational needs for more effective deployment of police personnel and, more specifically, police *patrol* personnel?

TEAM POLICING

The phrase "team policing" suggests a variety of organizational arrangements. For example, team policing is used to denote: (1) a basic plan;[15] (2) a selective enforcement program; (3) a group of senior and junior police officers; and (4) any number of other programs. In this instance, team policing includes, but is a significant modification of, the basic car program. The concept of team policing is explained as follows.

The basic car plan (BCP) operates in this manner: Based on workload, a minimum radio car plan is established and becomes the BCP for all watches. Basic radio cars are called "A" units. Nine officers assigned to each basic car include one lead officer, five senior officers, and three probationary officers. Each basic car is assigned to its own "basic car district." Three officers are assigned to the basic car district during each of the three watches. Additional radio cars are deployed during periods of increased work load; these cars are designated "X" units. Once a month, the nine officers of each basic car meet with citizens of their basic car district. The purpose of the meeting is to allow discussion of police problems between the officers and the citizens.

[15] The pioneering effort in field experimentation with team policing was referred to as the basic car plan (Los Angeles Police Department, 1970–71).

Basic cars are given priority on radio calls in their districts. In the event a basic car is not available for an urgent call, the call is assigned to an "X" unit. As a last resort, a neighboring basic car can be assigned, but basic cars are not assigned out of their district unless it is absolutely necessary. In the event of a tactical alert in another area, "X" units will be assigned to respond to the unusual occurrence before the basic cars.

The Goals of Team Policing

Team policing programs have generally adopted goals in the following areas:[16]

Organizational development
Officer role and responsibilities
Traditional law enforcement services
Police-community relations

ORGANIZATIONAL DEVELOPMENT

The organizational development of team policing has been aimed largely at one fundamental goal: decentralizing the delivery of law enforcement services. This is most frequently attempted by a downward shift of decision making and a tendency to increase the management and operational responsibility of team leaders and first-line supervisors. Further, in order to establish accountability for operations at the lowest level possible, team programs have encouraged participant decision making and the involvement of patrol officers in planning, investigative, and community relations activities. In addition, decentralization or service delivery usually includes assigning a clearly defined and relatively small geographic area of responsibility to each team.

OFFICER ROLE AND RESPONSIBILITIES

The organizational changes brought about by team policing have frequently generated new goals for the patrol officer. Team policing programs have tried to enhance the officer's role by expanding his responsibilities. They often stress the development of generalist officers who, although their primary responsibility may be responding to calls for service, perform some of the work traditionally assigned to specialists. Team officers have sometimes engaged in follow-up investigative work, taken responsibility for developing community relations contacts, and helped their sergeants plan and coordinate team activities. The model for many team programs has been a more professional officer who can capably perform a variety of tasks with a minimum of supervision. The expansion of the patrol offi-

---

[16] This section is taken in part from the monograph by William G. Gay, H. Talmadge Day and Jane P. Woodward, *Neighborhood Team Policing* (Washington, D.C.: U.S. Government Printing Office, 1977), pp. 8–12.

cer's role usually has two objectives. First, some teams assign the officer more responsibility in an effort to increase the level of service delivered by the offficer and the team. Second, enlarged job responsibilities have been viewed as a method by which to increase job satisfaction.

TRADITIONAL LAW ENFORCEMENT SERVICES

Police administrators have been seeking ways to more efficiently manage the patrol and investigative workload. Reducing crime is one of the most frequently stated goals of team policing programs. Most team leaders have attempted to reduce crime by demanding better quality preliminary reports, encouraging officer-investigator coordination, and permitting patrol officers to engage in some investigative work. A second goal of team administrators has been to more effectively manage the patrol workload by improving manpower allocation, increasing the number of dispatch calls serviced and decreasing response time without assigning additional personnel to the team area. Some have looked upon the decentralization of patrol and investigative activities to teams as a means of increasing the level of service delivered without appreciably increasing inputs.

POLICE-COMMUNITY RELATIONS

A final goal of most of the teams here has been to enhance the relationship between the police and the public. Team policing community relations objectives have usually included attempts to initiate crime prevention programs, improve police-citizen cooperation and encourage citizen involvement in and concern with public safety issues. Team policing administrators have attempted to improve police-community relations by making the patrol officer responsible for initiating police-citizen contacts and for carrying out activities designed to reduce police-citizen conflicts.

Team Organization

The organizational structure of the team is an important criterion for dividing the various team programs into types and developing a conceptual framework. Departments have organized their officers into teams responsible for either an area within the city on a twenty-four hour basis or for a spccific block of time during the day—usually an eight-hour shift. *Area Teams* are responsible for providing law enforcement services around the clock and are usually headed by a lieutenant. Twenty-four-hour responsibility permits a single team leader to coordinate all patrol activities in the team area. It has usually facilitated cross-shift planning and coordination. In addition, twenty-four-hour responsibility frequently gives the team leader considerable flexibility in deploying officers to meet the changing level of service demands experienced throughout the day. Area Teams generally have from seventeen to forty-nine officers and are larger than teams organized by shifts. *Shift Teams* are usually led by a sergeant or corporal and usually have from eight to twenty-two officers. Unlike the Area Team organization, no formal chain of command has been established to coordinate the various shifts serving a single area. The sergeant directing a shift team usually reports to a watch commander who, like the sergeant, is responsible for only a single shift within a twenty-four-hour period.

The permanent assignment of officers to the team is an important element in the decentralization scheme and has been a common feature of team policing programs. Unlike traditional patrol systems where officers are frequently dispatched throughout the city, team programs have attempted, not always successfully, to assign most calls for service in the team area to team officers. Permanent assignment has led police administrators to hold team officers accountable for the delivery of law enforcement services in the team area. All of the team programs feature permanent assignment, and most assign officers to a specific beat within the team area. The assignment to a specific beat has meant that the beat officer is responsible for preventive patrol in that beat and may participate in community relations, and investigative and traffic activities in the same area. Team policing has frequently been accompanied by efforts to decentralize management and planning functions to the team level. Most teams have made an attempt to establish procedures that would enable first-line supervisors and officers to plan and coordinate patrol strategies. Many team programs have also attempted to better coordinate investigative and community relations activities within the team area.

The primary mechanism for planning and coordinating has been regular and periodic meetings of team members. In most instances the traditional roll call has been replaced by less formal gatherings where team members and first-line supervisors can discuss and plan activities for the team area. These meetings also provide a mechanism for team members to participate in decisions made by team leaders and first-line supervisors.

Team Responsibilities

The organizational and managerial aspects of team policing described in the previous section provide the base upon which departments have decentralized the delivery of basic law enforcement services in the field. Most team programs have sought to replace random roving patrol with patrol activities designed to achieve specific objectives. Teams have been assigned additional duties so that when officers are not responding to service calls they can perform community relations, investigative, or crime prevention activities.

We have developed a functional typology to describe the kinds of services that various team programs have provided to citizens. Analysis of functional responsibilities of each team has made it possible to group the nineteen-team policing programs into four categories:

- Basic Patrol Teams
- Patrol-Investigative Teams
- Patrol-Community Service Teams
- Full Service Teams

BASIC PATROL TEAMS

The simplest form of team policing has involved the reorganization of departments into teams responsible for basic preventive patrol, radio dispatch service, and traffic duties. The cities utilizing this plan have viewed policing as an organizational form which could more efficiently deliver basic patrol services to the community. In these cities improved manpower allocation, reduced response time, and the clearance of service calls have been primary objectives. Unlike the other programs described in this report, the officers in the Basic Patrol Team do not have community relations or investigative responsibilities. Except for evidence technicians in Richmond, specialists have not been assigned to these teams. All three Basic Patrol Teams employ a shift organizational structure.

PATROL-INVESTIGATIVE TEAMS

The Patrol-Investigative Team combines the features of the Basic Patrol Team with the assignment of follow-up investigative responsibilities to the team. The single example of this system is Rochester, New York, where most investigative work has been decentralized. The Rochester reorganization has involved the transfer of approximately one-half of the centralized investigative bureau's detectives to teams. Although most of the team follow-up investigations are performed by detectives, patrol officers have been responsible for conducting more complete preliminary investigations and have occasionally been assigned investigative follow-ups. The Rochester team is an Area Team responsible for patrol and investigative duties around the clock.

PATROL-COMMUNITY SERVICE TEAMS

The Patrol-Community Service Team incorporates the features of the Basic Patrol Team with responsibility for community relations. By assigning community responsibilities to team officers, administrators have hoped to increase the level and kinds of service delivered to the community. The community relations focus of team policing has been an important step in replacing traditional reactive patrol with a more focused proactive patrol strategy.

Three departments—Albuquerque, Hartford, and New York—have adopted this approach. Although the San Diego experimental Community Profile Program emphasized individual officer rather than team responsibilities and organization, we have chosen to include it in this group because of the profile program's emphasis upon community service. Team officers in Hartford and San Diego have also been assigned some responsibility for traffic services. Although each team has performed community relations activities, personnel from the centralized community relations units of these departments have not been reassigned to the teams. Even in San Diego, for example, which has extensively enlarged the role of the team officers' community relations responsibilities, community service officers working in the team area are attached to the centralized community relations office and not to the team. Hartford, because of its satisfaction with team policing, has diminished the role of its centralized community relations units and has contemplated the transfer of community relations personnel to its teams. Albuquerque implemented a Shift Team while Hartford and New York implemented Area Teams.

FULL SERVICE TEAMS

The most complex team policing programs have involved the decentralization of patrol, investigative, and community relations responsibilities to the team. Eleven of the nineteen programs analyzed in this report have adopted this mode of team policing. A number of these programs have also decentralized some traffic duties to the team. The transfer of personnel from centralized bureaus to the team unit has usually involved detectives and to a lesser extent community relations and traffic personnel. The usual tendency has been to assign between three and four detectives to each team. Because of the relative size of the detective bureau in most agencies, the transfer of personnel from that bureau to the team has frequently had the most impact upon a department implementing team policing.

The Full Service Teams can be classified into two distinct groups by the types of specialist duties assigned to team members. Seven of the eleven teams—Arbor Hill in Albany, Charlotte, Cincinnati, Detroit, Los Angeles, Palo Alto, and St. Petersburg—have developed a Multi-Specialist approach. These agencies have deployed mixed teams of patrol officers and specialists (detectives and community relations officers) who are under the direction of the team leaders. Although team patrol officers frequently participate in investigative and community relations activities, the specialists assigned to the team have taken primary responsibility for these activities.

South End in Albany, Dayton, Holyoke, and Menlo Park have adopted a Generalist approach to team policing. In these agencies all team officers have been expected to perform both basic patrol and specialist duties. When the Generalist mode has been adopted, the number of personnel and functions assigned to centralized bureaus has been severely reduced. With the exception of Menlo Park and Palo Alto, the Full Service Teams have been organized as Area Teams.

THE ROLE OF THE PATROL OFFICER

We conclude this chapter with a NAC standard that we believe to be most pivotal. For, indeed, effective policing rests on effective patrol. And obviously, effective patrol means effective patrol officers. Their effectiveness depends to a large extent on their selection, development, rewards, self-esteem, and status. Hence, the urgent requirement to enhance their role.

Standard 8.2

ENHANCING THE ROLE OF THE PATROL OFFICER

Every local government and police chief executive, recognizing that the patrol function is the most important element of the police agency, immediately should adopt policies that attract and retain highly qualified personnel in the patrol force.

1. Every local government should expand its classification and pay system to provide greater advancement opportunities within the patrol ranks. The system should provide:

   a. Multiple pay grades within the basic rank;

   b. Opportunity for advancement within the basic rank to permit equality between patrol officers and investigators;

   c. Parity in top salary step between patrol officers and nonsupervisory officers assigned to other operational functions;

   d. Proficiency pay for personnel who have demonstrated expertise in specific field activities that contribute to more efficient police service.

2. Every police chief executive should seek continually to enhance the role of the patrol officer by providing status and recognition from the agency and encouraging similar status and recognition from the community. The police chief executive should:

   a. Provide distinctive insignia indicating demonstrated expertise in specific field activities;

   b. Insure that all elements within the agency provide maximum assistance and cooperation to the patrol officer;

   c. Implement a community information program emphasizing the importance of the patrol officer in the life of the community and encouraging community cooperation in providing police service;

   d. Provide comprehensive initial and in-service training thoroughly to equip the patrol officer for his role;

   e. Insure that field supervisory personnel possess the knowledge and skills necessary to guide the patrol officer;

   f. Implement procedures to provide agencywide recognition of patrol officers who have consistently performed in an efficient and commendable manner;

   g. Encourage suggestions on changes in policies, procedures, and other matters that affect the delivery of police services and reduction of crime;

   h. Provide deployment flexibility to facilitate various approaches to individual community crime problems;

   i. Adopt policies and procedures that allow the patrol officer to conduct the complete investigation of crimes which do not require extensive followup investigation, and allow them to close the investigation of those crimes; and

   j. Insure that promotional oral examination boards recognize that patrol work provides valuable experience for men seeking promotion to supervisory positions.[17]

---

[17] National Advisory Commission on Criminal Justice Standards and Goals, *Police* (Washington, D.C.: U.S. Government Printing Office, 1973), pp. 195, 196.

LEARNING EXERCISES

Issues to Be Discussed

1. In regard to the role (expected behavior/activities) of a patrol officer: What do we expect? What should we expect? Are there any differences between what the class currently expects versus what they prefer? If so, discuss the lack of congruity between the "is" and the "should."
2. What can be done to lessen the usual hostile reaction on the part of a citizen to receiving a traffic citation? As mentioned earlier, the majority of us seldom (if ever) appreciate the experience of being cited for a traffic law violation. As a consequence, poor police-community relations frequently result. What remedies might tend to alleviate this problem?
3. What does team policing mean to you? How is it distinguished from traditional forms of policing? What are the similarities between team policing and the traditional methods? Basically, why the present emphasis on team policing?

Group Activity

The class is to be divided into groups of six to eight members each. The focus of the group interaction is to center on ways of enhancing the position of *patrol* officer. In other words, precisely what steps ought to be taken in order to increase the self-esteem of the patrol officer within the police organization? Will the proposed steps, if taken, make the assignment to a position in patrol more attractive to a police officer? Indeed, will the patrol officer have equivalent, if not higher, status to those on specialized assignments (e.g., criminal investigation)?

Field Activity

Each member of the class is to briefly visit with an on-duty patrol officer. The conversation should deal with the officer's most recent activities (past two days). What type of services—and frequency—did the officer provide? How did he feel about the kinds of tasks expected of him? Written notes should be made *after* the interview. Subsequently, each student is to make a three-minute in-class presentation of the results of the interview.

Key Terms

Apprehension and detention
Called-for services: emergency
Called-for services: nonemergency
Community relations
Crime specific programs

Crowd control and civil disorder
Generalist
Information processing
Investigation
Modified workweek

Planned law enforcement patrol
Preventive patrol
Specialist
Team policing
Traffic

SUGGESTED REFERENCES

ADAMS, THOMAS F. *Police Patrol Tactics*. Englewood Cliffs, N.J.: Prentice-Hall, 1971.

BARD, MORTON. *Family Crisis Intervention: From Concept to Implementation*. Washington, D.C.: Law Enforcement Assistance Administration, 1973.

BLOCK, PETER B. *Equality of Distribution of Police Services: A Case Study of Washington, D.C.* Washington, D.C.: The Urban Institute, 1974.

———, AND SPECHT, DAVID. *Neighborhood Team Policing*. LEAA Prescriptive Package. Washington, D.C.: Law Enforcement Assistance Administration, 1973.

CRIMINAL JUSTICE COUNCIL, IACP. *Model Rules for Law Enforcement Officers: A Manual on Police Discretion*. Gaithersburg, Md.: International Association of Chiefs of Police, 1974.

Full-Service Neighborhood Team Policing: Planning for Implementation. St. Petersburg, Fla.: Public Safety Research Institute, 1975.

GAY, WILLIAM G.; DAY, H. TALMADGE; AND WOODWARD, JANE P. *Neighborhood Team Policing*. Washington, D.C.: U.S. Government Printing Office, 1977.

GOURLEY, G. DOUGLAS. *Patrol Administration*. 2nd ed. Springfield, Ill.: Charles C Thomas, 1974.

KELLING, GEORGE L., et al. *The Kansas City Preventive Patrol Experiment: A Summary Report*. Washington, D.C.: Police Foundation, 1974.

LARSEN, RICHARD C. *Urban Police Patrol Analysis*. Cambridge, Mass.: M.I.T. Press, 1972.

MILTON, CATHERINE H., et al. *Women in Policing: A Manual*. Washington, D.C.: Police Foundation, 1974.

NATIONAL ADVISORY COMMISSION ON CRIMINAL JUSTICE STANDARDS AND GOALS. *Police*. Washington, D.C.: U.S. Government Printing Office, 1973.

OSTROM, ELINOR; ROGER, B.; AND WHITAKER, G. P. *Patterns in Metropolitan Policing* (draft). Bloomington, Ind.: Indiana University Workshop in Political Theory and Analysis, 1976.

PRESIDENT'S COMMISSION ON LAW ENFORCEMENT AND THE ADMINISTRATION OF JUSTICE. *Task Force Report: The Police*. Washington, D.C.: U.S. Government Printing Office, 1967.

Project STAR: Police Officer Training. Sacramento, Calif.: California Commission on Peace Officer Standards and Training, 1974.

SCHELL, THEODORE H., et al. *Traditional Preventive Patrol: Phase-Summary Report*. Washington D.C.: U.S. Government Printing Office, 1976.

SHANAHAN, DONALD T. *Patrol Administration: Management by Objectives.* 2nd ed. Boston: Holbrook Press, 1978.

SHERMAN, LAWRENCE W., et al. *Team Policing—Seven Case Studies.* Washington, D.C.: Police Foundation, 1973.

U.S. DEPARTMENT OF JUSTICE. LEAA. *Allocation of Resources in Chicago Police Department.* Washington, D.C.: Law Enforcement Assistance Administration, 1972.

WHISENAND, PAUL M., AND CLINE, JAMES L. *Patrol Operations.* Englewood Cliffs, N.J.: Prentice-Hall, 1971.

WILSON, O. W., AND McLAREN, ROY C. *Police Administration.* 4th ed. New York: McGraw-Hill, 1977.

4

Program Operations: Specialist Units

Overview
The Need for Specialists
Criminal Investigation
Youth Services
Narcotics and Drug Abuse
Vice Control
Traffic Safety
Special Enforcement
Jail (Custody)
Crime Prevention/Community Relations
Civil (Court Support)
Learning Exercises
Suggested References

OVERVIEW

The police problems that require a specialized effort due to either their complexity or their longer time commitment require a specialist. A police specialist essentially has a particular purview within which he or she applies an acquired expertise. Organizations are too prone to create specialized assignments when, in fact, a generalist would suffice. A specialized assignment should be established and maintained only if it is repeatedly demonstrated that a generalist or another specialist cannot effectively handle a specific service.

Police specializations vary according to the size of the agency and the types of services provided. The more common specializations are: criminal investigation, youth service, narcotics, vice, traffic safety, special enforcement, jail, crime prevention, civil, and organized crime (the latter was covered in a preceding chapter under the label of intelligence). The omnipresent concern for police-community relations (PCR) is subsumed within the crime prevention unit. Although assigned to a single unit, PCR is in reality the responsibility of all the personnel comprising a police agency.

THE NEED FOR SPECIALISTS

As our law enforcement agencies experience accelerated complexity and change, they respond with specialized units or positions. Thus, over the years a number of specialist positions have grown out of the generalist's inability to perform certain functions, due to either lack of knowledge or time. Within today's urban police department one finds the police officer who, for one example, specializes in performing the tasks of a detective. The detective (specialist) is usually further specialized, let's say, in robbery. Moreover, the robbery detective can be even more specifically directed to handling bank robberies. In this chapter, the specialists we will discuss are assigned operational or program responsibilities.

The evolution of law enforcement specialization began in 1843, fifteen years after the first police department was formed in London, England. Detectives were organized into a specialized unit of the London Metropolitan Police Department. Similarly, when the Boston Police Department was created in 1854 it assigned about 2 percent of its total force as detectives.

The next major specialization was in the 1920s. This was in traffic control and enforcement. At about the same time, specialization in narcotics, vice control, and delinquency prevention also developed.[1]

---

[1] For additional history of police specialists, see Richard Ward, *Criminal Investigation* (Boston: Holbrook Press, 1975).

The complexities of modern police service demand highly specialized hardware and personnel, and considerable variation exists within each type of specialization. Each community has its own needs. The agrarian community will perhaps require less specialization than the metropolis. A successful strategy in one community may be a dismal failure in another of the same size but with diffferent ethnic makeup.

Police specialists are recognized as critical to the effective functioning of the department. At the same time, the question of how many and of what type arises. The nature and level of needed services determine the number and kinds of police specialists needed. However, far too often other factors tend to influence the decision concerning specialists. Most organizations seem to possess a natural tendency to create specialist positions. Some police managers are presently developing formulas to test the need for specialists more objectively. A rough rule of thumb: (1) Prove by an analytical study that the generalists are ineffective in the handling of a particular service; and (2) seek to relate the new specialization to an existing unit of a similar nature—in essence keep the specialization as broad as possible to limit the additional staff needed. The reason for this yardstick is as follows:

> In almost all large police departments there is a considerable amount of organizational fragmentation. Traditionally and almost universally, patrol and investigative forces have separate lines of command and tend to be isolated from one another; often they keep separate sets of records; frequently they work different shifts or are based in different places so that there is a minimum of contact between patrolmen and detectives. In addition, investigators are more often than not divided at both headquarters and precinct levels into squads—vice, robbery, burglary, fraud, homicide, and so forth—that may themselves keep separate records, use separate informants and remain more or less isolated from each other in other ways.
>
> At both the staff and the field levels, this overseparation of functions, or overspecialization, can have undesirable results. When intelligence is not centralized and coordinated, staff planning for the purpose of either apprehending specific criminals, or solving crime problems such as, for example, an outbreak of burglaries in some neighborhood, is almost impossible. When lines of command are kept rigidly separate, it is difficult to bring the full resources of a department to bear on crime solution. Also considerable conflict exists in many forces between uniformed branch officers and the detective division.[2]

The above also holds true for other specializations, as well—not only between the specialists and the generalist but also among the various specialized units. Interestingly, the following solution to the problem was offered in the same document. "The most promising means of overcoming this problem is to combine the patrol and detective field forces under a common supervisor."[3]

The more prevalent police specializations devoted to providing operational services are criminal investigation, youth services, narcotics, vice, traffic safety, special enforcement, jail, crime prevention. and civil. This chapter discusses each.

---

[2] The President's Commission on Law Enforcement and the Administration of Justice, *Task Force Report: The Police* (Washington, D.C.: U.S. Government Printing Office, 1967), p. 58.

[3] *Ibid.*

The order of presentation or amount of material discussed should not be interpreted as a ranking in terms of their importance to the department. Each specialization adds its own separate contribution to the overall objectives of the organization. Further, as covered in the previous chapter, the *intelligence* (organized crime) function is *supportive* of staff to the line specialists. Obviously, departments vary in relation to the kinds of services required of them. One community may have a large juvenile population, hence a sizeable juvenile services unit; another community may be suffering from extensive organized crime and thus considerable staff would be assigned to this unit. The following descriptions are, therefore, representative of medium- to large-scale police and sheriff's departments. Smaller agencies usually contain few, if any, police specialists.

The following NAC standard concludes this section by summarizing the above thinking concerning police specializations. Additionally, a NAC standard is used to open the subsequent section on the largest of all specialized assignments—criminal investigation.

Standard 9.1

SPECIALIZED ASSIGNMENT

Every police agency should use generalists (patrol officers) wherever possible and, before establishing any specialization necessary to improve the delivery of police service, specifically define the problem that may require specialization, determine precisely what forms of specialization are required to cope with this problem, and implement only those forms in a manner consistent with available resources and agency priorities.

1. Every police chief executive should define the specific problem in concise written terms and in doing so should consider at least:
    a. Whether the problem requires the action of another public or private organization;
    b. The severity of the problem:
    c. The period of time the problem is expected to exist; and
    d. The community's geographic, physical, and population conditions that contribute to the problem or which may affect or be affected by the specialization.
2. Every police chief executive should consider community perception of the problem: community awareness, and the attitudes based on that awareness.
3. Every police chief executive should—based on his definition of the problem, community perception of it, and the pertinent legal requirements—assess all resources and tactical alternatives available to the agency, and in doing so determine at least:
    a. Whether the problem requires specialization;
    b. The degree of specialization required;
    c. The manpower and equipment resources required by specialization;
    d. Which of the needed resources are available within the agency and which are available outside it;

e. The availability of necessary specialized training;
   f. The expected duration of the need for specialization; and
   g. The organizational changes needed as a result of specialization.
4. Every police chief executive should give special consideration to the impact of specialization on:
   a. The identified problem;
   b. Personnel and fiscal resources;
   c. Community attitudes toward the agency; and
   d. The agency's delivery of general police services.
5. Every police agency should develop an operations effectiveness review for each new specialization. This review process should be carried out:
   a. As a goal-oriented activity analysis; and
   b. On a specific schedule for the expected duration of the need.
6. Every police agency should terminate a specialized activity whenever the problem for which it was needed no longer exists, or can be controlled as well or better through other agency operations.[4]

CRIMINAL INVESTIGATION

Standard 9.7

CRIMINAL INVESTIGATION

Every police agency immediately should direct patrol officers to conduct thorough preliminary investigations and should establish in writing priorities to insure that investigative efforts are spent in a manner that will best achieve organizational goals.

1. Every police agency should recognize that patrol officers are preliminary investigators and that they should conduct thorough preliminary investigations. However, investigative specialists should be assigned to very serious or complex preliminary investigations when delay will not hamper the investigation.

2. Every police agency should establish only as many specialized criminal investigative units as needed, staffed only with the number of personnel necessary to conduct timely investigations that lead to organizational objectives. The thoroughness of preliminary investigations by patrol officers should be insured, to reduce followup investigative efforts.

3. Every police agency should establish investigative priorities according to the seriousness of the crime, how recently it was reported, the amount of readily available information about suspects, the availability of agency resources, and community studies.

4. Every police agency employing 75 or more personnel should assign full-time criminal investigators. Every agency with fewer than 75 personnel should assign criminal investigation specialists only where specific needs are present.

[4] National Advisory Commission on Criminal Justice Standards and Goals (NAC), *Police* (Washington, D.C.: U.S. Government Printing Office, 1973), pp. 210–211.

a. Specialization within the criminal investigation unit should take place only when necessary to improve overall efficiency within the agency.

b. Criminal investigation operations should be decentralized to the most effective command level. However, unusual cases or types of cases may be investigated by a centralized unit.

5. Every police agency should establish quality control procedures to insure that every reported crime receives the investigation it warrants. These procedures should include:

a. A followup report of each open investigation every 10 days and command approval of every continuance of an investigation past 30 days;

b. Constant inspection and review of individual, team, and unit criminal investigation reports and investigator activity summaries; and

c. Individual, team, and unit performance measures based at least on arrests and dispositions, crimes cleared, property recovered, and caseload.

6. Every police agency with 75 or more personnel should consider the use of a case preparation operation to insure that all evidence that may lead to the conviction or acquittal of defendants is systematically prepared and presented for review by the prosecuting authority. A technician should be employed to handle any or all of the functions listed, whenever an agency can improve the quality of case preparation at the same or reduced cost.

a. Policies and procedures should be developed in cooperation with representatives of the local prosecutorial and judicial systems, and should contain the information required by all three systems.

b. All police information on each case prepared for prosecution should be in a systematically prepared, written report that contains the following documentation: copies of the incident report, followup reports, identification and laboratory reports, and any other reports necessitated by the investigation.

c. Every case also should contain written documentation relating to all case disposition information and notification records.

d. The case preparation technician may: establish case files and insure their completeness; present case files to prosecutors; present subjects in custody for arraignment, or obtain a warrant and disseminate warrant information; represent the agency at all pretrial hearings; notify witnesses; document final dispositions of cases; and return the case report file to the originating unit for retention.

7. Every police agency should coordinate criminal investigations with all other agency operations. This coordination should be supported by:

a. Clearly defined procedures for the exchange of information between investigative specialists and between those specialists and uniformed patrol officers;

b. Systematic rotation of generalists into investigative specialties; and

c. Equitable publicity of the efforts of all agency elements.[5]

The criminal investigator (detective) is a police specialist who concentrates on the apprehension and conviction of adult criminal offenders. (Although adult and juvenile police work presently differ in many aspects, emerging trends seem to point

[5] *Ibid.*, pp. 233–234.

toward the consolidation of the two specializations.) The primary responsibilities of the criminal investigation unit are:

1. Identification of criminal offenders
2. Location of criminal offenders
3. Arrest of criminal offenders
4. Collection and preservation of physical evidence
5. Locating witnesses
6. Recovery and return of stolen property

Because the patrol officer is frequently in a position to initiate an investigation, often the process begins and ends with him. On occasion, either the nature or complexity of the criminal offense requires a specialist who has the time and approximate training to pursue the suspected culprit. However, the patrol unit must retain the principal responsibility for conducting preliminary investigations of crime, and, when feasible, complete investigations. The fact that it is an around-the-clock, jurisdiction-wide, mobile, radio-equipped unit makes it crucial for fulfilling this purpose. Patrol officers can conduct investigations at once, thus avoiding delays due to the dispatching of investigators. It also reduces the problem either of locating specialists, who may be on other assignments or of delaying cases for investigators who report for duty. Clearly, no other unit is as well suited as patrol to make direct investigation when a crime has been committed.

As related earlier, the detective specialists are frequently divided into other specializations or subunits. Typically, the investigation unit is organized into three subunits: (1) crimes against persons; (2) crimes against property; and (3) general assignment. Each is explained as follows:

> The crimes against persons unit would be charged with the responsibility of conducting investigations where a person is the victim of a crime—e.g., murder, forcible rape, robbery and assault. The crimes against property unit would be charged with the responsibility of conducting investigations involving loss of property—e.g., burglaries, larcenies, and auto thefts. The general assignment unit would be charged with the responsibility of conducting all investigations which the other two units do not handle, such as bad-checks cases, embezzlements, "con" games, and others. In larger cities a far greater degree of specialization may be needed. In any case, specialized units should be created only in response to real need and consolidated with other units when the need has passed or has ceased to be acute and continuous.[6]

It should be noted that each subunit in some agencies is subjected to even more divisions. For example, urban departments normally include such units as: homicide, robbery, missing persons, burglary, larceny, auto theft, arson, forgery, sex offenses, and fraud.

Detectives should be assigned equal workloads. Cases should be weighted in

[6] *Municipal Police Administration,* 7th ed. (Washington, D.C.: International City Management Association, 1969), p. 131.

terms of their seriousness, complexity, and estimated time of their completion. Thus, a number of minor cases would at a certain point be considered equivalent to a single, more serious case. Temporary imbalances of workload should be adjusted by reassignment of some work to investigators currently experiencing a lighter load.

Detectives must be mobile and flexible. With the emergence of team policing, a small but growing number of departments is assigning detectives to beats along with patrol officers. At the same time, the detectives retain an overall jurisdictional responsibility for functioning in any part of the community requiring investigative services. Hence, the detectives would have a fundamental beat area in which to conduct investigations, but would be on call to provide assistance in other beats. In some instances, departments find it necessary to elicit aid from other nearby agencies. The recognition of the need for improved cooperation among departments, and in particular investigative units, has led to three basic changes: (1) total consolidation of investigative services; (2) partial consolidation of investigative services; and (3) formalized mutual aid.

The total consolidation of criminal investigation is most apt to occur in areas where consolidation of law enforcement has been established. However, even where full consolidation of local police services into regional police services has not been achieved, the consolidation of investigative services has become an increasing reality.

Partial consolidation is being adopted by an expanding number of agencies. One variation has resulted in the assignment of federal, state, and local law enforcement officers to a team or "strike force" that concentrates on organized crime. Another form is seen in the Major Case Squad of the Greater St. Louis Area, which is comprised of investigators from both Illinois and Missouri local police departments. The investigators remain in the employ of their parent agency, but are assigned to the team, which through enabling legislation has police powers in more than a single jurisdiction. This and the former type of consolidation is currently assessed as having a number of operational advantages:

1. A small department rarely is sufficiently staffed or equipped to investigate a major case.
2. The perpetrator in many cases resides or takes refuge in an urban area while he operates in it and the smaller jurisdictions.
3. Witnesses, leads, and evidence may be found in more than one jurisdiction.
4. The general pooling of resources has proven to be a successful tactic in apprehending criminal offenders.

Mutual cooperation between agencies is common today and ranges from equipment and personnel support during periods of collective violence to the loan of needed police aircraft for search and rescue missions. In terms of criminal investigation, for example, the Los Angeles Sheriff's Department will, upon request, supply needed specialists to police departments and other surrounding agencies. Homicide, kidnapping, narcotics, vice, and other specialists in investigating are often provided to police agencies in need of such aid. At times, the smaller agencies find themselves in a position to assist the larger departments by loaning them personnel and equipment.

The selection and deployment of detectives naturally varies according to the problems confronted by the department. The selection of a detective and other specialists is based on one or more of the following: past performance as a police officer (high efficiency ratings as a patrolman, for example), need (sex crimes requiring the use of a policewoman, for example), and examination (written and/or oral tests). In most instances a promotion from generalist to specialist involves salary increases and clothes allowances.

Except in dangerous circumstances, investigators should be assigned to work alone. Most investigations may be made more effectively by one investigator, and the economy of using one investigator on a case should be apparent to the police administrator. When an investigator is involved in a dangerous investigation, one or more partners should be assigned to work the case.

The investigation of criminal offenses includes a series of interdependent phases that each provide the foundation for successfully accomplishing the next. First, the immediate action at the scene of the crime is most frequently performed by the patrol officer. Second, the patrol officer usually conducts the preliminary investigation. The officer seeks to secure the immediate area, and identify and locate victims, suspects, witnesses, and property. Also, field evidence technicians may come to the scene for detailed searches and the preservation of evidence. The technicians work in support of the detective but are best assigned to the patrol unit in order to assure rapid response, better coordination of services, and effective preliminary investigations. Third, the detective either responds to the scene of the crime or performs a follow-up on investigation as soon as possible. In the course of continuing an investigation beyond the preliminary stage, the efforts of the patrol division must be reviewed by the detective. Evidence that does not appear in the course of the initial investigation may be discovered later. Suspects and witnesses who have nothing of significant value to reveal when first questioned may have reflected on the events and established important connecting links between pieces of information previously considered unimportant. Each of the three phases contains a vast array of prescribed and proscribed rules and techniques that encompass confessions, search and seizure, notification of a suspect's legal rights, access to legal counsel, use of the polygraph, use of existing records pertaining to the crime and the suspects, and establishing the elements of the crime.

Although confronted with an enormous set of constraints and regulations, the detective is being furnished with an enlarged number of scientific and structural aids. These include: computer link-ups (that furnish investigative leads, criminal histories, and so on), aircraft (for surveillance, tailing, and so on), crime laboratories (blood tests, physical analyses, and so on), expanded jurisdictional authority (consolidation and cooperation), and improved training (frequent and in-depth training programs on legal changes and new techniques).

YOUTH SERVICES

Standard 9.5

JUVENILE OPERATIONS

The chief executive of every police agency immediately should develop written policy governing his agency's involvement in the detection, deterrence, and prevention of delinquent behavior and juvenile crime.

    1. Every police agency should provide all its police officers with specific training in preventing delinquent behavior and juvenile crime.

    2. Every police agency should cooperate actively with other agencies and organizations, public and private, in order to employ all available resources to detect and deter delinquent behavior and combat juvenile crime.

    3. Every police agency should establish in cooperation with courts written policies and procedures governing agency action in juvenile matters. These policies and procedures should stipulate at least:

        a. The specific form of agency cooperation with other governmental agencies concerned with delinquent behavior, abandonment, neglect, and juvenile crime;

        b. The specific form of agency cooperation with nongovernmental agencies and organizations where assistance in juvenile matters may be obtained;

        c. The procedures for release of juveniles into parental custody; and

        d. The procedures for the detention of juveniles.

    4. Every police agency having more than 15 employees should establish juvenile investigation capabilities.

        a. The specific duties and responsibilities of these positions should be based upon the particular juvenile problems within the community.

        b. The juvenile specialists, besides concentrating on law enforcement as related to juveniles, should provide support and coordination of all community efforts for the benefit of juveniles.

    5. Every police agency having more than 75 employees should establish a juvenile investigation unit, and every smaller police agency should establish a juvenile investigation unit if community conditions warrant. This unit:

        a. Should be assigned responsibility for conducting as many juvenile investigations as practicable, assisting field officers in juvenile matters, and maintaining liaison with other agencies and organizations interested in juvenile matters; and

        b. Should be functionally decentralized to the most effective command level.[7]

Of all the police-specialized responsibilities, that of handling juvenile problems is the most replete with change and confusion. A large group of agencies—public and private—are attempting to assist in abating juvenile delinquency without any coordination of their efforts. In many instances, the agencies find themselves either duplicating one another's endeavors or acting in ways counterproductive to each other.

Added to the large number of organizations currently providing services to

---

[7] NAC, *Police,* p. 221.

youthful offenders are far-reaching legal and philosophical changes. First, the agencies concerned with problems associated with juveniles are organizationally and in practice seeking to separate the delinquent from nondelinquent youth. This trend is leading to the juvenile unit being divided into two sections: one section to handle youthful offenders, and the other to aid children that are either potential delinquents or being victimized by others. The trend is also in other instances causing the juvenile criminal offender to be dealt with by the criminal investigation unit, with the youth services unit assuring responsibility for delinquency prevention and assistance programs. Here, we are discussing programs for both juvenile delinquency and youth in need of help as being combined within the same unit. Nevertheless, we recognize that as of this writing a stronger and more reasonable case can be made for including juvenile offenders in the criminal investigations unit.

Second, a concerted effort is being mounted by the criminal justice agencies to divert children and youth away from the juvenile courts so that their problems, which otherwise would be dealt with in a context of delinquency and official action, will be defined and handled in other ways.[8] It is premised on the idea that an excessive number of children are being processed by juvenile courts, that children are unnecessarily referred to juvenile courts, and that in many cases the harm done to children and youth by contacts with these courts outweighs any benefits thereby gained. Moreover, the interaction between child and court and unanticipated consequences of the processing of a child in many instances contributes to or aggravates the problem of delinquency.

Becoming delinquent is not a simple result of the effects of juvenile court experiences but rather a process in which parents, neighbors, teachers, school officials, and police, and environment as well, play significant roles. No less important is the "self-reaction" that youths make to these factors. Becoming delinquent is by no means a single or simple process; frequently it discloses a cumulative reinforcement of problems confronting a child in different social contexts. Parents may be loveless, punitive, or rejecting, or they may place the child prematurely on his own. The child may be labeled as the "bad one" or black sheep of the family; neighbors may focus hostility on such a child and make him a scapegoat. Teachers may add another facet to the child's disrepute with the designation of troublemaker, or a principal may insist that the child be removed from his school. The police, who are the main source of juvenile court referrals, form stereotyped judgments of the child based upon limited information from his family or his school record. Finally, if the child is growing up in an environment of delinquency—if his peer group is involved in the offenses that so often characterize very poor or very rich neighborhoods—chances are he will join in, in order to

---

[8] A documented example of a youth diversion project devoted to status offender processing ("status offender" denotes juveniles who have committed acts that would not be considered a criminal offense if perpetrated by an adult) is contained in the report by Roger Bacon and Floyd Feeney, *Juvenile Diversion Through Family Counseling* (Washington, D.C.: U.S. Government Printing Office, 1976).

be "accepted." Thus, while there is no agreement on the precise way a child becomes delinquent, much indicates that the process consists of predominant interactions in which the child's sense of honesty and moral worth are placed in question. This is most likely to happen when relationships of trust vital to personal growth are weakened or changed to those of distrust. When this occurs, wariness and surveillance replace the easy mutual acceptance of trust. There is little effort to normalize deviance or to see it as a problem capable of ordinary solutions.

Consequently, society in general and policy makers in particular are critically examining all agencies concerned with youth services. The criticisms levied against our criminal justice agencies have raised two issues: (1) whether some of the actions of children and parents now subject to definition as delinquent or unfit should be reinterpreted and either ignored or written off simply as part of the inevitable, everyday problems of living and growing up; and (2) whether many of the problems now considered delinquency or preludes to delinquency should not be defined as family, educational, or welfare problems, and diverted away from the juvenile court into other community agencies. If diversion is the appropriate answer, then the social policy makers must be certain that there is something better to divert to.

The police can and probably will play a major role in the diversion process. Police encounter youth problems more frequently than other community agencies; they meet the problems at the time of their occurrence, and they wield a great deal of coercive and symbolic authority to make deviance costly to juveniles and parents, as well as to define it on their own terms. Police methods, such as cautioning, counseling, supervision, dramatized hearings, and suspended action, usually proceed from relatively uncomplicated moral conceptions of right conduct and respect for law (authority), with a background knowledge of human behavior and its treatment. But the police should be expected to act in concert with other responsible agencies in order to more adequately deal with the scale and complexity of juvenile delinquency. (One urban police and probation department is now assigning their juvenile personnel to combined teams on which city and county field investigators are working in direct support of one another.) Although a large percentage of children and youthful offenders running athwart the police can be safely dismissed out of hand or after an interview or hearing, there are others whose problems are such that they may need help that police or paraprofessional workers cannot give. Furthermore, it is very doubtful whether certain kinds of problems now called delinquent tendencies, such as runaways, incorrigibility, and some types of sex problems, should ever be processed by the police at all. A more encompassing program that unites public and private welfare agencies or generates new agencies and services is preferable.

The primary responsibilities of the youth services unit are:

1. To prevent delinquency
2. To investigate and apprehend juvenile offenders
3. To aid children that are neglected or abused

The fulfillment of the first can be attempted through a variety of programs ranging from ride-along (allowing juveniles to ride in police vehicles while on routine patrol) to school resource officer programs (assigning an officer to teach in a public school and counsel students). The second objective is achieved in much the same manner described in the previous section. The officer's discretionary decision making is put to the full test in that essentially three choices can be made: (1) refer the offender to juvenile court; (2) refer (divert) the juvenile to other public or private agencies; or (3) release the youngster to his family or under his own recognizance. The third objective includes investigating complaints against adults or other juveniles regarding the psychological or physical health of a youth.[9]

In conclusion, one might reasonably predict that the nature and scope of the juvenile unit will significantly change, and the police will become an integral link in the diversion process. The first already can be seen in the transference of the duties for juvenile criminal investigation to the criminal investigation unit. Recent court decisions and procedural changes (right to counsel, bail, adversary proceedings, and so forth) underpin such an organizational transition. The second is readily apparent in the literature and is under development by an increasing number of criminal justice agencies. With all the flux and ambiguity surrounding police and youth, the only certainty is that the police will play an expanded role in youth problems ranging over criminal violations through prevention programs to protecting children from the harmful acts of others.

NARCOTICS AND DRUG ABUSE

Standard 9.10

NARCOTIC AND DRUG INVESTIGATIONS

Every police agency should acknowledge the direct relationship between narcotic and drug offenses and other criminal activity, and should have available a narcotic and drug investigation capability based on that acknowledgment.

    1. Every police agency should provide fundamental narcotic and drug investigation training to every officer during basic training.

    2. Every police agency should cooperate in and, where necessary, establish narcotic and drug abuse public awareness programs such as school system educational programs, civic group programs, multiagency community programs, and Analysis Anonymous programs.

---

[9] The details connected with the pursuit of each objective can be found in Edward Eldefonso, *Youth Problems and Law Enforcement* (Englewood Cliffs, N.J.: Prentice-Hall, 1972), pp. 64–91. A benchmark text on the subject should also be consulted: John P. Kenney and Dan G. Pursuit, *Police Work with Juveniles and the Administration of Justice*, 5th ed. (Springfield, Ill.: Charles C Thomas, 1975), and Malcolm W. Klein, ed., *The Juvenile Justice System* (Beverly Hills, Calif.: Sage Publications, 1976).

3. Every police agency employing more than 75 personnel should have a full-time narcotic and drug investigation capability. Personnel in smaller agencies may be assigned where justified by the local problem.

    a. The number of personnel assigned to the narcotic and drug operation should be determined by the local problem.

    b. Where appropriate in agencies with 75 or less personnel, drug and narcotic operations may be consolidated with vice operations.

    c. Drug and narcotic operations should be decentralized to the extent that the agency is; however, a central drug and narcotic unit should be maintained to coordinate the decentralized operations.

4. Every police agency should insure coordination and the continual exchange of information between officers assigned to narcotic and drug enforcement, vice enforcement, intelligence, and uniformed patrol.

5. Every chief executive should establish written policies and procedures requiring that every narcotic and drug complaint will be reported in writing and thoroughly investigated. These policies and procedures should provide that:

    a. All narcotic and drug complaints be distributed to the chief executive or his delegate, and to the central narcotic and drug unit;

    b. A written followup report of every open drug or narcotic investigation be prepared every 30 days to indicate the progress of the investigation;

    c. Individual, team, and unit narcotic and drug investigation reports and activity summaries be inspected and reviewed continually;

    d. Individual, team, and unit performance measures continually be applied to drug and narcotic operations. These measures should include arrests and dispositions; number of purchases by type of drug or narcotic, quantity and quality of seized narcotics and drugs, other crimes cleared, and working caseload.

6. Every police agency should provide narcotic operations with special funds and specialized equipment such as vehicles, electronic equipment, and vision devices necessary to conduct effective narcotic and drug operations.[10]

The narcotics and dangerous drug unit (NDD) typically develops as a separate specialization from the criminal investigation unit. In some instances, the vice and NDD units function in a similar manner to other overt investigative units, such as organized crime and vice. Besides functional similarities, the units are informationally interdependent. As with most problems that the police seek to resolve, the questions surrounding narcotics and drug abuse are equally monumental and perplexing. First, the documented increase in usage and trafficking in narcotics and dangerous drugs has alarmed nations and their local government jurisdictions.

The primary responsibilities of an NDD unit are:

1. Identification, location, and apprehension of illicit narcotic users and traffickers
2. Provision of prevention and education programs designed to lessen the probabilities of narcotic usage
3. Counseling of narcotic users in therapeutic centers

---

[10] NAC, *Police,* pp. 246–247.

Drug abuse growth patterns within our states and cities have caused NDD to become a top priority in terms of effecting criminal apprehension and preventive measures. While the federal government agencies focus on illicit drug traffic, the state and local police departments are endeavoring to enforce laws pertaining to traffic and usage. Further, state and local community treatment centers are being established by both public policy makers and volunteer organizations. At the same time, there are political movements (some have proven successful) designed to decriminalize certain drug offenses—primarily personal marihuana usage.

Narcotics control has become a socially and politically prominent issue. And, the police have been thrust into the center of the conflict. As mentioned earlier, a rapidly increasing number of community treatment centers and custom-designed educational programs have been established to complement the enforcement activity. Interestingly, due to his expertise the police specialist in narcotics is becoming actively involved in educational programs.

> The public has been bombarded with horror stories about the drug abuser, unsubstantiated claims of massive increases of drug use, and the emergence of sure-fire cures by an increasing number of social scientists. As a result, citizens are saturated with fear, misinformation, and unproductive nonsense about the way in which drug abuse evolves and is controlled. If this misinformation is to be replaced with factual knowledge, law enforcement officers have an important function in education. The education dispensed by law enforcement should basically be restricted to facts concerning their function in the drug abuse programs.
>
> Drug education may be approached in three steps: (1) the field officer as a teacher, (2) basic curriculum areas for officer involvement, and (3) the field officer as a community resource person for drug education.[11]

Essentially, there are two concepts about narcotic and dangerous drug addiction. The first looks at the drug problem as a sickness. The second is to use criminal detention to isolate the user from society. Enlightened police departments recognize the former method as a better approach to the problem and have moved to use available facilities for community medical care treatment of the user; these departments correctly view the "pusher" as the criminal. It should be noted that history records that political manipulation has been instrumental in making drug abuse a social rather than a medical problem. The closing of an unproved clinic system in the 1920s forced the drug user into a situation controlled by organized crime. Community prevention programs including education, medical, and psychological treatment have in most instances shown themselves to be of invaluable aid in coping with drug abuse problems.

Organizations such as the United Nations and Interpol, as well as various departments of the United States and foreign governments, are involved in the suppression and eradication of drug traffic. When these international and national efforts fail, state and local police find themselves confronted with an enormous enforcement and treatment problem. Hence, both control and an attack on the root

---

[11] Denny F. Pace and Jimmie C. Styles, *Handbook of Narcotics Control* (Englewood Cliffs, N.J.: Prentice-Hall, 1972), p. 70.

causes of drug abuse (therapy, education, and social conditions) are recognized as vital to any resolution of the existing problem.

Because of the mobility of the "pusher" and the addict, many agencies are consolidating their NDD units. A case in point is the Stark County Metropolitan Enforcement Group (MEG) Unit.[12] Stark County, located in northeastern Ohio, is characteristic of many of the smaller urban areas situated within a large megalopolis. The major city in the county, Canton, with a population of 110,000, represents approximately 30 percent of the county's total population of 372,000. The four remaining cities of Masillon, Alliance, North Canton, and Louisville represent an additional population of 80,000; fourteen villages with small police departments contain an additional 17,000 people. The remaining 165,000 persons live in the unincorporated areas of the county under the direct jurisdiction of the sheriff's department. Flourishing narcotics traffic and drug abuse posed a very special problem to law enforcement in the county. In 1969, actively assisted by the county prosecuting attorney's office, the chiefs of police of five cities and the sheriff started an informal, cooperative effort to combat narcotics and drug abuse growth. The program included a regular exchange of intelligence, the development of investigative techniques, and a concentration of attention on those persons identified as engaged in trafficking drugs and narcotics. The value of this program was demonstrated by almost immediate success in producing significantly increased arrests and convictions, primarily on possession charges. By early 1970, however, the results achieved from this cooperative effort had reached a plateau, indicating that a broader approach was necessary.

The MEG Unit furnishes a cogent illustration and example of consolidated and cooperative programs encompassing a variety of police specialists: criminal investigation, youth services, and so on. The reader desiring more exhaustive coverage of narcotics and drug abuse will immediately find a wealth of literature. It is recommended that the reader first consult The President's Commission on Law Enforcement and the Administration of Justice, *Task Force Report: Narcotics and Drug Abuse* (Washington, D.C.: U.S. Government Printing Office, 1967).

VICE CONTROL

Standard 9.9

VICE OPERATIONS

Every police agency should immediately insure its capability to conduct effective vice operations against illegal gambling, traffic in liquor, prostitution, pandering, pornography, and obscene conduct. These operations should be capable of reducing the incidence of vice crimes and related criminal activity.

---

[12] The description of the MEG program is taken in part from David D. Dowd, Jr., "The Stark County MEG Unit—A Response to Fragmented Law Enforcement," *FBI Law Enforcement Bulletin,* Vol. 41 (September 1972), pp. 13–15.

1. Every chief executive should establish written policies governing vice operations. These policies, consistent with existing statutes:
    a. Should reflect community attitudes toward vice crimes, the severity of the local vice problem, and the effect of the vice problem on other local crime problems.
    b. Should acknowledge that the patrol force is responsible for taking enforcement action against all vice violations they see.
2. Every police agency employing more than 75 personnel should have a full-time vice investigation capability. Every agency employing fewer than 75 personnel may assign vice operations specialists on a full- or part-time basis, depending on the local problem.
3. Every chief executive should insure close coordination and continual exchange of information between vice, narcotic and drug, patrol, and intelligence operations, and close liaison with other agencies conducting similar operations.
4. Every police agency should provide vice operations with special funds, specialized equipment, vehicles, vision devices, and any other physical support necessary to conduct effective vice operations.
5. Every chief executive should insure that every field commander reports in writing every 30 days to the chief executive, or his designee, the form and extent of the current vice problem in his area and the effort of vice operations on that problem. This report should contain:
    a. The number of vice arrests by type of offense and location;
    b. Information received on vice problems; and
    c. Current vice operations directed against area vice problems.
6. Every police chief executive should insure, through written policies and procedures, that every vice complaint received by his agency will be reduced to writing and investigated as thoroughly as possible. Vice complaint policies and procedures should provide that:
    a. All vice complaints be distributed to the chief executive or his designee, and to the vice unit;
    b. Every 10 days a written followup report on each vice complaint be made to indicate the progress of the investigation; and
    c. Every vice complaint investigation not completed within 30 days of its receipt be reviewed, and that all necessary steps be taken to expedite the investigation.[13]

Vice includes types and classes of personal or group conduct or activity that has been declared through legislation to be dangerous to the public welfare and subject to commercial exploitation. Vice is usually considered to include prostitution, illegal gambling, the use and sale of illegal alcoholic beverages and the illegal sale of legal alcoholic beverages, and the sale of obscene or pornographic material (as related earlier, narcotics sale and use enforcement is sometimes located in the vice unit). The primary responsibilities of the vice control unit are:

1. Prostitution
2. Gambling
3. Alcoholic beverages
4. Pornography

[13] NAC, *Police*, pp. 242–243.

Vice offenses differ from other crimes in a variety of ways, mainly because they are continuing offenses in both time and place. This occurs because vice offenders are providing a service and the clientele must know where it is being offered. Additionally, it involves a series of related acts, each of which is a separate violation. Clearly, a number of factors makes vice enforcement difficult. First, vice activities usually include two or more people as in the case of prostitution: madams, procurers, prostitutes, and clients. The difficulty occurs because the prostitute, gambler, and distributor of illegal material are generally visible, whereas the organizer of the operation is not. Second, vice is a victimless crime. In most crimes, there is a victim who complains. In vice offenses, on the other hand, the client is a willing participant who normally does not consider himself a victim. Third, profits are distributed throughout the vice organization and in particular tend to maintain the organizer. Fourth, profits are generous and thus available to pay for the exertion of corrupting influences (bribes). Fifth, public apathy makes the police task even more difficult. The police are severely hampered without the support of the large majority, which all too frequently acts in a passive role.

The most critical ingredient for a specialized vice-control unit to evidence a high degree of success is cooperation—internal and external. Within the department, all specialists and generalists should be held accountable for suppressing vice activities. Hence, in the absence of members of the vice unit, personnel of the investigations unit, for example, should take effective action when vice violations come to their attention. Furthermore, each patrolman should be held responsible for vice conditions on his beat. He should be required to take suitable action in line with departmental policy against all vice violations coming to his attention. He should be required to investigate and communicate the results on those vice complaints that do not seem to warrant assignment to the vice unit. Generally, the vice unit operates as the line unit responsible for vice, work that is normally beyond the ability and time restrictions of the patrol force. Undercover operators and the development of informers are two examples of vice activities best reserved for the assigned specialists.

Externally, at times it is necessary to request assistance from an outside agency. The training of local officers in the recognition of vice activities and in the enforcement of laws against them is often inadequate, and the needed training may be best supplied by outside assistance, as is the case also in other police training. Some departments are so small that lengthy vice investigations would divert manpower from needed patrol activities, as is the case with other criminal investigations. It is readily apparent that area-wide vice problems are interlinked with the problem of *organized crime*.

Every major investigation of such crime has concluded that there is need for greater cooperation among law enforcement agencies. Fortunately, units like MEG are being created to cope with vice activities. The states and the federal government are evidencing a greater interest in acting as the coordinative vehicle for integrating local, state, and federal law enforcement services. In some situations, the states have investigative components that take direct action in vice and narcotic problems.

In closing, we will add that a recent development and trend in vice control is intergovernmental coordination and cooperation.

TRAFFIC SAFETY

Standard 9.6

TRAFFIC OPERATIONS

Every police agency and every local government responsible for highway traffic safety should perform the basic functions of traffic law enforcement, traffic accident management and traffic direction and control.

1. Every police agency should perform the basic function of traffic law enforcement—the police activity specifically directed toward controlling traffic violations through preventive patrol and enforcement, case preparation, and court testimony. This function:

    a. Should include line patrol, area patrol, selective location patrol, and records and logistics; and

    b. Should be a fundamental responsibility of all uniformed officers.

2. Every police agency should perform the basic function of traffic accident management. This function relates to police activities connected with traffic collisions, and includes providing assistance to the injured, protecting the scene, preparing reports, taking necessary enforcement action, and conducting followup investigations. The function should include:

    a. Initial traffic accident investigation, followup investigation, traffic control at the scene, injury control, enforcement action, records, reports, and notifications; and

    b. On-scene investigations of all accidents involving a fatality, personal injury, or one or more vehicles that must be towed from the scene.

3. Every local government with responsibility for traffic direction and control should perform the basic function of traffic control and direction which has a direct and immediate effect on traffic flow. Such activities are those which have an immediate and direct effect. These activities:

    a. May include intersection control, parking control, pedestrian control, police escort, special event control, and hazard control;

    b. Should be transferred, wherever possible, from the police agency to another local government agency, or be undertaken by the police agency but assigned to nonsworn employees;

    c. Should not be performed by employees if the need can be anticipated in advance, and electronic traffic control devices can be installed, unless employees are cost-effective.

4. Every police agency should develop and implement written policies governing the investigation of traffic accidents, enforcement of State and local traffic laws and regulations, and traffic direction. Police chief executives should insure that these

policies are regularly communicated to all supervisors and line personnel. These policies should include guidelines on:

    a. Physical arrests, issuance of warnings and citations, and transportation of arrestees;

    b. Investigation of traffic accidents;

    c. Interjurisdictional responsibility and authority for traffic supervision; and

    d. Ancillary services that have an indirect effect on traffic flow.

5. Every State should assume complete responsibility for licensing all drivers of motor vehicles, vehicle registration, vehicle inspection, vehicle weight control, carrier and commercial regulation.

    a. Activities that do not require peace officer status should be assigned to nonsworn personnel.

    b. Observed failure to comply with driver licensing, vehicle registration, and equipment and safety regulations, should be subject to citation or reported to the appropriate agency through clearly established channels of communication.

6. Every police agency should employ, where necessary, specialized equipment operated by specially trained personnel to implement effective traffic programs.

7. Municipal police agencies employing more than 400 personnel should, consistent with an analysis of need, establish specialized accident investigation and traffic enforcement units. These units:

    a. Should be staffed with as few personnel as the local traffic problem will permit; and

    b. Should be functionally decentralized to the most effective command level.

8. Every police agency should make assignments for all traffic functions on the basis of traffic volume, accident experience, violation frequency, and congestion.

    a. Selective enforcement techniques should be implemented through assignment of men and equipment by time and location on the basis of demonstrated need.

    b. The establishment of a selective enforcement task force should be considered when the State or community accident death rate exceeds the national average or exceeds the average for the State or community for the last 3 years.

    c. Every police agency should have at least one employee specially trained in highway safety management and able to plan and evaluate effective traffic safety programs.

    d. Specialization should be limited according to need, and the major street traffic duties should be performed by patrol officers.

9. Every police agency should be capable of performing, or arrange for the performance of, activities necessary to support traffic line functions. These activities:

    a. May include administration, planning, budgeting, personnel management, research and analysis, public information, training, communications, transportation, records and identification, property control, equipment supply, and laboratory services; and

    b. Should enable the police agency to gather and analyze traffic information and to maintain records to guide the agency in the safe movement of traffic.

10. Every police agency should periodically release traffic safety information and traffic safety educational material to the general public, and should cooperate with appropriate educational institutions in the preparation and presentation of traffic safety educational programs.[14]

[14] NAC, *Police*, pp. 225–226.

The traffic safety unit is responsible for developing and maintaining a departmental program that is comprised of the following five responsibilities:

1. Enforcement
2. Education
3. Engineering
4. Investigation
5. Parking

It is seen that the services vary from law enforcement or order maintenance on through educational and technical planning projects. A traffic safety unit that avoids providing one or more of the five cited services will soon experience, at best, minimal effectiveness.

Departments that have established specialized traffic safety units in most instances reduce their traffic problems. However, certain basic features must be present in order to assure maximum success. First, as with all other specialized units, patrol units (generalists) must retain a responsibility for handling traffic situations that require police assistance or control. The traffic safety unit serves as an overlay and back-up to the more serious incidents. Second, the traffic specialist must be specifically trained in achieving the services mentioned above (obviously, the training should include the development of technical skills in accident investigation and traffic engineering support). Third, the unit should be furnished with the most modern equipment designed to assist in the performance of their duties. Examples are: audiovisual equipment, radar, alcohol and narcotic detection instruments, aircraft and/or helicopter, and sophisticated life-saving equipment.

Three final comments regarding enforcement, specialized enforcement, and interdepartmental relationships. Many citizens first and perhaps only meet their police "in action" during a traffic enforcement situation. The traffic citation, in other words, is a very common means for putting the police and his "client" together in a way that can easily lead to dissatisfaction on the part of the civilian. Hence, particular care should be afforded to making the enforcement of traffic laws and rule infractions as professional as is *humanly* possible.

Selective enforcement is simply the assignment of portions of or all the unit on specific problem areas. As with enforcement, the public should be apprised in nearly every instance of the reasons for selecting a given problem for intensified enforcement. To illustrate, frequent pull-overs would meet with less resistance if the public were informed that the department was going to make a concentrated effort to reduce drunk driving. Further, the traffic specialist should explain again and in detail the reasons for the stop to the operator of the vehicle. Interdepartmental coordination and information exchange is critical in order that planned changes in the streets and physical design of the community may be helpful to traffic flow and lessen the chances of accidents. Information exchange in terms of education is equally useful. In particular, police-student relationships tend to improve through an increased understanding by youth of the reasons behind enforcement practices.

SPECIAL ENFORCEMENT

Standard 9.8

SPECIAL CRIME TACTICAL FORCES

Every police agency employing more than 75 personnel should have immediately available, consistent with an analysis of its need, a flexible and highly mobile tactical force for rapid deployment against special crime problems.

1. Every chief executive should establish written policies and procedures that govern deployment of the tactical force against any problem. These policies and procedures should stipulate at least:

   a. That the tactical force will be deployed on the basis of current crime pattern analyses or validated current information on expected crime activity;

   b. That the tactical force will be deployed against a problem only when the regularly assigned patrol force is not adequate to be effective against that problem; and

   c. That tactical force deployment strategy will be based on an objective analysis of the problem: overt saturation as a highly visible preventive strategy, and covert saturation as a low visibility detection and apprehension operation.

2. Every police agency employing more than 400 personnel should consider maintaining a full-time tactical force, and every agency employing more than 75 but fewer than 400 should consider maintaining a full- or part-time tactical force, depending on local problems.

   a. The numerical strength of the tactical force should depend on agency needs and local problems.

   b. A full-time tactical force should include an analytical staff element.

   c. A part-time tactical force should use qualified personnel from anywhere within the agency.

   d. Every tactical force should have a central headquarters and should operate from that headquarters when deployed against a problem.

   e. Field commanders should be informed of tactical force activities within their area of responsibility. Tactical force activities should be consistent with the policies of the field commander of the area in which they are working.

   f. Every tactical force should be equipped with necessary specialized equipment, vehicles, radios, vision devices, and weapons.[15]

A special enforcement unit is usually found in the large urban sheriff's and police departments. It is responsible for supplementing any large police operation (patrol, traffic, investigation, and so on) within the jurisdiction that needs extraordinary manpower commitments. Situations typical of their involvement are high crime rate areas, major strikes, civil disturbances, large public events, and rescue. The primary responsibilities of the unit are:

   To provide temporary, supplemental patrol and investigative personnel

   To maintain order in large public gatherings

   To conduct special life-saving missions

[15] NAC, *Police,* p. 238.

The unit frequently has specialized equipment such as mobile command vehicles, trucks, and rescue gear. The special enforcement team is not to be confused with selective enforcement teams within the patrol division. The former is comprised of specialists that: (1) vary in assignments from saturation patrol, to vice, on through crowd control at public gatherings; and (2) are trained as technical specialists in such subjects as scuba diving, investigation, riot control, and so on.

The key to the effectiveness of the unit is twofold. First, the specialist must be highly trained over a wide range of subjects. Second, planning for deployment of the unit must be based on knowledgeable insight and accurate data. Finally, the use of a special enforcement unit commonly extends beyond the jurisdiction boundaries of the department. Other smaller departments often request the aid of the unit. The deployment of the unit in other governmental areas obviously requires extraterritorial arrest powers and a formalized mutual aid agreement that covers liability and monetary costs to both the sending and receiving agencies. The emerging developments and trends in specialized enforcements are the application of improved technological devices for controlling civil disturbances, and the use of data to predict more effective deployment patterns.

JAIL (CUSTODY)

Standard 12.4

THE DETENTION SYSTEM

Every police agency currently operating a detention facility should immediately insure professionalism in its jail management and provide adequate detention services. Every municipal police agency should, by 1982, turn over all its detention and correctional facilities to an appropriate county, regional, or State agency, and should continue to maintain only those facilities necessary for short term processing of prisoners immediately following arrest.

1. Every police agency that anticipates the need for full-time detention employees after 1975 should immediately hire and train civilian personnel to perform its jail functions.

2. Every municipal police agency currently operating its own detention facility should immediately consider using an easily accessible State or county facility for all detention except that required for initial processing of arrestees. Every agency should also consider using State or county facilities for the transfer of arrestees from initial processing detention to arraignment detention.[16]

The jail unit is responsible for the:

1. Custody, security, and care of all sentenced and presentenced prisoners
2. Accumulation, processing, and dissemination of information concerning inmate court appearances, physical location of the prisoner while in jail, and inmate bail, finding and releasing data

[16] NAC, *Police,* p. 313.

3. Storing the personal property and clothing of all prisoners
4. Maintaining the welfare and security of the inmate while in jail

The role of the jail is undergoing a sweeping change. To begin with, it is important to distinguish between municipal jail administration and county jail administration. The municipal responsibility is primarily exercised prior to hearings or trial. Those sentenced misdemeanants who may remain in custody for the duration of their sentence will probably be detained no longer than thirty to sixty days. County sheriffs, particularly in larger jurisdictions, more often assume a true custodial role after trial and sentencing for periods ranging upward to one year. These differences, of course, condition the type and extent of programs that can be offered.

Next, many city jails are being closed and at the same time the county jails are undersized and being expanded.[17] In many instances, sworn officers are being replaced by trained, nonsworn paraprofessionals.

Whether an agency makes use of a county or state facility, it should choose an easily accessible facility that provides a full range of detention services and meets the transportation, security, and welfare needs of prisoners. Under such a system, local detention standards can be raised and more efficient organization and administration made possible.

Finally, city and county jails are expending greater sums of money to improve the *quality* as well as the quantity of custodial care. Custody or detention is basically the setting in which the offender is placed and its primary concern is with the physical detention and orderly control of the inmate population. Moreover, treatment programs for sentenced and presentenced offenders are beginning to be found in many of the more advanced jail units. Predictive classification systems for handling special problems and program assignments are on the increase, providing the beginning linkage of a correctional continuum that extends from the local city jail, to county, state, and federal correction programs and facilities.

CRIME PREVENTION/COMMUNITY RELATIONS

Standard 3.2

CRIME PREVENTION

Every police agency should immediately establish programs that encourage members of the public to take an active role in preventing crime, that provide information leading to the arrest and conviction of criminal offenders, that facilitate the identification and recovery of stolen property, and that increase liaison with private industry in security efforts.

[17] To illustrate the growing size and importance of countywide jails, the Los Angeles Sheriff's Department currently operates the fourth largest jail system in the *nation*.

1. Every police agency should assist actively in the establishment of volunteer neighborhood security programs that involve the public in neighborhood crime prevention and reduction.

    a. The police agency should provide the community with information and assistance regarding means to avoid being victimized by crime and should make every effort to inform neighborhoods of developing crime trends that may affect their area.

    b. The police agency should instruct neighborhood volunteers to telephone the police concerning suspicious situations and to identify themselves as volunteers and provide necessary information.

    c. Participating volunteers should not take enforcement action themselves.

    d. Police units should respond directly to the incident rather than to the reporting volunteer.

    e. If further information is required from the volunteer, the police agency should contact him by telephone.

    f. If an arrest results from the volunteer's information, the police agency should immediately notify him by telephone.

    g. The police agency should acknowledge through personal contact, telephone call, or letter, every person who provides information.

2. Every police agency should establish or assist programs that involve trade, business, industry, and community participation in preventing and reducing commercial crimes.

3. Every police agency should seek the enactment of local ordinances that establish minimum security standards for all new construction and for existing commercial structures. Once regulated buildings are constructed, ordinances should be enforced through inspection by operational police personnel.

4. Every police agency should conduct, upon request, security inspections of businesses and residences and recommend measures to avoid being victimized by crime.

5. Every police agency having more than 75 personnel should establish a specialized unit to provide support services to and jurisdictionwide coordination of the agency's crime prevention programs; however such programs should be operationally decentralized whenever possible.[18]

There is a trend on the part of our police away from "telling" the public how good they are to "demonstrating" their worth. This trend has caused an emphasis on *crime prevention* and a de-emphasis on *police-community relations* (PCR). Let us explain further before someone misinterprets our commentary. We see the police and the public searching for program activities that reduce the probabilities of an individual being victimized. Additionally, we also see the police agency decentralizing and extending the accountability for PCR to all police and civilian personnel. Perhaps some local conditions dictate that specialized PCR units be sustained. Obviously local citizen needs should be given priority. In the meantime, however, we find the PCR responsibility and activity best disseminated throughout the entire organization. Consequently, PCR should be found in every unit. In particular, the crime prevention unit has a prime opportunity for building a positive *and supportive* relationship between the police and its community.

---

[18] NAC, *Police,* pp. 66–68.

Hence, this subsection will cover a number of crime prevention programs one of which is PCR. We begin with a brief overview of the purpose of crime prevention.

Crime Prevention: An Overview

Crime prevention can be interpreted in several ways depending upon the type of criminal behavior to be prevented. In some cases, it refers to the solution of social, psychological, and economic conditions that lead to the desire to commit crime. In others, it concerns the elimination of the opportunity for crime through the presence of police patrols and "hardening the site" to foil the commission of crime. Further, it involves systematic effort to meet both the general needs of the public, and the unique needs of special citizen groups (e.g., special interest groups such as senior citizens or minority groups such as ghetto or barrio residents).

While ultimate success or failure may well depend upon elimination of the conditions that foster crime, the presently overburdened criminal justice system may be relieved by placing obstructions in the way of potential criminals. Clearly an informed community that is supportive of their police acts as a *major threat to the criminal.* In addition, investigations can be aided by using the best methods of identifying criminal offenders and the property they steal.

Neighborhood Security Programs

In many cities, police agencies have involved the public in crime prevention efforts through neighborhood security and neighborhood watch programs. These programs are designed to encourage people to report suspicious circumstances in their neighborhoods to the police.

A typical program is the Neighborhood Security Program developed by the Nassau County, N.Y., Police Department. Based on a "brother's keeper" concept, the program began in May 1971. Since that time, 60 percent of the police district (approximately 320,000 families) have been contacted in connection with the program.

The Nassau County program includes several sound procedures that could be adopted by most agencies. Under this program, residents are forbidden to take enforcement action themselves; they are requested to report information about suspicious persons or circumstances by telephone to the local police precinct. The agency explains to residents that if it needs to contact them again it will telephone them instead of sending officers. Police units are dispatched directly to the scene of the incident rather than to the home of the person making the report.

The procedures should be incorporated in a memorandum or pamphlet prepared by the agency for participants so they will know what to expect if they provide information. Details of what kinds of information are helpful to the police should be included.

Police agencies should immediately notify volunteers by telephone when an arrest results from their information. Such recognition of volunteers' contributions generates enthusiasm for the program. Agencies should acknowledge any person providing information through a letter, telephone call, or a visit.

Identification Programs

Many neighborhood security groups have adopted a program pioneered by the Monterey Park, Calif., Police Department in 1963. Since the adoption of "Operation Identification," there have been only 25 burglaries in more than 5,000 participating households. In the remaining 6,000 homes in Monterey Park, there have been nearly 1,000 burglaries in the last three years alone. The agency buys electric marking tools and lends them to persons to mark their personal property with either their state driver's license number or their Social Security number. The agency provides decals for exterior windows to identify participants, as well as forms for listing factory serial numbers of personal property.

Both driver's license and Social Security numbers have been used in the various programs; however, the use of each identifying number has drawbacks. Using Social Security numbers creates problems because the Social Security Administration refuses to reveal the names the numbers identify. Using driver's license numbers presents problems with people who don't have a license or with duplicate numbers from different states.

Since police information systems would generally receive a number when an identified item is reported stolen, and would match that number, irrespective of origin, if the property is discovered and checked by police, it would not matter what type of identifying number is used as long as it is accurately reported when the item is stolen. Indianapolis uses this type of procedure in its Crime T.R.A.P. (Total Registration of All Property) program by supplying all identifying data from forms filled out by participants to its police computer to trace recovered or pawned stolen property.

Business, Trade, and Commercial Crime Prevention

Efforts by police agencies to reduce crimes against business establishments have traditionally consisted of warnings—once information is received or a trend is developed—to the particular businesses that may be victimized. Police agencies also frequently initiate chain-call warning systems operated by businessmen to alert others to shoplifters or bad check passers operating in the area.

Police agencies should establish or assist community programs that provide crime prevention protection to business establishments. Written material that describes both the program and potential crime hazards should be prepared and distributed to commercial establishments. Additionally, every time a police officer visits a commercial establishment or meets a businessman, he should be alert to opportunities for offering crime prevention advice.

Robberies of public transportation vehicles in many urban areas have been virtually eliminated through exact fare or cost rules that require customers to deposit fares in locked boxes that cannot be opened by either the vehicle operator or the potential robber. Similar techniques have been adopted by such robbery-prone establishments as all-night service stations. If the number of robberies justifies the inconvenience to the public, police agencies should consider recommending such programs.

All banking and lending institutions whose depositors are federally insured are required by federal law to maintain so-called bait money in their cash registers. Serial number lists have provided necessary evidence in identifying and convicting apprehended robbery suspects. Police agencies should encourage all robbery-prone establishments to keep a supply of such easily identifiable cash.

Minimum Security Ordinances

It has only recently been recognized that the police should fulfill a similar function in crime prevention to that of fire departments in fire prevention. A number of cities have enacted ordinances that require minimum security devices to prevent burglaries in buildings used for business. Such ordinances, which are generally made a part of the building code, authorize the police to enforce their provisions through routine inspections. The building department normally inspects for compliance with the building code during construction; thereafter, the police department enforces compliance.

The National Crime Prevention Institute at the University of Louisville trains police officers to develop crime prevention programs, especially those based upon minimum security ordinances. It recommends the enactment of general ordinances which can later be expanded to meet local conditions. For example, ordinances may be restricted initially to specific commercial buildings and later expanded to include all new buildings and existing commercial establishments.

Security Inspections

In several cities crime prevention officers routinely advise burglarized businesses on security measures to avoid further crimes. They conduct inspections of residences and businesses upon request. Programs such as these are within the capability of all police agencies, and are an excellent means of immediately improving relations between the public and the police.

Homeowners who participate in crime prevention programs may receive benefits beyond property security. A pilot one-year team-policing experiment in 1972 involved negotiation with insurance companies to lower homeowner insurance rates for persons who allow a security inspection of their home or apartment by team policemen, and who comply with suggested security improvements. The experiment resembles automobile rating reductions for persons who complete driver's training education, and fire insurance rates based upon local fire rating.

Coordinating Support Units

Although all police agencies should develop crime prevention programs, agencies with more than 75 personnel may find that some type of jurisdiction-wide coordination is required for training operational personnel, producing informational material, and inspecting large commercial and industrial sites. Nevertheless, crime prevention programs should be operationally decentralized in order that inspections and enforcement can be performed by police personnel familiar with the geographic area and its crime problems.

Police-Community Relations

Our concept of PCR is a twofold, continuing approach to building mutually supportive relationships between the police and their clientele. PCR is:

1. The responsibility of *all* personnel, sworn and civilian, in the department
2. Specialized efforts to redress alleged grievances, erase misunderstandings, improve knowledge of the role of the police, and abate the reasons for growing discontent on the part of certain select groups within the community

Thus, PCR is a sustained endeavor to meet the service needs of all clientele while simultaneously coping with the special problems of a few individuals. In other words, PCR is not crime prevention, it is not race relations, and it is not press relations. Although PCR may encompass bits and pieces of these three areas, it is presently emerging as a generalized effort for bringing the police and its community together in a supportive way.

Because of this twofold approach to PCR, this section covers it as a specialized or programmatic endeavor. Depending on the size of the agency, specialized PCR programs may be implemented by the chief, sheriff, an appointed police manager, staff assistant, or a group of police officers that have been trained as experts in PCR.[19] At this point PCR is discussed as a specialized function within the crime prevention unit. To reemphasize a point made earlier, PCR is and will remain the responsibility of all police employees!

[19] For a brief and highly relevant listing of PCR programs see Deborah Johnson and Robert J. Gregory, "Police-Community Relations in the United States: A Review of Recent Literature and Projects," *The Journal of Criminal Law, Criminology, and Police Science,* Vol. 62 (March 1971), pp. 94–103. A concise recap of the development of PCR can be found in the article by Gary A. Kreps and Jack M. Willer, "The Police-Community Relations Movement," *American Behavioral Scientist,* Vol. 16 (January–February 1973), pp. 402–12.

PCR: POLICY IMPLICATIONS

The police should adopt policy guidelines that provide direction to all personnel on the issues expressed below.[20]

PCR Guideline 1. As community managers and monitors of social change, the police should enforce the law as vigorously as possible but short of the point where vigorous enforcement produces more strain than the system can stand. The choice of areas of intensified law enforcement effort must be included in this policy statement. The types and locations of police intervention and reaction to or anticipating called-for services must be dealt with in such a policy.

PCR Guideline 2. The police should pursue a policy of increased communication aimed at reducing their isolation as exclusively enforcers of order. In essence, the police must be open to external comments. Moreover, they must provide feedback to clientele suggestions or problems. The police must operate in public and for the public. Easily stated, but anyone who has visited the real world of the police practitioner knows that numerous difficulties surround external directives. At best, public inclusion in police matters and practices is fundamental to any PCR program.

PCR Guideline 3. Communication to and from police about the special client groups should be improved. As with any profession, some clientele are in need of more service(s) than others. The police should identify those requiring special attention and, in turn, provide those services necessary to restore mutual support for one another.

PCR Guideline 4. Police should seek to increase the amount of general government service that they perform. Rather than adhering to the traditional "enforcer" notion, the police must diligently pursue the more expanded role of solving social problems—criminal and noncriminal. PCR is, therefore, responding to or anticipating police services that range from an *assault* to an *assist*.

THE "DO'S" OF PCR

United PCR Unit: "Do" Number 1. The responsibility for PCR must be assigned to a single unit or person.[21] Hence, full responsibility for mounting and sustaining a PCR program must be given to one person or one unit.

Clearly Identified Relationships: "Do" Number 2. First, in regard to central police administration, PCR units must have overt prestige and authority. Second, staff permitting, PCR officers must be assigned to each division or geographical unit.

---

[20] The so-called PCR policy implications were derived, with modifications, from a series of more concrete recommendations by David Bordua, "Comments on Police-Community Relations," *Law Enforcement Science and Technology II,* ed. S. I. Cohn (Chicago, Ill.: IIT, 1968), pp. 115–125.

[21] The following material is derived from Bruce T. Olson, "Police Preferences for Police/Community Public Relations Programs," *Police Chief,* Vol. 39 (September 1972), pp. 64–67.

Topside Support: "Do" Number 3. The authority and tasks of the PCR unit must be explicit in intent and means of accomplishment. The police manager is primarily responsible for manifesting the position and role of PCR within his agency.

Exertion of Influence: "Do" Number 4. The PCR unit must translate ideas into departmental practices. Therefore, the PCR group has to seek policies and personnel decisions that augment better police-citizen relationships. Such a "Do" ranges from assisting in the recruitment/selection of potentially competent police officers for the department-wide policies that in practice improve PCR.

Citizen Participation: "Do" Number 5. PCR units must draw forth citizen Interest, Input, and Involvement (I^3) in police matters. I^3 basically means participation by the clientele in determining the objectives and practices of their department.

CIVIL (COURT SUPPORT)

The civil unit is responsible for serving and enforcing civil and criminal processes submitted to them by the courts and providing bailiffs to maintain order in the courtroom. The basic responsibilities of the civil unit are:

>Serving civil and criminal court processes
>Providing sworn and civilian personnel to the court for maintaining order

Governmental jurisdictions vary considerably in the use of police to perform these functions. Typically, the county sheriff assumes the responsibility for the civil unit. The personnel assigned to the civil unit are either sworn or paraprofessionals (trained civilians). Until recently, the unit received little recognition for the services it furnished to the court. Of late, however, the unit is being regarded as a critical element in improving the coordination between the police and the courts, as well as the internal operations of the court subsystem. The new development and trend with the civil unit is the expanded use of local law enforcement personnel in direct support of court operations.

LEARNING EXERCISES

Issues to Be Discussed

1. The opening section of this chapter points out the natural tendency of a police agency to frequently add more or new types of investigative or other functional specialists. If this natural conditioning persists, why not permit it to enlarge the number of police specialists?
2. Where does team policing fit with police specializations? Drawing from the previous chapter, address the issue of coordinating the team policing plan with police specialists. How might both operate in support of one another?

Group Activity

Divide the class into groups of six to eight members each. Each group is to secure a police agency's organizational chart and staffing assignments. The groups are then to analyze each chart and staffing allocation in terms of the number of types of police specialists as compared to the number of patrol officers. Each group will subsequently present their data in both raw numbers and percentages. Comparisons between agencies are to be made. Attempt to surmise only why similarities or dissimilarities exist among the agencies.

Field Activity

Divide the class into groups of three or four members each. The groups are to seek an interview with a police supervisor or middle manager (e.g., sergeant or lieutenant) and inquire as to the basis (formula) for assigning and monitoring the case workload. Each group is to make a five-minute classroom presentation on their findings.

Key Terms

Civil (court support)
Crime prevention
Criminal investigation
Diversion
Generalists
Jail (custody)
Narcotics and drug abuse

Special enforcement
Specialists
Status offender
Traffic safety
Vice control
Youth services

SUGGESTED REFERENCES

BLOCH, PETER B., AND WEIDMAN, DONALD R. *Managing Criminal Investigations.* Washington, D.C.: U.S. Government Printing Office, 1975.

BRANDSTATTER, A. F., AND RADELET, LOUIS H. *Police and Community Relations: A Sourcebook.* New York: Macmillan-Glencoe, 1968.

GREENBERG, BERNARD. *Enhancement of the Investigative Function,* Vol. 1. Menlo Park, Calif.: Stanford Research Institute, 1973.

GREENWOOD, PETER W., AND PETERSILIA, JOAN. *The Criminal Investigation Process, Vol. 3: Summary and Policy Implications.* Santa Monica, Calif.: Rand Corporation, 1975.

KENNEY, JOHN P., AND PURSUIT, DAN G. *Police Work with Juveniles and the Administration of Justice.* 4th ed. Springfield, Ill.: Charles C Thomas, 1975.

KERNER COMMISSION. *Report of the National Advisory Commission on Civil Disorders: The Police and the Community.* Washington, D.C.: U.S. Government Printing Office, 1968.

NATIONAL ADVISORY COMMISSION ON CRIMINAL JUSTICE STANDARDS AND GOALS. *Police.* Washington, D.C.: U.S. Government Printing Office, 1973.

NEIDERHOFFER, ARTHUR, AND BLUMBERG, ABRAHAM, eds. *The Ambivalent Police Force: Perspectives and Police.* 2nd ed. Waltham, Mass.: Xerox Publishing Company, 1975.

PRESIDENT'S COMMISSION ON LAW ENFORCEMENT AND THE ADMINISTRATION OF JUSTICE. *Task Force Report: The Police.* Washington, D.C.: U.S. Government Printing Office, 1967.

——. *Task Force Report: Service and Technology.* Washington, D.C.: U.S. Government Printing Office, 1967.

——. *Task Force Report: Crime and Its Import—An Assessment.* Washington, D.C.: U.S. Government Printing Office, 1967.

——. *Task Force Report: Narcotics and Drug Abuse.* Washington, D.C.: U.S. Government Printing Office, 1967.

REISS, ALBERT J. *The Police and the Public.* New Haven, Conn.: Yale University Press, 1971.

SKOLNICK, JEROME H. *Justice Without Trial: Law Enforcement in a Democratic Society.* New York: John Wiley, 1966.

WARD, RICHARD. *Criminal Investigation.* Boston: Holbrook Press, 1976.

WHISENAND, PAUL M. *Crime Prevention.* Boston: Holbrook Press, 1977.

WILSON, O. W., AND MCLAREN, ROY C. *Police Administration.* 4th ed. New York: McGraw-Hill, 1977.

5

Police Administration

Overview
Management = Responsibility
The Management Component
Support Specialist Components
Learning Exercises
Suggested References

OVERVIEW

Management is synonymous with *responsibility*. Hence we find the police manager responsible for coordinating and directing the activities of the police agency. In doing so, the manager is not alone but commands a select group of professional specialists in his quest for goal attainment. Additionally, we see the police manager of today confronted with a number of issues or challenges that vary from ethical considerations through media relationships to that of the primary police mission—crime reduction.

The police manager seeks to buttress his position and role with some, if not all, of the following units: information, legal, planning, research and development, fiscal affairs, intelligence, and internal control. Together they form the management component of a police system.

Another component of a police organization is that of the support specialists. It comprises the following units: career development, information, crime analysis, evaluation, and criminalistics. They function in support of both the management and program components (patrol, detectives, traffic, etc.).

MANAGEMENT = RESPONSIBILITY

"The buck stops here" thinking applies to management. While all within and without the police system share some responsibility for achieving the assigned goals, the management component has the major accountability for getting the job done, and moreover, as Peter Drucker has asserted, for "getting the right things done."[1] Hence for the next few pages we will examine a variety of police management responsibilities, both external and internal.

Police Code of Ethics

The need for a statement of police responsibilities and conduct has been recognized and is summed up in the code of ethics adopted by the International Association of Chiefs of Police in 1957:

---

[1] "To be effective is the job of the executive. 'To effect' and 'to execute' are, after all, near-synonyms. Whether he works in a business or in a hospital, in a government agency or in a labor union, in a university or in the army, the executive is, first of all, expected to *get the right things done*. And this is simply that he is expected to be effective." Peter F. Drucker, *The Effective Executive* (New York: Harper & Row, 1966), p. 1.

As a law enforcement officer, my fundamental duty is to serve mankind; to safeguard lives and property; to protect the innocent against deception, the weak against oppression or intimidation, and the peaceful against violence or disorder; and to respect the Constitutional rights of all men to liberty, equality and justice.

I will keep my private life unsullied as an example to all; maintain courageous calm in the face of danger, scorn, or ridicule; develop self-restraint; and be constantly mindful of the welfare of others. Honest in thought and deed in both my personal and official life. I will be exemplary in obeying the laws of the land and the regulations of my department. Whatever I see or hear of a confidential nature or that is confided to me in my official capacity will be kept ever secret unless revelation is necessary in the performance of my duty.

I will never act officiously or permit personal feelings, prejudices, animosities, or friendships to influence my decisions. With no compromise for crime and with relentless prosecution of criminals, I will enforce the law courteously and appropriately without fear or favor, malice or ill will, never employing unnecessary force or violence and never accepting gratuities.

I recognize the badge of my office as a symbol of public faith, and I accept it as a public trust to be held so long as I am true to the ethics of police service. I will constantly strive to achieve these objectives and ideals, dedicating myself before God to my chosen profession . . . law enforcement.[2]

Adherence to such a code is the first step toward true professionalization of police service.

Changes in Problems and Methods

The only thing we can be certain of today is uncertainty! Change avalanches into our daily professional and personal lives. The shoot-out bank robberies of the 1930s are being replaced by barricaded suspects with hostages. To the radio ear is being added air mobile (helicopters and fixed-wing aircraft). To the simple line-item budget is being added the highly intricate zero-base budget. A single paragraph on change is obviously not sufficient when writers such as Alvin Toffler, author of *Future Shock,* have devoted entire books to the subject. The import of the message should be clear: Police management must be prepared to cope with change. Better yet, they should be seeking means for better anticipating the forms such change will take.

Higher Levels of Responsibility

The formulation of policy is complicated by the relative degree of control and responsibility exercised by officials at various levels of the governmental hierarchy. Unfortunately, many city/county charters or city/county ordinances are ambiguous on the question of control, and in some cases the management of a police or sheriff's department is simultaneously vested in a city/county council and/or po-

---

[2] Don L. Kooken, *Ethics in Police Service* (Springfield, Ill.: Charles C Thomas, 1957), p. 7.

lice commission, a mayor, a city manager or county administrator, a director of public safety, a chief of police, and a sheriff.

In few cities or counties has the solution for the problem originated with the legislative body, such as the city council or board of supervisors. To the elective and appointive political power structure is added a host of special interest groups that actively pursue their purposes. It is clear that management (especially police management) does not operate in a vacuum. On the contrary, police management is a pivotal function with high visibility and often conflicting pressures. Unfortunately, politics (the wielding of power) is often involved. The police manager is not and cannot be nonpolitical. Hopefully when competing for resources, sound judgment and expressed goals will serve as a guide for the city/county decision makers.

The Media

While the entire public must be kept informed, some individuals in the community exert such a powerful and widespread influence as to deserve special attention. The police chief and sheriff are frequently justified in taking them into their confidence and discussing their proposed plans with them in order to ensure their understanding and approval and to gain their assistance in informing and winning the support of others and in meeting opposition to the plan. Especially important is the support of the media. The chief or sheriff should discuss his plans candidly with members of the media in order to avoid criticisms that sometimes spring from ignorance of the purpose and nature of the operation and to obtain the active help of the printed and verbal media in disseminating information to the public.

Developing and Maintaining Community Support

The success of the agency's programs is dependent on a concerned and cooperative citizenry. In some instances the public may seek to question, if not resist, certain programs. If it is informed, then those programs *worthy* of implementation and public support will be viable. Similarly, rejection of certain programs will be based on reason rather than rumor or irrationality.

Community support is derived from understanding; the police cannot progress beyond the understanding of their superiors and the public. Everyone should be kept informed regarding the nature and purpose of police policies, plans, and programs. Public understanding, in turn, must be based on facts, and the first step is to disseminate those facts that were used in reaching department-level decisions so that they may be used to help others in reaching an understanding of the police purpose and method.

Initiating new legislation, policy making, and program implementation can be facilitated by a chief's or sheriff's use of or involvement in citizen surveys, neighborhood-police councils, regional planning units, civic associations, and social gatherings. Obviously we envision the police executive to be a highly visible and busy person. In a slightly different way, the executive should be as omnipresent as the patrol officer.

Consolidation and Regionalization of Police Services

> The existence of thousands of understaffed, ill-trained, and poorly equipped small police forces is a continuing major deficiency in police service in the United States. Some of the reasons for the collective deficiency of many smaller agencies can be identified. Foremost among them are problems relating to personnel quality, training, and standards. . . .[3]

In general, consolidation is most practical in the areas that are also relatively noncontroversial in terms of the exercise of local control. Few governmental officials or police administrators will question the desirability of pooling resources for the establishment of a consolidated or regional crime laboratory or training facility. On the other hand, there is much more apprehension about pooling patrol service and criminal investigation, which form the backbone of local policing. The following standard provides clear-cut direction in terms of what *ought* to be done to achieve greater levels of effectiveness. Political values, however, must be addressed when engaging in interjurisdictional changes.

Standard 5.2

COMBINED POLICE SERVICES

Every State and local government and every police agency should provide police services by the most effective and efficient organizational means available to it. In determining this means, each should acknowledge that the police organization (and any functional unit within it) should be large enough to be effective but small enough to be responsive to the people. If the most effective and efficient police service can be provided through mutual agreement or joint participation with other criminal justice agencies, the governmental entity or the police agency immediately should enter into the appropriate agreement or joint operation. At a minimum, police agencies that employ fewer than 10 sworn employees should consolidate for improved efficiency and effectiveness.

    1. Every State should enact legislation enabling local governments and police and criminal justice agencies, with the concurrence of their governing bodies, to enter into interagency agreements to permit total or partial police services. This legislation:

---

[3] O. W. Wilson and Roy C. McLaren, *Police Administration,* 4th ed. (New York: McGraw-Hill, 1977), p. 51.

    a. Should permit police service agreements and joint participation between agencies at all levels of government;

    b. Should encourage interagency agreements for and joint participation in police services where beneficial to agencies involved;

    c. Should permit reasonable local control or responsiveness to local needs.

    2. Every local government should take whatever other actions are necessary to provide police services through mutual agreement or joint participation where such services can be provided most effectively.

    3. No State or local government or police agency should enter into any agreement for or participate in any police service that would not be responsive to the needs of its jurisdiction and that does not at least:

    a. Maintain the current level of a service at a reduced cost;

    b. Improve the current level of a service either at the same cost or at an increased cost if justified; or

    c. Provide an additional service at least as effectively and economically as it could be provided by the agency alone.

    4. Every State, in cooperation with all police agencies within it, should develop a comprehensive, statewide mutual aid plan to provide for mutual aid in civil disorders, natural disasters, and other contingencies where manpower or materiel requirements might exceed the response capability of single agencies.

    5. Every State should provide, at no cost to all police agencies within the State, those staff services such as laboratory services, information systems, and intelligence and communications systems, which fill a need common to all these agencies and which would not be economical or effective for a single agency to provide for itself.

    6. Every local government and every local police agency should study possibilities for combined and contract police services, and where appropriate, implement such services. Combined and contract service programs may include:

    a. Total consolidation of local government services: the merging of two city governments, or city-county governments;

    b. Total consolidation of police services: the merging of two or more police agencies or of all police agencies (i.e., regional consolidation) in a given geographic area;

    c. Partial consolidation of police services: the merging of specific functional units of two or more agencies;

    d. Regionalization of specific police service: the combination of personnel and materiel resources to provide specific police services on a geographic rather than jurisdictional basis;

    e. Metropolitanization: the provision of public services (including police) through a single government to the communities within a metropolitan area;

    f. Contracting for total police services: the provision of all police services by contract with another government (city with city, city with county, county with city, or city or county with State);

    g. Contracting for specific police services: the provision of limited or special police services by contract with another police or criminal justice agency; and

    h. Service sharing: the sharing of support services by two or more agencies.

    7. Every police agency should immediately, and usually thereafter, evaluate its staff services to determine if they are adequate and cost effective, whether these

services would meet operational needs more effectively or efficiently if they were combined with those of other police or criminal justice agencies, or if agency staff services were secured from another agency by mutual agreement.

8. Every police agency that maintains cost-effective staff service should offer the services to other agencies if by so doing it can increase the cost-effectiveness of the staff service.

9. Every police chief executive should identify those line operations of his agency that might be more effective and efficient in preventing, deterring, or investigating multijurisdictional criminal activity if combined with like operations of other agencies. Having identified these operations, he should:

a. Confer regularly with all other chief executives within his area, exchange information about regional criminal activity, and jointly develop and maintain the best organizational means for regional control of this activity; and

b. Cooperate in planning, organizing, and implementing regional law enforcement efforts where such efforts will directly or indirectly benefit the jurisdiction he serves.[4]

Planning

This discussion best begins with (1) a quote from an organizational renegade and (2) a standard relative to the planning of enhanced cooperation within the system. First, the quotation:

> Once I was asked to head up a new long-range planning effort. My wife listened to my glowing description of my new job. Next evening she blew the whole schmeer out of the water by asking: "What did you plan today, dear?" Bless her.[5]

Second, the standard:

Every police agency should immediately act to ensure understanding and cooperation between itself and all other elements of the criminal justice system and should immediately plan and implement appropriate coordination of its efforts with those of other elements of the criminal justice system.[6]

The clarion call within and without police organizations is for more and improved "planning." We doubt that anyone would challenge its importance to the overall department. If for no other reason, planning is *theoretically* good. Regretfully, police planning, until very recently, has been paid primarily lip-service. Operationally speaking, the question remains for many, "Why police planning?" The answer that immediately comes to mind might be worded as follows: "While basically functional today, police management and, in turn, the police organizations are plagued with growing deficiencies that if left unchecked will cause them to

---

[4] National Advisory Commission on Criminal Justice Standards and Goals, *Police* (Washington, D.C.: U.S. Government Printing Office, 1973), pp. 108–109.

[5] Robert Townsend, *Up the Organization* (New York: Knopf, 1970), p. 146.

[6] National Advisory Commission on Criminal Justice Standards and Goals, *A National Strategy to Reduce Crime* (Washington, D.C.: U.S. Government Printing Office, 1973).

grind to a halt. And planning especially on the part of management seems to be the most reasonable alternative for coping with present and future difficulties."

The history and, for the most part, the present state of affairs in providing police services is centered around reaction. For the majority of police organizations, the daily burden of providing services does not permit the luxury of planning. Thankfully, police planning is no longer classified as a delicacy, but rather as an essential ingredient in the recipe for effective police operations. Because of this change, we are witnessing a growing and organized effort to *plan* in order to swing the system from reaction to proaction.

Currently, some states are in the process of regionalizing their planning activities. Similarly, LEAA has delegated considerable authority and responsibility to their ten regional offices. Thus, a discernable trend in planning and allocating federal funds is evident in the decentralization of decision making and enhanced participation at the community level. Obviously, the police are intimately involved in the planning efforts. Newly established or expanded planning and research units are in evidence in numerous local law enforcement agencies.

Two additional trends are worthy of note in police planning. One can observe, or at least feel, a broadening of the planning purview to encompass projects, people, and priorities. It has been within the past two or three years only that we have been successful in unlocking ourselves from "projectitis." In most instances, a myriad of police projects comprised the plan of action for agencies, the region, the states, and the nation. Consequently, the plan typically resulted in frustration, confusion, duplication, and wasted money. More will be said about this trend later. Finally, we have a strongly renewed interest in *research, development, evaluation,* and *planning.*

In summary, we believe that a reactive posture in police work is being replaced by a proactive one. This transition is occurring mainly due to police *planning.* Although criticism and pessimism has been directed at police planning and action, we cannot help but be optimistic for the near future. After all, within a relatively short period of time many police agencies have replaced a planning void with the construction of planning mechanisms that take into account *projects* (ideas), *people,* and (of late) *priorities.* Their integration and resulting output—viable plans—are coming to fruition. And on a larger scale, through the planning process and the plans, police agencies have provided a means for ensuring that this nation has a "system" as opposed to a "nonsystem" of criminal justice. Clearly, police planning is a major cornerstone in criminal justice planning.

Managing by Objectives/Participative Management

How one manages can very well determine if one will manage at all. The days of randomized and authoritarian managing are on the wane in our local police agencies. Replacing past practices are a number of newer and proven management styles and techniques. Foremost among them are management by objectives

(MBO) and participative management (PM). The responsibility of the police executive to manage also encompasses the responsibility to manage effectively. MBO and PM are two tools, borrowed from industrial organizations, that daily find more acceptance and utility within police management circles.

MBO essentially means that the manager defines a set of goals or objectives that his middle managers (captains and lieutenants) are to accomplish within a specified time period (e.g., reduce the burglary rate by 10 percent within six months). PM is a management style that seeks to promote openness, involvement, and trust among management and the employees. Out of the increased participation is expected greater commitment to the achievement of departmental goals. PM is not a democratic form of managing—the "buck" still stops with the manager. He can delegate authority *but not his responsibility*. To MBO and PM are linked a number of supportive tools such as the computer, word-processing devices, team-building programs, goal-setting laboratories, and so on.

Crime Reduction: Standards, Productivity, and Evaluation (the Bottom Line!)

If the 1960s become known as the decade of national commissions and police-community relations, then the 1970s will in every likelihood be associated with police standards. Significantly, from the consideration of police standards follow subsidiary issues of nearly equal importance: productivity and evaluation. The reason for emphasizing the fundamental value of identifying and adopting standards in police work is simply that they form the nucleus for any measurement of productivity and subsequent evaluation of performance. To repeat, the police must first decide on what standards they will adopt and adhere to. Next, indicators of productivity must be selected, which, in turn, provide a means for evaluating how well the police are performing in relation to the standards. All three serve as a means for determining if the police agency is fulfilling its prime mission—*the reduction of crime.*

The two standards that follow deal with the issue of *evaluation.* They are presented at this point because they are worthwhile standards, which although phrased in state-wide terms, are of direct application to the local police agency level.

> Each State Criminal Justice Planning Agency shall develop annually a specific evaluation strategy.
> A program shall be evaluated if it meets one of the following criteria:
> —If it proposes to reduce the incidence of a specific crime or crimes;
> —If it purports to produce quantifiable improvement of some aspect of the criminal justice system;
> —If there is potential for technology transfer.
> Evaluation shall be defined as determining whether the project or program accomplished its objectives, in terms of either preventing, controlling, or reducing crime or

delinquency or of improving the administration of criminal justice within the context of the state comprehensive criminal justice plan. Such evaluation shall include, whenever possible, the impact of the project or program upon other components of the criminal justice system.[7]

The following standard vividly shows the interdependent connection between police productivity and police evaluation. The American Bar Association refers to the following standard as one of evaluation. However, it is immediately noted that the standard for evaluation is comprised of a series of measures to determine police effectiveness. The standard begins by asserting that:

> The effectiveness of the police should be measured generally in accordance with their ability to achieve the objectives and priorities selected for police service in individual communities. In addition, the effectiveness of police should be measured by their adherence to the principles set forth in section 2.4. This means that, among other things, police effectiveness should be measured in accordance with the extent to which they:
>
> 1. Safeguard freedom, preserve life and property, protect the constitutional rights of citizens and maintain respect for the rule of law by proper enforcement thereof, and preserve democratic government;
> 2. Develop a reputation for fairness, civility, and integrity that wins the respect of all citizens, including minority or disadvantaged groups;
> 3. Use the minimum amount of force reasonably necessary in responding to any given situation;
> 4. Conform to rules of law and administrative rules and procedures, particularly those which specify proper standards of behavior in dealing with citizens;
> 5. Resolve individual and group conflict; and
> 6. Refer those in need to community resources that have the capacity to provide needed assistance.
>
> Traditional criteria such as the number of arrests that are made are inappropriate measures of the quality of performance of individual officers. Instead, police officers should be rewarded, in terms of status, compensation, and promotion, on the basis of criteria defined in this section which directly relate to the objectives, priorities, and essential principles of police service.[8]

Finally, Table 5-1 provides a more specific and easily developed list of productivity measures. It is predicted that our local law enforcement agencies will find themselves, as a few have already, adopting standards and evaluating their success in meeting them through the use of productivity and other related measures of effectiveness.

Recently, we are finding a sharper focus on the *cost* of crime reduction, as well as on the actual reduction of crime. Many of us are asking, What is it going to cost? And, some of us are realizing that we cannot afford to pay for all of the gov-

---

[7] *State of the States on Crime and Justice* (Frankfort, Ky.: National Conference of State Criminal Justice Planning Administrators, 1973), p. 62.

[8] American Bar Association, *Standards Relating to the Urban Police Function* (Washington, D.C.: American Bar Association, 1973), pp. 25-26.

TABLE 5-1 Productivity Measurements for the Police Crime Control Function

A. Currently Available

1. Population served per police employee and per dollar[b]
2. Crime rates and changes in crime rates for reported crimes (relative to dollars or employees per capita)
3. Clearance rates of reported crimes (relative to dollars or employees per capita)
4. Arrests per police department employee and per dollar[b]
5. Clearances per police department employee and per dollar[b]

B. Requiring Significant Additional Data Gathering

1. Crime rates, including estimates of unreported crimes based on victimization studies
2. Clearance rates based on estimates of unreported victimization studies
3. Percent of felony arrests that "survive" preliminary hearings in courts of limited jurisdiction
4. Percent of arrests that lead to convictions
5. Average response times for calls for service
6. Percent of crimes solved in less than "x" days
7. Percent of population indicating a lack of feeling of security
8. Percent of population expressing dissatisfaction with police services

[a] These (except for A-1, B-7, and B-8) should be aggregated by type of crime, with emphasis on the most "important" crime.
[b] Data on resource inputs should to the extent possible exclude resources expended on non-crime control functions such as traffic control.

Source: The National Commission on Productivity, *The Challenge of Productivity Diversity: Improving Local Government Productivity Measurement and Evaluation: Part 3, Measuring Police-Crime Control Productivity* (Washington, D.C.: The Urban Institute, 1972), p. 10

ernment, including police services, we believe necessary. Hence we see a trend toward setting realistic police standards, increasing police productivity, and evaluating the results. Zero-base budgeting is one technique currently being used to buttress this trend (see the fiscal affairs unit that follows). "The challenge of management in the 60s was creative use of expanding resources. The challenge of management in the 70s is how to say 'no!' "[9]

THE MANAGEMENT COMPONENT

Until very recently, the management component included only a few people. For example, one commonly found a chief of police or sheriff, an aide, and a secretary. The other managers (lieutenants, captains, and majors) were considered more as

[9] A. J. Wilson, "It Is Easier to Give Than to Take Away," *Public Management*, Vol. 59 (March 1977), p. 2.

parts of the operating components. Hence, there was no concept of a management team. Unfortunately, the notion of a management component has not been implemented by most police systems. However, the trend is in the direction of creating management components capable of more effectively steering the system. The component is comprised of a number of management specialists, many of whom can and should be professional civilians.

In order of presentation, the following elements are contained in the management component: information, legal advisor, planning, research and development, fiscal affairs, intelligence, internal affairs, and office of the administrator.

Departmental Information Unit

The departmental information unit (DIU) is comprised of specialists in gathering, processing, and disseminating information to the public and to the *other police components*. In the past, the DIU was responsible for building a good public image or public relations. The DIU presently has the enlarged responsibility of keeping the public informed of police plans, problems, and activities. Consequently, the DIU now: (1) assesses public needs and attitudes; (2) presents the various police programs and achievements in such a way to the public and press as to gain the maximum public relations benefit to the agency; (3) keeps the public, the press, and individual citizens informed of police activities that pertain to them; and (4) coordinates communications and furnishes news releases during periods of critical activity (riots, criminal homicide, and so on). An informed citizenry and informed public media are usually more supportive of their government. The reasons for certain policies, procedures, and problem areas are in most instances sufficient to elicit a person's cooperation. An ill-informed public or media, on the other hand, are more critical, suspicious, and resistant of police services. A DIU that adheres to an open, warm, and candid communication style is guaranteed a receptive public. A mix of sworn and professional civilians best staff the DIU. As an example, trained civilian journalists can be employed to develop news releases, internal newsletters, and create public relations messages.

Interestingly, some chiefs are beginning to draw upon the DIU skills in another related way. Large- and medium-scale police systems are often bothered by poor internal communications and thus "rumors fly" while "information creeps slowly" through the channels. As a part of the management component, the DIU is more and more being held responsible for quickly gathering and disseminating information within the system. The result is a better informed, and thus effective, officer. Newsletters, bulletins, and personal appearance meetings are all a part of constantly receiving and sending new and accurate information to other components and their memberships.[10] Thus, the DIU as a representative of the chief interacts externally (public and press) and internally with a vast number of

---

[10] Techniques for more effective, organization-wide communications are recommended by Anthony Downs, *Inside Bureaucracy* (Boston: Little, Brown, 1967).

audiences. The interactions cause improved understanding and support from both the public and the police.

Legal Unit

A fairly recent addition to the management component is the legal advisor or unit (LU). The rapidly growing number of court decisions, criminal and civil statutes, administrative regulations, and labor relations issues demands qualified legal assistance for the chief and other members of the management team. Clearly, the police manager is in need of sound, legal counsel during periods of collective negotiations with police associations and unions.[11] The issues, the decisions, and the challenges confronting management have never been more complex. Accurate and rapid advice is required on a daily basis in order to assure management that they are not inadvertently violating the law or a regulation in pursuit of a particular program. In an operational sense, the LU can keep the police officers updated as to new legal decisions. Further, the LU can be of direct assistance to a prosecutor before and during the presentation of a court case. Due to the importance of the LU, the police agency should seek to have its own legal advisor(s) rather than rely on the government's legal staff.

> Given the nature of police function, police administrators should be provided with in-house police legal advisors who have the personal orientation and expertise necessary to equip them to play a major role in the planning and the development and continual assessment of operating policies and training programs.[12]

Ideally, agencies of one hundred persons or more should have an LU. In most instances, the legal advisor should be a competent civilian attorney, although in some agencies we currently find sworn personnel with law degrees who are qualified for an assignment to the LU.

Planning, Research, and Development Unit

The activities of planning, research (grants management), and development should be contained within a single unit—PRDU. If any of the three activities is missing from the PRDU, the entire process of planning, researching, and developing needed resources will suffer. The function of grants management and development being added to the traditional planning and research unit is somewhat standard. The majority of plans and research ideas fail to become a reality due to an inability of the planners and researchers to follow through and put the ideas to

---

[11] The reader interested in police labor relations should consult John H. Burpo, *Police Labor Relations* (Springfield, Ill.: Charles C Thomas, 1972).

[12] Institute of Judicial Administration, *Standards Relating to the Urban Police Function* (New York: American Bar Association, 1972), p. 238.

work. Thus, by creating a PRDU, a continued responsibility for placing plans and research into action is maintained. As a part of the management component, the PRDU must have direct access to the chief in order to gain his concurrence and support.

The track record in public planning, researching, and idea development is poor, but improving. Planning is an attempt to predict future requirements, changes, and trends. Research is a *scientific inquiry* into present and/or future problem areas seeking alternative solutions. Development means the *implementation* of recommended plans and research solutions. The police are increasing their efforts to cope with "future shock."[13] To this end, federal (Law Enforcement Assistance Administration), state, and regional agencies are funding their own planning and creating PRDUs in police departments. In addition to staffing the unit, money is being allocated to establish the process.[14]

Similarly, the above-mentioned agencies are allocating larger sums of money to police research. PRDUs are researching problems of increasing effectiveness in crime prevention and deterrence, operations, and evaluation of programs. Hence, the staffing of the PRDU includes systems analysts, operations research scientists, statisticians, engineers, and social scientists. Obviously, most of the personnel will be civilian. The significance of a PRDU as a research unit is stated below:

> A research capability should be developed within Police agencies that will aid the police administrator in systematically formulating and evaluating police agencies and procedures and that will equip the administrator to participate intelligently in the public discussion of important issues and problems involving the police.[15]

Fiscal Affairs Unit

The fiscal affairs unit (FAU) encompasses budgeting, accounting, auditing, purchasing, and payroll. More specifically, the FAU prepares the agency's budget, maintains accounting records, audits the receipt and disbursement of funds, generates requisitions and purchase orders, and updates payroll and other related time cards. The fairly new responsibility of record keeping and auditing grants is part of the FAU also. This and the reemphasis on performance budgeting make the FAU a central part of any management component. Obviously, the FAU shares similar data requirements with the PRDU.

The most commonly used budgeting method is line-item budgeting. By combining the line items, the agency pieces together a departmental budget. There was a growing movement at all levels of government toward the adoption

---

[13] The term *future shock* is attributed to the thought-provoking book by Alvin Toffler, *Future Shock* (New York: Random House, 1970).

[14] For further details see G. F. Blake, D. C. Gibbons, J. L. Thimm, and F. Yospe, *Criminal Justice Planning—An Introduction* (Englewood Cliffs, N.J.: Prentice-Hall, 1977).

[15] Institute of Judicial Administration, p. 236.

of a planning, programming, and budgeting system (PPBS). The city and county governments selecting this more modern management tool eventually included the police. Briefly, PPBS means:

1. Determining the goals or objectives of a program or organization as well as the sub-goals and activities necessary to attain the primary goals.
2. Establishing alternative methods of attaining the goals and the cost of effectiveness of these methods.
3. Selecting the best alternative method or combination of methods for the achievement of the goals, based on the management information generated by the determination of goals and the establishment of methods to attain the goals with their corresponding costs and levels of effectiveness.[16]

A new and more advanced form of PPBS has been conceptualized and is in the process of being implemented—zero-base budgeting (ZBB).[17] The ZBB approach requires each organization to: (1) evaluate and review *all* programs and activities (current as well as new) systematically; (2) review activities on a basis of output or performance as well as cost; (3) emphasize managerial decision making first, number-oriented budgets second; and (4) increase the breadth and depth of analysis. The four steps to ZBB are: (1) identify "decision units," (2) analyze each decision unit in a "decision package," (3) evaluate and rank all decision packages to develop the appropriations request, and (4) prepare the detailed operating budgets reflecting those decision packages approved in the budget preparation. Essentially ZBB supports the police manager in selecting a level of services that fits the occasion and the resources of the governmental jurisdiction.

Intelligence Unit

The intelligence unit (IU) is to be viewed as comprised of public specialists who furnish support to both police management and operations.[18] Today, in most instances the IU emphasizes the combating of organized crime. This text presents a more encompassing role for the unit. Basically, the IU is considered a feeder of needed information to *all* specialist and generalist components within the police department. It serves, therefore, as an information center on criminal activities that are mainly "latent" (for example, vice, narcotics, and the like). The major responsibilities of the unit are:

---

[16] Additional details on PPBS are contained in the article by James J. Hennessy, "PPBS and Police Management," *The Police Chief,* Vol. 39 (July 1972), pp. 62–67.

[17] For a comprehensive review of ZBB, see Peter H. Pyhrr, "The Zero-Base Approach to Government Budgeting," *Public Administration Review,* Vol. 37 (January–February 1977), pp. 1–8.

[18] The majority of this section is taken from a benchmark document by E. Drexel Godfrey, Jr., and Don R. Harris, *Basic Elements of Intelligence,* Law Enforcement Assistance Administration, U.S. Department of Justice (Washington, D.C.: U.S. Government Printing Office, 1971), pp. 1–10.

1. Elicit, process, and supply information on criminal matters.
2. Advise the police management on issues involving strategic decisions.
3. Advise police operations on issues relevant to tactical decisions.[19]

Intelligence is the result of a complex process, sometimes physical and always intellectual. The end product is most often an informed judgment; it may also simply be a careful description of a state of affairs; it can be a single fact, or a good guess. The process that generates these judgments, descriptions, or facts and near facts is called the intelligence process. The intelligence process refers to data and their conversion into information useful for police purposes. The process includes the collection of data, the collation (or combining and storage) of data, the evaluation and analysis of the collected and stored data, and the dissemination of the analyzed and evaluated material. *Collection* and *storage* are traditional pursuits of law enforcement agencies. The *systematic exploitation* of raw data through the operation of the intelligence process can turn information into *intelligence*.

The most useful way of categorizing the differences in intelligence outcomes is to focus on the use of the material by consumers of intelligence. On this basis, there are two interrelated categories: tactical and strategic intelligence.

TACTICAL INTELLIGENCE

Tactical intelligence contributes directly to the success of an immediate law enforcement objective. It may be the supplying of a lead to a criminal investigator; it may be compilation of a list of potential surveillance subjects; it may be some small new fact supplied by an observant police officer who is aware that reports on the activities of a certain loanshark are being entered in a dossier on the subject. Clearly, tactical intelligence can take many forms.

STRATEGIC INTELLIGENCE

Strategic intelligence is the most vital form of the result of the intelligence process. It is a blending of facts and analysis to produce an informed judgment on a major aspect of a law enforcement agency's objectives. An example of strategic intelligence would be a report to the head of a police agency on the outcome of organized crime in a major sector of the urban area. Strategic intelligence differs from tactical in that it deals with the larger issues with which the police managers of the agency are concerned, not the nuts and bolts of intelligence support, which the investigator or patrol officer on the street must have to do his job.

POLICE MANAGEMENT AND ITS USE OF INTELLIGENCE

The police manager must not expect intelligence support on such matters to flow up to him automatically.[20] He must make clear what his needs are to his intelligence unit—how and when and in what format he expects to receive the finished intelligence product. If the police manager is preoccupied with the tactical

---

[19] *Ibid.,* p. 2.
[20] *Ibid.,* p.3.

details of enforcement activities, then he will only receive tactical intelligence from his subordinates instead of the broad interpretive material that can give him a perspective on the major planning moves he must make.

Internal Control Unit

All formal organizations are concerned with employees who would violate the rules, regulations, and norms of the agency. The need and type of control and sanctions vary according to the *accuracy* of the selection process and the ability to lead rather than direct. Control and discipline range from the glance of disapproval by a fellow worker or supervisor to the manager terminating an employee. The internal control unit (ICU) concentrates on the more critical and sensitive processes of coping with those who have deviated from the policies, rules, regulations, and norms of the department. However, any program of minimizing misbehavior must equally include attempts to reduce or eliminate the reasons for wrongful behavior.

> Most of the existing internal investigation units operate by the case method—tracking down and bringing to book individual officers who misbehave. However, they should also serve in a deterrent or preventive capacity. This means identifying the problems that cause police misconduct and the neighborhoods or situations in which such misconduct is most likely to occur; devising procedures that will help solve the problems; patrolling and scrutinizing the neighborhoods; and keeping track of situations. Ways must be found to rid police mores of the pervasive feeling that an allegation of misconduct against one officer is an attack upon the entire police force, and that to report a corrupt fellow officer is a detriment, rather than a benefit, to the department. Finally, an internal investigation unit should be responsible to a department's chief and to him alone. By these means it should be possible to bring police misconduct to a minimum.[21]

Formal procedures within all departments for the investigation of complaints against police officers are fundamental. Many departments now have procedures of some kind for dealing with charges of misconduct by their members, whether those charges originate inside or outside the agency. When such procedures are fairly used, they succeed both in disciplining misbehaving officers and deterring others from misbehaving, ensuring fairness and good community relations. There are numerous means through which competent police management of internal investigations should provide important information about the conduct of individual officers. Once the department has obtained information concerning alleged misconduct or violations of policies, it must give the same dedication and attention to further investigation and, when appropriate, punishment as it gives to other vital areas of police work. Fortunately, many police agencies have recognized this need and are seeking to meet it. But in many, the

---

[21] The President's Commission on Law Enforcement and the Administration of Justice, *Task Force Report: The Police* (Washington, D.C.: U.S. Government Printing Office, 1967), p. 50.

programs are seriously inadequate. Police departments have long faced problems in fighting corruption and the best agencies have responded by developing specialized investigative machinery to deal with them. The procedures for handling the violators of organizational rules and human decency include the following:

1. Receipt of complaint
2. Complaint investigation
3. Resolution of complaint
4. Publicizing the decision
5. Discipline (if warranted)

The growth and power of police associations has directly influenced the policies and practices of internal investigations. For example, a number of collective bargaining contracts negotiated during 1971 contained the "Policeman's Bill of Rights," a document extending broad protections to police officers during investigation interrogations. The substance of the Policeman's Bill of Rights was generally the same in all these contracts.[22] Following is an analysis of the Policeman's Bill of Rights:

1. *Time of interrogation.* The interrogation of an officer being investigated for a disciplinary violation must be at a reasonable hour.
2. *Identification of investigating officers.* The officer under investigation must be informed of the officer in charge of the investigation and the officer who will be conducting the interrogation.
3. *Information about the investigation.* The officer must be informed of the nature of the investigation before interrogation commences.
4. *Length of interrogation.* The length of an internal investigation must be reasonable.
5. *Use of coercion.* The officer cannot be threatened with transfer, dismissal, or other disciplinary punishment as a means of obtaining information regarding the incident under investigation.
6. *Presence of counsel.* The officer under investigation may have counsel or a representative of his employee organization present with him during an interrogation.
7. *Recording of interrogation.* The interrogation must be recorded, either mechanically or by a stenographer.
8. *Criminal rights warning.* If the officer is a suspect in a criminal investigation, he must be advised of his Miranda rights.
9. *Furnishing copy of interrogation.* The officer under investigation has the right to request an exact copy of any written statement he has signed or a copy of the recording of the interrogation.
10. *Refusal to answer questions.* The refusal of an officer to answer questions concerning noncriminal matters may result in disciplinary action.
11. *Refusal to answer questions.* An officer cannot be ordered to submit to a polygraph test for any reason unless the officer requests to do so.

---

[22] The majority of this section is drawn from an article by John H. Burpo, "The Policeman's Bill of Rights," *The Police Chief,* Vol. 39 (September 1972), pp. 18–26.

Internal investigations ought to adhere to the points of order expressed below:

1. A requirement that officers answer all questions.
2. Questioning must be limited to circumstances surrounding the employee's violation of rules of conduct.
3. The employee is specifically not given the right to counsel during an interview.
4. Questioning must be completed within a reasonable time.
5. An officer may be disciplined, including discharge, for refusing to answer questions or submit to a polygraph.[23]

The promulgation of a "Bill of Rights" has of late met with varying reactions. Many chiefs and sheriffs view it as extending "protection from personnel actions not afforded to any other public or private employee."[24] Indeed, it appears that minor infractions of a rule or law, previously handled as administrative discipline, will because of the exacting dictates of the "Bill of Rights" be pursued on a criminal basis. Management practice, case law, and police union decisions should in the coming years forge a meaningful balance between management prerogatives and employee rights.

Because of the increasing involvement of government officials in the lives of citizens, adequate procedures for the consideration of such individual grievances as citizens may have against such officials are essential. So far as possible, it is desirable that procedures for the consideration of citizen grievances against police officers be formally accepted and effectively resolved! The various kinds of external review are:

1. Government officials
2. Court
3. Civilian boards
4. Ombudsmen
5. Civil rights and other commissions

Regardless of the type of review, the intent remains constant—to ensure ethical police conduct and, when that is absent, to provide a legitimate means of legally removing or sanctioning those who have acted against their sworn oath of public office.

Office of the Administrator

The following quotes describe the role and responsibilities of the police administrator:

> In addition to directing the day-to-day operations of his agency, the police administrator has the responsibility to exert leadership in seeking to improve the quality of police service and in seeking to solve community-wide problems of concern to the

---

[23] *Ibid.*, p. 26.
[24] Duane R. Baker, "Police Officer's Bill of Rights," *Western City*, Vol. 53 (June 1977), p. 4.

police. The position of police chief should be recognized as being among the most important and most demanding positions in the hierarchy of governmental officials.[25]

A police administrator should be held fully responsible for the operations of his department. He should, therefore, be given full control over the management of the department; and *legislatures, civil service commissions, and employee associations should not restrict unnecessarily the flexibility that is required for effective management*.[26] [Emphasis ours.]

In the screening of candidates to assume leadership roles in police agencies, special attention should be given to the sensitivity of the candidate to the peculiar needs of policing in a free society; to the degree to which the candidate is committed to meeting the challenge of achieving order within the restraints of the democratic process; to the capacity of the candidate to deal effectively with the complicated and important issues that police administrators must confront in the decision-making processes that affect police operations; and to the overall ability of the candidate to manage and direct the total resources of the agency. A community should employ the best qualified candidate without regard to his present location or departmental affiliation.[27]

Clearly the above quotations evidence the central and important position and role that the chief administrator should fulfill in a police agency. The police administrator (chief) can be viewed as the "quarterback" of the above listed team members. Further, the other top and in some cases middle managers should be considered as a part of the management team. To continue the analogy, the units in the management component are the "backfield," and the other operational and support managers serve as "linemen." Together they comprise the administrators' *team*. The office of the administrator includes the chief or sheriff, sworn and civilian personnel, and clerical staff. As such they "call the plays" in order to move the team effectively in the direction of good attainment. Such notions as participative management and management by objectives can and should be the administrator's style or approach to directing the activities of his team.

Yet, the most important ingredient in any plan for organizational success is good leadership. And, good leadership means motivating others to form a management team, and then prudently leading the team. Further, good leadership assumes that a police administrator is prepared to devote a substantial portion of his time to effecting change. He must explain to the public the need and rationale for change and undertake a concerted effort to win its support. He must convince his supervisory personnel of the necessity for change and elicit their commitment to work for effective implementation. He must seek to develop innovations in police operations and prepare his community and his organization to accept some risks and some failures in experimenting with them. As a community leader, a police administrator should be in the forefront in support of the basic objectives and priorities to which the police are committed. It is, for example, in the interests of both the community and the police organization for the police chief to be a staunch supporter and protector of individual rights and basic freedoms.

---

[25] Institute of Judicial Administration, p. 20.
[26] *Ibid.*, p. 20.
[27] *Ibid.*, p. 21.

Because of the nature of the police function, the leader of a police agency must exert leadership in the accommodation and mediation of conflicting community interests. He should take the initiative in advancing proposals that serve to reduce conflict. By virtue of the kinds of problems with which a police agency must cope, police personnel come to recognize and identify what are essentially community problems when they are in their incipient stages. Police are among the first to realize, for example, that a serious narcotics problem is developing in the schools; that a racial conflict is developing in a neighborhood; or that the policies of a governmental agency or a private landlord are contributing toward the deterioration of a given area. Last, the police leader must assume a role in community planning. He should be involved in the development of preliminary plans for those building projects, transportation systems, or other programs that will either need policing or affect the department's work. Police chiefs and sheriffs should have extensive knowledge of the factors that create the problems with which they must commonly deal.

SUPPORT SPECIALIST COMPONENTS

Support specialists are those sworn personnel and civilian personnel assigned the responsibility for helping the operational components in the performance of their duties. One may wonder why the units cited earlier in the management component were not positioned here. Briefly, the units covered here are mainly *supportive* to the *operational units,* and those already mentioned are *supportive* to *management.* Hence, the two components are actually supportive in nature but they differ in terms of direction. The three supportive units are: career development, information services, and criminalistics.

Career Development Unit

Translated into organizational terms, the career development unit (CDU) is a dual-purpose personnel development system that is directed at both the organization and the individual. On one hand, it is concerned with productivity, efficiency, and effectiveness. On the other hand, it is concerned with improving the general level of employee job enrichment. The ultimate mission of CDU is to achieve the most effective and efficient utilization of human resources possible. There are three major areas that, when fulfilled, will accomplish the two purposes expressed above:

1. Identification of organizational needs—determining what jobs (tasks) are being performed and the demands of those jobs.
2. Identification of individual officer attributes and interests, including the maintenance of an ongoing assessment of personnel resources.
3. Interface the assessment of the organization's needs with the assessment of available human resources

THE FOUR ESSENTIAL INGREDIENTS
IN CAREER DEVELOPMENT

The four essential dimensions in any CDU program are as shown on page 176.[28] The diagram indicates the basic relationship of the various components. While individuals comprise the organization, they can also be considered apart from the organization. It is recognized that people affect the organization and vice versa. To begin with, organizational needs must be identified in terms of what demands are made on the department. A *position specifications catalog addressing each unique position within the department will provide necessary data to identify organizational and individual demands and training requirements.* This catalog of job descriptions will be of additional benefit for purposes of career planning, manpower planning, and budget preparation. Next, easily accessible information pertaining to overall and specific personnel capabilities, strengths, and weaknesses should be made obtainable via a personnel information system. Third, the linking component is a critical aspect of a career development system. At this point, it should be verified that organizational and individual needs are specifically identified based on informational input from the first two system components. The primary purpose of the linking system is to identify immediate, short-term, and long-range needs of the agency and its members and to work towards improving deficiencies and better utilization of assets. This process of identification, improvement, and utilization may be accomplished by implementing a career counseling program. Fourth, human resource development should be unique to the needs of each department. In many cases, ongoing training programs will satisfy the needs suggested by the system process. However, where the process indicates a need for increased or expanded training and development programs, changes should be made.

The functions of the CDU can be categorized as: recruitment, selection, training and education, assignment, promotion, career counseling, and health and welfare. The first five functions are typical and can be usually found in a CDU, personnel unit, or local civil service board. The latter two functions are new and in most cases experimental. Indeed, the very concept of a CDU is innovative. Each of the functions is briefly described below.

RECRUITMENT

Because of the ever-increasing and changing demands for competent police officers, police agencies find it not only convenient but mandatory that they individually or in concert with the civil service engage in recruiting capable officers. Rather than "wait and see who walks in for the job," many agencies are now adopting the position of "Let us go out, locate, and convince the types of people we need to join us." Recruitment teams can be seen on college campuses and in a

---

[28] The majority of the thinking reflected in this section is derived from a study by the Los Angeles Sheriff's Department.

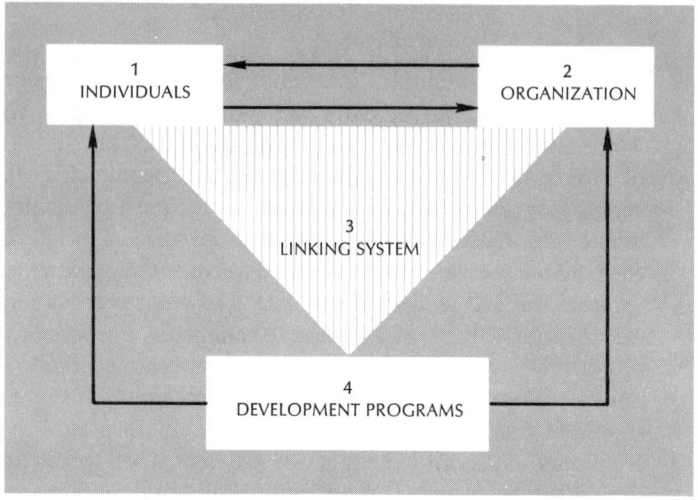

variety of other places actively pursuing and competing for the best in talent. Note the following.

> College graduates should be encouraged to apply for employment with police agencies. Individuals aspiring to careers in police agencies and those currently employed as police officers should be encouraged to advance their education at the college level. Communities should support further educational achievement on the part of police personnel by adopting such devices as educational incentive pay plans and by gradually instituting requirements for the completion of specified periods of college work as a prerequisite for initial appointment and for promotion. To increase the number of qualified personnel, police departments should initiate or expand police cadet or student intern programs which subsidize the education and training of potential police candidates.[29]

One particular focus is on increasing minority-group representation in police agencies.[30] To the traditional civil service standard of "only the best shall serve" has been added that of the civil rightists: "those that are representative shall serve." On the one hand, therefore, the goal of merit remains. On the other, however, we find a legal requirement and ethical norm for proactively recruiting minority groups and females into the ranks of our police service. Recruitment is fraught with frustration and uncertainty. Fortunately alert and imaginative police leaders are displaying good intent and innovativeness in *maintaining departmental effectiveness and promoting social justice.*

SELECTION

As the selection process goes, so goes the department. The input or selection of people to serve as police officers is the major determinant of an agency's success or

---

[29] Institute of Judicial Administration, p. 22.
[30] For specifics on this subject see the materials emanating from the Center for Criminal Justice and Minority Employment Opportunities, Marquette University Law School, Milwaukee, Wisconsin.

failure in appropriately serving the community. Unfortunately, the selection process and devices used to assist it—including paper and pencil tests, an oral examination, a medical examination, and a background investigation of the candidate—have been imperfect in predicting who will become a competent officer. More valid test processes and devices must be developed. Also, the techniques for using the end entry-level training program as a means for ferreting out those who are unsuited for the position of police officer should be improved. After all, the training period provides a considerably longer time frame to assess a person's ability to think and act in a police service role.

In order to assure themselves that they have effective police officers, the agencies are becoming actively involved in the selection process. Relevant and validated selection instruments are now an integral concern of police agencies dedicated to selecting the "right" people for the job and, thus, building the "right" organization. Although we have yet to scientifically ascertain who are the right people for a career in police work, the President's Commission on Law Enforcement and the Administration of Justice has asserted:

> Complexities inherent in the policing function dictate that officers possess a high degree of intelligence, education, tact, sound judgment, physical courage, emotional stability, impartiality, and honesty. While innumerable commissions and expert observers of the police have long recognized and reported this need, communities have not yet demanded that officers possess these qualities, and personnel standards for the police service remain low.
>
> The failure to establish high professional standards for the police service has been a costly one, both for the police and for society. Existing selection requirements and procedures in the majority of departments, aside from physical requirements, do not screen out the unfit. Hence, it is not surprising that far too many of those charged with protecting life and property and rationally enforcing our laws are not respected by their fellow officers and are incompetent, corrupt, or abusive. One incompetent officer can trigger a riot, permanently damage the reputation of a citizen, or alienate a community against a police department.[31]

While the issues surrounding personnel recruitment and selection are highly perplexing,[32] two basic criteria for selection tests are that they be *job-related* and *culturally unbiased*. Space does not permit an adequate coverage of these two testing requirements. Concisely, they mean that entry-level, promotional, and any other test procedures must directly pertain to the performance demands of the job and not unfairly discriminate against anyone due to their cultural heritage or gender.[33]

---

[31] The President's Commission on Law Enforcement and the Administration of Justice, *The Police,* p. 125.

[32] For those desiring an in-depth coverage of this subject, see David H. Rosenbloom and Carole C. Obrechowski, "Public Personnel Examinations and the Constitution: Emergent Trends," *Public Administration Review,* Vol. 37 (January–February 1977), pp. 9–18; and Winston W. Crouch, ed., *Local Government Personnel Administration* (Washington, D.C.: International City Management Association, 1976).

[33] In the past few years the "assessment center" method has become a part of personnel selection for some police agencies. Details can be found in George P. Tielsch and Paul M. Whi-

TRAINING AND EDUCATION

One sage commentator on the state of education in police work related that "It must be made clear as unambiguously as possible that education does count in police work."[34] Or, to paraphrase, "Good cops are well trained and educated." Some would spend considerable time arguing the differences between police training and police education. Obviously, some differences do exist. However, as compared to the importance of actually establishing effective, broad-gauged training/education programs, such debates appear trivial. Perhaps the most critical of all reasons to improve and expand police training and education is contained in the term "professionalization." Few would disagree that there is a strong interrelationship between professionalism in police service and appropriate training and education. Regretfully, to date many training and education programs fall short of enhancing police professionalization.[35] Encompassed in this allegation are the shortcomings of entry-level, in-service, and supervisory-management training efforts. However, major changes are being contemplated and created that will have a beneficial impact on police training and education.

Obviously at issue is a wide-sweeping examination and change of all police training and education. We can foresee for most police agencies during the coming decade:

1. Training academy entry-level programs being extended in duration to six months
2. Training curricula being expanded to include an emphasis on effectively resolving human conflict and other social or noncriminal problems
3. Closer union between the police academy and community and four-year colleges in regards to police education and the granting of academic credit
4. In-service (advanced officer) training/education programs being mandatory and conducted with greater frequency and with college credit offered
5. Supervisory and management training/education being mandatory and conducted with greater frequency and college credit being offered
6. Police professionalization being directly augmented through better and more training and education by academies and colleges
7. Training facilities and programs being consolidated on a regional basis with police agencies sharing in the use and funding of the academy
8. Academic pay incentive programs being abandoned
9. Entry-level and, in particular, promotional educational requirements being increased to two- and four-year college degrees, respectively
10. Less psychological stress in the academic portion of the training academy

---

senand, *Assessment Center Method in Police Personnel Selection* (Santa Cruz, Calif.: Davis Publishing Company, 1978).

[34] Egon Bittner, *The Functions of Police in Modern Society* (Chevy Chase, Md.: National Institute of Mental Health, 1970), p. 83.

[35] Robert F. Steadman, ed., *The Police and the Community* (Baltimore, Md.: Johns Hopkins University Press, 1972), p. 22.

At this point, two recommendations that seem to summarize this thinking are called to your attention:

1. Training programs should be designed, both in their content and in their format, so that the knowledge that is conveyed and the skills that are developed relate directly to the knowledge and skills that are required of a police officer on the job.
2. Educational programs that are developed primarily for police officers should be designed to provide an officer with a broad knowledge of human behavior, social problems, and the democratic process.[36]

ASSIGNMENT

For a few moments, think in terms of *job assignment* being synonymous with *job enrichment*—in other words, the police agency endeavoring to make the employee (sworn and civilian) more committed to performing his assigned duties and "happier" in doing so! We believe, as do others, that most jobs can be made more enriching for the individual. Proper job design and good supervision/leadership serve as a two-edged key to unlocking and solving the perplexities attached to job assignment. "I don't want to be locked into a low-prestige position in patrol" is being replaced with "I am a police officer, police supervisor, or police manager and will (without loss of status) serve in any assignment with dedication to the agency and the clientele alike." Job rotation, job enlargement, and counterbalancing decisions are being implemented that make police work in general and especially in patrol recognized as important and of equal status with other assignments. A reemphasis of the generalist-specialist (the compleat police officer) is at hand. To a limited extent *now,* and even more so in the *future,* job assignments will be treated as a career experience for a professional police officer.

PROMOTION

Career advancement is *not* the same as career development! The former means moving through the ranks, and the latter denotes individual growth within the occupation of police officer. Unfortunately, a few officers believe and behave as if the former only—career advancement—were important. How often have police agencies permitted, if not encouraged, competent police officers to be promoted into incompetent supervisors? Keep in mind that a successful patrol officer does not, once promoted, naturally become a successful supervisor or police manager. Far too often, police agencies rely on previous experience and seniority to determine who will be their supervisors and managers. Typically, the promotional formula includes weights being given to a written and oral examination, past performance ratings, and seniority.

Current promotion procedures should be altered in most departments. As

---

[36] Institute of Judicial Administration, pp. 19–20. Further, for those interested in a series of recommendations regarding the role of higher education in improving criminal justice organization, see the article by Richard A. Myren, "Decentralization and Citizen Participation in Criminal Justice Systems," *Public Administration Review,* Vol. 32 (October 1972), pp. 718–38.

stated previously, the period of seniority should be reexamined and in most departments greatly reduced. While there may be merit in requiring all candidates to take a competitive written examination, the results of such an examination should be only one of the many factors to be considered. Other factors should include: (1) an officer's prior performance and reputation in previous jobs as well as within the department and in the community; (2) an officer's educational achievement; and (3) an officer's demonstrated leadership potential and ability to assume greater responsibility. In order to ascertain prior performance and personal qualities, each department should adopt a system of rating personnel.[37]

Ideally, career tracking and counseling will eventually begin at every point in the police agency. Some officers will be counseled into supervision/management, and others will be counseled in line with a career in professional police work. The promotional selection formula will be totally changed and occur prior to actual appointment as a sergeant, lieutenant, and so on. The present system for promoting will be made more precisely predictive (one means for doing so would be to use a management training program—one to two weeks—as a means of assessing potential management capabilities). An extended and more definite probationary period is clearly needed. Where supervisory and management talent cannot be found within the agency, lateral entry of sworn and professional civilians (personnel, budgeting, data processing, and so on) must be fostered. The significance of qualified supervisory and management talent in local law enforcement was addressed in part earlier. The promotional process must be designed to facilitate the selection of those who wish to and *can* work to aid and control the activities of the professional police officer.[38]

CAREER COUNSELING

The notion of career counseling is just now being approached by our police agencies. Essentially, career counseling means a periodic conference with all police employees (sworn and civilian) concerning their job satisfaction and goal commitment. In the instance of small- to medium-sized agencies, external counselors may be used. Most large-scale agencies can afford a full-time counselor. The very concept and benefits of career development hinge on proper career counseling. Briefly stated, the counselors will assist in matching the needs of the organization with the needs of the individual. A career so vital to a hoped-for safe

---

[37] The President's Commission on Law Enforcement and the Administration of Justice, *The Police,* p. 142. A comparative analysis of existing promotional procedures in fifteen major police departments is presented by Richard G. Kohlan, "Police Promotional Procedures in Fifteen Jurisdictions," *Public Personnel Management,* Vol. 2 (May–June 1973), pp. 167–70.

[38] The vital role of job enrichment, career development, and mental and health programs in creating effective police services is covered in Robert F. Steadman, ed., *The Police and the Community* (Baltimore, Md.: Johns Hopkins University Press, 1972), pp. 12–50. As mentioned earlier, the assessment center method is becoming prevalent in the promotional selection process. For a description of the method see Paul M. Whisenand, "Assessment Centers: Situation-Based Testing," *Journal of California Law Enforcement,* Vol. 15 (April 1976), pp. 23–28.

society demands no less than guided career development and career advancement.

HEALTH AND WELFARE

Health and welfare units are a rarity. They provide credit services, help to an officer's family during an injury or after death, and other miscellaneous services. This unit can be created on a jurisdiction-wide basis or exclusively by the police agency. The duties often include mental and physical health programs, inservice benefits, and agency retirement programs. A total concern for the individual should be expressed via this unit—from entry to and beyond exit from the department. Most important, it should not be reactive (waiting until someone brings in a problem) but rather proactive in the sense that it wants to discover problem areas and resolve human difficulties.[39]

Information, Crime Analysis, and Evaluation Unit

The terms *information* and *crime analysis* are used to denote records, information processing, information analysis, and communication systems. The concept of *evaluation* means the assessment of the various police programs designed to control crime and maintain order. Technology and an understanding of the vital nature of accurate and timely management, analytical, and operational information have caused monumental changes in the area of information services, and the ability of a department to more fully analyze crime data and evaluate itself.[40] More specifically, police records should be viewed as a data base for supplying needed operational, analytical, and evaluative information on: wanted vehicles,

---

[39] Many agencies have developed a concern for the mental and physical health of their personnel. Occupational stress can lead to psychosomatic illnesses which in turn often cause disability retirements and prolonged sicknesses. The Los Angeles Sheriff's Department, for example, has in their full-time employ two clinical psychologists. Other departments have secured the services of consulting psychologists on a part-time basis. Still others have mounted stress reduction in-service training programs.

[40] Those interested in more information on the subject of police information systems should consult Tug Tamaru and Paul M. Whisenand, *Criminal Justice Information Systems* (Boston: Holbrook Press, 1979); the various reports published by Search Group, Inc., Sacramento, California; and the U.S. Department of Justice, 1976 Directory of *Automated Criminal Justice Information Systems* (Washington, D.C.: U.S. Government Printing Office, 1976). In regard to crime analysis see the *Police Crime Analysis Handbook* (Sacramento, Calif.: California Crime Technological Research Foundation, 1973). Finally, for those interested in the evaluation of police programs, review the monograph by Michael D. Maltz, *Evaluation of Crime Control Programs* (Washington, D.C.: U.S. Government Printing Office, 1972). Further, the literature on the impact of various police programs has grown immensely over the past few years. For one example, consult William G. Gay, H. Talmadge Day, and Jane P. Woodward, *Neighborhood Team-Policing: National Evaluation Program Phase 1 Summary Report* (Washington, D.C.: U.S. Government Printing Office, 1977).

property, persons, and investigative levels; manpower allocation information; planning information; budgetary information; and managerial statistics. Preferably, the above information should be located in a single and centralized data base that is secure from unauthorized access and physical damage! The field and other reports are usually generated elsewhere and transmitted to the Information, Crime Analysis, and Evaluation Unit (ICAEU) for further processing and storage for subsequent use.

A call for police service initiates the field reporting process, the need for supervisory and management information provides the stimulus for internal reporting. The reports are completed (handwritten or typewritten by the officer, or dictated by him to a machine, or directly to a stenographer) and usually reviewed for clarity and accuracy. The operational reports include arrests, criminal offenses, traffic accidents and citations, missing persons, injuries, and noncriminal incidents. The internal reports primarily deal with statistical data that assist supervisors and managers in their decision making. Next, the reports are indexed and stored. The indexing (by name, date, type of service, and report number) serves as a means of recalling the report for further analysis.

A comprehensive data base is nearly worthless without good communications. Sufficient high-grade voice channels connecting the police officers to their data base is imperative. The "need to know" if a subject is wanted, a vehicle is stolen, and so on is clearly basic to effective police work. To this is added the need for telephone linkages, intercom systems, and hand transceivers. Of late, audio and/or visual display communications have become a reality, so the police officer is able to interact directly with the data base. The advent of the computer and other electronic innovations has given rise to computerized command and control systems and computer-based information systems. The computerized command system is comprised of computer-assisted dispatching (based on the type and location of the called-for service, the computer furnishes a variety of information including the most logical car to be sent to the location), and car locators (through a series of transmitters the radio cars are kept constantly located on a status map). Computer-based information systems are of two types: batch and on-line/rapid-time (OLRT). Batch simply means that the data is processed and recalled in a relatively slow mode, and thus it is not immediately responsive to the inquiry. OLRT systems provide rapid (a few seconds) access to the entire data base and usually other larger data bases linked to it. Usually OLRT systems also process information not requested at once in a batch mode.

Local OLRT police information systems are linked to regional, state, and, in turn, national data bases. The types of information will vary somewhat in accordance with the potential geographical scope. In general, the following information can be found in the data bases: wanted persons, individual criminal histories, wanted vehicles, and wanted property. Besides the distinct advantages of more police data being made rapidly available to the police manager and supervisor, the strength of the computer has permitted police information systems to become linked (interfaced) and thus share data with other computer-based criminal justice (courts and corrections) information systems. Beyond all doubt, the age of the computer is here and will continue to have increasing impact on the quantity and quality of police services.

Criminalistics Unit

Police records and criminalistics seem to be running a close race for the title of being most neglected by local police agencies. The National Advisory Commission on Criminal Justice Standards and Goals expresses strong dismay at the sad conditions prevailing in criminalistics.

Criminalistics is defined as the application of physical and biological sciences to the control and prevention of crime. At times, forensic sciences and police science are substituted for the natural sciences. A pressing need for centralized, regional, and local criminalistics services has been confirmed. It has been proposed that the centralized laboratories be equipped to handle complex analysis and research and development projects. Such laboratories would be created in a single central location to furnish state-wide services. The medium-scale regional and small-scale local laboratories' levels of scientific expertness would vary according to their area and service demands. A full-service or central laboratory would contain the following capabilities: chemical analysis, biological analysis, physical examinations, ballistics, document examinations, photography, latent fingerprint identification, polygraph examinations, and research and development. The regional and local laboratories would be able to furnish only a part of these services and usually not to the same level of detail. Master planning and interagency cooperation is imperative in order to avoid duplication of services. Further, it is equally important that the laboratories receive adequate funding, staffing, and training through singular or joint-agency funding arrangements. The President's Commission on Law Enforcement and the Administration of Justice offered a set of recommendations designed to improve laboratory support of police operations:

> Basic laboratory services must be readily available within each locality or region to handle routine requests for service. Facilities for such services could be operated jointly by two or more jurisdictions with costs shared on an agreed basis. These facilities should perform only those scientific evaluations considered to be routine and not those requiring a heavy investment of limited-use equipment.
>
> Duplications in local facilities should be eliminated. States should provide central laboratory facilities capable of performing almost all complex and sophisticated scientific evaluations needed in police work. Local agencies would forward all complex work to this agency, and perform only routine work themselves. State services should be provided free of cost to all law enforcement agencies. Training of local personnel would be an important aspect of the State's laboratory's work. The FBI laboratory should continue to analyze the sophisticated evidence submitted to it.
>
> Well-developed police laboratories serving metropolitan needs should be continued, freeing State agencies to develop needed laboratory facilities in other parts of the State. Duplication of facilities between local and State agencies, and between local agencies in the same area, should be avoided.
>
> Consideration should be given to coordinating and consolidating laboratory services

for medical examiners and law enforcement, and related agencies, in one facility capable of serving all needs. In many areas such services could be provided on a local or regional basis.

Consideration should be given to placing all police laboratories in a State under the direction of a single administration, possibly an independent agency.[41]

We conclude with a quotation that is intended to summarize the critical role that police management must fulfill.

> The challenge to today's administrator at all levels in the organization is to cope with internal and external change simultaneously, to handle ambiguity and make decisions in the midst of confusion.[42]

LEARNING EXERCISES

Issues to Be Discussed

1. What are the major distinctions between the more traditional approach to organizing and the systems view?

2. What are two major changes of late in the problems confronting our police, and similarly, what are two major recent changes in policing methods?

3. Are there any close-at-hand examples of consolidation or regionalization of police services? List and describe them.

4. Review Table 5–1. Are there other measurements that can and ought to be made? If so, what are they?

5. One of the pivotal issues in police work today centers on recruitment and selection. Basically, how does a police agency maintain the standard of "only the best shall serve" in light of the requirement to make the personnel more representative of the community they serve (for example, in terms of race and sex)?

Group Activity

Secure the current budgets from three local police agencies. Divide the class into three groups for the purpose of analyzing each budget. (If the class is large, then obtain sufficient budgets in order to accommodate six to eight people per group.) A member from each group then makes a brief presentation on dollar amounts and percentages allocated to the various units and programs in the budget.

Field Activity

For one week each member of the class is to carefully review the media (newspapers, radio, and television) for any mention of local policing. A summary record (three-by-five-inch cards are convenient) of each observation is to be maintained. Notes should be

---

[41] The President's Commission on Law Enforcement and the Administration of Justice, *The Police*, p. 123.

[42] Victor I. Cizanckas and Donald G. Hanna, *Modern Police Management and Organization* (Englewood Cliffs, N.J.: Prentice-Hall, 1977), p. 57.

made on the content of the message, whether the information headlined or not, and whether it was favorable or negative in connotation. At the end of the week each student is to verbally summarize his notations to the class.

Key Terms

Administration
Career development unit (CDU)
Criminalistics unit (CU)
Departmental information unit (DIU)
Fiscal affairs unit (FAU)
Information, crime analysis, and evaluation unit (ICAEU)
Intelligence unit (IU)
Internal control unit (ICU)
Legal unit (LU)
Management
Management by objectives (MBO)
Manager
Office of the administrator (police chief and sheriff)
Operational generalists
Operational specialists
Organization
Participative management (PM)
Planning, research, and development unit (PRDU)
Support specialists
System

SUGGESTED REFERENCES

AMERICAN BAR ASSOCIATION PROJECT ON STANDARDS FOR CRIMINAL JUSTICE. *The Urban Police Function.* New York: American Bar Association, 1973.

ARGYRIS, CHRIS. *Integrating the Individual and the Organization.* New York: John Wiley, 1964.

BENNIS, WARREN G. *Changing Organizations.* New York: McGraw-Hill, 1966.

BITTNER, EGON. *The Functions of Police in Modern Society.* National Institute of Mental Health. Washington, D.C.: U.S. Government Printing Office, 1970.

BOPP, WILLIAM J. *"O.W." O.W. Wilson and the Search for a Police Profession.* Port Washington, N.Y.: Kennikat Press, 1977.

COHEN, BERNARD, AND CHARKEN, JAN M. *Police Background Characteristics and Performance: Summary Report.* New York: Rand Institute, 1972.

DRUCKER, PETER F. *Management: Responsibilities, Role, and Tasks.* New York: Harper & Row, 1975.

ENGELBERG, STEVEN L., AND GROVE, DANIEL G. *Interdisciplinary Criminal Justice Management Training Program.* Washington, D.C.: Georgetown University Law Center, 1974.

ETZIONI, AMITAI. *Modern Organizations.* Englewood Cliffs, N.J.: Prentice-Hall, 1964.

FOGELSON, ROBERT M. *Big City Police.* Cambridge, Mass.: Harvard University Press, 1977.

GARDNER, JOHN W. *Self-Renewal: The Individual and the Innovative Society.* New York: Harper & Row, 1963.

GARMIRE, BERNARD L., et al. *Municipal Police Administration.* 8th ed. Washington, D.C.: International City Management Association, 1977.

GOLDSTEIN, HERMAN. *Police Corruption: A Perspective on Its Nature and Control.* Washington, D.C.: Police Foundation, 1975.

HARRIS, RICHARD N. *Police Academy: An Inside View.* New York: John Wiley, 1973.

HERZBERG, FREDERICK. *Work and Nature of Man.* Cleveland, Ohio: World Publishing, 1966.

HOOVER, LARRY T. *Police Educational Characteristics and Curricula.* Washington, D.C.: U.S. Government Printing Office, 1975.

INTERNATIONAL CITY MANAGEMENT ASSOCIATION REPORT. "Police Unions." Vol. 8, No. 3 (March 1976), Washington, D.C.

KAST, FREMONT E., AND ROSENZWEIG, JAMES E. *Organization and Management: A Systems Approach.* 2nd ed. New York: McGraw-Hill, 1974.

Knapp Commission to Investigate Allegations of Police Corruption and the City's Anti-Corruption Procedures. New York: George Brazillier, 1973.

KUYKENDALL, JACK L. "Police Leadership: An Analysis of Executive Styles." *Criminal Justice Review,* Vol. 2 (Spring 1977), pp. 89–100.

LIKERT, RENSIS. *Conflict Management.* New York: McGraw-Hill, 1977.

MARCH, JAMES G., ed. *Handbook of Organizations.* Chicago, Ill.: Rand McNally, 1965.

MILTON, CATHERINE, et al. *Women in Policing: A Manual.* Washington, D.C.: Police Foundation, 1974.

NATIONAL ADVISORY COMMISSION ON CRIMINAL JUSTICE STANDARDS AND GOALS. *Police.* Washington, D.C.: U.S. Government Printing Office, 1973.

National Commission on Productivity Opportunities for Improving Productivity in Police Service. Washington, D.C.: U.S. Government Printing Office, 1973.

NICHOLAS, ALEX. *New York Cops Talk Back.* New York: John Wiley, 1976.

PRESIDENT'S COMMISSION ON LAW ENFORCEMENT AND THE ADMINISTRATION OF JUSTICE. *Task Force Report: The Police.* Washington, D.C.: U.S. Government Printing Office, 1967.

PRICE, BARBARA R. *Police Professionalism.* Lexington, Mass: Lexington Books, 1977.

SAUNDERS, CHARLES B., JR. *Upgrading the American Police.* Washington, D.C.: Brookings Institution, 1970.

SAYLES, LEONARD R. *Managerial Behavior.* New York: McGraw-Hill, 1964.

SCHWARTZ, ALFRED I., et al. *Employing Civilians for Police Work.* Washington, D.C.: Urban Institute, 1975.

STAHL, O. GLENN, AND STAUFENBERGER, RICHARD. *Police Personnel Administration.* Washington, D.C.: Police Foundation, 1974.

U.S. DEPARTMENT OF JUSTICE, LEAA. *Police Training and Performance Study 1970.* Washington, D.C.: U.S. Government Printing Office, 1970.

———. *Police Selection and Career Assessment 1976.* Washington, D.C.: U.S. Government Printing Office, 1976.

U.S. DEPARTMENT OF LABOR. *Collective Bargaining Agreements for Police and Firefighters.* Washington, D.C.: U.S. Government Printing Office, 1975.

WESTON, PAUL B. *Police Organization and Management.* Pacific Palisades, Calif.: Goodyear, 1976.

WHISENAND, PAUL M., AND FERGUSON, R. FRED. *The Managing of Police Organizations.* Englewood Cliffs, N.J.: Prentice-Hall, 1978.

WILSON, JAMES Q. *Varieties of Police Behavior.* New York: Atheneum, 1972 (paper).

WILSON, O. W., AND MCCLAREN, ROY C. *Police Administration.* New York: McGraw-Hill, 1977.

WOLFE, JOAN L., AND HEAPHY, JOHN F., eds. *Readings on Productivity in Policing.* Washington, D.C.: Police Foundation, 1975.

ZAGORIA, SAM, ed. *Public Workers and Public Unions.* Englewood Cliffs, N.J.: Prentice-Hall, 1973.

6
Community Crime Prevention

Overview
Crime Prevention and the Public
Citizen Responsiveness
The Delivery of Public Services
Community Crime Prevention Programs
Community Crime Prevention: An Epilogue—Placebo, Panacea, or Path?
Learning Exercises
Suggested References

OVERVIEW

Our communities have been perceived recently as being inextricably linked to the criminal justice system (CJS). In fact, the very success or failure of the CJS is now viewed as being dependent upon the involvement of the community in CJS efforts to reduce crime. Hence, the phrases "citizen involvement," "community participation," "citizen action," and "community representation" are omnipresent in CJS and administrative writings. Undoubtedly, the next decade will record a multitude of programs and an infinite number of activities intended to involve the public in preventing crime.

One of the programs that appears to be in line for increased resources and expansion is the youth service bureau concept. The youth service bureau is a single service center for children in trouble, about to cause trouble, or causing trouble. We shall also see drug abuse and treatment centers enhanced to better support the diversion of offenders out of the CJS and into community assistance programs. Further, employment and educational opportunities will be approached as they pertain to crime prevention. Recreation, religion, and improved physical designs for our cities will also be called upon to play a role in removing either the motivation or opportunity to commit a criminal act. In combination, such community and citizen action programs hold considerable hope for increasing our ability as a nation to prevent crime.

CRIME PREVENTION AND THE PUBLIC

Effective crime prevention is attainable only through broad-based community awareness and involvement. Indeed, if our country is to reduce crime, there must be a commitment on the part of every citizen to give of himself, his time, his energy, and his imagination to this end.[1] Additionally we can reasonably assume that *private* and *public agencies* outside the criminal justice system influence rises and declines in crime rates. Hence, a dominant concept of this chapter is that the more efficient and responsive the delivery of general services (education, manpower development, recreation, and other social services including drug abuse treatment and prevention programs), the less will be our feelings of alienation and the greater our confidence in public and private institutions, thus fostering our cooperation with these institutions—including those of the CJS.

---

[1] An example of this thinking is reflected in the article by George T. Hart, "Home Alert: Crime Prevention Through Police-Citizen Cooperation," *Crime Prevention Review,* Vol. 1 (July 1974), pp. 18–24.

Finally, crime prevention efforts must include benefits for institutions and agencies that have other primary goals, yet secondarily seek to reduce crime. Thus, an employer who sponsors a drug education or treatment program for his employees should anticipate both advances in his own economic interests and a decline in the incidence and dangers of drug abuse in his community. School-sponsored job counseling and referral services can reduce the number of dropouts, enabling many young people to avoid the idleness and boredom that can cause juvenile delinquency and classroom disruption. Churches and community clubs willing to make their facilities and personnel available on an extended basis can draw new members to their programs while providing enhanced recreational and social opportunities to many who typically are not interested.

Citizens, community organizations, agencies, and facilities must recognize that the degree of imagination, efficiency, and enthusiasm they bring to their own work has a direct impact on crime prevention. As a consequence, this chapter provides testimony to numerous cases in which communities already have recognized this fact and acted on it. Examples are cited of crime and delinquency prevention programs and other projects that have reduced crime, augmented existing criminal justice resources, found jobs for juveniles and ex-offenders, and influenced people to return to school and complete their educations. The remainder of the chapter is divided into four sections dealing with: (1) citizen and community participation in crime prevention efforts, (2) the CJS delivery system as it interacts with the citizen, and (3) programmatic efforts.

CITIZEN RESPONSIVENESS

Individual and collective responsiveness to crime prevention efforts is not a luxury for us but rather a fundamental ingredient in a concerted program to reduce crime.[2] However, this thinking on our part has merely resulted in limited and sporadic attempts by citizens to assist the criminal justice system in preventing crime. At the same time, the average citizen's response to the crime problem is a demand for more action by the police, courts, correctional institutions, and other government agencies. The citizen asks far too seldom what he can do to help; and when the public does decide to act, its activities often are short-lived outbursts in reaction to a particularly violent crime. Fortunately, this state of affairs is yielding to a citizenry that is more committed to the exertion of positive action in preventing crime. It is being recognized that while crime prevention may not be the main purpose of an organization, crime prevention opportunities still may exist. For example, tenant patrols may help prevent burglaries in apartment buildings, and cargo security councils formed and supported by local transportation companies may reduce the number of cargo thefts. Programs geared to increasing the employability of the jobless, furthering the education of the dropout, supplying ade-

[2] An expanded treatment of this subject can be found in *Marshaling Citizen Power Against Crime* (Washington, D.C.: Chamber of Commerce of the United States, 1970).

quate medical treatment for the alcoholic and drug addict, and providing adequate recreational and other constructive activities for youth are all preventive in nature. Moreover, group endeavors by citizens may focus on strengthening the crime prevention activities of government agencies (e.g., courts, corrections, and law enforcement agencies) or at supporting anticrime measures undertaken by the private sector. For instance, the focus of a block crime prevention association is often on self-help measures that are designed to improve the safety of persons and property over and above the protection afforded by local police. Other citizen groups, such as local chambers of commerce, may concentrate on the CJS by sponsoring surveys of police effectiveness, proposing more effective methods of selecting judges, or promoting support for community-based corrections facilities. Nevertheless, it remains that *organized efforts to reduce crime do not replace individual action; they result from it.* Organizations do not relieve a citizen of his crime prevention duty; they offer a most valuable vehicle for him to exercise it.

Dissipation of energies and resources can be avoided by organizing according to priorities. Thus, it becomes important to ascertain what others consider to be significant problems. The staffs of social agencies and of criminal justice agencies and clients of these agencies (e.g., poor people, persons held in pretrial detention, court witnesses, jurors, inmates, ex-offenders, and juvenile delinquents) can provide valuable insights on the major crime problems. Once the problems are identified, priorities must be selected, for the opportunities will outstrip the available resources of any organization. First, the course of action selected should fall within the scope of interest of the organization's members or potential members. Second, the problem selected for attack must be tractable within the organization's geographical base and its available manpower, funding, and other resources. A third concern in determining priorities is to be sure that the action program selected does not create more problems than it solves. Herbert Newburg supports the above thinking:

> Any suggested action in a crime prevention program should be first tested by determining if the objective of that action is obtainable and looking to see if the action will contribute effectively to the desired result. Attempts to solve unreachable problems at the outset is not only frustrating but will lead to the failure of the program.[3]

Word of mouth, publicity by media, and talks before community organizations are among the many ways the initial members of a crime prevention effort can elicit added manpower. Programs that seek to prevent specific crimes have fairly well defined recruitment targets. A campaign against shoplifting, for example, might require the involvement of merchants. Programs pertaining to self-help protection against burglary, for example, would enlist the participation of each neighborhood resident. It is advisable, however, that our citizens not be recruited for a crime prevention effort unless they have the time to fulfill these responsibil-

---

[3] Herbert B. Newberg, "Building Local Citizen Alliances to Reduce Crime and Create a Fairer and More Effective Criminal Justice System," *Journal of Urban Law,* Vol. 21 (February 1972), p. 470.

ities and unless they are prepared to serve for reasonable periods. High turnover and failure to be productive typically destroy the program.[4]

Citizen groups, far from regarding public officials as adversaries, usually attempt to work with them and rely on their assistance to achieve goals of common interest. In most cases, the relationship is mutually supportive and productive. Yet, it is alleged that although almost all citizen crime prevention organizations stress the need for cooperation and cordial relations with officials, there is substantial opinion that public servants should not be admitted as members.[5] At the same time, if official support is not acquired, then citizen action effort will be hampered. Other limiting factors are: (1) a lack of needed funds, (2) inadequate training of the volunteers, (3) waning enthusiasm once the project is established, (4) no means of evaluating their results, and (5) the absence of a feedback mechanism.

THE DELIVERY OF PUBLIC SERVICES

This section concentrates on the involvement of citizens in the delivery of government and social services to the community. Further, it focuses on the use of youth service bureaus as a primary vehicle for delivering social services to young people.

City Involvement in the Delivery of Public Services

Nearly every presidential or national commission report in recent years cites compelling arguments that citizen alienation, inaccessibility of governments, and the quality and quantity of the services provided are not conducive to respect for the laws of this nation. There is evidence to suggest that when governments are unresponsive to citizens' needs, there is a tendency to seek redress and to fulfill needs through extralegal means.[6] This is not to say that government may have caused the problems of the inner city, but most citizens feel that it is incumbent upon government to solve the cities' problems.

Most people now realize that the immediate priorities for improving the responsiveness of government must center on the aspect of government that will cause our citizens to view government in a positive light; namely, the delivery of services. To that end, the following goals are stated:

> To achieve equitable and more effective municipal services
>
> To improve methods of access to government services and program information
>
> To improve citizen complaint and grievance response mechanisms
>
> To promote maximum community involvement and participation in the governmental process

[4] *Ibid.*, p. 81.
[5] *Ibid.*, pp. 79–80.
[6] National Advisory Commission on Civil Disorders, *Report of the National Advisory Commission on Civil Disorders* (Washington, D.C.: U.S. Government Printing Office, 1968).

The methods of achieving these goals are reflected in the following recommendations, which include proposals for: reallocating resources, establishing complaint and information offices, utilizing the public media more effectively, improving channels of communications, decentralizing city halls, establishing multiservice centers, and developing partnership citizen councils.

Distribute public service on the basis of need.
Dispense government services through neighborhood centers.
Enact public right-to-know laws.
Broadcast local government meetings and hearings.
Conduct public hearings on local issues.
Establish neighborhood governments.
Create a central office of complaint and information.
Broadcast local Action Line programs.

Youth Services Bureaus

Neighborhood agencies or youth services bureaus which provide community services for our young people can be important elements in the prevention and reduction of crime and delinquency. An effective service delivery system, in addition to upgrading the quality of life for its clients, can reduce the feelings of alienation many of our citizens have, increase the confidence of these citizens in public and private institutions, and foster citizen cooperation with these institutions. Youth services bureaus (see Figure 6–1) for the most part were the result of a recommendation by the 1967 President's Commission on Law Enforcement and the Administration of Justice, which urged communities to establish these bureaus to serve both delinquent and nondelinquent youth referred by the police, juvenile courts, schools, and other sources.

We find that the youth services bureau concept seeks to resolve the problem of fragmented services by integrating the services available to the individual through a central intake unit, which analyzes the individual's needs and refers him to the appropriate agency. It is critical to the success of these programs that the clients be involved in the actual development and operation of the programs, both in an advisory role and as employees. The integrated nature of the youth services bureau approach and the multiple functions of the bureau are portrayed graphically in Figure 6–1. A youth can walk into the youth services bureau on his own or be referred by his family or by a number of community agencies. Figure 6–1 shows how the bureau itself utilizes a number of existing resources to help to develop a program appropriate to the individual youth. The program might involve direct assistance such as counseling, education, training, and health checks. Also, it might offer activities in which the youth can become involved, such as social or issue-oriented activities. For youth with particular difficulties, it involves utilization of drug programs, hotlines and crisis centers, and other resources.

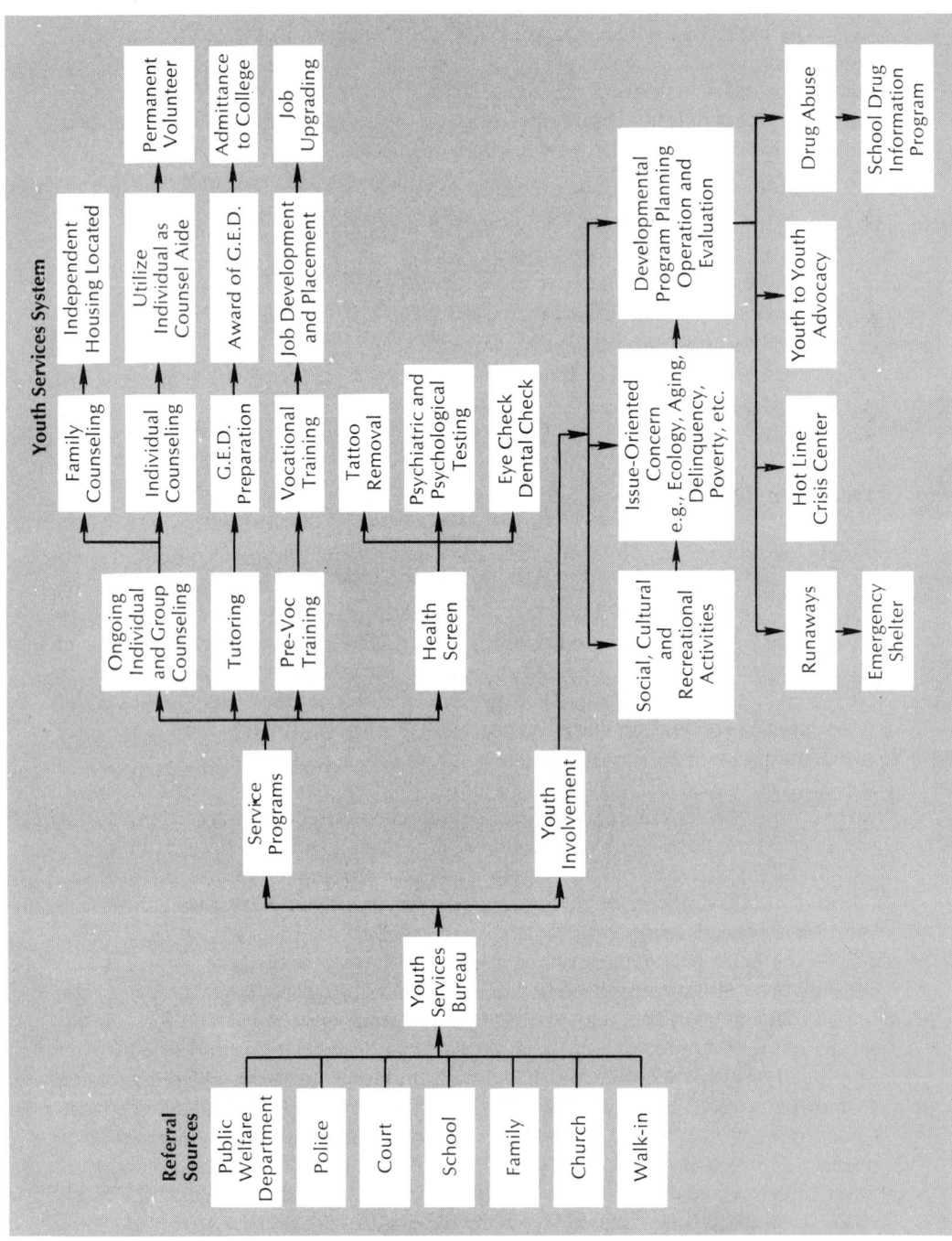

FIGURE 6–1 Youth Services Bureau

Source: Derived from material developed by the Youth Development and Delinquency Prevention Administration, U.S. Department of Health, Education and Welfare.

The goals for youth services bureaus suggested by the President's Commission in 1967 were primarily to establish and coordinate programs for our young people. As more bureaus have come into operation, the basic goals have been expanded.[7] Youth services bureaus have at least five goals. These include: (1) diversion of juveniles from the justice system, (2) provision of services to youth, (3) coordination of both individual cases and programs for young people, (4) modification of systems of services for emphasizing the needs of youth, and (5) involvement of youth in decisions that promote the development of individual *responsibility*. The following suggestions are in concert with the five goals:

Coordinate youth services through youth services bureaus.
Operate youth services bureaus independent of the justice system.
Divert offenders into youth services bureaus.
Provide direct and referral services to youths.
Hire professional, paraprofessional, and volunteer staff.
Plan youth program evaluation and research.
Appropriate funds for youth services bureaus.
Legislate establishment and funding of youth services bureaus.

COMMUNITY CRIME PREVENTION PROGRAMS

We find that a large number of crime prevention activities are aimed at what many view as the *infrastructure* of crime (e.g., insufficient education, inadequate job skills, and lack of recreational opportunities). Citizen action in these areas is brought to bear outside of the criminal justice system and is designed to reduce significantly the need to utilize the sanctions of that system. This section presents a series of programs that seek to attack the infrastructure of crime. The programs are: (1) drug abuse, (2) employment, (3) education, (4) recreation, (5) religion, and (6) physical design of the cities.

Drug Abuse

The concern here is primarily with treatment and prevention of drug abuse rather than with law enforcement efforts to prevent drug trafficking.[8] (While it is recog-

---

[7] William Underwood, *A National Study of Youth Service Bureaus,* U.S. Department of Health, Education and Welfare, Youth Development and Delinquency Prevention Administration (Washington, D.C.: U.S. Government Printing Office, 1972). Further, it should be noted that the youth services bureau concept is in concert with the growing movement to eliminate status offenses from the juvenile court. See Board of Directors, NCCD, "Jurisdiction over Status Offenses Should Be Removed from the Juvenile Court," *Crime and Delinquency,* Vol. 21 (April 1975), pp. 97–99.

[8] For those interested in a comprehensive overview of this subject, see the monograph by Alan L. Switzer, *Drug Abuse and Drug Treatment: Community-Center Drug Program* (Sacra-

nized that illicit trade must be stopped, the present discussion will be limited to abuse and treatment of the drug problem.)

The "multimodality" approach to drug treatment provides a broad range of services to treat all drug users. This approach permits addicts to be treated in programs suited to their individual health needs so that they may regain their status as functioning members of society. Consequently, a broad number of programs should be contained in a comprehensive drug treatment program. Among the elements of comprehensive drug treatment systems are:

- Crisis intervention and drug emergency centers
- Facilities and personnel for methadone maintenance treatment programs
- Facilities and personnel for narcotics antagonist programs
- Therapeutic community programs staffed entirely or largely by ex-addicts
- Closed and open residential treatment facilities as well as halfway houses staffed primarily by residents

Voluntary treatment of the addict-defendant before prosecution can be most helpful. Eligibility requirements should be liberal, and treatment made available early in the criminal justice process. Besides treatment programs, comprehensive drug abuse prevention programs should be developed. Children should be informed about drugs at an early age by parents and teachers. Peer-group influence also should be utilized in prevention strategies. Materials in prevention programs should focus on individuals as people, as well as on drugs and their effects. Young people also should be given alternatives to drug use, such as meaningful recreation and education programs. Communities desiring to establish a far-ranging drug treatment and prevention program should start by surveying the drug problem in their communities. A central agency to coordinate programs should be developed, and a study made of funding sources. States and local units of government should seek available aid from the federal government in designing their particular multimodality drug treatment and prevention centers. The following activities are suggested for a comprehensive program:

- Adopt multimodality drug treatment scene.
- Create crisis intervention and drug emergency centers.
- Establish methadone maintenance programs.
- Establish narcotic antagonist treatment programs.
- Create drug-free therapeutic community facilities.
- Organize residential drug treatment programs.
- Encourage broader flexibility in varying treatment approaches.
- Enable defendants to refer themselves voluntarily to drug treatment programs.

---

mento, Calif.: California Youth Authority, 1974). In a more comprehensive sense, the community is being asked to increase its responsibility for accepting sentenced criminals and *preventing* their return to the CJS. A case in point is the article by H. Richard Lamb and Victor Goertzel, "A Community Alternative to County Jails: The Hopes and the Realities," *Federal Probation*, Vol. 39 (March 1975), pp. 33–38.

Establish training programs for drug treatment personnel.
Plan comprehensive, community-wide prevention.
Coordinate drug programs through a state agency.
Coordinate federal, state, and local drug programs.

Employment

Opportunities for work are most often inequitably allocated among various groups. Hence, we see young people, members of minorities, residents of depressed urban areas, and individuals who have been denied a fair chance to obtain educational credentials or marketable work skills with higher unemployment rates, fewer opportunities for promotion or advancement, and lower earnings than other members of the community. Any success they achieve in the world of work is gained against great odds. Significantly, there are correlations between individual failure in the labor market and criminal behavior, and similar correlations between high local unemployment rates and high local crime rates ought to suggest that unequal economic status is a major cause of crime.[9]

The immediate institution of measures to eliminate unequal opportunity and to reduce economic deprivation is justified on the basis of "social fairness" alone. The prospect that such measures will also serve the self-interest of the community by reducing levels of crime indeed adds a special urgency to the need for them, and for committing the necessary resources in their design and implementation. Can it not be concluded therefore that changing labor market conditions are sufficient to explain increasing crime rates for youth? Crime rates could be explained not only by the raw unemployment rates but also by "participation rates" which represent the proportion of each age group in the labor force.[10]

It should be noted that the above material centered on the economic problems of particular groups in the community who pose high risks of criminal behavior. Just as present and potential offenders have problems that can be addressed by programs serving these individuals, so do neighborhoods display typical economic problems. To solve these problems it appears that two things are needed: (1) programs of systematic reform that will impact the levels of criminal activity of all residents, including those not singled out as members of any identified target group, and (2) more effective programs designed to reach the target groups by improving the environment in which program participants will make their venture into the world of work. A comprehensive program might involve the following efforts:

Expand job opportunities for disadvantaged youth.
Broaden after-school and summer employment programs.

[9] Robert Taggart, *The Prison of Unemployment* (Baltimore, Md.: Johns Hopkins University Press, 1972), pp. 502–3.
[10] Llad Phillips, Harold L. Votey, Jr., and Harold Maxwell, "Crime, Youth, and the Labor Market," *Journal of Political Economy*, May–June 1972, pp. 502–3.

Establish pretrial intervention programs.
Expand job opportunities for offenders and ex-offenders.
Remove ex-offender employment barriers.
Create public employment programs.
Expand job opportunities for former drug abusers.
Target employment, income, and credit efforts in poverty areas.
Require employers' compliance with antidiscrimination laws.
Increase support of minority businesses.
Alleviate housing and transportation discrimination.

Education

Unfortunately, the American educational system has not separated sufficiently its responsibility to provide learning conditions for the development of people from its concern with *operating schools*. It has not seen itself as part of a process of providing differential experiences for people maturing into adults. As a consequence, it has not perceived itself as a mechanism contributing to either the prevention or production of crime. It is readily apparent that very little is being done in the schools as a direct, intentional effort to discourage young people from criminal careers. Moreover, there is a definite impression that some of the existing conditions of our schools (which we often accept without question) actually create the antipathy, frustrations, and despair that lead people eventually to criminal acts.

The problems with our schools are chronic and profoundly complex.[11] The major problems are: (1) resistance to change, (2) a lack of specificity to the children's needs, (3) an overemphasis on college education, (4) needless competition, (5) poor parental participation, (6) inadequate democratic processes, (7) ambiguity over the learner's objectives and instructor qualifications, and (8) an absence of supportive relations between the schools and other parts of the community. These factors plus others directly bear on the ability of the school to favorably influence children in their conduct as responsible citizens.

The school plays an integral part in the socialization process and therefore is in a position to positively affect the predelinquent and delinquent behavior of youth. In seeking to direct individuals to socially acceptable roles, changes in the school system must continually be implemented. A willingness to experiment and evaluate must be a major responsibility of all school systems. A great deal is known about crime, what precipitates it, and what a large part learning and conditioning play in an individual's social behavior. Schools can exert a strong crime-preventing influence on their students through improvements in the learning environment. They can also influence family, peer group, and neighborhood environments, and indirectly influence others. Moreover, schools must become

---

[11] For details on the problems associated with education, see Charles E. Silberman, *Crisis in the Classroom* (New York: Random House, 1971).

more involved in the early years of students' lives. They need more information about their students; they need to design educational experiences that can adapt to the different needs, backgrounds, and environments of their students. The following recommendations are made in accordance with this thinking:

> Adopt teacher training programs for parents.
> Exemplify justice and democracy in school operations.
> Guarantee literacy to elementary school students.
> Provide special language services for bicultural students.
> Develop career preparation programs in schools.
> Provide effective supportive services in schools.
> Offer alternative education programs for deviant students.
> Open schools for community activities.
> Adopt merit training and promotion policies for teachers.

Recreation

In its *Task Force Report on Juvenile Delinquency and Youth Crime,* the President's Commission on Law Enforcement and the Administration of Justice cited a goal for recreation:

> If recreation programs are to have relevance in today's world, they must merge with others to create a total environment serving a central goal of human development. . . . It would appear that certain types of recreational opportunities may deter our young people from delinquency, but this effect is largely dependent on the nature of the activity and cannot be attributed to recreation as an entity.[12, 13]

In respect to the inconclusive relationship between recreation and delinquency prevention, an evaluation component should be included in recreation programs that attempt to prevent crime.

Recreation is common to all people and cultures. In its most fundamental sense, the term implies for us a pastime, a diversion, a respite from labor. Whatever serves to refresh or renew the person's physical or psychic energies is properly termed recreation and answers a completely human need. Recreation does have a part to play in the prevention or reduction of crime and delinquency, and recreational planners will need to weigh the social and economic aspects of making recreation a strategy of intervention.

Because recreation activities have a strong appeal for young people, delinquency is less likely to flourish in those communities where opportunities for wholesome recreation are abundant and attractive, as opposed to cities or neighborhoods where adequate facilities are lacking. Simply put, young people en-

---

[12] The President's Commission on Law Enforcement and the Administration of Justice, Task Force Report. *Juvenile Delinquency and Youth Crime* (Washington, D.C.: U.S. Government Printing Office, 1967), p. 339.

[13] *Ibid.,* p. 334.

gaged in recreation activities on the playground cannot at the same time be robbing a bank, breaking into a home, or perpetrating some other crime.[14] Yet, the provision of adequate recreation facilities is a minimum goal and will require aggressive followup in the form of innovative programming and flexible scheduling to attract and hold the interest of youth. Many recreation programs and facilities never reach the poor, the inner city resident, or the minorities; and while there is no statistical evidence to confirm a relationship between recreational deprivation and higher rates of delinquency among these groups, the existence and significance of such a relationship cannot be dismissed. Clearly, delinquency prevention programs must react to the specialized needs of those youths with special problems. Unfortunately, many of our youths are excluded from agency and institutional assistance if they have had behavior or academic problems in school, or have been disruptive in recreation groups. The delinquent population is thus excluded de facto from the programs it needs so much. Delinquent youths require special services and therefore constitute a special target group. However, providing specialized services while avoiding harmful labeling and stigma is a central dilemma in the delinquency prevention area.

Religion

The religious centers of our nation can well be a part of a massive new effort to reduce and prevent crime. The spiritual community is a significant part of society, and hence it has invaluable resources to commit. Indeed, religious institutions could list many other reasons that would reinforce the challenge to its members to become explicitly involved in crime prevention efforts. In responding to that challenge, these institutions have unique resources to apply in an effort against crime. In addition to their spiritual resources and moral influence, they have buildings in strategic locations, trained personnel with specific counseling skills, organizations with competency in planning and action, and access to large numbers of volunteers. The religious community also has facilities and equipment for educational and recreational activities; relationships with community organizations and communications networks; and links with state, regional, and national associations.

Most basically, the religious community should be encouraged to ask its congregations across the country what they can do to reduce crime, and more specifically, what individual members can do.[15] Such questions usually stimulate a

---

[14] George D. Butler, *Introduction to Community Recreation* (New York: McGraw-Hill, 1967), p. 26.

[15] The author would not want the reader to place a value judgment on the potential import of the religious community in preventing crime that is based on the space allocated to this subject. For one, personally I am convinced that the ethics and sense of justice professed by the various religions is directly applicable to the social problems at hand. If we emphasized moral obligations more, we would be able to lessen our emphasis on locks and a host of other items designed to protect us from those that are ignoring laws and the common good.

flow of ideas and an in-depth reassessment of the resources available in the crime prevention effort. Specifically, then, the religious community should:

> Enlist religious community participation in crime.
>
> Encourage religious institutions to educate their constituencies about the crime problem.
>
> Enlist religious institution support of crime prevention.
>
> Open church facilities for community programs.
>
> Promote religious group participation in the justice system.

Defensible Space

The reduction of the opportunity for a person to commit crime through control and design of the physical environment is an integral part of any crime prevention program. In this approach, crime must be seen not as a symptom of other factors to be corrected but as an act that must be prevented. Direct controls include only those that reduce environmental opportunities for crime, such as security hardware, street lighting, surveillance, and building design. The environment should be structured so that the individual considering a criminal act thinks that there is a good chance he will be seen and recognized, that he will be identified immediately as an intruder, that someone will take action, and he will be *apprehended*.

Physical targets can be made sufficiently crime-proof to deter an individual from perpetrating a crime. This approach, often referred to as "target hardening," involves use of security hardware. Proper use of such hardware can prevent some burglaries, or at least increase the time it takes to complete the criminal act (thereby increasing the chances of the offender's being detected and apprehended).

The physical design characteristics of residential complexes and housing—e.g., architectural features such as the grouping of dwelling units or the designs and placement of elevator doors and lobbies—can increase or decrease the probability that crimes will occur. The importance of building design in crime control was emphasized by the Violence Commission:

> Modern architectural features such as elevators, enclosed stairways, pedestrian underpasses, and underground parking garages, offer seclusion and screening from public view. Hence, they are often settings for violent behavior. This kind of problem can be overcome. In at least one case, the stairways of a public housing project were enclosed in glass and well illuminated. Crime in these stairways virtually ceased. Visibility also has been improved by selecting, locating, and trimming trees and shrubbery, by better street lighting, by using closed circuit television systems, and eliminating places of concealment.[16]

Many communities are currently trying to reduce residential and commercial crime through the adoption of security codes or the revision of building codes

---

[16] *Crimes of Violence,* A Staff Report to the National Commission on the Causes and Prevention of Violence, Vol. 12 (Washington, D.C.: U.S. Government Printing Office, 1969), pp. 710–11.

to include security measures. Some states are preparing state-wide security standards for most buildings. These codes can serve as guidelines for architects and physical planners, and can make security a primary consideration in the design and construction of buildings. For example, in 1971 the Governor of California signed into law Sections 14050 and 14051 to the California Penal Code. They require the State Department of Justice to develop and recommend to the legislature, and thereafter continually review, building security standards for the purpose of reducing the likelihood of burglary in California.

The Building Security Law was a legislative recognition of a strong feeling among many in law enforcement that serious target hardening could make burglary less desirable as a way of life. The regulations eventually adopted will appear in the State Administrative Code. They provide all of the necessary information for enforcement groups and for building owners. When considered together with technical guidelines developed by the California Crime Technological Research Foundation, they also provide sufficient information for producers to manufacture, construct, or assemble products to meet the regulations. Further, the purpose, scope, design specifications, and performance tests for each building component or system required under the new regulations will be specified, including drawings and technical references and descriptions where necessary for clarification. Detailed test reporting procedures for proprietary construction materials and equipment listings are also set forth. Each mandatory provision of these new requirements will be included as a part of the Minimum State Building Standards of the Administrative Code.[17]

Although the record of crime reduction due to these codes has not been totally confirmed, it is reasonable to assume that the codes can help prevent certain types of crime. In addition, security ordinances can:

> Lay the ground work to legitimize crime prevention as a responsibility of the community.
>
> Reassure the citizens of the responsiveness of government to their needs.
>
> Increase citizen awareness of different means of crime prevention.
>
> Bring pressure upon the security industry to improve its products.

It is recommended that:

> Buildings be designed to incorporate security measures
>
> Security requirements be included in building codes
>
> Street lighting be improved in high crime areas
>
> Shoplifting prevention techniques be adopted in retail establishments
>
> Car theft prevention programs be legislated
>
> Citizens be involved in law enforcement

---

[17] Donald R. Hughes and Eric E. Younger, "California's Answer to Building Security Legislation," *Crime Prevention Review,* Vol. 1 (January 1974), pp. 33, 38.

COMMUNITY CRIME PREVENTION: AN EPILOGUE—PLACEBO, PANACEA, OR PATH?

In closing Part 1, we encourage you to consider or reconsider a few dimensions that we believe crucial to ongoing effectiveness of the police service. To begin with, the police are a highly visible component in the criminal justice and general government systems. Second, policing has been and remains primarily a part of the local government delivery system of services. Third, it is essential that the police and community identify their common goals. Fourth, the police and the community must mutually support one another in the attainment of such goals. Fifth, the police should provide direction and technical assistance to the community for reducing the actual threat and fear of being victimized. Sixth, and finally, community crime prevention must not be used as a placebo. We must not think, for example, "The police department has a policy dealing with PCR, hence all must be OK now." Nor should it be looked upon as a panacea: "We now have a neighborhood watch program and thus crime will automatically disappear." On the contrary, a sound organizational design, competent personnel, a team policy deployment orientation, and community involvement must serve as a firm path upon which meaningful steps toward crime reduction can be taken.

LEARNING EXERCISES

Issues to Be Discussed

1. What are some of the practical considerations surrounding the involvement of the public in its defense against criminal acts? First, how does a police agency channel the public's active interest and sustained involvement to prevent crime? Second, what role should the police play? Third, is there any concern for *too* much responsiveness?
2. What are the main differences between the police department's juvenile control unit and a "youth services bureau"? What are the similarities? What is the principle interface among the two units (what links them together)?
3. Of the six crime prevention programs (drug abuse, employment, education, recreation, religion, and defensible space), which are the most feasible and which are the least feasible? Rank-order the six in terms of: (1) cost, (2) practicability, and (3) output (benefit). Create three separate lists, compare them, and discuss the rankings.

Group Activity

Divide the class into groups of six to eight members each. Each group is to prepare a four-minute speech on the reasons for activating public support for the various criminal justice agencies that either directly or indirectly increase the desire for crime reduction. Have each group select one of the six crime prevention tactics and center their proposal on it. One member of each group is to verbally present the speech. After each group has concluded its presentation the class is to vote on which proposal it ought to support (groups cannot vote for their own proposals).

Field Activity

The class is to be divided into six groups. Each group is assigned one of the crime prevention tactics. In turn, each group is to research what its particular assigned area is currently accomplishing (or planning) in the way of crime control and planning.

Key Terms

Community involvement (participation)
Defensible space
Drug abuse
Drug abuse treatment center
Youth services bureaus

SUGGESTED REFERENCES

BUTLER, GEORGE D. *Introduction to Community Recreation.* New York: McGraw-Hill, 1967.

GARMIRE, BERNARD L., ed. *Municipal Police Administration.* 8th ed. Washington, D.C.: International City Management Association, 1976.

KELLEY, THOMAS E., ed. *Community Crime Prevention and the Local Official.* Washington, D.C.: National League of Cities–United States Conference of Mayors, 1974.

Marshalling Citizen Power Against Crime. Washington, D.C.: U.S. Chamber of Commerce, 1970.

NATIONAL ADVISORY COMMISSION ON CIVIL DISORDERS. *Report of the National Advisory Commission on Civil Disorders.* Washington, D.C.: U.S. Government Printing Office, 1968.

NATIONAL ADVISORY COMMISSION ON CRIMINAL JUSTICE STANDARDS AND GOALS:
———*A National Strategy to Reduce Crime*
———*Police*
———*Community Crime Prevention*
Washington, D.C.: U.S. Government Printing Office, 1973.

NEWMAN, OSCAR. *Defensible Space.* New York: John Wiley, 1971.

PRESIDENT'S COMMISSION ON LAW ENFORCEMENT AND THE ADMINISTRATION OF JUSTICE:
———*The Challenge of Crime in a Free Society*
———*Task Force Report: The Police*

———— *Juvenile Delinquency and Youth Crime.* Washington, D.C.: U.S. Government Printing Office, 1967.

RADELET, LOUIS A. *The Police and the Community.* Beverly Hills, Calif.: Glencoe Press, 1973.

REISS, ALBERT J., JR. *The Police and the Public.* New Haven: Yale University Press, 1971 (paper).

SILBERMAN, CHARLES E. *Crisis in the Classroom.* New York: Random House, 1971.

TAGGART, ROBERT. *The Prison of Unemployment.* Baltimore, Md.: Johns Hopkins University Press, 1972.

UNDERWOOD, WILLIAM. *A National Study of Youth Service Bureaus.* Washington, D.C.: U.S. Government Printing Office, 1972.

WHISENAND, PAUL M. *Crime Prevention.* Boston: Holbrook Press, 1977.

WILSON, JAMES Q. *Thinking About Crime.* New York: Basic Books, 1975.

YONG HO CHO. *Public Policy and Urban Crime.* Cambridge, Mass.: Ballinger Publishing Co., 1974.

APPLYING YOUR KNOWLEDGE: LAW ENFORCEMENT

Case/Issue

CASE

Chief Jones is the head of a police department in a city of 250,000. The city has numerous ethnic groups located in its older sections. The city also has, in its outer reaches, prosperous middle- and upper-middle-class neighborhoods. Within the last year the crime rate rose startlingly in both areas. An analysis of the arrests made in the suburban areas revealed that over 90 percent of the offenders came from the inner city. The suburbanites asked the chief to set up heavily protected enclaves between the hours of 10 P.M. to 6 A.M. daily. The inner city groups protested. They maintained that their areas were even more vulnerable because of the greater number of crimes committed. The mayor said that the chief needed a more aggressive community relations program than the current public relations effort, and asked for plans within ten days. Jones acceded to this request but indicated that the situation demanded that he immediately review his own manpower requirements.

1. Drawing on your acquired knowledge of police organization and management, what are some of the alternatives that Chief Jones would have for making immediate manpower allocations and new manpower demands?
2. Assume you are Chief Jones. In answering the mayor, how would you sketch out a community relations program (general or crisis-oriented?) to address the problem?

ISSUE

Patrolmen should always be trained to be generalists in order to be able to handle both their professional crime-fighting tasks and the numerous citizen service functions (barking dogs, children playing in street, noisy parties, runaways), since almost 80 percent of current efforts are involved in such latter tasks.

1. What arguments would you put forth either in favor of greater specialization for the police professional functions, or for the generalist concept?
2. If the professional concept were to prevail, how would you propose to handle most of the service functions that most police now discharge?

Continuing CJS Project

This project is designed to evaluate the CJS system. At the end of each part of this text will be found specific directions for a progressive evaluation. Beginning with the law enforcement area here at the end of Part 1, establish a plan for analyzing law enforcement as a component of the criminal justice system. From your study of the previous chapters, related materials, and class discussions, prepare examples of areas where the law enforcement component appears to be:

1. Relating itself positively to the other components—courts and corrections—for system effectiveness.
2. At odds with other components either because of its own specific shortcomings or the difficulties thought by law enforcement officials to be due to the lack of response to its system needs by other components. Give examples.

PART II

Criminal Law and the Courts

7
Historical and Moral Perspectives on Criminal Law

Overview
The Development of Legal Systems
The Enactment of Crimes
Theories of Punishment
Classification of Crimes
Parties to Crimes
Act and Intent
The Rules of Evidence and the Jury System
Moral Considerations and Law
Summary
Learning Exercises
Suggested References

OVERVIEW

Citizens live under the rule of law. Law provides a balance for settling the conflicts among individuals. The essence of law is language. Such language has been embodied in two systems of law, civil law and common law, the latter having greatest influence on the United States. Criminal law attempts both to control individuals' behavior and to punish as a final measure against uncontrolled behavior. Punishment is usually employed to reform, to deter, or to prevent illegal behavior. In ordering crimes for purposes of imposing punishment, a classification system of felonies and misdemeanors has been developed and definitions established as to who are parties to crimes. Decisions about guilt are made through the jury system and rules of evidence. Other topics to be covered in this chapter include victimless crime, the cost of crime, organized crime, and the problems of decriminalization.

Law can be defined as a group of rules governing interaction; or, more specifically, a set of regulations governing the relationship between man and his fellow men, and between man and the state. An individual living in isolation does not need law, for his own habits govern his conduct. But a group of people living in a community or society must live under a set of regulations that serve as a means of social control, promoting the welfare of the entire group. The desires, needs, and wants of any individual differ from those of others. The law serves as a means of alleviating these conflicts or settling them in a manner most advantageous to the group. One means of viewing the law as a vehicle of social control is to say that law is simply a process of establishing communications among individuals and between individuals and their government, defining *communication* not merely as the conveyance of words, but, more properly, as the conveyance of words with the ability to make oneself understood. The more one studies and delves into the complexities of the law, the more one realizes the truth of the statement that language is the essence of law. The importance of being able to communicate in terms that mean the same thing to both the sending and the receiving parties cannot be overemphasized.

Throughout recorded history great legal scholars have attempted to define the nature and derivation of law. Varying schools of thought exist. Many philosophers have reasoned that man is essentially bad by nature, thus providing the rationale for the establishment of law. Others take an opposite position and view man as essentially good and law as a necessity to maintain that characteristic and to deal with exceptions. The issues and philosophies are more diverse and much more complex than this, but suffice it to say there is general agreement that law is neither a dormant nor a stagnant thing floating around in the sky, unseen and untouched by any human capabilities. Law, particularly man-made law, must be responsive to the ever-changing needs of a changing society.

As the reader undoubtedly has already gleaned and will continue to conclude while reading this book, not only the law but the whole criminal justice process is slow to react to the changing needs of society. Progress is slow but is being made.

THE DEVELOPMENT OF LEGAL SYSTEMS

There are two major legal systems that prevail throughout the majority of the civilized world. The *civil law system* can be traced back as far as the Roman Empire, where laws were written and codified by the rulers of the "state" and imposed on the people. Civil law has had some impact on the development of law in the United States, but the predominant legal influence in North America is the *common law system,* whose roots can be traced to England. Hence, it is prevalent in Great Britain, its dominions, and the North American continent.

The common law is an outgrowth of the habits of individuals and the customs of groups. These habits and customs became so entrenched in society that they became recognized as the acceptable norms of behavior. When court systems were developed, violations of these customs produced the cases heard. After courts began recording their decisions, judges, when confronted with new cases, started following previous court decisions to assist them in making their own decisions. This procedure is the basis for the following of precedents. The customs of the common people then became the source of the common law, the law of the common people.

This common law system, with its origins in Anglo-Saxon England, has had the greatest effects on the modern jurisprudence of the United States.

THE ENACTMENT OF CRIMES

Not all violations of the law are crimes. A crime is a public wrong. It is an act or omission forbidden by law for which the state prescribes a punishment in its own name. This means that a crime must be a wrong against the entire public, not merely against a particular individual. There are many laws in many jurisdictions governing the rights and duties of man in his relationship to other men. However, only those violations that wrong the public are considered criminal and make up the body of the substantive criminal law. Those wrongs that are private in nature—that hurt another person only—are civil wrongs. The determination as to whether a particular act is criminal or merely a civil wrong is a function of the lawmaking body of each jurisdiction. In tribal times, this decision was made by the people. They also considered criminal those acts that injured the welfare of the entire community. Today, this function rests with the legislatures of the states.

Crimes differ from civil wrongs in many respects, but the sole reason they differ is that the legislature says they differ. In other words, only a fine line distinguishes crimes from civil wrongs, and that line is drawn by the legislature where and when that body so desires within the limits of what the public will tolerate.

Crimes are prosecuted by the state in its own name. In a civil case, the action is instituted by the wronged individual. People convicted of crimes are punished by fines, imprisonment, or death; defendants who lose civil cases are usually ordered to pay the injured party. Punishment is prescribed for convictions of criminal acts, but there is no set amount of damages to which a wronged person is entitled in a civil suit. These are only a few of the major differences between crimes and civil wrongs, differences that exist solely as a consequence of the legislature having attached the label "crime" to one act and not the other. This is not to say that the legislature has only an "either-or" choice. The lawgivers may choose to declare a particular act both a crime and a civil wrong. In such a case, the victim may proceed against the defendant in a civil suit and the state may prosecute. Both avenues are open, and the outcome in one does not affect the proceedings in the other.

The purpose of the criminal law is twofold. First, it attempts to control the behavior of human beings. Failing in this, the criminal law seeks to sanction uncontrolled behavior by punishing the law violator. The cliché, "laws are made to be broken," is not philosophically or legally accepted even though laws are broken. Laws are made to protect individuals and society. Sanctions, in the form of punishment, are designed to prevent conduct that violates these rules of society. Human beings respond to a system of rewards and punishment. Freedom and liberty are the rewards; fine, imprisonment, and death have been the traditional modes of punishment ascribed to violations of the criminal law.

The criminal law is an offspring of personal vendetta. The concept of retributive justice—an eye for an eye—had its origins at least four thousand years ago. This idea of retribution has perhaps lost its original function in the criminal law, and now is the predominant philosophy underlying those legal wrongs that are outside the realm of crimes. In other words, the payment of damages in a civil suit is a type of retribution. Perhaps the one remnant of retributive justice in criminal law is capital punishment, where it still exists.

It is not individuals alone who may be charged and convicted of criminal activities. Groups of persons such as corporations may be criminally responsible. The usual punishment in such cases is a fine levied against the corporation.

THEORIES OF PUNISHMENT

There are at least three other widely accepted rationales for punishment. The *reformative* theory holds that the reform of the convicted offender is the purpose of punishment. This theory has several other names, including rehabilitation, correction, treatment, and education. Efforts to apply programs within the scope of reformation are obviously directed toward the individual offender.

The *deterrence* theory holds that punishment of one prevents others from committing the same evil deed as the individual whose life, liberty, or money is being held out as an example of the consequences. Of course, the success of the deterrence theory presupposes that people feel that crime does not pay; that the fear of being caught will deter sufficient numbers of people who are inclined toward committing criminal acts; and that the severity of the punishment is such as to reinforce that fear or respect for the consequences. The impact of deterrence is perhaps the most difficult one to measure because the success rate is based on those crimes that are not committed because of the potential punishment. It is like the police department whose effectiveness is truly measured by the amount of crime not committed in its jurisdiction. In this case, no manipulation of statistics is of value because none exist. Only the ineffectiveness of the deterrent theory is measurable, as illustrated in the classic common law example of the pickpockets who eagerly looked forward to the public hanging of one of their friends because it presented them with a real field day for fertile "pickings."

The *preventative* theory simply claims that the basic function of punishment is to protect society from those who commit crimes. Many programs exhibiting a combination of these philosophies are in existence. Some have more success than others. All have weaknesses, because all deal with the fallible human being.

Criminal law is a broad field of study. It is divided into substantive criminal law and procedural criminal law. Substantive criminal law endeavors to explain basic concepts and to define what constitutes the specific crimes that are dealt with by all phases of the criminal justice system. Procedural law encompasses such matters as the rules of evidence, constitutional law, and criminal procedure, all of which deal with means and methods by which the operations of the criminal justice system, particularly the judicial branch, function in a criminal proceeding.

CLASSIFICATION OF CRIMES

Crimes are classified in many ways. The most popular divides crimes into three categories: treason, felony, and misdemeanor. Although these categories may not be applicable in all states, they are perhaps the most workable.

Historically, treason has been considered such a serious offense that it has been set aside in a classification all by itself. In fact, treason is the only crime that is defined in the Constitution of the United States. Article III, Section 3 reads, "Treason against the United States, shall consist only in levying war against them, or in adhering to their enemies, giving them aid and comfort." Many state constitutional provisions or statutes also provide for the crime of treason against a state.

At common law, a felony was originally defined as any crime for which the perpetrator could be compelled to forfeit his property—both real and personal—in addition to being subjected to punishment through the normal procedures of death, imprisonment, or fine. Statutes have expanded the number of crimes now considered felonies, but the common law felonies were identified as murder, manslaughter, rape, larceny, robbery, arson, and burglary. The early distinguishing feature between felonies and misdemeanors was not in the punishment that could be imposed but that felonies required forfeiture.

The word *felony,* like misdemeanor, is just a label used to define a class of offense. Each jurisdiction is free to call criminal violations by any name it chooses and to impose such punishment for violation as it desires, providing the punishment does not violate the Eighth Amendment of the United States Constitution protecting individuals from cruel and unusual punishment. Today, the law does not require forfeiture of property for committing a felony. Therefore, the common law rule is no longer applicable. However, most jurisdictions still maintain the distinction between felonies and misdemeanors on the basis of where the imprisonment is to take place. Other jurisdictions use the length of imprisonment, and still a third group use a combination of both.

In the federal system, people convicted of crimes for which imprisonment is imposed are sentenced to federal prison. Thus, the distinction between felonies and misdemeanors on the federal level cannot be the place of imprisonment but rather must be based on the length of imprisonment. A felony under federal law is any crime the penalty for which is death or imprisonment for a time exceeding one year.

Whether a crime is a felony or a misdemeanor is governed by the maximum punishment that can be imposed by the courts for a conviction of the offense and not by the punishment that is actually imposed. The fact that an individual is placed on probation for the commission of an offense for which he may have been imprisoned for up to five years in the state prison, at the discretion of the judge, does not make him any less guilty of a felony, providing a five-year term of imprisonment constitutes a felony in that particular jurisdiction.

All crimes carrying penalties less than those imposed for the commission of felonies are called misdemeanors. Thus, by the process of elimination, it may be determined which crimes are misdemeanors in any particular jurisdiction.

PARTIES TO CRIMES

A person's mere presence at the scene of a crime during its commission will not support a criminal charge. The fact that a person is present, even though he may mentally support the commission of the criminal act, does not make him liable for the crime. To be liable, he must participate in some manner. At common law, parties to crimes were grouped into broad categories called principals and accessories. Each of these groups were further divided into principals in the first degree and principals in the second degree; and accessories before and after the fact. There were, however, two exceptions to this categorization at common law. All parties to the commission of treason or misdemeanors were treated as principals no matter how they participated. These distinctions were important only for felonies. The differences still exist in many states by statute, but in others they have been abrogated.

Principals in Crime—Common Law Definitions

A principal in the first degree is the actual perpetrator of the crime, that is, the person who, with his own hand or through some inanimate agency or some innocent human agent, commits the crime. A principal in the second degree is one who is either actually or constructively present at the commission of the crime and who aids and abets its commission even though he is not the actual perpetrator. Aiding and abetting is assisting the perpetrator by either doing some affirmative act or by providing advice. As used in this definition, *constructive presence* means being sufficiently near to render some type of assistance if necessary.

Accessories to Crime—Common Law Definitions

An accessory before the fact is someone who, although neither actually nor constructively present nor aiding or abetting in the commission of the crime, is a participant by his prior acts of procuring, counseling, or commanding.

As noted before, many states have combined these common law categories under their present statutes but still refer to the common law for definitional purposes. In essence, there is no distinction between the punishment for persons who participate by any of these methods.

One additional category exists that is generally treated separately. An *accessory after the fact* is defined as one who personally receives, relieves, comforts, or assists another, knowing that the person he is helping has committed a felony. The liability of an accessory after the fact does not arise until after the crime is completed. To convict someone as an accessory after the fact, the prosecution must show that a felony was in fact committed and that it was completed at the time the supposed accessory rendered assistance. He must also show that the accused knew a felony had been committed by the person he assisted.

ACT AND INTENT

Most crimes require the commission or omission of some act. However, the existence of an act that has been designated criminal, standing alone, is without worth unless it can be shown that the person accused of committing that crime conducted himself in a manner for which the law would hold him responsible; this includes deliberate actions and the existence of a particular state of mind. The prohibited conduct or act itself may lead to a variety of complex legal problems, which are beyond the scope of this book, but remember that the law will not punish anyone for merely thinking bad thoughts. Also, the law will usually not punish someone for committing prohibited acts unless it can be shown that an evil state of mind existed at the time. This concept is referred to in legal terminology as *actus reas*. Certainly, there are exceptions to this rule, as in the case of traffic violations, where the mere commission is all that is necessary to liability. The more serious crimes, however, require proof of a malevolent state of mind before a conviction can be had. It must also be shown that the illegal act and the state of mind existed concurrently. The several mental states that are considered malevolent by the law are all labeled *intent*. However, intent in its legal sense is only one of the several forms. Recklessness and negligence are also states of mind that may lead to criminal liability when coupled with a prohibited act. The legal terminology for the evil state of mind is *mens rea*.

The object of any court discussion of the defendant's mental state is to prove his liability for his actions. It must be recognized that it is impossible to look into a person's mind in a literal sense. The alternative is to resort to several legal tests to determine the apparent subjective mental state. This is accomplished by permitting the fact finders (jury) to presume or infer the accused's state of mind at the time he committed the act. This inference is based on what the accused allegedly did, what he said, and all the circumstances surrounding his act. Admittedly, this "Monday morning quarterbacking" is imperfect, but it is the best system available. There are constitutional, moral, and philosophical questions as to whether we ever want to be able to perfectly read a person's mind.

The reason for requiring proof of the evil state of mind, or criminal intent, in order to convict one of a crime can be traced to the development of the theory of responsibility. This theory holds that an individual's actions are an exercise of his own free will and not a result of something beyond his control. Because this is not always true, defenses to criminal liability are provided for by the law. Examples of these defenses include insanity, certain types of intoxication, infancy, mistake of fact, and entrapment.

Motive

Motive is often confused with intent. Motive, good or bad, is never an essential element of a crime. Neither the presence nor the absence of a motive ever has to be proved at trial regardless of the nature of the case.

Motive can be defined as those desires that compel or drive a person to intend to do something. Assigning a motive to an alleged perpetrator involves judgment, but we do not judge a person's motive for doing something. He may have the best of motives for committing an act—he may even have "done society a service"—but he is nonetheless guilty of a crime. Neither do we convict someone for doing an innocent act merely because he had an evil motive.

This is not to say, however, that motive has no use whatsoever in a criminal case. Proof of motive can assist a jury in determining the existence or absence of intent, although proving a motive is not sufficient to proving intent. The act of euthanasia (mercy killing) is an example of the difference between motive and intent. The motive may be good, but the criminal intent necessary to charge someone with homicide still exists.

THE RULES OF EVIDENCE AND THE JURY SYSTEM

The rules of evidence constitute an integral part of criminal justice processes. Like other rules that must exist for any society to function, the rules of evidence are designed to ensure a fair and impartial trial to those who find themselves charged with a criminal offense or defending a civil lawsuit.

Rules of evidence were not necessary to insure fairness and impartiality at trial until relatively recent times. The development of the jury to determine issues of fact in a case made necessary certain rules to ensure that its decisions were, in fact, impartial. It is on the basis of this move toward greater fairness that the rules of evidence began, and it is to this end that the rules remain directed.

Early Trial Methods and Evidence

Early methods of trial were violent and relied on "divine intervention" for determining truth. Predating the thirteenth century, three methods of trying individuals accused of crimes were most popular. *Trial by ordeal* was perhaps the most violent of the solutions. This type of "trial" required the accused to perform some ritual that, if successfully completed, showed his innocence of the crime charged. For example, the fire ordeal required the accused to walk over a bed of hot coals or pick up the wrong end of a hot iron without getting burned. Not too many innocent verdicts resulted from this kind of trial. Another favorite ordeal was to stick the arm of the accused in boiling water—he was innocent if his arm did not get scalded. The cold-water treatment, throwing the accused into a pool of water, gave the individual a better chance to "prove" his innocence. If he floated without swimming, he was guilty; if he could not float, innocence was assured. Of course, the fellow who could not swim at all was a real loser.

A second technique for conducting trials in less-enlightened times was *trial by combat*—the accuser and the accused battled to the death. Obviously, the winner was vindicated. If the accuser won, the accused was guilty. He was also dead. If the accused survived the battle, he was innocent. One would think that under this system, a person would be very sure of his facts before accusing another of a criminal offense. However, the opponents' physical size and weight often determined the quantity and nature of accusations; this abated somewhat when the law began to allow the accused and the accuser to select "champions" to do their fighting for them. Thus, we see the origins of the practice of choosing "seconds" to do battle and even traces of the advocate system.

Trial by compurgation, although nonviolent, was still another popular method of determining guilt or innocence. This early common law trial method allowed a verdict of innocence if the defendant could secure enough of his friends and neighbors to swear to his innocence. The theory underlying this system of trial was based on the belief that a person would jeopardize his immortal soul by swearing to a false belief under oath, and therefore anyone testifying would be telling the truth. The greater the number of compurgators an accused could secure to swear to their belief of his innocence, the better his chances of escaping punishment.

Regardless of which method of trial was selected for the determination of guilt or innocence, one fact stands out. All three methods placed heavy reliance on divine intervention for seeking the truth. Notwithstanding the physical attributes of the defendant, the belief was that the innocent would prevail. It is important to note that modern rules of evidence in the United States have not entirely discarded some characteristics of these early methods of trial; the present procedural practice of calling character witnesses on behalf of the defendant has evolved from compurgation.

The Evolution of the Jury System

The foundation of the English jury system (on which our present jury structure is based) can be traced to the French empire under the Carolingian kings. As part of their successful attempt to unite their empire, a procedure called the *inquisition* or *inquest* was devised. Carried out by representatives of the monarch, its purpose was to call together various groups of neighbors in order to ask questions and explain the sovereign's rights.

When the jury was in its inquisitional stage, it merely furnished information to an officer of the court. The inquisitors were expected to know about community affairs and the facts of the case and were disqualified for service if they did not, as contrasted with our present trial jurors who are challenged unless they are ignorant of the facts. Thus, the inquisition jury was the forerunner of our grand jury system, one of the functions of which is providing information to the court on matters of community affairs.

The Magna Carta, signed in 1215, had an impact on trial by jury. It was this document that established in England the procedure of trial by peers. Later in the thirteenth century, it appeared that it was not appropriate for the same jurors who found the bill of indictment (grand jury) to act also as a jury to try the accused for their own indictment. It was obvious that jurors would likely maintain in the second instance what they had sworn to in the first. It was seen that indictment and trial were two distinct functions, and therefore two juries were needed. This evolution ended in the establishment of the trial jury as a separate institution from the grand jury.

The initial experience of trial by peers left much to be desired, however, because during the first two hundred years or so after the signing of the Magna Carta the jurors picked were not very impartial. Selections of jurors were based upon their familiarity with the facts of the case and with the parties involved. During this period, it was felt that much time and effort could be saved if the jury were composed of people who already knew what happened. It was not until the sixteenth century that selection of jurors was made dependent upon their ignorance of the facts of the case and of the participants involved. It was at this time that juries had to begin depending solely on the testimony of others in making their decisions. Impartiality became the byword for effective jury trials.

In the United States, at the time of adopting the federal Constitution there was no definite conception of trial by jury, and thus the Constitution does not provide for any particular system to be used by the federal courts. Trial by jury in civil cases is not provided for in the Constitution. The Constitution does not even define what is meant by trial by jury, and, because states differed in their concepts of trial by jury and its practice, the federal courts chose to follow the common law of England rather than the practice of any particular state. The jury in American state courts plays a larger part than it does in either American federal courts or English courts. At the time America was being settled, the English judges under the control of the Stuarts were oppressing the people. The jury came to be regarded as the bulwark of liberty. This enthusiasm followed the jury to the New World and has been a persistent influence in judicial administration in the American states. Trial by jury has been a constantly changing institution. It has changed its purpose, its methods, and its functions. From being an instrument of the king, it has become an ally of democracy. It has supposedly become the protector of individual rights.

Reasons for Rules of Evidence

Experience was soon to reveal that impartial jurors were not always capable of separating fact from fiction during the course of the trial. Thus, to protect the jury from false or otherwise undependable testimony and to assure its impartiality, rules of evidence were evolved.

We might ask, "Why not allow the jury to hear all the testimony and all the other evidence and then be free to decide guilt or innocence?" The answer is simply that juries cannot really be entrusted with this responsibility. This is not intended as a derogation of the entire jury system, but rather points out that juries are made up of human beings and are thus subject to human weaknesses. Prosecutors and defense attorneys alike have but one objective when functioning within the courtroom—to persuade the jury to believe their client's side of the story. As a general rule, there are at least two sides in every criminal case. If this were not true, there would be no need for the type of system that we have. Because our juries today are selected on the basis of their lack of knowledge of the facts and the parties prior to the trial, they have enough difficulty deciding whose "truth" to believe, based upon honest differences of opinion, without having to be subjected to totally irrelevant matters and even deliberate falsehoods that might be put before them were there no rules of evidence. This is not to imply that there is no false information now being presented to juries, but the utilization of the rules of evidence attempts to minimize the opportunity for the commission of perjury, the making of mistakes, and the introduction of irrelevant evidence.

Judicial decisions have been the primary vehicle by which the rules of evidence have evolved. These decisions have been modified by court rule and, in some cases, by statutes. Among the initial problems confronting the courts during the developmental stages of the rules were the problems of determining which types of evidence would be admissible, what evidence the jury would be allowed to hear and see. Also, until this time, witnesses who appeared in a trial did so voluntarily, and therefore it was not difficult to elicit testimony from them. However, with the advent of the rules, witnesses were subsequently compelled to testify if it could be ascertained that they had knowledge of the facts involved in the case. This presented additional problems to the court because witnesses compelled to testify are more likely than voluntary witnesses to have particular biases and hostilities from which the jury must be protected.

MORAL CONSIDERATIONS AND LAW

As noted earlier, a crime differs from a noncriminal legal wrong only because someone (usually the legislature), at some time, said that the wrong was severe enough to warrant state action against the offender.

We must look behind this historical sketch to find the real issue. There are many types of laws. Some are natural laws, based on inherent human reasoning; some are divine laws, handed down by all Western religions; and some are man-made laws. It is this latter category that most concerns us. These man-made laws are just that—made by man. Thus, whenever a law is created someone has to make the decision regarding the need for such a law. On what basis is that decision made? The answer is simple. It is based upon what men consider to be right and wrong. The right/wrong determination is based on the accepted morality. In essence, then, all laws are to some extent and at one time or another based on the culture's morality.

Most acts that are considered major crimes today and those that were so labeled in the early English common law period were offenses involving some moral turpitude. The Latin phrase for those offenses that are not only legally prohibited but are also considered morally wrong is *mala in se*. Could any of us argue that murder, rape, robbery, burglary, and other serious crimes are not morally wrong? Of course not. But government, by its powers to protect the health, safety, and welfare of the citizens, may enact laws labeling certain acts crimes when the immorality of these acts is, at the very least, questionable. These offenses are often termed *mala prohibita* offenses; they are wrong only because they are prohibited. Many of these fall into the category called public welfare or police regulatory offenses and are enacted under the police power of the state. Most traffic violations, statutory rape, laws requiring a person who purchases exempt narcotics to sign a register, and so forth are examples of these types of laws.

Victimless Crimes

The question often asked by citizens today is, "Is it the function of society, acting through the agency of the law, to equate the sphere of crime with that of sin?" If not, then the realm of private morality is not the business of the law.

The basic function of the criminal law is not to intervene in the private lives of citizens. The function of the criminal law is and should be to preserve public order and decency, to protect citizens from what is offensive or injurious, and to provide sufficient safeguards against exploitation and corruption of others, *particularly* those who are especially vulnerable because they are young, weak in body or mind, or inexperienced.[1] As is readily ascertainable, it is sometimes impossible to protect such persons without intervening in their private lives and their private morality, just as it is impossible to protect them without regulating all citizens.

This dichotomy between moral considerations and law has made its impact. Vocal public opinion, pressures on legislative bodies, and contemporary criminal justice issues reflect concern about these "victimless crimes." The so-called victimless crimes of prostitution, homosexuality, fornication, adultery, pornography, obscenity, drunkenness, gambling, and narcotics use fall under the category of vice offenses. These offenses are given the generic label "victimless" because for the most part they are crimes voluntarily entered into by both parties, neither of which view themselves as victims under the traditional relationship found in most types of crimes. Instead, they are willing participants in an action that provides them with different degrees of pleasure and satisfaction.

Criticisms of Victimless Crimes

No other area of criminal law has come under such critical attack in recent years or been more instrumental in causing problems for the police and the courts as has the enforcement and adjudication of this particular class of offenses. Many legal scholars, criminal justice officials, criminologists, and health and welfare authorities have long contended that these offenses should be removed from the criminal codes as they are not true crimes. They argue that dealing with such violations by means of the criminal justice system is both ineffective and enormously expensive.

Those who advocate the abolition of victimless crime statutes point out rather convincingly that these laws have little or no impact upon controlling behavior. The laws on drunkenness, gambling, and narcotics abuse are universally disregarded. Alcoholics will still drink compulsively; people will still gamble; and addicts will continue to use drugs.

---

[1] Patrick Devlin, *The Enforcement of Morals* (New York: Oxford University Press, 1968), pp. 2–3.

Not only is the threat of imprisonment no deterrent, but reforming these offenders is almost certain to fail in the vast majority of cases when they are sentenced to jail or prison. Often, in fact, just the reverse happens. Instead of being reformed through incarceration, they return to society more embittered than when they first entered the institution. For the first time, they see themselves as "victims"; not of their original "crime," but victims of a capricious society whose moral standards as expressed by the law are hypocritical at best. An ever-growing group of reformers feel that what such offenders really need is the therapy and rehabilitative services of health or social agencies.

The most serious criticism of handling these offenders in the criminal justice process and the one that has generated the most urgent demands for change is that the existing effort to process these individuals through the agencies of justice drastically reduces the availability of manpower and resources of the police, as well as other agencies of criminal justice, to effectively deal with the serious crimes that are in fact a menace to life and property.

Magnitude and Costs

How significant a problem are these types of crimes as measured by their relative incidence? No one really knows. We do know, however, their magnitude in relation to all known arrests made by the police. Using the *Uniform Crime Reports* of the FBI, the total number of arrests annually reported by law enforcement agencies is nearing 10 million. Of this total, in excess of 30 percent are for offenses in this so-called victimless crimes category. This is a most conservative estimate. Drunkenness arrests alone account for almost 15 percent of the total. The statistics are in themselves appalling but the financial costs (not considering the unknown social costs) are staggering. The price tag for dealing with these offenders is well in excess of $2 billion annually.

This poses a crucial question to which we as a nation must address ourselves; that is, in light of our present crime problem and the growth in the incidence of serious offenses, does the preoccupation of our criminal justice system with victimless crimes represent anything in the way of a rational order of priorities?

The sanctions that make these types of acts illegal also have two serious social costs. Recognizably, the law and its agents have been unable to control to any significant degree the behavior of those who commit these offenses. This impossible task of trying to regulate moral conduct has undermined the respect for law that is necessary to control social interaction in a complex, civilized society. Increasing numbers of Americans, particularly the youth, ascribe no legitimacy either to the laws themselves or to the legal agents who are empowered to enforce them. This is a serious issue that strikes at the very foundation of any government purporting to act as an embodiment of the collective conscience and dictates of its people. This concept of *collective conscience* is important. Does *collectivity* mean that government and its laws are to be structured to ensure that majority interests only are to be acted upon, or does it mean that our legal institutions and the enforcers of our laws must also be cognizant of the interests of the minority? This argument has drawn the attention of social and legal philosophers throughout the history of Western civilization. Time, however, has not dimmed this topic as one of focal importance. It probably looms as the major domestic issue facing America today. Increasingly, active minority-group segments in the United States, as well as key members of the "establishment," are calling for major reforms in our criminal codes and the manner in which the criminal justice machinery reacts to these changing values and attitudes.

Acts that constitute crimes are being redefined most strikingly in the area of vice because of their very nature. The most critically outspoken are, for the most part unknowingly, expressing the same concern and argument that the great civil libertarian and scholar, John Stuart Mill, expressed over one hundred years ago. Mill set out to define "the nature and limits of the power which can be legitimately exercised by society over the individual."[2] He asserted one very simple principle that was to govern the amount of compulsion and control that society can rightfully exercise over the individual.

> . . . That the end for which mankind are warranted, individually or collectively, in interfering with the liberty of action of any of their number, is self protection. That the only purpose for which power can be rightfully exercised over any member of a civilized community, against his will, is to prevent harm to others. His own good, either physical or moral, is not a sufficient warrant. He cannot rightfully be compelled to do or forbear because it will be better for him to do so, because it will make him happier, because in the opinion of others, to do so would be wise, or even right.[3]

The Role of Organized Crime

Making these types of acts offenses is considered by many to be the seed of organized crime and the attendant problems of corruption of agencies of criminal justice that unfortunately are too often linked. Criminal syndicates exist to provide the services and goods that people cannot obtain legally, such as narcotics, gambling, prostitution, and illicit alcohol. Our success in trying to legislate morals and the consequence of such actions is best typified by the ill-fated passage of the Volstead Act, which ushered in prohibition. It is thought by a number of criminologists who have studied organized crime that the singular outstanding achievement of this particular piece of legislation was that it encouraged the formation of organized, criminal cartels. It displayed the value of an organized effort to provide the illicit commodities that people want as well as the need for and the success of continually bribing police and other authorities to permit uninterrupted operations. In addition, it provided organized crime with the working capital to build

---

[2] John Stuart Mill, *On Liberty,* ed. Currin V. Shields (Indianapolis, Ind.: Liberal Arts Press, 1956), p. 91.
[3] *Ibid.,* p. 97.

up their organizational operations and to branch out into other endeavors of both illegal and legal natures.

The impact of organized crime as a corrupting influence was documented in early studies of police behavior. The famous Wickersham Commission Reports of 1929 and 1931 focused on the impact of organized criminal activity as a major source of corruption among law enforcement personnel. Although these early studies pointed out that a strong correlation existed between the presence of organized crime and corruption, little if any inroads have been made in disassociating the two by launching an all-out attack on organized crime and raising police salaries, for example. The recent allegations of widespread corruption in the New York City Police Department tied to the problem of organized narcotics distribution in that city is just the latest in the many scandals that have rocked law enforcement agencies across the United States. It should be noted that since these allegations there has been an attack on organized crime in New York, the likes of which are unparalleled. Few corruption allegations have been made since this attack was mounted, perhaps because the city police are now considered "unreachable" by members of organized crime.

It is understandable, then, that an ever-increasing number of crime-control authorities are calling for the revocation of statutes pertaining to victimless crimes. Notable members from all the agencies of criminal justice who have studied and debated the phenomenon have reached the conclusion that the retention of these acts as punishable legal offenses is no longer justifiable.

Support for Victimless-Crimes Laws

However, there are those who feel just as adamantly that deleting victimless crimes from the statute books will only make an already bad situation even worse. The major thrust for this position also comes from notable people in all walks of life. There are many criminal justice officials, legislators, clerics, and average citizens who feel that repealing these statutes will plunge this country into increased lawlessness. Their major concern is that our society has already become too permissive and that sanctioning such acts through removal of the criminal prohibitions will in effect encourage a further decay of our moral standards and consequently our strength as a nation in the world community. These opponents are often quick to point out the history of earlier Western nations that have seemingly traveled the path of moral corruption and licentiousness that has led them to ignominious ends, which we, too, seem to be inexorably embarked upon.

Decriminalization—Pros and Cons

Table 7-1 presents in brief some of the more vocal arguments for and against the decriminalization of many of the so-called victimless crimes.

The table is by no means exhaustive in content or analysis. To a large extent,

TABLE 7-1

Offense	For Decriminalization	Against Decriminalization
Drunkenness	Enforcement is uneconomical. Arrest provides little or no deterrence. Condition should be treated as an illness rather than an offense.	Need to protect violators from inflicting harm to self or others.
Pornography	Difficult to define. Government should not regulate this area of private morality. Changing attitudes of society toward sex—no longer puritanical. Will adversely affect organized crime.	Protection of the moral well-being of society, particularly youth and others susceptible to suggestion. Exposure to pornographic matter heightens man's erotic desires and therefore leads to an increased incidence of sex offenses.
Gambling	Cannot be prevented and unenforceable. Is legal in some places, therefore not bad per se. Will adversely affect organized crime.	Weak and susceptible persons will be saved from themselves. Belief that it can be controlled. Corruptive influences gambling can have on public officials. "Fringed" by other illegal activities such as loan sharking.
Prostitution	Because of natural biological sex impulses, the availability of prostitutes will decrease the number of sex crimes and will remove psychological problems caused by the stigma of going to a prostitute. Unmeaningful enforcement and absence of deterrent effect. Will reduce associated criminal activity and adversely affect organized crime. Licensing would provide better control over spread of venereal disease.	Attracts other criminally and socially undesirable elements. Leads to demoralization of law enforcement and loss of respect for the law. Encourages promiscuity and fails to provide the moral leadership and example for youth.
Homosexuality	Unenforceable except in public places. Enforcement is a nuisance and unpopular with police.	It is sinful and thus should be illegal. Leads to child molestation. Leads to other criminal acts—e.g., assaults, robberies, and homicides. May lead to corruption of youth.
Fornication and adultery	Unenforceable but when rarely enforced usually done for political reasons. Not the business of the law—matters of private morality.	Morally wrong.

TABLE 7-1 (continued)

Offense	For Decriminalization	Against Decriminalization
Marijuana	Difficult to enforce and has little deterrent effect.	Leads to use of hard drugs and addiction.
	Engenders disrespect for the law and for law enforcement.	Loss of control of faculties, thus presenting danger—e.g., driving car.
	No proof that it leads to use of hard drugs or is associated with greater incidence of other crimes.	Associated with greater incidence of other crimes.
	Invites and leads to discriminatory enforcement against people deemed undesirable on other grounds.	

the arguments, both pro and con, are heaped with emotional overtones. Yet many states have moved toward decriminalization of some victimless crimes. The National Advisory Commission on Criminal Justice Standards and Goals in its 1973 reports urged all states to examine the issues very closely and consider the impacts on the criminal justice system. The question of priorities remains to be answered.

SUMMARY

Law is a means of regulating the relationship of individuals and governments in a society. Crimes are those wrongs which society has proscribed as being most injurious to its own welfare. The commission or omission of conduct deemed criminal must be coupled with some culpable state of mind for an individual to be held responsible. Motive is not an essential provable ingredient of a crime.

The jury system developed as a means of ensuring peer determination of whether conduct was injurious to society and the rules of evidence are designed to insure impartiality in a jury's decision.

All laws are to some extent founded on moral judgments. The so-called victimless crimes are among those for which the current propriety of moral judgments is being questioned.

LEARNING EXERCISES

Issues to Be Discussed

1. In society's attempt to define crimes through law, what factors should be involved in setting limits to those definitions?
2. Among the theories of punishment now current, which one might have the greatest potential for success in the coming year? Under what circumstances?

3. In your opinion what victimless crimes should be removed from criminal codes? How would you otherwise handle such cases?
4. Trace the development of the rules of evidence and describe their relationship to the development of the jury system.

Group Activity

Create two teams from the class representing the pro and con of the issue of decriminalization. Each team will be responsible for searching the relevant literature on the subject and presenting and debating the issue in a panel discussion before the class.

Field Activity

Create an issues analysis notebook for this section of the text on Criminal Law and the Courts. As a first effort scan newspapers and magazines, check radio and television, and note public speeches on either of the following subjects: (1) the nature of punishment or (2) moral issues and the demand to increase or decrease the number of acts deemed criminal. Develop a statement of from 100 to 200 words analyzing how the issue has been developed in the media and whether there is any indication of a decided trend.

Key Terms

Civil law
Common law
Criminal law
Decriminalization
Deterrence

Felony
Mens rea
Misdemeanor
Preventative punishment
Reformative punishment

SUGGESTED REFERENCES

ANDRENAES, JOHNANNE. *Punishment and Deterrence.* Ann Arbor, Mich.: University of Michigan Press, 1974.

BECKER, THEODORE L., AND FELLEY, MALCOLM M. *The Impact of Supreme Court Decisions.* 2nd ed. New York: Oxford University Press, 1973.

BERGER, RAOUL. *Government by Judiciary: The Transformation of the Fourteenth Amendment.* Cambridge, Mass.: Harvard University Press, 1977.

BLUMBERG, ABRAHAM S., ed. *The Scales of Justice.* New Brunswick, N.J.: Transaction Books, 1973.

CARDOZO, BENJAMIN N. *The Nature of the Judicial Process.* New Haven, Conn.: Yale University Press, 1949.

CHAMELIN, NEIL C., AND EVANS, KENNETH R. *Criminal Law for Policemen.* 2nd ed. Englewood Cliffs, N.J.: Prentice-Hall, 1975.

DONIGAN, ROBERT L., AND FISHER, EDWARD C. *The Evidence Handbook.* 2nd ed. Evanston, Ill.: Traffic Institute, Northwestern University, 1965.

GRUPP, STANLEY E., ed. *Theories of Punishment.* Bloomington, Ind.: Indiana University Press, 1971.

KLEIN, IRVING J. *Law of Evidence for Police.* St. Paul, Minn.: West Publishing Co., 1973.

KLOTTER, JOHN C., AND MEIER, CARL L. *Criminal Evidence for Police.* 2nd ed. Cincinnati: W. H. Anderson, 1975.

MILGRAM, STANLEY. *Obedience to Authority.* New York: Harper & Row, 1974.

NAGEL, STUART S. *Law and Social Change.* Beverly Hills, Calif.: Sage Publications, 1970.

PACKER, HERBERT L. *The Limits of Criminal Sanction.* Palo Alto, Calif.: Stanford University Press, 1967.

RAWLS, JOHN A. *A Theory of Justice.* Cambridge, Mass.: Harvard University Press, 1971.

SCHUR, EDWIN M. *Crimes Without Victims.* Englewood Cliffs, N.J.: Prentice-Hall, 1965.

VATTER, H. J., AND SILVERMAN, I. J. *The Nature of Crime.* Philadelphia: Saunders, 1977.

WESTON, PAUL B., AND WELLS, KENNETH M. *Criminal Evidence for Police.* Englewood Cliffs, N.J.: Prentice-Hall, 1971.

8

Survey of Constitutional Principles

Overview
The Development of the Constitution
The Constitution as a Grant of Power
Amending the Constitution
State Constitutions as a Limitation on Power
Constitutional Interpretation of Statutes
The Bill of Rights
The Evolution of the Fourteenth Amendment
The Bill of Rights and the Criminal Justice System
The Constitution and Criminal Justice
Summary
Learning Exercises
Suggested References

OVERVIEW

The Constitution of the United States embodies the highest law of the land. It also grants important powers to the Congress to make such additional laws as may be necessary, criminal laws being among those which Congress does enact. In the American historical process the Supreme Court developed into that federal agency which interprets the constitutionality of statutes enacted by Congress and the several states. Of particular importance to the criminal justice system is the interpretation of the Constitution by the Supreme Court under the Bill of Rights and the other amendments to the Constitution. The First, Fourth, Fifth, Sixth, and Eighth Amendments in relation to the Fourteenth Amendment are particularly applicable with particular reference to "due process" of law in criminal cases.

> We the People of the United States, in Order to form a more perfect Union, establish Justice, insure domestic Tranquility, provide for the common defence, promote the general Welfare, and secure the Blessings of Liberty to ourselves and our Posterity, do ordain and establish this Constitution for the United States of America.
>
> Preamble to the U.S. Constitution

The manner and substance of Supreme Court interpretations of the Constitution of the United States have been subjected to numerous and critical attacks in recent years, not only from within the criminal justice system but also from without. The criticism has not been unified. There are many who feel that recent decisions have upset the balance between protection of the rights of the individual and the rights of society in that the Supreme Court has neglected the welfare of society in order to protect individual freedoms. Others are of the opinion that insufficient protections have been guaranteed the individual and that much more must be done to ensure equal protection for all.

Certainly, the majority of feelings are founded in emotion rather than logic. But none could argue the fact that the United States Constitution is probably the finest, most noble, and most practical document for the governance of human society ever devised. These accolades can be justified simply by recognizing that the document has managed to exist for almost two centuries. This, in itself, is one of its most admirable characteristics. In spite of repeated attacks, the survival of the Constitution can be credited to the foresight and planning of its framers and to the courts that have interpreted it into a viable, contemporary instrument. A brief review of the history of the adoption of the Constitution will illustrate.

THE DEVELOPMENT OF THE CONSTITUTION

The people of the United States had survived a unique period of history at the time of the Constitutional Convention in Philadelphia. The latter half of the eighteenth century had been a time of war and unusual governmental control. The struggle for independence resulting in the Revolutionary War occurred because the American colonists felt they could no longer live under the domineering and oppressive reign of the English king's government. That form of government placed too many strict controls on the freedoms of the people.

The Articles of Confederation (the colonies' first attempt at self-government) were designed to unite the nation in its struggle against English dominance. To that end, a united nation did exist. But for other purposes, the loose confederation of states lacked the qualities needed for the maintenance of a strong central government. For one thing, the states, under the Articles, retained nearly complete sovereignty. They granted no significant governmental powers to the central government. This was due to the colonists' fear of a centralized government. Thus, the Articles of Confederation established nothing more than a league of sovereign and independent states with extremely loose, centralized control.

After the Revolutionary War, the colonies soon discovered that they could not continue to exist as a united nation under such a weak form of government. The Articles, reflecting the fears of the tyranny of a strong central government, created a country that was totally opposite from what they had fought against, but that was just as unworkable as the English system. The government had too little political control. The convention was called in Philadelphia for the purpose of revising the Articles of Confederation in a manner designed to compromise the two systems.

Within a week, it was agreed that revision of the Articles would be impractical, and the convention began to design a document that was to be the foundation of a new government that provided strong central control yet insured the necessary freedoms to the states and the people. Out of that convention came the United States Constitution.

Under the new system of government, each of the states was required to yield some of its sovereign powers to the centralized government. Thus, some powers that had previously rested entirely within the province of the several states were given exclusively to the national government. It was agreed that all powers not specifically granted to the federal government would be retained by the states. It is for this reason that the Constitution is often referred to as a "grant of power." The federal government has only those powers specifically granted to it by the states and by the people. It is a government of delegated and inherent powers.

The manner in which the states yielded sovereignty and power to the new government was by approving the Constitution, but ratification was not an easy task. Severe opposition to the Constitution grew during the process of ratification.

The chief criticism again was based on the fear of too much power becoming too remote from the citizens' control. Although a number of states did ratify the Constitution, demands were made for revisions or additions that would not only set out in the document the reservation of states' rights on matters over which the federal government was not exclusively given powers but also to provide a written guarantee of the rights of individual citizens of the United States. Thomas Jefferson was among those who spearheaded the drive to make these protections part of the Constitution. Thus, as a political compromise necessary to complete acceptance of the Constitution, a Bill of Rights was drafted and ratified as the first ten amendments to the Constitution.

THE CONSTITUTION AS A GRANT OF POWER

The concept of the Constitution as a grant of power is important in modern times. The criticisms of Supreme Court interpretation have, to some extent, centered on federal assumption of powers not granted in the Constitution and the resulting loss of states' rights. In legal theory, that argument is fallacious. The fallacy arises from the fact that the powers held by the federal government are those that have been granted it specifically by the people and the states and that ratification of the Constitution by the states was in full recognition of the fact that it was broadly worded in order to be open to interpretation. Thus, powers exercised by Congress in the passage of new legislation have existed as long as the Constitution itself, but because of the structure and needs of society they have never before been exercised. This is not an assumption of new powers not specifically enumerated. It is rather an illustration of a delayed use of those powers. If the welfare of society does not require the enactment of a particular law, there is no need to enact that law merely because the power exists to do so. Thus, the national government cannot control any activities within a state unless the states originally gave the federal government such powers by either ratifying the Constitution or accepting statehood. In summary, states' rights are still protected by the Constitution and are not subject to deprivation by the federal government.

The Constitution is often criticized as being too vague and too broad. These two words are not synonymous. The Constitution is broad in its language but it cannot be successfully argued that it is a vaguely written document. *Vagueness* denotes inability to understand while broadness refers to adaptability to a multitude of circumstances. The Constitution can be understood. It was drafted by the framers in such a manner as to be open to interpretation in light of the changing needs and complexity of society. The framers knew that the country would change; they realized that the problems and complexities of American society would be drastically different in the twentieth century than in the eighteenth century, but they could not possibly have foreseen the scope and magnitude of that change. In the 1780s, none could know what the United States would be like in the 1980s. So, they drafted the Constitution in broad language in order that it might remain flexible in changing times and yet be stable enough to continue as the basic governing document of the nation. Its stability can be measured by its life span. Had the Constitution been so specifically written as to cover only the needs of the times, it surely would have collapsed a long time ago as it would have held no application to a changing society. For these reasons, the Constitution is often called a stable yet flexible document.

Powers Granted to the Federal Government

The powers of Congress to enact legislation on specific matters, including those within the criminal realm, come through Supreme Court interpretation of the Constitution and by the "necessary and proper" clause found in Article I, Section 8, Subsection 18. That section says that Congress shall have the power "To make all laws which shall be necessary and proper for carrying into execution the foregoing powers [specified in previous sections of Article I], and all other powers vested by this Constitution in the Government of the United States, or in any department or officer thereof." Hence, specific pieces of legislation, so long as they are within the broad scope of the Constitution, are enacted under the authority of this section.

To illustrate, Article I, Section 8, Subsection 3, gives Congress the power to regulate commerce among the several states. *Commerce* has been interpreted to include people and goods for sale. By this authority, Congress has enacted legislation prohibiting the interstate transportation of a female for prostitution or other immoral purpose (Mann Act),[1] interstate transportation of a kidnapping victim (Federal Kidnapping Act, also known as the Lindbergh Law),[2] interstate transportation of a stolen motor vehicle (National Motor Vehicle Theft Act),[3] and civil rights legislation. The reason civil rights legislation falls under interstate commerce is that things such as segregated transportation, hotels, and restaurants can conceivably obstruct free interstate travel. This interpretation was the only way that Congress could enact civil rights legislation. Similarly, Article I, Section 8, Subsection 7, gives Congress the power to establish post offices. Through the "necessary and proper" clause, Congress has enacted legislation prohibiting the fraudulent use of the mails, use of the mails for obscenity, and other violations.

AMENDING THE CONSTITUTION

Supreme Court interpretation of the constitutionality of statutes such as those just described and all other federal legislation is an after-the-fact process that will be described later in this chapter.

[1] Title 18 U.S. Code § 2421 (1966).
[2] Title 18 U.S. Code § 1201 (1966).
[3] Title 18 U.S. Code § 2312 (1966).

As previously noted, many recent interpretations of the Constitution by the Supreme Court have drawn extreme criticism. Much if not all of the displeasure has been occasioned by emotional reaction to current issues. A reaction, when emotional, even when it exists among a majority of the people, does not necessarily reflect what is best for the country. Again, the foresight of the framers must be admired. They envisioned this possibility occurring and thus drafted the Constitution in such a manner as to require sufficient and calm thinking to amend it. The fact that less than thirty amendments were made in almost two hundred years, in view of the tremendous number of major emotional issues that this country has witnessed since the eighteenth century, is testimony to the fact that the procedure has worked.

Article V, Section 1, sets out the necessary procedure for amending the Constitution. It provides, "The Congress, whenever two-thirds of both houses shall deem it necessary, shall propose amendments to this Constitution, or, on the application of the legislatures of two-thirds of the several states, shall call a convention for proposing amendments, which in either case shall be valid to all intents and purposes as part of this Constitution, when ratified by the legislatures of three-fourths of the several States, or by conventions in three-fourths thereof, as the one or the other mode of ratification may be proposed by the Congress. . . ."

STATE CONSTITUTIONS AS A LIMITATION ON POWER

Because the United States Constitution is a grant of power, the purpose served by state constitutions presents a legitimate question. The states are free to exercise any control over their own people that has not been specifically granted away to the federal government through the Constitution. It is for this reason that state constitutions are referred to as "limitations on power." States really do not need a constitution to tell them what they can do because they have all powers not granted to the federal government. So why are there state constitutions? The purpose served by state constitutions is to further restrict activities that the state may undertake. State constitutions are a reflection of the desires of the state's people to limit the control their own state governments will have over their activities. Prior to the adoption of the Fourteenth Amendment, these limitations were essential to the protection of individual liberties. Of course, nothing contained within a state constitution may conflict with the United States Constitution. All state constitutions, state laws, and federal statutes are superseded by the Constitution.

CONSTITUTIONAL INTERPRETATION OF STATUTES

The federal government exercises its authority through acts passed by Congress. To determine the constitutionality of these acts, the courts look to the Constitution to see if the people gave the federal government the power to pass laws on the subject with which the congressional act deals. If the power and authority can be found in the Constitution, and if Congress acted within the limits set by the people in dealing with the subject of the act, it is constitutional. If Congress is without the authority or acting outside the scope of that authority, the act is unconstitutional.

It bears repeated mention that any powers not specifically granted to the federal government through the United States Constitution are reserved to the state or its people. Thus, the people, through their respective state constitutions, may limit the powers of the state legislature. They may prohibit their state from having an income tax or prohibit gambling, which would otherwise be permissible. State constitutions are therefore usually negative in their application, if not in their language. State legislatures may enact laws on any subject for which authority has neither been granted to the federal government nor prohibited to them by the people of the state.

To test the constitutionality of a state statute, the state courts first determine if the authority to legislate in a particular area has been granted exclusively to the federal government. For example, if a state enacted a criminal statute prohibiting the counterfeiting of money, the court would find that this power has been exclusively granted to the federal government. In this case, the state would not have the authority to pass such a law and the statute would be unconstitutional.

If the authority has not been granted to the federal government, the court must then look to the state constitution to determine if the people forbade the legislature to enact such a law. Finding no such prohibition, the court can declare the statute constitutional.

It is not intended to imply that the authority to enact laws on any particular subject rests either with the federal government or the state legislatures solely. There are times when both will have jurisdiction. However, federal legislation must apply uniformly to all states on any subject, but each state legislature can enact laws on the same subject pertaining only to its geographical boundaries. As a result, there are differences from state to state on the same subject.

In addition, it is a principle of law that courts will make every effort to hold statutes constitutional. Only when there is no way to do so, will they declare something unconstitutional.

One other principle governs the determination of the constitutionality of statutes. Because people are entitled to know what conduct is prohibited by the law, statutes cannot be written in such broad terms as to make unclear the type of conduct prohibited. Such statutes will be held unconstitutional for vagueness.

THE BILL OF RIGHTS

Those recent interpretations of the Constitution by the Supreme Court having a direct bearing on the operations of components of the criminal justice system have raised serious questions in the minds of the public concerning applications of the Bill of Rights to the states. It has raised questions concerning federal-state relationships and the preservation of states' rights.

A reexamination of the Constitution reveals that the powers yielded by the states were specifically granted for the purpose of establishing a national government. The Bill of Rights was added to protect the individual liberties of the people from potential oppression by the newly formed, powerful national government. Thus, the Bill of Rights restricts the actions of the federal government only and in no way applies to state governments. Similarly, the Bill of Rights does not protect citizens against abuses by other private individuals who are not government officials or acting on behalf of the government. For example, although the Fourth Amendment prohibits the government from conducting unreasonable searches and seizures and using evidence obtained as a result, a private citizen, as long as he is not acting on behalf of the government, may conduct an unreasonable search and turn over any evidence seized to government officials for use in a criminal prosecution. This does not mean that the individual may not be criminally prosecuted or held civilly liable for his acts, but the government will not be forbidden to use the evidence in court.

The liberties protected in specific clauses of the Bill of Rights are not necessarily exclusive guarantees. One of the clauses of the Fifth Amendment has been interpreted in such a way as to leave the door open for additional protections not spelled out in other clauses or amendments. That provision reads, ". . . nor [shall any person] be deprived of life, liberty or property without due process of law." The meaning of *due process* has long been the subject of judicial controversy. Like many other legal concepts, due process has no universally acceptable definition. Perhaps the closest one could come to an acceptable definition would be *fairness,* a concept that is one of the fundamental parts of the "American dream." The Court then has the latitude of interpreting the Constitution in any manner deemed to be fair and just under the American judicial system. However, prior to 1868, the federal courts were restricted to insuring fairness in federal criminal proceedings. In that year, the Fourteenth Amendment to the Constitution was ratified.

Before embarking on a discussion of the specific provisions of the Bill of Rights affecting the criminal justice system, it is necessary to examine the method by which provisions of the Bill of Rights are made applicable to the states.

THE EVOLUTION OF THE FOURTEENTH AMENDMENT

The Civil War was over. Slavery had been abolished. The Thirteenth, Fourteenth, and Fifteenth Amendments were all designed to guarantee the freedoms and equal protection of the laws for all citizens, especially the former slaves.

The interpretations given portions of the Fourteenth Amendment have established the foundation for much of modern criminal procedure in the United States today. The relevant provisions of the Fourteenth Amendment read, "No state shall make or enforce any law which shall abridge the privileges and immunities of citizens of the United States; nor shall any State deprive any person of life, liberty, or property, without due process of law; nor deny to any person within its jurisdiction the equal protection of the laws." The first three words of this quote supply the cornerstone to the foundation. Prior to the ratification of this amendment, the people of the nation had never before granted the federal government the power to tell the states what they could or could not do. It had always been the other way around. This reversal in roles presented a unique relationship between the federal government and the states.

But the impact of the Fourteenth Amendment cannot be fully understood without examining the first clause of Section 1 of the Amendment. That provision establishes the concept that has been popularly called "dual citizenship." The wording goes, "All persons born or naturalized in the United States, and subject to the jurisdiction thereof, are citizens of the United States and of the State wherein they reside." This section read with the remainder of the Fourteenth Amendment creates citizenship within the several states and then gives the federal government the power to tell the states they cannot abuse the freedoms of those people.

The Due Process Clause

Up to this point in history, the federal government could not protect the rights of citizens of the states by preventing abuses by the state governments. No part of the pertinent sections of the Bill of Rights, including the due process clause of the Fifth Amendment, was applicable to the states. But, the Fourteenth Amendment also contains a due process clause. A few years after ratification of the amendment in 1868 the Supreme Court was asked for a determination of the meaning of that clause.

In 1884, the case of *Hurtado v. California*[4] raised the question of the applicability of a portion of the Bill of Rights to the states by requesting an interpretation of the due process clause of the Fourteenth Amendment, contending that it included the guarantees contained in the first eight amendments of the Bill of Rights. *Hurtado* was charged with a capital offense upon information filed by the district attorney. He was convicted and sentenced to hang. The Fifth Amendment expressly requires that in capital cases there must be a presentment or indictment by a grand jury. Because Hurtado was being tried in a state court for a state violation, he could not claim a direct violation of his rights under the Bill of Rights, as he could if he were a defendant in a federal court. He asked the Court to declare that he was entitled to the same protections under the due process clause of the Fourteenth Amendment that he would receive under the Fifth Amendment were he being tried in a federal court for a violation of a federal criminal law.

This attempt to require carte blanche application of the first eight amendments to the states through the due process clause of the Fourteenth Amendment was rejected by a majority of the Court in *Hurtado,* and a line of cases presenting the same questions have resulted in similar decrees by the Court right up to the present time. The Court's theory in continually rejecting the "shorthand doctrine," as this has become known, is that if the people and the states had intended for the Fourteenth Amendment to encompass the rights protected in the Bill of

---

[4] 110 U.S. 516 (1884).

Rights and make them mandatorily applicable to the states, this would have been specified in the wording of the amendment. Because it was not, the Court felt, and still feels, it is under no compulsion to hold differently than the way it does.

In lieu of adopting the "shorthand doctrine," the Court has reviewed cases on a case-by-case basis, determining whether the particular issue of the case calling into question a clause of the Bill of Rights should be made mandatorily applicable to the states through the due process clause of the Fourteenth Amendment. In spite of the Court's rejection of blanket application, the truth is that today states have complied with most of the provisions by decree of the Supreme Court utilizing the due process clause of the Fourteenth Amendment. Notwithstanding this fact, it still remains a fundamental principle of constitutional law that a defendant in a state court cannot claim a denial of constitutional rights under the Bill of Rights but rather must use the due process clause of the Fourteenth Amendment as the vehicle for urging these rights. Figure 8–1 illustrates this procedure.

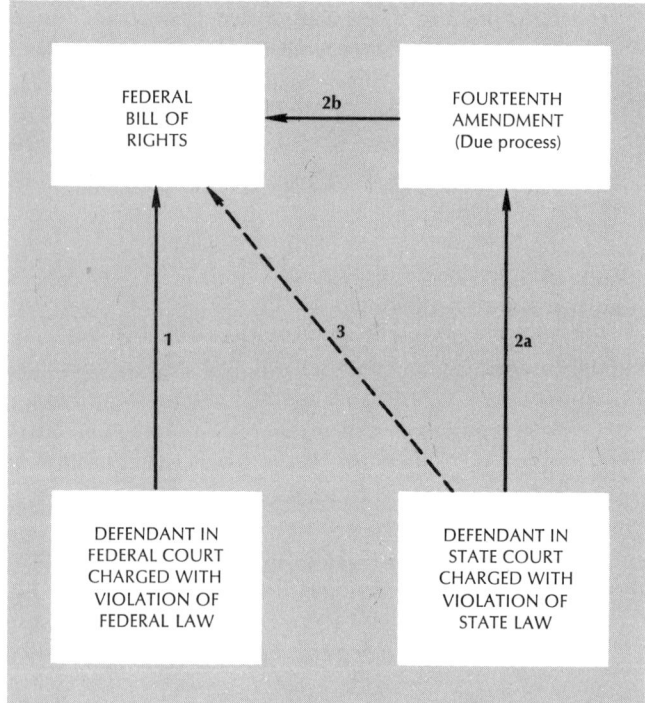

FIGURE 8–1   This chart represents the legal procedure a defendant would follow to claim violation of constitutional rights in a criminal case. Line 1 represents a defendant claiming his rights in federal court directly from the Bill of Rights. Lines 2a and 2b are the correct procedure followed by an accused in a state court. Line 3 would be an incorrect attempt by a defendant to claim violation of constitutional rights directly from the protections guaranteed in the Bill of Rights.

THE BILL OF RIGHTS AND THE CRIMINAL JUSTICE SYSTEM

With an understanding of how the Bill of Rights can have no direct effect on the states except through the due process clause of the Fourteenth Amendment, attention is now focused, in brief, on some specific applications which impact the criminal justice system at state and local levels. Where appropriate, conflicts and frustrations caused by differing police or correctional practices and judicial interpretations will be noted. Only the specific amendments of immediate concern to the criminal justice system are discussed.

First Amendment

AMENDMENT 1

Congress shall make no law respecting an establishment of religion, or prohibiting the free exercise thereof; or abridging the freedom of speech, or of the press; or the right of the people peaceably to assemble, and to petition the Government for a redress of grievances.

The First Amendment guarantees freedom of speech, press, assembly, and religion. All four freedoms have at one time or another been the subject of court interpretation. Of these, freedom of assembly and speech have impacted the most on the police and the rest of the criminal justice system. The right of the people to peacefully assemble is protected under the First Amendment. However, governments may impose reasonable regulations on assemblies such as demonstrations and protest marches, both of which have become prevalent in the past few decades, specifically in civil rights movements. Licensing and the granting of permits are permissible regulatory functions of governmental bodies used to ensure that there is no interference with the rights of others, as in the case of vehicular or pedestrian traffic. It is when demonstrations or assemblies become disorderly or disorder becomes imminent that the police usually are required to take official action. If the group cannot be pacified, arrests are sometimes necessary for such offenses as unlawful assembly, breaches of peace, inciting riots, or obstruction of traffic. Subsequent court cases usually examine the reasonableness of police action under the circumstances.

Freedom of speech and expression cases are perhaps the most litigated of all First Amendment guarantees. Not only are the police affected in their enforcement activities, but the corrections component of the system has been subjected to litigation as well. In addition, beginning in the late 1960s, a rash of state and federal court decisions intervening into the rule-making authority of primary and secondary school administrators began appearing. In large part these cases have addressed the application to students of First Amendment protections made applicable to the states through the due process clause of the Fourteenth Amendment. The types of First Amendment cases that have arisen in these areas involve the wearing of insignias, emblems, buttons, armbands, badges, and armpatches by students; production and distribution of literature; and issues related to dress and appearance, including a number of cases on hair length.

The issues are not much different from those which have arisen in correctional institutions in recent years. Numerous cases have arisen that mandate correctional authorities to become much more flexible in restrictions imposed on inmates. Courts have applied a general rule that an offender should retain all rights except those necessary to accomplish the basic purposes of incarceration or corrections. Thus, despite the basic arguments offered by correctional authorities in support of continued infringement of expression by inmates, cases have required the granting of freedom of speech, religious beliefs and practices, sending and receiving mail, more liberal visitation policies, access to the public through media, peaceful assembly, permission to belong to and participate in organizations, and maintaining individual identity through less stringent clothing and hair style requirements.[5] The major arguments put forth by correctional authorities to counter the position of the courts are : (1) ideas are a disruptive influence which tend to promote violence or other attacks on institutional authorities; (2) prisoners lie about conditions and bring unfair pressures on correctional institutions from the community; (3) ideas will offend others and the "troublemakers" will use this freedom to create tension; and (4) certain freedoms of expression are not conducive to a philosophy of rehabilitation. Each contention has been explained away or disregarded by the majority of the courts in reaching their decisions.[6]

One area of controversy over First Amendment rights that affects police from the enforcement standpoint, and the courts' adjudication processes, are cases involving obscene or pornographic material. The test of obscenity generally followed by American courts throughout the nineteenth and early part of the twentieth century was that if material was offensive to those people *most susceptible* to its effects, it was considered obscene. The first significant revision of this test occurred in 1933 when the federal courts were called upon to examine James Joyce's famous *Ulysses,* to determine if it was obscene. The U.S. Court of Appeals decided that it was not and instituted, by way of its decision, a new test. It abrogated the idea that obscenity was to be measured by its "effects on those persons most susceptible to it" and said that obscenity was to be measured by its "effect on the average person."[7] Thus, the delineation between obscene and nonobscene material became based upon the effect pornography might have upon those with average sexual propensities rather than upon those who because of age, sexual aberrations, and so on might be more easily aroused or disturbed by the content.

Another turning point for the courts, particularly for the Supreme Court, came in 1957 when some critical questions were raised in the area of constitutional guarantees under the provisions of the First Amendment as they related to the issue of pornography. In *Roth v. United States,* the defendant, who was in the

---

[5] National Advisory Commission on Criminal Justice Standards and Goals, *Corrections* (Washington, D.C.: U.S. Government Printing Office, 1973), pp. 58–69.

[6] *Ibid.,* pp. 59–60.

[7] *United States v. One Book Called "Ulysses,"* 5 F. Supp. 182 (1933).

business of publishing and marketing books, was indicted and tried under the provisions of the federal obscenity statute.[8] In a companion case, *Alberts v. California,* the defendant, who conducted a mail order business in California, was charged with the violation of that state's obscenity laws for having and displaying for sale obscene books.[9] The court was asked to rule upon the constitutionality of the two statutes in question in view of the First Amendment's guarantee of freedom of speech as made applicable through the due process clause of the Fourteenth Amendment.

The defendants contended that in addition to the violation of their constitutional rights, the wording of the respective statutes did not provide reasonably definite standards of guilt so that they could be understood and conformed to. The Court overruled their pleas by declaring the statutes constitutional and adding that not every form of speech or expression is protected by the Constitution. The Court felt that obscenity laws, designed to protect the morals of society, do not infringe on the area of protected speech or expression under the First Amendment. The Court went on to say that the test of obscenity is whether or not by applying contemporary community standards the material appeals to prurient interests of the average person.

Since this landmark decision in 1957, the Supreme Court has made some additional modifications. In *Manual Enterprises v. Day,* the Court held that the "appeal to prurient interest" in the *Roth* and *Alberts* cases was only part of the test and that the "patent offensiveness" of the material must also be considered.[10]

In *Jacobellis v. Ohio,* the Court faced the question of whether local or national community interests were to prevail in applying the test. The Court answered that national and not local standards were the proper criteria for considering the offensiveness of obscene material.[11]

During the period 1966–68, the Supreme Court again looked at the question of obscenity and in a number of decisions formulated additional guidelines. Besides showing that the material in question is "patently offensive" and "appeals to prurient interests," the state must also show that the material in question is also "without redeeming social value." The "variable standard," which stated that items not obscene for adults could be considered obscene for minors, was also added to the definition.

In 1969, in *Stanley v. Georgia,* the Court ruled that an individual has the right to read or observe in the privacy of his home what he pleases.[12] Even though an individual possesses obscene materials, in light of the various "tests" this mere possession for private use is not a crime. In 1971, the Court also affirmed lower court decisions that limit the power of the postal authorities to prohibit the mailing of obscene materials. The former decision seems to support the contention that consenting adults should choose their own moral standards as long as no one

[8] 354 U.S. 476 (1957).
[9] 354 U.S. 476 (1957).
[10] 370 U.S. 478 (1962).
[11] 378 U.S. 184 (1964).
[12] 394 U.S. 557 (1969).

else is hurt by them; the latter decision seems to weaken the protection of the nonconsenting person's privacy, while strengthening the purveyor's position.

The effect of public opinion is very readily apparent in the controversy over obscenity laws. Many times, the decisions of the Court had not been complied with and there were numerous incidences of local communities applying their own standards, which was in direct opposition to the Court's holding that national and not local community standards must apply.

Finally, in 1973 the Court ruled that it could not formulate a meaningful definition of obscenity. In a landmark decision, it overturned its own ruling and declared that each local community should apply its own standards.[13] Even the Court recognized that it still had not formulated an acceptable definition of obscenity although it had grappled with the problem for years.

Many cases have been decided since 1973 but the standard established in the *Miller* case continues to prevail.

Fourth Amendment

AMENDMENT 4

The right of the people to be secure in their persons, houses, papers, and effects, against unreasonable searches and seizures, shall not be violated, and no Warrants shall issue, but upon probable cause, supported by Oath or affirmation, and particularly describing the place to be searched, and the persons or things to be seized.

A quick reading of the Fourth Amendment would lead one to believe that its sole coverage is the topic of search and seizure. However, the authority for the laws of arrest also is derived from this amendment and is referred to in the last line as "persons . . . to be seized."

In criminal law terms, arrest may be defined as the taking of a person into lawful custody for the purpose of bringing him before a court of law to answer for a criminal charge. To accomplish an arrest, the law enforcement officer must generally (1) have an intention to arrest a particular person, (2) have authority to take the person into custody, and (3) bring the arrested person within the custody and control of the law either through voluntary submission or through the use of physical restraints. It is important to know exactly at what point in time a lawful arrest has taken place because this will often affect the admissibility of evidence obtained by a search and seizure.

By strict construction of the Fourth Amendment, the only time an arrest can lawfully be made is under the authority of a warrant. The courts have not been this stringent in their interpretation of the amendment. Although state statutes differ somewhat, generally it is recognized that a police officer may make an arrest without a warrant if a crime is committed in his presence or if he has probable cause to believe that a felony has been committed and the person being arrested

---

[13] *Miller v. California,* 413 U.S. 15 (1973).

has committed it. The term "probable cause" as used in the laws of both arrest and search and seizure is a very significant concept, for in order for a case to withstand judicial attack on the legality of the arrest or search, probable cause must have existed prior to the arrest or prior to the commencement of a search. Probable cause can best be defined as being more than suspicion but less than actual knowledge. It is suspicion plus facts and circumstances that would lead a reasonable man in the same situation to believe that a crime has been, is being, or is about to be committed. Figure 8–2 illustrates these relationships.

In all cases, it is preferable for an arrest or search and seizure to take place under the authority of a warrant issued by a judicial officer. In this manner a person who is trained in the law and is impartial toward the investigation can make a determination as to whether an arrest or search and seizure will be proper and will later stand up in a court of law. Police officers are always trained and advised to follow this procedure whenever practical.

Even though case law does allow police officers to make arrests and conduct searches without warrants under specific circumstances, the situations confronting police officers do not always lend themselves to a clear black-or-white answer as to whether a warrant is necessary. It is for this reason that police officers often get frustrated and confused with court decisions. But it is within the courts' prerogative to interpret the law as applicable to these "gray" areas.

A warrant is a judicial order, in writing, commanding the person to whom it is issued to arrest a particular person or to search a particular place and seize particular evidence and bring it before the court. The warrant must be supported by an oath or affirmation. Affirmation is a process undertaken by one who chooses not to swear but instead chooses to support his request for a warrant on the basis that he knows the importance of telling the truth and the penalties of perjury for failure to do so.

A warrant must contain a particular description. To obtain an arrest warrant it is necessary to particularly describe the person to be arrested. This is usually

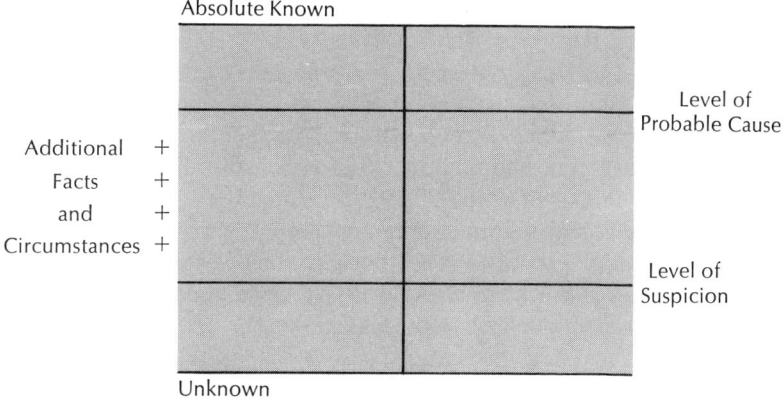

FIGURE 8–2 Probable Cause

done by using names, nicknames, aliases, residence, occupation, and physical characteristics. The purpose is to enable a police officer executing the warrant to specifically identify the person to be arrested. If an individual's name is not known, a "John Doe" warrant is appropriate, provided it contains a particular description of the individual to be arrested. However, "John Doe" warrants containing no particular description, but issued on the basis of knowledge that a crime was committed and therefore someone must have committed it, are totally invalid and unconstitutional. Such warrants would give the police too much opportunity for abuse of power and authority and are specifically what the Fourth Amendment was designed to prevent. Search warrants must specifically state a limited area in which the search may take place and the items to be seized. For example, if information known to the police indicates that evidence is located in the basement of a house, this must be specifically stated to the issuing judge. The warrant must be issued for that limited portion of the building and only for those items that the officers have probable cause to believe are contained therein. Again, if search warrants were written in more general terms, permitting searches of entire homes, without probable cause, there would be too much opportunity for abuse on the part of law enforcement officers contrary to the purpose of the Fourth Amendment.

The development of the law of search and seizure can best summarize the relationship described earlier between federal and state court systems and between the Bill of Rights and its application to the states through the due process clause of the Fourteenth Amendment.

At common law, an illegal search and seizure that produced incriminating evidence was allowed, and the evidence obtained was admissible in court. Surprisingly, federal law enforcement officers were permitted to follow the same rule as late as 1914. Up to that time, the search and seizure practices of federal officials had not been scrutinized in light of the wording of the Fourth Amendment. In 1914, the case of *Weeks v. United States*[14] was decided by the Supreme Court. Weeks was charged by federal agents with using the mails for transporting materials representing chances in a lottery. After his arrest for this federal offense, Weeks' room was searched twice without the authority of a valid search warrant. His arrest occurred at his place of employment. During the search, the officers found and took possession of various incriminating papers and articles. This evidence was admitted in his trial for the federal violation, and he was convicted. On appeal to the United States Supreme Court, the Court established what has now become known as the "Federal Exclusionary Rule." The Court held that any evidence unreasonably obtained by federal officers could no longer be admissible in federal prosecutions. They made it quite clear that because this was a federal case the decision was applicable only to federal officers and federal courts and in no way was applicable to the states. But the decision left unanswered an important question (most Supreme Court decisions do seem to create more unanswered

---

[14] 232 U.S. 383 (1914).

questions than are answered by the particular decision). Out of that unanswered question arose the famous "Silver Platter Doctrine." The Weeks decision prohibited federal officers from illegally seizing evidence, but it did not preclude unreasonable searches and seizures by state officers, who in turn could supply the tainted evidence to federal authorities for use in federal prosecutions. State officers would hand the evidence over on a "silver platter." This method of circumventing the Federal Exclusionary Rule remained unchallenged until 1960.

In *Elkins v. United States*[15] the Court prohibited the introduction in federal courts of all evidence illegally obtained by state officers in violation of the Fourth Amendment.

After the decision in the *Weeks* case, very few state jurisdictions voluntarily adopted their own exclusionary rule applicable within the state. It was not until 1949 that a serious attempt was made to seek mandatory application of the exclusionary rule to the states through the due process clause of the Fourteenth Amendment. In *Wolf v. Colorado*,[16] the defendant was charged with abortion. Based on suspicion of similar prior offenses, officers searched Wolf's office, arrested him, and seized certain documents that were later admitted into the trial. Wolf appealed his conviction contending that the unreasonable search and seizure was a denial of due process under the Fourteenth Amendment as it would be under the Fourth Amendment had he been in federal court. The Supreme Court held that unreasonable searches and seizures by state officials in state cases did not constitute a denial of Fourteenth Amendment due process but added that the Court did have the power to rule otherwise if they desired. The interesting point in this case seemed to be that the Court was giving the states fair warning that they disapproved of unreasonable searches by state authorities and that sooner or later they would rule in favor of incorporating the Fourth Amendment protection in the due process interpretation of the Fourteenth Amendment. Many states took the hint.

By 1961, only eighteen states had not adopted an exclusionary rule. In that year, the warning that the Supreme Court had given twelve years earlier in the *Wolf* case came to pass. In May 1957, three Cleveland police officers arrived at Dolree Mapp's residence in that city with information that a person who was wanted for questioning in a recent bombing was hiding out in her home and that there was a large amount of policy paraphernalia being hidden in the home. The officers knocked on the door and demanded entrance, but Miss Mapp, after telephoning her attorney, refused to admit them without a search warrant. The officers advised their headquarters of the situation and undertook a surveillance of the house. Some three hours later, the officers, with reinforcements, again sought entrance. When Miss Mapp did not come to the door immediately, one of the doors was forcibily opened and the officers gained entry. Miss Mapp demanded to see the search warrant. One of the officers held up a paper that he claimed was the

[15] 364 U.S. 206 (1960).
[16] 338 U.S. 25 (1949).

warrant. She grabbed the paper and placed it in her bodice. A struggle ensued in which the officers recovered the piece of paper and handcuffed Miss Mapp for her "belligerency" in resisting the attempt to recover the "warrant." A subsequent widespread search of the entire premises disclosed obscene materials for the possession of which she was convicted. No search warrant was ever produced at the trial. Following her conviction and the denial of her appeals in the state courts, her case was appealed to the United States Supreme Court. *Mapp v. Ohio*[17] was decided on June 19, 1961. The Supreme Court established the rule that any evidence unreasonably searched and seized would no longer be admissible in any court—state or federal.

Among the many unanswered questions created by the *Mapp* decision, the crucial question revolved around the definition of the word *unreasonable*. It did not take the state courts long to find the loophole and in order to avoid applying the decision in the *Mapp* case to instances arising in state courts, state officials merely called previously unreasonable searches and seizures reasonable searches. Because no standards had been set for determining what constitutes a reasonable or unreasonable search, many of the state courts felt free to make their own determination on this issue. In effect then, *Mapp* had little impact in these states. However, within two years of the *Mapp* decision, the Supreme Court had the opportunity to rule on the matter. The Court held in *Ker v. California*[18] that state court judges were still free to determine the reasonableness of searches but that in making those determinations they would now be guided by the same standards as had been followed by federal courts established in the line of cases decided since the *Weeks* case in 1914. In essence, the Court said that states would be held to federal standards in search and seizure matters.

The long line of state cases evolving since *Mapp* and *Ker* have essentially revolved around the single issue of what constitutes a reasonable search in instances where police officers act with or without a warrant. For example, the Supreme Court in 1969 in what is considered the landmark case of *Chimel v. California*[19] held that a search without a warrant conducted incident to a lawful arrest must be confined to the area "under the immediate control" of the arrestee and is only justified to prevent the arrestee from obtaining a dangerous weapon or to prevent the destruction of evidence.

Fifth Amendment

AMENDMENT 5

No person shall be held to answer for a capital, or otherwise infamous crime, unless on a presentment or indictment of a Grand Jury, except in cases arising in the land or naval forces, or in the Militia, when in actual service in time of War or public danger; nor shall any person be subject for the same offence to be twice put in jeopardy of life

[17] 367 U.S. 643 (1961).
[18] 374 U.S. 10 (1963).
[19] 395 U.S. 752 (1969).

or limb; nor shall be compelled in any criminal case to be a witness against himself, nor be deprived of life, liberty, or property, without due process of law; nor shall private property be taken for public use, without just compensation.

Double jeopardy, self-incrimination, and due process are issues addressed by the Fifth Amendment. Readers who recall earlier comments about the attitude of the American people at the time of the adoption of the Constitution and the Bill of Rights—their fears and concerns over the formation of a strong central government—will understand the rationale behind this amendment. The protection against double jeopardy, prohibiting continued harassment by government agents, was of paramount concern. Jeopardy attaches in a criminal trial when the jury is sworn. If the prosecution withdraws of its own volition after that point, prosecution cannot be recommenced. However, the state is also entitled to its day in court. Appeals from convictions by the defendant and hung juries do not violate double jeopardy protections. The concept of sovereignty also impacts the jeopardy issue. The guarantees of the Fifth Amendment only protect us from being twice put in jeopardy by the same soverign government. State and federal governments are separate sovereigns. Therefore, an act which violates both a state and federal law—e.g., robbery of a bank insured by the Federal Deposit Insurance Corporation—may be prosecutable in both jurisdictions without evoking double jeopardy. As a practical matter one jurisdiction will usually not try after a conviction in the other.

The same rationale does not hold true for offenses which violate both state law and local ordinance. Most counties are political subdivisions of the state. Home-rule counties and municipalities are creations of the state and may be abolished by state action. Hence, they are part of the same sovereign. Jeopardy does attach if an attempt is made to prosecute in both.

Few people are unaware of the Fifth Amendment privilege against self-incrimination and its application to a defendant's right not to testify against himself in a criminal case. But the privilege has broader implications and is affected by and impacts the search and seizure provisions of the Fourth Amendment and the Sixth Amendment guarantee of right to counsel. For example, in *Schmerber v. California*,[20] the Supreme Court addressed the issue of whether taking a blood sample from a suspect in a drunk driving case, in a hospital, without consent was an illegal search and seizure and violative of the self-incrimination protection. The Court held the procedure violated neither the Fourth nor Fifth Amendments as long as blood was drawn by a physician under sanitary conditions. Other cases holding no violation of self-incrimination involve fingerprinting, photographing, and compulsory handwriting specimens for identification purposes.

The courts have been more stringent in cases relating to the right to counsel and self-incrimination. The areas of concern are primarily focused on police interrogations and line-ups. In 1964, the Supreme Court decided the case of *Escobedo v. Illinois* in which it said:

---

[20] 384 U.S. 757 (1966).

> We hold, therefore, that where, as here, the investigation is no longer a general inquiry into an unsolved crime, but has begun to focus upon a particular suspect, the suspect has been taken into police custody, the police carry out a process of interrogation that lends itself to eliciting incriminating comments, the suspect has requested and been denied an opportunity to consult with his lawyer, and the police have not effectively warned him of his absolute constitutional rights to remain silent . . . the accused has been denied the assistance of counsel in violation of the Sixth Amendment of the Constitution as made obligatory upon the states by the Fourteenth Amendment . . . and that no statement elicited by the police during the interrogation may be used against him at a criminal trial.[21]

However, this ruling soon had to be clarified by the Court.

> The decision of the Supreme Court in the Escobedo case was so significant that state supreme courts tended to interpret it in a very narrow constitutional context by holding that it only applied where the suspect had been refused counsel after specifically requesting to consult with a lawyer, or when the attorney specifically requested to confer with his client. Hence, the Escobedo case left many questions unanswered. This condition existed in the state courts for a period of two years until 1966 when the Supreme Court again was asked to examine this procedure. In another five-to-four decision the court spelled out the requirements and procedures to be followed by officers when conducting in-custody interrogation of a suspect.[22]

In clarifying the requirements of Escobedo, the Court, in *Miranda v. Arizona,* felt compelled to include the Fifth Amendment requirements against self-incrimination in the decision. The guidelines require that after a person is taken into custody for an offense and prior to any questioning by law enforcement officers, if there is any intent to use a suspect's statements in court, he must first be advised of certain rights. These rights include:

1. The right to remain silent.
2. The right to be told that anything he does say, can and will be used against him in court.
3. The right to consult with an attorney prior to answering any questions and the right to have an attorney present during interrogation.
4. The right to counsel. If he cannot afford to pay for his own attorney, the court will appoint one to represent him.[23]

In 1967, the Supreme Court handed down several decisions extending the right-to-counsel provisions to police line-ups and on-the-street confrontations of the accused and the accuser for identification purposes. The decisions in *United States v. Wade*[24] and *Gilbert v. California,*[25] a companion case, held that such confrontations were a "critical stage" of the proceedings against an accused and that counsel is required under such circumstances. The reason for the decisions was to ensure that if the defendant were forced to participate in such an identification proceeding, he be guaranteed it was conducted fairly and impartially, so that im-

---

[21] 378 U.S. 478 (1964).
[22] Charles R. Swanson et al., *Criminal Investigation* (Santa Monica, Calif.: Goodyear, 1977), p. 147.
[23] 384 U.S. 436 (1966).
[24] 87 S.Ct. 1926 (1967).
[25] 87 S.Ct. 1951 (1967).

proper or tainted identifications were not made and that he not be required to incriminate himself by involuntarily participating.

Previous mention was made of the purpose of the due process clause in the Fifth Amendment. It is designed as a catch-all clause to ensure fairness in the treatment of those subjected to criminal processes by the government. Its inclusion in the Fifth Amendment was designed to ensure that other protections, not specifically spelled out in other clauses of the Bill of Rights, were afforded individuals.

Sixth Amendment

AMENDMENT 6

In all criminal prosecutions, the accused shall enjoy the right to a speedy and public trial, by an impartial jury of the State and district wherein the crime shall have been committed, which district shall have been previously ascertained by law, and to be informed of the nature and cause of the accusation; to be confronted with the witnesses against him; to have compulsory process for obtaining witnesses in his favor, and to have the Assistance of Counsel for his defence.

The Sixth Amendment guarantees defendants in criminal cases the right to a speedy trial, a public trial, the right to confront witnesses against them, the right of cross-examination, and the right of counsel. Although the right of public trial has not yet been made mandatorily applicable to the states through the due process clause of the Fourteenth Amendment, it is granted by state constitutional provisions in all jurisdictions. On the other hand, the right to a speedy trial has been decided at the federal level. In 1967, in the case of *Klopfer v. North Carolina*,[26] the Supreme Court made the right to a speedy trial applicable to the states through the due process clause of the Fourteenth Amendment. Since that time, court cases have established reasonable limits on what constitutes a speedy trial. Figures like 180 days and 90 days are used in state statutes and procedural codes. In 1974, Congress adopted the Speedy Trial Act[27] in which provisions were made for trial to begin within a specified period of time in federal cases. Failure to comply with the Act is grounds for release from charges. The Act provides for a transition period of declining lengths of time through June 1979, at which time a person held in pretrial detention for more than 125 days was required to be released without trial. In some instances the Act provides for freedom without trial if a person is not tried within 90 days from the time "continuous incarceration" begins.

The right of confrontation and cross-examination have long been recognized as essential to the conduct of criminal trials and are provided for in all jurisdictions, but the issue of the right to counsel was not raised until the early 1960s. The famous case of *Gideon v. Wainwright*,[28] decided by the Supreme Court in 1962, granted court-appointed counsel to people charged with felonies who could not afford to pay for their own attorneys. In a more recent case, the Su-

[26] 386 U.S. 213 (1967).
[27] 18 U.S.C. 1364.
[28] 372 U.S. 335 (1963).

preme Court declared that the right extends to persons who are charged with any crime for which prison is a potential penalty.[29] This line of cases does not mean that an imprisoned indigent must be represented by counsel at trial, as the defendant may waive that right. It does necessitate that the state at least provide the defendant with the opportunity to have free counsel.

Eighth Amendment

AMENDMENT 8

Excessive bail shall not be required, nor excessive fines imposed, nor cruel and unusual punishments inflicted.

The central contemporary issue involving the Eighth Amendment is capital punishment. In 1972, the Supreme Court in *Furman v. Georgia* held that state's death penalty law to be unconstitutional as violative of the Eighth and Fourteenth Amendments because the statute left too much uncontrolled discretion with the jury to either impose or withhold the death sentence.[30] This decision did not, as many erroneously believed, rule capital punishment unconstitutional. Rather, it held that statutes permitting too much discretion in their application constituted cruel and unusual punishment. Following the decision, many states desiring to retain capital punishment drafted new legislation, but no executions were carried out until the Court could rule on the constitutionality of the statutes. In fact, no one had been lawfully executed in the United States from 1964 until Gary Gilmore was killed by a firing squad in Utah early in 1977. Gilmore claimed he wanted to die and refused to pursue his avenues of appeal although many others made unsuccessful efforts on his behalf.

On July 2, 1976, the Supreme Court handed down capital punishment decisions in cases involving the constitutionality of newly passed statutes in five states. In the Georgia case, the court held that the use of the death penalty punishment for murder does not, per se, constitute cruel and unusual punishment in violation of the Eighth and the Fourteenth Amendments. It held that the new Georgia statute which requires the sentencing authority to focus its attention on the defendant and the circumstances of the crime and requires the state supreme court to compare each death sentence with sentences imposed on similarly situated defendants did not violate the holding of the *Furman* case which prohibited the death penalty from being imposed arbitrarily or capriciously.[31] The Court held in a Florida case that a statute which provided for the use of the death penalty as punishment for murder similar to the Georgia statute, but which provided that the trial judge always make the final determination of sentence, was not violative of the Eighth and the Fourteenth Amendments or the decision in the *Furman* case, even though

---

[29] *Argersinger v. Hamlin*, 92 S.Ct. 2006 (1972).
[30] 408 U.S. 238 (1972).
[31] *Gregg v. Georgia*, 19 CrL 3250 (1976).

the statute did not prescribe any particular form for the state supreme court to review the statute.[32]

The Court held that a North Carolina statute making the death penalty mandatory for a defendant convicted of first degree murder, which by statutory definition included a broad range of homicidal offenses, was violative of the Eighth and the Fourteenth Amendments.[33] Similarly, the Louisiana statute was ruled unconstitutional which made the death penalty mandatory for a defendant convicted of first degree murder even though, by statutory definition, that crime was limited to five categories of homicide.[34] But the use of the death penalty as punishment for murder under a Texas statute that limits capital homicides to intentional and knowing murders committed in five specific situations, and conditions the imposition of the death sentence on the jury's positive answers to specific questions propounded at the sentencing stage of the trial, is constitutional.[35]

THE CONSTITUTION AND CRIMINAL JUSTICE

This chapter has by no means presented an exhaustive analysis of the Constitution or its application to the criminal justice system. The Supreme Court in its supervisory powers over lower federal courts can determine the direction of criminal procedure in the federal system. Decisions in this vein do not seem to upset the vast majority of people. The powers of the Supreme Court to make decisions affecting all the states uniformly does often create an uproar. However, it must be remembered that the Supreme Court's power in dealing with issues of criminal procedure in the state courts is not supervisory, but rather is constitutional power—power that the people gave the federal government in 1868, when the states ratified the Fourteenth Amendment. In so doing, we yielded some additional sovereign powers and provided the federal government with the authority to say, "no state shall. . . ."

Every time the Supreme Court decides a case involving criminal procedure—whether that decision affects the police, the courts, community-based programs, or institutional correctional programs directly—the entire spectrum of criminal justice is touched. Whether those decisions are good or bad is often an academic question and one that must be answered on the basis of individual attitudes. What is crucial is recognition that maintenance of constitutional principles will continue to provide the bulwark of good government in the United States and that, in turn, will determine the quality of the criminal justice system.

Perhaps the necessity for maintenance of a good constitutional form of government can best be summed up in the words of the late Supreme Court Justice Louis D. Brandeis, who, in the case of *Olmstead v. United States,* said in 1928:

[32] *Proffit v. Florida,* 19 CrL 3276 (1976).
[33] *Woodson v. North Carolina,* 19 CrL 3287 (1976).
[34] *Roberts v. Louisiana,* 19 CrL 3301 (1976).
[35] *Jurek v. Texas,* 19 CrL 3282 (1976).

Decency, security, and liberty alike demand that governmental officials shall be subjected to the same rules of conduct that are commands to the citizen. In a government of laws, existence of the government will be imperiled if it fails to observe the law scrupulously. Our government is the potent, the omnipresent teacher. For good or for ill, it teaches the whole people by its example. Crime is contagious. If the government becomes a lawbreaker, it breeds contempt for the law; it invites every man to become a law unto himself; it invites anarchy. To declare that in the administration of the criminal law the end justifies the means—to declare that the government may commit crimes in order to secure the conviction of a private criminal—would bring terrible retribution. Against that pernicious doctrine this court should resolutely set its face.[36]

SUMMARY

The Constitution as the basic governing document of the United States has existed for two hundred years because of its stability and flexibility. It is capable of being interpreted in light of the needs of an ever-changing society. The Constitution is a grant of powers to a centralized government to operate a united group of states. Its formation is based on the assignment of certain powers granted by the people and by the states to this federal government. The Bill of Rights is designed to ensure certain guarantees of freedom to citizens of the United States. These freedoms were only applicable to citizens of the United States, not to the states, until the Fourteenth Amendment was adopted. The First, Fourth, Fifth, Sixth, and the Eighth Amendments contain clauses which apply to the states through the due process clause of the Fourteenth Amendment and which have the most impact on the operations of the criminal justice system. Practitioners and students alike must have an understanding of the role of the Constitution and its impact on the criminal justice system, for it is from this source that activities of the criminal justice system derive their authority.

LEARNING EXERCISES

Issues to Be Discussed

1. It has been argued that the Fourteenth Amendment was passed specifically to protect former slaves and subsequent decisions on "due process" by the Supreme Court vastly expanded its original purpose. In viewing what the Court has done up to the present related to the Bill of Rights, would you be in favor of a broad or a more strict interpretation of its powers of "due process" decisions in the future?
2. What is meant by the Constitution being a grant of power and how is this concept operationalized?
3. Describe the role of the Fourteenth Amendment in the application of Bill of Rights issues in criminal cases to the state.

[36] 227 U.S. 438 (1928).

4. List the topics relevant to criminal justice system problems addressed by clauses of the Bill of Rights.
5. Define probable cause, and discuss its application to cases of arrests and searches and seizures.

Group Activity

Select one recent Supreme Court decision such as *Mapp v. Ohio* (1961), *Escobedo v. Illinois* (1964), or *Miranda v. Arizona* (1966) and establish a panel to argue some citizen support of these decisions against a law enforcement agency's concern about their impact on limiting criminal justice procedures.

Field Activity

As a continuing project for the notebook on this section of the text, select one issue raised in the text as the result of a Supreme Court decision on one of the Bill of Rights Amendments and trace its implications for the criminal justice system. Use interviews with local law enforcement personnel or prosecutors, defenders, the media, or publications of the criminal justice field, particularly law journals.

Key Terms

Bill of Rights
Due process
Judicial review
Probable cause

SUGGESTED REFERENCES

BRANT, IRVING. *The Bill of Rights.* New York: New American Library, 1967.

FELKENES, GEORGE T. *Criminal Law and Procedure.* Englewood Cliffs, N.J.: Prentice-Hall, 1976.

KLOTTER, JOHN C., AND KANOVITZ, JACQUELINE R. *Constitutional Law for Police.* 3rd ed. Cincinnati: W. H. Anderson, 1977.

SWINDLER, WILLIAM F. *Court and Constitution in the Twentieth Century: The New Legality 1932-1962.* Indianapolis, Ind.: Bobbs-Merrill, 1970.

WRIGHT, LOUIS B. *Magna Carta and the Tradition of Liberty.* Washington, D.C.: U.S. Capital Historical Society, 1976.

9

Courts in the United States

Overview
The Development of Courts
The Supreme Court of the United States
The Supreme Court as a Political Entity
Lower Federal Courts
State and Local Courts
The Lower Courts
Juvenile Courts
Summary
Learning Exercises
Suggested References

OVERVIEW

The concept of a court as a place of judgment is almost as old as recorded history. The Supreme Court, as the highest federal court, has had a profound effect upon the criminal justice system, particularly in the last two decades. Within the federal judicial system there are other courts of special concern for the criminal justice system: the United States Courts of Appeals, the United States District Courts, and the United States Magistrates. The American judicial system is rounded out by the state and local courts whose designations vary from state to state. Many of the problems of the criminal justice system may be attributed to the court problems of excessive caseloads and inadequate facilities, personnel, and administrative procedures, all most acute in the lower courts. Of special and growing importance for criminal justice procedures, in view of the high crime rate among young people, is the structure and operations of the juvenile court system.

> ARTICLE III
>
> Section 1. The judicial Power of the United States, shall be vested in one supreme Court, and in such inferior Courts as the Congress may from time to time ordain and establish. The Judges, both of the supreme and inferior Courts, shall hold their Offices during good Behaviour, and shall, at stated Times, receive for their Services, a Compensation, which shall not be diminished during their Continuance in Office.

A dual court system exists in this country. On one hand are the federal courts ordained by Congress, and on the other are state court systems created by legislatures under the auspices of their respective state constitutions. The two systems are sovereign and often foreign to each other. Although the structure of the federal court system is uncomplicated and precise, no such simple universality exists in state court systems. Few states have identical courts with identical patterns of jurisdiction. Even within a state, it is often difficult to detect similarities between courts of the same title from county to county, or from judicial circuit to judicial circuit.

THE DEVELOPMENT OF COURTS

The word *court*, in its original meaning, signified an uncovered space within a residential yard (courtyard). It later was applied to the official residence of a ruler, and then finally expanded to include the ruler and members of his official household in whom the functions of government (executive, legislative, and judicial) were centered. Gradually, as the judicial function was separated from the others, *court* came to mean the institutions entrusted with judicial proceedings.

Perhaps the first center of civilization to have courts was China, about four thousand years ago. The emphasis is on *perhaps* because there is not a great deal of proof to this effect. In 2900 B.C., it is known that Egyptian kings had administrative officials who acted as local judges. In approximately 2050 B.C., King Hammurabi of Mesopotamia established courts in which judges heard religious disputes.

In the early Middle Ages in Europe, before the separation of the judicial function from the legislative and administrative functions the king and his chief counselors exercised all these functions at the palace, and so the household of the king was also called "the court." Because all judicial authority was derived from him, his presence was assumed in all specialized courts, each of which was regarded as the *curia regis* ("king's court").

The history of courts in England was one of steadily growing specialization, sometimes along lines of subject matter, sometimes of procedure. They were divided by certain features that can be summed up as follows: First, there was a distinction between superior and inferior courts—the former being the court of appeals and the high court of justice. The inferior courts were the local or district courts. Second, courts were distinguished as civil or criminal. Third, a distinction was made between courts of first instance and courts of appeal. The first hearing in any judicial proceeding took place in the former; judgment of the first court was brought under review in the latter.

Criminal courts in England include: (1) Magistrates' Court; (2) Courts of Quarter Sessions; (3) Courts of Assize; (4) Court of Criminal Appeal; and (5) the House of Lords. The civil courts are: (1) Magistrates' Court (having civil jurisdiction in a very few cases of small claims but very wide jurisdiction in cases of disputes between husband and wife); (2) County Court; (3) the Supreme Court; and (4) the House of Lords.

Court is used as a term for judicial settings within which judges and other officials sit, while the general public remains outside the *bar* (a railing) of the court. The word *bar* is also applied to the exams lawyers take to qualify to practice; they are permitted to come "within the bar of the court," thus, to become members of the bar. At first, the court and the bar were temporary structures in an open field; later, fixtures in a large room or hall.

The structure of court organization in the United States reflects the division of executive, legislative, and judicial functions characteristic of the federal government. When the thirteen original colonies declared their independence from England, each had an existing court system. The court systems were patterned on the English court system, and are maintained today.

THE SUPREME COURT OF THE UNITED STATES

Although Article III of the Constitution requires the establishment of a Supreme Court, it does not specify the organization or functions of the Court. These matters were left to the discretion of Congress. However, Article III does specify the extent of the judicial powers of the federal government in Section 2, Subsection 1.

The Supreme Court possesses two kinds of jurisdiction. *Original jurisdiction* is the power of the Court to sit as the first line of justice to determine the facts and law involved in a case. Subsection 2 of Section 2, Article III, mandates original jurisdiction residing in the Supreme Court: "In all cases affecting ambassadors, other public ministers and consuls, and those in which a State shall be a party. . . ." The remainder of the cases are heard by the Court acting in its capacity as an *appellate tribunal.* It hears and decides appeals from lower federal courts, territorial courts, and state courts of last resort when proper procedures have been followed. It is in this latter capacity that the decisions of the Court have a major influence on the criminal justice system.

THE SUPREME COURT AS A POLITICAL ENTITY

The mechanics of Supreme Court procedures are only the tip of the iceberg. Underneath, there is a maze of political and practical realities concerning staffing of the Court, selection of cases, decision making, jurisdiction, and the system of checks and balances.

Selection of Cases

REASONS FOR SELECTION

The original jurisdiction of the Supreme Court spelled out in the Constitution is rarely exercised. The primary functioning of the Court is in appellate cases. Appeals heard by the Supreme Court generally come from either a state court of last resort having jurisdiction in a case that has raised a substantial federal question or from a federal court of lower jurisdiction. Cases coming to the attention of the Court usually arise in one of three principal ways: an appeal as a matter of right; by a process known as certification; or on a writ of certiorari, the most used of the three methods.

APPEAL

Among the instances in which the Court is required by law to review a case are: (1) A state court of last resort has declared a federal law unconstitutional or has upheld a state law or provision of a state constitution against a challenge that it conflicts with federal law or the United States Constitution; and (2) when a United States Court of Appeals has invalidated a state law or state constitutional provision because of a conflict with federal law or the federal constitution.

CERTIFICATION

The process of certification is one by which a lower court asks the Supreme Court to review a case in order to decide a point of law that is presenting confusion in lower courts. For example, if courts of appeal in two different circuits were to hand down conflicting opinions on identical legal issues, the Supreme Court would be asked to grant certification in order to resolve the conflict.

CERTIORARI

The selection of cases under the certiorari procedure is discretionary with the Court. Although the Court's own Rule 19 states the purposes for which certiorari will be granted, on numerous occasions the Court has advised that it does not follow that rule strictly and decisions will be made on the basis of the social importance of the question raised in the particular case. The importance of the outcome of a particular case to the parties involved is not alone a sufficient ground for the Court to grant certiorari in a case. The Supreme Court never has been primarily concerned with the correction of errors in lower-court decisions or with the impact of the decision on the parties involved. The far-reaching impact of the Court's decisions is generally the initial concern in the selection of the case. In order to grant certiorari, the Court has for many years followed the rule that at least four of the justices must vote to accept the case. If certiorari is granted, the Court may either decide the case on its merits on the basis of the trial proceedings or it may schedule the case for argument in open court. Certiorari is the process usually followed by an individual who seeks to have his case reviewed by the Supreme Court. As indicated before, the process is not automatic.

CHANCES OF SELECTION

Each of us at one time has heard someone make the statement, "I'll take it all the way to the Supreme Court," be it an individual who is upset because his neighbor has put a fence up or because the neighbor's dog is running free, or a defendant in a criminal trial. However, the likelihood of any case reaching the Supreme Court is minimal for a number of reasons. First, the Court may not have jurisdiction over the case. Second, the case may not involve matters of law having significant social import to be considered by the Supreme Court. Third, the cost of appealing a case to the Supreme Court may run into the five-figure range and take anywhere from two to five years before the final decision, even if the case is accepted. Fourth, the case would probably be finally decided in a state court having jurisdiction over the matter.

The Supreme Court has jurisdiction to grant certiorari in cases arising in state courts only when all remedies in the state judicial process have first been exhausted. Thus, an individual who is tried for a crime on a state level may not seek certiorari to the Supreme Court until the entire appellate process available to him in the state has been exhausted and then only if the case involves a substantial federal question. In the case of state criminal trials, this usually means it must involve a question of federal constitutional procedures invoked by the police or the courts.

The Decision-Making Process

The Supreme Court tends to follow certain guidelines both in selecting the cases it will hear and in deciding those matters that have been selected. These rules have become known as the Doctrine of Judicial Restraint. They are guidelines that tend to restrict the types of cases selected and the bases on which decisions will be made. It is important to note these principles in order to fully comprehend the operations and motivations of the Supreme Court. Several of the rules have already been mentioned; specifically, that in any case for which review is sought in the Supreme Court, it must be shown that all available state remedies have been exhausted before the Court will take jurisdiction; and second, that the Court will only consider those cases that raise a substantial federal question that may have social import for the country.

The Supreme Court does not give advisory opinions. There must be an actual case or controversy involving parties on opposing sides of a legal issue before the Court will decide a case. They will not, for example, give an opinion to Congress as to whether proposed legislation might or might not be constitutional. As a corollary rule, the Supreme Court will not take the jurisdiction of moot cases. The case must be one in which the issue still has some direct impact on the parties involved. Only an individual or group having a direct interest in the outcome of the case has standing to seek review by the Supreme Court. One who does not have any personal involvement in the case or controversy would not be permitted to pursue this appellate procedure.

There is a presumption of constitutionality for every statute that is passed either by a state legislature or by Congress. The Court will make every effort to hold a statute constitutional when the statute is attacked on that basis, and wherever possible, the Supreme Court will decide a case on other than constitutional grounds, thus avoiding wholesale constitutional interpretation when that is unnecessary. If the Court finds that it lacks jurisdiction in the case or that the appealing party may not have exhausted all state remedies available to him, they will decide the case based on these procedural matters without mention of the constitutional issue involved. Constitutional issues are decided only when absolutely necessary.

The Supreme Court, like most other appellate courts, attempts to adhere to the principle of *stare decisis*. Although the Court is not bound to follow its own prior decisions, it is a fundamental principle of Anglo-Saxon law that past decisions will be followed if they are equitable and just wherever possible. The purpose of this is to attempt to maintain uniformity and simplification in legal matters. The Court will, however, drastically depart from *stare decisis* when it feels that precedence in a particular matter is no longer a socially acceptable solution or fails to guarantee the principle of fairness upon which our judicial system is based.

The Supreme Court, like all courts and all institutions devised by man, is subject to error. Occasionally, the Court has second thoughts about the wisdom of a decision. When this happens, several alternatives are available. The Court may await another case raising the same issue of law to reach them. In this instance, it may decide to reverse its decision in a prior case, thereby breaking with the doctrine of *stare decisis*. It may also decide to reconsider a case in which a decision has already been reached and possibly announced. The Court has been known to totally reverse itself on the same case.

Notwithstanding the separation of powers concept and the belief that courts do not make laws, it is somewhat unrealistic and academic to believe that lawmaking does not occur whenever the court renders a decision. Every constitutional interpretation, every declaration of statutory constitutionality or unconstitutionality makes law in the broadest sense of the word. It is true that courts do not enact laws in the same manner as legislatures and the Congress, but the impact of court decisions does set standards of social and legal policy.

Administering the Federal Judiciary

The authority of the Supreme Court to establish policy in state criminal courts is limited to the impact of its decisions interpreting the due process clause of the Fourteenth Amendment. The Court's authority is much more extensive over the federal judiciary than over that of the states because the Supreme Court serves also as the rule-making body of that system. The Court can, through the process of reviewing lower federal court decisions coming to them on appeal, establish guidelines in matters of criminal procedure that do not necessarily involve constitutional interpretation. The Court's decision in *McNabb v. United States* clearly enunciated this authority.

> In the view we take of the case, however, it becomes unnecessary to reach the Constitutional issue pressed upon us. For, while the power of this Court to undo convictions in state courts is limited to the enforcement of those "fundamental principles of liberty and justice" which are secured by the Fourteenth Amendment, the scope of our reviewing power over convictions brought here from the federal courts is not confined to ascertainment of Constitutional validity. Judicial supervision of the administration of criminal justice in the federal courts implies the duty of establishing and maintaining civilized standards of procedure and evidence. Such standards are not satisfied merely by observance of those minimal historic safeguards for securing trial by reason which are summarized as "due process of law" and below which we reach what is really trial by force.[1]

Thus, the Court held that a confession obtained from the defendant was inadmissible, not because it violated constitutional standards but because it felt that lower federal courts must be held to enforcing a more restrictive standard than that imposed by the Constitution and in compliance with federal law.

[1] 318 U.S. 332 (1943).

The Supreme Court and the Criminal Justice System

In the area of criminal procedure, the Supreme Court's rulings in the past few decades have evoked extensive criticism. It is often difficult yet absolutely essential to understand the manner in which Supreme Court decisions come to apply to the daily activities of those involved in the criminal justice system.

The Court's function is to construe and interpret the Constitution. The rulings of the Court take precedence over all other state and federal laws. But the protections that are afforded by the Constitution are only minimum protections that the federal government and the governments of the sovereign states must afford to their citizens. The fact that they are only minimum protections must continually be stressed. These are not maximum protections to which citizens are entitled. Every federal court is free to place more stringent requirements upon the agents of government (within the parameters of the rules set forth by the Supreme Court under its supervisory powers), and every state court and legislature can do the same. This is one reason that the application of a Supreme Court decision on a local level by state courts often appears to be totally disproportionate to the mandates of the Court's opinion. The states do have the right to extensively enhance the protections to the people.

A second reason for the apparent lack of similarity between the Court's pronouncements and the application of those decisions in state courts is clearly a problem of understanding the guidelines set forth in the opinions of the Court. Local and state courts are not to be held totally responsible for this dilemma. Even the most capable Supreme Court justices have not been particularly noted for their writing abilities. Thus, "cloudy" language can sow the seeds of controversy and misunderstanding which, in turn, often lead to misapplication of the law. The following anonymous quote is a good illustration and summary of this problem: "I know that you believe you understand what you think I said, but I am not sure you realize that what you heard is not what I meant."

Clarification is perhaps in order regarding a point of confusion and irritation to those not trained in the law. Most people are of the impression that when the Supreme Court decides a criminal case in favor of the defendant, the defendant "goes free," never again to be touched by the long arm of the law for that same forbidden act. This is a misconception, for the Supreme Court has no authority to make a final determination of any case in which it reviews judgments from state courts. The Court can only decide the federal issue on which the appeal was taken and then send the case back to the state court with directions for the court to proceed with the case *in a manner not inconsistent with the Supreme Court ruling*. This process of returning the case to the state court is called *remand*. The disposition of the case on the state level will be directly affected by the nature of the appeal to the Supreme Court. If the constitutionality of the entire proceeding against the defendant was struck down, the state court may have no alternative but to dismiss the case. On the other hand, if only a portion of the evidence used to convict the defendant was held inadmissible and additional evidence exists by which a conviction might be obtained, the state court may order a new trial in which the "bad" evidence cannot be used. Because it cannot generally be determined to what extent the jury considered the "bad" evidence in reaching its verdict in the initial trial, only a complete new trial with a new jury is acceptable under our system of law.

LOWER FEDERAL COURTS

The federal court system is basically a three-tiered system with the Supreme Court at the apex. The eleven United States Courts of Appeals are the intermediate-level courts, and the bottom of the pyramid consists of a large number of United States District Courts, which are the trial courts in the federal system. There are a number of other specialized courts on the federal level. You will recall that Article III, Section 1, of the Constitution mentions only one supreme court but also states that Congress may from time to time ordain and establish inferior courts (see Figure 9-1).

The United States Courts of Appeals (known as Circuit Courts of Appeals until 1948) and the United States District Courts were essentially established

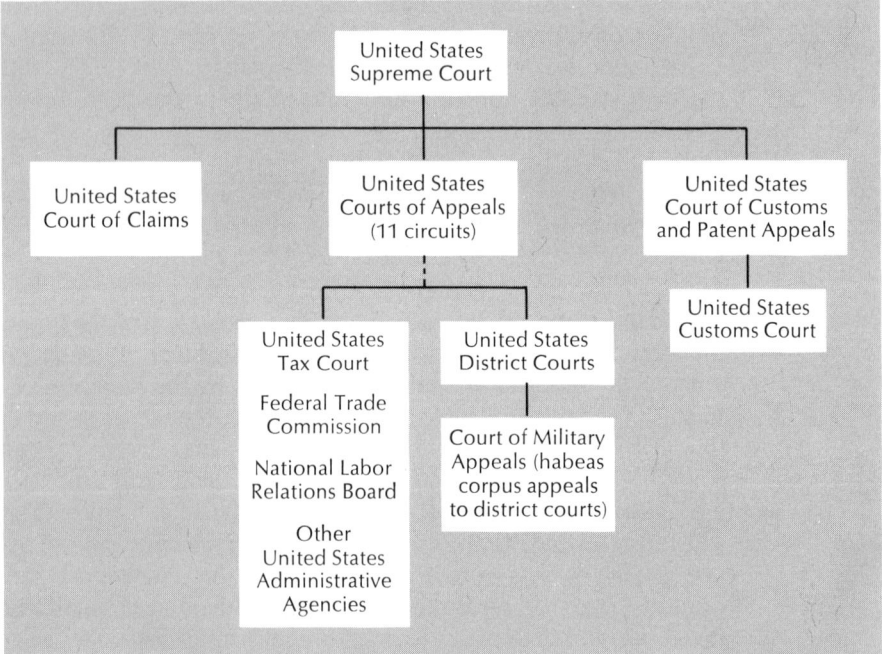

FIGURE 9-1 Federal Court Structure

under the authority of this constitutional article but were created by the Judiciary Act of 1789.

United States Courts of Appeals

The eleven United States Courts of Appeals, located throughout the United States, are each composed of from three to nine judges who are appointed for good behavior. A case in an appeals court may be heard by as few as two judges. Except in cases when the court of appeals has declared a state law to be in opposition to the laws and treaties of the United States or to the federal Constitution—in which case the Supreme Court must hear the appeal—the decisions of the court of appeals are generally final. These courts may be likened to the Supreme Courts of most states in this respect. In most cases in which the court renders decisions, appeals to the Supreme Court are made through the certiorari process.

The appellate jurisdiction of the courts of appeals extends to all federal cases, both civil and criminal, arising from lower federal courts, with three exceptions. First, when a three-judge district court has enjoined the enforcement or operation of a federal or state statute on grounds of unconstitutionality, the appeal goes directly to the Supreme Court and bypasses the court of appeals. The second instance are those cases in which by statute the decision of a district court declares a federal statute unconstitutional and the United States is a party to the act. These must go directly to the Supreme Court for final adjudication. The third instance is upon showing that a case requires immediate settlement because of imperative public importance.

The courts of appeals hear appeals from criminal cases arising through prosecution of federal crimes tried at the district-court level within its geographic jurisdiction. It is not uncommon for cases involving similar legal issues to be appealed to courts of appeals in different circuits and have opposite rulings handed down. To promote uniformity and standardization of federal law, the Supreme Court is often asked either through certiorari or certification to resolve these differences.

United States District Courts

The United States District Courts, some ninety-four strong, are the trial courts of the federal system. The district courts are located throughout the United States and its territories with at least one in each state. The larger states may have three or more districts, each with its own court. The district courts exercise original jurisdiction in noncriminal (civil) actions on patents, copyrights, postal problems, bankruptcy, and civil rights, and in almost all cases arising under the laws and treaties of the federal government and under the United States Constitution. It is in the District Courts that crimes against the federal government are tried. Federal crimes are those that constitute conduct prohibited by the Congress and punishable by the federal government.

United States Magistrates

The United States Magistrates, previously called United States Commissioners, are part of the federal judicial system. They perform on the federal level similar functions as committing magistrates do on the state level. Although the position is often not a full-time job for most of the magistrates, they presently have authority to issue warrants, fix bail, hold preliminary hearings for a determination of probable cause to hold the accused for trial, and to summarily decide guilt or innocence of one accused of minor criminal offenses when the defendant does not wish a trial in the United States District Court.

Other Specialized Federal Courts

There are a number of other courts in the federal system that are more restrictive in the scope of their jurisdiction than are the courts previously discussed. The titles of these courts, for the most part, define their respective specialized functions. These specialized courts are: United States Court of Claims (financial suits against the United States), United States Court of Customs and Patent Appeals, Tax Court of the United States, United States Customs Court, and the United States Court of Military Appeals. See Figure 9-1.

STATE AND LOCAL COURTS

As noted earlier, it is an impossible task to attempt a uniform explanation of state and local systems. The variances in functions, jurisdiction, and even titles are so great that no simple statement can have universal acceptance. Nevertheless, an attempt must be made to generalize. The court system in a particular state may consist of two, three, four, or more levels of courts. (See Figure 9-2, which shows how these levels may parallel the levels of the federal court system.) Where the levels are fewer, the functions and jurisdiction of each level may be broader.

Court of Last Resort

Each state does have one highest appellate tribunal that serves as its court of last resort on issues of state law. The term *Supreme Court* is avoided in this context because of variances in titles among the states. For example, the court of last resort is called "Court of Appeals" in the District of Columbia, Kentucky, Mary-

	State Court System	Federal Court System
Level 4	Court of Last Resort "Supreme Court" "Court of Criminal Appeals" "Supreme Court of Appeals" "Supreme Judicial Court," etc.	Court of Last Resort U.S. Supreme Court
Level 3	Intermediate Appellate Courts "Superior Court" "District Court of Appeals" "Appelate Court" "Supreme Court," etc.	Intermediate Appellate Courts U.S. Courts of Appeals
Level 2	Trial Courts (courts of general jurisdiction) "Circuit Court" "District Court" "State Court" "County Court," etc.	Trial Courts U.S. District Courts
Level 1	Lower Courts (courts of limited jurisdiction) "Municipal Court" "Justice of the Peace" "Small Claims Court" "Traffic Court" "Magistrate's Court," etc.	Lower Courts U.S. Magistrates and Specialized Courts

FIGURE 9-2 Parallels Between State Court Systems and the Federal Court System
Source: Harold J. Vetter, and Clifford Simonsen, *Criminal Justice in America: The System, the Process, the People* (Philadelphia: W. B. Saunders Co., 1976), p. 161.

land, and New York. "Supreme Court" is used by many states. Other titles used throughout the nation include: "Supreme Court of Appeals," "Supreme Court of Errors," "Supreme Judicial Court," and "Court of Criminal Appeals."

The court of last resort has final authority over issues of law within its state. Only in those rare instances (compared to the total criminal caseload handled by all states' appellate courts) where issues of federal law or federal constitutional principles are at stake can a case go beyond this court. The Constitution does not guarantee the right of an accused to appeal his case but all states have provided machinery for appeals and some have legislatively granted one guaranteed appeal to an appropriate court. With that exception, the court of last resort usually has discretionary power to choose the cases it will hear. The writ of certiorari is used in state court systems for this purpose as it is used by the United States Supreme Court.

Intermediate Appellate Courts

This level of courts, in those states that utilize this system, serves often as the final stage in most criminal cases. Except in cases where the court of last resort grants certiorari or is required by law to hear an appeal, the decisions of the intermediate appropriate court stand as law. In states having more than one court on this level, differences in legal decisions are settled by the high court of the state.

It should be noted here again that a generic description of these courts is used to avoid confusion. Many different titles are used. "Superior Court," "District Court of Appeals," "Appellate Court," and "Supreme Court" are just a few of the titles applied to intermediate appellate courts.

Trial Courts

Trial courts, sometimes referred to as courts of general jurisdiction, are not the lowest-level courts operating in the states, but they are the basic-level tribunal having original jurisdiction in most serious criminal cases. They may also be known by various names, often depending on the area covered by their territorial jurisdiction. Those courts covering only one county may be titled "County Courts." Multicounty trial courts may be known as "Circuit Courts," "Superior Courts," "District Courts," or "State Courts."

The subject matter under the jurisdiction of trial courts is usually only restricted in the case of petty offenses, jurisdiction over which may be given to a lower court under the laws of a particular state. Trial courts may, in addition to their original jurisdiction, have appellate jurisdiction over certain lower-court proceedings.

Courts of general jurisdiction are generally the lowest state-level court of record. Most cases heard by an appellate court are decided upon oral arguments of the attorneys representing the parties and upon the record of the proceedings made in the lower appellate and trial courts. This record, of course, is the transcript of the proceedings made by a court reporter. Some of the lower courts, particularly those operating only on a county or municipal level, do not transcribe their proceedings and are not courts of record. The consequence of all this is that when an appeal is taken from one of these courts, the court having appellate jurisdiction must hold a new trial (witnesses, jury where applicable, and the whole works) because there is nothing else upon which to base a decision. This new or second trial is called a trial *de novo*.

THE LOWER COURTS

The lower courts, some 12,500 strong, are courts of limited and special jurisdiction. They exist in rural as well as urban areas of the states. They most often serve as the entry point for those who become involved in the processes of adjudication in the criminal justice system. For those millions of Americans who are arrested for minor offenses, including traffic violations, these lower courts serve as the only contact with the judiciary. Ninety percent of all criminal cases are heard in these lower courts. Historically, the lower courts are most important to the criminal justice system because of sheer number of cases handled. They are also the portion of the American judicial system most visible to the public. It is in these courts also that employees of the criminal justice system perform most of their judicial functions. Yet these same courts function under deplorable conditions. The crisis is not new. For over a century, scholars, judges, study commissions, and others have stressed the importance of the lower courts and the need for reform.

Shortcomings of Lower Courts

Certainly, there are notable exceptions, but for the most part these courts operate under the pressures of impossible case loads, inadequate facilities, and untrained personnel. Formal procedures for the conduct of criminal proceedings are rarely, if ever, followed; little effort goes into preparation for trials or hearings, rules of evidence are ignored; and there generally exists an air of indifference to the principles of fairness, equality, and dignity usually attributed to a judicial setting.

The first-time observer is flabbergasted by the lack of concern for people and their problems exemplified in most lower courts, to say nothing of individual rights. New police officers find it hard to believe that they must also serve as prosecutors in their own cases. All criminal justice personnel are frustrated by the proceedings in these courts. There is very little in the process that instills respect for the system of criminal justice in the eyes of defendants, witnesses, criminal justice personnel, or observers. The following descriptive observations are taken from the 1967 report on the courts by the National Crime Commission in their discussion of lower courts:

> *Initial Presentment.* Following arrest, the defendant is initially presented in court, often after many hours and sometimes several days of detention. In theory the judge's duty is to advise the defendant of the charges against him and of his rights to remain silent, to be admitted to bail, to retain counsel or to have counsel appointed, and to have a preliminary hearing. But in some cities the defendant may not be advised of his right to remain silent or to have counsel assigned. In others he may be one of a large group herded before the bench as a judge or clerk rushes through a ritualistic recitation of phrases, making little or no effort to ascertain whether the defendants understand their rights or the nature of the proceedings. In many jurisdictions counsel are not assigned in misdemeanor cases; even where lawyers are appointed, it may not be made clear to the defendant that if he is without funds he may have free representation. . . . The judges have little time to give detailed consideration to the question of bail. Little is known about the defendant other than the charge and his prior criminal record. The result is that bail is based on the charge instead of on the circumstances of each case; high money bonds are almost invariably set by established patterns, and large numbers of defendants are detained.
>
> *Disposition.* The initial appearance is also the final appearance for most defendants charged with misdemeanors or petty offenses. While those who can afford to retain

counsel are released on bond to prepare for trial at a later date or to negotiate a disposition, a majority of defendants plead guilty immediately, many without advice of counsel. Pleas are entered so rapidly that they cannot be well considered. The defendant is often made aware that if he seeks more time, his case will be adjourned for a week or two and he will be returned to jail.

Trial. An observer in the lower criminal courts ordinarily sees a trial bearing little resemblance to those carried out under traditional notions of due process. There is usually no court reporter unless the defendant can afford to pay one. One result is an informality in the proceedings which would not be tolerated in a felony trial. Rules of evidence are largely ignored. Speed is the watchword. Trials in misdemeanor cases may be over in a matter of 5, 10, or 15 minutes; they rarely last an hour even in relatively complicated cases. Traditional safeguards honored in felony cases lose their meaning in such proceedings; yet there is still the possibility of lengthy imprisonment or heavy fine. . . . In some cities trials are conducted without counsel for either side; the case is prosecuted by a police officer and defended by the accused himself.

Sentence. Most defendants convicted in the lower criminal courts are sentenced promptly. Usually there are no probation services or presentence investigations. Unless the defendant has an attorney who has taken time to inquire into his background, little will be known about him. Sentence may be based on the charge, the defendant's appearance, and the defendant's response to such questions as the judge may put to him in the few moments allotted to sentencing. . . . Short jail sentences of one, two, or three months are commonly imposed on an assembly line basis. A defendant's situation can hardly be considered individually. When a defendant is fined but is unable to pay, he may be required to work the penalty off at the rate of $1 to $5 for each day spent in jail.

Petty Offenses. The conditions described above are found in more aggravated form in lower courts which handle petty offenses. Each day in large cities hundreds of persons arrested for drunkenness or disorderly conduct, for vagrancy or petty gambling, or for prostitution are led before a judge. Among the defendants are slum dwellers who drink in public and young men who "loiter" on street corners or "fail to move on" when ordered to do so. Typically, they have no private place to go, no money to spend, and no family or lawyer to lend them support.

Judges sometimes seem annoyed at being required to preside in these courts. Defendants are treated with contempt, berated, laughed at, embarrassed, and sentenced to serve their time or work off their fines. Observers have sometimes reported difficulty in determining what offense is being tried in a given case, and instances have come to light in which the disposition bears little relationship to the original charge.[2]

As noted earlier, the structure, functioning, and jurisdiction of these lower courts is so diversified that no system can be described as being typical, but the problems faced in and by lower courts seem to prevail whether these courts be part of a state system or supported and operated entirely on a local level. The problems are frequently aggravated rather than ameliorated by attempts to establish new courts with limited, specialized jurisdiction. One lower court is relieved of its jurisdiction over traffic offenses by the establishment of a traffic court, but as

---

[2] The President's Commission on Law Enforcement and the Administration of Justice, *Task Force Report: The Courts* (Washington, D.C.: U.S. Government Printing Office, 1967), pp. 30–31.

population increases, the caseloads of both courts again reach the point of unmanageability. Beyond that, the problems relating to lack of procedure, inadequate facilities, and untrained personnel still run rampant regardless of structure.

Insufficient numbers of personnel to handle the overbearing caseload contributes a great deal to the crowded dockets in lower courts. Not only judges, but prosecutors, defense attorneys, and probation officers, are in short supply. Those working in the courts have an impossible task. In 1964, three Atlanta municipal judges disposed of more than 70,000 cases.[3] In many of the courts facing similar problems, clearing the dockets becomes a prime objective. People end up being the ultimate losers. Cases get dismissed, guilty pleas that should not be are entered, plea bargaining is prevalent, facts are relegated to a level of secondary importance, and the rights of individuals are often not even recognized, much less protected.

The lack of sufficient numbers of people working in the lower courts is far from being the only problem. Those who do staff the courts are often unqualified, untrained, and show little concern. Many courts do not require the presiding judges to be lawyers. Yet, as in the case of many justices of the peace, they have the power to issue arrest and search warrants, fix bail, conduct preliminary hearings to determine if sufficient evidence exists to hold one accused of a crime for trial, and to summarily try and dispose of petty offenses when the defendant does not desire a jury trial. Even coroners, where they are still used, may not be required to be physicians. They have to hold inquests, a quasijudicial proceeding designed to investigate unnatural and suspicious deaths to determine whether a criminal agency caused the death.

Many states have abrogated the coroner system partially or entirely in favor of medical examiners, professionals trained in medico-legal aspects of death investigation. Their function lies entirely outside the judicial arena except insofar as they investigate unexplained or criminal deaths and report their findings to the appropriate authorities. The importance of the contributions made to the field of criminal justice by medical examiners and those specially trained in forensic pathology can never be overemphasized. Unfortunately, detailed coverage of these services are beyond the scope of this text.

The lower courts serve as a training ground for new, inexperienced prosecutors, public defenders, and legal aid attorneys. They gain their courtroom experience and are then promoted out of the lower courts up to the handling of felony cases in the courts of general jurisdiction. Many defense attorneys who practice only in the lower courts often fail to prepare cases adequately, give poor representation to their clients, and often are more interested in making money than in providing legal counsel. Those who are dedicated are poorly paid. The presence of probation officers assigned to the lower courts is a rarity except in some of the larger jurisdictions. Where probation services are used, it is not uncommon to find poorly trained and unqualified personnel performing these functions.

[3] *Ibid.*, p. 31.

The fee system also is one major handicap to the effective operations of lower court judicial administration. Justices of the peace in many states still are paid by a fee based on the number of cases handled, the number of convictions obtained, or a percentage of the revenue collected. Needless to say, the impartiality of the judiciary becomes questionable under this type of system. Although the fee system is still used, many states have abolished it and have placed all judges on salary.

The lower courts are faced with the same problems of administration as are higher courts. Administering the judiciary is no easy task. It takes time and talent. Setting dockets, assigning cases, and keeping records all decrease the amount of time a judge has for performing his judging functions. With the heavy volume of cases faced by the lower courts, this deficiency is even more pronounced than it is in courts of general jurisdiction or in appellate courts.

As deplorable as conditions in the lower courts are, the situation is not hopeless. We will discuss the efforts being made to reform the courts in Chapter 11.

JUVENILE COURTS

Juvenile courts deserve special mention at this point because they have received special attention from the higher courts over the past decade. Although juvenile courts generally fall within the broad definition of lower courts, they are usually discussed and treated in a different manner. Facilities are often better, caseloads are not so burdensome, and personnel are usually better trained and qualified. Since the advent of the first juvenile court in Cook County, Illinois, in 1899, every state has adopted some form of juvenile court system. Juvenile courts are designed to handle and dispose of cases involving juveniles in a manner more akin to treatment, with the welfare and the best interests of the child always of primary importance.

With the advent of the juvenile court system, a whole new vocabulary developed within the framework of criminal justice. Among the terms that gained popularity in this context were *petition* instead of complaint, *summons* instead of warrant, *initial hearing* instead of arraignment, *findings of involvement* instead of conviction, and *disposition* instead of sentence.

A juvenile is defined by chronological age limitations, but not all states agree what that age should be. Because each state is free to define and interpret its own juvenile court laws, many variations exist. The ages range from a child under fifteen years to one who has not yet reached his nineteenth birthday at the time he commits a prohibited act. Several states have taken the initiative in trying to treat rather than punish youths by creating Youth Aid Authorities, which deal with the child until he is twenty-one.

Even though all states have a juvenile court system, the makeup of the court may vary from area to area within the same state. This is dictated by population and economic factors. In the densely populated urban and suburban areas, there may be a separate staff, buildings, and other facilities serving as the juvenile court.

The court may be composed of one or more judges whose sole function is to serve in juvenile matters. In the less densely populated rural areas of the state, the court may work out of the same facilities and share the staff of other county offices. In fact, the judge may wear two or more hats. He may serve as the judge of one or more courts in the county and also serve as the juvenile judge. As a result, the quality of juvenile justice may vary greatly from one area of the state to another.

Jurisdiction

Juvenile courts generally have jurisdiction over four basic types of situations:

Delinquency—conduct engaged in by a juvenile that, if committed by an adult, would violate the penal laws of the state. Delinquency then is a "crime" committed by a juvenile.

Dependency—conduct usually committed by the parents or guardian of a juvenile which deprives the juvenile of the basic necessities of life. Dependency often involves situations where the parent or guardian is unable, although willing, to provide the basic necessities.

Neglect—cases of crimes committed against juveniles including situations of abused children, abandoned or homeless children. Neglect cases usually involve situations where the parent or guardian voluntarily does not wish to provide the basic necessities of life for the juvenile.

Status Offenses—a group of offenses which are directed specifically at juveniles and which would not be offenses were they to involve adults. This category includes such things as truancy and runaways. In 1974 Congress passed an amendment to the Safe Streets Act called the Juvenile Justice Delinquency Prevention Act which earmarked monies to address problems in the juvenile justice system. The priorities of the Law Enforcement Assistance Administration in administering this act have been directed at efforts to divert status offenders from juvenile court jurisdictions so that no stigma of court action attaches.

Not every child adjudged a delinquent is in fact delinquent. Most states have facilities in which delinquent children may be housed. As a matter of fact, any child adjudged a delinquent and not put on probation must be housed at these facilities. However, there is a glaring shortage of facilities and foster homes for dependent children. The facilities for delinquent children are not required to accept, house, feed, or clothe a dependent child. If there are no facilities available at the time a dependent child comes to court, the judge is in a dilemma. Some judges have chosen to classify dependent children as delinquents so that the children will have the basics of life. This abuse is decried, but until funding for juvenile courts is more adequate, the practice will continue.

Philosophy

Juvenile courts have operated, until recently, under a philosophy that their function was treatment and rehabilitation to prevent the youthful offender from involving himself in activities that would lead him into a life of crime in his adult years. Juvenile court proceedings were treated as civil in nature, not requiring all the constitutional safeguards of a criminal trial. This philosophy was called the doctrine of *parens patriae,* meaning that the court would act with the welfare of the child as its only goal. Recent court decisions have drastically affected the *parens patriae* concept as it applies to delinquency cases. Prior to these court decisions, the hearing in delinquency cases was conducted in an informal atmosphere. The hearing was attended by the child, the judge, the parents, and a juvenile counselor or caseworker, if one had been assigned to the case. No emphasis was placed on adhering to strict rules of evidence. The juvenile was entitled to have an attorney represent him if he wanted one but the court was under no obligation to afford the youth the services of legal counsel. The object of the hearing was to determine what happened, why it happened, and how to best dispose of the case in the interest of the juvenile. Disposition of the case could take any number of forms, ranging from dismissal to mild reprimand to committal to a boys' or girls' school. If the case came before the court on referral from a police officer, he, too, was present to disclose the circumstances surrounding his contact with the juvenile.

Due Process

Prior to 1966, the United States Supreme Court had reviewed few cases dealing with constitutional protections for juveniles. But, in that year, in the case of *Kent v. United States,* the Supreme Court stated that the *parens patriae* philosophy of the juvenile court was not an invitation to procedural arbitrariness.[4] This remark set the stage for the 1967 decision of *In re Gault.*[5] Among other points decided in the *Gault* case, the Supreme Court said that a juvenile was entitled to counsel, had the right to cross-examination and confrontation, and was permitted to invoke the self-incrimination privilege. This, of course, has unquestionably formalized the proceedings in juvenile courts, and it would now be more difficult to say that the hearing is civil in nature. With all the safeguards now provided, the hearing takes on the aura of a criminal trial.

The Supreme Court also found, in the *Gault* case, that the term *delinquency* had lost its intended function of preventing the stigma of criminality from attaching to the offender. Instead, the term had taken on a new meaning, a meaning that equated delinquency with criminality, juvenile delinquent with criminal. Also, the court recognized that some youths were being locked up in state youth facilities for longer periods of time than they could have served had they been convicted in adult courts with all the constitutional safeguards. This seemed incongruous and unfair. For these and other reasons, children were given many of the same rights as adults in court proceedings. Subsequent cases continue to show the development of a trend toward providing juveniles due process standing equal to their

[4] 383 U.S. 541 (1966).
[5] 387 U.S. 1 (1967).

adult counterparts. As yet, the transition is not complete. In a 1970 case, the Supreme Court held that due process requires, in a delinquency hearing, the prosecution to prove every fact necessary to establish the juvenile's delinquency "beyond a reasonable doubt."[6] This is the same degree of proof needed to convict an adult offender. Conversely, the Court in a 1971 case said that due process does not require an alleged delinquent be extended the right of trial by jury.[7]

The *Gault* decision and companion cases have not drastically affected the operations of juvenile courts in matters of dependency, neglect, or status offense cases. Once the court acquires jurisdiction over the parents, it may dispose of the case in a manner best suited to the welfare of the child. The *parens patriae* concept still operates in these instances.

Very often, in a dependency matter the child is taken from the parent or parents and placed in a foster home or committed to a state agency for placement until disposition of the case. The social worker in the case investigates the petition or complaint to determine the facts. The facts are presented by the social worker in a hearing. The judge and the parents are present at the hearing. Because this is basically a noncriminal proceeding to determine what would be best for the welfare of the child, the right to counsel has not yet been guaranteed in such hearings. If the parents have the means, they can be represented by counsel. After all sides are heard, the judge makes a disposition on the basis of the facts.

Dispositions

The court can usually do one of three things. First, it can determine that the facts do not warrant any action against the parents. In this case, the court removes the child from the foster home, returns the child to the custody of the parents, and dismisses the petition. Second, the court can find that, although the facts do not warrant permanently removing the child from parental custody, the child does require some supervision by the court. In this situation, the court will return the child to the custody of his parents but will retain jurisdiction by having a social worker periodically check on the child and his environment. Finally, the court may determine that extreme measures are warranted. In this case, custody of the child is taken away from the parent or parents and is assumed by the state. The child is not eligible for adoption, however, unless and until the parents consent of their own free will. The parents can, at a later time, petition the court to regain custody of the child. If the court deems that the circumstances have changed sufficiently to warrant returning custody to the parents, the court will remove the child from the foster home and place the child in his natural home. Very often, the parents are placed on probation. In any event, the welfare of the child and not the parents is paramount.

---

[6] *In re Winship,* 397 U.S. 358 (1970).
[7] *McKeiver v. Pennsylvania,* 403 U.S. 528 (1971).

SUMMARY

A dual court system exists in this country. The federal system is three-tiered, consisting of the Supreme Court at the apex, eleven courts of appeals in the middle, and the district courts at the lower, trial level. State courts, on the other hand, are organized in many different ways. There is no universality of structure. However, it is in state court systems, particularly in the lower courts, where most criminal justice cases are heard. The lower courts in the state systems are usually the entry point and most often the only contact the majority of the citizens have with the courts, and yet these courts have often been criticized for their impossible caseloads, inadequate facilities, and untrained personnel. Too often, formal procedures for the conduct of criminal proceedings are not followed and little effort goes into preparation for trials or hearings. Rules of evidence are often ignored and there generally exists an air of indifference to the principles of fairness, equality, and dignity usually attributed to a judicial procedure.

Juvenile courts generally have jurisdiction over four basic types of situations—delinquency cases, dependency, neglect, and status offenses. This latter group of offenses are those such as truancy and runaways which are specifically directed at juveniles and which would not be offenses were they to involve an adult. The Juvenile Justice Delinquency Prevention Act of 1974, a part of the programmatic responsibilities of the Law Enforcement Assistance Administration, is directing its efforts at diverting status offenders from juvenile courts. In delinquency cases, the Supreme Court has, since the middle 1960s, been developing a posture of granting many due process guarantees to juveniles in juvenile court proceedings.

LEARNING EXERCISES

Issues to Be Discussed

1. The operations of local state courts have often been described as confused, chaotic, disorganized, and unfair to defendents. Examine the literature or visit a local court and develop a short paper which reflects your views of the current problems of a local court.
2. Describe what is meant by the statement that the Supreme Court is a political entity.
3. Describe some of the more patent shortcomings of lower courts.
4. Discuss the rationale behind the development of due process guarantees in juvenile courts.

Group Activity

Create two panels from members of the class to discuss the issue regarding the handling of juveniles in the future. Should the concept of *parens patriae* prevail or should juveniles involved in more serious crimes be treated more like adults with the adult concepts of due process increasingly applied?

Field Activity

Continuing the individual notebook, prepare a 300-word analysis of your visit to any level court in your community. Describe the level of its activities and outline how individual cases were handled as your study of court procedure. This exercise covers a description of actual court operations. Under Issues to Be Discussed, the aim is to critically analyze the weaknesses and strengths of the system. One or two visits would suffice to address both of the exercise requirements.

Key Terms

Appeal
Certification
Certiorari
Court
Disposition

Initial presentment
Parens patriae
Stare decisis
Status offenses

SUGGESTED REFERENCES

ARTHUR, LINDSAY, AND GAUGER, WILLIAM A. *Disposition Hearings: The Heartbeat of the Juvenile Court.* Reno, Nev.: National Council of Juvenile Court Judges, 1974.

BAILEY, F. L., AND ROTHBLATT, H. *Fundamentals of Criminal Advocacy.* Rochester, N.Y.: Lawyers Cooperative, 1974.

BLUMBERG, ABRAHAM S., ed. *The Scales of Justice.* New Brunswick, N.J.: Transaction Books, 1973.

CALIFORNIA COMMISSION ON PEACE OFFICER STANDARDS AND TRAINING. *The Impact of Social Trends on Crime and Criminal Justice.* A Project S.T.A.R. publication. Published jointly by W. H. Anderson Publishing Co., Cincinnati, and Davis Publishing Co., Santa Cruz, Calif., 1976.

DORSEN, NORMAN, AND FRIEDMAN, LEON. *Disorder in the Court.* New York: Pantheon, 1973.

FOX, VERNON. *Handbook for Volunteers in Juvenile Court.* Reno, Nev.: National Council of Juvenile Court Judges, 1973.

GOLDMAN, SHELDON, AND JAHINGE, THOMAS P. *The Federal Courts as a Political System.* 2nd ed. New York: Harper & Row, 1976.

GRAHAM, FRED P. *The Due Process Revolution.* Rochelle Park, N.J.: Hayden Book Co., 1970.

HENSON, RICHARD A. *Court Administration.* Chicago: American Judicature Society, 1971.

INSTITUTE FOR COURT MANAGEMENT. *Courts and Personnel Systems: A Personnel Administration Handbook.* Denver: Institute for Court Management, 1973.

JACOB, HERBERT. *Urban Justice: Law and Order in American Cities.* Englewood Cliffs, N.J.: Prentice-Hall, 1973.

KALVEN, HARRY, JR., AND ZIESEL, HANS. *The American Jury.* Boston: Little, Brown, 1966.

LEVIN, M. A. *Urban Politics and Criminal Courts.* Chicago: University of Chicago Press, 1977.

NATIONAL ADVISORY COMMISSION ON CRIMINAL JUSTICE STANDARDS AND GOALS. *Courts.* Washington, D.C.: U.S. Government Printing Office, 1973.

———. *Juvenile Justice and Delinquency Prevention.* Washington, D.C.: U.S. Government Printing Office, 1976.

NORTH, ARTHUR A. *The Supreme Court: Judicial Process and Judicial Politics.* New York: Appleton-Century-Crofts, 1966.

PFEFFER, LEO. *This Honorable Court: A History of the Supreme Court.* Boston: Beacon Press, 1965.

PRESIDENT'S COMMISSION ON LAW ENFORCEMENT AND THE ADMINISTRATION OF JUSTICE. *Task Force Report: The Courts.* Washington, D.C.: U.S. Government Printing Office, 1967.

ROSEN, PAUL L. *The Supreme Court and Social Science.* Urbana, Ill.: University of Illinois Press, 1972.

U.S. DEPARTMENT OF JUSTICE, LAW ENFORCEMENT ASSISTANCE ADMINISTRATION. *National Survey of Court Organization.* Washington, D.C.: U.S. Government Printing Office, 1973.

10
The Processes of Criminal Justice

Overview
Pretrial Processes
Trial Processes
Post-trial Processes
Summary
Learning Exercises
Suggested References

OVERVIEW

The criminal justice system is a process with various stations in the system that handle the flow of offenders into, through, and out of the system, beginning with police actions and ending with correctional procedures and a return to society. The initial stage—that is, the point of entry—is exceptionally important since many of the recent court cases have involved actions at this point. Bail procedures, right to counsel, and care of the indigent are matters of concern. The later judicial process involving the courts again is a step-by-step procedure leading to trial or to plea bargaining and to sentencing—all important decisions. There are numerous individuals involved in the judicial process, from the judge and jury members down to the court reporter, each having a distinct role to play in the proceedings. These court proceedings are prescribed and the patterns followed in courts are essentially the same for most state and local courts. The title of this chapter reflects a systemic approach within the operations of criminal justice. Processing a case through the judicial system must begin with an input element and conclude with output. The term *input* as used here refers to the knowledge that a crime has been committed. Most often, this identification of input is the role of the police. The process element is that portion of the flow involving judicial aspects of a case, and output refers to the correctional component.

Input occurs when a crime is committed and its commission is somehow made known. The reporting of crimes can be accomplished in a variety of ways. A crime may be observed by a private citizen who reports its commission to the police; a police officer may observe the commission of a crime; a grand jury may discover the commission of a crime based upon an investigation undertaken of its own initiative; or it may be discovered in a variety of other ways. Regardless of the manner in which a crime is made known, that fact must occur before the criminal justice system even becomes involved. Yet, not all crimes are reported to governmental authorities.

In studies done by the National Opinion Research Center of the University of Chicago for the President's Commission on Law Enforcement and the Administration of Justice in 1965, and by numerous victimization studies conducted in the 1970s by the Law Enforcement Assistance Administration, it is evident that a large number of crimes are never reported; hence, official action cannot be and is not taken. In fact, the surveys reveal that the actual amount of crime in the United States today is several times greater than the amount actually reported and reflected in police statistics. Thus, the first input step in engaging the processes of criminal justice is the reporting of criminal activity to officials charged with the responsibility of formally dealing with crime. (The reader may find the figure on the inside corner of this text useful as a reference for following the processes discussed in this chapter.)

The second and obvious phase of input is the identification of the offender. This may require no effort, as in the case of a crime being committed in the presence of a police officer, or it may take days, weeks, months, or years. In many cases, the offender will never be identified, but unless and until identification is made, the processes of criminal justice will not come into play. Once identification has been made, the processes of criminal justice may commence.

The exact time sequence involving the commission of an offense, the identification of the probable offender, and the initiation of the process can frequently be a crucial legal issue due to the statutes of limitations. These are legislative enactments specifying a length of time after the commission of a crime within which proceedings must be commenced against an offender. Failure to take action within that time period will bar the state from subsequent prosecution. Each state usually has statutes of limitations applicable to all crimes except capital offenses or murder in non-capital-punishment states. The lengths of the statutory provisions may vary but usually specify two or three years. If the processes are not begun within that time, which starts to run at the moment of the commission of the crime, the offender cannot later be prosecuted. The rationale underlying statutes of limitations is that after a period of time, witnesses forget, die, disappear, or otherwise are of little value; evidence is lost or destroyed; and, in general, it becomes a waste of time, effort, and money to attempt to prosecute.

The initiation of process against one identified as the offender is the only thing that can prevent the statute of limitations from running out. Once process is initiated, the time stops running (statute is tolled)—when an indictment is issued by a grand jury, an arrest warrant is issued charging a named person with the crime, or the offender is in custody. It can be seen that the essential ingredient of commencing the processes of criminal justice is identification of one who is believed to be the culprit. Hence, "John Doe" warrants for unknown persons, issued simply on the theory that a crime was committed and that someone must have committed it, are not only worthless for purposes of tolling the statute of limitations but are also totally and unequivocally unconstitutional. On the other hand, if a description of the person exists sufficient to arrest him and satisfy the requirements of the Fourth Amendment of the Constitution but his name is unknown, a "John Doe" warrant describing the suspect is perfectly valid.

PRETRIAL PROCESSES

As may be seen from the preceding paragraphs, arrest may or may not be the first step in the pretrial processes of criminal justice. Depending upon the method by which the existence of a crime and the identification of the offender is made known, an arrest may be preceded by an indictment or presentment issued by a grand jury, based upon information presented to it or discovered after its own investigation, or upon the issuance of an arrest warrant. In some instances, especially those of a less serious nature, an arrest may not occur. Instead, a substitute for arrest in the form of a written summons may serve to initiate the pretrial processes. A summons is a written document that notifies an individual that he has been charged with an offense and orders him to appear in court at a certain time and date to answer the charge. It is a substitute for arrest and, where used, serves as a matter of convenience not only to the police officer but to the citizen as well. It also keeps people from having to spend unnecessary time in jail. Usually, the summons is used only on occasions involving minor offenses, and then only when it appears that there is no risk of the offender not appearing for court. A summons can only be issued if and when a police officer would have the legal authority to arrest the individual instead of issuing the summons.

When an arrest does occur, particularly in the event of serious felonies, it is usually thought of as the initiation of pretrial processes.

Initial Action

Arrest is one of those legal concepts that escapes adequate definition. Many descriptive phrases are offered; all are acceptable; none are entirely accurate or satisfactory. We prefer the following: An *arrest* is the taking of a person into the custody of the law for purposes of answering to a court of law for a crime with which he is charged. Although an arrest must be legally made in order to withstand attacks in court, the legality of the arrest has no direct relationship to the ultimate determination of the guilt or innocence of the accused. Rather, the legality of the arrest depends on whether the arresting officer followed proper procedures in bringing the person into the custody of the law, such as whether he made a warrantless arrest for a crime committed in his presence, or if he had probable cause to believe that the person he is arresting has committed a felony, or whether his arrest warrant, issued by a judge, is valid.

To dispel any myths that persist regarding arrests, it must be noted that physically touching the person to be arrested is not essential to accomplish the arrest. If the person voluntarily submits to the custody of the law, the arrest is accomplished. Only under circumstances when voluntary submission is not forthcoming is physical restraint needed or, for that matter, justified. Force may be used to affect a lawful arrest only to the extent that it is reasonable and necessary.

Following a valid arrest, the alleged offender is taken to the police station, where he is booked. *Booking* is the official recording of the arrest in the records of the agency. At this time, all personal items found on the defendant are inventoried, recorded, and a receipt issued in the presence of the defendant. The accused is given a copy of this receipt and often is asked to sign it indicating his concurrence with the inventory. Booking also involves the recording of the accused's name, address, and other vital statistics, and the charge against him.

As a general rule, most jurisdictions require that the violation of a specific criminal statute be charged against the arrestee. Only a few states still recognize the validity of an "open charge" or a charge of "hold for suspicion of" or "investigation of."

During booking, the defendant is usually photographed (mugged) and fingerprinted. These procedures are conducted to confirm the identification of the arrestee. Then comes his initial incarceration.

If the local court system is functioning with any reasonable degree of efficiency (not necessarily effectiveness, however), the time spent in jail should be relatively short prior to the first appearance of the accused before a judicial officer. Constitutional interpretation and statutory provisions specify that the accused must be brought before a committing magistrate within either a specified or reasonable time.

During initial incarceration, additional investigative work may also be conducted by the police, including interrogations of suspects, interviews of witnesses, crime laboratory analysis and so forth.

First Appearance

The first appearance before a judge may serve one or several functions depending upon local procedure. A prime responsibility of the committing magistrate is to inform the accused of the charge against him and to advise him of certain constitutional rights, including his guaranteed freedom against self-incrimination and his right to have an attorney represent him.

Another significant event that usually occurs during the first appearance is the setting of an amount of bail bond. This is of critical and immediate importance, especially to the defendant.

The bail system in the United States determines whether an accused person in a criminal proceeding will be released or jailed in the period between his arrest and trial. The legal theory underlying this procedure is that the bail will be sufficient to ensure the appearance of the defendant at trial, which is the only way the money will be returned. If he is able to post bond in the bail amount, or pay a bondsman to post it for him, the accused is released. If he is financially unable to make bail, he is detained in jail.

Each year, the freedom of hundreds of thousands of persons charged with crime hinges upon their ability to raise the money necessary for bail. Those who go free on bail are released not because they are innocent but because they can buy their liberty. The balance are detained not because they are guilty but because they are poor. Though the accused be harmless, and have a home, family, and job that make it likely that if released he would show up for trial, he may still be held. Conversely, the habitual offender who may be dangerous to the safety of the community may gain his release.

The belief that a system should condition the accused's liberty solely on the amount of money in his pocket rather than on the likelihood that he will return for trial denies equal justice and interferes with the proper functioning of our criminal process. Bail reform requires careful inquiry into the nature of existing bail practices and the factors that underlie current decisions to release or detain. Experiments are being conducted in many areas seeking ways to diminish unnecessary pretrial detention without impairing the effectiveness of the community's law enforcement efforts.

Right to Counsel

The constitutional application of the Sixth Amendment guarantees of right to counsel were discussed in an earlier chapter but it may be useful to trace the evolution of public defender and legal aid programs.

PUBLIC DEFENDER AND LEGAL AID PROGRAMS

Until 1962, only a few jurisdictions had established community agencies under the titles of public defender or legal aid whose function was to provide free legal assistance in the defense of indigents charged with criminal violations. For the most part, when it was determined by a court that a defendant needed free legal counsel, the judge would generally appoint an attorney in private practice to the defense of the indigent. The attorney was required to provide this legal assistance. This is still a common method of providing defense counsel for indigent defendants. Generally, the judge would appoint a lawyer who happened to be in the courtroom on the day that the determination of indigency was made and, all too often, the attorney in private practice would not devote his full talents to the defense of the person charged with a crime who could not provide payment for his legal services.

The first public defender office created by statute was in Los Angeles in 1911. The public defender is a paid, public official charged with the task of defending indigents accused of crimes. This means that the same sovereignty seeking to prosecute is also providing defense services. Perhaps this illustrates our preoccupation with the concepts of justice, fairness, due process, and our steadfast belief in the presumption of innocence.

The public defender concept did not spread rapidly. But with the case of *Gideon v. Wainwright* in 1962, virtually every jurisdiction was compelled to devise some means for coping with the overwhelming increase in demands on the legal profession.

Organized legal aid began in New York in 1877, when an office was opened and a salaried attorney appointed to give legal assistance to German immigrants. There is a wide network of legal aid societies, in a large part organized and financed through voluntary effort, that provide legal services for the needy. Most are charitable corporations sponsored by the bar association. Usually, they are governed by community-representative boards of directors; a few are tax supported. Service is given by salaried staff and volunteer lawyers in private practice.

Volunteer service committees of local bar associations do operate in smaller communities not served by legal aid and defender offices. By the 1960s, there were more than 230 legal aid offices, about 115 defender offices, and over 125 volunteer service committees of bar associations. There is a National Legal Aid and Defender Association that coordinates and guides the services.

In 1920, the ABA established its first legal aid committee—the Special Committee on Legal Aid Work—which was the predecessor of the present Standing Committee on Legal Aid and Indigent Defendants.

In 1920, few legal aid agencies were operating, and those were financed on a shoestring. In 1921, the Special Committee authorized the previous year became the Standing Committee on Legal Aid Work, and by 1923 sixty-one legal aid offices were established.

To make legal assistance available, many localities began without staff and depended on volunteer services that were far from adequate. Slowly, the agencies were transformed into properly staffed operations, with financial backing from the bar and community.

In 1937, more than a quarter of a century before *Gideon,* the Committee on Legal Aid Work declared their belief that every man accused of a serious crime was absolutely entitled to counsel and that, if he was too poor to employ one, society must furnish one. In 1938, a survey was planned to determine legal aid needs and the ways to meet them.

This survey indeed found a need for legal aid. So, in 1940 a resolution was adopted by the association calling for the establishment of organized legal aid by such method and instrumentality, whether public or private, as may be determined by local conditions, needs, and wishes. The three objectives of the committee were: (1) establishment of civil legal aid and defender services throughout the country; (2) the encouragement of law school instruction on the importance of legal aid; and (3) the study and drafting of legislation to reduce the cost of legal remedies to the poor and to secure protection for them against special abuses.

Financing legal aid was always a major problem. Many lawyers and the country's leading industrial and financial institutions were persuaded to become annual donors to the cause, and their contributions played an important part in the buildup of legal aid.

Although both defender and legal aid programs provide legal counsel in criminal cases, the latter generally provides services of a much broader nature, including in noncriminal areas such as landlord-tenant relationships, automobile liability suits, domestic problems, and the rest of the range of civil problems.

Preliminary Hearing

The preliminary hearing is usually done before a committing magistrate, as is the initial appearance. The preliminary hearing serves a number of functions. These functions may vary depending on the nature and seriousness of the offense. In serious cases (usually felonies), the court's responsibility includes advising the defendant of specified constitutional rights and determining if sufficient probable cause exists to bind the defendant over to an appropriate trial court for trial. *Bind over* is referral of the case to a court with jurisdiction to try the defendant for the offense with which he is charged.

The probable cause hearing has often been looked at as a minitrial. Perhaps it should more accurately be referred to as a semitrial. Its purpose is not to determine whether the defendant is guilty, but rather if the prosecution can produce enough evidence to convince the court that it is more probable than not that the accused did commit the crime and that a trial is justified. The hearing thus serves as a screening device. It should be noted that the defendant has an option of waiving the preliminary hearing and proceeding directly to other pretrial processes at the trial court level. Most defense attorneys recommend against waiver for several reasons. The most important is that the hearing presents another opportunity for the defendant to be freed from the system by a dismissal of the case, resulting from a failure of the prosecution to show sufficient probable cause. A second justification for wanting the hearing is its use to the defense as a tool of discovery. Because the prosecutor must present at least some of the evidence he possesses in support of his case to prove probable cause, the defense may learn a great deal about the state's case: the evidence possessed against the accused and the theory of the case or manner in which the state will seek a conviction when the case comes to trial.

One of the most frequent reasons why one would waive the preliminary hearing is an intent to plead guilty to the crime charged. Because the committing magistrate generally does not have the authority to accept a plea in a felony case, it must be referred to the judge of a trial court anyway. Waiver thus avoids an unnecessary step in the process.

The hearing itself may be brief or extended. As indicated, the purpose is to determine if the prosecution has sufficient evidence to warrant a trial. The state need not present all its evidence or its entire case against the defendant. It is required only to show probable cause (this is called a *prima facie* case). Just as in the proceedings of a full-scale trial, the defense has the right and opportunity to cross-examine witnesses, examine evidence, and otherwise seek to defeat the contentions of the prosecution.

Unlike a trial, the defense usually does not present evidence and witnesses at the preliminary hearing, although it may if it so chooses. The prime function of the defense is to convince the court (the judge; the preliminary hearing is a nonjury proceeding) that the state has not shown probable cause. This accomplishes two things. First, it argues for a dismissal of the case against the defendant, and second, it forces the state into revealing as much of its case as is possible under the circumstances.

In the serious cases, if probable cause is found, the court will remand the defendant to custody or bail and bind the case over for trial. If no probable cause is found, the case against the defendant will be dismissed (at least temporarily). Because the preliminary hearing is a screening device, not a trial, the decision for dismissal is not final or binding nor does jeopardy, the Fifth Amendment prohibition against subjecting a person to being tried twice for the same crime, attach. In most jurisdictions, the prosecutor may file a direct information against the accused even after dismissal at a preliminary hearing. An *information* may be likened to a complaint, but it is filed by the prosecutor rather than the victim. It is used when the state is of the opinion that it does have sufficient evidence to convict in spite of the ruling at the preliminary hearing. The information is filed with the trial court of general jurisdiction.

The procedures followed in a preliminary hearing for a misdemeanor or other minor offenses may be the same as for a felony, with bind over or dismissal. The one basic difference is that for the minor offense the magistrate has the authority to accept a guilty plea or try the case if the defendant chooses to waive his right to trial by jury.

The Grand Jury

The grand jury originated with the process of inquisition whereby those who possessed knowledge of the facts surrounding the case were summoned forward to tell what they knew. It was thus an accusatory proceeding that had its origins around the twelfth century. In order that official action be taken, at least twelve had to agree on the accuracy of the accusation.

Today, a grand jury consists of from one to twenty-three persons. Its purpose is still one of accusation. In this regard, it functions similarly to the committing magistrate by examining facts surrounding a crime and determining if probable cause exists to order an accused held for trial. Sometimes, its jurisdiction overlaps that of the committing magistrate; in some states, it is limited to the most serious offenses, and the magistrate hears the remainder. The grand jury proceedings are secret. The defendant is not permitted to attend. The prosecution only presents its evidence. Confrontation and cross-examination are not recognized guarantees in the hearing. Jurors may ask any questions they wish, but questioning is usually handled by the prosecutor. Unanimity is not required for a decision.

The process by which the state seeks an accusation from a grand jury is called an indictment. If the jury decides there is sufficient evidence, it issues a "true bill." If it finds the allegations are unwarranted, it hands down a "no bill." Jury members are selected in the same manner as are trial jurors, generally from a list of eligible citizens from the community served by the court's jurisdiction.

Grand juries have an additional unique power. In addition to their function as an accusatory body, they are impowered to investigate matters of public interest or other possible infractions of the criminal laws and, if appropriate, seek criminal charges against violators. This investigatory function may be initiated by the jury on its own or at the request of another official or private citizen. The findings of the jury are referred to the presiding judge, under whose supervisions the grand jury functions, in the form of a presentment—a written report with recommendations.

Arraignment

The arraignment is the event occurring at the general trial court level, that formally initiates the trial process. It is the first official occasion at which the accused is given an opportunity to answer the accusation. It is the time when he is required to enter a plea. The arraignment is held in open court and generally begins with a formal reading of the indictment or information by which the accused is again formally advised of the charges against him. He is again advised of his constitutional guarantees of rights to counsel and protection against self-incrimination. He is then asked to answer the charge by entering a plea. The plea may take one of several forms.

He may plead guilty to the crime as charged or to a lesser offense. A plea of guilty to a lesser offense often results from plea bargaining. Although the defense attorney can never ethically tell his client how to plead, he can advise him. If it appears that the state's case against him is so strong that it is unlikely he will be found innocent by going to trial on the original charge, he can attempt, on behalf of the accused, to bargain with the prosecutor to accept a guilty plea in exchange for a reduced charge and save the time and expense to the state of going to trial. More often than not, the prosecutor will accept the offer because it frees him more rapidly to proceed with other important trial matters and also saves the state the expense of a trial. In many locales, as many as 90 percent of the cases are settled in this manner. Once a bargained agreement has been reached, the prosecutor, the defense attorney, and the defendant will go to the judge and ask him to accept the plea of guilty to the lesser charge. They must convince the judge that the defendant of his own initiative desires to so plead and that there has been no plea bargaining (remember that the practice is not officially approved of); that the plea is voluntarily made and that no promises have been made that the sentence would be lighter than if he chose to pursue his constitutional right to trial and was found guilty. If the judge is satisfied that the plea is voluntary and in accord with the true wishes of the accused, he may accept the plea.

A plea of guilty, even to the crime charged in open court, need not be accepted by the judge if he believes that the defendant was coerced into pleading guilty, or does not understand the significance of his plea, or really may not be guilty. If the guilty plea is accepted, the judge then sets a date and time for sentencing. It should be pointed out that under the laws of some states, a trial is required and a plea of guilty may not be accepted in a capital case.

Of course, the accused may plead not guilty, in which case the judge sets a trial date.

In some jurisdictions, the plea of *nolo contendere* is available. *Nolo contendere,* or no contest, is not an admission of guilt but rather a willingness to accept a declaration of guilt rather than go to trial. It is treated as a guilty plea but serves one purpose not served by a guilty plea. In a subsequent civil suit possibly arising out of the same event, a guilty plea is admissible as evidence against the defendant, but a plea of *nolo contendere* is not.

Several additional alternatives are open to the accused depending on the jurisdiction he is in. He may stand mute, say nothing, in which case a plea of not guilty is entered. This plea has the effect of preserving to the defendant the right to contest all irregularities that have occurred up to this point in pretrial stages preceding the arraignment. In some states, a claim of not guilty by reason of insanity is a form of plea, but in others it is a defense to be raised during trial.

Pretrial Motions

Inevitably, if the accused has remained in the system long enough to reach the trial stage, a series of pretrial motions will be the next order of business following arraignment. These motions are usually made by the defense attorney for the purpose of doing all in his power to have the charges dismissed, have evidence possessed by the state declared inadmissible, or find out as much as he can about the state's case in order that he may better prepare his defense. The motion might be for dismissal for lack of evidence possessed by the state, for suppression of evidence based on the claim of an illegal search and seizure, to learn more about the state's evidence, and so forth. The pretrial motions also serve two other purposes. They often delay the trial, which may benefit the defense. More important, they often answer many legal questions and allow the judge to render decisions on matters that, if decided at the time of trial, would be out of the hearing of the jury anyway and would cause additional delay and money. So, motions are also convenient and necessary to the efficient operation of the judicial system.

TRIAL PROCESSES

In every state, the right to trial by jury is provided the accused. He need not take advantage of the right. If he so desires, he may choose to waive his right to a jury trial and instead be tried before a judge. It is in the courts on the trial level that jury trials are usually permitted. The lower courts infrequently provide this protection.

Before commencing an explanation of the progress of a case through trial, it would be worthwhile to first look at the setting and the people involved.

The Setting—Jurisdiction and Venue

The fact that a court has a judge, a place to meet, and officers to enforce its commands does not automatically give that court the power to try a case. The court must have jurisdiction. Without jurisdiction, no court can validly try and sentence a man. Jurisdiction is the power of a court to handle a case. That some courts have power to dispose of some matters and are denied this power in dealing with others is simply a matter of convenience and order established by legislative action and constitutional mandate. There are three components of jurisdiction in criminal cases—territorial, personal, and subject matter.

Territorial jurisdiction simply refers to the proposition that no court of any state can attempt to adjudicate any criminal violation that occurred wholly outside that state and that no state can enforce or adjudicate the criminal laws or violations of any other state or the federal government. Just as the federal courts, as part of a separate sovereignty, are not superior to state courts in most instances, so, state courts are without authority to deal with criminal violations of the federal government or other states. Federal courts dispose of federal crimes. State courts dispose of state criminal violations. It may be interesting to note at this point purely as a statistical reference that state courts and lower courts within the states handle approximately 90 to 95 percent of all cases that reach the courts, and the remainder are disposed of at the federal level.

In order for a court to have jurisdiction over the accused person, the presence of the accused in the courtroom is all that is required. Voluntary appearance and arrest are the two most common methods of insuring his presence, the latter being predominant.

Jurisdiction over the subject matter is also determined by the legislature or prescribed by constitutional authority and is done as a matter of convenience. As was seen in Chapter 9, there are many different types of courts with different responsibilities. These responsibilities, in essence, are defined as subject matter jurisdiction. Only a court with trial jurisdiction in criminal cases can validly dispose of such a case. If any other court attempts to try such a case, the proceedings are totally invalid.

Venue is closely related to territorial jurisdiction. *Venue* is defined as the place where the crime was committed, the particular court having jurisdiction that sits in that locale, and the place (community) from where the jury is selected. Generally, a person has the right to be tried in the locale where the offense took place unless he waives that right. However, he may request a change of venue if he feels he cannot get a fair trial in that place for reasons such as adverse pretrial publicity.

The People Involved

There are numerous individuals who have functional roles in the conduct of any trial. Because procedural regularity is much more prevalent in the trial courts than in the lower courts, where laxness and informality tend to dominate, it is important to briefly review the functions of these individuals.

THE JUDGE

Under our adversary system, the function of the judge is to referee, mediate, and arbitrate the many differences between the prosecutor and the defense attorney. He is the authority on the law and makes determinations as to the admissibility of evidence, the validity of objections, and the determination of what the jury will be allowed to hear. In jury trials, his responsibility is to interpret the law for the jury while leaving them free to decide issues of fact. In nonjury cases, he also assumes the burden of deciding issues of fact, including guilt or innocence.

In carrying out these many roles, the judge has the responsibility for safeguarding both the rights of the accused and the welfare of society while maintaining impartiality at all times. He is responsible for ensuring that dignity and demeanor are kept at the highest level throughout the proceedings and should recuse (excuse) himself anytime there is doubt as to his own ability to impartially preside over a case.

The judge is an extremely powerful figure in the courtroom drama. His decisions on plea negotiations, admissibility of instructions, charging the jury, and sentencing convicted offenders can all dictate the ultimate decision on guilt or innocence and the final disposition of each case. Consequently, the judge who takes seriously his duties of conducting a fair and impartial trial is entitled to the utmost respect in the courtroom.

THE TRIAL JURY

The trial jury, or petit jury as it is sometimes called, serves as the trier of fact. Its responsibility is to weigh the evidence presented by both the prosecution and the defense, decide which is more believable, and determine the guilt or innocence of the accused. A trial jury in criminal cases generally consists of six or twelve members with possibly two alternates, depending on state law. The exact number is set by state statute and constitutional requirement, but there is no magic in the choice. Until recently, unanimity was generally required for either a conviction or acquittal. Inability to reach a unanimous decision resulted in a "hung jury" and a mistrial. Then, the whole trial would have to be reconducted with a new jury. Two recent Supreme Court cases held that unanimity is not constitutionally required and that each state can, by legislative action, allow for decisions to be reached by less than a unanimous verdict.[1]

The right to trial by jury is ingrained in the American judicial structure but its usefulness does not go unquestioned. Those who challenge the system contend that laymen who serve on a trial jury "of our peers" neither serve long enough nor are knowledgeable enough about the problems and functions of the criminal justice system to make decisions that may have quite far-reaching consequences for the defendant. Theoretically, a trial jury is supposed to decide issues of guilt or innocence based on the evidence presented in the case with the additional proviso that it may also consider the demeanor and appearance of witnesses in reaching decisions as to the believability of testimony. But, jury deliberations are held in secret; no one other than jurors may be present during deliberations. Consequently, the true reasons why jurors vote the way they do has always been an in-

---

[1] *Johnson v. Louisiana,* 406 U.S. 356 (1972); and *Apodaca v. Oregon,* 406 U.S. 404 (1972).

triguing question. One may ask a juror after a verdict why he voted a particular way but there is no guarantee of an accurate answer.

As important as is the role played by the trial jury, juries are only used in a small percentage of the cases that go to court. In the majority of criminal cases, the defendant either pleads guilty or the case is plea bargained. Even in those that go to trial, only about half are tried with a jury. Defendants often exercise the option of waiving a jury trial and having the case heard entirely by a judge who then becomes responsible for fact finding as well as deciding issues of law. The choice usually hinges on whether the defendant and his attorney believe they have a better chance of acquittal with a jury or with the judge alone.

Tampering with a jury by attempting to influence a juror's decision is a felony. To avoid this occurrence, in important cases, the jury may be sequestered. Sequestration is a decision by the judge to "lock up" the jury at night in a hotel to avoid any undue influence by friends, family, or the press. Sequestration has been known to go on for weeks or months during a trial. Even if sequestration is not ordered, jurors are instructed not to watch television, listen to radio, or read news accounts of the trial and are further instructed not to discuss the trial with anyone, including members of their families.

WITNESSES

Witnesses have varied personalities, backgrounds, and information, but they all appear in court for the same purpose—to present information of which they have knowledge for the consideration of the court and jury. Their function is not to be biased for or against one side of the case. They are not on the witness stand for the purpose of convicting or acquitting the accused but as impartial bearers of information.

Besides the defendant, witnesses are often in the most uncomfortable and unusual position within the courtroom. Unless the witness is an experienced one (such as a police officer), he often does not know what to expect when he appears in the courtroom. For most witnesses the experience of testifying in court is a relatively infrequent experience. Too often, they are reluctant participants in a courtroom drama. Even the most cooperative witness interviewed at the scene of a crime may feel put out or annoyed by having to appear in court. Too often, trials are scheduled for the convenience of judges and lawyers rather than witnesses and the inconvenience imposed upon witnesses to appear often creates a hardship. A witness may have to leave a business without pay, close down a business for a day or two while waiting to be called to testify, or round up babysitters to watch the children while sitting in the witness room waiting for his name to be called.

A number of studies and experiments have been conducted in recent years attempting to streamline the procedure and make the responsibility of being a witness less inconvenient. Attempts have been made to schedule the appearance of witnesses at an exact date and time so that waiting in the witness room will not be such a long drawn-out chore. Such experiments have proven somewhat successful. Dade County, Florida, and several other locations have attempted to implement similar procedures for calling police officers as witnesses. In this manner, officers are not forced to waste many precious hours of duty time or days off sitting in the witness room waiting to be called.

THE PROSECUTOR

Perhaps the most powerful figure in the entire criminal justice field (not excluding the police officer), the prosecutor often literally holds the power of life and death in his hands. He has much more discretion than any police officer. The decision whether to prosecute a case or to forget it is his. He may *nolle prosequi* (decide not to prosecute at this time) if he feels that the evidence is insufficient to gain a conviction, yet he wishes to hold the case open for further action if and when warranted. He is the individual who represents the state in criminal proceedings. He has the ultimate decision as to the charges brought against the accused. He, in effect, determines which cases will ever reach the courts for adjudication, and he can terminate the processing of any case anywhere within the system. Although he is perhaps the most autonomous individual in the system, he is an elected official, responsible to the people, and if he does not exercise his authority in good faith and in the best interests of the people, he can be replaced at the polls.

The prosecutor, exercising discretion in carrying out his role responsibilities, often experiences a dilemma. His position is one that is a part of the executive branch of government (like that of the police), and he often represents police in matters requiring legal advice, such as the preparation of testimony, the preparation of affidavits and warrants, and determinations as to the legality of police conduct. On the other hand, he is also a representative of the judicial branch of government with the responsibility of ensuring the rights of all the people. In the courtroom the prosecutor is often viewed as a representative of the state seeking a conviction of one charged with violating a criminal act. In theory, his function is not to convict but to ensure that justice is carried out in the best interest of the society he represents as well as to protect the rights of the accused. In actuality, it is known that the prosecutor, being a political animal, sometimes builds his own personal reputation in the furtherance of political goals from convictions obtained, particularly in major trials. Often these varying roles are in conflict with one another and prosecutors are often charged with "political motives" for exercising their vast discretion in a particular manner. In actuality, by virtue of the prosecutor's position, he cannot satisfy everybody all the time.

In a criminal case the prosecutor has the enormous burden of proving the guilt of a defendant beyond and to the exclusion of every reasonable doubt, an enormous burden that requires the state to prove the crime was committed by the defendant to a level which convinces each and every juror of the defendant's guilt.

For every case presented, the prosecutor must decide whether to charge for a specific crime, a lesser crime, or no crime at all. In the latter case, the prosecutor may also direct certain alternatives to prosecution, such as psychological treatment for offenders, or recommend other similar diversionary measures to the court. The prosecutor also plays a major role in plea negotiation cases, the number of which exceed those cases which actually go to court.

THE DEFENDANT

The defendant is the person who has the biggest stake in the outcome of the judicial process, yet, of all the participants, he has the least to do. Of course, the defendant has the right to be present during any and all criminal processes (except the grand jury proceedings). His prime function, however, is to serve as an advisor to his attorney and assist him in the preparation of the defense case.

In his role as an advisor to his defense counsel, the defendant may assist in selection of the jury by advising his attorney of reasons why a particular juror should or should not be accepted during the process of jury selection. He may possess certain information that may sway a particular juror. During the trial the defendant's primary responsibility is to listen to the testimony, observe the evidence, and advise his attorney of any contradictory or additional information which may be of value to his attorney in cross-examining witnesses or in explaining away certain evidence apparently against the defendant's interest.

THE DEFENSE ATTORNEY

Part of the defense attorney's role has already been discussed in the sections on pretrial motions and plea bargaining. Once the case has reached the trial stage, the function of the defense attorney is, by whatever legal, ethical, and tactical means are within his power, to persuade the jury of his client's innocence and of the weaknesses and holes in the state's case. His objective is an acquittal for his client. His tools are objections, cross-examination, closing arguments, and his personality.

At trial the responsibility of the defense attorney is to represent his client to the best of his ability within the bounds of state law and his professional ethics. His code of ethics does not permit him to select the cases he will defend on the basis of his belief in his client's innocence. Rather he has an obligation to provide defense to everyone entitled to legal defense whether guilty or not. He is required to counsel and advise his client but he is not obligated to violate the law by knowingly permitting false evidence or testimony to be delivered in the courtroom. His obligation is to learn all he can of the facts of the case from his client, then prepare the best defense that will appear most beneficial to his client. In doing this, he must cross-examine witnesses for the state and present evidence most beneficial to his client. Unlike the prosecutor who represents the people, the defense attorney represents only his client.

The role of the defense attorney often suffers from conflicting and erroneous images. One need only listen to stories about "ambulance chasers" or "mouthpieces for organized crime figures" to gain a poor impression of defense attorneys.

On the other hand, stories about well-known defense attorneys like F. Lee Bailey, Edward Bennett Williams, and Melvin Belli who are credited with the Perry Mason-type reputations are found at the other extreme. Although there are defense attorneys at both ends of the spectrum, the majority of lawyers who engage in defense practice are truly dedicated to ensuring that a proper job is done and that persons in need of defense services receive the best that can be afforded. The mercenaries and the superheroes are the exception, not the rule, and it is time that the proper role of the defense attorney be recognized for its contribution to maintaining our system of justice in America.

THE BAILIFF

The bailiff is an officer of the court. It is his responsibility to see that order is maintained. He is thus like a sergeant-at-arms. He is also responsible for the security of legalities surrounding the actions of witnesses and jurors. He must see to it that they do not discuss the case when they are not supposed to, that the secrecy of jury deliberations is maintained, and that appropriate accommodations are made for housing and feeding a sequestered jury.

THE COURT CLERK

The man responsible for handling the necessary paper work that accompanies a judicial proceeding is the clerk. He ensures that all files and documents are in order before trial may begin, and generally he is responsible for swearing witnesses before they testify. The clerk is also the individual who reads the indictment or information charging the accused with a crime.

THE COURT REPORTER

In all cases conducted in a court of record, a court reporter is present to record verbatim the proceedings. Some court reporters use a manual method of shorthand to record, but most use a stenographic recorder, which is a mechanical shorthand machine. After each trial or each day of a trial, the shorthand is transcribed and typed in longhand. Court reporters usually get paid based upon the length of the transcript rather than by the case or on a salary. As a consequence, it is not rare to find triple-spaced, wide-margined transcripts. Of course, they are also much easier to read this way.

Selection of the Jury

The selection of the jury can often be the most complex and time-consuming part of any jury trial because it is upon this group of people that both the prosecution and the defense must rely for a favorable decision. Consequently, both must be extremely careful and concerned with their selection of jurors.

A list of names is taken from the roles of eligible voters or taxpayers in the county (methods vary). This list forms the jury panel or *venire.* Veniremen are called to the court to serve on the panel from which the jurors are selected. They may be chosen to serve in criminal or civil cases. The length of service may vary but usually runs for about a week. Of course, if they are selected to sit upon a jury, they serve until that trial is disposed of regardless of duration. Anyone notified of his selection for jury duty is obligated to attend unless he can show cause why he is exempt by statute from jury duty, for example, that he is an attorney. Statutory exemptions vary among the states. Police officers are not necessarily exempted from jury duty, although they are very rarely seated on a jury. However, many have served in civil cases in both state and federal courts where the action did not involve police participation.

Once the veniremen assemble in court, they may explain why they feel they cannot serve, if they so desire. The court may excuse for a variety of business or personal reasons even though statutory exemption is not provided.

From the remaining veniremen, the names of prospective jurors are randomly selected. These individuals are seated as the prospective jury to hear a particular case. Then begins the process of *voir dire,* which literally translated means "to speak the truth." *Voir dire* is the procedure whereby the prospective jurors are questioned separately and as a group to determine their suitability to sit on the trial jury. They are asked if they know any of the participants (lawyers, judge, witnesses, defendant, and so on) in the case, whether they know or have heard anything about the case that would influence their ability to be impartial, and so forth. An affirmative response to any of these or similar questions is grounds for a challenge for cause and dismissal from the panel. Each side has an unlimited number of challenges for cause. The judge determines whether cause does exist for dismissing the prospective juror. Both the prosecution and the defense may question the juror on any matter that may bear on his ability or willingness to reach an impartial decision in the case. The judge also has the option of questioning prospective jurors. Dismissal from a jury panel in one case does not automatically exclude the venireman from being selected to sit on another jury in another case during his term of jury duty.

In addition to the unlimited challenges for cause, each side has a specified number of *peremptory* challenges—challenges for which no reason need be given. It may be that the prosecutor does not like the look in some prospective juror's eyes or that the defense "just gets a certain feeling" about a prospective juror that tells him that this person is likely to convict. Whatever the reason, he may ask that the juror be excused. The number of peremptory challenges varies, but usually the more serious the case, the greater the number of peremptory challenges allowed to each side.

After the requisite number of jurors have been selected, the entire panel is sworn. They then select one of their number as foreman to speak for them. Generally, it is at this time that jeopardy attaches, so that if for some reason the case is not completed because of some act on the part of the prosecutor, the defendant is protected by the Constitution from being subjected to double jeopardy. In a nonjury trial before a judge, jeopardy attaches when the first witness is sworn.

Opening Statements

Once the jury is empanelled, the trial begins. The first order of business is the opening statements. Both the prosecutor and the defense attorney have this opportunity to tell the jury the manner in which they intend to persuade the jury. The prosecutor explains his theory of the case and, in brief, what he intends to prove. The defense attorney briefly reveals how he plans to show the weaknesses in the state's case and convince the jury of his client's innocence.

Case for the Prosecution

The state always presents its case first. The prosecutor calls his witnesses and presents his evidence in an attempt to show, first, that a crime was committed and, second, that the defendant committed it. Those witnesses called by the prosecutor are subjected to direct examination to ascertain what they know. There are two predominant techniques used for conducting direct examinations. One is called the *narrative technique,* by which the prosecutor asks the witness to tell the jury the facts of which he has knowledge. The witness then tells his story in his own words. This technique is the least frequently used because witnesses often blurt out inadmissible evidence if they are not familiar with courtroom procedure and can jeopardize the case. Most frequently, the *question-answer technique* is used, which requires only short and to-the-point answers to questions put by the prosecutor.

After the prosecutor has elicited the information he desires from the witness, the defense attorney has the opportunity to cross-examine the witness. Generally, he must restrict the scope of his cross-examination to those matters covered in direct examination. The function of defense counsel in cross-examination is to destroy the credibility of the witness and/or his testimony in the minds of the jurors by attempting to show that the witness drew an erroneous conclusion from the things he perceived, is lying, is biased, or is just plain confused. When he attacks the credibility of the witness he attempts to *impeach* the witness, thus making anything said less believable.

When the defense attorney completes his cross-examination, the prosecutor may *redirect*. Redirect examination gives the prosecutor an opportunity to clarify the witness' testimony as to matters clouded by defense counsel on cross-examination and to attempt to rehabilitate the credibility of his witness in the eyes of the jury. Again, the defense attorney has another crack at the witness on recross-examination. He must ask questions confined to those matters covered in redirect examination. This process is followed with each witness called by the state until the state feels it has shown the guilt of the defendant to the satisfaction of the jury. It then rests its case.

Motion for Dismissal or Directed Verdict

Almost routinely, at the close of the prosecutor's case, the defense attorney will ask that the jury be removed and he will move for a dismissal of the case or a directed verdict of innocence from the judge on the grounds that the state has failed to show any number of things, such as (1) that a crime was committed; (2) that the defendant had anything to do with the commission of the crime; or (3) that the defendant's guilt has been shown beyond a reasonable doubt. Only rarely will such a motion be granted because generally the state will not even go to trial with the case if it is not convinced that it can show guilt beyond a reasonable doubt. However, if the motion is granted, the case is dismissed and the defendant freed. If the motion is denied, the defense counsel may put on his case.

Case for the Defense

The process for the defense case is the same as that for the state. The defense attorney directly examines those witnesses he calls and then offers them to the state for cross-examination. Remember that the defense is not required to prove the innocence of the defendant but rather to show that the state has not proved or cannot prove his guilt. However, this will have little bearing on the manner or degree with which counsel presents the defense case. When all witnesses have testified for the defense and all evidence has been presented, the defense attorney rests his case.

Rebuttal and Surrebuttal

The prosecutor, after close of the defense case, has the opportunity for rebuttal: to present additional witnesses to bolster his own case if it was weakened by the defense case. He may choose not to use the rebuttal. If he does, the defense may conduct surrebuttal to bolster its case.

Closing Statements

Closing statements, arguments, or summations allow both attorneys to summarize what they contend they have proven to the jury and the weaknesses in the case for the opposition. Although closing statements must be confined to the facts and evidence presented to the jury, they may often turn into quite a theatrical production tending to sway the emotions as well as the logic of the jury.

Instructions and Charge to the Jury

At this point in the trial, the judge undertakes his responsibility to instruct and charge the jury. Instructions may be both of the written and oral type and consist of the law that the jury must apply in determining whether the facts presented to them reflect guilt or innocence of the crime charged or of any other offense for which they may hold the defendant liable as a result of the evidence they have heard. The judge also charges them with the responsibility of rendering a true and just verdict.

Deliberations and Verdict

The jury then retires to the jury room to begin discussing and voting on their verdict. The deliberations are secret. No one is permitted to hear what is going on. The bailiff is responsible for maintaining the security of jury deliberations. The time it takes for the jury to reach a decision will vary. It is apparent that as a result of the *Johnson* and *Apodaca* cases, referred to earlier, deliberations will be shortened. If several days are needed the jury is sequestered. Jury members are housed and fed together and prohibited from reading newspapers or watching television news programs that might be publicizing the trial. Sequestration may also take place during the trial if the judge so orders.

When the jury has reached a verdict, they inform the bailiff who in turn informs the judge. The judge will reconvene court, have the jury brought in, and ask the foreman to either read the verdict or give it to the clerk who reads it in open court. Either attorney may request that the jury be *polled.* Each juror is asked in turn what his verdict was. If the verdict is not guilty, the case is dismissed and the defendant freed. If the verdict is one of guilt, the judge will usually ask for a presentence investigation.

POST-TRIAL PROCESSES

Presentence Investigation

The presentence investigation is usually conducted by a probation or (parole) officer. It is a compilation of the offender's history, including his family, socioeconomic background, mental and physical status, employment, criminal history, seriousness of the offense for which he was convicted, and any recommendations as to the most appropriate disposition the judge can make. This information is given to the judge in the form of a written report. The judge is not bound by the report or the recommendations in it. The report serves as a tool by which he may dispose of the case through sentencing in a manner that he feels will be most advantageous to the offender and society within the limits of the sentencing laws.

Motions

Prior to or during the presentence investigation, the defense attorney has the opportunity to move for a new trial based on any number of irregularities that he contends occurred during the trial. If the judge grants the motion, a mistrial is declared, and a new trial will be ordered. The presentence investigation will cease.

Sentence

If motions for a new trial are denied, the final phase of the trial process is the handing down of sentence. As critical as the sentencing responsibilities are, traditionally this has been that portion of the trial process to which the least amount of attention has been paid. Generally, sentence is imposed upon completion of the presentence investigation, which is designed, as noted above, to determine as much as possible about the offender and his offense, thus making the sentence more appropriate.

In actuality, there are a number of problems that exist in sentencing practices. The first issue concerns sentencing authority. The National Advisory Commission on Criminal Justice Standards and Goals reports that, in the mid-1970s, thirteen states still permitted the jury to impose sentencing in noncapital cases while in the remainder of the states this responsibility rests entirely with the judge. Second, although the range of sentencing alternatives can be broadly classified into six basic categories—fine, imprisonment, suspended sentence, pardon, probation, and execution—each of these alternatives has many ramifications which may or must be considered. Also complicating the issue is the historical fact that guidelines for the imposition of sentence have been few and far between. The alternatives selected in similar cases by differing judges under differing circumstances have caused an enormous disparity that has created problems for the criminal justice system. For example, the lack of uniformity in sentencing has long been a problem affecting not only the judiciary but also the lives of prison inmates. This is reflected in stories about cellmates who are both incarcerated for the same offense, one receiving a two-year sentence, and the other ten years. This disparity is not going to convince the inmates of "equal justice for all" in our criminal justice system, nor will it contribute much to the rehabilitation of the inmate who received the ten-year sentence.

Although there is a problem of disparity, it cannot be logically contended that there should be identical sentences imposed for identical crimes. There are many variables that must exist in any sentencing structure. For example, the presentence investigation should reflect factors regarding the nature and seriousness of the offense committed as well as the criminal and social history of the offender. These will and should impact on the severity of sentence imposed for conviction of a criminal act. In addition, types of sentencing alternatives such as the indeterminate sentence, which provides a minimum and maximum sentence; the determinate sentence, which specifies a maximum time of incarceration; mandatory sentences, which impose certain restrictions on the discretion of the sentencing authority; and habitual offender statutes, which provide more severe punishment for recidivist (repeater) offenders—all will have an impact on what appears to be a disparity in sentencing. The next chapter on judicial reform will explore some of the issues surrounding sentencing practices, and in Part 3 detailed attention will be devoted to implementation of sentencing through the corrections subcomponent of the criminal justice system.

Post Conviction Remedies—Appeal

Appeal is the next step in the process. The process of appellate review is one that usually is taken advantage of by the defendant in a criminal case who is convicted at trial. But there are certain instances where the prosecution may seek review of a lower court decision. The appellate process may be invoked by the defendant on a voluntary basis; it is not required, but in all jurisdictions, at least one appellate review is automatically allowed, thus guaranteeing that the final decision does not rest with a trial jury. As stated by the National Advisory Commission on Criminal Justice Standards and Goals:

> Because a conviction of crime imposes a serious stigma upon a person in the eyes of society and often results in the loss of liberty, there is a widely shared view that determining guilt and fixing punishment should not be left to a single trial court. The interest of both society and the defendant are served by providing another tribunal to review the trial court proceedings and to insure that no prejudicial error was committed and that justice was done.[2]

The National Advisory Commission notes that review is the final stage in a judicial process of determining guilt and fixing sentence and that, like the trial proceedings, it should be fair and expeditious. But the Commission goes on to state that in many jurisdictions upwards of 90 percent of all convictions are appealed by defendants and that most state and federal courts are being inundated with the review process. The procedures that have been established are antiquated, cumbersome, and fragmented, thus causing undue delay. Often, it is five, six, seven, or ten years from trial before a case is finally decided through appellate review. A great many of the difficulties arise because appellate review is confined to matters contained in the record of the trial, thus restricting the issues that can be raised regarding the entire process which led to the conviction of the defendant. Also complicating the issue is the fact that the defendant is not necessarily restricted to a one-time appeal but rather may seek multiple reviews of issues involved at the trial level.

[2] National Advisory Commission on Criminal Justice Standards and Goals, *Courts* (Washington, D.C.: U.S. Government Printing Office, 1973), p. 112.

The National Advisory Commission goes on to report that in state criminal cases the complicated review scheme may have as many as eleven procedural steps involved, some of which may be repeated.

> Although not every case goes through each of these steps, they are potentially available, and it is not uncommon for a defendant to pursue at least four or five. They are:
> 1. New trial motion filed in court where conviction imposed;
> 2. Appeal to state intermediate appellate court (in states where there is no intermediate appellate court the step would not be available);
> 3. Appeal to State Supreme Court;
> 4. Petition to U.S. Supreme Court to review state court decision on appeal;
> 5. Post conviction proceeding in state trial court;
> 6. Appeal of post conviction proceeding to state intermediate appellate court;
> 7. Appeal to State Supreme Court;
> 8. Petition to U.S. Supreme Court to review state court decision on appeal from post conviction proceeding;
> 9. Habeas corpus petition in federal district court;
> 10. Appeal to U.S. Court of Appeals;
> 11. Petition to U.S. Supreme Court to review Court of Appeals decision on habeas corpus petition.
>
> The actual operations and interplay of review proceedings are more complex than this listing suggests. Some convictions are not appealed at all, others are subject to a number of these steps several times over, and with respect to some convictions, review may proceed simultaneously in more than one court system.[3]

The recommendation of the National Advisory Commission is that there should be a single, unified review proceeding in which all arguable defects in the trial proceeding can be examined and settled finally, subject only to narrowly defined exceptional circumstances where there are compelling reasons to provide for a further review.

Although the right of the defendant to appeal a conviction is generally extremely broad, the prosecution's right of appeal is often more complex and more restrictive and the variations among states are significant. Texas and Georgia, for example, provide absolutely no right on the part of the state to appeal in criminal convictions. Other states may be found at the opposite extreme. Connecticut, Vermont, and Wisconsin basically allow the state to appeal questions of law arising from the trial of criminal cases, with the permission of the presiding judge, provided final judgment has not yet been rendered in the case. New York allows the prosecution to appeal in cases where an appeal may be taken by the defendant except where a verdict or judgment of not guilty has been rendered. Alabama permits appeal by the state only when the trial court has held unconstitutional a statute on which the indictment or information is based. Virginia prohibits appeal by the Commonwealth except in a case involving the violation of a law relating to state revenue.

[3] *Ibid.*, p. 113.

Most states do have broader authority for prosecution appeal in instances involving pretrial orders, as where an indictment, information, or complaint has been dismissed by a lower court, an arrest or search warrant has been quashed, or an order suppressing evidence or suppressing a confession or admission has been issued. None of these grounds is automatic. In each state, state law must be consulted. The basic concern about expanding the right of the state to appeal is that it might subject the defendant to double jeopardy. This, of course, is prohibited by the Constitution.

SUMMARY

If the reader accepts the proposition that a system requires input, process, and output, then despite arguments to the contrary both from within and without criminal justice, there does exist a system of sorts. The courts generally rely on the police for input; corrections relies on input from the courts; and corrections and its impact constitute the output portion of the system. Once the existence of a crime is known and reported to law enforcement authorities, the criminal justice system becomes operative. The judiciary becomes involved after an alleged offender is identified, arrested, and booked.

The defendant's first appearance before a member of the judiciary is for the purpose of informing him of the charges and advising him of certain constitutional rights, including protection against self-incrimination, right to counsel, and the setting of bail, if applicable. The second appearance is usually at a preliminary hearing at which time a determination is made if there is sufficient evidence to hold the)arrested person for trial. In capital cases and, in many states, major felony cases, an indictment by a grand jury is necessary for proceeding to trial. In other states and cases, the prosecutor may exercise his discretion by filing an information, a formal judicial charge leading to trial.

At arraignment the defendant is given the opportunity to enter a plea to the charge. Assuming that a plea of innocent is entered, trial date will be set. Normally, during the pretrial period, defense attorneys will file motions attempting to get the charge dismissed, have evidence ruled inadmissible, or gain additional information about the prosecutor's case so that they may prepare a better defense.

The first step in the trial process is the selection of the jury. Once this is accomplished, attorneys for both sides may make opening statements. The prosecutor then presents the case for the prosecution, attempting to convince the jury beyond a reasonable doubt that a crime was committed and the defendant committed it. As a matter of routine, upon completion of the prosecution's case, the defense attorney will file a motion for dismissal or directed verdict claiming that the prosecution has failed to prove either that a crime was committed or that the defendant committed the offense. If the judge is convinced that the prosecution has failed to make a case, he will dismiss the charges. Normally, however, he will allow that to remain a question for the jury to decide and ask the defense attorney to present his case. The defense attorney then calls witnesses in an attempt to show that the defendant is not guilty. Upon completion of the testimony, both sides have the opportunity for closing statements in which they attempt to summarize for the jury what they believe they have proved.

The judge then takes the responsibility of instructing and charging the jury as to what evidence they may consider and what verdicts they may reach. The jury is excused for its deliberation and verdict. If the jury decides the defendant is innocent, the defendant will be dismissed; if guilty, the judge will normally order a presentence investigation, establish a time period for the defense attorney to move for a new trial based upon irregularities or errors the defense attorney may contend occurred during the trial, and establish a date for sentencing. After sentencing, the defendant may pursue his appellate rights.

LEARNING EXERCISES

Issues to Be Discussed

1. Bail is often described as unfair to those with limited or no financial means since they are more likely to end up in jail because of such financial inabilities to pay a bail fee. Look carefully at some of the recent literature on bail and describe what in your opinion would constitute fair bail procedures.
2. Grand juries today are being criticized as mere tools of prosecutors, having lost much of their independent investigation powers. Undertake current readings on the system. Do you believe that this criticism is justified? Why or why not?
3. What purpose is served by the first appearance of the defendant before a judicial officer?
4. Describe the function of the preliminary hearing.
5. Describe the process of jury selection.
6. Briefly describe the purpose of a presentence investigation.

Group Activity

Set up a courtroom situation. Designate individuals who represent defendant, counsel, and all the principal court officials except jury members. Establish the principal stations from first appearance up to jury selection and trial to demonstrate through role-playing the important steps which lead to trial or plea bargaining. Participants should acquaint themselves, by reading and courtroom visits, with key issues surrounding their role and their tasks. This should be accompanied by a good rehearsal prior to class presentation.

Field Activity

Visit a courtroom in which there is an actual jury trial involving a criminal offense. Study the roles of each person involved and particularly the procedures. As part of your notebook activity, prepare a 300-word analysis of your observations, including comments on efficiency, fairness in procedure, and an evaluation in sum total of the trial itself.

Key Terms

Bail
Bondsman
Booking
Grand Jury
Information

Legal aid
Nolle prosequi
Nolo contendere
Venire

SUGGESTED REFERENCES

ALSCHULER, ALBERT W. "The Prosecutor's Role in Plea Bargaining." *University of Chicago Law Review,* Vol. 36 (1968), pp. 50–112.

———. *The Defense Attorney's Role in Plea Bargaining.* Washington, D.C.: U.S. Government Printing Office, 1973.

AMERICAN BAR ASSOCIATION, PROJECT ON MINIMUM STANDARDS FOR CRIMINAL JUSTICE. *The Function of the Trial Judge.* New York: Institute of Judicial Administration, Approved Draft, 1973.

———. *The Prosecution Function and the Defense Function.* New York: Institute of Judicial Administration, Approved Draft, 1971.

———. *Criminal Appeals.* New York: Institute of Judicial Administration, Approved Draft, 1970.

———. *Appellate Review of Sentences.* New York: Institute of Judicial Administration, Approved Draft, 1968.

———. *Post-Conviction Remedies.* New York: Institute of Judicial Administration, Approved Draft, 1968.

———. *Providing Defense Services.* New York: Institute of Judicial Administration, Approved Draft, 1968.

———. *Sentencing Alternatives and Procedures.* New York: Institute of Judicial Administration, Approved Draft, 1968.

———. *Trial by Jury.* New York: Institute of Judicial Administration, Approved Draft, 1968.

BOTTOMLEY, A. KEITH. *Decisions in the Penal Process.* South Hackensack, N.J.: Fred B. Rothman, 1973.

CALIFORNIA COMMISSION ON PEACE OFFICER STANDARDS AND TRAINING. *The Impact of Social Trends on Crime and Criminal Justice.* A Project S.T.A.R.

publication. Published jointly by W. H. Anderson Publishing Co., Cincinnati, and Davis Publishing Co., Santa Cruz, Calif., 1976.

CANNAVALE, FRANK J., JR., AND FALCON, WILLIAM D., eds. *Improving Witness Cooperation.* National Institute of Law Enforcement and Criminal Justice, Law Enforcement Assistance Administration, U.S. Department of Justice. Washington, D.C.: U.S. Government Printing Office, 1976.

CARLSON, RONALD L. *Criminal Justice Procedure for Police.* 2nd ed. Cincinnati: W. H. Anderson, 1977.

CARTER, ROBERT M. "The Presentence Report and the Decision Making Process." *Journal of Research in Crime and Delinquency,* Vol. 4 (July 1967), pp. 203–11.

DAVIS, KENNETH CULP. *Discretionary Justice.* Baton Rouge, La.: State University Press, 1969.

EDELBERTZ, HERBERT. *The Nature, Impact and Prosecution of White Collar Crime.* Washington, D.C.: U.S. Government Printing Office, 1970.

FRANKEL, MARVIN E. *The Grand Jury.* New York: Hill & Wang, 1977.

GROSMAN, BRIAN A. *The Prosecutor: An Inquiry into the Exercise of Discretion.* Toronto: University of Toronto Press, 1971.

JACOBY, JOAN E. *The Prosecutor's Changing Decision: A Policy Perspective.* National Institute of Law Enforcement and Criminal Justice, Law Enforcement Assistance Administration, U.S. Department of Justice. Washington, D.C.: U.S. Government Printing Office, 1977.

KATZ, LEWIS R., et al. *Justice Is the Crime: Pretrial Delay in Felony Cases.* Cleveland: Press of Case Western Reserve University, 1972.

LE GRANDE, JAMES L. *The Basic Processes of Criminal Justice.* Beverly Hills, Calif.: Glencoe Press, 1973.

MEADOR, DANIEL J. *Criminal Appeals: English Practices and American Reforms.* National Institute of Law Enforcement and Criminal Justice, Law Enforcement Assistance Administration, U.S. Department of Justice. Washington, D.C.: U.S. Government Printing Office, 1973.

MOORE, LLOYD E. *The Jury.* Cincinnati: W. H. Anderson, 1973.

NATIONAL ADVISORY COMMISSION ON CRIMINAL JUSTICE STANDARDS AND GOALS. *Courts.* Washington, D.C.: U.S. Government Printing Office, 1973.

NATIONAL COUNCIL ON CRIME AND DELINQUENCY. *Model Sentencing Act.* New York: National Council on Crime and Delinquency, 1963.

NATIONAL DISTRICT ATTORNEYS ASSOCIATION. *The Prosecutor's Manual on Economic Crime.* Chicago: National District Attorneys Association, 1977.

NATIONAL INSTITUTE OF LAW ENFORCEMENT AND CRIMINAL JUSTICE, LAW ENFORCEMENT ASSISTANCE ADMINISTRATION, U.S. DEPARTMENT OF JUSTICE. *A Guide to Juror Usage.* Washington, D.C.: U.S. Government Printing Office, 1974.

———. *A Study of Court Reporting Systems.* Washington, D.C.: U.S. Government Printing Office, 1971.

PRESIDENT'S COMMISSION ON LAW ENFORCEMENT AND THE ADMINISTRATION OF JUSTICE. *Task Force Report: The Courts.* Washington, D.C.: U.S. Government Printing Office, 1967.

ROSETT, ARTHUR, AND CRESSEY, DONALD R. *Justice by Consent: Plea Bargains in the American Courthouse.* Philadelphia: Lippincott, 1976.

THOMAS, WAYNE H. *Bail Reform in America.* Berkeley, Calif.: University of California Press, 1976.

TOBIAS, MARK W., AND PETERSEN, R. DAVID. *Pre-Trial Criminal Procedure: A Summary of Constitutional Rights.* Springfield, Ill.: Charles C Thomas, 1972.

ZIMRING, FRANKLIN E. "Measuring the Impact of Pretrial Diversion from the Criminal Justice System." *University of Chicago Law Review,* Vol. 41 (1974), pp. 224–41.

11
Toward Judicial Reform

Overview
Law Reform
Unification of State Court Systems
A Need for Better Administration
Improved State–Federal Court Relations
Quality of Personnel
Court Procedures and Practices
Summary
Learning Exercises
Suggested References

OVERVIEW

Some of the most persistent problems in the criminal justice system involve the courts component. There is a great need for court reform, particularly in state and local courts where most criminal case activity is concentrated. Many reform measures must come through legislative action based on sound studies of the current inadequacies of the court system. Action in court reform appears concentrated in the following areas: unification of state court systems; improvements in court management and administration; improvements in the quality of the judiciary through better selection procedures; and reexamination of the plea bargaining process, bail procedures, and sentencing practices. Such actions normally would have a favorable impact on the criminal justice system as a whole. The preceding chapters show that significant problems exist in the American judicial system. The courts are a vital component of our criminal justice system, yet they constitute only one segment of an interdependent whole.

The reforms needed include facilitation of administrative unification, management modification, increased financial responsibility, improvement of quality of judges and creation of standards for these positions, improvement of the bail system, development of better sentencing practices and alternatives, and establishment of a closer working relationship between state and federal courts. There is also a need to treat the system as a whole by recognizing the interdependence of the police, prosecution, courts, and correctional components even though custom, tradition, and other factors tend to accentuate and perpetuate the separateness and autonomy of these functions. The time has come for balanced consideration of the relationships of each element to the others and their collective impact on the public. As stated by the Advisory Commission on Intergovernmental Relations, "Courts are the balance wheel of our nation's criminal justice system, and the balance wheel is out of alignment."[1] The National Advisory Commission on Criminal Justice Standards and Goals agreed. Several years later it said:

> Two premises underlie the report of this Commission. The first is that crime in America is seriously interfering with the Nation's ability to attain economic, political, and social well-being for all its citizens. The second is that no attempt to alleviate this problem can succeed unless dramatic improvements are made in the ability of the courts to perform their critical role in the criminal justice system.[2] (See Figure 11–1 for flow.)

---

[1] Advisory Commission on Intergovernmental Relations, *For a More Perfect Union—Court Reform* (Washington, D.C.: U.S. Government Printing Office, 1971), p. 1.

[2] National Advisory Commission on Criminal Justice Standards and Goals, *Courts* (Washington, D.C.: U.S. Government Printing Office, 1973), p. 1.

The Litigated Case

SUMMARY OF COMMISSION RECOMMENDATIONS FOR STEPS TO ACHIEVE TRIAL IN A FELONY CASE WITHIN 60 DAYS OF ARREST.

In some felony cases, the Commission recommends that a summons or citation be issued in lieu of arrest. In such instances, there would be no first judicial appearance and the Commission calls for a preliminary hearing within 14 days of the issuance of citation or summons.

In felony cases in which there is a grand jury indictment, the Commission recommends that no preliminary hearing be held. The time limits and steps shown as following the preliminary hearing become applicable upon apprehension of the indicted individual or service of a summons following the indictment.

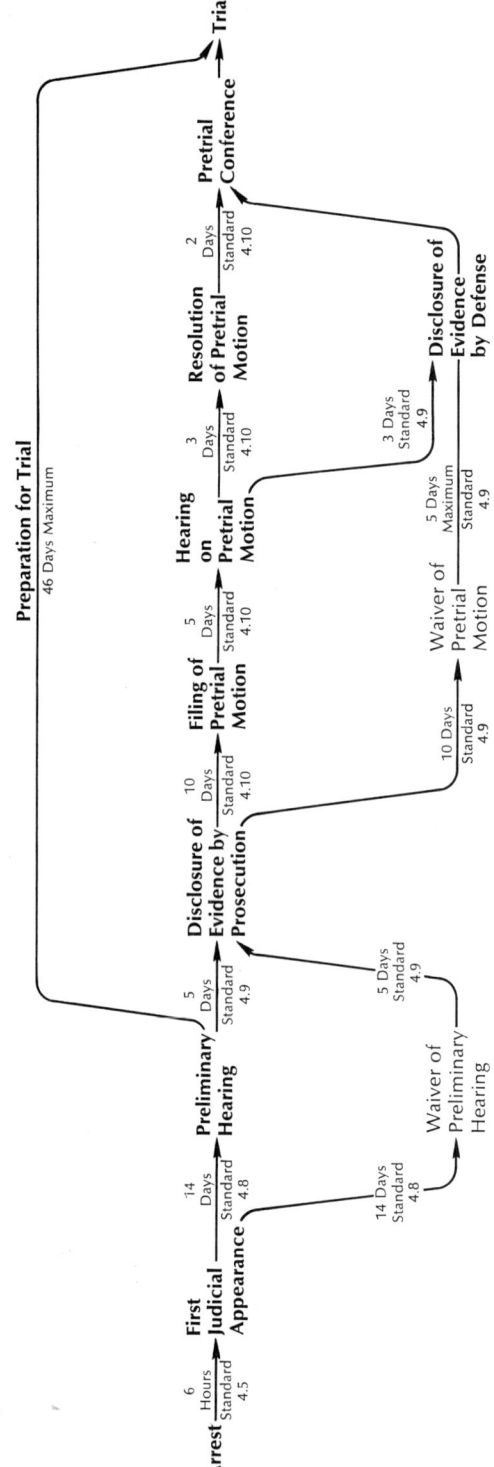

FIGURE 11–1 The Litigated Case
Source: National Advisory Commission on Criminal Justice Standards and Goals, Courts, pp. xx–xxi.

Many study commissions have examined the areas of concern and possible solutions to the court reform issue over the past five decades. Among the points of agreement reached by the various independent studies is that, because of the nature of our criminal justice system, the overwhelming majority of criminal court cases are heard and adjudicated by state and local court systems. It is in these systems, as opposed to the federal system, that the greatest need for reform exists.

State and local judicial systems are operating under an increasingly severe threat of collapse due to overwhelming case loads, lack of full-time judges, overlapping jurisdictions, and numerous administrative problems. The state is ultimately responsible for all the scattered courts, whether their authority comes from constitutional provisions, statutes, or from the powers delegated to local units of government. Because of the diverse categories of courts within the respective states, lines of authority become crossed and blurred. The problem, although existing on a nationwide basis, is most overt in urban areas where state, county, and municipal courts with overlapping jurisdictions may hear similar types of cases. This often imposes an unnecessary burden upon an arresting police officer by compelling him to make a choice between two or more different courts in which he may seek prosecution. And in some instances, because of the shortage of attorneys practicing in the lower courts, the police officer may end up prosecuting his own case.

LAW REFORM

The first step in reform of the courts must be initiated by legislative action. The problem of overwhelming caseloads that confronts the courts at all levels is compounded by the necessity to litigate or at least take action on offenses that realistically should be decriminalized, legalized, or disposed of by administrative rather than judicial action. The National Advisory Commission on Criminal Justice Standards and Goals has called for complete criminal law revision in jurisdictions that have not revised their criminal laws in the past decade.[3] This action alone can contribute much to increasing the effectiveness of the court systems by relieving some of the case load and forcing the judiciary to concentrate on realistic and contemporary problem areas of criminal activity.

UNIFICATION OF STATE COURT SYSTEMS

Many study commissions, including the Advisory Commission on Intergovernmental Relations, has called for the establishment of a unified state court system consisting of a supreme court, an intermediate court of appeals, and trial courts of general jurisdiction with special subdivisions to perform the duties of courts of

---

[3] National Advisory Commission on Criminal Justice Standards and Goals, *Criminal Justice System* (Washington, D.C.: U.S. Government Printing Office, 1973), p. 175

limited jurisdiction. By this method, duplication and overlapping of jurisdiction can be eliminated.[4] A number of states have already drastically revised their court systems in accordance with these recommendations and several others are seeking the necessary legislative and voter approval. Part of the unification process requires that all courts within a state be subject to administrative supervision and direction by the state supreme court or the chief justice of that court.[5]

In spite of the contention that courts of limited jurisdiction are the bulwark of democracy, accessible to the ordinary citizen who can come and receive justice, the quality of justice dispensed by many of these courts casts serious doubts on their responsiveness or accessibility, particularly in rural areas. A consolidated county court system utilizing qualified judicial personnel would provide both professionalism in the judiciary as well as greater accessibility and responsiveness to the public.

The National Advisory Commission on Criminal Justice Standards and Goals supports the call for unification and simplification of court systems. Standard 8.1 of the Commission's report on the courts perhaps sums up the need as follows:

Standard 8.1

UNIFICATION OF THE STATE COURT SYSTEM

State courts should be organized into a unified judicial system financed by the State and administered through a statewide court administrator or administrative judge under the supervision of the chief justice of the State supreme court.

All trial courts should be unified into a single trial court with general criminal as well as civil jurisdiction. Criminal jurisdiction now in courts of limited jurisdiction should be placed in these unified trial courts of general jurisdiction, with the exception of certain traffic violations. The State supreme court should promulgate rules for the conduct of minor as well as major criminal prosecutions.

All judicial functions in the trial courts should be performed by full-time judges. All judges should possess law degrees and be members of the bar.

A transcription or other record of the pretrial court proceedings and the trial should be kept in all criminal cases.

The appeal procedure should be the same for all cases.

Pretrial release services, probation services, and other rehabilitative services should be available in all prosecutions within the jurisdiction of the unified trial court.[6]

---

[4] *For a More Perfect Union—Court Reform*, p. 1.
[5] *Ibid.*
[6] National Advisory Commission, *Courts*, p. 164.

A NEED FOR BETTER ADMINISTRATION

The deficiencies existing in the quantity of judicial manpower, particularly in the lower courts in urban areas, along with weak administration and the increase in case volume, tend to increase the backlog of cases and the already lengthy periods between arrest and disposition. As the President's Commission stated:

> In those courts in which high volume interferes with the orderly movement of cases and creates tremendous pressure to dispose of business, one may observe concomitant delay in the disposition of cases and hasty consideration when these cases come to be heard.[7]

Delays in our court systems not only diminish the deterrent effect of the entire criminal justice system in the eyes of the potential offender but also undermine public confidence in the system's effectiveness. In most parts of the country, traffic, drunkenness, and drug abuse cases clog up the judicial system far more than felony cases. These types of cases place heavy demands not only on the police and the prosecutors but on judicial personnel as well. Moreover, the sanctions and remedies that the criminal justice system provides are frequently inappropriate, ineffective, and, to some degree, counterproductive, thus contributing to the overbearing volume of cases necessitating court appearances. Inflexibility in criminal procedures often excludes the use of more appropriate remedies.

The qualities of a good judge do not necessarily coincide with the skills of a good administrator. One of the major movements toward court reform has been accomplished in this country by the establishment of administrative offices in state court systems headed by a professional whose function is to assist in the administrative supervision and direction of the entire court system. The purpose of court administrators is to decrease the nonjudicial functions previously falling upon the shoulders of members of the judiciary, thus leaving them greater freedom to perform their functions as judges.

The functions that court administrators are able to perform include superintendence of court calendars, assignment of physical and personnel resources, collection of judicial statistics, management of the fiscal affairs of the courts, furnishing of supplies and equipment, and supervision of court personnel. The independence and autonomy of the judiciary creates a problem of resistance to change that has to be overcome. Many states are moving in this direction, and court administration is rapidly being recognized as an avenue toward court reform.

It has thus become obvious that the answer to court reform lies not solely in terms of dollars nor in the quantity of judges. Efficiency through the use of court administrators promotes more effective use of manpower and greater productivity through improved methods, improved machinery, improved management, and trained administrative personnel.

[7] President's Commission on Law Enforcement and the Administration of Justice, *Task Force Report: The Courts* (Washington, D.C.: U.S. Government Printing Office, 1967), p. 80.

Some years ago, Chief Justice Warren Burger proposed the establishment of an institute specifically designed to train individuals to become administrators of court systems. The Institute for Court Management has been operating at the University of Denver for several years now and has produced highly qualified individuals to assume positions in court administration. Many states are presently taking advantage of the talents of these young individuals. A number of other colleges and universities have instituted similar programs.

IMPROVED STATE–FEDERAL COURT RELATIONS

The need for closer relationships between state and federal court systems cannot be overemphasized. The problem lies in the dramatic increase in postconviction petitions of state prisoners to federal courts. Some state courts, federal district courts, and individual judges have developed informal relationships to deal with joint problems. Yet, much more could be done on a broader scale, especially as it relates to joint conviction petitions, judicial rules, and criminal codes. State and federal district judges, judicial officers, and bar associations have been urged to initiate and support the development of State–Federal Judicial Councils, composed of chief judges of state and appropriate courts, to cooperate and explore problems of joint concern. Chief Justice Warren Burger called for establishment of such bodies in 1970. Almost all the states have State Judicial Councils that serve to some degree as coordinating bodies among the various state courts. These councils could be building blocks for the establishment of closer state–federal judicial ties. The councils should have the longer-range goal of improving general communications between federal and state courts by stimulating and aiding in the development of more uniform criminal codes, sentencing procedures, judicial roles, and a forum for exchange of ideas and experience on the full range of judicial business.

QUALITY OF PERSONNEL

Despite the most modern administration and the most generous of funding, courts cannot stand on their own or function effectively as part of the criminal justice system if they are staffed by incompetent or unqualified judges. Among the most basic requirements characterizing a competent judge are that he have a basic knowledge of the law and that he be able to devote full time to his judicial functions. In sparsely populated areas of the nation, the problems related to the use of unqualified and part-time judges are most apparent because it is in these regions that it is most difficult to find adequately trained individuals and sufficient judicial business to employ them on a full-time basis.

Selection of Judges

The methods by which judges are selected has played an important role in obtaining and maintaining the services of those who are competent. Election and appointment have been the two choices in most areas of the United States as the alternatives for selecting judges.

Election of judges is a widely accepted practice within states. The duration of terms for elected judges varies from locale to locale, from as little as a one-year term to as much as twenty-one years in a few areas. In some states, the office seeker runs on a bipartisan ticket; in others, he is required to seek a nonpartisan election. It is not the electorate who always have the prerogative of electing judges. In some jurisdictions, judges are "elected" by the state legislature.

The advantages and disadvantages of the elective system can be summed up in the following simple statements: The election of judges allows for public input into the type of judiciary and judicial philosophy practiced in their communities but does not ensure the services of the most qualified individuals. An additional disadvantage is the common belief that one who is required to seek office in a partisan election would not be totally dedicated or impartial in his judicial capacity.

The pros and cons of the elective system would be equally applicable to the appointive system, but in reverse. Nevertheless, the appointive system is the exclusive method utilized for the selection of judges in the federal system and, to a far lesser extent, exists in some state jurisdictions. All federal judges are appointed by the president with a majority vote of concurrence by the Senate.

The appointive process is not entirely free of a political atmosphere and is often criticized because of accusations of "political appointments." On the other hand, those who favor selection of judges by appointment contend that those who appoint judges are themselves usually vulnerable at the polls should they make "bad" appointments.

It is clear that neither of these selection systems can satisfy everyone. Each has merit, and each has its shortcomings. Several attempts have been made to capitalize on the best of both.

The Missouri Plan

A third method of judicial selection, combining both the elective and appointive procedures, is rapidly growing in popularity among the states. Named after the state in which it had its inception, the *Missouri Plan* provides for a series of nonpartisan nominating boards consisting of judges, lawyers, and lay (nonlawyer) citizens who select three candidates for each vacant judgeship. The nominating boards have differing memberships depending upon the level in the court system in which the vacancy exists. Board members are appointed by the governor for staggered six-year terms with new appointments made in alternate years. This system prevents the governor from "packing" the boards because he cannot succeed himself in office after his four-year term. Board members receive no compensation for their services and, except for the member judges, cannot hold public office while serving as members, nor are they permitted to hold an official position in a political party.

The names of the candidates are given to the governor, who must select one of the three to fill the vacant judgeship. The individual chosen serves for one year and then must seek the approval of the electorate for a full term. The election is on an unopposed, separate, nonpartisan ballot that simply asks the voters if the judge should be retained in office. A yes or no answer is all that is required.

Professor Henry J. Abraham sums up the advantages of the Missouri Plan in his book, *The Judicial Process:*

> Generally deemed to be the most adult and most commendable system of judicial selection extant in the various states, the Missouri Plan combines a number of commendable features. It combines the democratic notion of accountability to the electorate with an intelligent method of selecting qualified candidates for judicial office. The necessity of facing the electorate on his record provides the judge with an incentive of judiciousness, and the fact that he runs on his own record rather than against that of an opponent allied with a specific political party goes far toward taking the courts out of the more crass aspects of politics. On the other hand, a case could be made for the contention that the awareness of establishing a "good record" for the electorate's eyes and ears may lead to timid and/or "popular" judgments. The results of the Missouri Plan in action, however, do not generally support that theory.[8]

Adoption of the Missouri Plan or similar programs for judicial selection would go a long way toward resolving the problems of the courts; yet, there are still twenty-five states in which judges must run for election.[9]

COURT PROCEDURES AND PRACTICES

Many cases are disposed of outside the judicial trial process. The methods vary, but the results are the same. A decision may be made not to charge a suspect with a criminal offense, the suspect may plead guilty, or the game of plea bargaining may be played.

Dropped Charges

Overburdened courts have come to rely upon these informal procedures for dealing with overpowering case loads. As a result, some cases are not prosecuted simply because sufficient resources are not available to pursue the trial process.

---

[8] Henry J. Abraham, *The Judicial Process* (New York: Oxford University Press, 1962), p. 37.

[9] *For a More Perfect Union—Court Reform,* p. 3.

Procedural regularity does not exist to any great degree in these informal dispositions. Facts bearing both on the offense and on the character of the offender are not systematically presented before decisions are reached in these nontrial dispositions. Nonpunitive alternatives (with the exception of dismissal of the case) are not often considered. Thus, one of the major difficulties in the present system of nontrial dispositions is that when an offender is dropped out of the criminal process by dismissal of charges, he usually does not receive the help or treatment needed to prevent recurrence of his prohibited conduct. Because of the absence of social agencies or the inability of these agencies to deal with the offender, such an individual is often discharged without prosecution in the expectation that his conduct will not be repeated. Yet, there is little assistance given by the community to insure that this expectation will become a reality. People who come in contact with the criminal process because of mental illness, youth problems, or alcoholism and who are not processed through the criminal justice system rarely are given any follow-up. Of course, these faults cannot be attributed entirely to failures of the judicial system because any practical solution to these problems would require a great deal of additional manpower and financial resources.

Plea Bargaining

A large percentage of guilty pleas are the product of negotiations between the prosecutor and defense counsel or the accused. Plea bargaining involves discussion to reach an agreement by which the accused will enter a plea of guilty in exchange for a reduced charge or a favorable sentence recommended by the prosecutor. The propriety of offering the defendant an inducement to surrender his right to trial becomes a fundamental problem with plea bargaining. Presentence reports and other investigations into the background of the offender usually are made after conviction and are unavailable at the plea bargaining stage.

The informality and wide variation in practice among prosecutors and trial judges regarding plea bargains often cause bewilderment and a sense of injustice among defendants. It often happens that the result may be excessive leniency for professional, habitual criminals who generally have expert legal advice and are best able to take full advantage of the bargaining opportunity. Equally true are the cases of marginal offenders who may be dealt with harshly and left with a deep sense of injustice, having learned too late the manipulations possible in the system. There is also the possibility that an innocent defendant may plead guilty because of the fear that he will be sentenced more harshly if he is convicted or that he will be subjected to damaging publicity because of a guilty charge.

Plea bargaining is not recognized, in most jurisdictions, as a valid method of ensuring justice in criminal cases. Yet it does happen. It is widely practiced and accepted. The plea bargaining system can be an effective and meaningful tool for easing the problems of the judicial system, provided certain procedural guidelines are established that would guarantee due process (fairness) in the disposition of cases and treatment of offenders. Of first magnitude would be ensuring that adequate counsel is given a defendant who faces a potentially significant penalty, that the plea is made voluntarily and intelligently, and that any promises made to the defendant be kept. Second, plea bargaining discussions between prosecutors and defense attorneys should deal explicitly with dispositional questions and the development of appropriate treatment programs for the offender. These priorities are by no means exhaustive and, of course, would require additional manpower, money, and interagency cooperation and dedication.

Plea bargaining does serve a number of important purposes. In reality most courts could not handle the increased caseload if they were required to try all cases upon which arrests were made and which normally would lead to ultimate judicial determination. In addition, it relieves both the prosecution and the defense of certain risks of going to trial and injects a degree of certainty and flexibility into the judicial system. Frequently, plea bargaining serves law enforcement needs by providing leniency in exchange for information, assistance, and testimony about other offenses and offenders. Plea bargaining is not used and should not be used simply as a means of disposing of criminal cases at minimal cost.

The most controversial and far-reaching standard or recommendation of the National Advisory Commission on Criminal Justice Standards and Goals is its position on the abolition of plea negotiation. In its Standard 3.1 the Commission said:

As soon as possible, but in no event later than 1978, negotiations between prosecutors and defendants—either personally or through their attorneys—concerning concessions to be made in return for guilty pleas should be prohibited. In the event that the prosecution makes a recommendation as to sentence, it should not be affected by the willingness of the defendant to plead guilty to some or all of the offenses with which he is charged. A plea of guilty should not be considered by the court in determining the sentence to be imposed.

Until plea negotiations are eliminated as recommended in this standard, such negotiations and the entry of pleas pursuant to the resulting agreements should be permitted only under a procedure embodying the safeguards contained in the remaining standards in this chapter.[10]

The Commission recognized that its recommendation would be controversial. When the reports were released, this recommendation received a lot of opposition. Many people within the criminal justice system believe that plea bargaining or plea negotiations is an indispensable practice and that its abolition would cause total chaos and collapse in the judicial process. What they proposed instead, and what the Commission agreed to in the interim, was that plea negotiations should be more aboveboard, out in the open, and formalized so that the process is subject to objective judicial and public review.

The manner in which this should be accomplished is by: (1) keeping records of all agreements reached in plea negotiations, the reasons for such negotiations,

[10] National Advisory Commission, *Courts,* p. 46.

and the basis for the pleas; (2) establishing uniform policies and practices in prosecutors' offices for engaging in plea negotiations; (3) prohibiting consideration of weaknesses in the prosecutor's case as the basis for plea bargaining; (4) establishing time limits within which plea negotiations may take place as a basis for freeing the trial docket; (5) requiring the defendant to have representation of counsel; (6) prohibiting the prosecutor from inducing guilty pleas by improper charging, overcharging, or threatening more severe sentences if the defendant chooses to exercise his right to trial; (7) prohibiting the prosecutor from failing to disclose information which may be exculpatory to the defendant; (8) ensuring that all pleas are voluntary, knowledgeable, and based on facts pointing to the defendant's guilt; and (9) prohibiting consideration of the plea as a factor in sentencing the defendant.

Sentencing

Judicial problems in the area of sentencing of convicted offenders are being addressed. Among the issues of concern are sentencing authority, disparity of sentences, legislative direction, and review of sentences.

As noted earlier, the National Advisory Commission on Criminal Justice Standards and Goals reports that thirteen states still permit sentencing by juries in noncapital cases. Both this Commission and the American Bar Association Project on Minimum Standards for Criminal Justice call for an abolition of jury sentencing practices. Despite arguments that the jury or some other nonjudicial entity should have the authority for sentencing and that the judiciary should be removed from the responsibility, such proposals have been rejected both by the National Advisory Commission and the American Bar Association. It is recognized that there is little training or experience in the background of the judge that prepares him for the immense task of sentencing convicted offenders, and problems do exist with sentencing disparities, but those who argue for sentencing authority to rest with the judiciary contend that jury sentencing is nonprofessional and would lead to greater disparity and more arbitrary decision making than exists in most states today. In addition, jury sentencing would allow little opportunity for the development of consistent sentencing policies.

To overcome some of the disparities in sentencing that do exist, several proposals have been made to promote more rational sentencing policies, including: the establishment of sentencing councils where judges discuss planned sentencing with each other prior to imposition, sentencing institutes to provide a forum for the exchange of new ideas and the development of criteria for the imposition of sentences, orientation sessions for new judges, and regular visitation of custodial and noncustodial facilities by judges.[11]

---

[11] American Bar Association, Project on Minimum Standards for Criminal Justice, *Sentencing Alternatives and Procedures* (New York: Institute of Judicial Administration, 1968), pp. 40–42.

Sentencing is not entirely the responsibility of the judiciary. At the outset, state legislatures must take the initial responsibility of establishing guidelines and parameters under which sentencing may occur. This statutory framework must take into consideration the basic purposes of correctional programs within the state as well as the needs of the offender and the welfare of society. It is urged that legislatures legislate, to some degree, the exercise of discretion in the imposition of sentencing. There are both advantages and disadvantages to different types of sentencing programs. The system where the determinate sentence is used and maximum sentences are structured has the advantage of working beneficially in a true punishment sense where time served is the objective of the system. On the other hand, where rehabilitation is the objective, maximum sentences are generally too long and counterproductive to rehabilitation. In the case of mandatory minimum sentences, a system used in certain cases (e.g., where a firearm is used in the commission of a crime) in some states, the advantage is that it removes such offenders from society. But, where rehabilitation is the goal, mandatory minimum sentences are unrelated to treatment programs and flexibility is lost. Those who oppose the use of mandatory minimum sentences contend that juries would be more hesitant to convict knowing a mandatory minimum sentence would be imposed and judges would be reluctant to sentence because it deprives them of the exercise of discretion in the imposition of sentence.

A final issue is appellate review of sentences. Appellate remedies practiced in our criminal justice system provide little opportunity for either the defendant or the state to appeal a decision solely based on the appropriateness of the sentence to the offense and the offender. If it is important to provide a review system of trial court proceedings to ensure the absence of prejudice, then opportunities for review of sentences must not be denied.

Sentencing cannot be relegated to an unimportant or inconsequential responsibility of the judiciary but, in fact, must be understood as the vehicle for smooth transition of a convicted offender from the courts to the corrections component of the criminal justice system.

Pretrial Detention—Bail

Normally, bail is a procedure for releasing arrested persons on financial or other consideration to ensure their return for trial. Recent bail reform has shown that careful fact gathering for pretrial release decisions, experimentation with standards for release without bail, and the mobilization of broad public and professional interest can change long-established practices. The National Conference on Bail and Criminal Justice, held in 1964, focused attention on the wastefulness and unfairness of the system. The system's major fault is exclusive reliance on the posting of money to ensure the defendant's return. A defendant with means can afford to pay bail or buy his freedom. The poor defendant languishes in jail for weeks or more before trial. Detainees are often indiscriminately mixed with persons convicted of crime with the result that the detainee might come out with greater criminal inclinations. Unnecessary detention costs the community more than jail expenses. A central fault of the existing system is that it detains too many people, with serious consequences for defendants, the criminal process, and the community. The aim of reform must be to reduce pretrial detention to the lowest level without allowing the indiscriminate release of persons who pose substantial risk of flight or of criminal conduct. The present bail system fails to promote decisions founded on facts about the accused.

The first step toward reform must be to introduce fact-finding procedures that will furnish, immediately after arrest, verified information about the accused and his community ties. With this information, a rational assessment of the risk can be made. Where there is no significant risk, the defendant can be released without bail.

Another step is to develop new methods to reduce the risk of flight where it is significant. The judge should be given authority to set certain conditions on release. The courts should clearly explain to him the defendant's duty to appear at trial at the time of his release and should notify him in advance of his scheduled return. The growing recognition of the need for reform of the bail system has led to impressive progress in many states.

Much More

Other factors cannot be overlooked. The legal, manpower, and financial needs for defense of the accused, the need for lawyers providing counsel for defendants unable to obtain adequate representation, adequate compensation of counsel, flexible standards of eligibility, and proper education and training in the criminal law are all worthy of consideration.

SUMMARY

There is a great need for reform in our judicial and court systems. Particular concentration must be placed on the state court systems and, more specifically, the lower courts. The first step in reform must come with complete criminal law revision in jurisdictions that have not revised their criminal codes in the near past. Many recommendations focus on the need for unified and simplified state court systems with central supervision. Well-trained court administrators are needed to perform functions of an administrative nature, thus allowing judges to concentrate on their judicial responsibilities. There is a need for closer working relationships between state and federal court systems, the sharing of ideas and opening of lines of communication. Quality of personnel in courts, particularly judges, must be improved. Courts should have full-time professional judges who have law degrees. It is highly recommended that the Missouri Plan be followed for selection of judges.

Court procedures and practices that need to be updated and streamlined include plea bargaining, sentencing practices, and bail procedures.

LEARNING EXERCISES

Issues to Be Discussed

1. There is considerable belief that professionally trained court administrators can materially increase the effectiveness and efficiency of court management and administrative procedures. Some contend, however, that the trend to better court management by this method is impeded by judges refusing to give up their own prerogative in this area. Examine the literature on this subject and if possible talk to a court administrator. Do you believe in the rapid expansion of the role of the court administrator? Why or why not?
2. Describe why the area of most needed reform in the judicial system is in the lower courts at the state level.
3. Why is the reform of criminal law a necessary first step in judicial reform?
4. Why is it necessary that there be established better relationships between state and federal judicial agencies and officers?

Group Activity

Establish a class panel on sentencing. One group will take the position for the need to retain indeterminate sentencing. The second will favor determinate or, in addition, flat sentencing. Study the concepts of each and the literature on the positions taken with respect to these types of sentences. Debate the issue in a panel discussion. Ensure that the moderator or panel members describe generally each type of sentencing.

Field Activities

1. Interview a public defender to obtain information on how he views the function of his office, his legal philosophy regarding public defense, and some of his most persistent operating problems.
2. Attend courtroom sessions where plea bargaining is in process and prepare your own critical analysis of the process.
3. As part of your continuing notebook record, prepare a 300-word evaluation of one of the above efforts.

Key Terms

Court administrator
Court unification
Missouri Plan

Plea bargaining
Pretrial detention

SUGGESTED REFERENCES

ADVISORY COMMISSION ON INTERGOVERNMENTAL RELATIONS. *For a More Perfect Union: Court Reform.* Washington, D.C.: U.S. Government Printing Office, 1971.

AMERICAN BAR ASSOCIATION. *The Improvement of the Administration of Justice.* Chicago: American Bar Association, 1971.

AMERICAN FRIENDS COMMITTEE. *Struggle for Justice.* New York: American Friends Committee, 1971.

CALIFORNIA COMMISSION ON PEACE OFFICER STANDARDS AND TRAINING. *The Impact of Social Trends on Crime and Criminal Justice.* A Project S.T.A.R. publication. Published jointly by W. H. Anderson Publishing Co., Cincinnati, and Davis Publishing Co., Santa Cruz, Calif., 1976.

DOWNE, LEONARD. *Justice Desired: The Case for Reform of the Courts.* New York: Praeger, 1971.

FRANKEL, MARVIN E. *Criminal Sentences: Law Without Order.* New York: Hill & Wang, 1973.

FRIEDMAN, LEE S. "The Evaluation of a Bail Reform." *Policy Sciences,* Vol. 7 (1976), pp. 281–313.

FRIESEN, ERNEST C.; GALLAS, E. C.; AND GALLAS, N. M. *Managing the Courts.* Indianapolis, Ind.: Bobbs-Merrill, 1971.

GOLLFREDSON, DON M.; WILKINS, LESLIE T.; AND HOFFMAN, PETER B. *Guidelines for Parole and Sentencing.* Lexington, Mass.: Lexington Books, 1977.

HAND, RICHARD C., AND SINGER, RICHARD D. *Sentencing Computation Laws and Practice: A Preliminary Survey.* Washington, D.C.: American Bar Association, Resource Center on Correctional Law and Legal Services, 1974.

HOGARTH, J. *Sentencing as a Human Process.* Toronto: University of Toronto Press, 1971.

INSTITUTE OF CRIMINAL JUSTICE AND CRIMINOLOGY, UNIVERSITY OF MARYLAND. *Reducing Court Delay.* National Institute of Law Enforcement and Criminal Justice, Law Enforcement Assistance Administration, U.S. Department of Justice. Washington, D.C.: U.S. Government Printing Office, 1973.

LEINERT, EDWIN M. *Social Action and Legal Change: Revolution Within the Juvenile Court.* Chicago: Aldine, 1970.

MERRILL, W. JAY; MILLES, MARIE N.; AND SENDROW, MARK. *Case Screening and Selected Case Processing in Prosecutors' Offices.* National Institute of Law Enforcement and Criminal Justice, Law Enforcement Assistance Administration, U.S. Department of Justice. Washington, D.C.: U.S. Government Printing Office, 1973.

NAGEL, STUART S. *Improving the Legal Process: Effects of Alternatives.* Lexington, Mass.: Lexington Books, 1975.

NATIONAL ADVISORY COMMISSION ON CRIMINAL JUSTICE STANDARDS AND GOALS. *Courts.* Washington, D.C.: U.S. Government Printing Office, 1973.

PRESIDENT'S COMMISSION ON LAW ENFORCEMENT AND THE ADMINISTRATION OF JUSTICE. *Task Force Report: The Courts.* Washington, D.C.: U.S. Government Printing Office, 1967.

SARRI, DAVID J. *Modern Court Management: Trends in the Role of the Court Executive.* Washington, D.C.: U.S. Government Printing Office, 1970.

SERILL, MICHAEL S. "Determinate Sentencing: History, Theory, Debate." *Corrections Magazine,* Vol. 3 (September 1977), pp. 3–13.

SEYMOUR, WHITNEY NORTH, JR. *Why Justice Fails.* New York: Morrow, 1973.

SINGER, RICHARD G. "Sending Men to Prison: Constitutional Aspects of the Burden of Proof and the Doctrine of Least Drastic Alternatives as Applied to Sentencing Determinations." *Cornell Law Review,* Vol. 58 (1972), pp. 51–89.

TWENTIETH CENTURY FUND TASK FORCE ON CRIMINAL SENTENCING. *Fair and Certain Punishment.* New York: McGraw-Hill, 1976.

VON HIRSCH, ANDREW. *Doing Justice: A Rationale for Criminal Sentencing.* Report of the Committee for the Study of Incarceration. New York: Hill & Wang, 1976.

WALKER, NIGEL. *Sentencing in a Rational Society.* New York: Basic Books, 1971.

WHINERY, LEO H., et al. *Predictive Sentencing.* Lexington, Mass.: Lexington Books, 1976.

WICE, PAUL BERNARD. *Bail and Its Reform: A National Survey.* National Institute of Law Enforcement and Criminal Justice, Law Enforcement Assistance Administration, U.S. Department of Justice. Washington, D.C.: U.S. Government Printing Office, 1973.

APPLYING YOUR KNOWLEDGE: COURTS

Cases/Issues

CASE

Ralph Williams was elected in November as county prosecutor for a four-year term on a promise to eliminate all plea bargaining in the county criminal courts. The local press had heartily endorsed him for office because a recently published study had indicated that the evidence behind many previous guilty pleas in exchange for lighter charges might not have held up in jury trials. The county judges refused to involve themselves in the election issue since they were not running for reelection in the recent voting. When Williams took office the administrative judge of the criminal courts contended that any phased reduction even of 10 to 20 percent in the pleas would almost double the workload of the courts. The citizens group for Equity in Court Procedures criticized the judge for being more interested in workloads than rights. The county commissioners grew alarmed at the possible strain on the county budget. The newspaper again reprinted the foundation findings and called for an end to plea bargaining.

1. How should prosecutor Williams prepare the way for his program? Does he have alternatives?
2. What arguments could be marshalled to demonstrate that plea bargaining is acceptable provided certain other reforms were undertaken in the court system?
3. Is plea bargaining cost effective?

ISSUE

Every offender sentenced to a correctional institution is entitled to know precisely, at the time of sentencing, how long the term of imprisonment will be if good behavior is maintained. Parole boards should then be abolished.

1. If you were a judge would you be in favor of an indeterminate or a determinate sentencing system? Why?
2. What actions might prosecutors and judges take under a determinate sentencing system if they believed the required sentence to be too harsh?
3. Is a determinate sentencing system, in your opinion, a deterrent to crime?

Continuing CJS Project

Refer back to the concluding pages of Part 1 of this text in which the project for system analysis was introduced. Follow the same pattern for courts. Consider the following:

1. What are good examples of areas where the courts component of the criminal justice system is impacting favorably on the other components? Where is it creating "system" problems for other components?
2. Who is the pivotal person in the judicial process, in your opinion, having the greatest impact on law enforcement and corrections activities? Why?
3. What are your recommendations for system improvements in courts, based upon your previous readings and discussions?

PART III

Corrections

12

Development of Corrections

Overview
History of Corrections
Emergence of Corrections
Keeping Criminals as Public Policy
Capital Punishment
Brief Review of Criminology—Theory and Research
Summary
Learning Exercises
Suggested References

OVERVIEW

The development of corrections can be traced back to primitive man when tribal punishments were imposed on those who offended the tribe or individual members. Ancient punishments among the Greeks, Romans, Sumerians, and Hebrews were specifically devised to fit the level of crime. Corrections as a concept arose out of the writings of eighteenth- and nineteenth-century European scholars who founded principally the Classical and Positive Schools. Prisons for the most part were later developments of the correctional system that was built on these concepts. Most of the ideas of indeterminate sentencing, probation, parole, and juvenile court were also nineteenth-century inventions, particularly in America. Capital punishment had primitive origins and the debate over its efficacy has grown more intense in very recent times. The field of professional study of crime causation and treatment of offenders and delinquents is generally referred to as criminology.

Corrections is the third and final phase of the criminal justice process. Beginning with law enforcement as the case-finding phase, the courts determine by trial under due process of law what cases shall proceed to the corrections phase. Corrections attempts to rehabilitate and neutralize the deviant behavior of adult criminals and juvenile delinquents.

The contribution of corrections to the criminal justice system is to process the people in whose lives the courts have given society the authority to intervene so that society can be protected and individual offenders may be safely released back into society. The successes and failures of the criminal justice system are measured in the field of corrections. The productivity of the entire criminal justice system is judged by the productivity of corrections.

There are probably more than 12 million major crimes committed in the United States each year. Recent victimization studies, particularly the National Crime Surveys (NCS),[1] indicate that most offenses are vastly underreported and that the real crime rate could be several times that high. The *Uniform Crime Reports* (UCR) are the official crime rates published by the FBI and contain those statistics voluntarily reported by law enforcement agencies. Some states have laws requiring these statistics to be reported by a state law enforcement agency, which improves their quality in those states. In 1976, the statistics based on 9,738 agencies and a total population of 196,156,000 indicated a total estimated number of offenses at 11,304,800.[2] There were 10,530,772 crimes reported, according to the

---

[1] Panel for the Evaluation of Crime Surveys, Bettye K. Eidson Penrick, ed., *Surveying Crime* (Washington, D.C.: National Academy of Sciences, 1976).

[2] *Crime in the United States, 1976—Uniform Crime Reports* (Washington, D.C.: Federal Bureau of Investigation, released September 28, 1977), p. 35.

UCR,[3] followed by 2,161,800 arrests for these major or Index Crimes[4] (Index Crimes are those reported most consistently—homicide, forcible rape, robbery, aggravated assault, larceny, and motor vehicle theft). There were 1,203,880 persons charged in court, with 60.3 percent (725,140) guilty as charged, 3.4 percent (40,932) guilty of lesser offenses, 18.7 percent (225,126) turned over to juvenile court, and the remainder (212,602) acquitted.[5] Approximately 20 percent of persons referred to juvenile court are subsequently adjudicated delinquent.

Although the corrections phase of the criminal justice system has considerably fewer clients than do either law enforcement agencies or the courts, corrections has its clients much longer. The average police contact with an offender may range from one day to a matter of weeks, depending upon the length of the investigation. The court contact generally ranges from a matter of weeks to several months, depending upon the severity of the case and the court load, even though a "speedy trial" is guaranteed by the Constitution of the United States and the penal code of the individual jurisdictions.

The recidivism rates per crime may be observed by the number of persons rearrested within four years after their releases in 1972, shown in Table 12–1. They may not have been rearrested for the same offense. Rearrest rates for all offenses average about 63 percent. The offenses most frequently involved in rearrests for the same previous offenses are auto theft, forgery, and larceny. Persons

TABLE 12-1 Repeaters by Type of Crime Released in 1972 and Rearrested Within 4 Years

Type of Crime	Percent of Offenders Who Are Repeaters
Burglary	81
Robbery	77
Motor Vehicle Theft	75
Rape	73
Assault	70
Stolen Property	68
Forgery	68
Larceny—Theft	65
Narcotics	65
Murder	64
Weapons	64
Fraud	63
Gambling	50
Embezzlement	28
Other	64

Crime in the United States, 1975—Uniform Crime Reports (Washington, D.C.: Federal Bureau of Investigation, released August 25, 1976), p. 45.

[3] Ibid., p. 146.
[4] Ibid., p. 173.
[5] Ibid., p. 217.

are seldom rearrested for the same offense in cases of murder, rape, and embezzlement.

The corrections caseload may be divided in several ways. The primary division is between the adult offenders and the juvenile offenders. Although state laws differ, a person is usually a juvenile until his eighteenth birthday, though he can be transferred to adult court generally around the fifteenth birthday at the discretion of the juvenile court judge. Other divisions are made between the felons and the misdemeanants, depending upon the seriousness of the offenses.

HISTORY OF CORRECTIONS

The development of our modern system of criminal justice was difficult and tedious to achieve. The corrections phase is the newest part of the criminal justice system—workhouses and county installations had their beginnings about 1553, only four centuries ago, and the prison or penitentiary had its beginning around 1773 and 1790, only two centuries ago.

Social control of some sort has existed since man organized into a society. It first began to be enforced by social disapproval and vengeance against the offender by the victim or his family. The development from early social reaction against offending individuals to the modern criminal justice system took a long time. Custom and folkways were the controls of primitive man. Ancient man developed his concepts of right and wrong and placed them into codes. Medieval man institutionalized them, and the church became central to social control. Modern man developed criminal laws at the end of the eighteenth century. An adequate understanding of corrections, as compared with law enforcement or the courts, requires a historical perspective of man's reaction to deviant behavior from primitive to modern times.

Ancient Punishments

The blood feud is the matrix of all law.[6] The blood feud and some primitive approaches such as trephination continued in ancient Egypt. In fact, the blood feud continues to modern times, but ancient man attempted to mitigate its social effects, as has modern man. Ancient man developed arbitration courts to replace the fighting that occurred in the blood feud. The first arbitration court, which was depicted on Achilles' shield in Homer's *Iliad,* probably existed around 2000 B.C. It was shown as being located at the gates of the city, suggesting that the offender was returned to the city or expelled from it, depending upon the verdict of the court. The decision of this court generally involved an indemnity to the victim or his family for two or three years or longer, depending upon the seriousness of the offense and the damage to the victim. An offender may have been indentured for life. There were several situations, other than offenses, that could result in this

---

[6] William Seagle, *The History of Law* (New York: Tudor, 1946), p. 36.

slavery, such as heavy indebtedness or being taken a prisoner of war. In any case, this system led to the establishment of a society of free men and slaves, of which Plato wrote in *The Republic*. This social system pervaded the ancient feudal era, the medieval feudal era, and continued for centuries. When the Mayflower arrived at Plymouth Rock in 1620, for example, there were 104 freemen, as distinguished from indentured persons who could not make the trip.

The ancient codes developed after writing by pictures emerged around 4000 B.C. The first were the Sumerian codes, which were developed about 3500 B.C. The Code of Hammurabi in Babylon, written in 1927 B.C., included suggestions for harsh punishments for many offenses. The Law of Moses developed between 1500 B.C. and 900 B.C. and became incorporated in the Old Testament, particularly in Exodus 21 and 22. The Ten Commandments appear in Exodus 20: 3–17. Manu, the Law-Giver, is supposed to have authored the Code of Manu in India probably in the sixth century B.C., but this code has been preserved only in a metrical recension made probably about 100 A.D. Manu had been warned by a huge fish to build an ark; after surviving the deluge, he became ancestor to mankind and so was able to decree laws. Confucius (Latinized form of K'ung Fu-tze) of China lived from 550 or 551 to 479 B.C. He never claimed divine relationships, but provided an ethical system, a system of philosophy, and the Golden Rule that influenced China for centuries. Although similar developments in social control were evolving throughout the civilized world, the codes of the Western civilizations became most important when, centuries later, colonialization spread European thinking and social arrangements around the globe.

The rise of the great religions influenced the entire world in terms of social control. Primitive peoples centered their social control around religion and the "bad luck to the tribe" concept. The witch doctor and the medicine man called on supernatural powers to dispel evil. With the rise of the great religions, however, the ethical systems and social control became more systematized. Most important to Western civilization was the Council of Nicaea in 325 A.D., where the relationship of Christ to God was settled by a close majority in favor of viewing Christ as divine rather than merely a prophet. Major developments occurred immediately on the side of church law and enforcement, which secular law was coerced to support. The vote of Nicaea was so close and the issues so emotional that the victors pressed their advantage harshly, zealously punishing and eliminating their opposition. Heresy became a major crime. Christianity ceased to be a sect of Judaism and became an independent religion. The subsequent development of the church was almost congruent with the history of the Middle Ages.

Medieval Punishments

After the fall of Rome in 476 A.D., Emperor Justinian I assumed the throne of the Eastern Roman Empire in 518 A.D. He appointed ten commissioners to go through all the existing constitutions and codes to select the valuable sections and render them useful to the empire. The resulting code was promulgated in 529. In the years that followed his death in 565, more revisions were made to the code. Four books were finally produced, roughly dated about 600 A.D., and they became the standard of law throughout Europe during the Middle Ages in the absence of any other standard. The common law, as it is known today—both English and European—is basically derived from the Code of Justinian.

With the fall of the Roman Empire, Europe was in chaos. The organized church was the only reliable political entity. Any Western secular ruler had to have the blessings of the Pope. Around 800 A.D., Charlemagne began to organize secular control of Europe, still in concert with the church. The Holy Roman Empire, established around 1200 A.D., was a secular organization in cooperation with the church, which adopted the entire Justinian Code as its legal structure.

There were a few isolated incidents of long-term confinement for punishment, however, beginning in the twelfth and thirteenth centuries, particularly in London, Venice, Paris, and Constantinople. These were humanitarian acts and were the exception, rather than the rule. Some thieves were incarcerated at Baulk House on High Street in Winchester (London area) in 1103, for example.[7] The first prisoner to die in the Tower of London was Rannulf Flambard in 1128, and a special facility was built by Brian Fitzcourt in 1128, called "Cloere Brien," to accommodate the famous William Martel.

Medieval jails were rarely housed in special buildings. The castle towers, the inn cellar, and, most frequently, the gatehouse to the abbey served as places of safe-keeping for prisoners. There was no adequate separation by age, character, or sex, and so contagious pestilence and moral corruption of every type went on undeterred. The construction of jails was first authorized by Henry II at the Assize of Claredon in 1166. Spain was the first to separate men from women in 1519. Most other countries did not make this separation until the late eighteenth century.

The medieval system of punishment was primarily based on compensation. Restitution, indentureship, and fines were common. Whipping and the pillory (stocks in which offenders were locked in public view) were usual. Capital punishment was not permitted under Canon Law, so the church turned some offenders over to secular courts in order to impose the death penalty. Other dispositions were commitment to working the mines, working in the galleys of war ships, and working on fortifications. Amputation of limbs was frequently used in northern Africa and the Middle East, and mutilation and branding for purposes of identification were common everywhere.

A method of expelling an offender from society in the late Middle Ages was to declare him an "outlaw"; this was done by the courts. While it is difficult to establish the beginnings of outlawry in Britain, it was in use prior to the Norman Conquest in 1066.[8] Outlawry remained a civil procedure in Britain until about 1879 and continued, in theory at least, in criminal cases until 1938. Many outlaws

---

[7] N. Vidmar and P. Ellsworth, "Public Opinion and the Death Penalty," *Stanford Law Review,* Vol. 26 (1974), pp. 1245–70.

[8] Anthony Babington, *The Power to Silence* (London: Robert Maxwell, 1968), p. 73.

formed gangs of three or four hundred and served as mercenaries for powerful barons who wanted to control towns or areas of the countryside.[9] The legendary Robin Hood, who was supposed to have lived in the last half of the twelfth century, was a supposed "outlaw."

As the feudal system broke down, indentureship became unprofitable, except in the trades. Consequently, with the expansion of commerce and industry, the feudal economic and social systems broke down, there were riots in the cities, and new methods of handling offenders had to be found. For 400 years before the Industrial Revolution, between the fourteenth and eighteenth centuries, punishments in England and in Europe were harsh and bloody, with corporal and capital punishments prevailing. Ingenious torture devices were developed.

In 1557, a workhouse was established at St. Bridgit's Well, shortened to Bridewell. Originally designed to hold recalcitrant apprentices, it soon housed prostitutes, beggars, vagrants, and minor offenders. By 1576, justices throughout England were required to provide one in every shire or county. The Rasp Huis, a similar institution, was established in Amsterdam in 1595. The purpose was to bring the offenders to good citizenship by the discipline of industry, education, and religious instruction. Gradually, however, the penal implications predominated, and industry as training gave way to hard labor as punishment. The early workhouses were operated by the warden, who purchased his position, and who used the workhouse and the prisoners as a business enterprise. Licensed keepers sold liquor to the prisoners and, despite the lack of privacy, prostitutes plied their trade in the institutions.

For the more serious offenders, however, the purpose of punishment was to eliminate them from society. In 1679, statutory sanction was given to transporting major English offenders to the American Colonies. The English Parliament in 1717 made the American Colonies the penal colony for England. By 1775, two thousand major offenders were being sent to America each year. Estimates were that up to 100,000 convicts were sent in chains from England to the American Colonies.[10] This practice continued until 1776, when the American Revolution began. After that, English prisoners were sent to Australia until exporting prisoners was stopped in 1854.

The Eighteenth Century

The eighteenth century was pivotal in the history of Western man. This period was the heyday of European colonialization, which spread the thinking, culture, philosophy, economics, and social and political arrangements of Europe across

---

[9] C. Hibbert, *The Roots of Evil: A Social History of Crime and Punishment* (Boston: Little, Brown), pp. 3–50.
[10] Harry Elmer Barnes, *The Story of Punishment,* 2nd rev. ed. (Montclair, N.J.: Patterson Smith, 1972, originally published by The Stratford Company, 1930), p. 71.

the world. It was in the eighteenth century that the slogan, "the sun never sets on the British empire," was coined.

The Industrial Revolution is generally dated at 1750, although the transition was a hundred years on either side of that date. The feudal system had broken down, and the capitalistic system of economy was emerging in Western civilization. Governmental reorganization followed the great revolutions. The American Revolution created a new and significant nation that was to contribute much to the history and culture of the world. The French Revolution revised the concepts of government on the continent.

In the area of social control, religion had been central from early primitive man until the eighteenth century. The priests and ministers had been the community leaders and a potent force in government. In the eighteenth century, however, the emergence of secular law replaced religion as the base of social control. Since the eighteenth century, industrial economies, capitalistic systems, and democratic governments became the foundations of Western society. Society's response to crime and its treatment of criminals had to be modified to accommodate this changing social thinking.

EMERGENCE OF CORRECTIONS

A review of the emergence of corrections must take into account the emergence of the criminal law. In 1764, Beccaria published his famous *Essay on Crimes and Punishments,* anonymously at first, in which a primary contention was that the punishment should fit the crime. Previous punishments were harsh and bloody far beyond equity, such as hanging for picking pockets. Further, Beccaria said that man was hedonistic, in that he sought pleasure and avoided pain, and if he knew the consequences of his crime, he might choose not to do it. A primary result of this thinking was that laws were passed and the punishments delineated so that offenders could know the consequences of criminal behavior. Previously, the court or the judge made adjudications on the "merits of the case."

Of course, the English Parliament had passed laws in the fourteenth and fifteenth centuries outlawing war against the king, forbidding serfs to leave the soil in search of work, and forbidding persons who did not own land from keeping dogs. During the sixteenth and seventeenth centuries, treason and heresy became capital crimes, as did swearing, adultery, and witchcraft. However, it was not until the late eighteenth century that the criminal law as it is known today was written. Previously, wrongs were heard on their own merit, and punishments were meted out according to the judgment of the court.

Early Prisons

While there had been places of detention in Greece in the seventh century B.C., in Jerusalem in the sixth century B.C., and in Rome (the Mamertine Prison) in the third century B.C., they were used for detention, rather than for long-term punishments. In the Middle Ages, the places of detention were not separate buildings, but facilities already there, such as a tower or the gate-house of an abbey.

The workhouse had been the first attempt at a prison approaching the modern definition. The Newgate Prison, built in London in 1769 and torn down in 1902, was also a place of detention, without a program. However, in the workhouse at Ghent in 1773 Jean Jacques Philippe Vilian developed businesslike methods that served as a pattern for later prison experimentation. Consequently, some have indicated that this workhouse at Ghent was really the first modern prison. Also in 1773, a prison was developed in Connecticut by constructing administration buildings over an old abandoned mine at Simsbury, about forty miles north of New Haven. Offenders were simply dropped down the shaft and lived in three parallel tunnels about eight hundred feet long, supplied by a single pool of fresh water. Not surprisingly, the first prison riot occurred there in 1774.

Maine soon constructed an underground prison using an abandoned quarry. However, the majority of the colonies constructed prisons above ground because underground construction was quite expensive. The first one west of the Alleghenies was at Frankfort, Kentucky. The construction began on this prison in 1797 and it received its first prisoners in 1800. These early prisons were not much different from the jails of the medieval period. Everybody was thrown in together. Men and women, children and adults, the sick and the healthy were put in the same tank. Liquor was freely available. In fact, the jail or confinement facility at Hartford, Connecticut, was under one roof with the town tavern.

In Philadelphia, a group of Quakers organized into the Philadelphia Society for Alleviating the Miseries of the Public Prisons. By 1790, they gained enough strength and influence to transform the old Walnut Street Jail into the first modern penitentiary. Consequently, the penitentiary movement was one of the first American contributions to the criminal justice system. The concept of "corrections" had been developed.

Early Prison Systems

The Pennsylvania System, incorporated in the old Walnut Street Jail, was one of solitary confinement to avoid spreading moral contamination from one prisoner to another. Everyone was given productive work to do in his cell. In addition, he had a Bible and received religious counseling. Each cell had its own small exercise yard. A person could remain in prison for years without associating with fellow prisoners. His only contact with other people was when the religious counselor visited him and when his meals were brought to him and slipped under the door.

In 1815, New York established a prison at Auburn that provided individual confinement at night, congregate work during the day in silence, and harsh discipline. Strong security measures were prominent in the Auburn System. The Auburn plan was more economical and administratively feasible than the Pennsylvania System. The factories or industries incorporated in the Auburn System provided productive work that brought income to the prison. Whipping was defended as the best approach to discipline because it supposedly eliminated long-term confinement that defeated the socialization process.

These two systems, the Pennsylvania System and the Auburn System, competed almost viciously for several years, at least into the 1850s. European observers adopted the Pennsylvania System, feeling it was more humanitarian. Consequently, the Pennsylvania System is prominent throughout Europe. The prison of the Commonwealth of Puerto Rico has a motto inscribed in Spanish over the entrance, "Abhor the crime, but have compassion for the criminal." Because of its greater economy, however, American penology adopted the Auburn System.

The early prisons were characterized by idleness, lack of discipline, and unsanitary conditions. The Pennsylvania system begun by the Quakers at the Walnut Street Jail in Philadelphia emphasized solitary confinement and meditation for the purpose of penitence, thereby becoming the first "penitentiary." The Auburn System in New York in 1815 emphasized congregate labor and silence.

By the mid-1800s, American prisons had become industrialized or had large farms. Some worked mines, such as Kansas, Tennessee, and Alabama. The majority of prisons in the 1800s leased the prisoners to the highest industrial bidder or contracted with him to furnish the raw materials to the prison and pay an agreed price for the finished product. By the twentieth century, however, most American prisons had gone to the state-account system, where prison-made goods were sold on the market, or the state-use system, where the prison made goods to be used by state agencies and institutions. In 1870, the first meeting of the National Congress on Penitentiary and Reform Discipline met in Cincinnati to discuss prison policy and grew into the American Correctional Association, which is today attempting to provide accreditation to prisons and other correctional programs. The two primary thrusts of the Congress were toward education and toward gradual release or parole. The indeterminate sentence is needed to institute parole. Michigan first passed an indeterminate sentence law in 1867. It remained for New York, however, to implement the gradual release or parole program at Elmira in 1876, which also was the first reformatory based on educational programs.

Other Corrections Developments

Probation was another American contribution to the criminal justice system. John Augustus, a shoemaker in Boston, spent some time visiting the courts. In 1841, he requested that the judge let him pay the fines and give him supervision of several minor offenders. By 1858, he had bailed out 1,152 men and 794 women and girls. He had also helped thousands of others. The first probation law was passed in Massachusetts in 1878 to enable the city of Boston to appoint a probation officer to replace John Augustus, who had died but who had established the need for probation. All states now have some form of probation, although the probation laws may differ from state to state.

Parole is a form of release under supervision after the prisoner has served some time in an institution. Parole was a contribution of England and Ireland, although it was first mentioned by Mirabeau in 1791 in a report designed to suggest improvements for the court in Paris. Captain Alexander Maconochie used it on Norfolk Island in 1840, when he thought some of the inmates who had been banished from England could safely return home. They were given a ticket-of-leave to cover their return. Parole was made part of the Irish system by Sir Walter Crofton in 1854.

The *juvenile court* was another American contribution to criminal justice. Inaugurated in 1899 in Illinois, it was the result of considerable work by the Women's Clubs of Chicago, which hired lawyers to draft a constitutional act. It is interesting that the two women who took initial leadership in the juvenile court movement in Chicago had organized the national PTA in Washington, D.C., in 1897. After unsuccessful attempts in Illinois to draft a constitutional juvenile court law in 1895 and 1897, the first juvenile court act became effective July 1, 1899. Since that time, countries all over the world have developed specific methods of handling children, some with juvenile courts, others with different laws handled by the same courts as adults, and still others handling children differently from adults on an informal basis only.

Corrections emerged, then, in the last part of the eighteenth century and throughout the nineteenth century. The early developments, of course, preceded the eighteenth century, such as jails and workhouses. Twentieth-century refinements have brought corrections to its present state.

KEEPING CRIMINALS AS PUBLIC POLICY

As technology improved and the old feudal system broke down in favor of commerce and the capitalistic system of economy, the food supplies improved and man's entire standard of living improved with it. As a surplus of food developed, moral values had greater holding power. It was at the time of this transition, around the time of the Industrial Revolution, that welfare programs were started (1601), prisons were initiated (1773), and public health programs (1797 in the United States) and mental health programs (late eighteenth and nineteenth centuries) were introduced to civilization.

The surplus of food and a higher standard of living has permitted man not only to support nonproductive citizens, but to try to diagnose and treat them so that they can become productive. It was at this pivotal turn in history, essentially the eighteenth century, that moral values became as important as economics in public policy. Consequently, the emerging public policy was that all programs designed to promote the general welfare, including prisons, be supported and promulgated by civilized society. In an affluent society, moral values can support "human rights," minimum welfare payments, and minimum standards for prisons. The philosophical determinants in modern prison administration have become important.

Slavery has been associated with criminal justice since ancient times. The ancient and medieval feudal systems approached criminal justice in private terms. A common disposition by the courts was enslavement as a factor in restitution and compensation into the sixteenth century continuing in the Old South in the United States until the Civil War. It is generally conceded that slavery has provided some of the basic ingredients for the modern penal system.[11] In 1891, the Supreme Court held that prisoners had no rights, that they were "slaves of the state," and that the Thirteenth Amendment prohibits involuntary servitude "except as a punishment for crime."[12] In 1978, the Texas Department of Corrections was compared to a slave plantation.[13]

In a democratic society, police, correctional workers, and all agents of social control in the criminal justice system must respond to the rights, needs, and desires of the constituency they serve, including the citizen offender. Otherwise, they risk violence, riots, strikes, adverse public opinion, and litigation initiated by inmates or civil liberties groups. Berkley has indicated that democracy is hard on the police and other agents of social control.[14]

CAPITAL PUNISHMENT

The death penalty has been in the criminal justice system from primitive to modern times. It was first seriously challenged by Marcus Porcius Cato (234–149 B.C.) in the Roman Senate. In the Middle Ages, the Church did not have capital punishment, but occasionally turned a serious offender over to the secular courts for that purpose.

Capital punishment was used extensively until the eighteenth century. During the reign of Queen Elizabeth (1533–1603), there were 72,000 Englishmen put to death. Whether a dent was made in the crime rate as a result depends on which account is read. At the least, the accounts are inconclusive. In the eighteenth century, the writings of Voltaire and Montesquieu in France, the influence of Jeremy Bentham and Samuel Romilly in England, and the significant contribution of Beccaria's famous *Essay on Crimes and Punishments* reduced the practice of legal executions. All African and Asian nations, as well as Communist states, retain the death penalty today. In contrast, most Western European countries, most South American countries, and sixteen states and territories of the United States had abolished it by 1972.

Since statistics on the death penalty began to be collected systematically in the United States in 1930, 3,859 people had been executed by July 2, 1967, when Luis José Monge died in the gas chamber at the Colorado State Prison. Of the

---

[11] J. Thorsten Sellin, *Slavery and the Penal System* (New York: Elsevier Publishing Co., 1976).

[12] *Ruffin v. Commonwealth*, 21 Grat. 760, Virginia, 1891.

[13] "Is TDC the Paragon of Prison Systems . . . or a Slave Plantation?" *Corrections Magazine*, Vol. 1 (March 1978), pp. 1–25.

[14] George Berkley, *The Democratic Policeman* (Boston: Beacon Press, 1969), p. 1.

3,859 executions, there were 1,731 white males, 20 white females, 2,054 black males, and 12 black females.

On July 29, 1972, the United States Supreme Court declared the death penalty unconstitutional in *Furman v. Georgia*[15] because it was applied in a discriminatory manner, since the indigent black male was executed in disproportionate numbers, making it cruel and unusual punishment. Due process and equal protection problems had to be met before a death penalty statute could be written so that it would apply equally to all and not be simply discretionary. Florida was first to pass such a statute on December 2, 1972. By July 1976, thirty-seven states had reinstated the death penalty and there were 572 men and 10 women on death row in thirty states, of whom 300 were black, 260 were white, 13 were Mexican-Americans, and 8 were Indians. Actual executions were held up, however, because of cases before the Supreme Court questioning the constitutionality of the death penalty statutes, mostly on due process, as had been the case in *Furman v. Georgia*.

On July 2, 1972, the Supreme Court validated the capital punishment statutes of Georgia, Florida, and Texas, and struck down those of Louisiana and North Carolina.[16] On July 6, 1976, the Supreme Court struck down Oklahoma's death penalty statute as cruel and unusual punishment in violation of the Eighth and Fourteenth Amendments.[17] On January 17, 1977, Gary Gilmore was executed by firing squad at the Utah State Prison, the first execution in nearly a decade after Luis José Monge in Colorado in July 1967.

By December 31, 1976, all states except Alaska, Hawaii, Iowa, Maine, Michigan, Minnesota, Washington, West Virginia, and Wisconsin had reinstated the death penalty, as had the United States at the federal level. There had been 125 persons on death row in North Carolina when its law was struck down, which eliminated the death penalty; the persons on death row reverted to life imprisonment. The states with the largest number of people on death row at that time were Florida (81), California (68), Ohio (67), Texas (53), Georgia (34), Tennessee (34),

The public favors capital punishment. The 1972 "straw vote" on the California ballot in November was overwhelmingly in favor of the death penalty. In June 1973, 59 percent of the public favored the death penalty.[19] Simultaneously, 57 percent of the public considered life sentence without parole as an effective deterrent.[20]

---

[15] *Furman v. Georgia,* 408 U.S. 228 (1972).

[16] *Gregg v. Georgia,* 44 U.S.L.W. 5230 (1976); *Proffit v. Florida,* 44 U.S.L.W. 5256 (1976); *Jurek v. Texas,* 44 U.S.L.W. 5262 (1976); *Woodson v. North Carolina,* 44 U.S.L.W. 5267 (1976); *Robertson v. Louisiana,* 44 U.S.L.W. 5281 (1976).

[17] *Green v. Oklahoma,* 44 U.S.L.W. 3761 (1976).

[18] *Capital Punishment, 1976—National Prisoner Statistics Bulletin, Advance Report* (Washington, D.C.: National Criminal Justice and Statistics Service, LEAA, April 1977), pp. 2-3.

[19] Louis Harris and Associates, *Current Opinion* (Williamstown, Mass.: Roper Public Opinion Research Center), Vol. 1, p. 80.

[20] *Ibid.,* p. 81.

Attitudes toward the death penalty are a function of social orientation and personality that determine the value systems of people from which these attitudes emerge. Conservatives in social orientation tend to favor the death penalty while liberals tend to desire its abolition. Authoritarian personalities with strong antioffender attitudes, punitive approaches to social problems, intense power-oriented feelings, and controlling policies exist everywhere.[21] These people favor the death penalty almost automatically, while nonauthoritarian people are more tolerant and oppose the death penalty. Significant personality differences by a variety of tests show that these two opposite personality groups differ widely on measures of dogmatism, moral judgment, and other tests of personality. Studies of these authoritarian personalities with regard to jury selection have indicated significant differences between two groups—those who could return a verdict of guilty in a capital case and those who could not.[22] There is a tendency for less-educated people, including prison inmates, and some in the professional levels of law, law enforcement, engineering, and medicine, to be less tolerant and more authoritarian, while people in the social and behavioral sciences tend to be less authoritarian. The authoritarian personalities in society provide a strong base for capital punishment.

The most recent strong debates on this topic have occurred in the Canadian Parliament, where a moratorium on the death penalty was imposed between 1968 and 1973. The debate was finally—or temporarily—settled in 1976 with abolition of the death penalty. The arguments used by Cato in the Roman Senate two centuries before Christ and the arguments in the Canadian Parliament are surprisingly similar.

The historical arguments concerning the death penalty can be divided into utilitarian or empirical arguments based on fact and traditional sentiments and beliefs. From the debates of Cato in the Roman Senate to the recent debates in the Canadian Parliament, the death penalty has never been argued successfully either way on the utilitarian basis.

The most successful arguments have come from traditional sentiments and beliefs. The primary arguments have been (1) that the death penalty deters others from committing serious crimes; (2) that the death penalty eliminates at least one dangerous criminal; (3) that the revenge motive is espoused by Mosaic Law (Exodus 21: 12, 16, 17, 24, 25, and 29; also Exodus 22: 1–9, 18, 19) and is sufficient to retain it; and (4) that the satisfying of social anger is functional. The first and second arguments are based on attempts to show positive effect. Historically, the third and fourth arguments have really been most effective, with deterrence as a

---

[21] T. W. Adorno, Else Frenkel-Brunswick, Daniel J. Levinson, and R. Nevitt Stanford in collaboration with Betty Aron, Marcia Hertz Levinson, and William Morrow, *The Authoritarian Personality* (New York: Harper Brothers, 1950).

[22] Robert E. Thayer, "Attitude and Personality Differences Between Potential Jurors Who Could Return a Death Verdict and Those Who Could Not," *Proceedings of the Annual Convention of the American Psychological Association, 1970* (Washington, D.C.: American Psychological Association, 1971), pp. 445–46.

rationalization. There have been many other arguments advanced, of course, but they seem to be peripheral and secondary to the four main arguments.

Religious arguments have ranged from the vengeance of the Mosaic Law in the Old Testament to the question of humaneness and brotherly love. Although these other arguments have been used, the four fundamental arguments remain deterrence, elimination, revenge, and satisfying social anger.

Studies by Sellin[23] and others[24] have indicated neutral results when the death penalty has been used for deterrence. On the other hand, a recent study by Ehrlich, an economist, suggests that it is a deterrent,[25] but other researchers point to his narrow data base and questionable research methodology. In his dissent in *Furman v. Georgia,* Chief Justice Burger called the evidence on deterrence by the death penalty an "empirical stalemate."

By December 31, 1976, forty-one states and the United States government had reinstated the death penalty and there were 444 people on death rows. States without the death penalty were Alaska, Hawaii, Iowa, Michigan, Minnesota, New Hampshire, Oregon, West Virginia, and Wisconsin. The largest number on death row at that date was 81 in Florida, which rose to 87 by July 1977.

BRIEF REVIEW OF CRIMINOLOGY—THEORY AND RESEARCH

The serious study of criminal justice, criminal law, and its practical application in corrections began with Beccaria in 1764. The criminal law emerged with the impetus given by Cesare Beccaria (1738-94) in his *Essay on Crimes and Punishments,* first published in 1764, and with the active participation of William Blackstone (1723-80), Samuel Romilly (1757-1818), and Jeremy Bentham (1748-1832) in codifying English criminal law and procedure between the time of the American Revolution and the War of 1812. Known as the Classical School of Criminology, the key approach was equality of sentencing under the slogan, "Let the punishment fit the crime." The underlying correctional philosophy was the utilitarian concept of the greatest good for the greatest number. Prevention was more important than punishment, the need for open and speedy trials was noted, the watchword was deterrence rather than revenge, and there was increased use of imprisonment in humane physical quarters. The Classical School remains the basis of the legal approach to crime control and correction.

With the rise of biology as a science in the mid-nineteenth century (the term *biology* having first been used in 1837), the influence of Charles Darwin and other famous biologists on other fields of knowledge was unmistakable. In criminology, Cesare Lombroso (1836-1909) developed the Positivistic or Positive School of Criminology by placing emphasis on the appraisal of criminality in scientific

[23] Thorsten Sellin, *Capital Punishment* (New York: Harper & Row, 1967).
[24] See a fairly well-balanced collection of studies in James A. McCafferty, ed., *Capital Punishment* (Chicago and New York: Aldine-Atherton, 1972).
[25] Isaac Ehrlich, "The Deterrent Effect of Capital Punishment: A Question of Life or Death," *American Economic Review,* Vol. 65 (1975), p. 397.

terms. In 1836, Lombroso published the thesis that the typical criminal can be identified by certain physical characteristics, that behavior was a function of structure, and that the criminal was born as an atavistic animal who could not be civilized.[26] His "born criminal" concept was subsequently refuted by the work of Charles Goring in his study of *The English Convict,* which was published in 1913, but Lombroso's influence was great in the late nineteenth and early twentieth centuries. His primary constructive contributions were in focusing corrections on the offender himself and in applying scientific method in the field of criminology.

Two diverse views, then, entered into the field of criminal justice, criminology, and corrections. The Classical School focused upon the crime. The Positive School focused on the individual offender. While Lombroso may have been wrong about the "born criminal," he did introduce the determination to assess criminality in scientific terms, focusing on the individual. This approach, while enlarged to include social and environmental factors impinging on the individual, has prevailed in criminal justice in the twentieth century.

Criminology became identified with sociology after World War I when Maurice Parmelee pointed out strongly that the research in criminology that had been published in scholarly journals between 1900 and 1919 had been done primarily by sociologists.[27] Subsequently, most colleges and universities developed courses in criminology and in juvenile delinquency in their departments of sociology. After World War II, separate programs in criminology and criminal justice began to develop. Previously, August Vollmer, chief of police at Berkeley, was influential in getting a police program begun at the University of California in 1929 that became formalized in 1931 as the School of Criminology, and Michigan State had a police program supported by the Michigan State Police in 1935. Washington State University began a law enforcement program in 1941. Florida State University began the first correctional program in 1952, which became a broad criminal justice program offering a Ph.D. in 1957 and is now a School of Criminology. Southern Illinois University at Carbondale began a corrections program in the early 1960s and the Texas legislature established a program at Sam Houston State University in Huntsville with the intent that the Texas Department of Corrections be served. The funds from the LEAA have given considerable impetus to the development of college and university programs in criminal justice since 1968.

Criminology Research

The first large-scale, significant research in criminology and its application to corrections was developed in the late 1920s at the University of Chicago under the leadership of Ernest Burgess, Henry D. McKay, and Clifford Shaw. Although

---

[26] See Gina Lombroso Ferero, *Criminal Man, According to the Classification of Cesare Lombroso* (New York: Putnam, 1911).

[27] See Maurice F. Parmelee, *The Principles of Anthropology and Sociology in Their Relations to Criminal Procedure* (New York: Macmillan, 1908); and Maurice F. Parmelee, *Criminology* (New York: Macmillan, 1922).

Sam Warner had previously done the first study of parole prediction (prediction of success or failure on parole) in 1923 in Massachusetts, most of the subsequent work in this field was done in Illinois. The Chicago Area Project was initiated by Clifford R. Shaw in 1926 and contributed to research and knowledge in the field for decades afterward. By 1959, there were twelve Chicago neighborhoods with projects under a central board. Other cities emulated in principle these projects for the study and prevention of delinquency. The New York City Youth Board, established in 1947, is probably the outstanding example.

In 1935, the Cambridge-Somerville Youth Study was begun under the leadership of Richard C. Cabot to prevent delinquency and develop stability in children. There is general agreement that the possibilities for providing sound research for good social policy in the field are encouraging.[28] Sheldon and Eleanor Glueck of Harvard University have been prolific in their research since the 1930s, although some of it, like their Delinquency Prediction Scale,[29] has been questioned. Their contributions, nevertheless, have been significant. They, more than other theorists, probably remained in their own frame of reference, having essentially paid little attention to the research and theories of others in the field while developing a voluminous contribution of their own.

The first major theory was that of differential association, presented by Edwin H. Sutherland in 1937. Simply stated, it means that the delinquent learns delinquent behavior from his associates. Sutherland's students have developed modifications of his theory. Daniel Glaser developed a theory of differential identification. Donald R. Cressey has refined and defended the original theory. David Matza and Gresham Sykes developed a theory of neutralization, which holds that unfavorable predispositions toward delinquency can be negated. Walter C. Reckless, originally from the Chicago School, has proposed a containment theory in which inner self-concept and outer containment provide pressures that may or may not result in criminal behavior. Robert Merton has refined Emile Durkheim's sociological theory of *anomie,* or alienation from society, and applied it to crime causation. Albert Cohen has based an interpretation of delinquent behavior on social class and delinquent subcultures, which several sociologists have done, such as Walter Miller and others. Richard Cloward and Lloyd Ohlin have tried to combine these approaches into a theory of opportunity. Various combinations of these concepts comprise contemporary criminological theory.

SUMMARY

Corrections has developed from practically nothing prior to the late eighteenth century to a full-fledged segment of the criminal justice system in the nineteenth and twentieth centuries. The emergence of corrections provided the base for com-

---

[28] William McCord and Joan McCord, *Origins of Crime* (New York: Columbia University Press, 1959); and Daniel Glaser, *Adult Crime and Social Policy* (Englewood Cliffs, N.J.: Prentice-Hall, 1972).

[29] Sheldon and Eleanor T. Glueck, "Early Detection of Future Delinquents," *Journal of Criminal Law, Criminology, and Police Science,* Vol. 47 (1956), p. 175.

paratively sophisticated approaches to treatment in the 1970s. Correctional functions exist in other noncorrectional agencies, such as the family, school, church, police, and courts, that are involved with behavior development long before formalized correctional programs come to bear on the individual. Only about one-sixth of the people arrested by law enforcement agencies ever become a part of the corrections caseload. Corrections is the smallest, but the longest and most difficult part of the criminal justice system.

LEARNING EXERCISES

Issues to Be Discussed

1. There is some evidence that tends to show that the Positive School which has emphasized the individual in the criminal equation and which predominated in the past fifty years has given way to the Neo-Classical. This latter school focuses on the crime itself, swift and sure punishment, determinate sentencing only, and a selective use of rehabilitation. Study all the schools of punishment and present your views of what appears to be the best method for meeting the problems of the next decade.
2. Why is the blood feud referred to as "the matrix of law"?
3. When and how did the penitentiary develop?
4. Why does modern society keep its criminals, supporting them with tax funds, rather than enslaving them or eliminating them?

Group Activity

Prepare a class panel to argue the issue of capital punishment. Include historical development, modern criticisms, court decisions, and moral issues involved.

Field Activity

Check the local city directory for private or public organizations dealing with problems of ex-offenders, capital punishment, rehabilitation of prisoners—schooling, jobs, etc.—and interview a staff member on the aims and purposes of the organization as it relates to the criminal justice system. Elicit from your interviewees the current problems and what they see as the future needs of the criminal justice system in their own areas of concern. Prepare as part of your continuing notebook a 300-word critical summary of your interview.

Key Terms

Auburn System
Beccaria
Classical School
Code of Hammurabi

Justinian Code
Law of Moses
Pennsylvania System
Positive School

SUGGESTED REFERENCES

BARNES, HARRY ELMER. *The Story of Punishment.* Boston: Stratford Co., 1930.

BEDAU, HUGO A., ed. *The Death Penalty in America.* New York: Anchor Books, 1967.

———, AND PIERCE, C. M. *Capital Punishment in the United States.* New York: AMS Press, 1976.

GAROFALO, RAFFAELE. *Criminology.* Montclair, N.J.: Patterson Smith, 1968.

LOMBROSO, CESARE. *Crime and Its Causes.* Montclair, N.J.: Patterson Smith, 1968.

MANNHEIM, HERMANN. *Pioneers in Criminology.* Chicago: Quadrangle, 1960.

MENNINGER, KARL. *The Crime of Punishment.* New York: Viking, 1966.

NATIONAL ADVISORY COMMISSION ON CRIMINAL JUSTICE STANDARDS AND GOALS. *Corrections.* Washington, D.C.: U.S. Government Printing Office, 1973.

ROTHMAN, DAVID J. *The Discovery of the Asylum: Social Codes and Disorder in the New Republic.* Boston: Little, Brown, 1971.

RUBEN, SOL. *The Law of Criminal Correction.* 2nd ed. St. Paul, Minn.: West Publishing Co., 1973.

SCHAEFER, S., AND KNUDTEN, R. D., eds. *Criminological Theory.* Lexington, Mass.: Lexington Books, 1977.

SHORT, JAMES F., JR., ed. *Delinquency, Crime and Society.* Chicago: University of Chicago Press, 1976.

TAPPAN, PAUL W. *Crime, Justice and Correction.* New York: McGraw-Hill, 1960.

WRIGHT, ERIK O. *The Politics of Protest.* New York: Harper & Row, 1973.

ZIMRING, F. E., AND HAWKINS, G. *Deterrence: The Legal Treat to Crime Control.* Chicago: University of Chicago Press, 1973.

13

Jails

Overview
Jails and Stockades
Jail Administration and Operation
Lockups
Misdemeanants
Volunteers in Jail
Jail and Release on Own Recognizance
Houses of Correction
Summary
Learning Exercises
Suggested References

OVERVIEW

Jails have been established since ancient times as places for individuals awaiting trial or disposition. Today they are still considered places of limited detention—again for awaiting trial or for incarceration for periods of less than one year. Because the jail is a catchall, it has special problems involving the adequacy of the facility, training of personnel, budget for essential services, and methods for handling inmates. Jails are normally supervised by a sheriff and his staff, who are normally county based. Most jail inmates are confined for victimless crimes such as prostitution, drunkenness, and drug abuse. Jail reform for the future involves not only problems of staff and facility but also the increased services to be made available to inmates, such as personal counseling, help from various community sources, and bail assistance during the period of confinement.

The jail is the oldest of the institutions in the criminal justice system. In accordance with the tenets of the Code of Justinian that confinement should never be used as punishment, the jail historically has been a place for detention awaiting trial. By the twelfth and thirteenth centuries, English law provided for royal commissions to hold general and special assizes (sessions) to deal with treasons, murders, felonies, and other offenses. The commissions were also charged with "jail delivery," which required them to try every prisoner in jail, regardless of the offense, and make disposition in order to get them out of the jail. Frequent dispositions were flogging, branding, mutilation or amputation, and stock and pillory, although more extreme offenses resulted in banishment, exile, or death.

There were no separate buildings for detention prior to the Assize of Claredon in 1166. At that time, under Henry II, the jury system was formalized in much the same way it still functions, the duties of the sheriff were delineated, and jails were authorized to be constructed. Prior to this and in many jurisdictions afterwards, available buildings and facilities were used for detention.

Jails were the only places designed for detention until the development of workhouses in the middle and late sixteenth century. In the sixteenth century jails or local institutions began to be used for the punishment or care of minor offenders. Major offenders were still banished, exiled, or put to death.

In the United States jails are considered to be those local facilities that can be used to hold offenders or accused persons for forty-eight hours or longer, according to the LEAA and the United States Bureau of the Census when the *1970 National Jail Census* was taken. The four functions of jails are (1) to hold accused persons awaiting trial; (2) to hold convicted persons serving short-term sentences; (3) to hold convicted persons awaiting sentence or execution of a long-term sentence, such as transfer to a prison; and (4) to hold material witnesses as needed.

Some stockades could be considered in this group. Stockades are viewed in at least three different ways: (1) a county facility used like a jail for persons who can work under minimum security conditions; (2) the same county facility sometimes used to house accused offenders who have not been tried and who cannot "be worked"; and (3) the confinement facility on military posts. Lockups are short-term detention facilities found in almost any police station where persons cannot be legally held more than forty-eight hours.

The *1970 National Jail Census* reported 4,037 locally administered jails with authority to detain prisoners for forty-eight hours or longer, excluding the state-operated jail systems of Connecticut, Delaware, and Rhode Island. The number of jails in the country is difficult to count accurately, partly because jails are local institutions, with no central point for reporting. Also, it is frequently difficult to determine whether a person can be held in an installation for more than forty-eight hours, which generally differentiates a jail from a lockup. Estimates of the number of lockups have ranged from 15,000 to 41,000, depending upon what definition is used.

The jails surveyed in the *1970 National Jail Census* held 160,863 inmates on March 15, 1970, of whom 7,800 were juveniles.[1] About half (50.9 percent) of the adults had not been convicted, and about two-thirds (66.1 percent) of the juveniles had not been adjudicated delinquent. Recreation facilities were reported by 13.6 percent of the jails, educational facilities by 10.8 percent, medical facilities by 51.0 percent, visiting facilities by 74.0 percent, and 98.6 percent of the jails reported having toilet facilities. By 1972, the number of local jails had been reduced to 3,921, with 141,588 inmates.[2] This was apparently due to the condemning of existing jails, such as in Des Moines, and failure to build new ones, combined with the use of ROR (release on own recognizance) and other diversion projects.

JAILS AND STOCKADES

Jails and stockades are frequently considered to be correctional institutions, though many correctional administrators and law enforcement administrators have difficulty in viewing them as such. It is generally agreed that lockups are a part of police protection rather than corrections. There have been poorly defined relationships and some antagonism and strain between law enforcement, such as the National Sheriff's Association, and correctional people, such as the American Correctional Association, as to proper programming of jails.[3]

---

[1] Law Enforcement Assistance Administration, *1970 National Jail Census* (Washington, D.C.: U.S. Government Printing Office, 1971), p. 19.
[2] *The Nation's Jails: A Report on the Census of Jails from the 1972 Survey of Inmates of Local Jails* (Washington, D.C.: National Criminal Justice and Information Service, LEAA, May 1975), pp. 22–25.
[3] W. S. Brent, "The National Jail Association, Inc.," *American Journal of Correction,* Vol. 27, No. 4 (July–August 1965), p. 43.

The Literature

Probably one of the best guides to jail construction has been the *Handbook of Correctional Institution Design and Construction* published in 1949.[4] The first significant book on jails in the United States was published in 1944.[5] The second noteworthy book on jails was published in 1957.[6] Prior to that, the Wickersham Report in 1931 included a report by Hastings H. Hart about jails, including the comment that there were fully 3 million different persons committed to jails each year, with some being committed several times.[7] The National Sheriff's Association published a *Manual of Jail Administration* in 1970.[8] Two excellent presentations of jail standards are the *Manual* of the Illinois Department of Corrections' Bureau of Detention Facilities and Jail Standards, which includes an excellent bibliography, and *Jail Evaluation: A Standard Report* by Culbertson and Mayra.[9]

The United States Bureau of Prisons developed a correspondence course for jailers in the 1940s and 1950s. A new course has been developed by the bureau, with the assistance of the University Extension Service of the University of Wisconsin, under a grant by the LEAA. Its excellent basic text is titled *The Jail: Its Operation and Management*.[10]

The National Sheriff's Association published five excellent pamphlets on jails in 1974: *Inmates' Legal Rights; Food Service in Jails; Jail Security, Classification, and Discipline; Jail Programs;* and *Sanitation in the Jail*. Another one in 1975 was published on *Jail Architecture*. Beginning in January 1978, the Washington Crime News began publishing a monthly compilation of jail news under the title, *Jail Administration Digest*.

Limitations and Problems of Operation

The safe and successful operation of a jail depends on the ability of staff members to follow established procedures when dealing with prisoners. Procedures are aimed at meeting the goals of (1) protection of the safety of jail personnel; (2)

---

[4] *Handbook of Correctional Institution Design and Construction* (Washington, D.C.: Federal Prison Industries, Inc., 1949), pp. 168–87.

[5] Louis N. Robinson, *Jails: Care and Treatment of Misdemeanant Prisoners in the United States* (Philadelphia, Pa.: Winston, 1944).

[6] Myrl Alexander, *Jail Administration* (Springfield, Ill.: Charles C Thomas, 1957).

[7] *Report of the National Commission on Law Observance and Enforcement,* No. 9 (Washington, D.C.: U.S. Government Printing Office, 1971), p. 329.

[8] *Manual of Jail Administration* (Washington, D.C.: National Sheriff's Association, 1970, rev. 1973).

[9] *Illinois County Jail Standards* (Springfield, Ill.: Illinois Department of Corrections, 1971); Robert G. Culbertson and Randy Mayra, *Jail Evaluation: A Standards Report* (Lansing, Mich.: Michigan Council on Crime and Delinquency, 1976).

[10] Nick Pappas, ed., *The Jail: Its Operation and Management* (Washington, D.C.: United States Bureau of Prisons in cooperation with University Extension Service of the University of Wisconsin, LEAA Grant #373, 1970), p. 153.

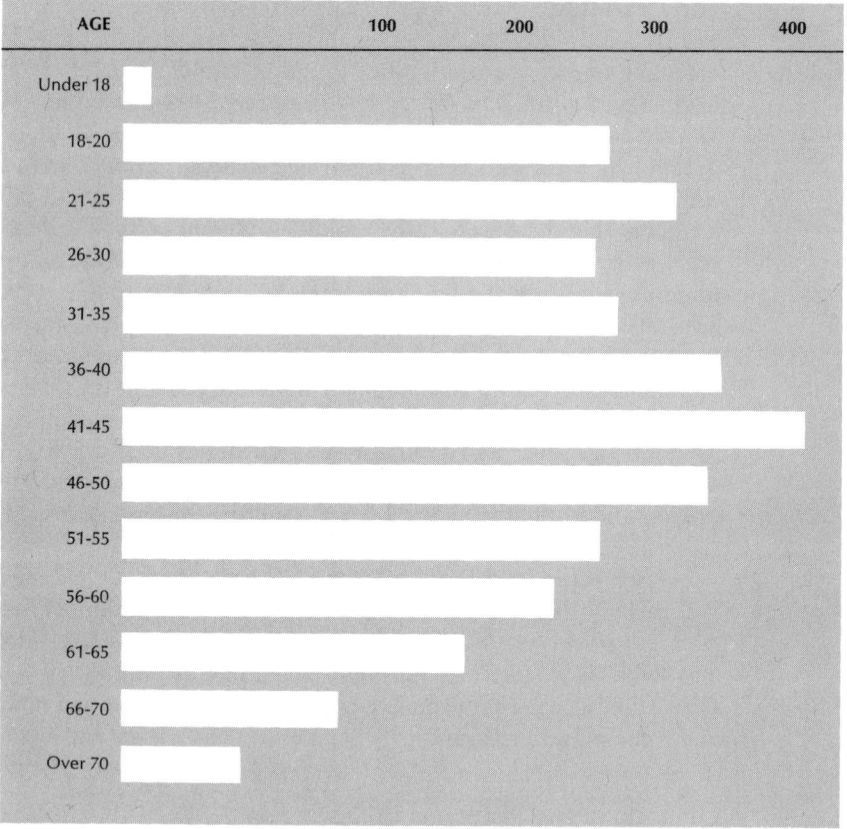

FIGURE 13-1 Age: Total Bookings, San Joaquin County, California
Source: Nick Pappas, ed., *The Jail: Its Operation and Management* (Washington, D.C.: United States Bureau of Prisons in cooperation with University Extension Service of the University of Wisconsin, LEAA Grant #373, 1970), p. 153.

safe-keeping and welfare of prisoners; and (3) protection of society by prevention of escapes.[11]

The jail receives many unusual persons because it deals with people in trouble from a variety of approaches. The special prisoner most seen by the jailer is the drunk, although some seemingly drunk people may be diabetics lapsing into a coma and therefore in need of immediate medical attention. Psychotics, medical problems, mental retardates, drug addicts, users sometimes in withdrawal, head injuries, and suicides are only a few of the problems jails have to handle.[12] In

---

[11] Alice Howard Blumer, *Jail Operations: A Training Course for Jail Officers, Programmed Instruction Book II: Jail Operations* (Washington, D.C.: United States Bureau of Prisons, LEAA Grant #373, 1971), p. 1.

[12] Alice Howard Blumer, *Jail Operations: A Training Course for Jail Officers, Book VI: Special Prisoners* (Washington, D.C.: United States Bureau of Prisons, LEAA Grant #373, 1971), p. 6.

Dade County, Florida, 60 percent of jail inmates in 1972 had experience with drugs and 18 percent were charged with drug offenses.

The ages of persons booked in jail is distributed fairly evenly between eighteen and fifty-five, though the largest single age group is in the age forty-one to forty-five category.[13] The number of persons under eighteen years of age who are booked in jail is almost negligible in comparison with the total number. The number of bookings begins to decrease in the age fifty-six to sixty category, decreases rather sharply in the sixty-six to seventy category, with a further decrease in the over-seventy age group. The ages of prisoners booked in San Joaquin County, California, in 1969, which are typical of the national averages, appear in Figure 13–1. The grade completed in school by inmates booked in the same facility at the same time is shown in Figure 13–2. This results in programming problems for a nonhomogeneous clientele.

The problem of discipline is a very important part of jail programs, and must be handled with considerable discretion.[14] It is important to recognize what

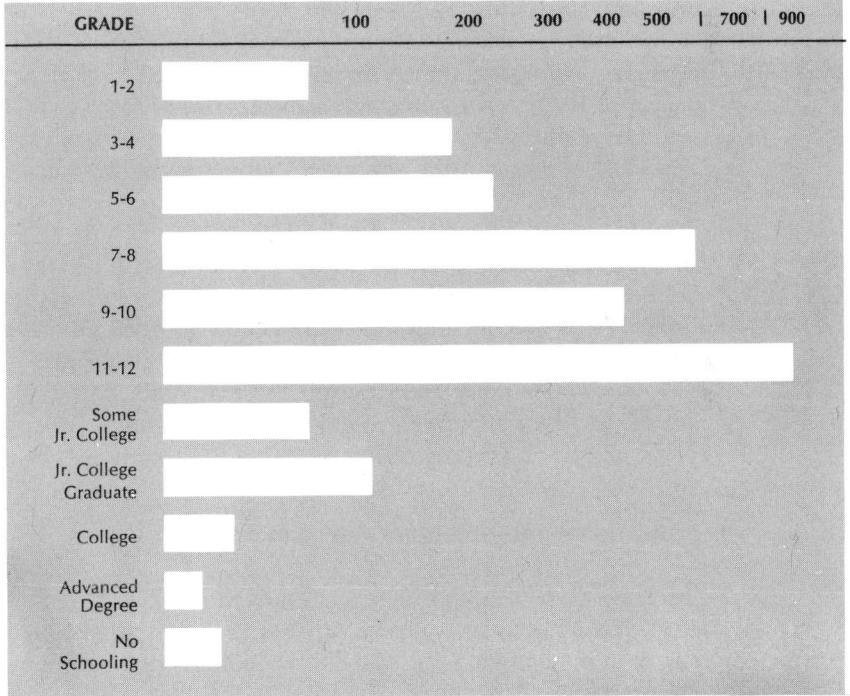

FIGURE 13–2 Last Grade Completed: Total Bookings, San Joaquin County, California

Source: Nick Pappas, ed., *The Jail: Its Operation and Management* (Washington, D.C.: United States Bureau of Prisons in cooperation with University Extension Service of the University of Wisconsin, LEAA Grant #373, 1970), p. 153.

[13] Pappas, *The Jail*, p. 153.
[14] Alice Howard Blumer, *Jail Operations: A Training Course for Jail Officers, Book V: Discipline* (Washington, D.C.: United States Bureau of Prisons, LEAA Grant #373, 1971), p. 39.

situations require disciplinary actions and what situations do not, and then choose the correct disciplinary action needed. Some positive factors of discipline include teaching self-control, setting standards of proper behavior, and correcting improper behavior consistently and fairly. Some of the negative actions are taking away some of the prisoners' "good times," taking away privileges, or assigning prisoners to solitary cells.

Jail Services and Personnel

There have been several outstanding surveys of jail services. The Missouri jail survey in 1939 was one of the earliest of the adequate surveys. The Illinois jail survey of 1969 was one of the most recent and probably the best.[15] In that survey, wide discrepancies were found within the state as to what or even whether records were kept in jails. Two-thirds of the jails fingerprinted everyone. Some kept the prints within the jail, rather than sending them to the FBI in Washington for recording, classifying, and reporting.

It is not unusual for county jails anywhere in the country to be accused of neglecting medical treatment for inmates who need it, of allowing night jailers to require sexual favors from female inmates, and of misuse of jail labor by sheriffs or county commissioners. Inadequate personnel who do not know or care what is legal or ethical tend to be permitted to function in these manners in a similarly inadequate political climate.

Recruiting jail personnel is most important because historically the jail has been staffed by the most inadequate personnel available to the sheriff. In the past, the staff frequently consisted of people who could not meet the public well. Jail employees in modern times must be people of good character and reputation, competent enough to forestall many incipient jail problems.[16]

Work-release has been instituted in many jails on a county-wide basis. Although the first work-release law, known as the Huber Law, was passed in Wisconsin in 1913, it was not really used until the second half of the century.

Professional and Volunteer Associations

The National Jail Association was founded in 1939. It included sheriffs, police chiefs, law enforcement officers, jail wardens, and others interested in jails. It is now an affiliate of the American Correctional Association. It meets annually with the American Correctional Association and has a column in the bimonthly *American Journal of Correction,* the house organ of the American Correctional Association. Its purpose is to provide a forum for the exchange of information

---

[15] Illinois Department of Corrections, "The Current Status of County, City Jails in Illinois," *New Horizons in Detention,* Vol. 2, No. 1 (January 1972).

[16] Alexander, *Jail Administration,* p. 17.

among jail administrators and personnel and to generally upgrade the contribution of the jail to the criminal justice system.

There are several volunteer organizations that serve jails. An example is the Offender Aid and Restoration group called O.A.R. of Virginia, Inc. (414 Fourth Street, N.E., Charlottesville, Virginia 22901). These volunteer organizations have proved to be most helpful in improving conditions by providing service or by communicating to the political leadership the real problems and needs of the jail. Much of the contribution of volunteer programs has been directly or indirectly effective in improving budgets and standards for the jail.

JAIL ADMINISTRATION AND OPERATION

The typical American jail is a county institution supervised by the sheriff and his staff. In large urban centers, the jail may be operated by a county department of corrections or a competent administrator appointed by the sheriff. Many of the jail's staff are relatively unskilled guards. Frequently they are those of the law enforcement staff who have had difficulty in meeting the public on the streets. On occasion, also, the jail has been used to discipline patrolmen or deputies who are good enough to keep on the force, but who may need "punishment time" and so serve in the jails.

Jail Population

Many different types of people appear in jails, but some present special problems, such as the juvenile offender, the female offender, the drug addict, the alcoholic, the mentally ill, the escape-minded prisoner, the suicide risk, the handicapped prisoner, the homosexual, the epileptic, the diabetic, and all other possible classifications found in the jail-prone strata of society.[17]

Rights of Prisoners

The jail administrator and his staff must be aware of the prisoner's constitutional and civil rights, as well as the legal processes by which they are implemented. No prisoner can be held *incommunicado,* although some jails have violated the spirit of the law by permitting only one telephone call, thereby meeting the letter of the law. No person can be denied access to counsel at any time.

Persons held in jail awaiting trial have many problems in which assistance is needed. If the prisoner is employed, for example, adequate contact with his employer must be arranged so the prisoner can arrange a leave of absence or termination, rather than just dropping out of sight. Arrangements for the family to

[17] *Unusual Prisoners in the Jail,* Correspondence Course for Jailers, Nick Pappas (ed.): Vol. 8 (Washington, D.C.: United States Bureau of Prisons, 1970), p. 12.

receive welfare payments as well as assistance for other family problems, perhaps including adoption or foster placement of the children, have to be followed through. In some cases, business transactions, such as arranging for deferred payment of installment loans, will help prevent a prisoner from losing everything he has accumulated. The vast majority of persons held in jail, whether awaiting trial or for misdemeanors, are from the lower socioeconomic strata and may not have accumulated much, so the little they have accumulated becomes all the more important to them.

Although the Constitution guarantees the right to a speedy trial, some jail prisoners awaiting trial prefer to wait long periods of time to avoid holding a "speedy trial" while all the witnesses are still in town and available, with memories and tempers still fresh. Not having a speedy trial is considered by some offenders as a good defense.

The general public has tended to disregard or remain totally unaware of the problems or activities of the jail. A jail administrator can develop and encourage community involvement and interest in the problems of the jail to assist in the search for financial support and solutions to these problems.[18]

Other Problems and Goals

One of the primary problems of the jailer is that he works in a field that lies between law enforcement and corrections, and thus becomes "a person of divided loyalties and split philosophies."[19] However, many people contend that the philosophies are not divided, but can incorporate the spectrum of viewpoints and broader perspective of the total criminal justice system. The jail is considered to be a part of corrections by the United States Bureau of Prisons.[20] A policy of "firmness and fairness," rather than punishment, is the official policy regarding jails used by the United States Bureau of Prisons.

Before an inmate goes to court for trial, corrections can begin gathering information for a possible presentence investigation report, psychological testing, and other information-gathering procedures.[21] Another important phase of the correctional process is the family counseling to enhance the family's understanding and ability to cope with this new situation. This is important because, despite

---

[18] Alice Howard Blumer, *Jail Management: A Course for Jail Administrators, Book IV: Community Relations* (Washington, D.C.: United States Bureau of Prisons, LEAA Grant #373, 1971), p. 1.

[19] Nick Pappas, ed., *Instructor's Guide to the Jail: Its Operation and Management* (Washington, D.C.: United States Bureau of Prisons, LEAA Grant #373, 1971), p. 1.

[20] Alice Howard Blumer, *Jail Operations: A Training Course for Jail Officers: Programmed Instruction Book 1: Correctional History and Philosophy* (Washington, D.C.: United States Bureau of Prisons, LEAA Grant #373, 1971), p. 42.

[21] *Task Force Report: Corrections*, p. 74, after the New York State Commission on Corrections, *Thirty-seventh Annual Report, 1963* (Albany, N.Y.: State Printing Office, 1964), p. 485.

the heavy rate of repeated offenses and contacts with the jail, the fact remains that about half (49.62 per cent) the inmates in the state of New York, for example, are in jail awaiting trial, and may be released legally innocent but socially damaged.

The treatment program of a jail must aim toward (1) developing job skills in the unskilled; (2) improving educational achievement in the undereducated; and (3) treating personal problems such as alcoholism, personality deficiencies, marital and financial difficulties, and other problems frequently found in the social groups confined to jails.[22]

Programs in jails have been shown to be worthwhile in most areas, from financial gain through programmed and self-improvement of inmates to improved recidivism records, although there is much room for improvement.[23] Offenders in these jails have been found to be chronologically mature, but emotionally and psychologically immature, undereducated, and from unstable backgrounds. Studies of self-concept aspects also indicated that those who accept themselves as criminals are more difficult to correct. Of course, continued exposure to the criminal justice system could lead the inmates to begin to accept themselves as criminals.

LOCKUPS

Lockups are places of temporary detention generally available to every police department or other jurisdictional unit in the country. With more than 40,000 police jurisdictions and over 1,000 other special jurisdictions, such as military installations and specialized state and federal agencies, it has been estimated that there may be as many as 41,000 lockups and other facilities used as lockups in the country. Generally, a lockup is considered to be a facility for confinement for a period of less than forty-eight hours.

There are generally no programs at all in lockups. In fact, feeding the prisoner and meeting his basic needs constitute the major problem in lockups other than security. Only persons arrested or taken into custody on the streets or elsewhere in the community are supposed to be held in lockups, and then only for temporary detention.

MISDEMEANANTS

Misdemeanants are in a legal classification defined by the statutes. Although there is some general agreement as to the offenses included in this category, such as drunkenness, disorderly conduct, petty larceny, assault and battery, other simple

---

[22] Alice Howard Blumer, *Jail Management: A Course for Jail Administrators, Book III: Jail and Community Corrections Programs* (Washington, D.C.: United States Bureau of Prisons, LEAA Grant #373, 1971), p. 1

[23] Alvin Rudoff and T. C. Esselstyn, *Jail Inmates at Work* (San Jose, Calif.: San Jose State College, 1969).

assaults, vagrancy, vandalism, some drug laws, gambling, carrying or possessing weapons illegally, prostitution and commercialized vice, and some family offenses, there is room for considerable variation from jurisdiction to jurisdiction as to many other categories of offenses that might be considered misdemeanors.

Misdemeanant arrests in 1976 were as follows:[24]

Offense	Number of Arrests
Drunkenness	1,297,800
Driving under the influence	1,029,300
Disorderly conduct	657,500
Narcotic drug laws (including felonies)	609,700
Other assaults	428,000
Liquor laws	369,700
Vandalism	211,800
Runaways	202,600
Curfew and loitering law violations	106,300
Gambling	79,000
Offenses against family and children	72,406
Prostitution and commercialized vice	62,600
Suspicion (not included in total)	37,600
All other offenses (except traffic)	1,619,100

The largest single group of misdemeanants are those arrested for some form of drunkenness, constituting about half the jail population that has been convicted. Arrests vary widely according to the policy of the police, city, and the system of justice. Public intoxication is a crime in almost every jurisdiction in the United States. Chronic drunkenness offenders are generally excessive drinkers who may or may not be alcoholics. There are no studies that clearly differentiate the alcoholic from problem drinkers in the chronic drunkenness offender group. Much of the differentiation depends upon variations in definitions. There are over 2 million arrests for drunkenness each year in the United States serious enough to bring people to jail. This places a heavy load on the court system and on the jail. Some persons have been arrested for drunkenness more than one hundred times and have served ten to twenty years in jail in a long series of short-term sentences.

The detoxification unit in St. Louis is an example of what can be accomplished by a concerted treatment program.[25] Police pick up drunks and take them to the detoxification unit where they are placed in bed, nourished, and given medical treatment for seven days and referred for follow-up counseling. The drinking problem of those so treated has generally lessened, along with improvement in employment, health, and housing. This is a considerably better result than that achieved by the traditional drunk tank in a jail.

[24] *Crime in the United States, Uniform Crime Reports—1976* (Washington, D.C.: Federal Bureau of Investigation, 1977), p. 173.

[25] *The St. Louis Detoxification and Diagnostic Evaluation Center* (Washington, D.C.: Law Enforcement Assistance Administration, Grant #284, 1970).

Police have an unusual strategic position to identify human behavioral pathology early, and alcohol and family disturbance calls are indices of problems. Police can play a critical role in the criminal justice system. Sensitive and skillful police intervention in family disturbances has reduced the occurrence of family assaults and homicides. While maintaining their professional identity as officers of the law, they can also acquire the skills and techniques of the helping professional.[26]

VOLUNTEERS IN JAIL

Volunteers have been used in jails as far back as 1800, when Quakers in Philadelphia established a program of counseling jail inmates by lay leaders, although most of the counseling consisted of religious instructions. Volunteers or "lay visitors" have historically been part of jail programs in England. The Salvation Army and other religious organizations traditionally hold religious meetings on Sundays in the jails.

During recent years, professionally coordinated volunteers have been active in counseling in many jails in the United States. A primary advantage is that volunteer participation in jail programs develops an interest on the part of the community in the jail so that the problems and needs become public information for use in budget hearings and other policy formulations. Volunteers can be trained in the realistic objectives to be accomplished in counseling and working with the inmates.

JAIL AND RELEASE ON OWN RECOGNIZANCE

The use of bail has long been a method of lightening the jail population. Bail is the money paid by an alleged offender who is released from jail before his trial, and it establishes security that the accused citizen will appear for arraignment and trial. Article VIII of the Constitution of the United States guarantees that "excessive bail shall not be required, nor excessive fines imposed, nor cruel and unusual punishment inflicted." In recent years, release on one's own recognizance (ROR) has been established. Misdemeanant probation is also used to keep many offenders out of jail. In both cases, bail is paid, but ROR misdemeanants are not supervised, and probation misdemeanants have to report to an officer at frequent intervals before their trials to account for their whereabouts.

Defendants frequently lose their jobs during long periods of incarceration awaiting trial. Release before trial is also associated with the outcome of the case, whether by causation or by selectivity. In a Philadelphia study of 946 cases, 52 percent of the bailed defendants were convicted as compared with 82 percent of

---

[26] Morton Bard, *Training Police as Specialists in Family Crisis Intervention* (Washington, D.C.: Law Enforcement Assistance Administration, 1970), p. 65.

those who had been jailed awaiting trial.[27] Also, 22 percent of those who had been on bail received prison sentences, and 59 percent of those who remained in jail received prison sentences.[28] These statistics do not prove that bail influences the outcome of the trial; they probably reflect which people get out on bail (proving only ineptitude or resources on the part of individuals), and which people provide defense as opposed to pleading guilty. In New York City alone, defendants have been detained in jail prior to trial for a total of 1,775,778 man-days in one year at a daily average cost of $6.25 per man or over $10 million per year,[29] dramatically highlighting the advantages of the ROR system.

HOUSES OF CORRECTION

Houses of correction constitute a large group of county correctional institutions. They trace their history to the establishment of workhouses in England and Europe. These county institutions still remain in some of the older colonial sections of the country, particularly in New York and Pennsylvania. The Westchester County Penitentiary, Albany County Penitentiary, New York City Reformatory on Riker's Island, and the New York City Correctional Institution for Men in Queens are examples in New York State. In Pennsylvania, the Allegheny County Workhouse, Allegheny County Prison, Bucks County Prison and Rehabilitation Center, Erie County Prison, and Lancaster County Prison are examples. In Michigan, the Detroit House of Correction is an example of this local institution. Other county institutions include county road prisons (of chain-gang fame) frequently found in the South, as well as separate penal farms, such as the Shelby County Penal Farm near Memphis, Tennessee.

These houses of correction are generally for offenses referred to as "high misdemeanors," or misdemeanors of the first degree, which are relatively serious offenses but still less than a felony. The general sentence may be one or two years, though it is more frequently six months to a year. The clinical services and programs in these institutions lie somewhere between the jail and the state or federal prison or penitentiary. Most are unable to afford a full program, but can offer more than the jail.

SUMMARY

Jails, lockups, stockades, and other similar facilities are generally for short-term detention. Jails and houses of correction have been used for holding people for short-term sentences of a year or more. At the present time, jails are inadequate,

---

[27] Daniel J. Freed and Patricia M. Wald, *Bail in the United States* (Washington, D.C.: U.S. Government Printing Office, 1965).

[28] Anne Rankin, "The Effect of Pre-Trial Detention," *New York University Law Review*, Vol. 39 (June 1964), pp. 631–55. Also, Daniel J. Freed and Patricia M. Wald, p. 46.

[29] *Pre-Trial Release,* American Bar Association Project on Minimum Standards for Criminal Justice, Institute for Judicial Administration (March 1968), p. 3.

partially because the gradual movement of the population from rural to urban areas has decreased the sheriff's law enforcement duties and increased his political patronage over the jail.[30] It is frequently asked why jails have been permitted to exist for so long, particularly in their present condition. The reasons jails exist have been indicated as follows:

1. Because the tax-paying public wants them and permits them to exist.
2. Because they ostensibly serve the purpose of protecting society, that same tax-paying group, from the depredations of those awaiting court action, or those serving sentences, usually as misdemeanants.
3. Because society seemingly has no alternative for the housing of varied misdemeanants, alcoholics, drug users, vagrants, mentally incompetents, and other assorted misfits—most of whom are not and should not be committed as violators of the criminal law.
4. Because in far too many areas, jails mean jobs (44,298 in 1972), power, and political influence.
5. Because tradition demands, if not dictates, that many holdovers from ancient days be continued.[31]

The jail is really a holding operation at this time. It could, of course, serve those beginning longer terms and offer effective rehabilitation. Because they are the initial contact with the prevailing authority for people in trouble, lockups, jails, stockades, and houses of correction tend to set the tone and will raise the offender's defenses for self-protection or will lower his defenses for subsequent acceptance of rehabilitation, depending upon the manner and attitude with which he is initially held.

LEARNING EXERCISES

Issues to Be Discussed

1. Jails have been branded as the most disgraceful element of the criminal justice system, perhaps the area most in need of reform. Yet it is argued that some way-station is needed, no matter how chaotic, to delay, keep, and sort out offenders until other elements of the criminal justice system make determinations, particularly the courts. In this view, since everything is temporary, the need for reform, while it exists, is not as urgent as in some other parts of the criminal justice system. Which position do you support and why?
2. What are the functions of jails?
3. Describe the procedure followed by jails after commitment of people to them.
4. For what misdemeanors are people held in jails most frequently?
5. What are the functions of volunteers in jails?

[30] Richard A. McGee, "Our Sick Jails," *Federal Probation,* March 1971, p. 4.
[31] Roberts J. Wright, "Why Do Jails Exist?" *Proceedings of the 101st Annual Congress of Correction of the American Correctional Association, Miami Beach, Florida, August 15-20, 1971* (College Park, Md.: American Correctional Association, 1972), p. 177.

Group Activity

In a role-playing situation establish the positions of sheriff and deputy sheriff and two jail inmates—one awaiting trial, another under a misdemeanor sentence for drug abuse of six months. The issue is prisoner rights and prisoner assistance. Have the sheriffs present their views after the inmates have made their case. Let a discussion evolve, then move in a consultant to ask neutral questions and develop a meeting of minds for reform.

Field Activity

Arrange for limited group visits to a local jail. After these visits, hold a class discussion on class findings with respect to observations on administration and management and staff discussions of important problems.

Key Terms

Code of Justinian
Commitment procedure
Detoxification unit
Drunk tank

Huber Law
Lockups
Misdemeanants

SUGGESTED REFERENCES

AMERICAN BAR ASSOCIATION. *Survey and Handbook on State Standards and Inspection Legislation for Jails and Juvenile Detention Facilities.* 3rd ed. Washington, D.C.: American Bar Association, 1974.

AMERICAN CORRECTIONAL ASSOCIATION. *Manual of Standards for Adult Local Detention Facilities.* Rockville, Md.: Commission on Accreditation for Corrections, American Correctional Association, 1977.

CULBERTSON, ROBERT G., AND RANDY MAYRA. *Jail Evaluation: A Standards Report.* Lansing, Mich.: Michigan Council on Crime and Delinquency, 1976.

GOLDFARB, RONALD L. *Jails: The Ultimate Ghetto.* New York: Doubleday, 1975.

NATIONAL CRIMINAL JUSTICE INFORMATION AND STATISTICS SERVICE. *National Jails: A Report on the Census of Jails from a 1972 Census of Inmates.* Washington, D.C.: U.S. Government Printing Office, 1975.

NATIONAL SHERIFF'S ASSOCIATION. *Food Service in Jails.* Washington, D.C.: National Sheriff's Association, 1974.

———. *Inmates' Legal Rights.* Washington, D.C.: National Sheriff's Association, 1974.

———. *Jail Architecture.* Washington, D.C.: National Sheriff's Association, 1975.

———. *Jail Programs.* Washington, D.C.: National Sheriff's Association, 1974.

———. *Jail Security, Classification, and Discipline,* Washington, D.C.: National Sheriff's Association, 1974.

———. *Sanitation in the Jail.* Washington, D.C.: National Sheriff's Association, 1974.

PAPPAS, NICK, ed. *The Jail: Its Operation and Management.* Washington, D.C.: U.S. Bureau of Prisons, 1970.

14
Probation

Overview
Presentence Investigation
Supervision of Probationers
Probation Subsidy Legislation
Conclusions
Learning Exercises
Suggested References

OVERVIEW

Probation is an alternative to sentencing. It involves the supervision of offenders within the community, allowing for continued employment and the use of community services. It is much less costly than incarceration. Probation officers prepare presentence reports and supervise the probationers to ensure maintenance of probation conditions and to assist them in counseling, job placement, and other rehabilitative services. Service is augmented by volunteers who often help to reduce the probation officer's heavy caseload problems. Probation officers have a dual role as both an enforcement officer, to ensure that parole is not violated, and as a counselor, to facilitate readjustment to community life.

Probation is the out-of-jail supervision of the convicted offender by an officer of the court. It is one disposition available to the judge, the other being sentencing to a prison or correctional institution. Probation is used more frequently than any other disposition, both for juveniles and adults. There were 923,064 adults and 328,854 juveniles on state and local probation as of September 1, 1976.[1] In addition, there were 64,246 persons under Federal probation.[2]

Conditions of probation are relatively standard, although special conditions may be imposed. Keeping regular hours, maintaining gainful employment, avoiding public drunkenness, supporting one's family, and not leaving the jurisdiction are a few of the more standard rules. Rules of probation may vary more widely than parole rules, the latter being administrative release under supervision from an institution. Because probation is a judicial concern, each judge may impose special conditions. The usual length of probation averages three years, though it may be as long as five years. Probation given as the result of conviction of misdemeanors, as opposed to felonies, is generally for one year. Supervision in juvenile courts varies according to circumstances. Juvenile court jurisdiction can technically extend to the twenty-first birthday, but such lengthy supervision very rarely occurs.

There are economic and rehabilitative advantages to probation. It costs ten to thirteen times more to maintain a person in an institution than it does to supervise him in the community. In addition, the social situation can be better handled

---

[1] *State and Local Probation and Parole Systems,* Washington, D.C.: Law Enforcement Assistance Administration, 1978, p. 3.

[2] "Persons under supervision of the Federal Probation System, by type of supervision, circuit, and district, on June 30, 1976," *Administrative Office of the United States Courts, 1976, Annual Report of the Director,* pp. 1–50.

in the community, including working with the offender's family. Commitment to institutions involves "social surgery," as the person is completely removed from his social setting. It is more effective to work constructively with his social relationships when the objective is to help the offender adjust to his environment. Unwholesome or unhealthy social relationships can be somewhat subdued by the probation officer, and constructive relationships can be supported, thereby improving the social acceptability of the offender. Even though probation has been usually understaffed and poorly administered, the success rate ranges between 60 and 90 percent.[3] The probation officer, as an agent of the court, investigates people to be sentenced, prepares a report, and then supervises those on probation.

The sentencing judge decides, generally upon the recommendation of the probation officer, who will be on probation and who will be sent to an institution. The probation officer has two functions: (1) the preparation of the presentence investigation (PSI); and (2) the supervision of probationers. During the preparation of the presentence investigation, the probation officer recommends probation or sentencing, depending upon whether he thinks he can work with the convicted person.

The number of probation and parole officers in the United States at the end of 1975, both juvenile and adult, is shown in Table 14–1.

TABLE 14–1 Number of Probation and Parole Officers in the United States

State	Federal Officers	State Officers			Local Officers			Total
		Probation Only	Parole Only	Probation and Parole	Juvenile only	Adult only	Juvenile and Adult	
Alabama	39	—	—	121	180	—	13	353
Alaska	4	—	—	—	—	—	65	69
Arizona	31	—	69	—	279	100	30	509
Arkansas	13	—	31[a]	39	90	—	—	173
California	207	—	541	—	241	202	7,896	9,060
Colorado	17	—	69	—	155	116	70	427
Connecticut	12	225	43	—	—	—	—	280
Delaware	4	48	20	53	—	—	—	125
District of Columbia	53	134	64	—	—	—	—	251
Florida	66	—	—	1,524	—	—	—	1,590
Georgia	39	—	—	636	215	125	1	1,016
Hawaii	7	—	—	—	—	32	91	130

[3] Ralph W. England, Jr., "What Is Responsible for Satisfactory Probation and Post-Probation Outcome?" *Journal of Criminal Law, Criminology and Police Science,* Vol. 47 (March–April 1967), pp. 667–76.

TABLE 14-1 (continued)

State	Federal Officers	State Officers			Local Officers			Total
		Probation Only	Parole Only	Probation and Parole	Juvenile only	Adult only	Juvenile and Adult	
Idaho	3	—	—	90	24	15	9	141
Illinois	75	—	264	—	322	124	346	1,131
Indiana	29	—	76	—	135	92	197	529
Iowa	8	—	61	116	161	—	10	356
Kansas	15	—	—	53	85	16	57	226
Kentucky	28	—	—	128	23	—	—	179
Louisiana	29	—	—	366	105	—	—	500
Maine	2	—	—	48	—	—	—	50
Maryland	35	—	—	922	—	22	—	979
Massachusetts	23	—	200[b]	—	116	377	277	993
Michigan	61	—	—	175	522	525	—	1,283
Minnesota	14	—	—	106	27	2	496	645
Mississippi	13	—	—	162	56	—	—	231
Missouri	36	—	44[a]	248	594	—	—	922
Montana	6	—	17	28	46	—	—	97
Nebraska	5	—	28	—	23	21	52	129
Nevada	10	—	—	85	40	—	—	135
New Hampshire	2	15	4	—	—	—	14	35
New Jersey	38	—	211	—	—	—	1,279	1,528
New Mexico	11	—	—	62	77	20	—	170
New York	117	121	543	—	19	16	2,270	3,086
North Carolina	44	211	—	464	—	—	—	719
North Dakota	3	—	—	12	24	—	—	39
Ohio	49	121	234	—	503	426	155	1,488
Oklahoma	21	—	—	153	83	—	—	257
Oregon	14	—	—	139	263	26	—	442
Pennsylvania	68	—	—	281	224	215	565	1,353
Rhode Island	3	—	—	64	—	—	—	67
South Carolina	22	—	24[a]	125	82	—	3	256
South Dakota	6	—	—	33	5	—	48	92
Tennessee	30	—	—	266[c]	121	—	—	417
Texas	113	—	159[d]	—	422	421	231	1,346
Utah	5	78[a]	—	69	—	—	—	152
Vermont	3	—	—	55	—	—	—	58
Virginia	37	—	—	198	634	204	—	1,073
Washington	26	—	93[a]	213	389	2	10	733
West Virginia	9	71[a]	—	31	9	10	—	130
Wisconsin	8	—	—	281	292	—	31	612
Wyoming	3	—	—	23	—	—	—	26
Total	1,516	1,024	2,795	7,369	6,559	3,109	14,216	36,588

[a]Juvenile only. [b]Includes 120 juvenile. [c]Includes 118 juvenile. [d]Includes 69 juvenile.

Source: *Probation and Parole Directory, Seventeenth Edition, 1976* (Hackensack, N.J.: National Council on Crime and Delinquency, 1976), p. xxii.

PRESENTENCE INVESTIGATION

The presentence investigation (PSI) is conducted by the probation officer in order to learn about the offender, his family, and his social background and to assess his strengths and weaknesses with a view toward working out a treatment program. The presentence investigation report is prepared and presented to the judge after the offender has been convicted, but before he has been sentenced. It is done to guide the judge in the disposition. It generally includes an evaluation of the offender's background, social relationships, occupational strengths and weaknesses, school background, criminal history, and other factors pertinent to the problem. There are several books available that discuss the presentence investigation report in detail.[4]

The presentence investigation report (1) aids the court in determining the appropriate sentence; (2) assists institutions in planning the classification and treatment programs in the institutions; (3) furnishes the parole board with information pertinent to the offender's release on parole; (4) aids the probation officer in his rehabilitative efforts in probation supervision, as well as on parole supervision after the offender's release from prison; and (5) serves as a source of information for systematic research. The report can be helpful to the judge in reviewing the social background of the offender, assessing the recommendation of the probation officer, and arriving at an appropriate sentence.

Decisions Made by the Probation Officer

During the preparation of the presentence investigation report, the probation officer assesses whether a recommendation for probation or for a sentence would be best for the offender and for society. Many probation officers believe that there are no real objective criteria for this decision, so it frequently becomes a matter of whether or not the probation officer thinks he can work with the offender. Prison sentences have been recommended on this basis, but they are also recommended when the previous criminal history of the offender indicates the need for something stronger in terms of external controls. Sometimes, the probation officer's caseload is already too heavy to add another case, so that persons who would otherwise have been placed on probation may have to go to prison.

In making decisions regarding recommendations for probation, the items shown in the following table were considered in their order of importance by probation officers in a California study.

Relatively few items actually seem to enter the probation officer's decision to recommend probation or imprisonment. From those items listed in Table 14–2,

---

[4] For example, see Paul W. Keve, *The Probation Officer Investigates* (Minneapolis: University of Minnesota Press, 1960).

TABLE 14-2 Probation Criteria

Item	Percentage of Times Selected
Offense	100.0
Prior record	100.0
Psychological/psychiatric	79.7
Defendant's statements	69.6
Defendant's attitudes	62.3
Employment history	60.9
Age	53.6
Family history	52.2
Marital status	42.0
Medical history	29.0
Education	21.7
Military history	17.4
Alcoholic involvement	15.9
Homosexuality	15.9
Drug usage	13.0
Interests and activities	13.0
Family criminology	11.6
Plea	7.2
Confinement status	7.2
Residence data	4.3
Religion	4.3
Legal representation	0.0
Place of birth	0.0
Race	0.0

Source: Carter, "The Pre-sentence Investigation Report," in Carter and Wilkins, eds., *Probation and Parole*, p. 135.

the following were among the first three selected by the group of probation officers responding to the inquiry:

TABLE 14-3 Most Selected Probation Criteria

Item	Percentage of First Three Times Selected
Offense	97.1
Prior records	68.1
Defendant's statement	31.9
Family history	26.1
Psychological/psychiatric	21.7
Plea	7.2
Defendant's attitude	2.9
Alcoholic involvement	2.9
Employment history	1.4
Marital status	1.4

Source: Carter, "The Pre-sentence Investigation Report," in Carter and Wilkins, eds., *Probation and Parole*, p. 135.

Decisions Made by the Judge

The presentence investigation report is of considerable value to the judge in the sentencing procedure. The only contact the judge might have with an offender would be as the judge in the trial, where his primary concern is to rule on the admissibility of evidence and maintain orderly procedure. After the adjudication, however, most judges believe that sentencing procedures must be based on a broader view of the person as a functioning or nonfunctioning member of society, considering the psychological, sociological, economic, and cultural factors.

It is estimated that judges follow the recommendations made by probation officers in the presentence investigation reports more than 95 percent of the time. The probation officer is the "professional" in this particular area, has made a close social study of the convicted offender, and works for the judge. The judge might be working with a probation officer in whom he had confidence or, due to a staff turnover, with a new probation officer. Some judges have said that "nobody knows for sure what to do in most cases, unfortunately, and everybody guesses based on some knowledge. My guess comes last—and it is *my* guess that counts!" As politicians, some judges are better attuned to the attitudes of the power structure within their communities or jurisdictions than are many career "professionals," so they may alter the disposition of some cases to avoid critical editorials in the local newspaper or critical public opinion.

SUPERVISION OF PROBATIONERS

Supervision of probationers is the most important part of probation. Although the presentence investigation report is a necessary basic tool for the judge in sentencing and is of assistance to supervision of and working with the offender in prison and on parole, the supervision of the probationers is the means by which their life styles are altered sufficiently to let them exist peacefully in society.

The Role of the Probation Officer

Supervision includes not only case work and counseling assistance in employment and personal planning but enforcement functions as well. It is a type of treatment-supervision. People are changed by other people. The supervision of probationers must be based on mutual confidence and trust. Many offenders have difficulty in developing this trust in persons with authority. The probation officer has some advantage in gaining the trust, in that he selected his caseload while doing the presentence investigation and, therefore, recommended that the offender be placed on probation. He therefore kept the offender out of prison. This frequently becomes an opener for developing trust and confidence, particularly when the judge tells the offender he is being placed on probation "upon the recommendation of your probation officer."

As with other jobs in the criminal justice system, the probation officer investigates, counsels, and enforces. He has to find the balance between changing people and controlling people. It is unfortunate but true that most controlled people do not stay controlled when the controller is gone, which means that the probation period has to be used effectively to change the probationer while the opportunity exists. This tenuous balance will shift as the probationer responds favorably and needs less and less control. There are four general principles that usually are basic for obtaining this balance:

1. Change comes from within the person; therefore, a probationer must be a participant in any treatment program designed to help him.
2. The needs, problems, capacities, and limitations of the individual offender must be considered in planning a program with him.
3. Legally binding conditions of probation are essential and in the best interests of the offender and the community.
4. The goal of supervision is to help the offender understand his own problems and enable him to deal adequately with them.[5]

Probation's most important objective is not to control the offender but to help him understand himself and gain independent control over his own behavior. Special counseling may be necessary for some offenders, such as in the case of alcoholism, mental illness, or other deviation that might appear in the probation caseload. Sometimes, the offender simply needs a stabilizing and supporting authoritative figure nearby. Employment counseling and assistance in finding jobs is always a major part of the probation officer's work. This is a major problem and a major need because people in correctional caseloads generally have not developed good work habits.

The Role of Volunteers in Probation Supervision

Volunteers have recently been used effectively in the probation process. Some have taken a few special problem cases in which they could be effective, and others have served as "linkers" in high-crime neighborhoods where they can make contacts with offenders in a way that would be nearly impossible for the probation officer. Still others concentrate on finding jobs in employment counseling for several probation officers. Many have served in assisting the probation officer with administrative detail, clerical help, by being receptionists, and with similar functions. Volunteers can do many of the time-consuming chores, filling out reports and doing other tasks that drain the time of the probation officer from his counseling and supervision of probationers.

---

[5] *Manual of Correctional Standards* (Washington, D.C.: American Correctional Association, 1966), p. 107.

Caseload Size

Overloading the officers appears to defeat the concept of probation. When the worker has to strain even to partially cover his caseload, he cannot apply professional techniques. Rather, he is forced to do the minimum supervision essential to keep the process going and then to go to somebody else in his caseload. The situation means that everybody provides supervision in the same way, regardless of his education and qualifications, and none of the supervision is adequate. This is why some correctional administrators have said that they have seen uneducated and untrained people do as good a job as that done by some of the educated people. The fact is that they *are* doing the same kind of job because of overwork and overload, but the professional people *can* do a better job, all else being equal, if given the opportunity.

The National Council on Crime and Delinquency has recommended a fifty-unit method of controlling caseload size. Each case under supervision is worth one point and each presentence investigation report a month is worth five points. If a probation officer supervises a caseload of fifty, then he can make no further presentence investigation reports, which in itself would not be good probation practice. If he supervises twenty-five cases, he can then do five presentence investigation reports each month. This appears to be a good operational caseload size.

PROBATION SUBSIDY LEGISLATION

California initiated legislation in 1966 that provided for the state to give the counties up to four thousand dollars for every individual that could have been sent to state institutions prior to that time, but was instead kept on probation in the community. Initiated by the Youth Authority with offenders prior to their twenty-first birthdays, it has since been extended to adult offenders. With this subsidy money, probation services have been expanded. The counties are required to demonstrate a commitment to improve probation services, with the result that individual caseloads have been reduced to fifty offenders per officer, sometimes less. The increasing number of drug-related offenses are posing a problem for probation because these offenders are more likely to violate probation than others. The program has perceptibly reduced the prison population in California and has contributed to preparing the way to the planned phasing out of the California State Prisons at San Quentin and Folsom.

Subsidy caseloads on probation include persons who would ordinarily have been sent to prison, but can be retained in the community on probation by benefit of the money returned by the state for that purpose. In forty-one counties in California on December 31, 1970, the regular probation caseload constituted 33.5 percent of the total probation caseload, including 7.5 percent with prior prison records. On the other hand, the subsidy caseload constituted 42.6 percent of the total caseload, with 9.1 percent of the total having prior prison records.[6] The remaining probationers were juveniles, some of whom were also subsidy cases, and misdemeanants. Based on its success in California, the State of Washington passed a Probation Subsidy Act in 1970.

CONCLUSIONS

Probation is probably the most successful phase of corrections, partially because it does not remove the offender from the community. The "social surgery" of removal from the home and community severs the constructive social ties as well as those that are harmful. A competent probation officer can support the positive and constructive social relationships for an individual, while discouraging and diminishing the unwholesome ties. This is important because one of the basic problems among offenders in any correctional caseload is that, however well they may manipulate others, they tend to have difficulty in maintaining stable and meaningful relationships. Taking a person out of the community is almost like removing a person from the water so he can be taught to swim. In summary, probation is one of the most economical and most successful of the correctional approaches.

LEARNING EXERCISES

Issues to Be Discussed

1. It has been argued that probation has been less effective than it could be because the probation officers are overloaded with casework. Since presentence reports bring them closest to the judge, they give more priority to this function in the midst of their caseloads. Look into the literature of probation, particularly in the past issues of the publication *Federal Probation,* to determine the extent of this issue. What steps would you take to alleviate the condition of an overabundance of casework?
2. What are the economic and rehabilitative advantages to probation?
3. What is the role of the probation agent or officer in the supervision of probationers?
4. How does the probation agent find the balance between controlling behavior and changing behavior among people in his or her caseload?

Group Activity

Establish a class role-playing activity involving three individuals: the probation officer, a volunteer, and a new probationer. Have the three act out a session in which the probationer states his problems and the probation officer explains his official duties and the

---

[6] *Characteristics of Adults and Juveniles in Regular and Subsidy Caseloads on December 31, 1970* (Sacramento, Calif.: California Department of Justice, Bureau of Criminal Statistics, 1971), p. 17.

manner in which he or she and the volunteer can otherwise assist. Have the session work out a plan of action for the probationer based upon his qualifications and problems.

Field Activities

1. Establish an interview with a probation officer, a volunteer worker, or an organization that assists probationers. Look at the manner in which they view their function, and what they consider to be their problems and their best practices. Prepare a 300-word evaluation report.
2. Prepare what you would consider to be a model presentence report based upon examination of some reports and report forms.

Key Terms

Caseload
Presentence investigation report

Probation services
Probation subsidy

SUGGESTED REFERENCES

DRESSLER, DAVID. *Practice and Theory of Probation and Parole.* 2nd ed. New York: Columbia University Press, 1969.

POTTER, JOAN. "Shock Probation: A Little Taste of Prison." *Corrections Magazine,* Vol. 3 (December 1977), pp. 49–55.

UNIVERSITY OF CALIFORNIA CENTER ON ADMINISTRATION OF CRIMINAL JUSTICE. *An Evaluation of California Probation Subsidy Program. Vol. VI: A Summary.* Davis, Calif.: University of California, 1977.

15

Prisons and Correctional Institutions

Overview
Types of Institutions
Objectives of the Institution
Organization and Administration
Custody
Court Intervention in Prisons
Treatment
Conclusions
Learning Exercises
Suggested References

OVERVIEW

Prisons are the institutions within the criminal justice system to which individuals are removed from society to serve terms imposed in the sentencing procedures. The nature of the offense and the disposition of the offender largely determine the type of custody institution in which the individual will reside—a maximum, medium, or minimum custody institution. The amount of control exercised in prisons depends upon the warden's views on administration and the character of the prison population. Prisons vary in emphasis on custody and treatment. The degree to which emphasis is given to either or both determine how a prison is organized and staffed.

Prisons and correctional institutions comprise the last resort of the criminal justice system. Offenders are sent to prisons and correctional institutions when probation and other community-based correctional programs are unable to handle them. At the end of the line is the maximum security prison, with its own solitary confinement, the "jail within a prison." The criminal justice system is constructed so that everybody will get along somehow, even if he has to be placed in a box or solitary confinement cell.

The historical significance of prisons in developing the total correctional phase of the criminal justice system should not be underestimated. Because the prison represents the hard-core base of the correctional process, the prison system has frequently affected the philosophy and approach of the other correctional programs within a state. Parole developed from the prison, as evidenced by the ticket-of-leave introduced by Captain Alexander Maconochie of Norfolk Island Penal Colony in 1840 and implemented in the Irish System in 1854 by Sir Walter Crofton. It was the discussion of the Irish System at the first meeting of the National Congress on Penitentiary and Reformatory Discipline in Cincinnati in 1870 where, along with education, the parole principle of the Irish System received considerable attention and influenced American thinking. Probation developed in Boston about 1843 when a volunteer shoe cobbler, John Augustus, habitually visited the courts and paid the fines and accepted supervision of many offenders to give them a "second chance," a diversion from jail or prison. Even the juvenile corrections field split off from the adult prison during the period between 1847, when state juvenile institutions were constructed in New York and Massachusetts, and 1899, when the juvenile court in Chicago separated children from adult offenders.

Approximately 80,000 felons were received in adult correctional institutions in the United States in 1965.[1] There were 221,597 felons already in correctional institutions at that time.[2] At the same time, there were 257,755 felons on probation, and there were 102,000 felons on parole.[3] One-third of the total felony caseload in corrections is in prisons and correctional institutions.

A new record high prison population of 250,000 was unofficially reported at the end of 1975,[4] and that population had risen to 283,000 by the end of 1976.

TYPES OF INSTITUTIONS

General Types

There are several different types of institutions in the United States today. The *maximum security* prison is the hard-core, last-resort institution to hold older or more difficult offenders. The reformatory has been developed to house and care for younger offenders or first-termers.

In addition, several specialized types of institutions have emerged. For example, the United States Bureau of Prisons and several states have specialized institutions for juvenile and youth offenders. Examples are the most recent Robert F. Kennedy Youth Center at Morgantown, West Virginia, opened in 1968; the Federal Youth Center opened in 1940 at Ashland, Kentucky; and another at Englewood, Colorado, also opened in 1940. Correctional institutions at state levels have been opened in the past generation or so as minimum security and better-programmed institutions, frequently for first-termers or offenders who do not present a serious security risk. The first such institutions opened in the federal system were at La Tuna, Texas, in 1932; at Milan, Michigan, in 1933; and at Tallahassee, Florida, in 1938.

Prison camps developed more recently in the federal system, although the first federal prison camp was opened in Montgomery, Alabama, in 1930. The prison camp system has been used in the Midwest and the West primarily for providing labor for forestry and conservation work and, simultaneously, providing the inmates with fresh air in a "relaxed" environment. The prison camps in the South, of course, had a different development. In the South, many prison camps emerged after the Union Army left in 1877, and the highest bidder

---

[1] The President's Commission on Law Enforcement and the Administration of Justice, *Task Force Report: Corrections* (Washington, D.C.: U.S. Government Printing Office, 1967), p. 178.

[2] *Ibid.,* p. 45.

[3] *Ibid.,* p. 27.

[4] Steve Gettinger, "U.S. Prison Population Hits All-Time High," *Corrections Magazine,* Vol. 2, No. 3 (March 1976), p. 9.

operated them. Most were turpentine and lumber operations, frequently under the control of new, northern owners. The abuses of the lease system and the introduction of railroads and automobiles resulted in the termination of this lease system, the early use of prisoners in building and maintaining railroads, and later in building and maintaining roads and highways. More recently, the southern road prisons have been in the process of being transformed into community-based correctional programs. A discussion of the methods of security classification in these institutions appears later in this chapter.

Specialized Types

This broad variety of types of institutions within the same system, both federal and state, has provided greater possibilities for differentiation of treatment of offenders. The first reformatory was at Elmira, New York, in 1876, based on a program of education for younger offenders. Similar institutions and programs have developed in the United States Bureau of Prisons. They provide for an easy separation of the younger first-termers from the older and more intractable offenders. The introduction of correctional institutions and prison camps has provided an even wider selection of types of institutions that permits greater differentiation among offenders.

In addition, the medical center idea has been implemented for special psychiatric and medical cases in some jurisdictions, probably the most important being the California Medical Facility at Vacaville and the United States Medical Center at Springfield, Missouri. Special institutions and programs have also been constructed for the criminally insane, the first having been built at Ionia, Michigan, in 1885. The first separate institution for women was constructed at Indianapolis, Indiana, in 1873. The various types of institutions available today offer a much wider selection of correctional programs and institutions than were available in the original prisons in the nineteenth century. With this diversification of institutions and facilities comes greater flexibility in programming.

Security Classifications

Prisons and correctional institutions are classified for purposes of security into four broad and sometimes overlapping categories: maximum, medium, minimum, and community custody. Although there is considerable overlapping and one central institution may have all types of custody available, these divisions into security classifications permit the assignment of prisoners with great security risk into the maximum custody institutions and those with little or no security risk into the minimum or community custody institutions, with graduations available within categories.

Maximum custody institutions can have walls, cell blocks with inside cell construction, or back-to-back construction with each cell facing an exterior wall, armed guard towers, wall towers, and similar security measures. In recent years, the high walls have given way to two or three exterior fences with appropriate security measures, such as electric fences, dogs, armed towers, electronic devices, or some combination of them. The advantage of walls is that they preclude visibility and signaling, but the cost outweighs this advantage. The last wall of any significance was built at the State Correctional Institution at Graterford, Pennsylvania, opened in 1928 as a branch of the Eastern State Penitentiary. The wall there cost $1.25 million—about half the cost of the entire institution.

A medium custody institution generally has a fence rather than a wall, a strong perimeter with guard towers, but with generally less restriction inside the fences or in the compound. A minimum custody institution frequently possesses a single fence or no fences, no towers, and no obvious security measures. A community custody institution is one constructed, or frequently rented, in the center of the city. Because these facilities will be discussed in the chapter on community-based corrections, however, discussion in this chapter will focus on maximum, medium, and minimum security institutions only.

Prisoners can be classified according to the degree of security they need and are then sent to the appropriate institution within the prison system. The different types of institutions with their various types of programs and security offer the total prison system a wide flexibility that permits greater individual treatment than has ever been possible before.

OBJECTIVES OF THE INSTITUTION

The objectives of prisons and correctional institutions are sometimes difficult to identify in practice. Theoretically, the protection of society is a generalized objective, but how that protection shall be achieved ranges from harsh discipline to minimum or community security, education, therapy through peer groups or a clinical staff, and other treatment approaches. The majority of the public knows or cares little about what goes on behind those high prison walls. Some consider only that they are being protected by the confinement of convicted offenders. The general public is favorably disposed to education and religious training for inmates, but there is little consensus about anything else. Riots and escapes tend to produce apprehension for the safety of residents in the area of the prison and for the civilian personnel within the prison.

Correctional Architecture

The relationship between correctional architecture and correctional philosophy lies in the degree of flexibility that the physical space permits in the interrelationships between groups of people, particularly inmates or residents and staff in an institution. Ideally, the correctional philosophy should be worked out first and then the physical plant should be designed to house that philosophy. In progressive penology, the overall atmosphere conveyed by a physical plant built with aesthetic taste is more conducive to normal living than the old prison discipline represented by rows of barred cells housed within gray walls.[5] Space should be made available for small groups to function institutionally much as the family unit does in outside society. Joint undertakings of prisoners participating with the staff in the duties and responsibilities of running the institution provide an atmosphere built on sound democratic principles. Security is primary, but not dominant. A strong perimeter can contain a therapeutic community. The architectural atmosphere can help to reduce the traditional security-treatment conflict by such techniques as replacing bars with detention windows that are attractive but too narrow to permit escape, such as those built in several of the Metropolitan Community Centers constructed by the United States Bureau of Prisons. Correctional officers who are in contact with residents should work in groups with professional staff and inmates to permit group meetings and discussions. Multiple dining rooms allow small-group principles to function. Use of community programs helps to reduce the barriers between the correctional institution and the community.

Architecture has the capacity to contribute to correctional programs at four significant levels.[6] First, it can provide adequate space in which program activities can be conducted. Second, depending on whether it permits or does not permit flexibility, it has the potential for positive or negative impact on activity patterns. Third, architecture has an impact on organizing relationships between people: The very location of the facility permits or limits visits by the family, specialized services, and community reintegration; internally, architecture determines the spatial organization of human interaction, just as the presence or absence of a civic center expands or limits sporting and other entertainment events in a city; and identification of residential clusters or modules may provide a reference place that contributes to the identity of the individuals living there. Fourth, architecture has impact on the communications patterns of the correctional environment in which hostile-appearing physical environments may carry threatening connotations to the activities attempted in that setting and impede efforts at rehabilitative methods. In summary, architecture should provide adequate space for the program, permit flexibility in design to accommodate new programs, provide settings that permit outside contacts and inside positive identification, and provide nonthreatening environments that permit positive communication of socially approved values and attitudes.

---

[5] Howard B. Gill, "Correctional Philosophy and Architecture," *Journal of Criminal Law, Criminology and Police Science,* Vol. 53, No. 3 (September 1962), pp. 312–22.

[6] Fred Moyer, *Correctional Environments* (Urbana-Champaign, Ill.: National Clearinghouse on Criminal Justice Planning and Architecture, 1973).

Program Priorities

On an everyday basis, the desires of employees in specific areas might well control policy or provide a measure for the priorities of specific objectives. Priorities for future training programs as stated in a 1969 survey of 1,282 correctional personnel employed by the Illinois Department of Public Safety, now the Illinois Department of Corrections, are shown in Table 15-1.

TABLE 15-1 Priorities for Training Requested by Illinois Correctional Personnel

Topics	Percentage of Requests
Security measures	86
Riot control	66
Rehabilitation and treatment	65
Institutional procedures	64
Techniques of supervision	64
Institutional rules	60
Working with groups	51
Inmate's personality and so on	36
Counseling	21
Personnel code	20
Corrections law	20
Criminal justice system	14

Source: *The Correctional Trainer—Newsletter for Illinois Correction Staff Training* (Carbondale, Ill.: Southern Illinois University), Vol. 1, No. 3 (July 1969), p. 9.

The high priorities of security measures and riot control, with rehabilitation and treatment seen almost on a par with riot control, suggest the philosophy of line staff. The high priority of institutional procedures, techniques of supervision, and institution rules also suggest the predominant issues in their thinking. Concern for changing behavior of offenders is generally low as far as line staff is concerned. In recent years, inmate militancy in litigation and violence have increased the concerns of line personnel for security.[7]

Recent efforts to involve line staff, particularly the correctional officer, in treatment efforts have mitigated this philosophy in some smaller institutions. When correctional officers are involved in treatment procedures, they become interested in correctional procedures. Most progressive prison systems are moving toward involvement of the correctional officer in treatment.

---

[7] James B. Jacobs, *Stateville: The Penitentiary in Mass Society* (Chicago: University of Chicago Press, 1977), p. 208.

ORGANIZATION AND ADMINISTRATION

The organization and administration of a prison or correctional institution varies with its size, purpose, population, and degree of custody. The largest prison in America is the State Prison of Southern Michigan, which held 6,500 prisoners in the early 1950s, but now holds less than 5,000 because of increased use of probation and parole. At the other extreme, southern road prisons and northern and western forestry and conservation camps may hold only forty or fifty inmates. Halfway houses in the community, of course, may hold as few as ten offenders.

Administrators

The chief administrator's function is complex. As a public relations man, he appears before civic groups, at conferences, and at other places where it is advantageous for the work of the prison to be interpreted. The presentations may range from image making to honest and substantive discussions of problems and needs. Many prison administrators have become defensive, particularly in times of trouble, and have barred the press from their institutions. Others open the gates of the prison to newsmen and let them have free access to everything. The warden or superintendent often determines public relations policy, although his superiors in the central office or the governor may give him other directives.

The warden or superintendent must present the budget to the budget commission, director, or other fiscal agent of the executive department. Subsequently, he may have to defend it before legislative committees. He is responsible for personnel policies. He makes policy decisions when members or factions within his institution conflict over issues.

The deputy warden or associate warden focuses on the administration of programs within the institution. In the traditional prison, the deputy warden is primarily responsible for custody—for the safety and security of the institution. After World War II, there was a move toward adding a second deputy warden or associate warden in charge of treatment with equal rank to the deputy or associate warden in charge of custody. Today, many state prison systems and the United States Bureau of Prisons use this two-deputy system for custody and treatment. The deputy warden for custody is in charge of the custodial force made up of correctional officers. His function is to prevent escapes and to maintain the safety and security of the institution without interfering inordinately with the treatment program of the institution. The deputy warden in charge of treatment is responsible for the classification program, education, religion, recreation, and other programs designed to bring services to the inmates in an effort to change their behavior constructively.

Prison Departments and Personnel

The important departments in the prison are (1) custodial; (2) school programs; (3) classification system; (4) chaplain and the religious program; (5) hospital and dental services; (6) industries; (7) farm; (8) chief engineer and maintenance department; (9) business manager, who generally also has charge of the kitchen and dining room, clothing issue, and laundry because of their frequent and continuous purchases; (10) psychiatric and mental health services, which sometimes include a psychiatric ward; (11) recreation; (12) library, which is sometimes independent and sometimes within the school program; and (13) administrative services, such as accounting, personnel, and record office where court papers and institutional records are filed. The heads of these various departments may report to the deputy warden or, too frequently, wonder to whom they are supposed to report. In a maximum security institution, the department head knows that when any custodial personnel, from the lowest officer to the deputy warden, "suggests" something for the safety and security of the institution, he had better act on it. The custodial function has been considered to be the most important function in the traditional prison.

CUSTODY

Custody, with major concern for the safety and security of the institution and the prevention of escapes, is of primary concern among correctional administrators. The institution cannot treat inmates if it does not have them. Further, the type of treatment provided an inmate is sometimes debatable, but security has seldom been so. Any discussion of institutional procedures must include custody, both in terms of the institution and of the inmate.

Traditional custody involves well-known, established procedures such as counting the inmates, shaking down cells, tower duty, making disciplinary reports, and other procedures that can be taught easily and in which the correctional officer can be expert. The newer view of custody, however, is in "mass treatment," by which the application of external controls may be gradually relaxed as internal controls are impressed upon each inmate. Enlightened custody attempts to provide only that amount of external control which is immediately necessary and to reduce that external control as the individual is able to function in society on his own devices. Although this function also exists in the family, the school, the gang, organized and unorganized recreation, the church, and throughout all society, custody in prisons and correctional institutions is a distinct and separate specialized function of which all other departments in the institution must be aware and within which their own functions must be coordinated.

Custodial Techniques and Duties

The techniques by which custody is maintained can be classified broadly as (1) segregation of inmates and (2) controlling movement of inmates. In the most secure prisons, each inmate is in a separate cell. Some prisons have two or more inmates in a cell, and many correctional institutions use the dormitory concept.

Segregation is used administratively for discipline and to isolate problems. All prisons have their troublemakers, agitators, or quarrelsome people who cannot get along with others. Some prisons isolate these troublemakers in a single unit; other prisons distribute them throughout the population and permit informal inmate control to handle some of the problems. Most prison wardens seem to favor the diffusion of problems, rather than their concentration in one place, reserving the latter for the few who cannot be controlled by the other inmates. Isolation or solitary confinement is generally reserved for (1) disciplinary problems with inmates who have violated institutional rules and regulations and (2) administrative segregation to prevent inmates from assaulting or being assaulted by other inmates and to control extreme homosexual activity.

The controlled movement of inmates within the prison is important in maintaining order. Movement of inmates from cell blocks to central dining halls and back must be worked out, as well as movement to work and back. The majority of institutions use informal lines accompanied by correctional officers, but a few, such as some institutions in New York, still use the military approach and divide the inmates into quasi-military companies. Many minimum security institutions have no rigid controls, for example, permitting the inmates to go from their domicile or work assignments to the dining hall by themselves within a two-hour or shorter time period. The inmates or residents may come to the dining hall at their convenience during the prescribed time period. Count procedures are very important in prison. Having the exact number of inmates in custody and on record at any given time is most important to the prison or correctional institution. One inmate too few results in an escape alarm, notification of the appropriate law enforcement agencies, and a manhunt. One or more in excess of what there should be could result in litigation and, certainly, embarrassment of the administration. The control room is the central headquarters of this custodial operation. Counts in the cell blocks and on work assignments are relayed to the control room for synchronizing into a single count.

Control of the yard and of the institution as a whole is a custodial duty. As far as movement of inmates is concerned, a system of passes and details (group passes) to cover work assignments and special calls is used. Control of property is generally by manifests (itemized lists) to cover property going in and out of gates, listing of contraband, and frequent shakedowns or searches of inmates and of cell blocks.

Searches and shakedowns of cell blocks or dormitories are regular routines in security-minded institutions and are made on a spot-check basis in minimum custody institutions. A maximum custody institution might have a shakedown once or twice a month and more frequently on an irregular basis. To protect the morale of the institution, a trusted inmate is frequently assigned to make the bed and put the cell back in order after a correctional officer has "torn it up" to search it. This means that the cell is left as the officer had found it so that the inmate occupying that cell will not have a mess to clean unnecessarily. This helps keep tempers cool.

Tool and key control are important in maximum custody institutions because stolen tools and keys can be used in escape attempts and in making weapons. The basic factor in tool control is a rigid check system with receipts signed by the inmates for the tools in the shop and a classification system for differential storage of tools. For example, class A tools are those which can cut steel, such as welding torches, and must be stored in the arsenal overnight, to be checked out by the supervisor or instructor each morning. Class B tools need to be stored in the machine shop under close scrutiny. Class C tools, such as screwdrivers and pliers, need observation, but do not require unusual surveillance. Keys are generally on rings. Key rings are stored in the control room arranged according to the tour of duty of each correctional officer. When a key is lost the only recourse is to change the locks and issue new keys to the affected areas.

Supervision of work assignments is a primary custodial duty. The correctional officer in charge of the assignment has a function to get the job done, to prevent escapes, and to keep counts. If the job assignment is outside the walls, he must prevent contact with the public, prevent the "trafficking service" in contraband items and underground mail, and prevent a "messenger service" between the outside and inside of the prison.

Escapes and disturbances are also central to the task of custody. Most escapes are "walk-aways," generally after nine o'clock at night. Although a manhunt frequently results in apprehension, a quick notice to interested law enforcement agencies is essential. Notifying the FBI office in Washington, where the inmate's fingerprints are filed, will bring notification to the institution if the escapee is ever arrested anywhere else and fingerprinted. Consequently, escapes are not the problem today that they were prior to World War II. The number of successful escapes has gone down, a reflection of modern society's system of social security numbers, birth certificates, identification cards, driver's licenses, and other documents that make up "the wallet card cage." This decline is also reflected in the increased use of minimum custody institutions and community-based correctional programs.

Reduction of custody is the gradual removal of the external controls imposed by prisons. For example, a maximum custody prisoner must be kept under lock at all times and be accompanied by an officer, frequently handcuffed, whenever he leaves the cell for any purpose. A close custody prisoner is one who locks (lives) inside the walls and can work in gangs under supervision inside the walls. A medium security prisoner is one who can lock inside the walls, work in gangs outside the walls, or work alone inside the walls, which makes him an "inside trustee" in some institutions. A minimum custody prisoner can live inside the walls and work alone outside the walls. A community custody prisoner can go downtown to work on a work-release program and return to the prison at night, or he may live in a halfway house or in a community-based correctional center. Reduction of custody refers to moving the inmate from maximum or close custody to minimum and to community custody as rapidly as possible. The purpose is to provide no more custody than the individual needs, both for the purposes of economy and from the standpoint of rehabilitation.

Advantages and Disadvantages of Custody

The irritating factors of prison discipline are (1) restriction on individual behavior, (2) regimented movement of groups from place to place, (3) complete lack of privacy, (4) constant supervision by uniformed officers representing authority, (5) restricted social contacts with friends and relatives outside by limitations placed on correspondence and visits.

The constructive factors in prison discipline are that it (1) allows inmates to experience the desirable results of obedience to rules for the common good; (2) permits various recreational and other pursuits that, through training, may teach inmates the advantage of cooperation with others; (3) produces a general atmosphere of order and system that includes regular living; (4) helps inmates to acquire recreational habits that might be transferred to the community later; and (5) neutralizes the negative effects of prison life as much as possible by controlling and reducing some disturbing elements, such as inmates bullying and terrorizing each other.

In summary, the custodial function can be a constructive influence in the treatment of offenders, as well as protecting the public by preventing escapes and maintaining peace and order within the institution. More and more, the correctional officer with a primary concern for custody is becoming concerned with treatment and rehabilitation as he becomes involved in the treatment process.

COURT INTERVENTION IN PRISONS

Prior to the 1960s, procedures within the prison were considered to be beyond judicial review. In 1891, a Virginia case held that prisoners had no rights and that the Thirteenth Amendment prohibits involuntary servitude "except as punishment for a crime."[8] In 1954, the courts were held to be without power to supervise prison administration or to interfere with the ordinary rules or regulations.[9] In the 1950s, there were approximately 500 lawsuits filed by inmates against correctional administrators each year. By the mid-1970s, there were about 19,000 such suits annually.

[8] *Ruffin v. Commonwealth,* 21 Grat. 760, Virginia (1891).
[9] *Banning v. Looney,* 213 F. 2d 771, 10th Circuit (1954).

The first real confrontation between inmates and the prison administration occurred in *Fullwood v. Clemmer*[10] in 1962 when the Black Muslims sought recognition as a legitimate religion under the First Amendment. At the annual meeting of the American Correctional Association in Philadelphia in 1961, a resolution was passed indicating that the Black Muslims were not a religion, but were a social group intent on creating disruption and disturbances in American prisons. The court decided in favor of the Black Muslims and the administration of the District of Columbia Youth Center at Lorton, Virginia, had to accommodate to the finding by eliminating pork from the diet, permitting a Black Muslim chaplain to participate in classification meetings, and other accommodations.

Most prisons were developing law libraries in the 1950s and 1960s or, at least, providing access to law books in accordance with the requirements for access to counsel in the Sixth Amendment and equal protection in the Fourteenth Amendment. Most prisons had rules, however, against an inmate working on the case of another inmate because of the development of obligations between inmates and the resulting potential for conflict and disturbance or other problems involved in "paying off" the obligation. In *Johnson v. Avery* in 1969,[11] however, the court held that regulations banning all inmate assistance in the preparation of writs of habeas corpus and other legal work were unconstitutional. This was upheld in *Novak v. Beto* in Texas in 1971.[12] In 1969 and 1970, courts began considering taking over jurisdiction of prisons or closing them. In 1969, Judge Henley threatened to close Cummins, the main unit of the Arkansas Prison System, if conditions were not changed.[13] Conditions there involved mental abuse and corporal punishment in violation of the cruel and unusual punishment clause of the Eighth Amendment. This case came close to providing the inmates the "right to treatment" and indicated that when the state has deprived an individual of his liberty, it has a constitutional duty to use ordinary care to protect his life and safety while in prison. The *Morris v. Travisono* case[14] in Rhode Island in 1970 was a significant case in which the court assumed jurisdiction of the prison for eighteen months to allow the state time to correct the cruel and unusual conditions in the facility at Cranston.

Several court cases in the 1970s emphasized the introduction of due process standards in disciplinary hearings within the institutions. *Landman v. Royster*[15] declared that bread and water diets were unconstitutional, the use of chains and other restraint equipment was banned, no inmate could be kept nude longer than necessary to secure a doctor, no inmate could be placed in a solitary cell with another inmate except in emergency, minimum due process standards must be implemented immediately, and access to counsel through confidential mail and

---

[10] 206 F. Supp. 370, D.D.C. (1962).
[11] 393 U.S. 483 (1969).
[12] No. 3116 U.S. Ct. Apt. 5th Cir., opinion 12-9-7.
[13] *Holt v. Sarver,* 300 S. Supp. 825, E.D. Arkansas (1969).
[14] Civil action 4192, U.S. Dist. Ct. for the Dist. of Rhode Island (1970).
[15] 333 F. Supp. 621 E.D. Virginia (1971).

interview cannot be abridged. *Clutchette v. Procunier*[16] held that the disciplinary procedures at San Quentin failed to meet due process requirements and instituted minimum due process procedures.

Probably the most significant case in the due process area was *Wolff v. McDonnell*,[17] which established due process in the federal prisons. This includes (1) advanced written notice of the charges, (2) written statement of the decision as to evidence and reasons, (3) right of the inmate to call witnesses and prevent documentary evidence, (4) cross-examining adverse witnesses when permitting the inmate to do so would not be unduly hazardous to institutional safety or correctional goals, and (5) use of counsel or counsel substitute for those who cannot understand the proceedings. The *Wolff v. McDonnell* principles have been referred to in other disciplinary cases.

By the mid-1970s, the courts were involved in many areas other than disciplinary procedures and conditions, such as transfers, inmate classification within the institution, punitive isolation, and handling of emergencies. There are several cases affecting transfer of inmates from one institution to another. A good example would be *Carroll v. Sielaff*,[18] which held that whether a prisoner had suffered a grievous loss as a result of transfer depends upon the actual differences between the institutions at the time of the transfer, reasons for the transfer, and the basis for segregation of transferees. If there is a loss of relative freedom, which might involve punitive segregation in a more secure institution, then the *Wolff v. McDonnell* due process principles must apply. Further, *Tai v. Thompson*[19] held that if there were overtones of disciplinary action or deprivation of liberty or equality of treatment in an out-of-state transfer of a state prisoner, then *Wolff v. McDonnell* principles apply. *Aikens v. Lash*[20] held that if an inmate is subject to a hearing that might result in transfer from the state reformatory to the penitentiary, then minimum due process principles apply.

Court intervention in classification procedures also appeared in the mid-1970s. Several cases are on the record. An example is *Daigle v. Hall*,[21] in which it was held that any classification within the institution that imposes an adverse change in conditions of confinement because of behavior are subject to minimum standards in due process. Placing prisoners in disciplinary units is subject to due process, meaning advance warning of at least twenty-four hours, written statement of evidence, inmate provided opportunity to present documentary evidence and call witnesses, inmate permitted to cross-examine adverse witnesses with adequate justification in terms of the security and safety of the institution and its inmates if permission for such cross-examination is denied, and representation by

---

[16] No. C-70, 2497 AJZ, U.S. Dist. Ct., Northern Dist. of California, opinion 6-21-71.
[17] 418 U.S. 593 (1974).
[18] 514 F. 2d 415, Illinois (1975).
[19] 396 F. Supp. 196 (1975).
[20] 514 F. 2d. 55, Indiana (1975).
[21] 387 F. Supp. 652 (1975).

another staff member or inmate if the inmate is illiterate or faced with complex issues. Transfer of a prisoner to a different wing of the prison with more stringent conditions has been declared a serious deprivation and requiring due process in the case of *Carol v. Gunter*.[22] Transfer to less restrictive custody is the prerogative of the staff, rather than the right of the inmate, according to *Russell v. Oliver*,[23] but once reduced security or other privileges are granted, they are subject to due process when taken away, according to *Sands v. Wainwright*.[24]

Punitive isolation is not unconstitutional, but inmates can communicate with attorneys and the courts, according to *McCray v. Sullivan*.[25] According to *Gregory v. Wyse*,[26] the common element in finding violations of the Eighth Amendment is deprivation of the basic elements of hygiene and when the punishment offends the evolving standards of decency that mark the progress of a maturing society. In *Batt v. Twomey*[27] it was decided that deprivations associated with institutional deadlock (sometimes called top-lock or keep-lock), including a twenty-four-hour confinement in cells and curtailment of all associations, exercises, and normal activity, constitute dislocation of the prisoner's normal conditions and a grievous loss that requires minimum procedural protections, particularly when the status is prolonged.

Transfers can be made in emergency situations, such as riots, without prior notice or warning, but they must be followed with due process standards.[28] According to *Adams v. Carlson*,[29] prison officials may segregate inmates who are dangerous to the staff but must give due process later.

Courts may interfere in prison management only when deprivations of prison confinement impose conditions of such onerous burdens as to be of constitutional dimensions, according to *McNeil v. Latney*.[30] According to *Burke v. Levi*,[31] the courts do not have the power under the guise of protecting constitutional rights to usurp the responsibility that rests with the executive branch for the management of the prisons. The position of the courts was well stated in *Thompson v. Montemuro*,[32] which held that prison officials had wide discretionary authority to exercise disciplinary control over the inmates but that inmates have a constitutional right to be free from physical abuse and seek vindication under the Constitution and civil rights acts.

---

[22] 520 F. 2d. 1293, Massachusetts (1975).
[23] 392 F. Supp. 470 (1975).
[24] 357 F. Supp. 1060 (1973).
[25] 509 F. 2d. 1332 (1973).
[26] 512 F. 2d 378 (1975).
[27] 513 F. 2d. 641 (1975).
[28] *Robbins v. Kleindienst*, 383 F. Supp. 239, Dist. of Columbia (1974).
[29] 375 F. Supp. 1228, Illinois (1974).
[30] 382 F. Supp. 161 (1974).
[31] 391 F. Supp. 186 (1975).
[32] 383 F. Supp. 1200, Pennsylvania (1974).

TREATMENT

Treatment in prisons and correctional institutions refers to those programs that bring socializing influences to bear on the inmate or resident population. These programs are viewed broadly because the narrow sense of *treatment* as used in psychiatry and casework is almost nonexistent in American prisons. Treatment in prison really refers to those processes ordinarily found in the normal socialization of people in the free community, such as schools, religion, recreation, hospitals and medical attention, as well as the psychological, psychiatric, and social work services that might be available. Treatment in prison even includes industries and farms where work habits and skills might be learned.

Classification for Treatment

Classification in prisons is an organized procedure to promote the best possible coordination, integration, and continuity in providing the inmates with the best distribution of services within the institution and to provide the manpower needed to operate and maintain the institution. Formerly classification referred only to the separation of inmates by a variety of criteria. The modern concept of classification, however, includes assignment of work, school, and special programs designed to be part of the treatment process. It is the "delivery system" by which inmates are assigned to different institutions and different programs within the institutions as part of the treatment program best suited to them. The presentence investigation report done by the probation officer is especially helpful in this process. The admission summary done by the classification officer or counselor in the prison draws heavily from available presentence investigation reports, which appear in less than half the cases received in prison. In effect, the classification officer or counselor does the missing presentence investigations in a majority of cases after the prisoners are received. Consequently, the majority of admission summaries are based on correspondence, available records, interviews, and tests administered to the inmate after he arrives in the prison system. The inmate is generally interviewed after the other data have been collected. Although many factors enter into the classification procedure, the primary factors have always been age and criminal history.

Classification in American prisons has thus far gone through six distinct stages of development, as follows:

1. Preprofessional
2. Traditional
3. Integrated
4. Professional
5. Team treatment
6. Functional unit management

PREPROFESSIONAL

Classification as it is known today probably had its beginnings with the Borstal system of minimum security in England and in separate treatment approaches in Belgium, both developing around 1908. New Jersey introduced classification as it is now known in the United States in 1937, and most of the larger states had classification by the beginning of World War II. The annual Congress on Correction sponsored by the American Correctional Association, then the American Prison Association, had its first major section on classification in 1936, when Dr. F. Lovell Bixby explained the New Jersey System. This gave impetus to classification in most American prison systems. The first systems were preprofessional, in that there were no social workers, psychologists, or other professional personnel available in most prisons. The administrative and helping staff of the prison comprised the classification committee, including the deputy warden, director of classification, director of education, chaplain, industries superintendent, farm superintendent, medical officer, and others, usually making a committee of ten to fifteen members. This committee recommended assignments of prisoners who had come in during the previous month.

TRADITIONAL

The second system became traditional with the addition of a sociologist, a social worker, or a psychologist, who prepared the social history or admission summary for the committee, but essentially the same committee made the assignments.

INTEGRATED

The third system of classification really integrated the classification procedure into the institutional program. Prior to this, the classification committee recommendation was exactly that—a recommendation—that the deputy warden could implement or ignore, according to his discretion. The integrated committee's decision became an order that could not be reversed or altered. This made the classification committee's deliberation an order that became an integral part of the prison procedure.

PROFESSIONAL

The fourth, or professional committee, was much reduced in size, including generally the director of classification, a high-ranking custodial officer, and the inmate's counselor or other professional person who had prepared his social history or admission summary. The advantages of this committee were that it did not immobilize most of the administrators in the prison for two half-days a week, and it still accomplished the classification objective in an expeditious manner.

TEAM TREATMENT CONCEPT

The fifth approach developed a "team" or an individual classification committee for each inmate or resident in the prison. Generally, it included one correctional officer, one educator or other staff member, and one classification person, such as a counselor. These three people served as the inmate's team throughout his incarceration and were responsible for his treatment and frequently his disciplinary or behavioral problems. This approach has the enormous advantage of involving the correctional officer visibly and tangibly in the treatment process.

FUNCTIONAL UNIT MANAGEMENT

Functional unit management refers to the placing of the treatment team in a living unit on a permanent basis. A unit manager, an administrative assistant, two counselors, two correctional officers, and a secretary frequently comprise the team or "unit." All problems, counseling, and other affairs of the residents of the unit are taken care of by this group. It is a decentralized system, with the unit manager becoming tantamount to a "sub-warden" in his unit, thereby bringing the decision-making and treatment resources as close to the inmates or residents as possible.

In 1969, the United States Bureau of Prisons implemented the "RAPS" system of classification according to diagnoses that could be computerized.[33] On the basis of the staff's experience in placing offenders into intensive, selective, or minimal treatment categories according to the likelihood of change, further systematization was considered to be logical. The new RAPS system developed a code that could be translated into categories (I) intensive, (II) selective, or (III) minimal, depending upon whether there should be great, medium, or no expenditure of resources above the essential level of service. The *R* (rehabilitation potential or rating) in the code is based on the staff's professional opinion or rating regarding the prospects of change. The *A* refers to age as under thirty, thirty to forty-five, or over forty-five years of age. The *P* is the number of prior sentences ranging from none, one or two, or more. The *S* refers to the sentence in terms of special classification (for example, the Federal Juvenile Delinquency Act, Youth Center Act, or Narcotic Addict Rehabilitation Act) or length of sentence. The combinations fed into the computer categorize inmates into I, II, or III classifications to be used as guidelines in the expenditure of resources for treatment. Category I inmates are reviewed every thirty days and have first priority on assignments. The treatment team makes all assignment changes and the caseworker sits in disciplinary action procedures. Category II prisoners are reviewed every six months and do not have first priority on assignments, but have priority in what is left over from Category I inmates. The caseworker is advised regarding assignment changes and disciplinary action in this category. Category III inmates are reviewed annually, have last

---

[33] *United States Bureau of Prisons Policy Statement on the Case Management System* (Washington, D.C.: United States Bureau of Prisons, 1969).

priority on assignments, are routinely assigned to the labor pool, are used as needed to maintain the institution, and are processed by regular procedure in disciplinary action.

Education

Education became the primary treatment approach in the last decade of the nineteenth century, and it represented a shift in the emphasis on religiously oriented moral rehabilitation, which had been dominant in the penitentiary movement since its inception in 1790. Security and work, of course, had always been major concerns. The reformatory movement, based on academic and vocational education, began in Elmira in 1876. The first meeting of what is now the American Correctional Association in Cincinnati in 1870 had focused discussion on education in prisons and the idea was started. The prison population in the United States averages about three grades behind the general public in academic achievement. Consequently, academic education in prison is important. Almost half the prisoners in the country are considered to be functionally illiterate by school people, and the vast majority do not have high school diplomas. Therefore, academic education in prison focuses on making literate those who cannot read or write and achieving a high school diploma or its equivalent for those literate prisoners who do not already have one. Cultural demands for entry into most jobs in America make a high school diploma a minimum requirement.

Vocational training is a popular phase of educational programs. It receives more popular support than most other types of programs. What an institution may have in the form of vocational training would be dependent upon a combination of factors, including resources, the demand for skills in the area where the prisoner is located, the availability of instructors, and resistance from labor unions.

Teaching in prisons is a difficult task. Not only are the majority of offenders academic dropouts and underachievers but they are also not well known for their work and study habits. To complicate the situation further, prisons do not begin their semesters in September, like public schools and universities, but must be prepared to accept any new inmate at any time at his own level. Consequently, it is difficult to have classes in the same manner as does the public school. Most teaching in prison is individual tutoring or the monitoring of a group of people who are at different levels, providing individual assistance where it is needed. This is somewhat like modern "open classrooms," but it is not as organized.

Religion

Religion has been essential to the correctional process since the first penitentiary was introduced in Philadelphia in 1790 by the Quakers, who organized the Society for Alleviating the Miseries of the Public Prisons. The chaplain has always had access to all parts of the prison. Historically, the chaplain was the first treatment man. In fact, he spearheaded other treatment programs in the institution. The original function of the chaplain as seen by the prison administrator was to convince the inmates that their sentences were just, thereby keeping up the morale of the prison population.

The chaplain is and always has been an indispensable part of the correction program. He has always been *the* person interested in individuals and their rehabilitation. In summary, the chaplain has contributed more throughout the history of prisons than any other person or position in the treatment process.

Counseling, Casework, and Clinical Services

Counseling, casework, and psychological and psychiatric services do exist, however small in number, in a majority of prisons and correctional institutions. Where they exist, the patterns vary widely in terms of numbers of professional personnel and the manner in which the services are used. Professional personnel in most classification departments *process* prisoners—they do not *counsel* them.

Casework includes professional services in (1) obtaining case histories and descriptions; (2) solving immediate problems involving family and personal relationships; (3) exploring long-range problems of social adjustment; (4) providing supportive guidance for the inmates about to be released; and (5) providing supportive guidance and professional assistance to probationers and parolees.[34] This service appears to some extent in most prisons and correctional institutions.

Group therapy methods have been introduced into the prison program since World War II. New Jersey has developed an extensive, professional group-methods program. California, on the other hand, has used line officers and staff in an extensive group-counseling program. Group methods appear to be the coming phase in correctional treatment. They are economical in that they allow one leader to handle more than one client at a time. Further, they dilute the threat of authority that occurs in a one-to-one relationship between a counselor and a client. The use of peer groups appears to be even more helpful.

The peer group has been found to be more influential than the family in determining whether or not a person drinks, is more powerful than other agencies or social units in controlling excessive drinking, and has a tendency to bring the self-image of the individual into line with the expectations of his group.[35] Most studies have shown that the influence of the peer group after puberty is sustained. This is why group programs making use of peer pressure have been demonstrated to be effective.

[34] "Counseling, Casework, and Clinical Services," *Manual of Correctional Standards,* 3rd ed. (Washington, D.C.: American Correctional Association, 1966–69), p. 423.

[35] George S. Rothbart, "Deviant Career Patterns of College Drinkers," *Report by the Scientific Advisory Council on the Alcoholism Research Grant Program, 1960-1969* (New York: Licensed Beverage Industries, Inc., 1970), pp. 109–10.

Recreation

Recreational pursuits in prison are generally comprised of programmed athletics, either varsity or intramural. The majority of prisons and correctional institutions have athletic teams in football, basketball, and baseball that may play outside teams. Some fraternity teams from nearby colleges and semiprofessional teams frequently play the prison teams. Recreation can be one of the most important parts of the correctional process. People generally do not get into trouble while they are working or sleeping—rather, it is during their leisure time. Consequently, a recreational program providing interesting recreational procedures that can be transferred to legitimate and nonhazardous areas in the outside world could contribute much to the correctional process.

Library

As recreational pursuits in prison have considerable potential, the library as a source of recreation and self-improvement is potentially helpful but difficult to promote. The importance of the library has generally been underestimated by many correctional administrators. On the other hand, correctional personnel have observed that libraries, particularly in youthful institutions, are not used much because academic dropouts do not read much.

Most prisons have libraries that are in locations almost inaccessible to inmates or that are in the schools. The supply of books is generally donated by women's clubs or other outside sources. The construction of a library similar to outside public libraries, from which books can be checked out and where the books are kept contemporary and of interest to the inmates, could contribute much to rehabilitation of many inmates.

Many postadolescent inmates who are not athletic and who are withdrawn and isolated will read if the opportunity presents itself. When a public library is an unfamiliar entity, however, so that he does not even know how to check out a book, he is not very likely to go to the library. The prison library service, if handled properly, could acclimate him to library procedure and dispel his fear of embarrassment, enabling him to go into a public library after release from prison. At the same time, the understanding of experience of others, whether fictional or real, helps him better understand himself. Reading is also of great benefit to any educational program and to most job functions.

Medical and Dental Services

Medical and dental services are very important to the prison because the correctional caseload generally comes from deprived socioeconomic strata. The incidence of tuberculosis, venereal disease, dental decay, and other conditions resulting from lack of medical and dental care are pervasive in the prison population. Cosmetic surgery that can remove scars, straighten crossed eyes, take bumps out of noses, remove tattoos, and bring persons back to normal appearance also contribute immeasurably to the rehabilitation of individuals, as they no longer need to put up a strong, defensive front to ward off jokes about their appearance or to explain away a remnant of a previous crime.

CONCLUSIONS

The average cost per inmate per year varies widely with the prison system. The general estimate in 1977 was that it cost about $8,500 annually to keep a single man in prison, and about $13,000 to keep a married man when the family has to be supported by welfare. New York costs were around $9,000 per year per inmate. Some state schools cost around $45,000 to keep a juvenile for a year, such as the Connecticut School for Boys at Meriden, and some private schools may double that figure. A person could be sent to Harvard or any of the finest universities in the land for that amount of money. Consequently, it is to the economic advantage of society, as well as to its social advantage, to improve the correctional program so that recidivism can be reduced. In 1978, a New York City Council Committee recommended that the Spofford Juvenile Detention Center in the Bronx that houses 175 children between the ages of 10 and 16 be closed because there is no professional assistance, no adequate custodial supervision, the children are subject to assault and rape, and it costs $65,277 per child each year to keep them there.[36]

The total treatment program and a treatment-oriented custodial staff can produce therapeutic institutional environment. Correctional officers participating in team treatment can contribute immeasurably to the therapeutic community. In fact, correctional officers really determine the tone of the institution because they constitute approximately 65 percent of the personnel in American prisons and correctional institutions. At the same time, they are exposed to the inmates, and the inmates are exposed to them virtually twenty-four hours a day all year.

Inmates *are* affected by the correctional officer, whether good, bad, or indifferent, more than by any other staff member, because of his availability. When he is brought into the treatment process he can augment and support the treatment procedures. Unfortunately, most modern prisons and correctional institutions are still "deep-freezing," "warehousing," or just "processing" prisoners as was the case a century ago. In a period when there is concern about overpopulation and overcrowding, there is a serious manpower shortage in corrections. Education, training, and cooperation toward the treatment objectives are very important in American prisons and correctional institutions. A therapeutic community can be a reality when all personnel augment and support the treatment objective and pro-

[36] Edward Ranzal, "Council Panel Asks Closing of Spofford," *The New York Times*, March 22, 1978, Section B, p. 3, column 8.

gram. As a matter of public policy, 97 percent of all inmates are released at some time, the average stay being twenty-one months. For the protection of society, it is just common sense to promote the therapeutic community in American prisons and correctional institutions.

LEARNING EXERCISES

Issues to Be Discussed

1. Treatment programs in correctional institutions have been criticized as being quite ineffective since they do not appear to materially reduce recidivism rates. The Neo-Classicists hold that proven treatment programs should be voluntary. Their completion should not be used as a basis for extending stay beyond the date of eligibility for parole. Review the literature to determine the extent of the criticism of the treatment process. If you were a director of corrections for a state, what policy statements would you issue regarding treatment programs?
2. What are the three broad attitudes toward handling offenders in prison as taken by the public and political leaders?
3. What are the five general approaches to prison administration found in the United States?
4. What are the systems of classification and treatment used in most prisons and correctional institutions?
5. What services are generally provided in an institution?

Group Activity

Establish a panel discussion group to debate the issue: Prisons are for punishment not rehabilitation, thus serving time with reasonable things to occupy daily attention will suffice. Costly treatment staffs can thus be eliminated.

Field Activity

Arrange, if possible, for a visit to or have a personal appearance at class of one or more of the following: a deputy warden for custody; a deputy warden for treatment; a custodial officer; a counselor; or a psychologist. Discuss with them their roles as they see them.

Key Terms

Classification for treatment
Custody
Maximum security
Medium security

Minimum security
Prison departments
RAPS
Treatment

SUGGESTED REFERENCES

AMERICAN CORRECTIONAL ASSOCIATION. Resource Document No. 3. *The Mutual Agreement Program, a Planned Change in Correctional Service Delivery.* College Park, Md.: American Correctional Association, 1973.

ATKINS, BURTON M., AND GLICK, HENRY R. *Persons, Protest and Politics.* Englewood Cliffs, N.J.: Prentice-Hall, 1972.

CARROLL, LEO. *Hacks, Blacks and Cons.* Lexington, Mass.: Lexington Books, 1974.

CONRAD, JOHN P. "Corrections and Simple Justice." *Journal of Criminal Law and Criminology,* Vol. 64 (1973), pp. 208–17.

FLANAGAN, JOHN. "Crisis in Prison Populations." *American Journal of Corrections* (November–December 1975), pp. 20–36.

GOLDFARB, R. L., AND SINGER, L. *After Conviction.* New York: Simon & Schuster, 1973.

HALLECK, SEYMOUR L., AND WITTE, ANN D. "Is Rehabilitation Dead?" *Crime and Delinquency,* Vol. 23 (October 1977), pp. 372–82.

HARDY, RICHARD E., AND CULL, JOHN G. *Introduction to Correctional Rehabilitation.* Springfield, Ill.: Charles C Thomas, 1973.

HAWKINS, GORDON. *The Prison: Policy and Practice.* Chicago: University of Chicago Press, 1976.

IRWIN, JOHN. *The Felon.* Englewood Cliffs, N.J.: Prentice-Hall, 1970.

JOHNSTON, NORMAN. *The Human Cage: A Brief History of Prison Architecture.* Philadelphia: The American Foundation, 1973.

KASSENBAUM, G.; WARD, D.; AND WILNER, D. *Prison Treatment and Its Outcome.* New York: John Wiley, 1971.

LYSTON, D.; MARTINSON, R.; AND WILKES, JUDITH. *The Effectiveness of Correctional Treatment: A Survey of Treatment Evaluation Studies.* New York: Praeger, 1975.

MINTON, ROBERT J., JR., ed. *Inside: Prison American Style.* New York: Vintage Books, 1971.

NAGEL, WILLIAM. *The New Red Barn: A Critical Look at the Modern American Prison.* New York: Walker, 1973.

NEW YORK SPECIAL COMMISSION ON ATTICA. *Attica: The Official Report.* New York: Bantam, 1972.

ORLAND, LEONARD. *Justice, Punishment, Treatment. The Correctional Process.* Riverside, N.Y.: Free Press, 1973.

―――. *Prisons: Houses of Darkness.* Riverside, N.Y.: Free Press, 1975.

Program for Prison Reform, Final Report of the Annual Chief Justice Earl Warren Conference on Advocacy in the United States. Cambridge, Mass.: Roscoe Pound–American Trial Lawyers Foundation, 1972.

SCOTT, EDWARD M., AND SCOTT, KATHRYN L., eds. *Criminal Rehabilitation Within and Without Walls.* Springfield, Ill.: Charles C Thomas, 1973.

SERRILL, MICHAEL S. "Is Rehabilitation Dead?" *Corrections Magazine,* Vol. 1 (May–June 1975), pp. 1–32.

U.S. CONGRESS. HOUSE SELECT COMMITTEE ON CRIME. *American Prisons in Turmoil.* Hearings, 92nd Congress. Washington, D.C.: U.S. Government Printing Office, 1972. 2 volumes.

YOCHELSON, SAMUEL, AND SAMENOW, STANTON. *The Criminal Personality,* Vols. 1 and 2. New York: Jason Aronson, 1977.

16

Institutional Society

Overview
The People
Society
Culture
The Factions
Customs and Folkways
Staff Society
Effects of Institutionalization
Conclusions
Learning Exercises
Suggested References

OVERVIEW

A prison is a closed community possessing a singular social structure. Compared to other institutions it is unnatural, authoritative, and isolated. Prisons house people who are in conflict, whose one objective is to leave the institution. To understand the prison population it is necessary to look at social and environmental factors, personality makeup, and cultural origins. Especially important is the study of recidivists. Inmates generally run the administrative routines of prison. Racial tensions are one of prisons' most persistent problems. Frequently conflict occurs within the institution among custodial, treatment, and inmate personnel, with the inmates often being in the position of manipulators in carrying out prison folkways. The impact of institutional society on inmates upon returning to civilian life or upon their personal adjustment is generally negative.

The prison or correctional institution is similar to the city in that both have residences, schools, hospitals, kitchens, water and power supply, sewage disposal, and other facilities and services to maintain the population. There ends the similarity, however, because most prisons and correctional institutions are unisexual communities housing people whose legal status is either felon or misdemeanant. The social formation and interaction within institutions differ considerably from that in free society.[1] Although the city has a nucleus of permanent population with many transients that give a quality of dynamic movement, the prison has a permanent population, or the feeling of one, only. Nobody is "just passing through" in the same overnight sense as is possible outside. The prison is a closed community.

The maximum custody institution, where the differences from outside society are greatest, has been compared to a totalitarian state in miniature.[2] Even the least secure, minimum custody institution follows the same patterns, but not to such an extreme. Regimentation for purposes of optimum economy and efficiency in providing the necessities of life, possession of weapons and use of force by the custodial force and administration, constant presence of uniformed authority imposing varying degrees of control, complete lack of privacy, and the forceful social influence of other inmates with whom a prisoner lives are only a few of the significant factors that make institutional society different from free society outside a prison. These differences contribute to the definition of prison society as "unnatural," however "natural" it might be under similar circumstances anywhere else. It is difficult to find those "similar circumstances" in a democratic society.

---

[1] Erving Goffman, *Asylums* (Chicago: Aldine, 1962), p. 1.
[2] See James B. Jacobs, *Stateville: The Penitentiary in Mass Society* (Chicago: University of Chicago Press, 1977).

This unnatural society has a significant impact on the people who live in it, the people who work in it, and the people who administer it. Power orientation within a relatively small area tends to develop among people who are exposed to the system over a period of time. The authoritarian atmosphere induces people to narrow their social functioning for their own protection. Inmates and staff alike develop life styles that permit them to do their "own time."

THE PEOPLE

The people in prison have one characteristic in common—conflict with authority. They have one objective in common—to get out of prison and stay out. The means by which the objective *is* achieved is really less important than the means by which it *might be* achieved.

Prison populations differ from most other populations receiving public care or support. Welfare clients or those receiving public assistance may be poor managers and unable to compete effectively in the economic system, but they are generally prosocial and law abiding. Patients in mental hospitals are "insane," which is a legal status relating to incompetence but, with the exception of the few criminally insane, they are law abiding. Even among the criminally insane, most hospital staffs consider that the patients were insane first and criminal second when their behavior was labeled. Clients of community mental health clinics, of private psychiatrists, and of other counseling agencies frequently show neurotic patterns and are sufficiently anxiety motivated to actively seek help, often paying a fee to the clinic or a private counselor or psychiatrist. The offender who comes to the prison, however, is most frequently within the "normal" range in terms of the deviant clinical classifications, although many may be neurotic, psychotic, antisocial personalities[3] or other clinical classifications, but their *conflict with authority* in committing crimes differentiates them from other groups of people receiving public aid or care.

Because crime is a sociopolitical phenomenon rather than a clinical classification, it would be very difficult to attempt to diagnose criminal behavior on the basis of personality. There is no such thing as a "criminal personality." Nevertheless, there are some common factors observed in most prison populations that differ from the average in the general population. In this sense, we can consider some differences in the prison population without coming up with the concept of a criminal personality. There are people in the general population with essentially similar problems, but who are not in prison. For example, there were 7,179,000 high school graduates in 1975, and there were 3,271,000 dropouts in the United States.[4] Because there are slightly over 287,000 prisoners in federal and state pris-

---

[3] The clinical classification best known as the *psychopath* has had several names. In 1952, the American Psychiatric Association changed their nomenclature from *psychopath* to *sociopath*. In 1969, that Association changed the terminology again from *sociopath* to *antisocial personality disorder*.

[4] U.S. Department of Labor, Bureau of Labor Statistics, *Special Labor Force Report, Nos. 66, 155, 168, and 180* (Washington, D.C.: U.S. Government Printing Office, 1976).

ons (as of 1977), it is obvious that the majority of dropouts are not in prison. Nevertheless, in the general population these dropouts constitute a minority of the population, but they constitute a heavy majority of the prison population. Part of the prisoner's profile, then, would be academic retardation followed by dropping out of school. Other factors may be viewed similarly.

When diagnosing any behavior, two questions have to be asked. First, how stressful is the environment? Second, how stable is the personality bearing that stress? Environmental factors in family, neighborhood, socioeconomic status, and level of power and influence in the state or nation or, conversely, the level of powerlessness and futility, are only a few of the factors in the environment with which people have to cope. Standards of conduct, levels of enforcement, parental expectations, and many other social pressures encroach on the freedom of the individual. How the individual responds to these environmental and social pressures is dependent upon the environmental and social factors. Consequently, it is important to examine the personality, environmental and social factors, and the culture from which the prison population came, and compare those with the average for the general population.

Personality Development

Normal personality development begins after birth with close and warm interaction between the infant and his mother. During the first year and a half or thereabouts, mother cares for all his physical needs, plays with him, elicits smiles, and interacts with the infant in generally happy and supportive demeanor. It is during this period that the mother develops in the child the capacity to relate emotionally to other people. This capacity for emotional reciprocity is subsequently used in the socialization process. Toilet training is the first imposition of social control over the functioning of the individual. After toilet training, the "do's" and "don't's" come rapidly. Regardless of whether the interpretation is sociological, psychiatric, psychoanalytic, or theological, the function is the same, though it may be referred to in different terminology. For example, the values of the culture are learned from mother during preschool childhood. Sociologists may call it an internalized system of values, experimental psychologists may call it conditioning, psychiatrists may call it superego, and theologians may call it conscience. Regardless of the terminology, the function is the same.

When the internalized system of values is strong enough to withstand conflict (psychiatrists refer to ego strength), then the child is old enough to go to school. When he arrives at school, he encounters other children with different value systems from different homes and with different ways of handling stress and problems. While at school, the child must reinforce the personal defenses that work, abandon those that do not, and modify those that have possibilities of success. The basic defense pattern has been formed, however, and the refinement process is beginning to take place with expanded social contacts in school and neighborhood.

As the child approaches puberty, the father or father substitute becomes important. Although mother's world is more home-centered, according to still-strong cultural definitions, and the value system is learned there, the integration of that value system into the power structure of the community is a function of the father. The boy learns the tools of masculinity from his father or father substitute as the influence of his mother diminishes (psychiatrists refer to this as the resolving of the Oedipus situation). The girl goes through similar developmental changes, but concentrates on "how mother handles the old man" and sometimes learns more about manipulation of others than do boys. It is at this stage when adolescence begins with the struggle for independence and "fighting it out" with authority.

Studies of family relationships have shown that when this normal pattern is not followed, several problems may arise. For example, if the mother has not developed the child's capacity to relate during infancy, then the capacity to relate emotionally never develops and the possibility of antisocial personality is increased. Personality can "learn" to relate later, but it does not have the same emotional depth as has a person who enjoyed normal infancy and warm mother-child relationships.

The father is even more important in determining whether an individual becomes criminal or delinquent. There is a difference between the presence or absense of the mother when comparing groups of delinquents or nondelinquents, but it is not statistically significant. There is a difference between the presence or absence of the father when comparing groups of delinquents and nondelinquents, also, but this difference *is* significant.[5] In summary, paternal deprivation has been found to be most significant in the development of criminal and delinquent offenders.[6]

Common Personality Traits

Underachievement is a primary characteristic of the prison population. The prison population is at least as intelligent as the population from which it is drawn.[7] The correctional client, however, is estimated to be about three grades retarded in school. It would be erroneous, however, to suggest that education is the area of deficiency. Rather, the deficiency is across the total psychological and social spectrum, as mentioned in the previous chapter. Poor work and study habits, lack of

---

[5] Ruth Shonle Cavan, *Juvenile Delinquency*, 2nd ed. (Philadelphia: Lippincott, 1969), p. 187. Also, Thomas P. Monahan, "Family Status and the Delinquent Child: A Reappraisal and Some New Findings," *Social Forces*, Vol. 35 (1957), pp. 250–58.

[6] Gustave Newman and Sidney Denman, "Felony and Paternal Deprivation: A Socio-Psychiatric View," *The International Journal of Social Psychiatry*, Vol. 17, No. 1 (1971), pp. 65–71.

[7] Fabian L. Rourke, "Recent Contributions of Psychology to the Study of Criminal Genesis," *Journal of Criminal Law and Criminology*, Vol. 41, No. 4 (November–December 1950), pp. 446–55.

motivation, inadequate internalization of the social values, and deficient social comprehension have also been shown to be characteristic of prisoners. Education can be focused upon because it is easiest to measure. It is only an index, however, of a total cultural deprivation and underachievement. To expect to treat this deprivation through education alone would be a serious oversimplification.

Defense mechanisms frequently ascribed to prison populations are *projection* and *denial.* Projection is frequent in that a prisoner often assigns blame for his plight to "the system." Many people have done worse than he, according to his thinking, but *"they arrested me!"* The caught and the uncaught make up the prisoner's concept of society. The offender frequently considers himself to be one of the unlucky ones who was caught. Denial is also a frequent defense of prison inmates. "That is not the way it happened!" arises frequently. The inmate's version of the offense and the official version are seldom congruent. Many parole boards make an issue of the fact that offenders will not admit their guilt after having been convicted and having served their sentences. Even prisoners who had pleaded guilty in court maintained that their plea had been bargained so they would not be "nailed" for an even more serious offense. Denial of guilt, blame, and responsibility, combined with projection of blame to the system, is characteristic in prison populations.

A succession of failures throughout life, underachievement, and "getting the short end of the stick" leads to the development of a *self-concept of worthlessness.* Many offenders have finally accepted and identified with this status. Many have tattooed on their chest and arms the slogan "Born to Lose." It becomes their identity. This self-concept introduces feelings of futility and drains motivation. The offender becomes a "victim of circumstances," he is "born to lose," underachieves, denies reality, and projects blame.

The general attitude that some people get "the breaks" and others do not and that some people are "born to lose" and others are born "with silver spoons in their mouths" leads to dependence upon luck. This is the reason that much *gambling* goes on among prison populations and the outside populations from which they were drawn. The chances of winning in the "numbers," "bolita," or similar lotteries are very slim, but nickel, dime, and quarter gambling in the large urban ghettos runs into millions of dollars in many large cities. There is always the hope of getting a "long shot." Frequent losses do not deter gambling because the "law of averages" should eventually provide that long shot.

Emotional immaturity is characteristic of most prison populations, and this comment appears frequently in the reports of prison psychologists. In normal development, a child operates on the pleasure principle, seeking pleasures and avoiding pain.[8] As he matures, he learns to postpone immediate gratification for future reward. Expending time and effort in school to obtain an education is an example of his more mature functioning on the reality principle. More than the general population, the prisoner population has not made this maturity shift suc-

---

[8] Leon Joseph Saul, *Emotional Maturity* (Philadelphia: Lippincott, 1947), p. 1.

cessfully. Many still function on the pleasure principle and cannot postpone gratification for future reward. Normal maturation can be shown in statistics of insurance rates and arrest rates. There is a significant drop in arrests in the middle thirties, probably around thirty-five years of age. Insurance companies have found that there is a similar drop in the risks in the general population in the middle twenties, probably around twenty-five years of age. This is reflected in automobile insurance rates for men, which go down dramatically after the twenty-fifth birthdate. It becomes apparent that emotional maturation is a real factor in crime.

Repeat Offenders

There are many "repeaters" of crime in prison. The crimes that are repeated most often are forgery, auto theft, robbery, and burglary, and these offenders constitute a large number of the prison population. In any prison at any given time, probably burglary offenders would outnumber the others because of the longer sentences imposed for this crime. As indicated in Table 12-1, the rearrest rates average about 63 percent in a 4-year period. Further, approximately 32 percent of new offenders received in prison are first-termers, while about 68 percent have been in prison before.

SOCIETY

Society is the interaction between people and groups of people. Illustrations of social interaction or behavior can be demonstrated in experiments on the pecking order of chickens.[9] In one experiment, a flock of chickens was identified individually with leg tags and then observed. Chicken A pecked everyone in the flock, but nobody pecked Chicken A. Chicken B pecked everyone in the flock, except Chicken A, and Chicken A pecked Chicken B. Chicken C pecked everybody in the flock except Chickens A and B, and on through the flock until the pecking order was charted. In elementary school, many boys work out the "pecking order" at recess. When a new boy comes to town, they find out where he places in the pecking order by antagonizing him until he asserts himself. Any group of people has a pecking order. "Heavyweights" and "lightweights" appear in legislatures, universities, prisons, and any social organization. In the city ghetto, many of the people who are in the criminal justice system, either delinquent or criminal, have been at the lower end of the "pecking order" and have therefore considered themselves as having been "born to lose." What occurs is that these people have

[9] R. H. Masure and W. C. Allee, "The Social Order in Flocks of the Common Chicken and the Pigeon," *AUK,* Vol. 51 (1934), pp. 306–27; R. H. Masure and W. C. Allee, "Flock Organization of the Shell Parakeet Melopsittuacus Undulatus Shaw," *Ecology,* Vol. 15 (1934), pp. 388-98; and A. M. Ghul, "The Social Order of Chickens," *Scientific American,* Vol. 194, No. 2 (1956), pp. 42–46.

no one in their "flock" to "peck," so they turn on strangers or society at large in order to assert themselves.

An interesting experiment that can be applied to the city ghetto, to prisons, and other human society was done by John Emlen at the University of Wisconsin.[10] In the first part of the experiment, 250 grams of food were supplied for a colony of house mice. When the number of mice became greater than the number that the 250 grams per day could support, some mice left the colony—the weaker ones. Subsequently, the emigration occurred at about the same rate at which new mice were born. A second phase was a repetition of the experiment, but the mice were confined and prevented from emigrating. When the food shortage developed, the birth rate of mice declined so that the population size and food supply reached equilibrium. In the third part of the experiment, the food was not allowed to become scarce, but the space was held constant. Emigration was prevented as the population increased, so there was a decrease in the space and the available nest locations per mouse. When the colonies became crowded, chasing, fighting, and biting occurred. The females ceased to take proper care of their young. Finally, cannibalism developed even in the presence of an adequate food supply. This social phenomenon without culture can be observed to a lesser extent in urban ghettos and in prisons. A study of 37 institutions in the United States Bureau of Prisons in the fiscal years 1973 to 1976 supports the contention that population density and misconduct reports are correlated in prisons.[11]

This interaction, almost devoid of culture, occurs in prisons, particularly in maximum security prisons. It is a dog-eat-dog, survival-of-the-fittest existence. One learns to protect himself by various means in such a society.

CULTURE

The culture of a prison is characterized by deprivation. Methods of protecting one's self become a real part of the culture. In a culture of deprivation, simple things become important. The day's menu, identifying the movie that is to be shown in the auditorium Saturday or Sunday afternoon, a letter, a visit, and a tour by a college class, all became important, some just by virtue of breaking the monotony of tedious and regimented living.

The "inmate code," frequently discussed in books on penology, is that one does not communicate information, nor does he expose a fellow inmate to discipline. It is really difficult to define the inmate code, as it is unwritten and not repeated to authorities, except in very hypothetical terms. Any group of people

---

[10] Reported in *Biological Science, Molecules to Man,* by the Biological Sciences Curriculum Study, American Institute of Biological Sciences (Boston: Houghton Mifflin, 1963), pp. 606-8.

[11] Peter L. Nacci, Hugh E. Teitelbaum, and Jerry Prather, "Population Density and Inmate Misconduct Rates in the Federal Prison System," *Federal Probation,* Vol. XXXXI, No. 2 (June 1977), pp. 26-31.

under stress or oppression, real or imagined, reacts similarly. In New York City in the middle 1960s, for example, the newspapers carried the now-famous story of Kitty Genovese, who was raped, stabbed, and killed while thirty-eight people watched. The offender escaped on foot. Subsequent interviews by police and the press revealed that these people simply did not want to "get involved." This behavior is identical to the inmate code, which applies in prisons, of course, but is not confined to prisons.

Structure by Coercion

The social structure of the inmate body within a prison involves many factors. The "heavyweights" assume positions of leadership, while the "lightweights" hide or follow, for all practical purposes, rather than have to fight more powerful inmates. Otherwise, they are victimized in various ways, such as being forced to provide sexual services or to give up their property.

Women Prisoners

Women's prisons are culturally different from men's prisons for several reasons. Obviously, vocational training and interests in personal grooming are different. Some other differences emanate from the fact that there is considerable selectivity of women offenders for imprisonment, meaning that inmates in a women's prison would be relatively more hard-core than would those in a men's prison.[12] The percentage of persons serving time for murder in women's prisons, for example, is higher than that in men's prisons, though the actual numbers are less. Generally one woman is arrested for every five men, one woman is indicted for every nine men, one woman is convicted for every seventeen men, and one woman is sentenced to prison for every twenty-seven men.

Emotional development is different, also, with the result that there are more minor fights in women's prisons when they "fly off the handle." Homosexual relationships are stronger, too, since women need to be needed more than do men. One former warden of a women's prison writes:

> Probably the most significant difference between men and women in this regard is that women are socialized in the language of love before they learn about sex, while men are socialized in the language of sex before they learn about love.[13]

A significant concern in women's prisons arises because more than half of the inmates are (or are about to be) mothers of young children.[14] Separation from minor children already born takes on dramatic and traumatic consequences for

---

[12] Phyllis Haslam, *The Woman Offender* (Toronto: John Howard Society of Ontario, 1972), p. 2.
[13] Joy S. Eyman, *Prisons for Women* (Springfiled, Ill.: Charles C Thomas, 1971), p. 135.
[14] *Ibid.*, p. 119.

the children when mother goes to prison. The ramifications in terms of normal psychosexual development of the children are staggering. Their physical care while the mother is in prison can be handled easier by foster home placement or by placement with relatives. In addition, many women are pregnant when they arrive in prison. The first three years of a child's life are critical in terms of relationships with mother, particularly the first year of life. Some prisons allow mothers to keep their children in the prison nursery for a year or more and permit daily visits. Other prisons insist on immediate placement of the child outside the institution. Certainly, joint planning between the correctional institution, child-caring or welfare agency, and the mother are minimum requirements for the benefit of the child and of society. It is one very important way to break the vicious cycle of crime.

The significant increase in female crime in 1975 over 1960, combined with recent feminist movements, have focused concern of the criminal justice system on the female offender. During this fifteen-year period, crime for females eighteen years of age and under increased 253.9 percent and for females over eighteen, the increase was 101.7 percent.[15] Because of their traditionally low representation in the offender population, the institutions for females have been undifferentiated and have received fewer facilities and resources than male institutions.[16] The April 1977 issue of *Crime and Delinquency,* published by the National Council on Crime and Delinquency, was devoted to this issue, with a subheadline, "Criminal justice to women: NOT FAIR!" In 1973, there were 6,175 females in state and federal institutions, of whom more than half had children and were their sole support.

Summary

According to scholars who have studied prison life, inmate culture can be summarized as follows:

1. Don't be nosey.
2. Don't suck around.
3. Be sharp.
4. Don't break your word.
5. Don't welch on bets.
6. Don't steal from cons (highjacking in the yard, and so on).
7. Don't interfere with inmates' interests.
8. Refrain from quarrels with fellow inmates.
9. Maintenance of self is important.

[15] *Crime in the United States, 1975—Uniform Crime Reports* (Washington, D.C.: Federal Bureau of Investigation, released August 25, 1976), p. 183.

[16] National Advisory Commission on Criminal Justice Standards and Goals, *Task Force Report: Corrections* (Washington, D.C.: U.S. Government Printing Office, 1973), p. 279.

10. Don't give respect to guards, to "thy brother's keeper." What kind of a guy would be his brother's keeper?[17]

The prison culture is designed as an accommodation to regimented living in a world characterized by deprivation and authority.

THE FACTIONS

There are factions in all large organizations. The prison has at least three built-in factions. The administration and the custodial force are interested in keeping the prisoners in and maintaining peace and order at all costs. The treatment personnel are interested in a relaxed atmosphere so that the interpersonal barriers are down, thereby permitting casework and psychotherapy to function better. The inmates want a relaxed atmosphere for easier living, and they want to get out and stay out. Because the treatment people want the same things as do the inmates, if for different reasons, administration and custody generally see the treatment people as being "on the side" of the inmates. This makes for divisiveness.

CUSTOMS AND FOLKWAYS

There are many different customs and folkways that are peculiar to the maximum security prison. The special language or argot has been a matter of interest to several writers. Calling the correctional officer a "screw" is probably the most usual word. The disciplinary unit is called different names in different areas, such as the "Klondike" at San Quentin, the "Cuba" at South Carolina State Penitentiary, the "Flat-top" at the Florida State Prison. Of course, it is referred to as the "hole" in almost all prisons. Other words and phrases developed in prison and adopted by prisoners result in ready recognition after release on parole by others with the similar "language."

It is the inculcation of these prison "folkways and customs" that is termed as *prisonization*. The institutionalized personality that has almost completely internalized the prison value system finds it difficult to stay outside. Unfortunately, many long-term staff as well as the inmates are "institutionalized."

STAFF SOCIETY

Prison staff have much interaction with each other and with inmates. Many large prisons are constructed in rural areas away from urban communities, resulting in the prison frequently providing housing for many of the staff, particularly administrative and other key staff. Mutual distrust frequently exists between officers and inmates. Many prison personnel have "done more time" than many of the in-

---

[17] Gresham Sykes and Sheldon Messinger, in "Theoretical Studies in Social Organization of the Prison," Social Science Research Council Pamphlet, No. 15, New York, 1960, p. 7.

mates and, after constant exposure to paranoid thinking over a period of years, they find themselves struggling with the temptation to overuse their authority in the interests of control for the safety and security of the institution and its personnel.[18] It becomes so natural for prison personnel to socialize with their fellow workers who "understand the situation" that a gradual "institutionalization" of many staff members is understandable.

Another effect of their exposure to paranoid thinking over a period of years is the development of pessimistic attitudes in many prison personnel, the feeling that they are committed to and involved in a hopeless venture. When correctional personnel experience the "burn-out syndrome," they lose their enthusiasm and optimism, thereby reducing their efforts to day-to-day "processing" of prisoners, rather than exhibiting their earlier enthusiastic mission to help their fellow man.

Sherman has suggested several problematic factors that are constant in police work, and many of these may tend to affect prison people even more: (1) discretion to arrest (discipline) someone or not, which has numerous bases, both legitimate and illegitimate; (2) low managerial visibility of the line officer; (3) low public visibility; (4) peer group secrecy and mutual support that makes peer visibility useless as a control; (5) managerial secrecy to avoid hurting a "brother," almost no matter how serious an offense may be; and (6) status problems associated with low pay relative to their powers and responsibilities, complexity of their tasks, and even their low prestige, itself.[19] These factors also apply to correctional personnel in the prison, probably even to a greater extent than police. The phenomenon of staff society in prisons is a significant part of the criminal justice system.

EFFECTS OF INSTITUTIONALIZATION

The effects of institutionalization are significant to the people who experience them. Certainly, attitudes toward socialization, law, and moral judgment all are more consistently unfavorable in the prison population than in the general population as represented by labor unions or even probationers.[20] Although there may have been some selection of persons with unfavorable attitudes in these areas, the prison population reinforces these unfavorable attitudes by a tendency for an unfavorable or abnormal value system to be imposed. With time, it seems to become more acceptable and normal to the individual exposed to institutionalization.

There is currently a debate as to whether or not rehabilitation actually works. The attempt to use psychiatric, psychological, and social work approaches

---

[18] Bruno M. Cormier, *The Watcher and the Watched* (Montreal and Pittsburgh: Tundra Books, 1975), p. 12.

[19] Lawrence W. Sherman, *Police Corruption: A Sociological Perspective* (Garden City, N.Y.: Anchor Press/Doubleday, 1974), p. 5.

[20] Walter C. Reckless, "The Development of a Criminality Level Index," in Walter C. Reckless and Charles L. Newman, eds., *Interdisciplinary Problems of Criminology: Papers of the American Society of Criminology, 1964* (Columbus, Ohio: Ohio State University, 1965), p. 75.

in prisons began after World War II when clinical psychology found its first firm base in the universities almost as an assistant to psychiatry. The mental health model was reflected in large grants for education in these fields from the National Institute of Mental Health. In order to introduce the new approaches, correctional administrators requested budgets to finance them. However, correctional budgets did not enjoy favor, not even from the National Institute of Mental Health, until the late 1960s when some educational grants were provided psychology and social work in the correctional field. In the meantime, although lip service was given the mental health and rehabilitative ideal while requesting budgetary implementation, leaders in the correctional field, such as Dr. E. Preston Sharp, Executive Director of the American Correctional Association, said repeatedly in the late 1960s and the 1970s that corrections was merely "ware-housing and deep-freezing" inmates. The facilities to implement the rehabilitation ideal were not available. The "Martinson Report,"[21] published in 1975, contended that rehabilitation had not worked and further literature stated that rehabilitation was a failure, based on a survey of the literature between 1945 and 1967. The conclusion was that some corrections programs showed positive results, some showed negative results, and most showed neutral results. Intense controversy rose around the findings, well summarized in a brief publication by the National Council on Crime and Delinquency written by Martinson, Palmer, and Adams.[22] A survey by *Corrections Magazine* done in 1975 showed that 63 percent of correctional administrators still supported the rehabilitative ideal, 15 percent argued that there was not enough evidence to support a decision, and 12 percent wanted to go to flat sentencing because rehabilitation did not work.[23]

There is also debate about prisons, themselves. Many writers want to abolish prisons.[24] Others want to imprison more people and keep them longer in order to make society safe.[25] Some moderates want smaller prisons for fewer people.[26] While this debate has gone on for a long time, the prison populations reached a new high of 287,000 people in 1977.

Constructive changes that could take place in the present inmate system in maximum custody institutions include (1) reduction of the deprivation that ac-

---

[21] Douglas Lipton, Robert Martinson, and Judith Wilks, *The Effectiveness of Correctional Treatment* (New York: Praeger Press, 1975).

[22] Robert Martinson, Ted Palmer, and Stuart Adams, *Rehabilitation, Recidivism, and Research* (Hackensack, N.J.: National Council on Crime and Delinquency, 1976).

[23] "Editor's Notebook: Rehabilitation?" *Corrections Magazine,* Vol. 1, No. 5 (May/June 1975), p. 2.

[24] See Joseph Wilson, *Are Prisons Necessary?* (Philadelphia: Dorrance Press, 1950); Karl Menninger, *The Crime of Punishment* (New York: Viking Press, 1969); American Friends Service Committee, *Struggle for Justice* (New York: Hill & Wang, 1973).

[25] James Q. Wilson, *Thinking About Crime* (New York: Basic Books, 1975); Ernest van den Haag, *Punishing Criminals: A Very Old and Painful Question* (New York: Basic Books, 1975), Andrew von Hirsch, *Doing Justice* (New York: Hill & Wang, 1976).

[26] Norval Morris, *The Future of Imprisonment* (Chicago: University of Chicago Press, 1974); Gordon Hawkins, *The Prison: Policy and Practice* (Chicago: University of Chicago Press, 1976).

companies confinement; (2) changes in the communication patterns between inmates and staff so that vertical communication is facilitated; and (3) programs of staff training and education designed to offset the patterns of accommodation that the more antisocial inmates adopt and that influence their positions of power and visibility by the prison social structure.[27]

There is no relationship between custody and rehabilitation.[28] The type of custody of a prisoner or how he is viewed as a security risk in the institution has no relationship to his rehabilitation and his potential adjustment to free society.

CONCLUSIONS

The modern maximum security prison has become a substitute for the banishment of two hundred years ago. As a closed society based on caste (inmates and free personnel) and class (social hierarchy among inmates and staff), the prison becomes a microcosm of a broader society. Characterized by deprivation, the prison is as close to a society without culture as could be found in Western civilization. Much of the culture that exists results from inmate attempts to protect themselves from oppression by staff or to "buy in" for favors, such as recommendations to the parole board. In a culture of deprivation, simple items become important, such as the menu or the Saturday movie.

The institutional society varies, of course, with the age and composition of the inmate body and with the size and security of the institution. A large, maximum security institution would have more institutionalized inmates than a small, minimum custody, or community-based correctional facility for young first offenders would have. Nevertheless, the trends of an institutional society are present in every institutional setting. The results of institutionalization in a deprived, closed, unisexual, abnormal society have not as yet provided many examples of successful rehabilitation in prisons.[29]

LEARNING EXERCISES

Issues to Be Discussed

1. It is claimed that there is no such phenomenon as a criminal personality. At the same time scholars feel that certain traits can be isolated which give clues to understanding many prison inmates. Look carefully at some of the recent literature and in a 200- to

---

[27] Stanton Wheeler, "Role Conflict in Correctional Communities," in *The Prison*, ed. Donald R. Cressey (New York: Holt, Rinehart & Winston, 1961), pp. 229–59.

[28] Daniel Glaser, "Isolation Promotion and Custody Grading," Chap. 7 in his *The Effectiveness of a Prison and Parole System* (Indianapolis: Bobbs-Merrill, 1964), pp. 149–71.

[29] Walter C. Bailey, "An Evaluation of 100 Studies of Correctional Outcome," *Journal of Criminal Law, Criminology and Police Science,* Vol. 52, No. 2 (June 1966), pp. 153–60; and in Norman Johnston, Leonard Savitz, and Marvin E. Wolfgang, eds., *The Sociology of Punishment and Correction,* 2nd ed. (New York: John Wiley, 1970), pp. 773–842.

300-word paper summarize the findings that have been useful in arriving at some classification of personality traits among criminals.
2. How do prisoners differ from other populations receiving public care and support?
3. What two general questions have to be answered to explain behavior?
4. Describe the prison culture.
5. How are women's prisons different from institutions for men?
6. Describe the built-in conflicts in prisons.
7. What are the effects of institutionalization?

Group Activity

Develop a role-playing skit to highlight the institutional conflict between custodial, treatment, and inmate personnel. Have the inmate set the stage by his demands regarding his treatment-work program which will precipitate conflict situations. Study the results for tentative solutions to such problems.

Field Activities

1. Plan a visit to a prison to examine the physical structure of the prison from the viewpoint of how it controls, in part, institutional life. Determine how near it is to a city within itself. View it not from contact with inmates but from the physical elements—workshops, dining areas, recreational spots, kitchens, boiler rooms, etc.
2. Plan to interview a former prison inmate and develop a short paper on evaluating the ex-offender's views on the impact of prison on his personal and social adjustment.

Key Terms

Defense mechanisms
Emotional immaturity
Inmate code
Recidivist

Self-concept of worthlessness
Society
Underachievement

SUGGESTED REFERENCES

ALPER, BENEDICT S. *Prisons Inside-out: Alternatives to Correctional Reform.* Cambridge, Mass.: Ballanger Publishing, 1974.

AMERICAN BAR ASSOCIATION. Resource Center on Correctional Law and Legal Services. *A Survey of Prison Disciplinary Practices and Procedures.* Washington, D.C.: American Bar Association, 1974.

JACOBS, J. B. *Stateville: The Penitentiary in Mass Society.* Chicago: University of Chicago Press, 1977.

KASSENBAUM, G.; WARD, D.; AND WILNER, D. *Prison Treatment and Its Outcome.* New York: John Wiley, 1971.

KEVE, PAUL W. *Prison Life and Human Worth.* Minneapolis: University of Minnesota Press, 1974.

KWARTLER, RICHARD, ed. *Behind Bars.* New York: Vintage Books, 1976.

NATIONAL COUNCIL ON CRIME AND DELINQUENCY. *A Model for the Protection of Rights of Prisoners.* New York: National Council on Crime and Delinquency, 1972.

OHLIN, LLOYD E. *Prisoners in America: The American Assembly.* Englewood Cliffs, N.J.: Prentice-Hall, 1973.

PETERSEN, DAVID M., AND FRUZZI, MARCELLO, eds. *Criminal Life: Views from the Inside.* Englewood Cliffs, N.J.: Prentice-Hall, 1972.

RADZINOWICZ, SIR LEON, AND WOLFGANG, MARVIN E. *Crime and Justice: The Criminal in Confinement,* Vol. 3. New York: Basic Books, 1977.

U.S. BUREAU OF PRISONS. *Female Offenders in the Federal Prison System.* Washington, D.C.: U.S. Government Printing Office, 1977.

WEISS, KAREL, ed. *Prison Experience: An Anthology.* New York: Delacorte Press, 1976.

17

Community-Based Corrections

Overview
Diversion Programs
Halfway Houses
Work Release, Study Release, and Furloughs
Ex-Offender Groups
Private Community-Based Corrections
Conclusions
Learning Exercises
Suggested References

OVERVIEW

The concept of community-based corrections generally holds that offenders can profit more in rehabilitation and personal adjustment through assignment to agencies within their own community. Such proximity to family and community resources could facilitate more favorable adjustment within a less-structured and less debilitating environment than the formal prison. Community-based agencies, however, have faced hostility from some law enforcement agencies and from citizens who have seen them as threats to community stability. However, they afford opportunities for judges to divert individuals away from formal prisons and allow correctional authorities to release offenders to civilian life gradually through halfway houses and programs such as work and study release and furlough. Community-based facilities have grown in both the public and the private sectors.

Some type of "community-based corrections" has existed since the beginning of criminal justice itself, as indicated by the first court depicted on the shield of Achilles in Homer's *Iliad* about 2000 B.C. and in the Code of Hammurabi in 1927 B.C. Even before that, primitive man handled most of his offenders within the community or tribe. In the absence of institutions, all those not banished or executed remained in the community subject to local social responses to their offenses. With the beginning of prisons in the period from 1773 to 1790 and with their further development in the early 1800s, community-based corrections came to consist of private participation through lay visiting to prisons and the formation of prisoners' aid societies.

In 1787, the Quakers started the Philadelphia Society for Alleviating the Miseries of the Public Prisons, and this organization was responsible for the beginning of the "penitentiary" movement in 1790. The name was changed to the Pennsylvania Prison Society in 1887, as it remains today. The Correctional Association of New York was formed in 1844. The Prisoner's Aid Association of Maryland was formalized in 1869, but its beginning goes back to 1829 when the rector of Saint Paul's Episcopal Church in downtown Baltimore provided housing and other assistance to men leaving the penitentiary. The John Howard Society was first established in England in 1866 and has spread to most English-speaking countries. The Massachusetts Correctional Association was established in 1889 as a John Howard Society. Today, there are private societies interested in prisons and corrections around the world, most of them listed in the *International Directory of Prisoners' Aid Societies.*[1]

---

[1] *International Directory of Prisoners' Aid Societies* (Philadelphia: International Prisoners' Aid Association, 1970).

The first halfway houses were established in New York, Pennsylvania, and Massachusetts in the early 1800s.[2] These early halfway houses were self-contained and isolated from official correctional programs and personnel. A halfway house was established in Boston in 1864 and operated for twenty years. In New York City in the 1880s, the Quakers opened the halfway house for women that remains today as the Isaac T. Hopper House. They also opened the House of Industry in Philadelphia in 1889, which still receives prisoners released from Pennsylvania prisons.[3] Maud Booth, whose Volunteers of America had split from the Salvation Army, opened Hope Hall with her husband in 1896 in the Washington Heights section of Manhattan. It came under police harassment to the extent that Mrs. Booth appealed directly to President Theodore Roosevelt for assistance.[4]

Settlement houses began to appear in the 1880s. The first was Toynbee Hall in London in 1884; the Neighborhood Guild was patterned after it in New York in 1897. The purpose of these settlement houses was more generalized than that of the halfway houses. They assisted in the improvement of deteriorated neighborhoods by working for better economic conditions, employment, recreation, lighting, social welfare, and other social goals. Probably the most famous of these early settlement houses was Hull House, founded in Chicago in 1889 by Jane Addams and Ellen Gates Starr, who rented a house built by Charles G. Hull at 800 South Halsted Street. Hull House operated until 1967 when the land was taken over by the University of Illinois at Chicago Circle. In 1967 the original Hull House was declared a National Historical Landmark, supervised by a curator, and the functions of the Hull House organization were decentralized and now operate from several bases in Chicago.

The Chicago Area Project was begun in 1932 as a research project of the Department of Sociology at the University of Chicago. The thesis was that delinquency developed in the neighborhood and could be controlled there. Subsequently, there were area projects set up in various places, including the Cambridge-Somerville Youth Study in Boston. It was begun in 1935 and was originally intended to last ten years, but was cut off in 1941 because of World War II. As a result of the Great Depression, low-cost housing projects were begun in the late 1930s in the administration of President Franklin D. Roosevelt. There tended to be a merging between the settlement house and the area projects in this situation, in which both became primarily interested in delinquent behavior. In fact, settlement houses existed almost as area projects in most of the low-cost housing projects in large cities, such as the Brewster Housing Project in Detroit in 1939.

Residential community centers continued to grow in the 1950s for a variety

---

[2] Oliver J. Keller and Benedict S. Alper, *Halfway Houses: Community-Centered Correction and Treatment* (Lexington, Mass.: D. C. Heath, 1970), p. 7.

[3] Edwin Powers, "Halfway House: An Historical Perspective," *American Journal of Correction,* Vol. 21 (July–August 1959), p. 35.

[4] Keller and Alper, *Halfway Houses,* p. 7.

of purposes. Synanon House was established in Santa Monica, California, for drug addicts in 1958. Daytop Village was established in New York in 1963 for the treatment of narcotics offenders and drug addicts.

Work release for misdemeanors was begun in Wisconsin in 1913 under the Huber Law, but had been used informally in Vermont as early as 1907. North Carolina extended work release to felons in 1959 as a result of economic pressures. Furloughs have since been gradually extended from emergency furlough for funerals and serious illness when offenders would go home in the company of an officer to the current participation in home visits without supervision for a period ranging from eight hours to a week, most frequently a forty-eight-hour weekend.

Historically, community-based corrections has been difficult for official programs, administrators, and personnel to accept. It was considered to be run by "meddlers" who might be soft-hearted and were surely "soft-headed." Police were suspicious because they represented a concentration of known offenders in one place in the community. In 1965, however, the Congress passed the Prisoners Rehabilitation Act, which provided for community-based corrections, including work release and community treatment centers. The President's Commission on Law Enforcement and the Administration of Justice recommended an increase in community-based corrections in their major publication in 1967.[5]

The Proceedings of the American Correctional Association in reporting on its Annual Congress on Correction traditionally had a section on "Community Services and Citizen Particitation" to cover the area of community services, halfway houses, and similar activities. By 1968, however, a major section entitled "Community-Based Treatment" covered this area.[6] By 1969, the section on citizen participation had disappeared and the section on community-based corrections had become a standard section. Community-based corrections had become an accepted integral part of the correction system, having been given greatest impetus by the congressional action of 1965.

Modern community-based corrections refers to the mobilization of community resources to assist offenders in reintegrating back into society commensurate with the public safety. It is not meant to incorporate the traditional correctional services already in the community, such as jail, juvenile court, probation, or parole. Rather, community-based corrections augments and supports these traditional programs. The community services officers or programs can provide valuable assistance to existing probation and parole agents, to jail programs, and to the juvenile court.

---

[5] The President's Commission on Law Enforcement and the Administration of Justice, *The Challenge of Crime in a Free Society* (Washington, D.C.: U.S. Government Printing Office, 1967), p. 132.

[6] *Proceedings of the Ninety-Eighth Congress of Corrections of the American Association, San Francisco, 1968* (Washington, D.C.: American Correctional Association, 1968), pp. 50–59.

DIVERSION PROGRAMS

Diversion programs include (1) pretrial intervention without taking the case to court, which is similar to the informal handling of minors by the juvenile court; (2) diversion from jail or from posting of bail; and (3) deferred sentencing. Offenders eligible for these diversion programs are generally property offenders who are not dangerous and who are first offenders. Diversion is accomplished after agreement between prosecution, defense, and judge, and with the consent of the police and the victim. Diversion of persons from the criminal justice system, of course, has been common in the United States for a long time. It has generally been a part of the discretionary action of the police and the prosecutors when they did not consider a case worth going through the criminal justice system. Screening out of less serious cases has always occurred, but it has become more widespread and publicly recognized in recent years.

Pretrial intervention is generally the function of a special program supported by funds from a federal agency, such as the Department of Labor or LEAA, or a private foundation. In some states, such as Massachusetts, it functions under state-wide legislation, while in other states, such as New Jersey, it functions under a state-wide court order. The United States District Courts and some other programs referred to this diversion as "deferred prosecution," which is the most frequently used term. Some states, such as Florida, have used "probation without adjudication." Pennsylvania uses "Accelerated Rehabilitative Disposition" (ARD). The procedures generally follow this order: (1) referral, (2) personal interview, (3) investigation, (4) approval by the judge, (5) prosecuting attorney's consent, (6) determination of period of participation, (7) first recommendation to prosecuting attorney, (8) exit interview for successful determination, and (9) complete follow-up. Supervision is generally the function of probation personnel and, sometimes, special arrangement with other agencies. Pretrial intervention has been seen generally in a positive manner.[7] On the other hand, there have been some suggestions that many people admit to guilt who could have been acquitted in court; pretrial intervention, therefore, becomes a court "overreach" of the law.[8] The weight of consensus appears to be in favor of this type of diversion from the criminal justice system.

Diversion from jail and bail began formally in New York City when the

---

[7] Robert F. Leonard, "Deferred Prosecution Program," in *Source Book in Pretrial Criminal Intervention Techniques and Action Programs* (Washington, D.C.: National Pretrial Intervention Service Centers of the American Bar Association Commission on Correctional Facilities and Services, May 1974), pp. 43–45; *Manpower Administration* (Washington, D.C.: U.S. Department of Labor, 1972); Richard T. Nimmer, *Diversion: The Search for Alternative Forms of Prosecution* (Chicago: American Bar Foundation, 1974), p. 33.

[8] Nancy E. Goldberg, *Pre-trial Diversion: Bilk or Bargain?* (Chicago: World Correctional Services Center, reprinted from the *National Legal Aide and Defender Association Briefcase*, 1973); R. W. Balch, "Deferred Prosecution: The Juvenilization of the Criminal Justice System," *Federal Probation,* Vol. 38, No. 2 (1974), pp. 46–50.

Vera Foundation reorganized into the Vera Institute of Justice in 1961. It launched the Manhattan Jail Project in cooperation with the New York University Law School in 1961. Justice William O. Douglas had asked the previous year in *Bandy v. United States*[9] whether an indigent man could legitimately be denied his freedom in cases where a wealthy man would not, simply because he does not have the property to pledge his freedom. The following year, Douglas said in *Bandy v. Chambers*[10] that no man should be denied release because of indigency when he could be released on his own "personal recognizance." The Manhattan Bail Project was implemented as an experiment to test the validity of such release without bail, subsequently called "Release on Own Recognizance" (ROR), as Justice Douglas had called it. Soon afterward, legislation encouraging the use of release without bail or a nominal or cash bail was passed in many states. In the federal system, changes in pretrial release procedures and resources were reflected in (1) the bail reform act of 1966 (Public Law 89-467), (2) the District of Columbia Bail Agency Act (Public Law 89-519), and (3) amendments to Rule 46 of the Federal Rules of Criminal Procedure adopted by the Supreme Court and transmitted to Congress to be effective in July 1966. Since that time, ROR or other substitutes for jails have increased. The well-known Des Moines Project is an outstanding example of such a project that includes ROR and a residential facility as a substitution for the jail.[11] ROR is used in most cases, but a few who need residential care live in a barracks that was part of an old cavalry fort, and its security derives from relationships with the staff rather than locks and bars. The Des Moines Project has been adopted by several other cities. The recent emphasis on diversion is due to (1) the increase in recognition of the deficiencies in the system of justice, (2) the rediscovery of the ancient truth that the community, itself, has a significant impact upon behavior, and (3) a growing desire of the citizenry to be more active in the affairs of government.[12]

HALFWAY HOUSES

The early history and development of the halfway house is discussed on p. 416. The halfway house began to develop more strongly in the 1930s.[13] The term *halfway house* had been used informally for some time before its first appearance in the mental health literature in 1953.[14] It was not until 1953 when Dismas Resi-

---

[9] 81 S.Ct. 197, 198 (1960).

[10] 82 S.Ct. 11, 13 (1961).

[11] Harry Woods, Jr., *Fort Des Moines Residential Corrections Facilities* (Des Moines, Iowa: Fifth Judicial District, mimeograph, 1971), p. 1.

[12] Robert M. Carter, "The Diversion of Offenders," *Federal Probation,* Vol. 36, No. 4 (December 1972), pp. 31–36.

[13] Negley K. Teeters and John Otto Reinemann, *The Challenge of Delinquency* (Englewood Cliffs, N.J.: Prentice-Hall, 1950), p. 78.

[14] Lewis E. Reik, "The Half-Way House: Role of Laymen's Organization in the Rehabilitation of the Mentally Ill," *Mental Hygiene,* Vol. 37, No. 4 (October 1953), pp. 615–18.

dence in Wilmington, Delaware, became the beginning of today's halfway house movement.[15]

Many halfway houses are for people who have problems that are too serious to allow them to remain at home, but not sufficiently serious to require them to be institutionalized away from the community. One of the tasks of corrections is to build or rebuild an individual's life within the community, thereby facilitating his or her reintegration into community life. Institutionalization away from the community would result in a type of "social surgery" by cutting all social contacts, both positive and negative. By using a halfway house in or on the outskirts of the community, an offender does not lose contact with his family or with community services. These halfway "in" houses are a type of diversion from the more secure institutions in the criminal justice system. While there is no uniform prototype of the halfway house, and the personnel and program differ widely, a halfway house is generally a small residential facility in or near the community. These centers have also been called (1) reintegration centers, (2) community corrections centers, (3) alcohol detoxification units, (4) restitution shelters, and other names.

WORK RELEASE, STUDY RELEASE, AND FURLOUGHS

Work release, study release, and furloughs are programs that permit offenders to leave prisons or other correctional facilities to work, go to school, or visit home or friends. Work release began with the Huber Law in Wisconsin in 1913, permitting misdemeanants to leave jails to work in the community. Many county facilities in Wisconsin have Huber dorms as part of the jail complex. Work release was first extended to felons in North Carolina in 1959 and has since been extended to forty-four states and the United States Bureau of Prisons. Work releasees pay a stipulated amount for board and room and for transportation to and from work, besides supporting their families. While less than 5 percent of the felons in the United States are participating in work release, it is considered to be a desirable program.

Study release is similar to work release, except that the offenders attend school. They usually attend vocational training courses, junior colleges, and universities, but there is really no limit on their study programs. In the NewGate program, begun in Oregon in 1967 and supported by the Office of Economic Opportunity, professors come to the prison to teach classes and, when the residents can be placed on study release, they may leave the prison or live in a community center and study. There are six states with NewGate programs. Some other states, such as South Carolina, permit trusted residents to study at any college or university that will accept them.

Furloughs are available on a selective basis in most states. They range from eight hours to forty-eight hours, generally, although Mississippi permits fur-

---

[15] Keller and Alper, *Half-Way Houses*, p. 8.

loughed prisoners to go home for Christmas for two weeks. Furloughs are considered to be helpful because children do not have to visit their fathers in prison and the social contacts tend to keep the family together. Of course, furloughs are used for special purposes, also, such as job-hunting prior to release and in case of emergencies in the family.

EX-OFFENDER GROUPS

Ex-offender groups have been increasing since World War II. In the late 1940s and early 1950s, several groups of Convicts Anonymous appeared in Detroit and other major cities. Most parole rules forbid association of parolees with other ex-offenders, which may be unrealistic because many have brothers and fathers with criminal records. However, many ex-offenders consider the mutual support of other ex-offenders to be worth the risk. Using the same basic mutual help approach as Alcoholics Anonymous, these groups were reported by the ex-offenders and by some parole agents to be useful. Other programs for ex-offenders have developed more recently, such as their use as probation aides in the Los Angeles County Probation Department and elsewhere. Some are now used as counselors in community correctional centers and in other correctional programs.

The first large ex-offender organization was the Seven Steps program initiated in 1963 on the West Coast by Bill Sands.[16] It subsequently spread eastward and a chapter was organized in 1963 at the Kansas State Penitentiary. Today, there are chapters in sixteen states and in many prisons and correctional institutions. The purpose of these centers is to help ex-offenders reintegrate into the community by helping them find employment and providing supportive counseling and other direct services. The organization is now incorporated as The 7th Step Foundation with headquarters in Cincinnati (28 East 8th Street, Cincinnati, Ohio 45202).

The Fortune Society was begun in 1967 by David Rothenberg, who was at that time producing a play about prison experiences entitled *Fortune and Men's Eyes.* After several performances, audiences were invited to stay and discuss the play. The interest in it was so great that Rothenberg organized this group.[17] By 1975, it had helped between 4,000 and 5,000 people located in the Lower East Side of Manhattan. It serves offenders and ex-offenders in and near New York City.

Ex-offender groups provide face-to-face counseling and assistance for participants, finding jobs for them and helping them in other ways, such as using community resources in health, education, welfare, and other matters. There are many ex-offender groups in major cities around the country, most of them small, and their services are primarily "in-house," without publicity, and, in fact, at-

---

[16] Bill Sands, *My Shadow Ran Fast* (Englewood Cliffs, N.J.: Prentice-Hall, 1964).

[17] "The Fortune Society—Championing the Ex-Offender," *Corrections Magazine,* Vol. 1, No. 5 (May–June 1975), pp. 13–20.

tempting to function quietly without attracting public notice. By 1974, for example, there were thirty-five to forty identifiable ex-offender groups functioning in the Chicago area alone.[18]

PRIVATE COMMUNITY-BASED CORRECTIONS

Private groups historically have taken the lead in advances in the criminal justice system. Religious organizations traditionally have provided assistance to strangers, vagabonds, and people in trouble.[19] We have mentioned the Quaker-organized Philadelphia Society for Alleviating the Misery of the Public Prisons that established the first "penitentiary" at the old Walnut Street Jail. The Salvation Army has been most active in slum and ghetto neighborhoods and in jails and prisons in assisting people in trouble in various ways, particularly through their Bureau of Correctional Services and Bureau of Missing Persons. The Volunteers of America, who split from the Salvation Army in 1896, perform similar services with probably a heavier emphasis on maintaining halfway houses and drug abuse programs. Other examples of religious groups that provide services for persons in trouble include the Juvenile Rehabilitation Ministry of the Home Mission Board of the Southern Baptist Convention; Youth for Christ, founded by the Rev. Billy Graham; and many other religious organizations.

Prisoners' aid societies have provided direct and indirect services to the criminal justice system for a long time. Direct services refers to counseling ex-offenders, helping them get jobs, and other services to reintegrate them into society. Indirect services refers to efforts in prison reform, advising legislatures in criminal justice matters, and generally attempting to improve the criminal justice system. The Philadelphia Association for Alleviating the Miseries of the Public Prisons, organized in 1797, still exists as the Pennsylvania Prison Society (311 South Juniper Street, Philadelphia) and provides direct and indirect services. The Correctional Association of New York, formerly known as the New York Prison Society, was founded in 1844. The Prisoners' Aid Association of Maryland was formally organized in 1869. There are many other private associations providing direct and indirect services to ex-offenders and the criminal justice system.

CONCLUSIONS

Community-based correctional programs have no single or uniform pattern. They tend to reflect the personalities operating the programs. Most people engaged in community correctional programs are enthusiastic and dedicated to the work of

---

[18] Patrick B. McAnany, Dennis Sullivan, William Kaplan, and Edward Tromanhouser, *Final Report: The Identification and Description of Ex-Offender Groups in the Chicago Area* (Chicago: University of Illinois at Chicago Circle, mimeograph, August 1974), p. 68.

[19] C. J. Ribton-Turner, *A History of Vagrants and Vagrancy and Beggars and Begging* (London: Chapman & Hall, 1887; reprinted Montclair, N.J.: Patterson Smith, 1972), pp. 1–33.

helping their fellow man in trouble to reintegrate into the community. Skoler identified seven innovative programs in the early 1970s as being in the forefront of corrections, and they were all community-based: (1) youth services bureaus, (2) court diversion projects, (3) volunteer paraprofessional services, (4) community custody, (5) community or regional correctional centers, (6) foster care or subsidy homes, and (7) new uses for correctional manpower.[20]

The evaluations of community-based programs have ranged from positive to neutral; none are negative. On the basis of evidence available, the use of community-based programs will expand. It is apparent that the most optimistic way of working with offenders and ex-offenders in their readjustment to society lies in community-based corrections.

LEARNING EXERCISES

Issues to Be Discussed

1. Ex-offender groups have been providing adjustment services, including counseling services, to former inmates and, if permitted, to those in prisons about to be released from prison. Among some correctional personnel there is adverse feeling about permitting ex-offender services within an institutional environment. Study some of the literature on this subject and visit, if possible, a local organization. What are your views on the use of ex-offenders in readjustment programs?
2. On what basis were Synanon House, Daytop Village, and many other drug programs established?
3. What has been the function of prisoners' aid societies?
4. What are The 7th Step Foundation and The Fortune Society and what do they do?

Group Activity

Develop a panel discussion on the subject: Designing a model community-based correctional program. What should be the criteria and procedure for establishing such an activity?

Field Activity

Visit in small groups different community-based programs and in a 300-word paper summarize your evaluation of the program.

[20] Daniel Skoler, "Future Trends in Juvenile and Community-Based Corrections," in Gary R. Perlstein and Thomas R. Phelps, eds., *Alternatives to Prison: Community-Based Corrections* (Pacific Palisades, Calif.: Goodyear, 1975), pp. 3–15. Originally published in *Juvenile Court Judges Journal,* Vol. 21 (Winter 1971), pp. 98–103.

Key Terms

Diversion
Furloughs
Halfway house
Pretrial intervention

ROR
Study release
Work release

SUGGESTED REFERENCES

HAHN, PAUL H. *Community-Based Corrections and the Criminal Justice System.* Santa Cruz, Calif.: Davis Publishing Co., 1975.

KELLER, OLIVER J., JR., AND ALPER, BENEDICT S. *Halfway Houses: Community-Centered Corrections and Treatment.* Lexington, Mass.: Lexington Books, 1970.

KULINGER, GEORGE G., AND CROMWELL, PAUL F., eds. *Corrections in the Community: Alternatives to Imprisonment. Selected Readings.* St. Paul, Minn.: West Publishing Co., 1974.

RUDOLPH, ALVIN T.; ESSELSTYN, T. C.; AND KIRKHAM, GEORGE L. "Evaluating Work Furlough." *Federal Probation,* Vol. 35 (March 1971), pp. 34–38.

SCHOEN, KENNETH. "Port: A New Concept of Community Based Correction." *Federal Probation,* Vol. 36 (September 1972), pp. 35–40.

SCULL, ANDREW R. *Decarceration, Community Treatment and the Deviant: A Radical Review.* Englewood Cliffs, N.J.: Prentice-Hall, 1977.

SEITER, RICHARD P. *Halfway Houses.* Washington, D.C.: U.S. Government Printing Office, 1977.

WARREN, MARGUERITE Q. *Correctional Treatment in Community Settings.* Washington, D.C.: U.S. Government Printing Office, 1972.

18

Juvenile Corrections

Overview
Juvenile Detention
Juvenile Training Schools
Juvenile Aftercare
Juvenile Justice and Delinquency Prevention Act of 1974
Conclusions
Learning Exercises
Suggested References

OVERVIEW

Juvenile corrections follows the pattern set in juvenile courts in which the courts become *parens patriae*. Institutions for confining juvenile delinquents are normally set apart from adult institutions, having their own unique programs and procedures adapted to the needs of different age groups. Court decisions regarding due process for juveniles have sharpened the procedures for handling juveniles. At the same time the rising crime rate among juveniles means that judges need to have an increasing number of correctional agencies to which juveniles can be sent appropriate to both the degree of offense committed and the delinquent's personality traits. Thus detention homes, training schools, and aftercare programs, in terms of their purpose, organization, staffing, and operational problems, loom large in the handling of juveniles.

Juvenile corrections and the juvenile court were the culmination of centuries of growing interest in the welfare of children. The ancient Roman father had power of life and death over his children and, in fact, over his family, as did other primitive and ancient peoples. Killing children as human sacrifice among primitive and ancient peoples was not uncommon. Even Abraham was ready to sacrifice Isaac, his only son (Genesis 22:1). In ancient Carthage (near the present-day city of Tunis), where children were sacrificed to the goddess Tanith and the god Baal Amun, there remains a gravestone depicting a priest offering a human child. After the rise of the great religions and the acceptance of the soul that made every person worthwhile, infanticide slowed, but abandonment increased and became a problem in Europe in the Middle Ages. The first permanent asylum for wandering children was built in Paris in 1648 by St. Vincent de Paul.

The first institution for wayward youth was built in 1704 in Rome by Pope Clement XI, and called the Hospice of San Michele (Ospizio di S. Michele). It was used to house youths under twenty sentenced by the courts for crime and for incorrigible boys who could not be controlled by their parents. Floggings were used as penalties for past mistakes and for infractions of the rules. While there were other institutions constructed for children for domiciliary care, the first House of Refuge for problem children was built in Danzig in 1824 and the second in New York City in 1825. Private institutions for problem children were built throughout the nineteenth and twentieth centuries. The first state training school for boys was opened in Massachusetts in 1847. Known as the Lyman School, it was not closed until 1972. By the time the juvenile court was instituted in 1899, other states had built training schools and there was a rather elaborate network of private and state training schools. The procedure for commitment to these schools was for the courts to withhold prosecution and informally commit children to these schools without proceeding through conviction.

In the meantime, the state was taking more and more interest in children. The famous Napoleonic Decree of 1811 held that the state was responsible for the welfare of its children. In England, the House of Lords heard the case of the nephew of Lord Wellesley in 1828 and gave custody of the nephew to his family on the basis of *parens patriae,* the doctrine that the state has responsibility for the welfare of its children.

Because many parents were bringing writs of habeas corpus against the informal commitments of their children to institutions as deprivation of liberty without due process of law, such as in *Ex parte Bucknell,*[1] a way had to be found to develop a juvenile court that could meet the constitutional test. Illinois had passed a juvenile court law in 1895, but it was declared unconstitutional by the Illinois Supreme Court. Another law was passed in 1897, but it was ruled unconstitutional by the Illinois Attorney General. A juvenile court was established in the school system in Denver, effective April 1, 1899, with Judge Ben Lindsey presiding, but it was not really in the judiciary. With the assistance of the Cook County Women's Clubs, which had mounted an intensive campaign, the Chicago Bar prepared a bill that was passed by the Illinois legislature finally establishing the Juvenile Court effective July 1, 1899. Juvenile courts were eventually established in all states using that model.

The juvenile court became constitutional because it was voluntary. A person accused of a crime and who was within juvenile court age could consent to be heard in juvenile court or not. If he did not, then he could be certified to the criminal court or handled in other ways. This has been implemented in three ways: (1) a waiver signed by the juvenile, as in the Federal Juvenile Delinquency Act and some other jurisdictions; (2) review by a higher court in case of ignoring lack of consent, which is usual; or (3) writ of certiorari to certify the case to the proper court. The juvenile court was still challenged. In 1905 in *Commonwealth of Pennsylvania v. Fisher,*[2] the principle of *parens patriae* was established in juvenile court, meaning that the state has responsibility for the welfare of its children and that this is more important than the constitutional guarantees in criminal cases that are waived in order for a case to be heard by juvenile court. Juvenile court proceedings became "in the interests of the child," rather than the adversary *State v. John Doe.*

Variations between judges and courts became a problem and due process became central to the debate in the 1960s. In *Kent v. United States*[3] in 1966, counsel was introduced at the point of the waiver, so the child could be well advised as to whether or not to be heard in juvenile court. The landmark *Gault* case[4] had an immense impact on the juvenile court, introducing counsel at all stages of the juvenile court proceedings to ensure civil due process. It lengthened juvenile court procedure from at least two hearings (adjudicatory and disposition) to three hear-

---

[1] 119 California 496, 51 Pac. 692 (1897).
[2] 213 Pa. 48, 62 Atl. 198 (1905).
[3] 383 U.S. 541, 556 (1966).
[4] *In re Application of Gault,* 387 U.S. 1, 8 S.Ct. 1428 (1967).

ings (detention or exploratory, adjudicatory, and disposition). Juvenile court procedure became more cumbersome and some predicted the demise of the juvenile court, altogether. The result has been that more juveniles are handled administratively and informally without going to juvenile court, reserving juvenile court for the most serious cases. Since that time, significant changes in the handling of status offenses (offenses such as truancy and violation of curfew laws that would not be offenses were the juvenile an adult) have tended to move their handling from the juvenile court to other agencies, such as Youth Services or Family Services (welfare). The *Winship* case[5] moved the burden of proof in juvenile court from "preponderance of evidence" as in civil cases to "beyond a reasonable doubt" as in criminal cases. On the other hand, the *McKiever* case[6] held that the right to trial by jury did not apply to juvenile court.

There were 1,143,700 juvenile delinquency cases in the United States in 1973.[7] This is a rate of 34.2 per 1,000 children aged 10 through 17 in the United States, which, despite more informal handling of juveniles in recent years, represents the highest proportion of juvenile cases in the history of the juvenile court. This is congruent with arrest trends. While the largest number of arrests in the mid-1960s was in the twenty–twenty-two age range, the largest single age of arrests in 1975 was 16, well within juvenile court age in all jurisdictions.[8]

Juvenile corrections includes voluntary police supervision and informal probation by the juvenile court, for which there are no estimates available as to numbers of juveniles. Figures show that there were 522,000 juveniles adjudicated delinquent in 1973.[9] Simultaneously, there were 158,000 children declared dependent and neglected in 1973,[10] but more were undoubtedly cared for by child-caring and welfare agencies, both public and private. As of June 30, 1974, there were 31,270 adjudicated delinquents in state and federal institutions.[11] Further, there were 7,373 juveniles being held pending disposition by a court, 4,644 juveniles declared in need of supervision (status offenses), and 1,635 awaiting transfer or other disposition.[12] There were 9,874 delinquents in private institutions, such as the Starr Commonwealth for Boys at Albion, Michigan; Berkshire Farms in New York; and other private institutions. There were 7,635 voluntary commitments and 7,104 dependent and neglected commitments.[13] The remaining 2,167 juveniles were

---

[5] *In re Winship*, 397 U.S. 358 (1970).

[6] *McKiever v. Pennsylvania*, 403 U.S. 528 (1971).

[7] *Juvenile Court Statistics, 1973* (Washington, D.C.: Office of Youth Development, U.S. Department of Health, Education and Welfare, 1975), p. 10.

[8] *Crime in the United States—1975 Uniform Crime Reports* (Washington, D.C.: Federal Bureau of Investigation, released August 25, 1976), p. 196.

[9] *Juvenile Court Statistics, 1973*, p. 11.

[10] *Ibid.*, p. 13.

[11] *Children in Custody: Advance Report on the Juvenile Detention and Correctional Facility Census of 1974* (Washington, D.C.: National Criminal Justice Information and Statistics Service, U.S. Department of Justice, February 1977), p. 4.

[12] *Ibid.*

[13] *Ibid.*, p. 5.

awaiting disposition by another court or transfer to another jurisdiction.[14] There were more children sent to private schools and military schools financed by parents.

JUVENILE DETENTION

There are approximately 250 juvenile detention homes in the United States to serve 3,071 counties. Less than 10 percent of the courts, then, have juvenile detention facilities. Most of the courts without facilities either leave the alleged delinquent at home, place him in a foster home, make use of county-operated group homes, or place him in a juvenile section of the jail. The courts with detention facilities serve probably 85 percent of the delinquent children because the detention facilities that do exist are in middle-sized and larger urban centers.

Programming for detention homes varies quite widely depending upon the philosophy and resources of the jurisdiction. Several detention facilities, both in large urban areas and in rural or sparsely populated areas, have virtually no program at all, so the facility becomes a "juvenile jail." On the other hand, there are several detention facilities in large urban areas that use available resources to develop sophisticated programs. Some detention homes in rural and sparsely populated areas invest their resources, which include "hard money" allocated by the county commissions, "soft money" or grant funds from federal agencies or private foundations, and considerable volunteer activity, to produce excellent programs. In general, however, most juvenile detention homes function with minimal programs as a holding operation awaiting the disposition of children by the court.

Primary problems in juvenile detention have been (1) misuse and long stays; (2) substandard care; (3) insufficient community resources; and (4) lack of state responsibility and minimum standards.[15] The detention center is simply too easy to use and too easy to neglect to provide effective programming in many cases. It becomes an expediency with insufficient resources. Whether it is a "juvenile jail" or a progressive and well-programmed detention home for growing children depends upon its leadership.

JUVENILE TRAINING SCHOOLS

Organization

Whether public or private, the internal organizations of juvenile-corrections institutions are similar, frequently with (1) a department of cottage life; (2) the educational director, who has charge of the schools and educational programs; and (3) a

[14] *Ibid.*
[15] Sherwood Norman, *Think Twice Before You Build or Enlarge a Detention Center* (New York: National Council on Crime and Delinquency, 1968), p. 16.

program or clinical director, who has charge of social services and general program. The kitchen, food services, clothing, and other administrative affairs including accounting are generally left to the business manager. The superintendent is frequently away from campus in his public relations capacity, so the assistant superintendent, most frequently the educational director, generally runs the institution on the day-to-day basis.

The approaches used in training schools vary. The inspirational-repressive philosophy with a religious and moral reeducation theme is used in many schools, particularly private training schools with religious support and many public training schools with superintendents having a religious background. The operant conditioning or punishment-and-reward theme is used in many schools. The education, hard work, and discipline approach is the most frequent. The orthopsychiatric approach that includes psychiatric, psychological, and social work services is used in a few outstanding schools. Research comparisons between these systems indicate that the orthopsychiatric approach is best, though it costs more than any of the other approaches.

Results

The juvenile training school has been an enigma to correctional people for a long time. The recidivism rate is higher than it is in adult institutions, giving rise to the notion that the earlier a person gets into the criminal justice system, the longer he will stay in it. Whether by selection of the poorest risks for socialization or by conditioning in associating intimately with other delinquents for long periods of time, the principal holds true. There is reason to believe that both occur, reinforcing each other.

In 1972, the Massachusetts Division of Youth Services simply abolished the training schools on grounds that they were doing more harm than good. It is apparent that the decision challenging society in this field is whether society should invest sufficient resources to make them useful or abandon the effort. At the present time, juvenile training schools with funds to implement good clinical programs seem to be helpful; other schools seem to be processing children to the adult criminal justice system.

JUVENILE AFTERCARE

There are three general patterns of follow-up for aftercare of children when they leave training schools in the United States. The most prevalent and probably the least effective is to place the responsibility of aftercare on the juvenile court that committed the child in the first place. Lack of staff and the fact that released children may now be of age and thus beyond jurisdiction of the original court generally result in the court focusing its efforts on its new cases and ignoring aftercare.

A second pattern is to make another agency whose primary duty is not in this particular field furnish supervision for children released from training schools, such as the Department of Public Welfare. Probably the best state system is the parental agency, in which training schools and aftercare services are in the same department, such as in California, Mississippi, Massachusetts, Florida, and several other states.

Some of the better programs are in private training schools in the New York City area, such as Children's Village at Dobbs Ferry, Berkshire Farms, and Wiltwyck School. In these programs, the caseworker has offices in the institution and downtown. He may spend two days working in one office and three in the other. He works with children in the institution, with their families outside, and assists in the transition from institution to home again, continuing supervision and thereby maintaining the continuity of relationships and security in that relationship.

JUVENILE JUSTICE AND DELINQUENCY PREVENTION ACT OF 1974

The Juvenile Justice and Delinquency Prevention Act of 1974 (Public Law 93-415, 42 U.S.C. 5601) was signed by President Ford on September 7, 1974, for the purpose of coordinating efforts in the area of juvenile delinquency. Evaluation of all federally assisted juvenile delinquency programs and technical assistance to public and private agencies, institutions, and individuals in developing and implementing delinquency programs were primary objectives of the act. Further objectives were to establish training programs in this field, to centralize research efforts, to implement national standards for the administration of juvenile justice, assist states and local communities with resources to develop and implement programs to keep students in elementary and secondary school and prevent unwarranted and arbitrary suspensions and expulsions, and to establish a federal assistance program to deal with the problems of runaway youth. Congress was motivated to focus on the problems of juvenile delinquency because juveniles accounted for almost half the arrests for serious crimes in the United States at the time the act was passed and existing facilities were considered to be inadequate to cope with the juvenile delinquency problem.

The Office of Juvenile Justice and Delinquency Prevention (OJJDP) was established in the Law Enforcement Assistance Administration (LEAA) within the Department of Justice. The act provided for the development of a comprehensive plan for federal juvenile delinquency programs with particular emphasis on the prevention of juvenile delinquency and the development of programs and services that encourage increased diversion of juveniles from the traditional juvenile justice system. The OJJDP was authorized to make grants or contracts with any public or private agency, institution, or individual to carry out the purposes of the act. A Coordinating Council of Juvenile Justice and Delinquency Prevention was established to coordinate all federal juvenile delinquency programs. This council is composed of the Attorney General; Secretary of the Department of

Health, Education and Welfare; Secretary of the Department of Labor; Director of the Special Action Office for Drug Abuse Prevention; Secretary of Housing and Urban Development; or their respective designees; as well as the Assistant Administrator of the OJJDP; the Deputy Assistant Administrator of the Institute for Juvenile Justice for Delinquency Prevention; and representatives of other agencies as the President may designate. A National Advisory Committee for Juvenile Justice and Delinquency Prevention was established to make recommendations with respect to planning, policy, priorities, operations, and management of all federal juvenile delinquency programs. The National Institute for Juvenile Justice and Delinquency Prevention was designed to provide training for federal, state, and local law enforcement officers, teachers and other educational personnel, juvenile welfare workers, juvenile judges and judicial personnel, probation personnel, correctional personnel, and others connected with the treatment and control of juvenile offenders. The Institute serves as an information bank by systematically collecting and synthesizing the data and knowledge obtained from studies and research by public and private agencies, institutions, or individuals. It is to serve as a clearinghouse and information center for the preparation, publication, and dissemination of all information regarding juvenile delinquency.

The implementation of the OJJDP was slow because the economic situation in the country made Congress and the administration reluctant to fund new programs. While the act authorizing the establishment and functioning of the OJJDP had passed, the appropriation bills funding it were slower and smaller than its sponsors had hoped. The 1974 act did make some grant funds available to assist state, local, and private juvenile justice programs, but it also required that within two years the states had to develop systems ensuring that status offenders be removed from jails and other detention facilities housing youths convicted of serious crimes.

In 1977, a similar act was passed by Congress and signed into law by President Carter. To be eligible for funds from the OJJDP, status offenders or those persons who have not committed crimes cannot be processed with delinquents. Many states still send children who are truant or incorrigible to training schools with delinquents. The extension of the OJJDP for three years also extended the period in which states must comply with the deinstitutionalization for status offenders for three years. By December 31, 1978, at least 75 percent of all status offenders would no longer be housed in security detention alongside juvenile delinquents. The 1977 act authorized $525 million and Congress appropriated $100 million in 1977.

Runaway Youth Act

The Runaway Youth Act was incorporated as Title III of the Juvenile Justice and Delinquency Prevention Act of 1974. It provides for grants to develop local facilities to deal primarily with the immediate needs of runaway youth in a manner that is outside the law enforcement structure and the juvenile justice system. The problem of runaway youth has increased substantially and is significantly endangering the young people who are without resources and live on the street. The exact nature of the problem is not well defined because national statistics on the size and profile of the runaway youth population are not tabulated, although it is estimated there are over one million runaway children each year. Because of their age and situation, many of these people are urgently in need of temporary shelter and counseling services. The problem of locating, detaining, and returning runaway children must be the responsibility of the federal government because of the interstate nature of the problem. In the extension of the Runaway Youth Act, together with the extension of the Juvenile Justice and Delinquency Act in 1977, for three more years, Congress authorized $24 million in 1977 to fund it through fiscal year 1980.

CONCLUSIONS

Juvenile corrections, in accordance with the philosophy of the juvenile court, is based on the principle of *parens patriae,* which means that it is "in the interests of the child," and the responsibility of the state is with the welfare of its children. Education, counseling, and casework are emphasized in varying degrees in the state and private training schools and in probation and other community programs for juveniles. As previously stated, the purpose of the juvenile court and juvenile corrections is not the protection of society, but the welfare of the child. If the juvenile is a clear and present danger to society, then he is certified to a criminal court and tried as an adult for the protection of society. Those retained in the juvenile justice system are judged to be not sufficiently dangerous to turn over to the adult criminal system. The basic philosophy of juvenile corrections, then, is not punishment, but rehabilitation and reform approaches to help the child grow into a self-supporting, tax-paying, law-abiding adult citizen.

LEARNING EXERCISES

Issues to Be Discussed

1. The arrest trends over a fifteen-year period from 1960 to 1975 reveal an alarming rise in juvenile (i.e., those under 18 years of age) participation in major crimes, indicating serious problems among the nation's youth. Study some of the juvenile literature, such as the National Advisory Committee on Standards and Goals publication *Juvenile Justice and Delinquency Prevention* (1976). What are the proposed remedies for the problem? How would you set priorities?
2. There is a trend established in Massachusetts for the deinstitutionalization of all formal state juvenile institutions. Would you be in favor of this trend toward community-based corrections only? Why?

3. What are the primary problems in juvenile detention?
4. How is a juvenile institution generally organized?
5. What are the patterns of juvenile aftercare?

Group Activity

Establish a panel discussion on the topic: The juvenile crime rate has grown so alarmingly and the court's insistence on due process has become so urgent that it would be best to abolish juvenile courts and set up correctional programs that treat juveniles exclusively as adults.

Field Activities

1. Visit a juvenile community-based facility, either private or public, and evaluate its program for juvenile delinquents.
2. Visit an agency that is engaged primarily with the prevention of juvenile delinquency—i.e., intervening before youth become part of the criminal justice system—and evaluate the techniques or programs it utilizes.

Key Terms

Aftercare

Detention home

Gault case

Training school

SUGGESTED REFERENCES

ADAMS, GARY B., et al., eds. *Juvenile Justice Management.* Springfield, Ill.: Charles C Thomas, 1973.

CHAPMAN, CHRISTINE. *America's Runaways.* New York: Morrow, 1976.

CIRCOUREL, A. V. *The Social Organization of Juvenile Justice.* New York: Russah and Co., 1976.

CRESSEY, DONALD R., AND WARD, DAVID A. *Diversion from the Juvenile Justice System.* Ann Arbor, Mich.: National Assessment of Juvenile Corrections, 1973.

ELDEFONSO, EDWARD. *Youth Problems and Law Enforcement.* Englewood Cliffs, N.J.: Prentice-Hall, 1972.

FERDINAND, THEODORE N., ed. *Juvenile Delinquency: Little Brother Grows Up.* Beverly Hills, Calif.: Sage Publications Inc., 1977.

GERMIGNANI, ROBERT J. *Diversion of Juvenile Offenders from the Juvenile Justice System.* Washington, D.C.: U.S. Government Printing Office, 1973.

KORN, RICHARD R., AND McCORKLE, LLOYD W. *Children in Custody.* Washington, D.C.: U.S. Government Printing Office, 1972.

LEMERT, EDWIN M. *Instead of Court: Diversion in Juvenile Justice.* Washington, D.C.: U.S. Government Printing Office, 1971.

LERMAN, PAUL. *Community Treatment and Social Control: A Critical Analysis and Juvenile Correctional Policy.* Chicago: University of Chicago Press, 1975.

MANN, DALE. *Interviewing with Convicted Serious Juvenile Offenders.* Santa Monica, Calif.: Rand Corporation, 1976.

MILHAM, SPENCER; BULLOCK, ROGER; AND HOSIE, KENNETH. *Locking Up Children.* Lexington, Mass.: Lexington Books, 1977.

NATIONAL ADVISORY COMMITTEE ON STANDARDS AND GOALS. *Juvenile Justice and Delinquency Prevention.* Washington, D.C.: U.S. Government Printing Office, 1976.

PAUL, J. T. *Child Advocacy Within the System.* Syracuse, N.Y.: University of Syracuse Press, 1977.

PLATT, ANTHONY M. *The Child Savers.* 2nd ed., enl. Chicago: University of Chicago Press, 1976.

RUTHERFORD, ANDREW. *The Dissolution of Training Schools in Massachusetts.* Columbus, Ohio: Academy for Contemporary Problems, 1974.

SANDERS, WILLIAM B. *Juvenile Delinquency.* New York: Praeger, 1976.

SARGENT, FRANCES W. *Community Based Treatment for Juveniles in Massachusetts.* Washington, D.C.: U.S. Government Printing Office, 1973.

TEITELBAUM, LEE E., AND GOUGH, ANDREW R. *Beyond Control: Status Offenders in Juvenile Court.* Cambridge, Mass.: Ballanger, 1977.

U.S. NATIONAL INSTITUTE FOR JUVENILE JUSTICE AND DELINQUENCY PREVENTION. *Juvenile Correctional Reform in Massachusetts.* Washington, D.C.: U.S. Government Printing Office, 1977.

19

Parole and Other Release Procedures

Overview
Selection for Parole
Prerelease Programs
Supervision of Parolees
Combined Probation and Parole Services
Problems with Parole
Other Releases from Prison
Summary
Learning Exercises
Suggested References

OVERVIEW

Parole permits correctional officials to release persons from prison with continued supervision in the community environment. Parole boards make the decision within the sentence prescribed by the court as to when such release can be made. Parole helps prison management, morale, and discipline and the regulation of prison capacity. Criteria for selection follow no set patterns among states. Such matters as readiness of the prisoner, future housing and employment, and family relationships are important. Parole administration has institutional conflict problems as well as parole supervision difficulties. Some are due to structure of the prison and the parole organizations, others to the quality and training of those in the parole establishment.

Parole is the supervision of persons released from prisons and correctional institutions to assist them in their reentry into free society. Parole is an executive function of government, as compared with the judicial function of probation, and is controlled and served from the central office of each state's correctional program. Parole involves supervision, in contrast to other types of releases from prison, such as discharge, conditional release, expiration of sentence, and mandatory release. Release by court order, pardon, or escape, of course, do not involve parole supervision.

In 1972, of approximately 110,000 persons released from state and federal prisons, about two-thirds were by parole, the remainder being primarily by expiration of sentence.[1] As of June 30, 1974, there were 215,284 persons on parole.[2] Over 40,000 persons are released from correctional institutions and prisons annually without supervision. Historically, states that parole the highest proportions are California, which abolished parole and went to determinate sentencing in 1977, Hawaii, Kansas, Michigan, New Jersey, New York, New Hampshire, Nevada, Ohio, Pennsylvania, Utah, Washington, and Wisconsin. States that have been historically conservative in paroling policies are Delaware, Maryland, Missouri, Nebraska, Oklahoma, Oregon, Tennessee, Texas, South Carolina, and Wyoming. Maine abolished parole in 1976 and went to flat sentencing, California and Indiana followed suit in 1977, and then Illinois in late 1977. Abolition of parole continues to be debated in several states and in the United States Congress.

[1] *Uniform Parole Reports Newsletter,* National Council on Crime and Delinquency, National Probation and Parole Institute, Davis, California, April 1974, p. 2; *Statistical Reports, Fiscal Year 1973* (Washington, D.C.: U.S. Department of Justice, Federal Bureau of Prisons, 1975), p. 27.

[2] *Uniform Parole Reports Newsletter,* National Council on Crime and Delinquency, National Probation and Parole Institute, Davis, California, January 1975, p. 2.

The idea of parole began developing soon after the establishment of the penitentiary. Mirabeau (1749–91), a French statesman, suggested the function of parole in one of his last reports to the Court in Paris in 1791, just prior to his death. His suggestions were based on his observations on penal practice while he was in prison for espousing tax reform and other governmental changes. A form of "parole," the French for a "word of honor," was used in the early 1800s when prisoners of war were released on their word that they would not take up arms against the French again. Captain Alexander Maconochie was generally credited with implementing the idea of parole for the first time when he provided a ticket-of-leave to prisoners in Norfolk Island Prison Colony, beginning in 1843, so that they could earn their return to England. Sir Walter Crofton began using the idea in 1854 as part of the grading system in Irish prisons. The Irish system had a great impact on American corrections, as shown in the report of the First National Conference in America devoted to the field of corrections in 1870.[3] Massachusetts was the first state to appoint an agent whose function was to secure employment, tools, clothing, and transportation for released prisoners.[4] By 1910, thirty-two states had parole systems.

The primary functions of parole boards are (1) selection for parole, (2) preparole preparation, and (3) supervision of parolees. Selection for parole is the identification of the persons who should be released from prisons and correctional institutions under supervision. This selection is usually made by a parole board on the basis of good institutional records. Preparole preparation is a series of lectures, films, and other types of instruction to prepare persons who have been in institutions for the decisions and self-discipline needed for resuming life in the free community. It is a kind of "debriefing" or a "decompression" experience from a social viewpoint. Supervision of parolees is a long-term supervision treatment in the home community by a parole agent or parole officer. All phases are needed for an adequate parole function.

SELECTION FOR PAROLE

Selection for parole is the determination as to who shall be paroled from among those prisoners eligible for parole. This has been done by a variety of methods and by a wide range of criteria. There was much criticism including charges of corruption prior to World War II, when single commissioners appointed by the governors selected prisoners to be paroled using various criteria, some questionable. The parole service regained its respectability after World War II by using boards of several persons with a more professional approach to the selection process. The two principle structures that have been adopted in most states have been a parole

---

[3] E. C. Wines, ed., *Transactions of the National Congress on Penitentiary and Reformatory Discipline* (Albany, N.Y.: Weed, Parsons and Company, 1871).

[4] George G. Killinger, "Parole and Other Release Procedures," in Paul W. Tappan, ed., *Contemporary Corrections* (New York: McGraw-Hill, 1951), pp. 361–62.

board independent of the prison system or a parole board within a broader department of corrections that includes the prison system. In both cases, a majority of states have full-time parole boards consisting of three to eight members, many selected for their professional competence and some by examination.

Parole policies vary quite widely in selection for parole, preparole preparation, and the supervision of parolees. Twelve states customarily parole more than 80 percent of their releases from prison, some paroling all before the end of their sentences to provide some supervision for everybody. On the other hand, ten states parole less than 20 percent of their releases. The national average generally ranges between 58 and 63 percent of the releases being on parole. The trend is toward releasing more and more people under parole supervision. It seems paradoxical to select the "best" prisoners for parole supervision while releasing the most dangerous ones at the end of their sentence without such supervision. An observation might be that boards in politically mature and more stable areas tend to parole more than do those in less politically mature or stable areas. One reason would be that there is a public relations hazard in letting offenders out too early, but there is no public relations hazard in keeping them in too long.

There is considerable debate in the field of corrections as to the proper role of the parole board. Supporters of the parole board in its present form hold that objectivity in decision making can best be achieved by a parole board independent of the rest of the correctional system. There is some opposition by those who feel that releases can best be judged by institutional personnel who know the prisoner best, similar to the "staffing" in most mental institutions in which the professional staff meets to determine whether a patient is ready for release or furlough. A suggestion has been made that the role of the parole board should be changed to that of an appeal board, with the institutional staff making the decisions and calling in the parole board for assistance in marginal cases, with the parole board serving as a grievance committee on prison conditions and as an appeal board for prisoners denied parole by the institutional staff.[5]

The advisability of parole has been challenged by several writers and by the American Bar Association's Joint Committee on the Legal Rights of Prisoners. On the other hand, it has been supported by other writers and researchers. Some writers in the field of criminal justice have said for a long time that parole itself is desirable, but the way it has been administered and implemented has left it open to many criticisms. The field of criminal justice has to decide whether it wants to keep parole or clean it up! Maine abolished parole in 1975, effective March 1, 1976, and California and Indiana abolished parole effective July 1, 1977. Other states seriously considering it include Illinois, Minnesota, and Washington, as well as the United States Department of Justice. The greatest movement toward abolishing parole appears to be in the eastern states from Maine to Delaware and Washington, D.C., with pockets in the Midwest (Indiana, Illinois, and Minnesota) and the West Coast (California and Washington).

[5] F. Lovell Bixby, "New Roles for Parole Boards," *Federal Probation*, Vol. 34, No. 2 (June 1970), pp. 24–28.

Criteria for Selection

Criteria for parole selection vary. Many parole board members look for the development of good work habits, completion of a school program that may range from learning to read and write to high school graduation or learning a trade. Some other parole board members may look for participation in religious services and pay more attention to the chaplain's report and other similar evidence. The question parole board members are trying to answer, essentially, is: How has this person changed so that he will not again respond in a criminal way when he encounters a stress situation similar to that which resulted in his original crime? How has he changed so that he will not look for a criminal solution to his problems?

The information on which the parole board bases its decision is generally (1) preparole progress report prepared by the institutional staff; (2) the presentence investigation prepared by the probation officer after conviction and prior to sentence; (3) the institutional file that reflects misconduct reports, school record, work record, medical history, and other institutional information; and (4) an interview with the inmate. The preparole progress report is generally prepared by institutional personnel, counselors, social workers, classification officers, or similar personnel. The preparole progress report includes reports from cell-block officers, work assignment supervisors, school personnel, the chaplain, and other personnel within the prison who may have had contact with the inmate. It includes a narration of the inmate's adjustment in the prison, what he has accomplished, and what he has not accomplished. It ends with a recommendation for or against parole, together with the reasons for the recommendation. This preparole progress report is furnished to the parole board approximately thirty days prior to the inmate's parole hearing, which is approximately thirty days prior to the release date.

Constant litigation has followed the *Morrissey v. Brewer* case (408 U.S. 471, 1972) that established due process procedures in parole revocation. The United States Board of Parole, now the United States Parole Commission, adopted the Salient Factors guidelines for parole in 1973 and 1974, which replaced judgment of an offender's institutional record with factors not related to the institution, such as number of previous convictions, previous incarcerations, age, whether the offense involved auto theft, any previous parole revocations, no history of heavy drugs, completion of high school or GED, verified employment or school attendance for six months during the last two years in the community, and whether the release plan involves living with spouse or children. Deviations must be defended. Legislation effective May 14, 1976 (Public Law 94-233) changed the name to the United States Parole Commission and established a nine-member Commission with no less than five regions. These regions are headquartered in Philadelphia, Atlanta, Kansas City, Dallas, and Burlingame, California (near San Francisco). Hearing examiners interview proposed parolees and make recommendations, that are implemented at the regional level. The headquarters office in Washington is responsible for administrative management of the Commission. The National

Appeals Board is also headquartered in the main office in Washington. The legal office of the Commission has concentrated on the development of procedures to balance the interests of the public and of the individual prisoner in his claims for procedural rights in both parole and revocation hearings.[6] Several states are in the process of modifying their procedures in response to litigation concerning due process somewhat in the direction of the federal model.

Criteria for parole selection varies widely, as mentioned before, with the background of the inmate being very important to board members in the paroling process.[7] Many parole board members "re-try" the original case on which the offender was convicted. If an inmate continues to deny his guilt, many parole board members refuse to release him, the suggestion being that he is deliberately antisocial and is practically calling the judge and jurors liars. Other parole board members consider this process to be double jeopardy. Realistically, most decisions are based on (1) the offense and the inmate's attitude toward it; (2) prior criminal history; (3) age; (4) work habits and employment history; and (5) prison record.

The Selection Process

Some state systems have based their decisions on the record alone, without interviewing the inmate. New Jersey, for example, has traditionally simply based its paroling practices on the record. This, also, has created morale problems for the prisoners.

Some systems have interviewed the inmate with a majority of the board present so the decision could be made at that time. This interviewing, termed *en banc,* appears to be the most therapeutic approach to parole procedures. Although some systems have sent the inmate out of the room while confidential discussions were taking place, probably the most therapeutic approach would be to interview *en blanc* with discussions taking place in the presence of the inmate. When the inmate hears a decision at the time of the hearing and knows what went into the decision, he has a better opportunity to use the information he learned for his own self-improvement. At least he knows what the parole board thinks and the procedure they were using. Holding these discussions in front of the inmate would eliminate extraneous arguments against parole by a board member who just does not like the "looks" of a prisoner. The arguments would have to be logical and based on concrete facts. In most of the prison riots during the last few decades, parole policies have been prominent in the listed causes. Knowing how the parole board functions and on what basis they arrive at decisions is important for the morale of prisoners. They are going to talk about the parole board in the yard, anyway. It is

---

[6] *Report: The United States Parole Commission* (Washington, D.C.: United States Department of Justice, July 1, 1973, to September 30, 1976, transmitted to Attorney General Griffin Bell March 30, 1977), p. 15.

[7] Lloyd E. Ohlin, *Selection for Parole* (New York: Russell Sage Foundation, 1951), p. 28.

much better that they have a greater understanding of the parole process. A response to a question loses its significance and value with delay. In early 1972, the United States Parole Board agreed to provide reasons for denial of parole in a few institutions by May 1 and in the system by July 1. This policy had a broad impact,[8] but was subsequently discontinued because of administrative difficulties.

Some scientific examination of the parole process began in the 1920s. Warner in 1923 and Burgess in 1928 developed the first parole prediction tables. The parole prediction table by Burgess became the prototype for most parole selection because it used only existing records. Laune based a prediction study on the analysis of hunches by fellow inmates.[9] In this study, Laune pointed out that the inmates at the Illinois State Penitentiary at Stateville had been able to predict success or failure on parole better than the parole board members. This research was an attempt to analyze the factors that went into the hunches by inmates. It is interesting that "inmate X," who was Nathan Leopold, assisted materially in the statistical methodology involved in developing the "truth group" among the inmates for this study.

PRERELEASE PROGRAMS

Prerelease preparation has taken many forms, but the common objective is to assist the inmate to make an adequate adjustment in leaving the prison and reentering society. Traditionally, the institutional parole officer (IPO) handles the prerelease program, though some states do not have an IPO. The IPO has the role of maintaining liaison between the institution and the parole board in matters concerning the release of prisoners, including prerelease preparation.

Alcohol and Women

The two main problems during the inmate's first few weeks out of prison involve alcohol and women. When a person has been locked in prison for years, he has lost some of his tolerance for alcohol or, as alcoholics say, he has "dried out." Still, he remembers the taste of alcohol and is attracted to it by advertisements and memories. This is why many parolees who leave the prison without a family or supervision are picked up the same day for drunkenness. They walk into a bar for a drink while waiting for the bus, cannot handle it, and are soon arrested. It is well to advise prospective parolees of this problem and to suggest methods of handling it. If they are going to drink, they should take a bottle of their favorite beverage or six-pack of beer home and test their tolerance in private. A general rule-of-thumb

---

[8] *The Wall Street Journal,* Vol. 189, No. 11, p. 1.
[9] Ferris Laune, *Predicting Criminality* (Evanston, Ill.: Northwestern University Press, 1937).

is not to attempt to drink in public for about four weeks or a month after release from prison.

Women are important. After having been locked up for years, there is danger that an inmate will be indiscriminate in his attempt to "make up for lost time." This frequently results in difficulties ranging from venereal disease to unfortunate marriages. This is the reason for the standard parole rule that an inmate cannot marry without the permission of the parole officer.

Employment

Employment is always important to the offender as well as to the parole officer. Personnel managers in most industries have had experience with parole officers and hiring ex-offenders. The general practice is that the personnel manager knows who an ex-offender is, but nobody else knows. Unfortunately, however, mannerisms and other "tell-tale clues" identify the ex-offender to other ex-criminals who have been in the same institution. Vocabulary or distinctive tattoos may identify ex-offenders. It is important that the prerelease program cover the areas of "unlearning" some of the prison jargon and characteristics.

Housing

The place of residence of a parolee is important. Generally, parole boards like to have their parolees live with the parental family or their wives and family. This provides the social ties so important in the socialization process. During the first weekend after release, for example, the parolee may be "jittery" on Saturday night and may indicate that he is going to the drugstore for a package of cigarettes. The parolee's father tells him to wait a minute so he can accompany him. Both the inmate and the father know that he is not going to the drugstore for cigarettes, but may have something else in mind. The fact that the father is interested enough in the offender to risk his hostility in order to protect him represents the social ties upon which the paroling authorities are depending. This human interest could also be what the parolee is looking for.

Parolees can live with relatives as a second choice, maintain their own apartments as a third choice, can stay in a boarding house as a fourth choice, or may rent a hotel room on a temporary basis as a last resort. Generally, they are not permitted to stay in friends' homes because they were not very judicious in selecting their friends in the first place. The presence of social ties is important in the board's decision to approve a residence.

Authoritarian Relationships

Parole rules are generally reviewed and discussed thoroughly in the preparole preparation sessions. The rationale behind the rules and the reasons for their existence must be thoroughly explained so that the parolees understand and all their questions are answered. Most rules include working steadily, supporting the family, meeting obligations, violating no laws, and keeping reasonable hours. Rules that are restrictive may be that parolees may not leave the county or jurisdiction of supervision without permission of the parole officer, not leave the state without permission of the paroling authority, and may not marry or own and drive an automobile without consent of the parole officer.

In one study of a California prerelease program, one hundred inmates were asked to select from a list of subjects usually covered in prerelease those topics that interested them the most. The responses are shown in Table 19–1. These survey results may provide some idea as to the attitudes of prisoners being released and how they view the problem areas of the free community.

The adjustment of a person newly released from prison is much more difficult than the adjustment of persons demobilized from the military services. Although unemployment rates, some health problems, and considerable maladjustment occurs among veterans released from the army and other services after demobilization, the problems faced by ex-prisoners are considerably more serious.

TABLE 19–1 Subjects Desired to Be Covered in Prerelease Preparations by 100 Prisoners

Item	Percent
Did not want to participate in a prerelease program at all	47
Would like to participate in the program	53
Parole agents to discuss problems of parole	47
Parole agents to discuss conditions of parole	43
Driving privileges on parole	43
Parolees to discuss parole problems	36
How to buy a used car	36
California Department of Employment representative	32
Labor union policies toward parolees	30
Applying for a job	29
Purchasing clothes	27
Income tax	26
Vocational rehabilitation	25
Social Security benefits	23
Family welfare aid	22
Certificate of rehabilitation	20
Budgeting your money	20

Source: Norman Holt and Rudy Renteria, *Pre-release Program Evaluation: How Effective Are Prerelease Programs?* Research Project No. 30 (Sacramento, Calif.: California Department of Corrections, October 1968), p. 7.

SUPERVISION OF PAROLEES

Parolees are more difficult to supervise than probationers, generally, if success in casework or treatment-supervision is the criterion. Although probationers have the authority's assurance and hopeful outlook because they have not been sent to prison, parolees have been sent to prison as poor risks for probation. In addition, they have been conditioned by an average of twenty-one months of institutionalization in an adult prison or correctional institution. The parolee has learned to "play the nods" in prison, acquiescing to authority on a superficial basis, while his basic behavioral pattern remains essentially unchanged. Many parolees have learned to manipulate their way through social situations and official contacts with authority. They have already been selected as too difficult for probation, subsequently conditioned by the prison experience, and have learned the poker-faced, staid, social veneer that makes diagnosis and evaluation difficult. They regard the parole officer as "another screw."

Parties Responsible for Success of Parole

Effective supervision involves casework services with the parolee and his family, a good relationship with the police, and a thorough knowledge of all the available employers in the area who will hire parolees. Labor unions can be effective in supervision. Some labor unions have indicated that since the Taft-Hartley Act went into effect, the closed shop has prohibited them from having any say in hiring. Consequently, juvenile delinquents and others have not been able to get into the working force because of extremely high standards set up by employers.[10] The unions may have a shared responsibility for discrimination against ex-offenders at times.

The size of parole caseloads varies from around 20 in some experimental intensive supervision situations to 100 and more in some areas where probationers and parolees are supervised together. One state has reported a probationer-parolee caseload of 314, with very few problems. Each United States probation officer has a caseload of about 110 on the average, including probationers and parolees. The caseload recommended by the National Council on Crime and Delinquency is 50 or less, but most progressive parole systems range around 80 under supervision by each parole officer.

A good parole officer does not *enforce* the parole rules but rather bases his progress on casework and counseling. When it becomes obvious that a parolee is not responding and is in danger of becoming involved in further trouble, the parole officer may recommend revocation of parole on the basis of violation of rules. He uses the rules as tools, rather than as limits. Many decisions for recommending

---

[10] *The Young Offenders—Citizen or Outcast?* Community Services Activities Committee, Massachusetts State Labor Council, AFL-CIO, and Labor Relations and Research Center, University of Massachusetts, 1966.

revocation of parole are dependent upon the visibility of parolees' violations to the parole officer or the police. Sometimes, the officer may have to place the parolee in jail for a week or so without recommending revocation if the use of authority is necessary to reestablish meaningful communication with the parolee.

The primary problems employers have had with parolees are absenteeism and problems associated with alcohol or drugs.[11] Lack of skill is seldom a problem, although poor work habits have been a persistent problem. Parole violations drop as incomes rises, which could be a circular phenomenon because more effective people tend to earn more and stay out of trouble better.[12]

Studies on inmate family relationships support the strong and consistent positive relationship that exists between parole success and maintaining strong family ties while in prison.[13] Although prisoners are less likely to be married than the average male in the general population, the family remains an important socializing factor. Frequent visits do not improve the inmate's institutional behavior, but do lead to better plans and a better chance of success on parole. Family visiting and temporary release programs are strongly supported by the inmate body and elicit negative reactions from those who cannot participate.

Revocation of Parole

Revocation of parole is a procedure by which the parole officer makes recommendations to the parole board and the prison to put the parolee back in prison. He must state reasons. Technical violations involve a violation of the rules. Many violations, however, are the commission of new offenses. In recent years, public hearings that permit the parolee to have legal counsel are part of the revocation procedure.

COMBINED PROBATION AND PAROLE SERVICES

More than half the states and the federal system have combined probation and parole services in the same offices. A United States parolee-probation officer prepares presentence reports and probation reports and supervises probationers and parolees. These systems have generally started in the more settled areas where probation services varied so widely that they were present in urban areas and completely absent in rural areas. By combining the services on the state level,

---

[11] Robert M. Dickover, Verner E. Maynard, and James A. Painter, *A Study of Vocational Training in the California Department of Corrections*, Administrative Abstract No. 40 (Sacramento, Calif.: California Department of Corrections, January 1971).

[12] *Training Needs in Correctional Institutions* (Washington, D.C.: United States Department of Labor Manpower Administration, 1966), p. 8.

[13] Norman Holt and Donald Miller, *Explorations in Inmate-Family Relationships* (Sacramento, Calif.: California Department of Corrections, January 1972).

probation could technically be provided in all counties, whether or not there were local personnel. For example, one state with over 2 million people and 1,500 prisoners has sixteen probation and parole officers to handle all probation and parole services in the state, and probation and parole services are reported in surveys to be available to all counties. There are other states in even more unfavorable positions. The advantage of the combined probation and parole systems is apparently that state parole officers could be made available to prepare presentence investigations for the local judges. Supervision in these systems generally goes to parolees.

PROBLEMS WITH PAROLE

Parole has had probably more problems than most other phases of the correctional system. The first paroling authority in America was Zebulon R. Brockway, first superintendent of the Elmira Reformatory in New York in 1876 when the reformatory movement and the indeterminate sentence came together to permit parole. Soon, the selection of persons to be paroled by the superintendent of the institution brought criticism based on favoritism and an outside, supposedly objective, parole commissioner was appointed. Over the years, abuses of the one-man commissioner system, generally serving at the pleasure of the governor, brought challenges of corruption. Probably the best-known such incident occurred in 1936 when Howard Gill accused Governor Ely of Massachusetts of selling paroles, was fired, and was subsequently supported by a legislative investigation. These rumors were common prior to World War II, but after the war multiple-member parole boards replaced the single commissioner and charges of corruption decreased significantly. Subsequently, the charges became incompetence, well expressed by Richard McGee, who, in 1969, predicted that "parole boards will change to include better people."[14] In the meantime, many of the causes ascribed to prison riots included "parole board policies." Parole board members and institutional personnel were in frequent conflict.

Concerning the future of corrections, McGee predicted in 1969 that parole boards may disappear.[15] Bixby predicted in 1970 that the role of the parole board, at least, may be changed.[16] There have been many calls for the abolition of parole.[17] Fogel has suggested the abolition of parole in favor of flat sentencing which allowed some good time to be earned and not forfeited for misbehavior, as well as some other embellishments.[18] He has testified in many legislative hearings around

[14] Richard A. McGee, "What's Past Is Prologue," *The Annals—The Future of Corrections,* Vol. 381 (January 1969), pp. 9–10.

[15] *Ibid.,* p. 10.

[16] F. Lovell Bixby, "A New Role for Parole Boards," *Federal Probation* (June 1970), pp. 24–28.

[17] Herman Schwartz, "Let's Abolish Parole," *Reader's Digest* (August 1973), pp. 185–90.

[18] David Fogel, ". . . *We Are the Living Proof . . .": The Justice Model for Corrections* (Cincinnati: W. H. Anderson, 1975).

the country when these bodies have considered abolition of parole. The American Bar Association has also recommended abolition.[19]

Maine was first to abolish parole in 1975, effective March 1, 1976, after which the parole board was given new duties, the courts were empowered to reduce sentences, and the supervision of persons already on parole was to continue until expiration. Indiana and California abolished parole effective July 1, 1977, but those already on parole will be supervised until expiration. Illinois, Minnesota, and Washington were debating the issue in 1977. The Arizona Supreme Court in 1977 ruled that a victim opposing parole of an offender could sue parole board members individually or collectively for negligence or capriciousness in paroling offenders.

On the other hand, parole has been supported by several responsible sources. Martinson and Wilks have pointed out that abolition of parole supervision would result in substantial increases in arrests, convictions, and returns to prison.[20] In fact, the Florida legislature debated the issue in 1976 and 1977, but dropped it when the projected increase in prison populations that would result from it made the prospective costs prohibitive. Niethercutt has indicated that the evidence is overwhelming in favor of parole supervision increasing the chances of successful reintegration of offenders into the community and, simultaneously, doing it with considerably less cost than imprisonment.[21] It has been apparent to many persons in the field for a long time that there is nothing wrong with parole per se, but its administration has frequently been less than desirable.[22]

OTHER RELEASES FROM PRISON

There are several methods besides parole that allow the release of inmates. The recidivism rate of discharged persons is significantly higher than those released on parole. Release on expiration of sentence, therefore, appears to be undesirable in terms of keeping the offender out of subsequent difficulty and out of prison. Casework and counseling have been more helpful than financial aid.

Mandatory Conditional Release

Several states have mandatory release laws that provide for the release of all prisoners or those prisoners designated by prison officials six months or more prior to expiration of their sentences. This type of conditional release affords a short pe-

---

[19] *The American Criminal Law Review,* Winter 1977, American Bar Foundation; summarized in "ABA Panel Urges Extension of Inmate Rights," *Criminal Justice Newsletter,* Vol. 8, No. 10 (May 9, 1977), pp. 5–6.

[20] "Martinson Defends Parole Supervision," *Criminal Justice Newsletter,* Vol. 8, No. 15 (July 18, 1977), p. 7; Robert Martinson and Judith Wilks, "Save Parole Supervision," *Federal Probation,* No. 3 (September 1977).

[21] M. G. Niethercutt, "Parole Legislation," *Federal Probation,* Vol. 41, No. 1 (March 1977), p. 26.

[22] Harry Elmer Barnes and Negley K. Teeters, *New Horizons in Criminology,* 3rd ed. (Englewood Cliffs, N.J.: Prentice-Hall, 1959), p. 572.

riod of supervision in the community, regardless of parole action. Mandatory release also occurs at the expiration of sentence, but the term *mandatory release* is generally reserved for a mandatory *conditioned* release permitting some type of supervision. The usage of the term, of course, can be easily confused because release at the expiration of sentences is also mandatory.

Expiration of Sentence

Approximately two-thirds of all prisoners released from American prisons and correctional institutions are those who have completed a sentence. It is unfortunate that no supervision is afforded these people. Because they were never granted parole they are generally considered to be the worst cases, and therefore in the greatest need of supervision.

Prisoners' aid societies seem to be the best source of information as to what happens to the discharged prisoner. Those who do not get into difficulty tend to gravitate toward assistance from prisoners' aid societies, the Salvation Army, and other private agencies. Their experience has been that counseling, assistance in employment, and providing a stable source of emotional or social support is most important. Most prisoners' aid societies do not have funds for financial aid.

Pardons

There are several types of executive clemency, including pardons, commutations, and amnesty. A pardon is official forgiveness by the executive or judicial branch of the government and revocation of the inmate's sentence. A conditional pardon depends upon the performance of the recipient out of jail and therefore can be revoked. Commutation is an executive reduction of sentence. For example, a frequent type of commutation is reducing a life sentence to a specific number of years or the death penalty sentence to a life sentence. Amnesty is a general pardon offered to groups of individuals, such as participants in an insurrection.

The purpose of pardons varies quite widely. The first and original purpose was to undo obvious miscarriages of justice. The modern "technical pardon" has been used to avoid deportation of persons under the Immigration Act as undesirable aliens. This pardon makes the deportation unnecessary. Restoration of civil rights has also been accomplished by pardons.

The use of pardons and commutations has frequently been misused by politicians, particularly prior to World War II. It was not uncommon in the 1930s for a governor going out of office to commute as many as a thousand sentences between election day and the last of December. This type of misuse for political purpose gave pardons a poor reputation at that time. In the 1970s, however, and since World War II in general, the use of pardons and commutations has been better controlled. In many jurisdictions, such procedure needs the recommendation of a board, or, in some cases, the paroling authority. Pardons today are used more for constructive social purposes.

SUMMARY

Release from prison can be by parole, by discharge, by conditional or mandatory release, by pardon or general amnesty, or by expiration of sentence. Two-thirds of first releases are generally by parole, almost one-third by expiration of sentence, and the other types of releases are insignificant at present. Approximately 61 percent of first releases from the American prison have been traditionally by parole.[23] Two-thirds of *all* releases are by expiration of sentence. Many of these people had been previously paroled. Approximately 5 percent are by conditional or mandatory release, with slightly over 34 percent by expiration of sentence. In 1978, the Uniform Parole Reporting Project of the National Council on Crime and Delinquency in San Francisco reported that paroles of first releases had risen to 70 percent in 1978 and to 78 percent in 1977, despite the move in some places to abolish parole. It should be noted, too, that while parole has been abolished in Maine, California, Indiana, and Illinois, some type of supervision, probably like that in mandatory conditional release, has been retained in three of these States, with Maine being the only State that did not retain some supervision.

The persons released by discharge are usually those who are the most difficult to rehabilitate and have therefore been denied paroles. Some jurisdictions do not discharge without supervision because gradual reentry into society is most needed by the difficult offenders and society needs some protection until they are adjusted. All types of parole and other release procedures, of course, are designed to return the offender from the prison or correctional institution to the free community and keep him there.

LEARNING EXERCISES

Issues to Be Discussed

1. There is a persistent criticism of the parole officer's function: He must be a policeman with powers of revocation and a counselor handling adjustment and personal problems of ex-offenders. Do you believe that the two roles are incompatible? Why or why not?
2. What have been the criteria used by parole boards to select prisoners for parole?
3. Describe prerelease programs.
4. Discuss the problems experienced with parole systems.
5. What is mandatory conditional release?
6. Discuss the use of pardons to release offenders.

---

[23] *National Prisoner Statistics 1966* (Washington, D.C.: United States Bureau of Prisons, 1968), p. 9.

Group Activity

Set up a parole board hearing with three parole board members and the inmate. Have a small committee initially draw up a preparole progress report and a presentence investigation report, with copies made available to the board and to the inmate so that he knows the full conditions of his incarceration for discussion. Have the board interview the inmate and make a decision to be critiqued by the class.

Field Activity

Engage one or several parole officers to come to the class to discuss the problems that parole officers face in their community activities, and their views on the subject of elimination of parole under determinate sentencing and the combining of probation and parole services.

Key Terms

en banc	Preparole report
IPO	Presentence investigation
Parole board	Revocation

SUGGESTED REFERENCES

AMERICAN BAR ASSOCIATION, RESOURCE CENTER ON CORRECTIONAL LAW AND LEGAL SERVICES. *Survey of Parole Conditions in the United States.* Washington, D.C.: American Bar Association, 1973.

CARTER, R., AND WILKINS, L., eds. *Probation, Parole and Community Corrections.* New York: John Wiley, 1976.

CITIZENS' INQUIRY ON PAROLE AND CRIMINAL JUSTICE. *Prison Without Walls: Report on New York Parole.* New York: Praeger, 1975.

"COP OR COUNSELOR? A DAY IN THE LIFE OF A PAROLE AGENT." *Corrections Magazine,* Vol. 3 (September 1977), pp. 57–63.

LENIHAN, KENNETH J. *The Financial Resources of Released Prisoners.* Washington, D.C.: Bureau of Social Science Research, Inc., 1974.

NEWMAN, CHARLES L. *Sourcebook on Probation, Parole and Pardons.* 3rd ed. Springfield, Ill.: Charles C Thomas, 1972.

O'LEARY, VINCENT, AND NUFFELD, JOAN. *The Origin of Parole Systems in the United States.* Hackensack, N.J.: National Council on Crime and Delinquency, 1972.

PARKER, WILLIAM. *Parole: Origins, Development, Current Practices and Statutes.* American Correctional Association Parole Corrections Projects, Resource Document No. 1. College Park, Md.: American Correctional Association, 1975.

SCHMIDT, JANET. *Demystifying Parole.* Lexington, Mass.: Lexington Books, 1977.

STANLEY, DAVID T. *Prisoners Among Us: The Problem of Parole.* Washington, D.C.: The Brookings Institution, 1976.

STUDT, ELLIOT. *Reintegration of the Offender into the Community.* Washington, D.C.: Law Enforcement Assistance Administration, June 1973.

WALLER, IRWIN. *Men Released from Prison.* Toronto and Buffalo: University of Toronto Press in association with Center of Criminology, 1974.

WILSON, ROB. "Release: Should Parole Boards Hold the Key?" *Corrections Magazine,* Vol. 3 (September 1977), pp. 47–55.

20

The Criminal Justice System in Transition

Urban Policy Development and the Criminal Justice System
The Reality and Mythology of the Criminal Justice System
The Manpower Base for Criminal Justice Operations
The Impact of Standards and Goals
Policing at the Crossroads
Gathering in the Wayward Juvenile
The Perplexities of Prisons and Jails
The Propriety of the Way the Law Is Ruled

The criminal justice system as it has been presented in this volume appears as an enormously complex organization whose operations and their accompanying problems seem unending. It is one of the most dynamic, volatile, and frequently the most frustrating system in the public service galaxy. Although the President's Commission on Law Enforcement and the Administration of Justice of more than a decade ago focused attention on its manifold difficulties, the pace involved in solving its problems has been slow. The burgeoning crime problems of the inner city and nearby suburbs, especially among juveniles; the uncertainties of the real role of policing in modern society; the unhappy circumstances of presentence pleading; the gross disparities in the sentencing process; the overcrowding of jails and prisons; the uncertainties of the community as a base for assisting offenders; and the public demands for swift and sure justice and the more vigorous control of career criminals—all have conspired to bring into sharp focus the unique complexities of a system that often does not appear to be functioning as a system.

A suggested diagram of the relation of the criminal justice system to society as a whole is presented in Figure 20-1. As operational, specialist, and management jobs get tougher throughout a system plagued by a kaleidoscopic number of pressures, there will be continuous efforts to advance the skills and knowledge of those who must operate and manage the system—from patrol and correctional officers to chiefs, superintendents, and judges. All the compounding difficulties must also be considered in reference to tighter municipal and state budgets. These conditions tend to emphasize the need for the federal government to reappraise most carefully the priorities for assisting local and state governments and to focus on the critical decision points throughout the system where improvements in operations are most urgent.

While change in the criminal justice system has been slow, the progress since the President's Commission in 1967 has been perceptible. Advances have been most noticeable in the police area. Since the police are always at the cutting edge, or the front line of human troubles, hardships, and altercations, they have been forced more rapidly to develop new procedures and new methods to cope with many of society's aberrations and divergencies as criminal law has defined them. At the same time police and other components of the criminal justice system, its critics infer, have tended over time to isolate themselves from the community. The more the system became detached and removed, the more power seemingly accrued to it, based upon its singular legal foundations. However, with the steady increase in numbers of those who collide with the law, with the constant appearance of new and more serious problems in the packed urban areas of the nation, and with the battle for resources to cope with growing dilemmas, the system now

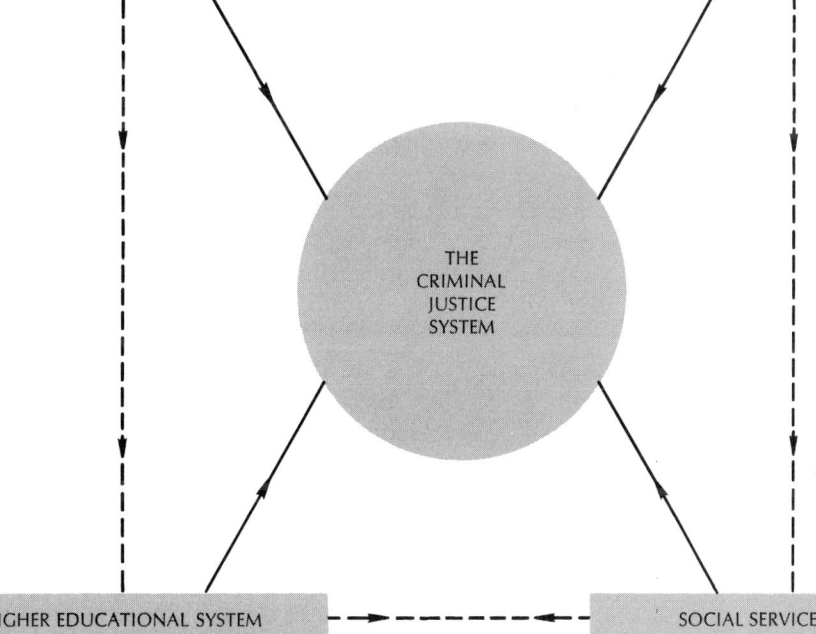

FIGURE 20–1   Interrelationship of the Criminal Justice System with Society
Source: *A Summary of the Comprehensive Criminal Justice Plan for Crime Prevention and Control* (Boston: Massachusetts Committee on Law Enforcement and Administration of Criminal Justice, 1970), p. 29.

appears to be seeking alternative ways of discharging its current responsibilities by looking more toward community involvement. The eminent British criminologist, Sir Leon Radzinowicz, put the basic dilemma this way:

> The spread of traditional crime breeds public apathy and defeatism. The police fall behind in bringing the offender to justice, their temptations to cut corners increase, dangers of corruptions rise. The courts, endlessly bogged down by long waiting lists, are under heavy pressure to hurry cases through, to accept devices which offer shortcuts, and to neglect legal protections. Penal institutions, overcrowded with the untried as well as the sentenced, see tensions mount and standards deteriorate. All those who have to deal with offenders are frustrated by the widening gap between what is expected of them and what they can hope to achieve.[1]

This final sentence announces the call for urgent assistance.

While this final chapter—with its attempt to peek over the horizon into the future—cannot hope to cover all of the criminal justice system's issues and trends, the reader is invited to ponder a few of those of major significance.

URBAN POLICY DEVELOPMENT AND THE CRIMINAL JUSTICE SYSTEM

Ever since the sociologist Durkheim propounded the theory, it has been widely argued that crime will always be a component of society, even a good, in that it helps society to reappraise and reconstitute its moral structure continuously. The criminal justice system, built for crime control, is, in effect, the argument continues, a reactor, an enforcer of what society in its moral judgment defines as criminal laws. True crime reduction, it is maintained, can only come about by the alteration of society itself. Meanwhile the criminal justice system cannot indulge too long an immersion in this bewildering long-range problem. It must execute the government's will in the real world, now, by enforcing the law and managing offenders through the established system.

The criminal justice system at present suffers from the lack of well-defined urban policies within which it should operate. Such policies should approach problems of crime causation and control within the context of their interrelationship with other urban community problems and necessities. They should view the community as a system, of which the criminal justice system in turn is a component, and help to define more succinctly the revised role of the criminal justice system in the community setting.

The establishment of urban policies imply goal setting. Appropriate goals include the following: (1) a vigorous employment program; (2) a restructuring of federal programs that may affect a city; (3) a rediscovery of the "human-scale neighborhood" as a basic building block in the renewal of cities; (4) the realistic planning of land, housing, and energy resources; (5) the lessening of state-imposed restrictions; (6) the reorganization of fragmented local government to elimi-

---

[1] Sir Leon Radzinowicz and Joan King, *The Growth of Crime: The International Experience* (New York: Basic Books, 1977), pp. 323–24.

nate overlapping bureaus and contending officials; (7) the decentralization of governmental operations, including the possibility of establishing paragovernments to deal with very special problems; (8) the restoration of the financial vigor of cities where there now exist grave disparities in revenue allocations; and (9) the possible financially supported movement of the unemployed from the urban ghettos to other areas where employment opportunities are greater.[2]

Basically the problems related to urban policy planning are political, not technological. The question for the future is: What do people desire to be accomplished? The route for such decision making is political.[3] Pressures upon the criminal justice system may, in the coming years, be relieved with political decisions that place responsibilities for handling many alienated people and their manifold problems on community activities that are not necessarily a part of the criminal justice system. The more the criminal justice system is asked to cope with problems beyond its capacities, the more pressure is required to develop such urban policies that will direct responsibilities, through the political process, elsewhere. While the criminal justice system contends with all the current problems outlined in this book, states and municipalities are challenged to concentrate, not scatter, resources on the most urgent societal problems, such as those that breed crime. This issue is not new. The current disarray of American cities makes the issue likely to be even more compelling for the next two decades. In summary, the effectiveness and efficiency of the criminal justice system will in the future be bound inexorably to the development of a national urban policy.

THE REALITY AND MYTHOLOGY OF THE CRIMINAL JUSTICE SYSTEM

Many of the issues and operating problems discussed in this book clearly indicate that there is a perceptible cleavage between how the criminal justice system really operates and what is considered optimal or desired. A basic issue for the future is to recognize what now works well and to design new methods through management decisions or research in order to achieve the desired goals. At the same time, it will be important to continue to identify the critical points characterized by malfunction, sluggishness, and incongruity. Part of the problem is beyond the system's own capacity to improve and lies, rather, in the broader issue of the need for a new urban policy.

On the other hand, the progressive identification of problem areas at the

---

[2] Congressman Henry S. Ruess, "To Save a City," Committee Print, Sub-Committee on the City, Committee on Banking, Finance and Urban Affairs, House of Representatives, 93rd Cong., 1st Sess. (Washington, D.C., September 1977), pp. iii–v, 11–13; William E. Ewald, Jr., ed., *Environment and Policy: The Next Fifty Years* (Bloomington, Ind.: Indiana University Press, 1968), pp. 291–92, 423–42; Daniel P. Moynihan, "Toward a National Urban Policy," in *Violent Crime: The Report of the National Commission on the Causes and Prevention of Violence* (New York: George Braziller, 1969), pp. 1–30.

[3] Daniel Bell, *The Coming of Post-Industrial Society* (New York: Basic Books, 1973), p. 337.

really most critical decision points—such as those more susceptible to better management practices, more creative available resource allocations, or more realistic goal setting—can be accomplished by more adequately preparing those who can influence changes in the criminal justice system. Such agents of change are those who are professionally trained and possess the talent and insights to move the system forward. Much of the talent already latent in the system or now flowing into it should be afforded the opportunity for more specific education in the areas most needing critical attention, such as management, research and evaluation, and planning.

Shrinking revenues as a change agent within the system have forced criminal justice agencies to cooperate more closely, bringing greater competency to their operations. The New York City experience is an example of where the paper myth of the criminal justice system operating as a system was turned into a reality. Because of the financial pinch and manpower shortage, the Manhattan District Attorney's Office eliminated the assembly line system where some assistants handled complaints, others arraignments, and others trials. Under "verticle integration," cases are handled by one assistant from complaint through to final disposition. Delays dropped from forty-four weeks to seventeen weeks. A companion move, the establishment of an "early assessment bureau," determined immediately the kind of charge which was to be brought against the defendant at arraignment. Sixty percent of cases are settled at this stage. This innovation enabled the courts in turn to plan to speed up their case handling. The criminal courts adopted a "front loading" disposition approach by getting minor cases, such as Class B misdemeanors (six months or less in jail) out of the way first by fines, probation, and suspended sentences, thus getting rid of one-half of the arrests at the time of arraignment. Such a move meant concentrating manpower—a team of judges—to handle the innovation and speed up case disposition. The decision of the courts to front load in turn reduced the burden on the Department of Corrections by reducing the daily census of prisoners from 13–14,000 in 1972 to 7,000 in 1977. The whole system now affords a greater opportunity to concentrate on the career criminal and reduce the "crime-school effect of prisons."[4]

For the future there appear to be at least two avenues of approach to making the system work as a system: a concentrated effort toward systems analysis under a predetermined plan, or a forced program, such as instituted in New York, where officials admit that reduced resources oblige them to seek better means to accomplish their tasks and work together. With tax dollars dwindling in the future, the latter approach appears to be a necessity but the former should have better long-range results. Moreover, conscientiously planned efforts will undoubtedly proceed along a track parallel to forced changes in order to avoid endless crisis management. The increasing use of system modeling should accommodate this desired planning posture. Budget preparation, operations analysis, decision making, legis-

[4] For the details of the New York City experience, see Richard Harris, "Crime in New York," *The New Yorker,* September 26, 1977.

lative impact on the system, manpower planning, case management, and offender management are all susceptible to the analytic approaches—computer simulation, operational gaming or group judgment, or other procedures in modeling.[5] This tool, now used more effectively in business enterprise, will be introduced more widely in criminal justice planning in the next decade.

The success of such planning, in which modeling is but one tool, will depend upon at least two factors in the future. One is the establishment of professional high-level state criminal justice planning agencies to develop attainable criminal justice standards and goals within the broader state and urban policies. The other involves the ordering of a new professional structure in criminal justice which can undertake extended systems planning and conduct research according to the demands of a more organized criminal justice science. The pressure on the criminal justice higher education system to train such personnel can be decisive.

Finally, the matter of bringing more reality to the concept of criminal justice system functioning as a system will depend upon the increased readiness of citizens to extend their interest in greater community volunteer efforts and to make more positive demands upon their political processes. When taxes rise, there is greater citizen uneasiness. Consequently, there is an increasing urge for the executives, legislatures, and councils to foster greater system cooperation through the budget and management process. It can be expected that the criminal justice system will fall under more close scrutiny in the future.

THE MANPOWER BASE FOR CRIMINAL JUSTICE OPERATIONS

The staffing of the system to perform the varied tasks demanded will, in the future, depend upon a number of factors. Among these are the state and municipal budgets, the increased use of truly functional technology, the formulation of urban policies that permit the alternative use of community services not within the criminal justice system, federal program development and support, system planning and management improvement, population and crime trends, the consolidation of criminal justice efforts, and the redistribution or reduction in efforts occasioned by such actions as decriminalization, deinstitutionalization, or diversion.

Budget restrictions and a projected lessening of crime in the decade of the 1980s, in part due to the shrinking of the youth population and the projected reduction in national unemployment rates, may affect the overall criminal justice manpower employment picture. While the past two decades showed a rapid growth in law enforcement employment as a result of riots, violence, and growth in crime rates, there probably will be a greater acceleration in demands for courts and corrections personnel in the 1980s. All growth is relative. Overall system im-

---

[5] For examples, see Department of Justice, Law Enforcement Assistance Administration, *Criminal Justice Models: An Overview* (Washington, D.C.: U.S. Government Printing Office, 1976).

provement, a drop in overall crime rates, a shift to community agency responsibilities for one-time offenders, and increased diversions from the system could affect the numbers needed. However, to be meaningful manpower requirements must be broken down into specific areas. Given about the same rate of flow through the courts, the need for additional prosecutors and defense personnel is expected to show a very distinct increase. For example, the Supreme Court rulings with respect to right to counsel for both adults and juveniles, especially for the indigent, are still being implemented, some observers believe, too slowly because of the shortages in counsel among public indigent defense agencies. On the prosecutorial side, plea bargaining will remain under constant attack. On the other hand, Supreme Court Chief Justice Burger has maintained that only a 10 percent reduction in plea bargaining would double the manpower needs of the court system.

Given current trends, some increases in employment for the 1980s are likely to appear in probation and parole agencies as new sentencing practices come into play, and in community-based juvenile agencies as state deinstitutionalization occurs. Parole agency needs, however, could show a gradual reduction if states adopt determinate or mandatory minimum sentences in which all offender obligations would be satisfied through the time served in the institution alone. The parole situation reflects how greatly system changes affect manpower needs.

The 1977 Uniform Crime Report showed that 16 percent of the employees in law enforcement were civilian personnel in 1976. As law enforcement agencies increase their use of technology in overall management and personnel support, communications, and other nonoffender contact operations, this percentage is likely to increase, especially among the professional, technical, and administrative occupations for which specialized training in support skills will be required.

Generally, there are few new criminal justice occupations projected for the near future. The trend appears to be toward a refinement of existing occupations and a redefinition of roles, with an increasing number of women in policing. The most intense activity in the latter area will probably continue to focus on the patrol officer in the continuing debate over his or her role as a specialist or generalist and the definition of their duties and their discretionary powers. While a number of police agencies already employ a police legal advisor, the use of this occupation is expected to increase in support of police efforts to interpret new laws and determine the implications of criminal legal interpretations by the Supreme Court, and in the preparation of arrest cases that will meet prosecutor requirements. Changes will also occur in court administrative support personnel, in the expanded role of the correctional officer, and in treatment, counseling, and other professional support personnel in the correctional system. Again, in these areas the number of women occupying these positions is expected to increase.

Generally it can be expected that if occupations are to be refined, their tasks must be better identified and training and education established to help perform such tasks. For example, while the positions of the chief in law enforcement and the superintendent in corrections will remain the same, the duty demands on the positions will require, in addition to the basic administrative skills, training in such areas as budget and resource management, personnel administration, collective bargaining, and community relations. Consequently, throughout all of the criminal justice system—law enforcement, courts, corrections—the demand for increased management training is likely to persist into the future. Such training and education demands are in turn likely to spur specialist training in management support areas such as planning, data management, communication, and related technologies and research. As police and correctional officer roles are redefined and tasks regrouped, training and education are expected to keep step.

In summary, manpower demands for criminal justice are dependent upon a variety of factors, among which budget, crime rates, and court decisions are highly relevant. The trend in demands for the 1980s appears to be upward, with proportionate increases probably greater in courts and corrections. Occupationally, positions already extant in the criminal justice system will be subject to redefinition rather than new entities created. Changes in the responsibilities of the criminal justice system will also require the education and training system to increase the opportunities to acquire technical, professional, and specialized skill and knowledge to meet these new demands. Thus initial and in-service training and education programs are expected to accelerate within resource capabilities.

THE IMPACT OF STANDARDS AND GOALS

For almost a decade the criminal justice system has been involved in an intensive effort to put its own house in order by beginning at the top. These exertions are illustrated by the National Advisory Commission on Standards and Goals Projects and the American Bar Association's related effort in goals development, both covering an extensive portion of the criminal justice system; the American Correctional Association's effort to establish accreditation standards for correctional institutions; the Academy of Criminal Justice Sciences production of standards for accrediting college and university criminal justice education programs; and the federal and state endeavor to promulgate standard sentencing guidelines.[6] All of these efforts, as illustrated in this volume, have covered most of the principle issues in criminal justice and have, consequently, created serious debates with regard to the appropriateness of certain standards and goals. Such examination for the present and future is considered healthy, for it affords an opportunity for an extended critical analysis of the whole system. It is expected that standards and goals will continue to be adopted selectively, depending upon legislative and executive decisions, the size of the jurisdictions, the priorities related to problems within state or municipality, the bureaucratic initiatives, the ability to change in some cases without too great an organizational upheaval, and the costs of imple-

---

[6] For an example of the educational program envisaged, see Victor G. Strecher, "Integration of Instruction, Research and Service for the Professional Education System," *Police Chief* (August 1977), pp. 69–71.

mentation.[7] Debates in the future will revolve around specific goals or standards and even go to the extreme of challenging the whole system of standards and goals. For example, the National Commission recommends the consolidation of all police departments with fewer than ten sworn officers to increase the effectiveness of the overall law enforcement effort. Some critics object to the destruction of the person-to-person knowledge and contacts that the small force provides. Again, it is argued that standards and goals are not grounded on scientific knowledge. It would be more appropriate to provide "general explanatory principles" as a basis for policy determination and planning. Criminal justice agencies are diverse in their operations and are subject to changing problems, so that scientifically derived principles are better than subjective, fixed goals as guidelines.[8] Standards and goals will, however, continue to be given urgent consideration. They will continue to be the basis for bringing critical criminal justice issues to the legislatures and executives, not excluding the courts where standards could weigh heavily in court decisions. These bodies, in turn, can selectively review standards and goals with criminal justice officials for the adoption of those which address critical priorities.

POLICING AT THE CROSSROADS

Policing is the most studied activity in the criminal justice system. It is indeed the front-line function of that activity, the one that comes closest to the citizenry with the greatest visibility and possesses society's authority for initial action against those who would break the law. One of the most persistent issues of policing in the future will be the maintenance of this authority-bound law enforcement requirement to protect society against serious assault, and, at the same time, render to the public those day-by-day services that consume the bulk of time in extended community service.

The basic problem is that police are the only real twenty-four-hour domestic "troops" that citizens possess to handle an overwhelming variety of personal emergency needs. The professional model of policing, some observers believe, runs counter to the desire to provide this variety of social services. Thus the future seems to demand a continuous rethinking of the police function. One author suggests that the police have greater affinity toward operations outside the criminal justice system; that is, the bulk of citizen contacts occur before the criminal justice system is invoked. These include crowd handling, protection of demonstrators, resolution of often minor conflicts, and day-by-day assistance to the elderly, the

[7] An example of cost analysis can be found in Department of Justice, LEAA, *Cost Analysis of Correctional Standards Institutional-Based Programs and Parole,* Vols. 1 and 2 (Washington, D.C.: Law Enforcement Assistance Administration, 1976).
[8] Daniel Glaser, *Strategic Criminal Justice Planning,* Center for Studies of Crime and Delinquency, National Institute for Mental Health (Washington, D.C.: U.S. Government Printing Office, 1975).

young, and others in solving minor problems. Thus, the police role as a major administrative unit of local government is much broader than the more narrowly defined role within the criminal justice system itself.[9] If such a position is to be given serious attention in the future, then it probably must be reviewed within the context of the broader urban policy development discussed earlier in this chapter.

Regardless of the resolution of this larger issue, attempts to define more clearly the role of the patrol officer within the criminal justice system will continue. It is at the patrol level that the more defined law enforcement tasks and the more amorphous service tasks come together. The professional approach to policing would tend to allow greater discretion on the part of the patrol officer on the beat and an opportunity for participating in a variety of decision-making activities, such as neighborhood team policing, crime scene investigations, family crisis intervention activities, decoy programs, and sting operations.[10] But the persistent issue for the future will remain in defining the limits of discretion. Some departments have issued guidelines that include procedures which (1) interpret the Supreme Court decisions, as well as statutes and ordinances, for the patrolman in many of his actions, or (2) limit his discretion in order to keep departments away from serious troubles.

Another major emphasis in the future will be on the measurement of police productivity.[11] Policing is a highly labor-intensive activity. Manpower costs eat up the bulk of police budgets. The situation is exacerbated by the growth of unions and collective bargaining agreements that affect manpower utilization in such areas as duty hour limitations, overtime pay and restrictions, one- and two-man car patrols, shift agreements, and—a new development—union-developed apprentice training standards for police recruits.[12] Productivity of the uniformed police is expected to be further increased by greater civilianization of certain tasks in communications, ambulance and emergency services, and other support activities. Major efforts will be made to perfect case preparation, to screen out weak arrest cases in order to save court time, to arrange more viable duty shifts, to revise

---

[9] Herman Goldstein, *Policing a Free Society* (Cambridge, Mass.: Ballanger, 1977), pp. 32–33.

[10] For a discussion of the Washington, D.C., sting operations, see Ron Shaffer and Kevin Klose, *SURPRISE! SURPRISE!: How the Lawmen Conned the Thieves* (New York: Viking Press, 1977).

[11] Productivity measures utilized by police, such as management organization and analysis; workflow analysis; workload planning, scheduling, and control; labor planning, scheduling, and control; and labor- and cost-saving equipment, are covered in Rackham S. Fukuhara, *Productivity Improvement in Cities* (Washington, D.C.: International City Management Association, 1977); James R. Mandish and Laurie S. Frankel, "Personnel Practices in Municipal Police Service: 1976," in *The Municipal Yearbook* (Washington, D.C.: International City Management Association, 1977); Joan L. Wolfe and John F. Heaphy, eds., *Readings on Productivity in Policing* (Washington, D.C.: Police Foundation, 1975).

[12] Ilene Bergsmaann, *Police Unions* (Washington, D.C.: International City Management Association, March 1976); U.S. Department of Labor, Bureau of Labor Statistics, *Collective Bargaining Agreements for Police and Firefighters* (Washington, D.C.: U.S. Department of Labor, 1975).

booking procedures, and to institute crime prediction patrol and crime pattern analyses, especially in assault and robbery cases.

The increased participation of the community in police services may be considered a major trend within the next decade. Community relations have occupied police for the past quarter of a century. Much of this, critics and police themselves have argued, has tended more toward a public relations program than a participation effort. But obtaining the right relationship is often a difficult exercise. It has been found that departments with a high quality of police service possessed the best community relations. Ability to assess tensions and respond to community crises, ensuring that police training programs in community dynamics are established, encouraging individual and unit accountability that stresses service rather than conflict in street relationships—these appear to be proper building blocks in a sound community program.[13] What may be crucial for the future of policing, especially in the large cities, is the more positive involvement of the citizenry in the development of policies to combat crime.

Victimization studies have generally indicated that victim failure to notify police was based on a belief that nothing could be done,[14] that the police would not follow through anyway, or that victims feared the possible treatment they would receive at the hands of the police or the possible reprisal from their previous assailant or his friends. In the central cities neighborhood watch groups, tenant monitors, and other activities have sprung up, with the more aggressive taking on the characteristics of vigilantes. The police policy problem for the future will be how to encourage community self-protection through police-community councils without encouraging actions which are quite properly police responsibility in law enforcement. Crime scene reporting by direct dialing from pay telephones, meetings with social groups, school classes, and senior citizens concerning their specific roles in crime prevention and reporting, and making marking tools available on loan from local libraries for labeling important household articles—these are a few of the current procedures in enlarging citizen envolvement. But beyond the police professional actions—special task forces, crime prediction patrol and crime pattern analysis, rapid responses to calls, crisis intervention, neighborhood team policing, and procedures for citizen crime prevention and reporting—lies concern about the amount of police involvement in the political infrastructure, the specter of corruption, the differential handling of various classes of citizens, and the traditional authoritarian image. These remain some of the imponderables in the police-citizen relationships. It would appear imperative for the future, given budget restraints and manpower pinches as well as the impact of collective bargaining on police operations, that a far closer relationship between these two elements must come about. Perhaps the route involves making the community the organic element of the whole criminal justice system. In this way not only policing

[13] U.S. Department of Justice, LEAA, *Improving Police/Community Relations* (Washington, D.C.: U.S. Government Printing Office, 1973), pp. 5–6.
[14] U.S. Department of Justice, LEAA, *Victimization in the United States: A National Crime Survey Report* (Washington, D.C.: U.S. Government Printing Office, 1976).

but also community-based corrections and court probation or diversion activities could be interrelated in the community setting. If the trend among all sectors of the criminal justice system is to enhance crime prevention and control and to offer more assistance to both offender and victim, it would then appear that criminal justice leaders have before them a decade of planning challenges and implementation initiatives.

GATHERING IN THE WAYWARD JUVENILE

Although projections into the 1980s indicate a decline in the youthful age groups and thus the likelihood of a lessening crime rate among juveniles, the decade ahead still compels extensive study. The Juvenile Justice Act of 1974, as amended, set in motion a federal attempt to isolate juvenile delinquency within the whole criminal justice system to facilitate more aggressive and appropriate actions. A fundamental issue for the future, however, is: How much of the juvenile justice system should continue to belong in the criminal justice system at all?

There is a compelling need to look at alternatives to keep first offenders, particularly in crimes against property and self, such as drug addiction, in minimum contact with the system at all. The U.S. Senate observed:

> On any given day, there are close to 8,000 juveniles held in jail in the United States. It is estimated that 100,000 youths spend one or more days each year in adult jails or police lockups. In addition, the average daily population held in juvenile detention facilities is over 12,000, with close to 500,000 youths being placed annually in these facilities.[15]

These figures introduce a new dimension. The youth represented in the Senate study were placed into custody prior to any conviction and often for no crime except for the offense of running away. The problem here, extending into the future, is one of putting such youth into crimogenic situations by the experience of incarceration.

Part of the present situation is a matter of history. The American juvenile system is included within the criminal justice system, the juvenile court being pivotal. In contrast, the Scandanavian countries' method of treatment grew out of their poor laws. The treatment of juveniles became the responsibility of an administrative agency, a youth services bureau comprising people trained in counseling, psychology, social work, and the law. This action permitted juveniles to be screened in terms of needs, with only serious offenders moved up into court channels. The trend in America appears to be moving in this direction, although the number and seriousness of crimes committed by juveniles against persons have led to a hardening of public attitude in favor of treating youths as adults. In the future we will probably see an expansion of the youth service bureaus now growing in the nation, many of which are beyond the jurisdiction of the criminal justice

---

[15] Report of the Committee on the Judiciary, U.S. Senate, on S.1021, Juvenile Justice Amendments of 1977, 96th Cong., 1st Sess., May 14, 1977, p. 34.

system and are dealing with counseling, adjustment, schooling, and employment as a matter between the youth and the agency and perhaps the family.

Critics of the present system maintain that more juveniles get locked up than adjudicated and more detained than placed on probation in many jurisdictions. The system is thus structured more toward bringing juveniles conveniently into the criminal justice system than toward meeting the more urgent challenges of complete diversion from the system. The Massachusetts move to deinstitutionalize juvenile activities has been cited as a move toward eliminating part of this problem. In looking over the horizon, however, we see once again the need for broad urban policies that incorporate goals for communities to assume greater responsibilities in furnishing alternative means for handling juveniles within community service agencies. However, according to a 1974 survey, juvenile court judges view their major problems as centered on their inability to locate enough community agencies and resources to divert juveniles from the system.

The great debate over the *Gault* decision of the Supreme Court, which established procedural safeguards for juveniles during the adjudication stage and introduced the due process element of adult courts, involved the fear of converting the juvenile court into a criminal court. Later, the Supreme Court also expressed its growing concern by turning away from jury trials in juvenile courts. Thus the issue is one of ensuring fair treatment in adjudicatory proceedings in handling cases of juveniles charged with an act that would be considered a crime if committed by an adult. At the same time, there is an attempt to lessen the impact of the court proceedings on others by choosing some diversion route away from institutions and detention facilities. In the future we will see a further differentiation of disposition for those who commit serious crimes, particularly in an effort to derail the career of repeating juvenile offenders; those who are involved in less serious crimes; and those who are status offenders.

Any future decision making about court structure would perhaps need to take into account that raising the level of the juvenile court implies society's concern for its children. The consequent desire to further increase procedural safeguards might lead the court to protect the juvenile offender by more extensive legal procedures rather than the less-structured court acting in the parent relationship upon which the concept of the juvenile court was originally based. In the future the juvenile court may be utilized only as the ultimate decision maker when all community resources have been exhausted. In other words, the Scandinavian concept of the community-based, professionally manned youth service bureau might be expanded from its current status in the United States to handle much of the necessary assistance, help, and screening, thus easing police problems in handling minor offenders or status offenders, and in diverting juveniles from jails and detention centers. Such centers are particularly convenient when there are no other agency alternatives and no real detention standards.[16]

---

[16] The problem of detention is dealt with in "The Detention and Jailing of Juveniles," Hearings before the Subcommittee to Investigate Juvenile Delinquency of the Committee on the Judiciary, U.S. Senate, 93rd Cong., 1st Sess., September 10–12, 1973.

THE PERPLEXITIES OF PRISONS AND JAILS

Corrections is, and probably will continue to be, the most bewildering component of the criminal justice system. Law enforcement and court agencies have a variety of choices for dealing with offenders. The freedom to select among alternative courses of action (in deciding who to include or exclude in the system) can ease tensions within the agencies and often lessens some operational pressures. The correctional agencies have no such alternatives. They are receptacles whose flow-in is regulated only by capacity, by riot conditions, or perhaps by action of a judge who is suddenly appalled by overflows and breakdowns in elementary human facilities within the prison and shuts off further entry, thus precipitating legislative action. In the future, as states examine and implement correctional standards and goals and institutional accreditation becomes a reality, there is some likelihood that the often chaotic character of correctional institutions will change. Some logical predictions for the future of corrections have been made as follows:[17]

1. Fewer offenders will be confined for long periods in custodial institutions.
2. Institutional programs will place greater emphasis on preparation for release and less on escapes and economic production.
3. New institutions will be smaller.
4. There will be less of a sharp dichotomy between incarceration and parole or probation supervision.
5. Probation services will be expanded to include hostels, group homes, training programs, job placements, sheltered workshops, psychiatric services, and specialized counseling.
6. Postinstitutional supervision or parole will exhibit changes and come closer to probation.
7. The character, composition, and function of parole boards will change to include better people for other decision-making tasks. As a matter of fact, parole boards may disappear.
8. New forms of disposition from courts as substitutes for conventional sentencing will be developed (probably similar to the Youth Authority and Adult Authority in California or other treatment boards).
9. Community-based programs will make more and more use of related community services, both public and private.
10. More and more attention will be given to developing information systems, making use of computer technology to assist in decision-making tasks.
11. Empirical research methods will be employed to assess the effectiveness of programs.
12. Professional, competent assistants will be provided at all levels so the long-term needs of public protection will be better served.

We can expect that corrections will (1) stop building fortress prisons and take a look at the alternatives—smaller secure prisons for the hard core, smaller institutions for those for whom short incarceration is believed necessary, and

---

[17] Richard A. McGee, "What's Past Is Prologue," *The Future of Corrections: The Annals,* Vol. 381 (January 1969), pp. 9–10.

broader community residential programs; (2) look at treatment programs that work for offenders within the institution or facility as a major step toward reducing almost endless recidivism; (3) take positive steps to loosen the strains and stresses within prison by extending legal counsel facilities, recognizing constitutional rights, addressing grievances, extending outside communication privileges, providing safety guarantees and developing more definitive prerelease programs such as job counseling and placement, and equivalent unemployment compensation benefits for tiding over until employment is found;[18] and (4) decide more positively what minimum standards prisons must maintain to function properly within the criminal justice system.

It is in this latter area where the struggle in the future will be most intense. The issue takes many forms: Who shall go to prisons in the future and for what purpose? What shall prisons do with those sent? What must be the extent of the quest for real alternatives to incarceration? What community-based facilities can be expanded or developed, provided society is willing to bring more offender assistance closer to their urban homes? What must be correctional sciences' new contributions to the art of rehabilitation wherever it is designated to take place? What training and education must correctional staffs possess to make a realigned system work? To what ends must correctional science research be redirected to undergird positive change?

A powerful trend in the future will be to limit the purpose of prison to the imposition of punishment in relation to the criminal act. Prisoners will be swiftly and surely punished in relation to the intensity of the crime. They will know upon entrance when they will be released, subject to good behavior, and, at the beginning of entry, they will work out by mutual agreement with authorities the institutional program that is believed best to pursue during the period of incarceration. Such conditions of imprisonment would eventually eliminate parole. The alternative would perhaps be a continuation in prison as presently administered of those rehabilitation programs which research has proven will work. The greater emphasis will, however, be upon community-based rehabilitation and community assistance services. The latter movement could probably include a conversion of probation and parole services to one-stop community-operated assistance centers comparable to those operated by agencies such as the Veterans Administration.

If the smaller prisons of the future are to be related more toward the urban community—near inmates' homes, closer to a trained manpower pool for staffing, with job training programs definitely related to the home job market[19]—then the overall urban policy development discussed earlier in this chapter will become in-

---

[18] A Department of Labor study indicated that a financial aid program could result in a 27 percent reduction in the potential number of arrests for economically motivated crimes. Department of Labor, Employment and Training Administration, *Unlocking the Second Gate: The Role of Financial Assistance in Reducing Recidivism Among Ex-Prisoners* (Washington, D.C.: Department of Labor, 1977).

[19] Daniel Glaser, "The Prison of the Future," in George C. Kellinger and Paul F. Cromwell, Jr., ed., *Penology* (St. Paul, Minn.: West Publishing Co., 1973).

creasingly important. Community-based corrections, urban-related prisons, social services outside the correctional system as alternatives to probation and parole, as well as recidivism prevention programs—all will largely depend upon how those urban policies define the role of corrections within the community and indicate the resources necessary to effect this tremendous shift in locus for the major part of the corrections effort.

What is desired in the future is an end to jails as a camping ground for those who cannot make bail; those who are juveniles, such as runaways for whom there is no other available facility; those held without bond pending disposition; those who have committed petty victimless crimes; and those who have been sentenced—a startling heterogeneous group simply dumped in an unstructured holding detachment awaiting some decision by someone. Perhaps jails can be developed into entirely separate and exclusive compartments to contain (1) those held in pretrial detention; (2) those sent for classification and referral to a social service agency or unit that offers social, legal, education, job training, and medical services to those gathered in with specific problems; and (3) those who are already entered into a community, correctional program and are domiciled in the institution.[20] One organizational change in the future will involve making all jails a part of the unified state correctional system in order to ensure uniform standards of operation, as well as the continuing establishment of community resources offering viable alternatives to jail for those to whom bail is a problem and for those whose offenses are of victimless nature. This will require the formulation of clear policies about what resources outside the criminal justice system will be created and sustained to handle specific categories of people whose offenses do not merit, or require, system entrance.

THE PROPRIETY OF THE WAY THE LAW IS RULED

America lives in a society of law overkill. Some critics feel that the proliferation of laws defined as criminal reflects the true desires not of society as a whole but only of those who control social policy. While this is a debatable theoretical question, the federal government gave recognition to the problem by mandating a new codification of federal criminal law via the Federal Criminal Act of 1978. It is hoped that the states will follow through during the 1980s with similar actions. A better ordering of criminal statutes will in turn enable the establishment of uniform state sentencing practices. The centerpiece of the recent Federal Criminal Act includes guidelines for sentencing and the creation of a U.S. Sentencing Commission to establish sentencing policies and procedures and to measure sentencing and correctional practices in terms of how well they meet the purposes of sentencing. California became the first state to initiate its own sweeping changes in criminal

---

[20] Ronald Goldfarb, *Jails: The Ultimate Ghetto of the Criminal Justice System* (New York: Anchor Press/Doubleday, 1975); Benedict S. Alper, *Prisons Inside Out: Alternatives in Correctional Reform* (Cambridge, Mass.: Ballanger, 1974).

sentencing. The trend is now established to bring equity and fairness into sentencing power, thus eliminating its current disparities.

There has been equally severe pressure for the elimination of plea bargaining. Since 90 to 95 percent of all criminal convictions are by pleas of guilty, the practice of plea bargaining is more the rule than the casual practice. Given the loads in many courts and the current manpower demands against even these loads, we cannot expect the elimination of the process in the near future, despite the recommendations of the National Advisory Commission on Criminal Justice Standards and Goals, which called for an end to plea bargaining by 1978. Instead, the process will probably be refined and regularized to provide for full participation by defendants, counsel, prosecutor, and judge under more formal procedures. There are, however, earnest efforts within some large and small jurisdictions to move gradually toward elimination, which will continue in the next decade. Reform in court administration, changes in criminal law, opportunities for greater diversion upon the part of police and prosecutors, and a better distribution of court manpower will probably afford a greater opportunity to limit substantially the current practice or dispense with it in many jurisdictions.

The nationalization of the Bill of Rights during the 1960s, carrying with it substantial increases in due process and the reduction in police power, has greatly changed the state systems for handling offenders or would-be offenders over the past decade. Previous discussions in this book have already identified the extent of this revolution in making the Bill of Rights binding on the separate states. However, during the decade of the 1970s the trend of the Supreme Court has been to define these rights more narrowly and to permit a more flexible use. Police power, for example, has been upheld in blocking illegal aliens with or without a search warrant; searching of cars impounded for traffic regulations and use of evidence for unrelated charges; and by restraining a federal court on the issue of federalism from issuing orders to institute new procedures for handling complaints of police misconduct. Whether this trend will continue is often dependent upon the makeup of the Supreme Court itself and the issues it is willing to consider. However, it has been argued that the Supreme Court has set standards that are not strictly legal standards but rather public policy because the other two branches of government did not move to initiate rules and laws that would guarantee rights under due process of law.[21] Given the intense activity in establishing standards and goals, it can probably be expected that, in the future, the greater initiatives to recognize rights as well as criminal justice operational needs with respect to serious crime control will be taken by executives and legislatures to ensure a balanced system based on evenness and fairness. Such actions may then reduce the need for frequent court decisions affecting the operation of the criminal justice system.

---

[21] Paul L. Murphy, *The Constitution in Crisis Times: 1918–1969* (New York: Harper & Row, 1972), p. 466.

A FINAL WORD

We conclude somewhat as we began. The criminal justice system is an endlessly provocative and stimulating system, frustrating and bewildering, awesome and fearful, respected and scorned, authoritative and benevolent, filled with seemingly imponderable issues but enjoining and enticing a whole array of manpower to work on its fascinating and manifold problems and to carry forward its growing operational requirements.

APPLYING YOUR KNOWLEDGE: CORRECTIONS

Cases/Issues

CASE

The Westhaven Community Services Group received a five-year private grant to establish two service centers, one for adult offenders and one for juvenile delinquents, in a city of 750,000. The grant stipulated that the offender center should serve as a halfway house and the juvenile center afford an alternative to formal institutionalization of juveniles, providing them with food and shelter and the use of community facilities for training-schooling programs and other individual needs. It further required the director, Mary Stevens, to locate both facilities in areas within or at the fringes of the suburban areas and definitely not within blighted areas themselves. Director Stevens immediately surveyed possible areas and, anxious to move the project along, made arrangements to purchase two large older homes in fringe areas at different locations. Some realtors learned of the intended purchases and broke the news to the local press. Citizens in the areas affected protested the invasion of "undesirables." Director Stevens, when called upon by reporters, stated that she would move ahead with her plans.

When one of Mary Stevens' staff heard of her decision, he commented: "She is right, you must move fast, cut through all the red tape, and by a highly effective program prove to the opposition that being contiguous to a center is not a catastrophe." Do you agree? Why? If not, what is your procedure?

ISSUE

Rehabilitation programs for adult offenders under determinate sentences in correctional institutions should be voluntary, with the officials and the offender working out the agreement upon entry as to the kind of program to be pursued.

1. Do you favor a mutual agreement program between inmate and officials concerning the kind of training and/or rehabilitation program to be pursued on entry? Why?
2. What are your views about sentencing offenders to a correctional facility solely as punishment and not for the purposes of rehabilitation?

3. As a matter of policy, where do you believe rehabilitation efforts should take place?

Continuing CJS Project

If you will refer back to the concluding pages of the Law Enforcement and Courts parts of this text, you will find suggested approaches to an evaluation of the criminal justice system. Your analysis should now extend to Corrections as the concluding phase. Some principle guidelines are:

1. Where does corrections impact favorably on law enforcement and court activities?
2. Where does corrections impact negatively on other components of the system?
3. In what areas can corrections improve its own system performance?

The CJS Summary Evaluation Report

At the conclusion of your analysis of the Corrections portion of the system, gather together all three of your evaluations and prepare a substantial summary of your efforts to look at criminal justice as a *system*. Include the following:

1. Which component has the greatest impact on system effectiveness, positively or negatively? Why?
2. Considering all three components, what are the best examples for demonstrating how each is presently working well in its relationships with the others?
3. Where, for each, are the most glaring defects in their performance?
4. Prepare in summary form comments on those areas where you believe system effectiveness can be improved for one or all three of the components, together with your recommended actions for such improvement.

APPENDIX

The Constitution of the United States

PREAMBLE

We the people of the United States, in order to form a more perfect Union, establish justice, insure domestic tranquility, provide for the common defence, promote the general welfare, and secure the blessings of liberty to ourselves and our posterity, do ordain and establish this Constitution for the United States of America.

ARTICLE I

SECTION 1. All legislative powers herein granted shall be vested in a Congress of the United States, which shall consist of a Senate and House of Representatives.

SECTION 2. [1] The House of Representatives shall be composed of members chosen every second year by the people of the several States, and the electors in each State shall have the qualifications requisite for electors of the most numerous branch of the State legislature.

[2] No person shall be a representative who shall not have attained to the age of twenty-five years, and been seven years a citizen of the United States, and who shall not, when elected, be an inhabitant of that State in which he shall be chosen.

[3] [Representatives and direct taxes shall be apportioned among the several States which may be included within this Union, according to their respective numbers, which shall be determined by adding to the whole number of free persons, including those bound to service for a term of years, and excluding Indians not taxed, three-fifths of all other persons.] The actual enumeration shall be made within three years after the first meeting of the Congress of the United States, and within every subsequent term of ten years, in such manner as they shall by law direct. The number of representatives shall not exceed one for every thirty thousand, but each State shall have at least one representative; and until such enumeration shall be made, the State of New Hampshire shall be entitled to chuse three, Massachusetts eight, Rhode Island and Providence Plantations one, Connecticut five, New York six, New Jersey four, Pennsylvania eight, Delaware one, Maryland six, Virginia ten, North Carolina five, South Carolina five, and Georgia three.

Note.—The part of this clause relating to the mode of apportionment of Representatives was changed after the Civil War by Section 2 of the Fourteenth Amendment and as to taxes on incomes without apportionment, by the Sixteenth Amendment.

[4] When vacancies happen in the representation from any State, the executive authority thereof shall issue writs of election to fill such vacancies.

[5] The House of Representatives shall chuse their speaker and other officers; and shall have the sole power of impeachment.

SECTION 3. [1] [The Senate of the United States shall be composed of two senators from each State, chosen by the legislature thereof, for six years; and each senator shall have one vote.]

Note.—This provision has now been changed by the Seventeenth Amendment to the Constitution.

[2] Immediately after they shall be assembled in consequence of the first election, they shall be divided as equally as may be into three classes. The seats of the senators of the first class shall be vacated at the expiration of the second year, of the second class at the expiration of the fourth year, and of the third class at the expiration of the sixth year, so that one third may be chosen every second year; [and if vacancies happen by resignation, or otherwise, during the recess of the legislature of any State, the executive thereof may make temporary appointments until the next meeting of the legislature, which shall then fill such vacancies.]

Note.—That part of the above paragraph in brackets was changed by the Seventeenth Amendment.

[3] No person shall be a senator who shall not have attained to the age of thirty years, and been nine years a citizen of the United States, and who shall not, when elected, be an inhabitant of that State for which he shall be chosen.

[4] The Vice President of the United States shall be President of the Senate, but shall have no vote, unless they be equally divided.

[5] The Senate shall chuse their other officers, and also a president pro tempore, in the absence of the Vice President, or when he shall exercise the office of the President of the United States.

[6] The Senate shall have the sole power to try all impeachments. When sitting for that purpose, they shall be on oath or affirmation. When the President of the United States is tried, the chief justice shall

preside: and no person shall be convicted without the concurrence of two-thirds of the members present.

⁷ Judgment in cases of impeachment shall not extend further than to removal from office, and disqualification to hold and enjoy any office of honor, trust or profit under the United States: but the party convicted shall nevertheless be liable and subject to indictment, trial, judgment and punishment, according to law.

SECTION 4. ¹ The times, places and manner of holding elections for senators and representatives, shall be prescribed in each State by the legislature thereof; but the Congress may at any time by law make or alter such regulations, except as to the places of chusing senators.

² [The Congress shall assemble at least once in every year, and such meeting shall be on the first Monday in December, unless they shall by law appoint a different day.]

Note.—This provision of the Constitution has been superseded by the Twentieth Amendment.

SECTION 5. ¹ Each House shall be the judge of the elections, returns and qualifications of its own members, and a majority of each shall constitute a quorum to do business; but a smaller number may adjourn from day to day, and may be authorized to compel the attendance of absent members, in such manner, and under such penalties as each House may provide.

² Each House may determine the rules of its proceedings, punish its members for disorderly behaviour, and, with the concurrence of two-thirds, expel a member.

³ Each House shall keep a journal of its proceedings, and from time to time publish the same, excepting such parts as may in their judgment require secrecy; and the yeas and nays of the members of either House on any question shall, at the desire of one-fifth of those present, be entered on the journal.

⁴ Neither House, during the session of Congress, shall, without the consent of the other, adjourn for more than three days, nor to any other place than that in which the two Houses shall be sitting.

SECTION 6. ¹ The senators and representatives shall receive a compensation for their services, to be ascertained by law, and paid out of the Treasury of the United States. They shall in all cases, except treason, felony, and breach of the peace, be privileged from arrest during their attendance at the session of their respective Houses, and in going to and returning from the same; and for any speech or debate in either House, they shall not be questioned in any other place.

² No senator or representative shall, during the time for which he was elected, be appointed to any civil office under the authority of the United States, which shall have been created, or the emoluments whereof shall have been encreased during such time; and no person holding any office under the United States, shall be a member of either House during his continuance in office.

SECTION 7. ¹ All bills for raising revenue shall originate in the House of Representatives; but the Senate may propose or concur with amendments as on other bills.

² Every bill which shall have passed the House of Representatives and the Senate, shall, before it becomes a law, be presented to the President of the United States; if he approve he shall sign it, but if not he shall return it, with his objections to that House in which it shall have originated, who shall enter the objections at large on their journal, and proceed to reconsider it. If after such reconsideration two-thirds of that House shall agree to pass the bill, it shall be sent, together with the objections, to the other House, by which it shall likewise be reconsidered, and if approved by two-thirds of that House, it shall become a law. But in all such cases the votes of both Houses shall be determined by yeas and nays, and the names of the persons voting for and against the bill shall be entered on the journal of each House respectively. If any bill shall not be returned by the President within ten days (Sundays excepted) after it shall have been presented to him, the same shall be a law, in like manner as if he had signed it, unless the Congress by their adjournment prevent its return, in which case it shall not be a law.

³ Every order, resolution, or vote to which the concurrence of the Senate and House of Representatives may be necessary (except on a question of adjournment) shall be presented to the President of the United States; and before the same shall take effect, shall be approved by him, or being disapproved by him, shall be repassed by two-thirds of the Senate and House of Representatives, according to the rules and limitations prescribed in the case of a bill.

SECTION 8. The Congress shall have power ¹ To lay and collect taxes, duties, imposts, and excises, to pay the debts and provide for the common defence and general welfare of the United States; but all duties, imposts, and excises shall be uniform throughout the United States;

² To borrow money on the credit of the United States;

³ To regulate commerce with foreign nations, and among the several States, and with the Indian tribes;

⁴ To establish an uniform rule of naturalization, and uniform laws on the subject of bankruptcies throughout the United States;

⁵ To coin money, regulate the value thereof, and of foreign coin, and fix the standard of weights and measures;

⁶ To provide for the punishment of counterfeiting the securities and current coin of the United States;

⁷ To establish post offices and post roads;

⁸ To promote the progress of science and useful arts, by securing for limited times to authors and inventors the exclusive right to their respective writings and discoveries;

⁹ To constitute tribunals inferior to the Supreme Court;

¹⁰ To define and punish piracies and felonies committed on the high seas, and offenses against the law of nations;

¹¹ To declare war, grant letters of marque and reprisal, and make rules concerning captures on land and water;

¹² To raise and support armies, but no appropriation of money to that use shall be for a longer term than two years;

¹³ To provide and maintain a navy;

¹⁴ To make rules for the government and regulation of the land and naval forces;

¹⁵ To provide for calling forth the militia to execute the laws of the Union, suppress insurrections and repel invasions;

¹⁶ To provide for organizing, arming, and disciplining, the militia, and for governing such part of them as may be employed in the service of the United States, reserving to the States respectively, the appointment of the officers, and the authority of training the militia according to the discipline prescribed by Congress;

¹⁷ To exercise exclusive legislation in all cases whatsoever, over such district (not exceeding ten miles square) as may, by cession of particular States, and the acceptance of Congress, become the seat of the government of the United States, and to exercise like authority over all places purchased by the consent of the legislature of the State in which the same shall be, for the erection of forts, magazines, arsenals, dock-yards, and other needful buildings; —and

¹⁸ To make all laws which shall be necessary and proper for carrying into execution the foregoing powers, and all other powers vested by this Constitution in the government of the United States, or in any department or officer thereof.

SECTION 9. ¹ The migration or importation of such persons as any of the States now existing shall think proper to admit, shall not be prohibited by the Congress prior to the year one thousand eight hundred and eight, but a tax or duty may be imposed on such importation, not exceeding ten dollars for each person.

² The privilege of the writ of habeas corpus shall not be suspended, unless when in cases of rebellion or invasion the public safety may require it.

³ No bill of attainder or ex post facto law shall be passed.

⁴ [No capitation, or other direct, tax shall be laid, unless in proportion to the census or enumeration herein before directed to be taken.]

Note.—This provision was changed in 1913 by the Sixteenth Amendment to the Constitution.

⁵ No tax or duty shall be laid on articles exported from any State.

⁶ No preference shall be given by any regulation of commerce or revenue to the ports of one State over those of another: nor shall vessels bound to, or from, one State be obliged to enter, clear, or pay duties in another.

⁷ No money shall be drawn from the treasury, but in consequence of appropriations made by law; and a regular statement and account of the receipts and expenditures of all public money shall be published from time to time.

⁸ No title of nobility shall be granted by the United States: and no person holding any office of profit or trust under them, shall, without the consent of the Congress, accept of any present, emolument, office, or title, of any kind whatever, from any king, prince, or foreign State.

SECTION 10. ¹ No State shall enter into any treaty, alliance, or confederation; grant letters of marque and reprisal; coin money; emit bills of credit; make anything but gold and silver coin a tender in payment of debts; pass any bill of attainder, ex post facto law, or law impairing the obligation of contracts, or grant any title of nobility.

² No State shall, without the consent of the Congress, lay any imposts or duties on imports or exports, except what may be absolutely necessary for executing its inspection laws: and the net produce of all duties and imposts, laid by any State on imports or exports, shall be for the use of the Treasury of the

United States; and all such laws shall be subject to the revision and controul of the Congress.

³ No State shall, without the consent of the Congress, lay any duty of tonnage, keep troops, or ships of war in time of peace, enter into an agreement or compact with another State, or with a foreign power, or engage in war, unless actually invaded, or in such imminent danger as will not admit of delay.

ARTICLE II

SECTION 1. ¹The executive power shall be vested in a President of the United States of America. He shall hold his office during the term of four years, and together with the Vice President, chosen for the same term, be elected as follows:

² Each state shall appoint, in such manner as the legislature thereof may direct, a number of electors, equal to the whole number of senators and representatives to which the State may be entitled in the Congress: but no senator or representative, or person holding an office of trust or profit under the United States, shall be appointed an elector.

[The electors shall meet in their respective States, and vote by ballot for two persons, of whom one at least shall not be an inhabitant of the same State with themselves. And they shall make a list of all the persons voted for, and of the number of votes for each; which list they shall sign and certify, and transmit sealed to the seat of the government of the United States, directed to the president of the Senate. The president of the Senate shall, in the presence of the Senate and House of Representatives, open all the certificates, and the votes shall then be counted. The person having the greatest number of votes shall be the President, if such number be a majority of the whole number of electors appointed; and if there be more than one who have such majority, and have an equal number of votes, then the House of Representatives shall immediately chuse by ballot one of them for President; and if no person have a majority, then from the five highest on the list the said House shall in like manner chuse the President. But in chusing the President, the votes shall be taken by States, the representation from each State having one vote; a quorum for this purpose shall consist of a member or members from two-thirds of the States, and a majority of all the States shall be necessary to a choice. In every case, after the choice of the President, the person having the greatest number of votes of the electors shall be the Vice President. But if there should remain two or more who have equal votes, the Senate shall chuse from them by ballot the Vice President.]

Note.—The clause enclosed in brackets was superseded by the Twelfth Amendment.

³ The Congress may determine the time of chusing the electors, and the day on which they shall give their votes; which day shall be the same throughout the United States.

⁴ No person except a natural born citizen, or a citizen of the United States, at the time of the adoption of this Constitution, shall be eligible to the office of President; neither shall any person be eligible to that office who shall not have attained to the age of thirty-five years, and been fourteen years a resident within the United States.

⁵ In case of the removal of the President from office, or at his death, resignation, or inability to discharge the powers and duties of the said office, the same shall devolve on the Vice President, and the Congress may by law provide for the case of removal, death, resignation or inability, both of the President and Vice President, declaring what officer shall then act as President, and such officer shall act accordingly, until the disability be removed, or a President shall be elected.

⁶ The President shall, at stated times, receive for his services, a compensation which shall neither be encreased nor diminished during the period for which he shall have been elected, and he shall not receive within that period any other emolument from the United States, or any of them.

⁷ Before he enter on the execution of his office, he shall take the following oath or affirmation:—"I do solemnly swear (or affirm) that I will faithfully execute the office of President of the United States, and will to the best of my ability, preserve, protect and defend the Constitution of the United States."

SECTION 2. ¹The President shall be commander in chief of the army and navy of the United States, and of the militia of the several States, when called into the actual service of the United States; he may require the opinion, in writing, of the principal officer in each of the executive departments, upon any subject relating to the duties of their respective offices, and he shall have power to grant reprieves and pardons for offences against the United States, except in cases of impeachment.

² He shall have power, by and with the advice and consent of the Senate, to make treaties, provided two-thirds of the Senators present concur; and he shall nominate, and by and with the advice and consent of the Senate, shall appoint ambassadors, other public ministers and consuls, judges of the Supreme Court, and all other officers of the United States,

whose appointments are not herein otherwise provided for, and which shall be established by law: but the Congress may by law vest the appointment of such inferior officers, as they think proper, in the President alone, in the courts of law, or in the heads of departments.

³ The President shall have power to fill up all vacancies that may happen during the recess of the Senate, by granting commissions which shall expire at the end of their next session.

SECTION 3. He shall from time to time give to the Congress information of the state of the Union, and recommend to their consideration such measures as he shall judge necessary and expedient; he may, on extraordinary occasions, convene both Houses, or either of them, and in case of disagreement between them, with respect to the time of adjournment, he may adjourn them to such time as he shall think proper; he shall receive ambassadors and other public ministers; he shall take care that the laws be faithfully executed, and shall commission all the officers of the United States.

SECTION 4. The President, Vice President, and all civil officers of the United States, shall be removed from office on impeachment for, and conviction of, treason, bribery, or other high crimes and misdemeanors.

ARTICLE III

SECTION 1. The judicial power of the United States shall be vested in one Supreme Court, and in such inferior courts as the Congress may from time to time ordain and establish. The judges, both of the Supreme and inferior courts, shall hold their offices during good behaviour, and shall, at stated times, receive for their services, a compensation, which shall not be diminished during their continuance in office.

SECTION 2. ¹ The judicial power shall extend to all cases, in law and equity, arising under this Constitution, the laws of the United States, and treaties made, or which shall be made, under their authority;—to all cases affecting ambassadors, other public ministers and consuls;—to all cases of admiralty and maritime jurisdiction;—to controversies to which the United States shall be a party;—to controversies between two or more States; between a State and citizens of another State;—between citizens of different States;—between citizens of the same State claiming lands under grants of different States, and between a State, or the citizens thereof, and foreign States, citizens or subjects.

² In all cases affecting ambassadors, other public ministers and consuls, and those in which a State shall be a party, the Supreme Court shall have original jurisdiction. In all the other cases before mentioned, the Supreme Court shall have appellate jurisdiction, both as to law and fact, with such exceptions, and under such regulations as the Congress shall make.

³ The trial of all crimes, except in cases of impeachment, shall be by jury; and such trial shall be held in the State where the said crimes shall have been committed; but when not committed within any State, the trial shall be at such place or places as the Congress may by law have directed.

SECTION 3. ¹ Treason against the United States, shall consist only in levying war against them, or in adhering to their enemies, giving them aid and comfort. No person shall be convicted of treason unless on the testimony of two witnesses to the same overt act, or on confession in open court.

² The Congress shall have power to declare the punishment of treason, but no attainder of treason shall work corruption of blood, or forfeiture except during the life of the person attainted.

ARTICLE IV

SECTION 1. Full faith and credit shall be given in each State to the public acts, records, and judicial proceedings of every other State. And the Congress may by general laws prescribe the manner in which such acts, records and proceedings shall be proved, and the effect thereof.

SECTION 2. ¹ The citizens of each State shall be entitled to all privileges and immunities of citizens in the several States.

² A person charged in any State with treason, felony, or other crime, who shall flee from justice, and be found in another State, shall on demand of the executive authority of the State from which he fled, be delivered up, to be removed to the State having jurisdiction of the crime.

³ No person held to service or labour in one State, under the laws thereof, escaping into another, shall in consequence of any law or regulation therein, be discharged from such service or labour, but shall be delivered up on claim of the party to whom such service or labour may be due.

SECTION 3. ¹ New States may be admitted by the Congress into this Union; but no new State shall be formed or erected within the jurisdiction of any other State; nor any State be formed by the junction of two or more States, or parts of States, without the consent of the legislatures of the States concerned as well as of the Congress.

² The Congress shall have power to dispose of and make all needful rules and regulations respecting the territory or other property belonging to the United States; and nothing in this Constitution shall be so construed as to prejudice any claims of the United States, or of any particular States.

SECTION 4. The United States shall guarantee to every State in this Union a republican form of government, and shall protect each of them against invasion; and on application of the legislature, or of the executive (when the legislature cannot be convened) against domestic violence.

ARTICLE V

The Congress, whenever two-thirds of both Houses shall deem it necessary, shall propose amendments to this Constitution, or, on the application of the legislatures of two-thirds of the several States, shall call a convention for proposing amendments, which in either case, shall be valid to all intents and purposes, as part of this Constitution, when ratified by the legislatures of three-fourths of the several States, or by conventions in three-fourths thereof, as the one or the other mode of ratification may be proposed by the Congress; Provided that no amendment which may be made prior to the year one thousand eight hundred and eight shall in any manner affect the first and fourth clauses in the ninth section of the first article; and that no State, without its consent, shall be deprived of its equal suffrage in the Senate.

ARTICLE VI

¹ All debts contracted and engagements entered into, before the adoption of this Constitution, shall be as valid against the United States under this Constitution, as under the Confederation.

² This Constitution, and the laws of the United States which shall be made in pursuance thereof; and all treaties made, or which shall be made, under the authority of the United States, shall be the supreme law of the land; and the judges in every State shall be bound thereby, any thing in the Constitution or laws of any State to the contrary notwithstanding.

³ The senators and representatives before mentioned, and the members of the several State legislatures, and all executive and judicial officers, both of the United States and of the several States, shall be bound by oath or affirmation to support this Constitution; but no religious test shall ever be required as a qualification to any office or public trust under the United States.

ARTICLE VII

The ratification of the conventions of nine States shall be sufficient for the establishment of this Constitution between the States so ratifying the same.

Done in Convention by the unanimous consent of the States present the seventeenth day of September in the year of our Lord one thousand seven hundred and eighty-seven, and of the independence of the United States of America the twelfth. In Witness whereof we have hereunto subscribed our names.

_____[Names omitted]

Articles in addition to, and amendment of, the Constitution of the United States of America, proposed by Congress, and ratified by the legislatures of the several States pursuant to the fifth article of the original Constitution.

Amendments
First ten amendments passed by Congress
Sept. 25, 1789.
Ratified December 15, 1791.

AMENDMENT I

Congress shall make no law respecting an establishment of religion, or prohibiting the free exercise thereof; or abridging the freedom of speech, or of the press; or the right of the people peaceably to assemble, and to petition the government for a redress of grievances.

AMENDMENT II

A well regulated militia, being necessary to the security of a free State, the right of the people to keep and bear arms, shall not be infringed.

AMENDMENT III

No soldier shall, in time of peace be quartered in any house, without the consent of the owner, nor in time of war, but in a manner to be prescribed by law.

AMENDMENT IV

The right of the people to be secure in their persons, houses, papers, and effects, against unreasonable searches and seizures, shall not be violated, and no warrants shall issue, but upon probable cause, supported by oath or affirmation, and particularly describing the place to be searched, and the persons or things to be seized.

AMENDMENT V

No person shall be held to answer for a capital, or otherwise infamous crime, unless on a presentment or indictment of a grand jury, except in-cases arising in the land or naval forces, or in the militia, when in actual service in time of war or public danger; nor shall any person be subject for the same offence to be twice put in jeopardy of life or limb; nor shall be compelled in any criminal case to be a witness against himself; nor be deprived of life, liberty, or property, without due process of law; nor shall private property be taken for public use, without just compensation.

AMENDMENT VI

In all criminal prosecutions, the accused shall enjoy the right to a speedy and public trial, by an impartial jury of the State and district wherein the crime shall have been committed, which district shall have been previously ascertained by law, and to be informed of the nature and cause of the accusation; to be confronted with the witnesses against him; to have compulsory process for obtaining witnesses in his favor, and to have the assistance of counsel for his defence.

AMENDMENT VII

In suits at common law, where the value in controversy shall exceed twenty dollars, the right of trial by jury shall be preserved, and no fact tried by a jury shall be otherwise re-examined in any court of the United States, than according to the rules of the common law.

AMENDMENT VIII

Excessive bail shall not be required, nor excessive fines imposed, nor cruel and unusual punishments inflicted.

AMENDMENT IX

The enumeration in the Constitution, of certain rights, shall not be construed to deny or disparage others retained by the people.

AMENDMENT X

The powers not delegated to the United States by the Constitution, nor prohibited by it to the States, are reserved to the States respectively, or to the people.

AMENDMENT XI

The judicial power of the United States shall not be construed to extend to any suit in law or equity, commenced or prosecuted against one of the United States by citizens of another State, or by citizens or subjects of any foreign State.

RATIFIED JANUARY 8, 1798.

AMENDMENT XII

The electors shall meet in their respective States, and vote by ballot for President and Vice President, one of whom, at least, shall not be an inhabitant of the same State with themselves; they shall name in their ballots the person voted for as President, and in distinct ballots the person voted for as Vice President, and they shall make distinct lists of all persons voted for as President, and of all persons voted for as Vice President, and of the number of votes for each, which lists they shall sign and certify, and transmit sealed to the seat of the government of the United States, directed to the President of the Senate;—The President of the Senate shall, in presence of the Senate and House of Representatives, open all the certificates and the votes shall then be counted;—The person having the greatest number of votes for President, shall be the President, if such number be a majority of the whole number of electors appointed; and if no person have such majority, then from the persons having the highest numbers not exceeding three on the list of those voted for as President, the House of Representatives shall choose immediately, by ballot, the President. But in choosing the President, the votes shall be taken by States, the representation from each State having one vote; a quorum for this purpose shall consist of a member or members from two-thirds of the States, and a majority of all the States shall be necessary to a choice. And if the House of Representatives shall not choose a President whenever the right of choice shall devolve upon them, before the fourth day of March next following, then the Vice President shall act as President, as in the case of the death or other constitutional disability of the President. The person having the greatest number of votes as Vice President shall be the Vice President, if such number be a majority of the whole number of electors appointed, and if no person have a majority, then from the two highest numbers on the list, the Senate shall choose the Vice President; a quorum for the purpose shall consist of two-thirds of the whole number of Senators, and a majority of the whole number shall be necessary to a choice. But no person constitutionally ineligible to the office of President shall be eligible to that of Vice President of the United States.

RATIFIED SEPTEMBER 25, 1804.

AMENDMENT XIII

SECTION 1. Neither slavery nor involuntary servitude, except as a punishment for crime whereof the party shall have been duly convicted, shall exist within the United States, or any place subject to their jurisdiction.

SECTION 2. Congress shall have power to enforce this article by appropriate legislation.

RATIFIED DECEMBER 18, 1865.

AMENDMENT XIV

SECTION 1. All persons born or naturalized in the United States, and subject to the jurisdiction thereof, are citizens of the United States and of the State wherein they reside. No State shall make or enforce any law which shall abridge the privileges or immunities of citizens of the United States; nor shall any State deprive any person of life, liberty, or property, without due process of law; nor deny to any person within its jurisdiction the equal protection of the laws.

SECTION 2. Representatives shall be apportioned among the several States according to their respective numbers, counting the whole number of persons in each State, excluding Indians not taxed. But when the right to vote at any election for the choice of electors for President and Vice President of the United States, representatives in Congress, the executive and judicial officers of a State, or the members of the legislature thereof, is denied to any of the male inhabitants of such State, being twenty-one years of age, and citizens of the United States, or in any way abridged, except for participation in rebellion, or other crimes, the basis of representation therein shall be reduced in the proportion which the number of such male citizens shall bear to the whole number of male citizens twenty-one years of age in such State.

SECTION 3. No person shall be a senator or representative in Congress, or elector of President and Vice President, or hold any office, civil or military, under the United States, or under any State, who, having previously taken an oath, as a member of Congress, or as an officer of the United States, or as a member of any State legislature, or as an executive or judicial officer of any State, to support the Constitution of the United States, shall have engaged in insurrection or rebellion against the same, or given aid or comfort to the enemies thereof. But Congress may, by a vote of two-thirds of each House, remove such disability.

SECTION 4. The validity of the public debt of the United States, authorized by law, including debts incurred for payment of pensions and bounties for services in suppressing insurrection or rebellion, shall not be questioned. But neither the United States nor any State shall assume or pay any debt or obligation incurred in aid of insurrection or rebellion against the United States, or any claim for the loss or emancipation of any slave; but all such debts, obligations, and claims shall be held illegal and void.

SECTION 5. The Congress shall have power to enforce by appropriate legislation, the provisions of this article.

RATIFIED JULY 28, 1868.

AMENDMENT XV

SECTION 1. The right of citizens of the United States to vote shall not be denied or abridged by the United States or by any State on account of race, color, or previous condition of servitude.

SECTION 2. The Congress shall have power to enforce this article by appropriate legislation.

RATIFIED MARCH 30, 1870.

AMENDMENT XVI

The Congress shall have power to lay and collect taxes on incomes, from whatever source derived, without apportionment among the several States, and without regard to any census or enumeration.

RATIFIED FEBRUARY 25, 1913.

AMENDMENT XVII

The Senate of the United States shall be composed of two senators from each state, elected by the people thereof, for six years; and each senator shall have one vote. The electors in each State shall have the qualifications requisite for electors of the most numerous branch of the State legislatures.

When vacancies happen in the representation of any State in the Senate, the executive authority of such State shall issue writs of election to fill such vacancies: Provided, That the legislature of any State may empower the executive thereof to make temporary appointments until the people fill the vacancies by election as the legislature may direct.

This amendment shall not be so construed as to affect the election or term of any senator chosen before it becomes valid as part of the Constitution.

RATIFIED MAY 31, 1913.

AMENDMENT XVIII

SECTION 1. [After one year from the ratification of this article, the manufacture, sale, or transportation of intoxicating liquors within, the importation thereof into, or the exportation thereof from the United States and all territories subject to the jurisdiction thereof for beverage purposes is hereby prohibited.

SECTION 2. The Congress and the several States shall have concurrent power to enforce this article by appropriate legislation.

SECTION 3. This article shall be inoperative unless it shall have been ratified as an amendment to the Constitution by the legislatures of the several States, as provided in the Constitution, within seven years from the date of the submission hereof to the States by Congress.]

Note.—The Twenty-first Amendment to the Constitution repealed the Eighteenth Amendment.

RATIFIED JANUARY 29, 1919.

AMENDMENT XIX

The right of citizens of the United States to vote shall not be denied or abridged by the United States or by any State on account of sex.

Congress shall have power to enforce this article by appropriate legislation.

RATIFIED AUGUST 26, 1920.

AMENDMENT XX

SECTION 1. The terms of the President and Vice President shall end at noon on the 20th day of January, and the terms of Senators and Representatives at noon on the 3d day of January, of the years in which such terms would have ended if this article had not been ratified; and the terms of their successors shall then begin.

SECTION 2. The Congress shall assemble at least once in every year, and such meeting shall begin at noon on the 3d day of January, unless they shall by law appoint a different day.

SECTION 3. If, at the time fixed for the beginning of the term of the President, the President elect shall have died, the Vice President elect shall become President. If a President shall not have been chosen before the time fixed for the beginning of his term, or if the President elect shall have failed to qualify, then the Vice President elect shall act as President until a President shall have qualified; and the Congress may by law provide for the case wherein neither a President elect nor a Vice President elect shall have qualified, declaring who shall then act as President, or the manner in which one who is to act shall be selected, and such person shall act accordingly until a President or Vice President shall have qualified.

SECTION 4. The Congress may by law provide for the case of the death of any of the persons from whom the House of Representatives may choose a President whenever the right of choice shall have devolved upon them, and for the case of the death of any of the persons from whom the Senate may choose a Vice President whenever the right of choice shall have devolved upon them.

SECTION 5. Sections 1 and 2 shall take effect on the 15th day of October following the ratification of this article.

SECTION 6. This article shall be inoperative unless it shall have been ratified as an amendment to the Constitution by the legislatures of three-fourths of the several States within seven years from the date of its submission.

RATIFIED JANUARY 23, 1933.

AMENDMENT XXI

SECTION 1. The eighteenth article of amendment to the Constitution of the United States is hereby repealed.

SECTION 2. The transportation or importation into any State, Territory, or possession of the United States for delivery or use therein of intoxicating liquors in violation of the laws thereof, is hereby prohibited.

SECTION 3. This article shall be inoperative unless it shall have been ratified as an amendment to the Constitution by conventions in the several States, as provided in the Constitution, within seven years from the date of the submission thereof to the States by the Congress.

RATIFIED DECEMBER 15, 1933.

AMENDMENT XXII

SECTION 1. No person shall be elected to the office of the President more than twice, and no person who has held the office of President, or acted as President, for more than two years of a term to which some other person was elected President shall be elected to the office of the President more than once. But this Article shall not apply to any person holding the office of President when this Article was proposed by the Congress, and shall not prevent any person who may be holding the office of President, or acting as President, during the term within which this Article becomes operative, from holding the office of President or acting as President during the remainder of such term.

SECTION 2. This article shall be inoperative unless it shall have been ratified as an amendment to the Constitution by the legislatures of three-fourths of the several States within seven years from the date of its submission to the States by the Congress.

RATIFIED FEBRUARY 26, 1951.

AMENDMENT XXIII

SECTION 1. The District constituting the seat of Government of the United States shall appoint in such manner as the Congress may direct:

A number of electors of President and Vice President equal to the whole number of Senators and Representatives in Congress to which the District would be entitled if it were a State, but in no event more than the least populous State; they shall be in addition to those appointed by the States, but they shall be considered, for the purposes of the election of President and Vice President, to be electors appointed by a State; and they shall meet in the District and perform such duties as provided by the twelfth article of amendment.

SECTION 2. The Congress shall have power to enforce this article by appropriate legislation.

RATIFIED APRIL 3, 1961.

AMENDMENT XXIV

SECTION 1. The right of citizens of the United States to vote in any primary or other election for President or Vice President, for electors for President or Vice President, or for Senator or Representative in Congress, shall not be denied or abridged by the United States or any State by reason of failure to pay any poll tax or other tax.

SECTION 2. The Congress shall have power to enforce this article by appropriate legislation.

RATIFIED FEBRUARY 4, 1964.

AMENDMENT XXV

SECTION 1. In case of the removal of the President from office or of his death or resignation, the Vice President shall become President.

SECTION 2. Whenever there is a vacancy in the office of the Vice President, the President shall nominate a Vice President who shall take office upon confirmation by a majority vote of both Houses of Congress.

SECTION 3. Whenever the President transmits to the President pro tempore of the Senate and the Speaker of the House of Representatives his written declaration that he is unable to discharge the powers and duties of his office, and until he transmits to them a written declaration to the contrary, such powers and duties shall be discharged by the Vice President as Acting President.

SECTION 4. Whenever the Vice President and a majority of either the principal officers of the executive departments or of such other body as Congress may by law provide, transmit to the President pro tempore of the Senate and the Speaker of the House of Representatives their written declaration that the President is unable to discharge the powers and duties of his office, the Vice President shall immediately assume the powers and duties of the office as Acting President.

Thereafter, when the President transmits to the President pro tempore of the Senate and the Speaker of the House of Representatives his written declaration that no inability exists, he shall resume the powers and duties of his office unless the Vice President and a majority of either the principal officers of the executive department or of such other body as Congress may by law provide, transmit within four days to the President pro tempore of the Senate and the Speaker of the House of Representatives their written declaration that the President is unable to discharge the powers and duties of his office. Thereupon Congress shall decide the issue, assembling within forty-eight hours for that purpose if not in session. If the Congress, within twenty-one days after receipt of the latter written declaration, or, if Congress is not in session, within twenty-one days after Congress is required to assemble, determines by two-thirds vote of both Houses that the President is unable to discharge the powers and duties of his office, the Vice President shall continue to discharge the same as Acting President; otherwise, the President shall resume the powers and duties of his office.

RATIFIED FEBRUARY 10, 1967.

AMENDMENT XXVI

SECTION 1. The right of citizens of the United States, who are eighteen years of age or older, to vote shall not be denied or abridged by the United States or by any State on account of age.

SECTION 2. The Congress shall have power to enforce this article by appropriate legislation.

RATIFIED JULY 1, 1971.

Glossary of Frequently Used Terms in the Criminal Justice System

A

Adjudication (criminal): the judicial decision terminating a proceeding by a judgment of conviction (guilt) or acquittal (innocence), or a dismissal of the case.

Adjudication (juvenile): the juvenile court decision terminating an adjudicatory hearing, that the juvenile is either a delinquent, status offender, or dependent, or that the allegations in the petition are not sustained.

Aftercare: the supervision of youth released from training schools.

Appeal: a request by either the defense or the prosecution that a case be removed from a lower court to a higher court in order for a completed trial to be reviewed by the higher court.

Arraignment: the appearance of a person before a court in order that the court may inform him of the accusation against him (formal indictment or information) and enter his plea.

Arrest: taking a person into custody by authority of law, for the purpose of charging him with a criminal offense or for the purpose of initiating juvenile proceedings, terminating with the recording of a specific offense.

Assigned counsel: an attorney, not regularly employed by a government agency, assigned by the court to represent a particular person in a particular criminal proceeding.

Attorney, lawyer, counsel: a person trained in

A substantial portion of this glossary is extracted from *Dictionary of Criminal Justice Data Terminology* (Washington, D.C.: U.S. Government Printing Office, 1976) for the Law Enforcement Assistance Administration. The purpose of this directory is to standardize terminology for the criminal justice system. This glossary attempts to further this effort.

the law, admitted to practice before the bar of a given jurisdiction, and authorized to advise, represent, and act for other persons in legal proceedings.

Auburn System: the prison system established in Auburn, New York, in 1815, providing individual confinement at night, group work during the day in silence, and harsh discipline.

B

Backlog: the number of pending cases which exceed the capacity of the court, in that they cannot be acted upon because the court is occupied in acting upon other cases.

Bail: *see* Release on bail.

Booking: a police administrative action officially recording an arrest and identifying the person, the place, the time, the arresting authority, and the reason for the arrest.

C

Capital punishment: providing the death penalty for serious offenses.

Case: at the level of police or prosecutorial investigation, a set of circumstances under investigation involving one or more persons; at subsequent steps in criminal proceedings, a charging document alleging the commission of one or more crimes, or a single defendant; in juvenile or correctional proceedings, a person who is the object of agency action.

Case (court): a single charging document under the jurisdiction of a court; or a single defendant.

Case law: law created by court decisions made on previous cases (e.g., Supreme Court decisions). Differs from statutory law, which is law created by duly designated lawmaking bodies (e.g., the Congress or state legislatures).

Caseload (corrections): the total number of clients registered with a correctional agency or agent during a specified time period, often divided into active and inactive, or supervised and unsupervised, thus distinguishing between clients with whom the agency or agent maintains contact and those with whom it does not.

Caseload (court): the total number of cases filed in a given court or before a given judicial officer during a given period of time.

CCH: computerized criminal history; a criminal history or record of information concerning an identified offender or alleged offender contained in an automated file.

Charge: a formal allegation that a specific person has committed a specific offense.

Charging document: a formal written accusation, filed in a court, alleging that a specified person has committed a specific offense.

Citation (to appear): a written order issued by a law enforcement officer directing an alleged offender to appear in a specific court at a specified time in order to answer a criminal charge.

Classical School: the school of criminology that focuses attention on the crime to provide an adequate and appropriate sentence for punishment.

Classification: an organized procedure to separate offenders by sex, age, criminal history, and other factors, so as to facilitate better use of available programs in a corrective facility.

Close custody (of prisoners): a security status that means that the person is locked inside the walls and may work in groups under supervision inside.

Commitment: the action of a judicial officer ordering that an adjudicated and sentenced adult, or adjudicated delinquent or status offender who has been the subject of a juvenile court disposition hearing, be admitted into a correctional facility.

Community-based corrections: the mobilization of community resources to assist offenders in reintegrating back into society commensurate with the public safety.

Community facility: a correctional facility from which residents are regularly permitted to depart, unaccompanied by any official, for the purpose of daily use of community resources such as schools or treatment programs, and seeking or holding employment, and then return at night or weekends.

Community relations: the development and maintenance of supportive relations between the major components of the criminal justice system and the citizens they serve.

Complaint: a formal written accusation made by any person, often a prosecutor, and filed in a court, alleging that a specified person has committed a specific offense.

Conviction: a judgment of a court, based either on the verdict of a jury or a judicial officer or on the guilty plea of the defendant, that the defendant is guilty of the offense for which the defendant has been tried.

Correctional facility: a building or area enclosing a set of buildings operated by a government agency for the custody and/or treatment of adjudicated and committed persons, or persons subject to criminal or juvenile justice proceedings.

Correctional institution: a generic name for those long-term adult confinement facilities often called "prisons," "federal or state correctional facilities," or "penitentiaries," and juvenile confinement facilities called "training schools," "reformatories," "boys' ranches," and the like.

Corrections: a generic term which includes all government agencies, facilities, programs, procedures, personnel, and techniques concerned with the investigation, intake screening, custody, confinement, supervision, or treatment of alleged or adjudicated adult offenders, delinquents, or status offenders.

Court: an agency of the judicial branch of government which has the authority to decide upon controversies in law and disputed matters of fact brought before it.

Court of appellate jurisdiction: a court which does not try criminal cases, but which hears appeals.

Court of general jurisdiction: of criminal courts, a court which has jurisdiction to try all criminal offenses, including all felonies, and which may or may not hear appeals.

Court of limited jurisdiction: of criminal courts, a court of which the trial jurisdiction either includes no felonies or is limited to less than all felonies and which may or may not hear appeals.

Crime, criminal offense: an act committed or omitted in violation of a law forbidding or commanding it for which an adult can be punished, upon conviction, by incarceration and other penalties or a corporation penalized, or for which a juvenile can be brought under the jurisdiction of a juvenile court and adjudicated a delinquent or transferred to adult court.

Crime prevention: a specialized assignment for police officers responsible for providing the public with information and technical assistance designed to lessen their vulnerability to criminal acts.

Crime-specific programs: the allocation of a select group of police officers to accomplish a specified mission, e.g., reduce robberies in a given area.

Criminal investigation: a specialized assignment for police officers responsible for the identification, location, and apprehension of major offenders against persons or property.

Criminalistics: the application of scientific technology to assist in the solution of crimes (e.g., biology, chemistry, anthropology, physics).

Criminal justice agency: any government agency whose principal functions or activities consist of the prevention, detection, and investigation of crime; the apprehension, detention, and prosecution of alleged offenders; the confinement or official correctional supervision of accused or convicted persons; or the planning or administrative or technical support of the above functions.

D

Defendant: a person against whom a criminal proceeding is pending.

Defense attorney: an attorney who represents the defendant in a legal proceeding.

Defensible space: a crime prevention concept

that concentrates on the identification and implementation of physical and technical barriers to criminal acts, e.g., gatehouse and security guard in an apartment complex which is fenced.

Delinquent: a juvenile who has been adjudicated by a judicial officer of a juvenile court as having committed a delinquent act, which is an act for which an adult could be prosecuted in a criminal court.

Detention facility: a generic name for those facilities which hold adults or juveniles in confinement, and in some instances postadjudicated juveniles, including facilities called "jails," "county farms," "work camps," "road camps," "detention centers," "shelters," "juvenile halls," and the like.

Deterrence: an indication of impending sure and swift punishment as a means of deflecting individuals from committing an initial or repeated criminal offense.

Disposition, court: the final judicial decision which terminates a criminal proceeding by a judgment of acquittal or dismissal, or which states the specific sentence in the case of a conviction.

Diversion: the official halting or suspension, at any legally prescribed processing point, of formal criminal or juvenile justice proceedings against an alleged offender, and referral of that person to a treatment or care program administered by a nonjustice agency, or a private agency, or no referral.

Docket: a record or log of proceedings in a judicial case.

Drug abuse (treatment) center: a specialized health care center designed to provide comprehensive drug therapy.

Drug Enforcement Administration (DEA): a unit established in 1973 within the U.S. Department of the Treasury which operates both nationally and internationally to enforce the laws pertaining to the traffic and use of dangerous drugs.

Due process: a term used in the Fifth and Fourteenth Amendments to the Constitution of the United States and the Bill of Rights and which is part of the Constitution in nearly every state of the Union. In its strictest meaning, due process dictates that regular procedure or fairness must be followed before one can be convicted of a crime or punished in any way.

E

En banc: the process by which a parole board hears an inmate as an entire body, or majority of the board, and a parole decision can be made immediately, rather than waiting for executive session after a one-man interview.

Ex-offender groups: organizations of former offenders for the purpose of self-help, direct assistance to other ex-offenders in the form of finding jobs or other assistance; sometimes providing suggestions for penal reform.

Expiration of sentence: release from prison at the expiration of sentence without parole. No supervision required.

Expungement: a procedure by which first offenders who have maintained a subsequent good behavior record for several years after serving a sentence can go back to court and have their sentence removed from the record.

F

Felony: a criminal offense punishable by death, or by incarceration in a state or federal confinement facility for a period of which the lower limit is prescribed by statute in a given jurisdiction, typically one year or more.

Flat sentence: a sentence that is definite and does not have a minimum and maximum. The modern concept of flat sentencing contains provisions for good time to be earned that may reduce the sentence, but it remains a flat sentence without parole.

Forensic pathology: the study of tissues of the body and their impact on legal cases.

Furlough: a process permitting an offender to leave the prison or other facility for home visits, generally eight hours to forty-eight hours in length.

G

Group home: a nonconfining residential facility for adjudicated adults or juveniles, or those subject to criminal or juvenile proceedings, intended to reproduce as closely as possible the circumstances of family life, and at minimum providing access to community activities and resources.

H

Halfway house: a nonconfining residential facility for adjudicated adults or juveniles, or those subject to criminal or juvenile proceedings, intended to provide an alternative to confinement for persons not suitable for probation, or needing a period of gradual readjustment to the community after confinement.

Hearing: a proceeding in which arguments, witnesses, or evidence are heard by a judicial officer or administrative body.

Homicide: the killing of one human being by another human being, whether lawful or unlawful.

I

Incarceration: imprisonment; confinement in a jail or penitentiary.

Indeterminate sentence: a sentence given by the courts that contains a maximum term and a minimum term, leaving time for parole supervision.

Index Crimes: those serious crimes most constantly reported, including homicide, forcible rape, robbery, aggravated assault, burglary, larceny, and motor vehicle theft, in the FBI Uniform Crime Report.

Indictment: a formal written accusation made by a grand jury and filed in a court, alleging that a specified person has committed a specific offense.

Indigent: one who is needy and poor, or one who has not sufficient property or money to furnish him a living or to pay for legal representation.

Information: a formal written accusation made by a prosecutor and filed in a court, alleging that a specified person has committed a specific offense.

Inmate code: a self-protective life style in which inmates do not cooperate with administrative staff, do not "squeal" on fellow inmates, and generally identify with the inmate body.

Institutional parole officer (IPO): a person who works for a parole board but is housed in an office in the institution for the purpose of assisting in prerelease programs and other liaison between the institution and the parole board.

Intake: the process during which a juvenile referral is received and a decision is made by an intake unit either to file a petition in juvenile court, to release the juvenile, to place him under supervision, or to refer him elsewhere.

Investigation: the search by police for evidence and/or suspected offenders, witnesses, and victims that in turn will disclose the necessary facts in a criminal matter.

J

Jail: a confinement facility usually administered by a local law enforcement agency, intended for adults but sometimes also containing juveniles, which holds persons detained (normally for more than forty-eight hours) pending adjudication, and/or persons committed after adjudication for sentences of a year or less.

Judge: a judicial officer who has been elected or appointed to preside over a court of law, whose position has been created by statute or by constitution, and whose decisions in criminal and juvenile cases may only be reviewed by a judge of a higher court and may not be reviewed de novo.

Jurisdiction: the power of a court to render a valid judgment; usually has application to the person (who must be before the court), the subject matter (within the power of the court to decide), and the territory (the geographical area from which the court may hear cases).

Jury (grand): a body of persons (generally one to twenty-one) who have been selected and sworn to investigate criminal activity and the conduct of public officials and to hear the evidence against an accused person to determine whether there is sufficient evidence to bring that person to trial.

Jury (trial), jury, petit jury: a statutorily defined number of persons selected according to law, sworn to determine certain matters of fact in a criminal action and to render a verdict of guilty or not guilty.

Juvenile: a person subject to juvenile court proceedings because a statutorily defined event was alleged to have occurred while his age was below the statutorily specified limit of original jurisdiction of a juvenile court.

Juvenile court: a special court which has original jurisdiction over persons statutorily defined as juveniles and alleged to be delinquents, status offenders, or dependents, with variations between jurisdictions between ages twelve and eighteen and in some cases to age twenty-one.

Juvenile justice agency: a government agency whose functions are the investigation, supervision, adjudication, and care or confinement of juveniles whose conduct or condition has brought or could bring them within the jurisdiction of a juvenile court.

L

Law enforcement agency: a federal, state, or local criminal justice agency of which the principal functions are the prevention, detection, investigation of crime, and the apprehension of alleged offenders.

Law Enforcement Assistance Administration (LEAA): a unit established within the U.S. Department of Justice in 1968 to provide grants, policy, guidance, and technical expertise for states and local government in police services, courts, corrections, and juvenile delinquency.

Lockup: a local detention facility which can hold persons for less than forty-eight hours, generally used to hold persons for interrogations.

M

Management: a dynamic process intended to rationally direct the organization in line with effectively achieving its goal(s).

Management by objectives (MBO): a management style that is based on expressed and specific objectives to be attained within a given time-frame by a certain work group.

Mandatory conditional release: releasing a prisoner with only a few months left on his maximum sentence, not on parole, but by supervision of parole officers in order to assist in his reintegration into society.

Maximum security (institution): a facility with strong perimeter security with guard towers, high walls or other strong security, rigid control in the inside, frequent counts, and generally secure regimentation and control.

Maximum security (prisoner): a person locked in an individual cell who is not permitted out unless in company with an officer, generally with hand restraint equipment.

Medium custody (institution): a facility with secure perimeter, usually with fences and towers, but relatively relaxed inside.

Medium security (prisoner): a person who can lock (live) inside the walls and work in groups under supervision outside the walls or may work alone inside the walls as an "inside trusty."

Minimum security (institution): a facility with little perimeter security which may or may not have a fence, relaxed inside, and probably counts at meal times and bed check.

Minimum security (prisoner): a person who can work alone without supervision, including work inside or outside the walls of a minimum security facility.

Misdemeanor: an offense (e.g., drunkenness, gambling, petty larceny) usually punishable by incarceration in a local confinement facility, for a period of which the upper limit is prescribed by statute in a given jurisdiction, typically limited to a year or less.

Mistake of fact: a mistake not caused by the neglect of a legal duty on the part of the person making the mistake but consisting of an unconscious absence of knowledge about the fact.

Moot case: a case in which the issue originally raised is no longer of controversy but has been settled by other means prior to reaching the court determination stage.

N

Narcotics and drug abuse: a specialized assignment for police officers responsible for the identification, location, and apprehension of offenders who either use or traffic in illegal and dangerous drugs.

Nolo contendere: a defendant's formal answer in court to the charges in a complaint, information, or indictment, in which he states that he does not contest the charges, and which, while not an admission of guilt, subjects him to the same legal consequences as a plea of guilty.

O

Organization: a collection of people who are linked to each other by a set of authoritative relationships.

P

Parens patriae: a principle that holds that the state is responsible for the welfare of its children and that is one of the bases of the constitutionality of the juvenile court.

Parole: the status of an offender conditionally released from a confinement facility prior to the expiration of his sentence, and placed under the supervision of a parole agency.

Parole agency: a correctional agency whose principal function is the supervision of adults or juveniles placed on parole.

Parole authority: a person or a correctional agency which has the authority to release on parole adults or juveniles committed to confinement facilities, to revoke parole, and to discharge from parole.

Participative management (PM): a management style that fosters the involvement of the employees in the various decisions that affect them.

Penitentiary: synonymous with the prison; originally developed by the Quakers in 1790 as a place of penitence.

Pennsylvania System: a system of imprisonment characterized by solitary confinement to avoid spreading moral contamination, productive work to develop good work habits, religious counseling, and meditation.

Perjury: a crime of deliberately swearing falsely or of asserting under oath, as true, that which the swearer does not know to be true.

Plea: a defendant's formal answer in court to the charges brought against him in a complaint, information, or indictment.

Plea bargaining: the exchange of prosecutorial and/or judicial concessions, commonly a lesser charge, the dismissal of other pending charges, a recommendation by the prosecutor for a reduced sentence, or a combination thereof, in return for a plea of guilty.

Positivistic School: the school of criminology that focuses attention on the individual and varies sentences, punishment, and/or treatment in accordance with the needs of the individual offender.

Postconviction petitions: legal action taken by attorneys after sentence is rendered in a criminal case to secure a new trial or to pursue the appeal process on behalf of the defendant or the state in appropriate circumstances.

Precedents: previous decisions of courts, which are a source of law in all courts; the following of earlier case decisions on similar issues of fact and law.

Predisposition report: the document resulting from an investigation undertaken by a probation agency or other designated authority, which has been requested by a juvenile court, into the past behavior, family background, and personality of a juvenile who has been adjudicated a delinquent, a status offender, or a dependent, in order to assist the court in determining the most appropriate disposition.

Presentence investigation report (PSI): the document resulting from an investigation undertaken by a probation agency or other designated authority, at the request of a criminal court, into the past behavior, family circumstances, and personality of an adult who has been convicted of a crime, in order to assist the court in determining the most appropriate sentence. May also be used by prison personnel, parole agencies, and others in contact with the offender in the correctional system revocation of parole.

Presentment: a formal statement made by a grand jury of some condition of affairs which has been brought to their notice and which, in their opinion, requires corrective action within the community.

Pretrial intervention: removing cases from the criminal justice system by informal handling, such as deferred prosecution, probation without adjudication, and other ways in which cases are handled informally without going through courts.

Prison: a confinement facility having custodial authority over adults sentenced to confinement for more than a year.

Prisonization: the acceptance of customs, folkways, attitudes, and the general customs of the prison.

Private policing: individuals employed by nongovernmental organizations to perform police functions in a prescribed area but with delimited powers.

Probation: the conditional freedom granted by a judicial officer to an alleged offender, or adjudicated adult or juvenile, as long as the person meets certain conditions of behavior.

Probation agency: a correctional agency of which the principal functions are juvenile intake, the supervision of adults and juveniles placed on probation status, and the investigation of adults or juveniles for the purpose of preparing presentence or predisposition reports to assist the court in determining the proper sentence or juvenile court disposition.

Probation officer: an employee of a probation agency whose primary duties include one or more of the probation agency functions.

Probation subsidy: a sum of money paid by the state to counties for every individual that could have been sent to state institutions prior to the subsidy plan, but were instead kept on probation in the community.

Procedural law: the rules and legal methods by which substantive law is made effective within the machinery of the process of justice. Substantive law defines the manner of conducting oneself. Procedural law prescribes how behavior which is unlawful is to be dealt with.

Prosecutor: an attorney employed by a government agency whose official duty is to initiate and maintain criminal proceedings on behalf of the government against persons accused of committing criminal offenses.

Public defender: an attorney employed by a government agency whose official duty is to represent defendants unable to hire private counsel.

R

Recidivism: the act of relapsing into former criminal behavior, causing a return to a correctional facility after processing through the criminal justice system.

Referral to intake: in juvenile proceedings, a request by the police, parents, or other agency or person, that a juvenile intake unit take appropriate action concerning a juvenile alleged to have committed a delinquent act, status offense, or to be dependent.

Reformatory: generally a smaller correctional institution for younger first offenders, focusing on education programs.

Release on bail: the release by a judicial officer of an accused person who has been taken into custody, upon his promise to pay a certain sum of money or property if he fails to appear in court as required.

Release on own recognizance (ROR): the release, by a judicial officer, of an accused person who has been taken into custody, upon his promise to appear in court as required for criminal proceedings.

Residential treatment center: a government facility which serves juveniles whose behavior does not necessitate the strict confinement of a training school, often allowing them greater contact with the community.

Revocation: an administrative act performed by a parole authority removing a person from parole, or a judicial order by a court removing a person from parole or probation, in response to a violation on the part of the parolee or probationer.

Role: the expected behavior of an occupant of a position/assignment, e.g., police officer.

S

Special enforcement: a specialized assignment for police officers responsible for tactically and swiftly abating acute crime problems.

Standards and goals: an effort to establish measures or yardsticks of quality and a desired future state of affairs for a more effective criminal justice system. This effort has been a continuing work of such organizations as the National Commission on Standards and Goals and the American Bar Association.

Stare decisis: to stand by decided things; the following of precedents or earlier case decisions on similar facts and issues of the law. (*See also* Case law.)

Status offenses: behavior that would not be offenses were the individual of adult age, such as truancy from school, incorrigibility, curfew violation, running away, drinking, and similar behavior that are offenses only because the individuals involved are juveniles.

Sting operations: a police-established and -operated fence activity in which stolen goods are bought by incognito police officers, with the consequent roundup and arrest of all identified offenders.

Study release: a program in which offenders living in a prison or a community facility go to school at a vocational school, junior college, high school, university, or any other type of school.

Substantive law: that law which determines and regulates the rights, duties and obligations of persons within a community (*cf.* Procedural law).

Support specialists: those individuals assigned the responsibility for providing technical backup to management and field personnel in such areas as communications and data processing.

System: an administrative approach to organizing and managing that emphasizes mutually supportive relationships (internal and external), efficiency and effectiveness, and constant change.

T

Team policing: the grouping of patrol officers (and in some cases specialists) into teams that are permanently deployed and responsible for all the police services provided in an assigned geographical area.

Traffic safety: a specialized assignment for police officers responsible for the enforcement of traffic codes, investigation of traffic accidents, traffic engineering decisions, public education programs, and parking control.

Treason: the crime of levying war against the United States or a state or in adhering to their enemies, giving them aid and comfort.

Trial: the examination of issues of fact and law in a case or controversy, beginning when the jury has been selected in a jury trial, or when the first witness is sworn or the first evidence is introduced in a court trial, and concluding when a verdict is reached or the case is dismissed.

Trial *de novo:* new trial.

U

Uniform Crime Report (UCR): official crime rates published by the FBI containing those statistics voluntarily reported by law enforcement agencies.

V

Venue: the geographical area from which the jury is drawn and in which trial is held in a criminal action.

Vice control: a specialized assignment for police officers responsible for the identification, location, and apprehension of offenders who engage in illegal acts of gambling, pornography, alcoholic beverages, and prostitution.

Victimization studies: national surveys conducted in selected cities to determine through citizen inquiries more precisely the extent to which individuals within a specified limit have been subjected to some criminal offense, with special inquiries into those they have not previously reported.

Volunteers: private citizens who assist official workers, generally in probation, juvenile court, and jail.

W

Warrant (bench): a document issued by a judicial officer directing that a person who has failed to obey an order or notice to appear be brought before the court.

Warrant (search): a document issued by a judicial officer which directs a law enforcement officer to conduct a search for specified property or persons at a specific location, to seize the property or persons, if found, and to account for the results of the search to the issuing judicial officer.

Workhouse: a local institution initially designed primarily to hold minor offenders, debtors, beggars, and others needing public care and continued today as local prisons and correctional institutions above the level of the jail, but below the level of the state prison.

Work release: a program in which offenders are housed in a prison or other facility, frequently a halfway house, but who work on regular jobs in the community.

Y

Youth services bureaus: a central intake and multiservice community operated center to analyze and assist delinquent and nondelinquent youth who are referred from other sources (police, courts, schools, etc.).

Index

A

Abortion, 221
Abraham, Henry J., 314
Academy of Criminal Justice Sciences, 461
Accelerated Rehabilitative Disposition (ARD), 418
Accessories to crime, 215
Accessory after the fact, 215
Accessory before the fact, 215
Act and intent, 215–216
Actus reas, 215
Adams, Stuart, 410
Adams v. Carlson (1974), 387
Addams, Jane, 416
Adjudication, defined, 484
Administrators
  court, 311–312
  prison, 380
Adultery, 221, 225
Advisory Commission on Intergovernmental Relations, 3, 307, 309
Affirmation, 243
Aftercare of juveniles, 430–431
  defined, 484

Aggravated assault, 31
Aiding and abetting, 215
Aikens v. Lash (1975), 386
Aircraft, 129
Aircraft patrol programs, 108–109
Air security, 68
Alabama, 74, 116, 300
Alberts v. California (1957), 241
Albuquerque Police Department, 115
Alcohol, 137
  and parolees, 443
Alcohol detoxification units, 420
Allocation of police resources, 106–107
Amendments to the Constitution of the United States
  Eighth, 230, 250–251, 339, 385, 387
  Fifteenth, 236
  Fifth, 230, 236, 237, 246–249, 285
  First, 230, 239–242, 385
  Fourteenth, 230, 234, 236–238, 241, 249–251, 260, 339, 385
  Fourth, 230, 236, 242–247
  Sixth, 4, 230, 247, 249–250, 282, 385
  Thirteenth, 236, 338, 384
  See also Bill of Rights

American Bar Association (ABA), 5, 72, 163, 283, 317, 440, 448, 461
American Correctional Association (ACA), 336, 348, 352, 385, 389, 391, 410, 461
American Journal of Correction, 352
American Prison Association, 389
American Revolution, 231, 334
American Samoa, 38, 69
Amnesty, 449, 450
Annual Congress on Correction, 417
Anomie, 9–10, 343
Antipollution laws, 59
Appeal, 257, 299–301
  defined, 484
Appellate tribunal, 257
Appointive system of judge selection, 313
Arbitration courts, 330–331
Architecture, correctional, 377–378
Area teams, 113
Arraignment, 286–287
  defined, 484
Arrest, 101, 242–246, 279–280
  defined, 484
  for victimless crimes, 222
Articles of Confederation, 231
Assault, 24
Assemblies, 239
Assigned counsel, defined, 484
Assignment of police officers, 179
Assize of Claredon, 332, 347
Attorney, defined, 484–485
Auburn system, 335–336
  defined, 485
Augustus, John, 336, 374

B

Babylon, 331
Backlog, defined, 485
Bail Agency Act, 419
Bailiff, 293, 297
Bail Reform Act of 1966, 419
Bail system, 281–282, 318–319, 357
Bandy v. Chambers (1961), 419
Bandy v. United States (1960), 419
Banking, 148
Basic car plan (BCP), 111
Basic patrol teams, 115
Batch system, 182
Batt v. Twomey (1975), 387
Beat plans, 107
Beccaria, Cesare, 334, 338, 341

Bench warrant, defined, 493
Bentham, Jeremy, 338, 341
Bill of Rights, 4, 230, 232, 235–238, 470
  and criminal justice system, 239–251
Bind over, 284
Biological approach to crime causation, 7–8
Bixby, F. Lovell, 448
Black Muslims, 385
Blackstone, William, 341
Blood feud, 330
"Bobbies," 52
Bondsman, 281
Booking, 280, 281
  defined, 485
Booth, Maud, 416
"Born criminal" concept, 342
Borstal system of minimum security, 389
Boston, 53
Boston Police Department, 122
Bow Street Horse and Foot Patrol, 51
Brandeis, Louis D., 251–252
Breaches of peace, 239
Brewster Housing Project (Detroit), 416
Bridewell, 333
Brockway, Zebulon R., 447
Budgeting in police subsystem, 167–168
Building design and crime control, 201–202
Building Security Law, 202
Building security standards, 201–202
Bureau of Correctional Services (Salvation Army), 422
Bureau of Missing Persons (Salvation Army), 422
Burger, Warren, 312, 341, 460
Burgess, Ernest, 342
Burglary, 31, 38, 214
Burke v. Levi (1975), 387
Business and crime prevention, 147–148

C

Cabot, Richard C., 343
California, 202
California Crime Technological Research Foundation, 202
California Division of Law Enforcement, 83–84
California Highway Patrol, 105
California Medical Facility at Vacaville, 376
California Penal Code, 202
Called-for patrol services, 100–101
Cambridge-Somerville Youth Study, 343, 416

Corrections (*cont.*)
  defined, 491
  misdemeanant, 357
  presentence investigation, 366–368
  subsidy legislation, 370–371
  supervision, 368–370, 444
  releases other than parole
    expiration of sentence, 449
    mandatory conditional, 449
    pardons, 449–450
Corrections Magazine (1975), 410
Council of Nicaea, 331
Counsel
  defined, 484–485
  right to, 282–283
Counseling in prisons, 392
County courts, 266
County jail, 144
County sheriffs, 144, 151
Court case, defined, 485
Court clerk, 293
Court of last resort, 264–266
Court reporter, 293
Courts, 18–20, 22, 41, 255–274, 309, 312
  of appellate jurisdiction, defined, 486
  caseload, defined, 485
  defined, 486
  development of, 255–256
  intervention of in prisons, 384–387
  judicial reform, 307–320
    court procedures and practices, 314–319
    improved state-federal relations, 312
    need for better administration, 311–312
    quality of personnel, 312–314
    unification of state system, 309–310
  lower courts
    juvenile, 4, 39, 131, 132, 270–273, 337, 426–428, 430, 466, 489
    shortcomings of, 267–270
  lower federal courts, 262–264
    specialized courts, 264
    United States Courts of Appeals, 240, 255, 257, 262, 263
    United States District Courts, 255, 262–264
    United States Magistrates, 255, 264
  police civil unit, 151
  state and local courts, 264–266, 288, 307
    court of last resort, 264–266
    intermediate appellate courts, 266
    trial courts, 266
  Supreme Court, 3, 4, 12, 27, 256–263, 460, 466, 470
    administering federal judiciary, 260

Courts (*cont.*)
  on capital punishment, 339
  constitutional interpretations, 230, 233–235, 237–238, 240–242, 244–252, 338
  and criminal justice system, 261–262
  decision-making process of, 259–260
  on jury unanimity, 289
  on juveniles, 272, 273
  on presidential power, 62
  selection of cases, 257–258
  See also Processes of criminal justice
Courts of Assize (England), 256
Courts of general jurisdiction, 266
  defined, 486
Courts of limited jurisdiction, defined, 486
Cressey, Donald R., 343
Crime
  accessories to, 215
  act and intent, 215–216
  approaches to causation, 6–12
  vs. civil wrongs, 211–212
  classification of, 213–214
  defined, 486
  fear of, 22–24
  female, 407
  morality and, 220
  motive, 216
  organized, 58, 63–64, 135, 138, 168, 223–224
  parties to, 214–215
  prevalence of, 2–3
  prevention of, 25–26, 144–151, 189–203, 486
  rate of, 23–24
  reduction, 27–31, 36–41, 162–164
  victimless, 138, 221–226
  violent, 3, 38
Crime Commission Report (1967), 95
Crime and Delinquency (April, 1977), 407
Crime specific programs, 109–110
  defined, 486
Crime T.R.A.P. program (Indianapolis), 147
Criminal adjudication, 484
Criminal investigation, 125–129
  defined, 486
Criminalistics, defined, 486
Criminal justice agency, defined, 486
Criminal justice system, 454–471
  and Bill of Rights, 239–251
  and communities, 189
  and Constitution of United States, 230, 251–252
  and corrections, 328
  expenditure tables, 32–35
  goals and objectives, 12–14, 21–22
  impact of standards and goals, 461–462

Criminal justice system (*cont.*)
  manpower base for, 459–461
  processes of, 278–301
  program planning, 37–38
  reality and mythology of, 457–459
  societal expectations of, 26
  study of, 5–6
  subsystems of, 18–20
  and Supreme Court, 261
  and urban policy development, 451–457
  See also Corrections; Courts; Jails; Police subsystem; Prisons; Processes of criminal justice
Criminal laboratories, 87, 129, 183–184
Criminal law, 26, 216
  basic function, 221
  federal, 469
  origin, 334
  purpose, 212
Criminal offense, defined, 486
Criminal procedures, 27
Criminology, 5
  approaches to crime causation, 6–12
  theory and research, 341–343
Crofton, Sir Walter, 337, 374, 438
Cross examination, 295
Culture of prisons, 405–407
Custody, 143–144, 381–384

D

Daigle v. Hall (1975), 386
Daughters of the American Revolution of Virginia, Inc., 353
Dayton, Ohio, 116
Daytop Village, 417
Death penalty, *see* Capital punishment
Decentralization of police services, 112–116, 149, 161
Decriminalization of victimless crimes, 224–226
Defendant, 292
  defined, 486
Defense, case for, 296
Defense attorney, 292–293
  defined, 486
Defense mechanisms, 403
Defensible space, defined, 486–487
"Deferred prosecution," 418
Deferred sentencing, 418
Delaware, Maryland, 77
Deliberations of jury, 297
Delinquency, theories of, 343
  See also Juvenile delinquency

Delinquency Prediction scale, 343
Delinquency programs, 63
Delinquent
  defined, 487
  and personality development, 402
Demonstrations, 239
Denial, 403
Departmental information unit (DIU), 165–166
Dependency, 271
Des Moines Project, 419
Detectives, 126–129
Detention, 101, 143–144
  juvenile, 429
  pretrial, 249, 318–319
Detention facility, defined, 487
Determinate sentencing, 438
Deterrence theory of punishment, 213
  defined, 487
Detoxification unit, 356
Detroit, 116
Differential association, 10
Differential opportunity, 10
Direct examination of witnesses, 295
Directed verdict, 296
Discipline
  in jails, 351–352
  in prisons, 384
Dismas Residence, 419–420
Disposition, court
  defined, 487
  in juvenile courts, 273
District of Columbia, 38, 67
District Courts, 266
  See also United States District Courts
Diversion, defined, 487
Diversion programs, 418–419
"Divine intervention," 217
Docket, defined, 487
Doctrine of Judicial Restraint, 259
Double jeopardy, 441
Douglas, William O., 419
Dropped charges, 314–315
Drucker, Peter, 155
Drug abuse, 58, 59, 64–66, 70, 133–136, 417
  community programs, 195–197
  defined, 490
Drug abuse treatment center, defined, 487
Drug Enforcement Administration, 60, 64–65, 68, 70, 71, 487
Drug Enforcement Assistance Administration, 28
Drunkenness, 221, 225, 356, 443

"Dual citizenship" concept, 237
Due process
   defined, 487
   in juvenile courts, 272–273
   procedures, 440
   rights, 27
   standards in prison, 385–386
Due process clause, 230, 236–238, 247, 249
Durkheim, Emile, 343
Dyer Act, 57

E

Early assessment bureau, 458
Economic approach to crime causation, 9
Education
   community programs, 198–199
   of police officers, 178–179
   in prisons, 391–392
Edward I, 50
Egypt, 256, 330
Ehrlich, Isaac, 341
Eighth Amendment, 214, 230, 250–251, 339, 385, 387
Election of judges, 313
Elkins v. United States (1960), 245
Ely, Governor, 447
Emergency called-for services, 100
Emlen, John, 405
Emotional immaturity, 403–404
Employment
   community programs, 197–198
   of parolees, 443
En banc, 441–442
   defined, 487
England, 211
   courts in, 256
   early law enforcement, 49–51
   industrialization of, 51–53
   jury system, 218
English Convict, The (Goring), 342
Escobedo v. Illinois (1964), 4, 247–248
Essay on Crimes and Punishments (Beccaria), 334, 338, 341
Euthanasia, 216
Evidence, rules of, 217
   reasons for, 219–220
Ex parte Bucknell (1897), 427
Executive clemency, 449
Ex-offender groups, 421–422
   defined, 487
"Expenditure and Employment Data for the Criminal Justice System" (1978), 28

Expiration of sentence, 449
   defined, 487
Expungement, defined, 487

F

Federal Aviation Administration, 68
Federal Bureau of Investigation, 24, 28, 56–57, 59, 60, 65, 67, 68, 70, 71, 87, 222, 328, 329
Federal court system, 262–264, 312
Federal Criminal Act of 1978, 469
Federal criminal law, 469
Federal Criminal Procedure rules (Supreme Court, 1945), 27
Federal Exclusionary Rule, 244, 245
Federal government, 22, 27, 28, 56–59, 138
   areas of cooperation, 67–68
   assistance activities, 68–71
   commissions, 3–4, 71–73
   Drug Enforcement Administration, 60, 64–65, 68, 70, 71, 487
   investigation, 65–66
   juvenile delinquency, 63
   Law Enforcement Assistance Administration, 24, 37–38, 58–60, 67, 69–71, 161, 167, 271, 278, 431, 489
   organized crime, 63–64
   policing of, 59–60
   powers of, 60–62, 231
   response to crime, 31–59
Federal Justice Research Center, 69
Federal Juvenile Delinquency Act, 427
Federal Kidnapping Act, 56, 233
Federal Meat Inspection Act, 66
Federal Omnibus Crime Control and Safe Streets Act of 1968, 73
Federal Youth Center, 375
Fee system, 270
"Feedback loop," 19
Felony, 27, 213–215
   defined, 487
Field evidence technicians, 129
Fifteenth Amendment, 236
Fifth Amendment, 230, 236, 237, 246–249, 285
Findings of involvement, 270
First Amendment, 230, 239–242, 385
Fiscal affairs unit, 167–168
Fitzcourt, Brian, 332
Flambard, Rannulf, 332
Flat sentence, defined, 487
Florida, 339

Fluid patrol, 107
Fogel, David, 448
Foot patrol programs, 107–108
Ford, Gerald, 431
Forensic pathology, defined, 487
Fornication, 225
Fortune and Men's Eyes, 421
Fortune Society, 421
Fourteenth Amendment, 230, 234, 241, 249–251, 260, 339, 385
  evolution of, 236–238
Fourth Amendment, 4, 230, 236, 242–247
France, 49
French Revolution, 334
Fugitive Felon Act, 56
Fullwood and Clemmer (1962), 385
Functional unit management, 390–391
Furlough, 417, 420–421
  defined, 487
Furman v. Georgia (1972), 250, 339, 341

G

Gambling, 137, 138, 225
  in prisons, 403
Gault case, 4, 272, 273, 427, 466
General preventive patrol, 98–99
Generalist approach in team policing, 116
Genovese, Kitty, 406
Georgia, 300
Ghent, 335
Gideon v. Wainwright (1963), 4, 249, 282
Gilbert v. California (1967), 248
Gill, Howard, 447
Gilmore, Gary, 250, 339
Glaser, Daniel, 343
Glueck, Eleanor, 343
Glueck, Sheldon, 343
Golden Rule, 331
Goring, Charles, 342
Graham, Billy, 422
Grand jury, 285
  defined, 488–489
  forerunner of, 218
Grants management in police subsystem, 166
Gregory v. Wyse (1973), 387
Group home, defined, 488
Group therapy methods in prisons, 392
Guam, 38, 69
Guilty pleas, 286
Gun Control Act of 1968, 66

H

Halfway house, 416, 419–420
  defined, 488
Hammurabi, King, 256
Handbook of Correctional Design and Construction, 349
Hart, Hastings H., 349
Hartford Police Department, 115, 116
Hawaii, 56, 74
Health and welfare units in police subsystem, 181
Hearing, defined, 488
Helicopter patrol, 100, 108–109
Henry II (England), 334, 347
High-fear crimes, 31
High Impact Anticrime Program, 58
High priority crimes, 37
Highway patrol, 73, 77
Hobbs Act, 56
Holyoke, 116
Homer, 330, 415
Homicide, defined, 488
Homosexuality, 221, 225, 282
  in prisons, 406
Hoover, J. Edgar, 56
Hope Hall, 416
Hospice of San Michele, 426
Household burglary, 24
House of correction, 358
House of Industry in Philadelphia, 416
House of Lords (England), 256, 258
House of Refuge for problem children, 426
Housing of parolees, 443–444
Huber Law, 352, 417, 420
Hull House, 416
"Hundred," 50
Hung jury, 289
Hurtado v. California (1884), 237

I

Identification programs, 147
Iliad (Homer), 330, 415
Illinois, 128
Illinois jail survey (1969), 352
Immigration Act, 450
Immigration and Naturalization Service (INS), 65
Impeachment of witnesses, 295

Incarceration
  continuous, 249
  defined, 488
  initial, 281
Indeterminate sentence, 336
  defined, 488
Index crimes, 329
  defined, 488
India, 331
Indianapolis, 147
Indictment, defined, 488
Indigent person, defined, 488
Industrial Revolution, 51, 334
Industrialization in England, 51–53
Infanticide, 426
Information, 285
  defined, 488
Information, crime analysis, and evaluation unit in police subsystem, 181–183
Information processing, 104–105
Initial hearing, 270
Initial incarceration, 281
Inmate code, 405–406
  defined, 488
Input in criminal justice system, 279–280
Inquest, 218
Inquisition, 218
In re Gault (1967), 4, 272, 273, 427, 466
Inspector General, Office of, 66
Inspirational-repressive approach in training schools, 430
Institute for Court Management, 312
Institutional deadlock, 387
Institutionalization, 420
  of staff, 408–409
  effects of, 409–410
Institutional parole officer (IPO), 442
  defined, 488
Instructions and charge to jury, 297
Intake, defined, 488
Intelligence division of Internal Revenue Service, 65–66
Intelligence unit in police subsystem, 168–170
Interagency agreements in federal governments, 67–68
Intermediate appellate courts, 266
Internal control unit of police subsystem, 170–172
Internal Revenue Service, 65, 68
International Association of Chiefs of Police, 155
International Directory of Prisoners' Aid Societies, 415

Interpol, 135
Interstate commerce, 233
Investigation
  criminal, 125–129
  defined, 488
  narcotic and drug, 133–136
  of patrol officer, 101
Irish system, 337, 374, 438
Isaac T. Hopper House, 416

J

Jacobellis v. Ohio (1964), 241
Jails, 143–144, 347–359
  administration and operation, 353–355
  defined, 488
  functions, 347
  houses of correction, 358
  limitations and operational problems, 349–352
  literature on, 349
  local, 87
  lockups, 348, 355, 489
  medieval, 332
  misdemeanants, 355–357
  professional and volunteer associations, 352–353
  reasons for existence, 359
  release on own recognizance, 357–359, 419, 491
  services and personnel, 352
  volunteers in, 357
Jail Administration Digest, 349
Jail Evaluation: A Standard Report (Culbertson and Mayra), 349
Jail (The): Its Operations and Management (University of Wisconsin), 349
Jerusalem, 334
Jesus Christ, 331
Job assignment of police personnel, 179
"John Doe" warrants, 244, 279
John Howard Society, 415
Johnson v. Avery (1969), 385
Joint Committee on the Legal Rights of Prisoners (ABA), 440
Joyce, James, 240
Judges
  defined, 488
  function, 288–289
  instructions and charge to jury, 297
  presentence investigation report, 368
  selection of, 313–314
  sentencing, 268, 317–318

Judicial Process, The (Abraham), 314
Judicial reform, 307–320
   administration, need for better, 311–312
   court procedures and practices, 314–319
      dropped charges, 314–315
      plea bargaining, 315–319
      pretrial detention and bail, 318–319
      sentencing, 317–318
   improved state-federal court relations, 312
   law reform, 309
   quality of personnel, 312–314
   unification of state court systems, 309–310
Judiciary Act of 1789, 263
Judiciary powers, 62
Jurisdiction, 287–288
   defined, 488
   in juvenile courts, 271
Jury
   defined, 488–489
   deliberations and verdict of, 297
   evolution of, 218–219
   instructions and charge to, 297
   selection of, 293–295
   sentencing by, 317
   trial, 289–290
Justices of the peace, 50–52
Justinian, Emperor, 331
Juvenile, defined, 484
Juvenile adjudication, defined, 484
Juvenile corrections, 426–433
   aftercare, 430–431
   detention, 429
   future directions, 465–466
   history, 426–428
   Juvenile Justice and Delinquency Prevention Act of 1974, 431–433
   training schools, 429–430
Juvenile courts, 4, 39, 131, 132, 270–273, 337, 430, 466
   defined, 489
   development of, 426–428
   dispositions in, 273
   due process in, 272–273
   jurisdiction in, 271
   philosophy of, 271–272
Juvenile delinquency, 58, 63, 271, 431, 432, 445
   federal assistance in combatting, 70
   in future, 465
   prevention of, 38–39
   rate of, 428
   theories of, 343
Juvenile Delinquency Prevention and Control Act of 1968, 63
Juvenile Justice Act of 1974, 465
Juvenile justice agency, defined, 489
Juvenile Justice Delinquency Prevention Act, 271, 431–433
Juvenile police operations, 130–133
Juvenile Rehabilitation Ministry of the Home Mission Board of the Southern Baptist Convention, 422
Juvenile status offenses, 39

K

Kansas City, Missouri Police Department, 99, 105
Keep-lock, 387
Kent v. United States (1966), 427
Klopfer v. North Carolina (1967), 247

L

Labeling approach to crime causation, 11
Laboratory system, 78
Labor-Management Services Administration, 68
Labor unions, 445–446
Landman v. Royster (1971), 385
Larceny, 24
Larceny-theft, 2
Law
   civil vs. criminal, 26
   defined, 210
   federal criminal, 469
   and moral considerations, 220–221
Law enforcement in American colonies, 53
Law enforcement agency, defined, 489
Law Enforcement Assistance Administration (LEAA), 24, 37–38, 58–60, 67, 69–71, 161, 167, 271, 278, 431, 489
Law of Moses, 331, 340
Law reform, 309
Lawyer, defined, 484–485
Legal aid programs, 282–283
Legal systems, development of, 211
Legal unit in police subsystem, 166
Lending institutions, 148
Leopold, Nathan, 443
Library in prisons, 393
Lindbergh Law, 233
Lindsey, Ben, 427
Line-item budgeting, 167
Literature on jails, 349

Local government, 28, 30, 57
  police function of, 80–81
Lockup, 348, 355
  defined, 489
Lombroso, Cesare, 341–342
London, England, 122
Los Angeles, 116
Los Angeles County Sheriff's Department, 105, 128
Lower courts
  federal, 262–264
    specialized courts, 264
    United States Courts of Appeals, 240, 255, 257, 262, 263
    United States District Courts, 255, 262–264
    United States Magistrates, 255, 264
  juvenile, 4, 39, 131, 132, 270–273, 337, 426–428, 430, 466, 489
  shortcomings of, 267–270
Lyman School, 426

M

McCray v. Sullivan (1973), 387
McCulloch v. Maryland (1819), 61
McGee, Richard, 447, 448
McKay, Henry D., 342
McKiever v. Pennsylvania (1971), 428
McNabb v. United States (1943), 260
McNeil v. Latney (1974), 387
Maconochie, Alexander, 337, 374, 438
Magna Carta, 218
Major Case Squad of the Greater St. Louis Area, 128
Mala prohibita offenses, 220
Mamertine Prison, 334
Management, defined, 489
Management component of police subsystem, 164–174
  administrator, 172–174
  departmental information unit, 165–166
  fiscal affairs unit, 167–168
  intelligence unit, 168–170
  internal control unit, 170–172
  legal unit, 166
  planning, research, and development unit, 166–167
Management by objectives (MBO), 161–162
  defined, 489
Mandatory conditional release, 449
  defined, 489
Manhattan Bail Project, 419

Manhattan Jail Project, 419
Mann Act, 233
Manu, the Law Giver, 331
Manual Enterprises v. Day (1962), 241
Manual of Jail Administration (National Sheriff's Association), 349
Mapp v. Ohio (1961), 4, 246
Marijuana, 59, 64, 135, 225
Martel, William, 332
Martinson, Robert, 410, 448
Martinson Report, 410
Massachusetts, 5
Massachusetts Correctional Association, 415
Massachusetts Division of Youth Services, 430
Matza, David, 343
Maximum custody institution, 376–377, 382–383
  defined, 489
Maximum security institution, 375, 405, 408
  defined, 489
Maximum security prisoner, defined, 489
Media and police, 159
Medical and dental services in prisons, 393–394
Medium custody institution, 377
Medium security prisoner, defined, 489
Menlo Park, 116
Mens rea, 216
Mental health programs, 337
Merton, Robert, 343
Michigan State Police, 105
Mill, John Stuart, 223
Miller, Walter, 343
Minimum security institution, 377
  defined, 489
Minimum security ordinances, 148
Minimum State Building Standards of Administrative Code, 202
Minority groups, recruitment of, 176
Mirabeau, Comte de, 438
Miranda v. Arizona (1966), 4, 248
Misdemeanants, 355–357
Misdemeanor, 27, 214
  defined, 489
Missouri Crime Commission, 57
Missouri jail survey (1939), 352
Missouri Plan, 313–314
Mistake of fact, defined, 489
Modified Workweek Program, 110–111
Monge, Luis José, 338, 339
Monterey Park, California, Police Department, 147
Moot case, defined, 490
Morality and law, 220–221

Morris v. Travisono (1970), 385
Morrissey v. Brewer (1972), 440
Motions, 198
  for dismissal, 296
  pretrial, 287
Motive in crime, 216
"Multimodality" approach to drug treatment, 196
Multi-specialist approach in team policing, 116
Municipal jail, 144
Murder, 2
Mutual Pledge system, 50, 51, 53

N

Napoleonic Decree of 1811, 427
Narcotic Addict Rehabilitation Act of 1966, 67
Narcotics, defined, 490
  See also Drug abuse
Narcotics offenders, 417
Narrative technique of direct examination, 295
Nassau County, New York, Police Department, 146
National Advisory Commission on Civil Disorders, 3
National Advisory Commission on Criminal Justice Standards and Goals, 12, 31, 38, 45–46, 72–73, 77–78, 80, 183, 226, 298–300, 307, 309, 310, 316, 317, 470
  combined police services, 158–160
  crime prevention, 144–145
  criminal investigation, 125–126
  detention systems, 143
  enhancing role of patrol officer, 117
  juvenile operations, 130
  narcotics and drug abuse, 133–134
  police function, 45–46
  special crime tactical forces, 142
  specialized assignment, 124–125
  state specialists, 79–80
  traffic operations, 139–140
  vice operation, 136–137
National Advisory Commission on Standards and Goals Projects, 461, 462
National Appeals Board, 441
National Bank Robbery Act, 56–57
National Bureau of Standards, 67–68
National Commission on the Causes and Prevention of Violence (1969), 3
National Commission on Reform of Federal Criminal Laws, 4
National Conference on Bail and Criminal Justice, 318
National Congress on Penitentiary and Reform Discipline, 336, 374
National Council on Crime and Delinquency, 370, 407, 410, 446
National Council on Organized Crime, 63
National Crime Commission, 267
National Crime Information Center, 68, 70
National Crime Prevention Institute at the University of Louisville, 148
National Crime Surveys (NCS), 328
National Institute of Correction, 69
National Institute for Juvenile Justice and Delinquency Prevention, 432
National Institute of Law Enforcement and Criminal Justice, 67
National Institute of Mental Health, 67, 410
National Jail Association, 352
National Jail Census (1970), 348
National Legal Aids and Defender Association, 283
National Motor Vehicle Theft Act, 233
National Opinion Research Center, University of Chicago, 278
National Sheriff's Association, 348–349
National Stolen Property Act, 56
National Training Institute (DEA), 64–65
National Victimization Survey, 24
Necessary and proper clause, 233
Neglect, 271
Neighborhood Guild, 416
Neighborhood security programs, 146
Newgate Prison, 335
Newgate program, 420
New York, 53, 77, 300
New York City Police Department, 109, 115, 116, 224
New York City Youth Board, 343
New York Prison Society, 422
Niethercutt, M.G., 448
Nightwatch system, 51, 53
Nolle prosequi, 291
Nolo contendere, 286
  defined, 490
Noncriminal services of criminal justice system, 21, 46
Nonemergency called-for services, 100–101
North Carolina, 74
North Carolina, federal correctional facility at, 5
Novak v. Beto (1971), 385

O

Obscenity, 240–242
Office of Intelligence (DEA), 64
Office of Juvenile Justice and Delinquency Prevention (OJJDP), 431, 432
Ohio, 136
Ohlin, Lloyd, 343
Oklahoma, 74
Old Testament, 331
Olmstead v. United States (1928), 251–252
Omnibus Crime Control and Safe Streets Act of 1968, 37, 69
On-line/rapid-time (OLRT) system, 182
Opening statements, 295
Operant conditioning, 430
Organization, defined, 490
Organized crime, 58, 63–64, 135, 138, 168
  role of in victimless crime, 223–224
Organized Crime Control Act of 1970, 58, 66, 67
Organized Crime and Racketeering Section of Department of Justice, 58, 68
Original jurisdiction, 257, 263
Orthopsychiatric approach, 430
Outlawry, 332–333

P

Palmer, Ted, 410
Palo Alto, 116
Pardons, 449–450
Parens patriae, 272, 273, 426, 427
  defined, 490
Parmelee, Maurice, 342
Parole, 336–337, 374, 421, 437–450
  combined probation and parole services, 447
  defined, 490
  functions of boards, 438
  prerelease programs, 442–444
  problems, 447–448
  selection for, 439–442
  supervision, 444–447
Parole agency, defined, 490
Parole authority, defined, 490
Parole boards, 437, 440, 441–443, 448
  functions of, 438
Parole officer, 443, 446
  institutional, 442, 488
Parole prediction tables, 443
Parolees, supervision of, 444–447
Participative management, 162
  defined, 490

Paternal deprivation, 402
Patrol, *see* Police subsystem, patrol
Patrol-community service teams, 115–116
Patrol-investigative teams, 115
"Pecking order," 404–405
Peel, Sir Robert, 52
Peer group in prisons, 392
Peer pressure, 9
Penal colony, 333
Penitentiary, defined, 490
Penitentiary movement, 335, 415
Pennsylvania, 56
Pennsylvania Prison Society, 415, 422
Pennsylvania System, 335–336
  defined, 490
Peremptory challenges, 294
Perjury, defined, 490
Personality development, 401–402
Personality traits of prison populations, 402–404
Personal vendetta, 212
Petition, 270
Petit jury, 289
  defined, 489
Petty offenses in lower courts, 268
Philadelphia, 53
Philadelphia Society for Alleviating the Miseries of the Public Prisons, 335, 415, 422
Physical environment, community programs in, 201–202
Physiological approach to crime causation, 7
Pillory, 332
Planned law enforcement patrol, 99
Planning in police subsystem, 160–161
Planning, programming, and budgeting system in police subsystem, 168
Planning, research, and development unit in police subsystem, 166–167
Plato, 331
Plea, defined, 490
Plea bargaining, 27, 286, 315–317, 460, 470
  defined, 490
Police, 18–20, 22, 40–41
  costs of, 30
  federal assistance to, 69–70
  and First Amendment guarantees, 239, 240
Police Code of Ethics, 155–156
Police-community relations (CR)
  and crime prevention, 144–151
  and team policing, 113, 115–116
Policeman's Bill of Rights, 171, 172
Police line-ups, 248

Police regulatory offenses, 220
Police standards commissions, 80
Police subsystem
    federal policing, 59-60
    future directions, 462-465
    goals, 46-48
    history, 49-57
    local policing, 81
        county sheriff, 87
        private, 87-90
        services, 81-87
    management component, 155-184
        administrator, office of, 172-174
        career development unit, 174-181
        code of ethics, 155-156
        community support, 157-158
        consolidation and regionalization of services, 158-160
        crime reduction, 162-164
        criminalistics unit, 183-184
        departmental information unit, 165-166
        fiscal affairs unit, 167-168
        information, crime analysis, and evaluation unit, 181-183
        intelligence unit, 168-170
        internal control unit, 170-172
        legal unit, 166
        managing by objectives, 161-162
        and media, 157
        planning, 160-161
        planning, research, and development unit, 166-167
    modernization, 57
    patrol, 95-117
        apprehension and detention, 101
        called-for services, 100-101
        civil disorder, 103-104
        community relations, 104
        crowd control, 103-104
        foot patrol programs, 107-108
        general preventive, 98-99
        helicopters and fixed wing aircraft programs, 108-109
        importance, 95-98
        information processing, 104-105
        investigation, 101
        Modified Workweek Program, 110-111
        planned law enforcement, 99
        police function, 45-46
        radio-car patrol programs, 108
        resource allocation, 106-107
        role of officer, 116-117
        team policing, 111-116

Police subsystem (cont.)
        traffic, 102-103
        types of programs, 105-106
    specialist units, 122-151, 174-184
        civil (court support), 151
        crime prevention/community relations, 144-151
        criminal investigation, 125-129
        jail, 143-144
        juvenile police operations, 130-133
        NAC standards on, 124-125
        narcotics and drug abuse, 133-136
        need for, 122-124
        special enforcement, 142-143
        traffic safety, 139-141
        vice control, 136-139
    state policing, 73-81
        assistance to local police, 77-81
        regulatory power, 73-74
        services, 74-77
Polling of jurors, 297
Pornography, 137, 221, 225, 240-242
Position specifications catalog, 175
Positivistic school of criminology, 6, 341-342, 490
Postal Inspection Service, 66, 67
Postconviction petitions, defined, 490
Postconviction remedies, 299-301
Post-trial procedures, 297-301
    appeal, 299-301
    motions, 298
    presentence investigation, 297
    sentence, 298-299
Precedents, 211
    defined, 490
Predisposition report, defined, 490
Preliminary hearing, 283-285
Preparole progress report, 440
Prerelease programs, 442-444
Presentence investigation report (PSI), 297, 366-368, 388, 440
    defined, 490
Presentment, 285
    defined, 491
President, powers of, 62
Presidential Crime Commission (1967), 72
Presidential Riot Commission (1968), 72
President's Commission on Campus Violence, 4
President's Commission on Law Enforcement and the Administration of Justice (1967), 3, 37, 136, 177, 183, 193, 195, 199, 278, 311, 417, 454
Pretrial detention, 318-319

Pretrial intervention, 418
  defined, 491
Pretrial motions, 287
Pretrial processes, 279–287
  arraignment, 286–287
  first appearance, 281–282
  grand jury, 285
  initial action, 280–281
  motions, 287
  preliminary hearing, 283–285
  right to counsel, 282–283
Preventative theory of punishment, 213
Prima facie case, 284
Principals in crime, 215
Prison camps, 375–376
Prisoner Rehabilitation Act, 417
Prisoners
  classification of, 383–384
  rights of, 353–354
  women as, 406–407
Prisoner's Aid Association of Maryland, 415, 422
Prisoners' aid societies, 422, 449
Prisonization, 408
  defined, 491
Prisons, 374–395
  changes in, 410–411
  court intervention in, 384–387
  culture, 405–407
  custody, 381–384
  customs and folkways, 408
  defined, 491
  early, 334–335
  early systems of, 335–336
  effects of institutionalization, 409–410
  factions, 408
  future predictions, 467–469
  objectives, 377–399
  organization and administration, 380–381
  population, 400–404
  recidivism, 39
  society, 404–405
  staff society, 408–409
  treatment, 388–394
  types, 375–377
Private policing, 87–90
  defined, 491
"Probable cause," 243, 284
Probable cause hearing, 284
Probation, 336, 363–371, 374
  caseload, 446
  combined probation and parole services, 447

Probation (*cont.*)
  defined, 491
  misdemeanant, 357
  presentence investigation, 366–368
  subsidy legislation, 370–371
  supervision, 368–370, 444
Probation agency, defined, 491
Probationers, supervision of, 368–370
Probation officers, 368
  caseload size, 370
  decisions made by, 366–367
  defined, 491
  functions, 364
  supervisory role, 368–369
Probation subsidy, defined, 491
"Probation without adjudication," 418
Procedural criminal law, 213
  defined, 491
Proceedings of the American Correctional Association, 417
Processes of criminal justice, 278–301
  post-trial, 297–301
    appeal, 299–301
    motions, 298
    presentence investigation, 297
    sentence, 298–299
  pretrial, 279–287
    arraignment, 286–287
    first appearance, 281–282
    grand jury, 285
    initial action, 280–281
    motions, 287
    preliminary hearing, 283–285
    right to counsel, 282–283
  reducing delays in, 40
  trial, 287–297
    case for defense, 296
    case for prosecution, 295–296
    closing statements, 296
    deliberations and verdict, 297
    instructions and charge to jury, 297
    jurisdiction and venue, 287–288
    jury selection, 293–295
    motion for dismissal or directed verdict, 296
    opening statements, 295
    people involved, 288–293
    rebuttal and surrebuttal, 296
Program planning, 37–38
Prohibition, 223
Project on Minimum Standards for Criminal Justice (ABA), 317
Projection, 403

Promotion of police personnel, 179–180
Prosecution, case for, 295–296
Prosecutor, 291–292
  defined, 491
Prostitution, 137, 138, 221, 225
Psychiatric approach to crime causation, 8
Psychological approach to crime causation, 8
Public defender, 282–283
  defined, 491
Public health programs, 337
Public services, delivery of, 192–195
Public transportation vehicles, 148
Public welfare offenses, 220
Puerto Rico, 38, 69, 336
Punishment
  ancient, 330–331
  medieval, 331–333
  theories of, 212–213
  See also Capital punishment
Punishment-and-reward theme, 430

Q

Quakers, 335, 336, 357, 391, 415, 416, 422
Question-answer technique of direct examination, 295

R

Racial tensions in prisons, 399
Radio-car patrol programs, 108
Radzinowicz, Sir Leon, 11, 12, 456
Rape, 24, 31, 214
"RAPS" system of classification, 390
Rasp Huis, 333
"Rattlewatch," 53
Real crime rate, 328
Rebuttal, 296
Recidivism, 38, 39, 329, 449
  defined, 491
  in juvenile training schools, 430
Reckless, Walter, 343
Recreation
  community programs, 199–200
  in prisons, 393
Recruitment of police officers, 175–176
Redirect examination, 295
Referral to intake, defined, 491
Reformative theory of punishment, 212
Reformatory, 375, 376
  defined, 491

Regional planning councils, 38
Rehabilitation, debate over, 409–411
Reintegration centers, 420
Releases
  on bail, 491
  on own recognizance, 357–358, 419, 491
  from prisons, 449–450
  See also Parole
Religion
  community programs, 200–201
  in prisons, 391–392
  and social control, 331, 334
Remand, 261
Repeat offenders, 404
Reporting process in police subsystem, 182
Reports of the National Advisory Commission on Criminal Justice Standards and Goals, 4
Republic, The (Plato), 331
Research and technology, 70–71
Residential treatment center, 416–417
  defined, 491
Restitution shelters, 420
Revenue Cutter Service, 56
Revocation of parole, 446–447
  defined, 492
Richmond Police Department, 115
Right to counsel, 282–283
Riots in prison, 448
Robbery, 2, 24, 31
Robert F. Kennedy Youth Center, 375
Rochester, New York, 115
Role, defined, 492
Rome, 211, 331, 332, 334
Romilly, Samuel, 338, 341
Roth v. United States, 240
Rothenberg, David, 421
Rules of evidence, 217
  reasons for, 219–220
Runaway Youth Act, 432–433
Russell v. Oliver (1975), 387

S

Safe Streets Act of 1968, 66, 80, 271
St. Petersburg, 116
St. Vincent de Paul, 426
Salvation Army, 357, 416, 422
San Diego experimental Community Profile Program, 115–116
Sands, Bill, 421
Schmerber v. California (1966), 247
Search and seizures, 242–246

Search warrant, 244–246
  defined, 493
Secret Service, 66
Securities and Exchange Commission, 68
Security classifications of prisons, 376–377
Security contract forces, 88
Security hardware, 201
Security in-house forces, 88
Security inspections, 148–149
"Selective enforcement," 109, 141
Selective patrol, 99
Self-concept of worthlessness, 403
Sellin, Thorsten, 341
Senate, 313
Sentencing, 298–299, 317–318
  deferred, 418
  determinate, 438
  establishing guidelines for, 469–470
  expiration of, 449, 487
  flat, defined, 487
  indeterminate, defined, 488
  in lower courts, 268
Sequestration, 290
Settlement houses, 416
Seventh Step Foundation, 421
Sharp, E. Preston, 410
Shaw, Clifford, 342, 343
Sheriffs, 50, 53, 74, 87, 144
Sherman, Lawrence W., 409
Shift teams, 113–114
"Shire," 50
"Shire-reeve," 50
Shorthand doctrine, 237–238
Silver Platter Doctrine, 245
Sixth Amendment, 4, 230, 247, 249–250, 282, 385
Slavery, 337–338
Social Security Administration, 147
Social services, improving delivery of, 39
Society for Alleviating the Miseries of the Public Prisons, 391
Society and prisons, 404–405
Sociological approach to crime causation, 8–9
Solitary confinement, 335, 336
Sovereignty and double jeopardy, 247
Special Committee on Legal Aid Work (ABA), 283
Special enforcement, 142–143
  defined, 492
  teams, 109–110
Specialist units, *see* Police subsystem, specialist units
Specialization in law enforcement, history of, 122
  See also Police subsystem, specialist units

Special police, 89
Speck, Richard, 7
Speedy Trial Act, 249
Standards and goals, 37
  defined, 492
Standing Committee on Legal Aid and Indigent Defendants (ABA), 283
Stanley v. Georgia (1969), 241
Stare decisis, 259, 260
  defined, 492
Stark County Metropolitan Enforcement Group Unit, 136, 138
Starr, Ellen Gates, 416
State-account system, 336
State Administrative Code, 202
State constitutions, 234–235
State criminal justice planning agency (SPA), 38
State-Federal Judicial Councils, 312
State government, 27, 28, 30, 57–59, 73, 138
  police function of, 80–81
State Judicial Councils, 312
State and local courts, 264–266, 288, 307
  court of last resort, 264–266
  intermediate appellate courts, 266
  trial courts, 266
  unification of, 309–310
State Planning Agencies, 69, 73, 80
States' rights, 231, 232, 235
State training school for boys, 426
State-use system, 336
Status offenses, 271
  defined, 492
Statutes of limitations, 279
Sting operations, defined, 492
Stockades, 348
Strategic intelligence, 169
Street crime, 38
Study release, 420
  defined, 492
Subject matter jurisdiction, 288
Substantive criminal law, 26–27, 213
  defined, 492
Sumerian codes, 331
Summations, 296
Summons, 270
  defined, 280
Superior Courts, 266
Support specialist component in police subsystem, 174–184
  career development unit, 174–181

Support (cont.)
　criminalistics unit, 183–184
　defined, 492
　information, crime analysis, and evaluation unit, 181–183
Supreme Court, see United States Supreme Court
Surrebuttal, 296
Sutherland, Edwin H., 343
Sykes, Gresham, 343
Synanon House, 417
System, defined, 492
System modeling, 458

T

Tactical intelligence, 169
Taft-Hartley Act, 445
Tai v. Thompson (1975), 386
"Target hardening," 201, 202
Task Force Report on Juvenile Delinquency and Youth Crime (President's Commission on Law Enforcement and the Administration of Justice), 199
Tax Court of the United States, 264
Teaching in prisons, 391
Team policing, 111–116
　defined, 492
　goals of, 112–113
　organization of, 113–114
　responsibilities of, 114–116
Team treatment concept, 390
Technical pardon, 450
Television, 106
Ten Commandments, 331
Territorial jurisdiction, 288
Texas, 300
Texas Rangers, 56
Thirteenth Amendment, 236, 338, 384
Thompson v. Montemuro (1974), 387
Tithing, 50
Top-lock, 387
Tower of London, 332
Toynbee Hall, 416
Traffic and patrol officer, 102–103
Traffic safety, 139–141
　defined, 492
Training of police officers, 178–179
Training schools, juvenile, 429–430
Treason, 213
　defined, 492
Treasury/Internal Revenue Service Narcotics Traffickers Program, 66

Treatment in prisons, 388–394
　classification for, 388–391
　counseling, casework, and clinical services, 392
　education, 391
　library, 393
　medical and dental services, 393–394
　recreation, 393
　religion, 391–392
Trephination, 330
Trial
　defined, 492
　by combat, 217
　by compurgation, 217–218
　courts, 266
　de novo, 266, 492
　by jury, 489
　　development of, 218–219
　　right to, 289
　in lower courts, 268
　by ordeal, 217
　by peers, 218
　processes of, 287–297
　　case for defense, 296
　　case for prosecution, 295–296
　　closing statements, 296
　　deliberations and verdict, 297
　　instructions and charge to jury, 297
　　jurisdiction and venue, 287–288
　　jury selection, 293–295
　　motion for dismissal or directed verdict, 296
　　opening statements, 295
　　people involved, 288–293
　　rebuttal and surrebuttal, 296
　system of, development, 217–219
Tucson Plan, 107

U

Ulysses (Joyce), 240
Underachievement, 402
Uniform Crime Report, 24, 222, 328, 460, 492
United Nations, 135
United States Board of Parole, 440–441
United States Bureau of Alcohol, Tobacco, and Firearms, 60, 65–68, 70, 71
United States Bureau of the Census, 67
United States Bureau of Customs, 65, 66
United States Bureau of Prisons, 67, 349, 354, 375, 376, 378, 380, 390, 405, 420
United States Code, 61
United States Commissioners, 264

United States Courts of Appeals, 240, 255, 257, 262, 263
United States Court of Claims, 264
United States Court of Customs and Patent Appeals, 264
United States Court of Military Appeals, 264
United States Customs Court, 264
United States Department of Agriculture, 66
United States Department of Commerce, 67
United States Department of Defense, 58, 70
United States Department of Health, Education, and Welfare, 39, 67, 70
United States Department of the Interior, 66
United States Department of Justice, 38, 58, 60, 65, 67, 68, 69, 431
United States Department of Labor, 68
United States Department of the Treasury, 60, 65, 67, 68, 70
United States District Courts, 255, 262–264
United States Magistrates, 255, 264
United States Marshals Service, 68
United States Medical Center at Springfield, Missouri, 376
United States Park Police, 66
United States Parole Board, 442
United States Parole Commission, 440–441
United States Postal Service, 66, 68
United States Secret Service, 65, 68
United States Sentencing Commission, 469
United States Supreme Court, 3, 4, 12, 256–263, 460, 466, 470
   administering federal judiciary, 260
   on capital punishment, 339
   constitutional interpretations, 230, 232–235, 237–238, 240–252, 338–340
   and criminal justice system, 261–262
   decision-making process of, 259–260
   Federal Criminal Procedure rules, 27
   on jury unanimity, 289
   and juveniles, 272, 273
   on presidential power, 62
   selection of cases, 257–258
United States v. Wade (1967), 248
University of Denver, 312
Unlawful assembly, 239
Urbanization in United States, 53–55
Urban policy development, and criminal justice system, 456–457

V

Venire, 294
Veniremen, 294
Venue, 288
   defined, 492
Vera Foundation, 419
Vera Institute of Justice, 419
Verdict of jury, 297
Vermont, 300
Vertical integration, 458
Vice control, 136–139
   defined, 492
Victimization studies, 24, 464
   defined, 493
Victimless crimes, 138, 221–226
   criticisms of, 221–222
   decriminalization of, 224–226
   magnitude and costs, 222–223
   and organized crime, 223–224
   support for laws of, 224
Vilian, Jean Jacques Philippe, 335
Violence Commission, 201
Violent crime, 38
   perpetrators of, 3
Virginia, 300
Virgin Islands, 38, 69
Vocational training in prisons, 391
Voir dire, 294
Vollmer, August, 342
Volstead Act, 223
Volunteers
   defined, 493
   in jails, 352–353, 357
   in probation supervision, 369
Volunteers of America, 416, 422

W

Walnut Street Jail, 335
Warner, Sam, 343
Warrant, 242–246, 279
   defined, 493
Washington Crime News, 349
"Watch and ward," 50
Weeks v. United States (1914), 244, 245, 246
Welfare programs, 337
White Slave Act, 56
Wickersham Commission, 57, 71–72, 224, 349
Wilks, Judith, 448
Wilson, James Q., 97
Winship case (1970), 428
Wisconsin, 300
Witnesses, 290–291
Wolf v. Colorado (1949), 245
Wolff v. McDonnell (1974), 386

Women
  and parolees, 443
  as prisoners, 406–407
Women's Clubs of Chicago, 337
Workhouse, 335
  defined, 493
Work release, 352, 417, 420
  defined, 493
Workweek, modification of, 110
World War II, 108
Writ of certiorari, 258, 259, 263, 265, 427

Y

Youth Aid Authorities, 270
Youth Authority, 370
Youth for Christ, 422
Youth Development and Delinquency Prevention Administration, 70
Youth services bureaus, 189, 193–195
  defined, 493
  goals of, 195

Z

Zero-base budgeting, 164, 168

The Criminal Justice System

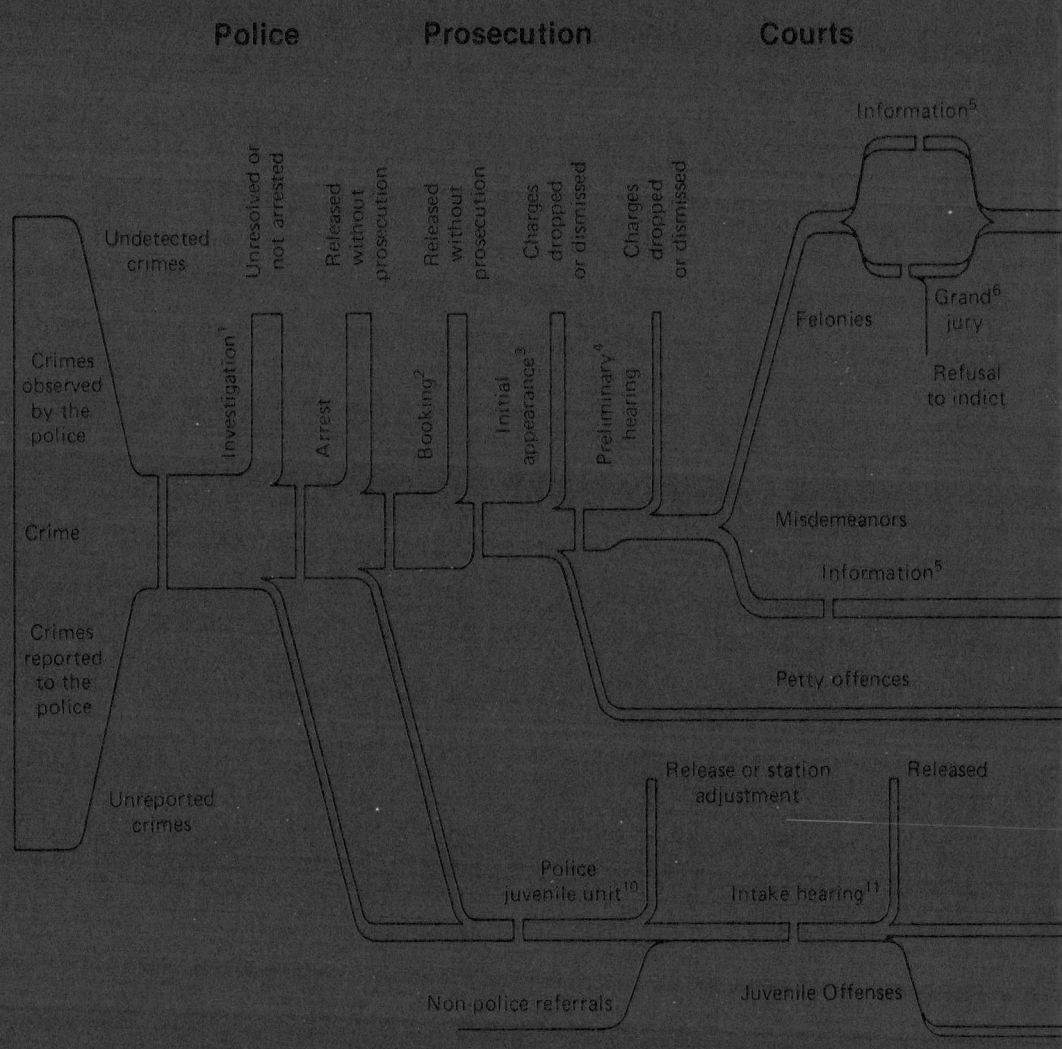

1. May continue until trial.

2. Administrative record of arrest first stage at which temporary release on bail may be available.

3. Before magistrate, commissioner, or justice of peace, formal notice of charge, advice of rights, Budget Summary trials for party offenses usually conducted here without further processing.

4. Preliminary testing of evidence against defendent. Charge may be reduced. No separate preliminary hearing for misdemeanors in some systems.

5. Charge filed by prosecutor on basis of information submitted by police or citizens. Alternative to grand jury indictment often used in felonies, almost always in misdemeanors.

6. Reviews whether government evidence sufficient to justify trial. Some states have no grand jury system, others seldom use it.